Do More

McGraw-Hill Connect Student Quick Tips for Blackboard Users

Use this McGraw-Hill Connect Student Quick Tips for Blackboard Users guide for a quick and easy start with your assignments within McGraw-Hill Connect or ConnectPlus. You'll get valuable tips on doing assignments, accessing resources, and support.

"Register Now" or "Sign In"

TIP: To start using Connect assignments within Blackboard, you will be asked to "Register Now" or "Sign In" the first time you click on a Connect assignment. Consider these points as you make your selection:

- If this is your first experience with a McGraw-Hill Connect assignment in Blackboard, select "Register Now" and follow the prompts to establish an account

- If this is not your first experience with a McGraw-Hill Connect assignment, simply select "Sign In" and enter the email address and password that you used for previous McGraw-Hill Connect assignments

- Enter the Connect Access Code purchased with your new textbook or choose "Buy Online" to purchase access online.

TIP: If you are creating a new account with McGraw-Hill, please choose your Security Question and Answer carefully. We will ask you for this information if you forget your password.

TIP: If you do not have an access code, or have not yet secured your tuition funds, you can click "Free Trial" during registration. This trial will provide temporary Connect access (typically three weeks) and will remind you to purchase online access before the end of your trial.

Home (Assignments)

TIP: If you are unable to begin an assignment, verify the following:

- The assignment is available (check start dates and due dates)

- You have not exceeded the maximum number of attempts for the assignment

- You have not achieved a score of 100%

NOTE: If an assignment contains questions that require manual grading, you can attempt to complete the assignment again if your instructor has enabled multiple attempts; however, you won't receive credit for the manually graded questions until the instructor reviews and enters a grade.

Do More

TIP: If you are unable to complete your assignment in one sitting, utilize the "*Save & Exit*" button to save your work and complete it at a later time. Once you have completed your assignment, utilize the "*Submit*" button in order for your assignment to be graded.

TIP: There may be limitations on your assignment, based on your instructor's settings. You may encounter the following limitations when working on your assignment(s):

- Ability to "Print" an assignment

- Once you begin a timed assignment, the timer will not stop

Library

TIP: For shortcuts to various resources, go to the **My Connect Section** under the McGraw-Hill Higher Education link in the "Tools" area.

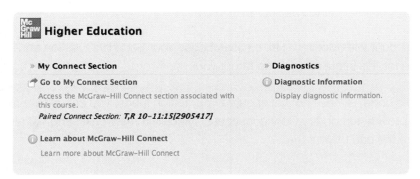

- If you purchased ConnectPlus, you will see an eBook link, which can also be accessed from the course section information widget of the "Home" tab

- Recorded lectures can be accessed if your instructor is using Tegrity Campus to capture lectures. You may also access recorded lectures when beginning an assignment by clicking on the projector icon in the navigation bar

- Many McGraw-Hill textbooks offer additional resources such as narrated slides and additional problem sets, which are accessible via the "Student Resources" link

Do More

Grades

TIP: Your grades and results are available in the **Grade Book** immediately.

NOTE: Your instructor has the ability to limit the amount of information (e.g. questions, answers, scores) you can view for each submitted assignment

Need More Help with Connect Assignments?

CONTACT US ONLINE:

Visit us at:

www.mcgrawhillconnect.com/support

Browse our support materials including tutorial videos and searchable knowledge base. If you cannot find an answer to your question, click on Contact Us to send us an email.

GIVE US A CALL

Call us at:

1-800-331-5094

Our live support is available:
Mon-Thurs:	8 am – 11 pm CT
Friday:	8 am – 6 pm CT
Sunday:	6 pm – 11 pm CT

TENTH EDITION

FIT & WELL

Core Concepts and Labs in Physical Fitness and Wellness

Thomas D. Fahey
California State University, Chico

Paul M. Insel
Stanford University

Walton T. Roth
Stanford University

Oregon State University Edition

McGraw Hill Education

Copyright © 2013 by McGraw-Hill Education. All rights reserved. Printed in the United States of America. Except as permitted under the United States Copyright Act of 1976, no part of this publication may be reproduced or distributed in any form or by any means, or stored in a data base retrieval system, without prior written permission of the publisher.

1 2 3 4 5 6 7 8 9 0 DOW DOW 15 14 13

ISBN-13: 978-1-259-21850-7
ISBN-10: 1-259-21850-3

Learning Solutions Consultant: Michelle Payne
Project Manager: Vanessa Arnold

BRIEF CONTENTS

CONTENTS

6

7

8

THE *FIT & WELL* LEARNING SYSTEM

The *Fit & Well* learning system utilizes innovative technologies to personalize the science of fitness and wellness and to motivate students to build research skills, critical thinking skills, and behavior change skills for lifelong wellness.

The new edition of *Fit & Well* is better than ever, thanks to a set of innovative digital teaching and learning tools, including:

- The **LearnSmart adaptive testing program**, which creates individualized study plans for each student, helping to build a strong foundation of knowledge.

- New **College Health Video** activities that discuss topics—like tattoos, tanning salons, DUIs, and stress—relevant to today's students.

- **Connect activities and assessments** that can be seamlessly integrated with your school's course management system.

- The **Tegrity lecture capture system**, which enables instructors to create their own videos and upload them into Connect.

FIT & WELL WORKS FOR INSTRUCTORS

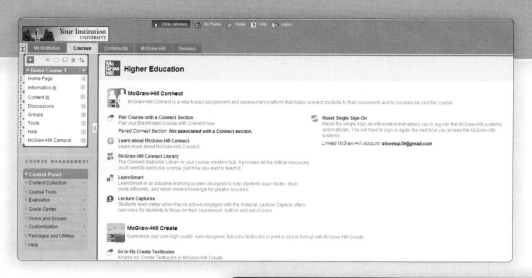

Through McGraw-Hill Campus, **Connect Fit & Well** can be easily integrated with Blackboard or other course management systems. Among other things, this integration enables **Connect** activities, assessments, grades, and other content to appear within your university's system. Setup is fast, easy, and flexible.

New and existing print and digital resources, activities, and assessment in the *Fit & Well* learning system give instructors the tools to challenge students to take small, measurable steps toward achieving a fitness or wellness goal. The result is a program that students can customize to achieve their unique goals.

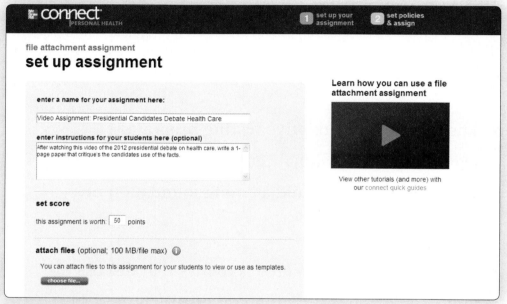

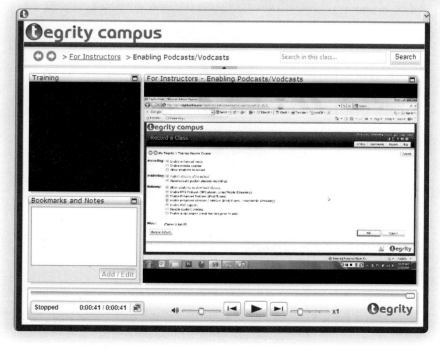

The new Tegrity lecture capture system enables instructors to create and upload into **Connect Fit & Well** their own video lectures.

FIT & WELL WORKS FOR STUDENTS

LearnSmart for Fit & Well:
LearnSmart, an unparalleled adaptive testing program, diagnoses students' knowledge of a subject and then creates an individualized learning path to help them master fitness and wellness concepts. Field studies show that college students who use *LearnSmart* demonstrate a 5% improvement in test scores over students who study without it.

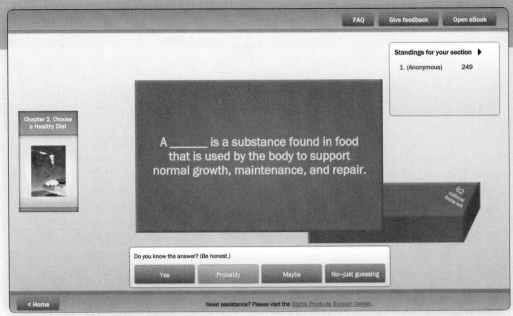

Connect Engages: *Connect Fit & Well* gives students access to a wealth of online interactive content, online fitness labs and self assessments, new College Health Report video activities, a fitness and nutrition journal, a behavior change workbook, and practice quizzes with immediate feedback.

Connect Personalizes. Connect for Fit & Well lets students learn their own way—online, interactively, at their own pace, on their own time.

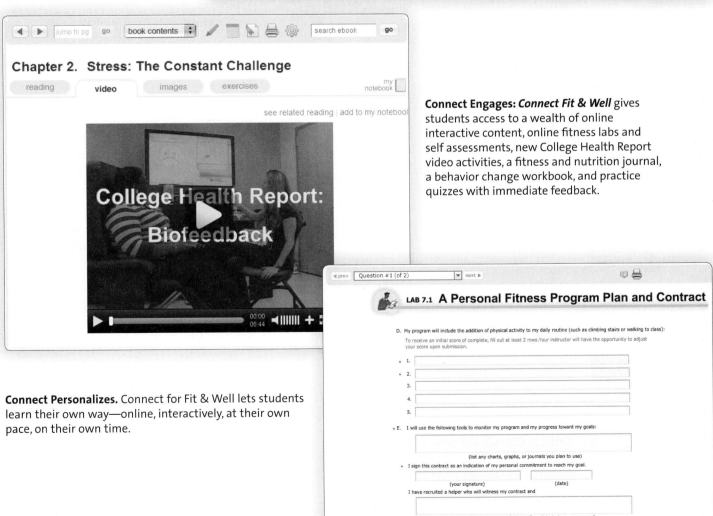

KEY FEATURES AND LEARNING AIDS

The *Fit & Well* learning system continues to provide the information students need to start their journey to fitness and wellness. *Fit & Well's* authoritative, science-based information is written by experts who work and teach in the field of exercise science, physical education, and health education. *Fit & Well* provides accurate, reliable, current information on key health and fitness topics while also addressing issues related to mind-body health, research, diversity, gender, and consumer health. Text features and interactive activities include self-assessments and fitness labs, videos on timely health topics such as tattooing and tanning beds, exercise demonstration videos, a daily fitness and nutrition log, sample programs, and a wealth of behavior change tools and tips.

New **Fitness Tips** and **Wellness Tips** catch students' attention and get them thinking—and doing something—about their fitness and wellness.

New **Wellness in the Digital Age** sections focus on the many new fitness- and wellness-related devices and applications that are appearing every day, from the Wii Fit system to iPhone apps to digital calorie counters and push-up coaches.

New **Personal Challenge** activities challenge the student to do something immediately to assess and enhance their fitness or wellness.

Evidence for Exercise sections show students that physical activity and exercise recommendations are based on solid scientific evidence.

Critical Consumer boxes provide reliable consumer information and help students hone their critical thinking and health literacy skills.

In Focus sections explore current trends and topics in fitness and wellness, such as high-interval training and exercising with kettlebells, stability balls, and medicine balls.

Hands-on lab activities give students the opportunity to assess their current level of fitness and wellness and to create their own individualized programs for improvement.

Exercise photos and online videos demonstrate exactly how to perform exercises correctly.

Behavior change tools take students through the behavior change process step by step.

Color Transparency inserts offer a visually enhanced presentation of key structures and processes, including circulation in the heart and lungs, the deep and superficial muscles, and muscle hypertrophy.

CHAPTER-BY-CHAPTER CHANGES

Chapter 1, "Introduction to Wellness, Fitness, and Lifestyle Management"

- The book's key message—that students need to take responsibility for their own fitness and wellness—has been given a new emphasis throughout this chapter, in strong but subtle terms.
- The **In Focus** feature ("Financial Wellness") complements the discussion of the six widely recognized dimensions of wellness and focuses on the importance of mastering basic personal financial skills. The feature has been expanded since the last edition, and includes especially relevant information for students on the dangers of becoming dependent on credit cards.
- The discussions of the Healthy People 2020 and Healthy Campus 2020 initiatives have been refined to focus on the newest round of objectives and the latest statistics on Americans' progress toward meeting those goals.
- All of the chapter's considerable statistical material has been updated to reflect the latest information on morbidity, mortality, and measures of quality of life.

Chapter 2, "Principles of Physical Fitness"

- Includes the most recent statistics available from the CDC on the physical activity and exercise habits of Americans.
- The **Evidence for Exercise** feature ("Is Exercise Good for Your Brain?") has been revised to make it more relevant to students.
- The discussion of exercise recommendations has been refined to show how the Physical Activity Guidelines for Americans (2008) are in line with recommendations from other agencies.
- Significant new points have been added on the health benefits of weight training, weight training safety, and the effects of weight training on the body's metabolism.

Chapter 3, "Cardiorespiratory Endurance"

- All statistics have been updated to reflect the latest data from authoritative sources, including the American Heart Association's Heart Disease and Stroke Statistics, 2011.
- New information has been added about the health benefits of combining strength training with aerobic conditioning.
- The chapter presents a wide variety of activities that benefit one's cardiorespiratory health, and challenges students to pick the activity that would best fit with their daily routine.

Chapter 4, "Muscular Strength and Endurance"

- The chapter presents several basic strength and endurance exercises that students can easily use to assess their fitness level, and challenges them to pick one exercise and set goals for improvement.
- Enumerates more ways than ever to develop muscular strength and endurance without going to the gym.
- Introduces weight training videos and discusses their usefulness.
- Discusses the specific benefits of doing multiple sets of weight-training exercises.

Chapter 5, "Flexibility and Low-Back Health"

- Reflects the latest recommendations for the minimum and maximum amounts of time to hold a stretch.
- Includes new statistics on the prevalence of osteoporosis, low bone mass.
- Presents a set of basic exercises one can do at home to strengthen the lower back and prevent or alleviate back pain.

Chapter 6, "Body Composition"

- Makes further distinctions between overweight and obesity.
- Includes newly updated statistics on the prevalence of overweight and obesity in the U.S., from the National Center for Health Statistics.

- Includes new data on the prevalence of metabolic syndrome among Americans, and expands the definition of metabolic syndrome.
- Explains the potential link between obesity and infertility.
- Provides new statistics on the prevalence of all types of diabetes, including prevalence among specific ethnic groups.
- Challenges students to record their weight every day, especially if they are trying to lose weight.

Chapter 7, "Putting Together a Complete Fitness Program"

- Introduces research indicating that runners may benefit from including stretches in their pre-workout warm-up, contrary to other research indicating stretching should be done after working out.
- Provides new sources and updated data on the benefits and drawbacks of incorporating a stability ball into one's training program.
- Promotes the use of resistance bands as an easy way to incorporate weight training into a total workout program.
- Introduces a variety of motivational programs for use with smart phones, which can help beginning exercisers stick with a program.
- Provides updated research into the benefits and drawbacks of drinking bottled water, and the product's effects on the environment.

Chapter 8, "Nutrition"

- The overview of nutrients has been expanded and several key terms have been added.
- The entire chapter has been updated, where applicable, to discuss the 2010 Dietary Guidelines for Americans.
- The discussion of sodium intake has been updated to reflect the CDC's latest recommendation that most Americans—not just those with risk factors for heart disease—reduce their sodium intake to 1500 mg per day.
- The discussion of MyPyramid has been replaced with an introduction to the USDA's new MyPlate program, and explains the program's recommendations.
- The discussion of dietary supplements has been expanded to help students understand when

supplements may be necessary and when they can be most effective.

Chapter 9, "Weight Management"

- Reiterates the latest statistics on overweight and obesity in the U.S., and breaks down the prevalence of overweight and obesity by gender and ethnicity.
- Challenges students to examine their own weight, think of reasons they may have gained weight, and list ways they can begin reducing their weight right away.
- Provides new data about the effects of exercise on metabolic rate and resting calorie consumption among college-age men.
- Explains how very simple, small steps—such as cutting back on soda—can have a direct impact on weight loss.
- Discusses high-tech weight management tools and how students can incorporate them into a weight loss program.
- Introduces new data on the impact of psychosocial factors on weight loss among college students.

Chapter 10, "Stress"

- The definition of "stress" has been clarified and simplified.
- The chapter more clearly defines and differentiates the concepts of "acute stress" and "chronic stress."
- New art illustrates the mechanics of sleep apnea.
- Explains the effects of chronic stress on the body's aging process.
- Expands the discussion of stress's effect on the body's immune system.
- Provides updated statistics on stress from the 2010 Stress in America survey.
- A new section, titled "Relationships and Stress," explores the way our personal and intimate relations with others can be a significant source of stress in our lives.

Chapter 11, "Cardiovascular Health"

- All statistics have been updated to reflect the latest data from authoritative sources, including the American Heart Association's Heart Disease and Stroke Statistics, 2011.

- Introduces easy-to-use and inexpensive digital blood pressure monitors and heart rate monitors that anyone can use at home.
- Provides warnings about the negative effects of weight training on blood pressure.
- Expanded discussions of heart disease risk factors such as C-reactive protein.
- Updated coverage of the benefits of aspirin therapy in some people.
- Instructions for recognizing a heart attack, stroke, and cardiac arrest have been updated to reflect the latest recommendations from the American Heart Association.

Chapter 12, "Cancer"

- All statistics have been updated to reflect the latest data from authoritative sources, including the American Cancer Society's Cancer Facts and Figures, 2011.
- Discusses the possible links between breast cancer, inactivity, and obesity.
- Provides updated guidelines for Pap tests.
- Outlines new federal regulations of sunscreens and sunscreen labeling.
- A new section, "Detecting and Treating Cancer" focuses on the importance of early detection in successful cancer treatment, and provides more detail than past editions on specific types of cancer treatments.
- The chapter includes all the latest cancer screening guidelines from the American Cancer Society, as well as the ACS's updated guidelines for performing breast self-exams.

Chapter 13, "Substance Use and Abuse"

- Statistics on drug use and abuse have been updated, based on the latest data from sources such as the Minding the Future Survey, the National Survey on Drug Use and Health, the Youth Risk Behavior Survey, and others.
- The overview of addiction has been revised for clarity and now focuses on addiction in particular and less on habituation.
- Statistics on alcohol use and abuse have been updated, based on the latest data from sources such as the Minding the Future Survey, the National Survey on Drug Use and Health, the Youth Risk Behavior Survey, and others.

- Statistics on alcohol-related accidents, injuries, deaths, and arrests have been updated.
- The new **Personal Challenge** feature challenges students to track their drinking habits daily for two weeks, to get a clear picture of their actual alcohol intake.
- Statistics on tobacco use have been updated, based on the latest data from sources such as the National Survey on Drug Use and Health, the Youth Risk Behavior Survey, the American Cancer Society, and others.
- The Food and Drug Administration's new regulatory authority over tobacco products is described.

Chapter 14, "Sexually Transmitted Diseases"

- Statistics throughout the chapter have been updated to reflect the latest available information from sources such as the CDC, WHO, Guttmacher Institute, and others.
- The overview of the major STDs, including HIV/AIDS, has been streamlined for easier retention.
- The **Dimensions of Diversity** feature ("HIV/AIDS Around the World") reflects the latest global prevalence estimates from the Joint United Nations Programme on HIV/AIDs.

Chapter 15, "Environmental Health"

- Current statistics and other information have been gleaned from authoritative sources such as the World Health Organization, World Wildlife Fund, United Nations, and many others.
- The chapter emphasizes ways individuals can take personal responsibility for improving the health of the environment and ensuring that their personal health is not negatively affected by the environment.
- Introduces the concept of sustainability, including sustainable energy and sustainable development, and the potential positive impact of sustainable practices on the environment.
- A **Take Charge** feature on compact fluorescent light bulbs (CFLs) has been expanded to discuss new and prospective state-level legislation regarding their manufacture, use, and disposal.
- The discussion of radiation includes new concerns about cell phone radiation and steps users can take to minimize their exposure.

TEACHING AND LEARNING

FIT & WELL
in Loose Leaf Format

McGraw-Hill has done a considerable amount of research with college students, not only asking them questions about how they study and use course materials, but also using ethnographic research tools to observe how they study. During the course of this research, students told us they want books and online learning systems that are:

- light and easy to carry
- engaging and relevant to their own lives
- inexpensive
- supported by digital activities that help them learn and succeed in their course

Based on what we heard from students, we are introducing *Fit & Well* in a *three-hole punched, loose leaf* format that is portable, flexible, and cost-effective. *Fit & Well* in loose leaf format offers these advantages:

- Students will need to carry only the portion of the book that's being covered in class with them.
- In addition to the print version of the book, students will receive an integrated multimedia eBook including videos and links to other resources.
- For the same price, students will also receive an access code to *Connect Fit & Well* and *LearnSmart*, providing a number of interactive, multimedia tools that will help them learn.

Would you still like your students to have a bound book? You will be able order one through our *Create* system. While you're at it, we can pull out any of the chapters of the book you don't assign. This ensures that students are purchasing only the content that is being assigned to them, making the book 100% relevant to your course, more affordable for students, and lightweight and portable.

Create, because Customization Matters

Design your ideal course materials with McGraw-Hill's *Create* **www.mcgrawhillcreate.com**! Rearrange or omit chapters, combine material from other sources, and/or upload your syllabus or any other content you have written to make the perfect resource for your students. Search thousands of leading McGraw-Hill textbooks to find the best content for your students, then arrange it to fit your teaching style. You can even personalize your book's appearance by selecting the cover and adding your name, school, and course information. When you order a *Create* book, you receive a complimentary review copy. Get a printed copy in 3 to 5 business days or an electronic copy (eComp) via e-mail in about an hour.

Register today at **www.mcgrawhillcreate.com**, and craft your course resources to match the way you teach.

WITH *FIT & WELL*

Tegrity Campus

Tegrity Campus is a service that makes class time available all the time by automatically capturing every lecture in a searchable format for students to review when they study and complete assignments.

With a simple one-click start-and-stop process, you capture all computer screens and corresponding audio. Students replay any part of any class with easy-to-use browser-based viewing on a PC or Mac.

With Tegrity Campus, students quickly recall key moments by using Tegrity Campus's unique search feature. This search helps students efficiently find what they need, when they need it across an entire semester of class recordings.

Help turn all your students' study time into learning moments immediately supported by your lecture.

To learn more about Tegrity watch a 2-minute Flash demo at **http://tegritycampus.mhhe.com**

McGraw-Hill Campus

McGraw-Hill Campus is the first-of-its-kind institutional service providing faculty with true single sign-on access to all of McGraw-Hill's course content, digital tools, and other high-quality learning resources from any Learning Management System (LMS). This innovative offering allows for secure and deep integration enabling seamless access for faculty and students to any of McGraw-Hill's course solutions such as McGraw-Hill Connect®, McGraw-Hill Create™, McGraw-Hill Learn-Smart™, or Tegrity®. McGraw-Hill Campus includes access to McGraw-Hill's entire content library, including eBooks, assessment tools, presentation slides and multimedia content, among other resources, providing faculty open, unlimited access to prepare for class, create tests/quizzes, develop lecture material, integrate interactive content, and more.

ONLINE LEARNING CENTER

The *Fit & Well* Online Learning Center (**www.mhhe.com/fahey10e**) provides many resources for instructors:

- Course Integrator Guide
- Test bank
- PowerPoint Slides
- Image bank
- Web links

STUDENT RESOURCES

Resources for student available with *Fit & Well* include the following:

- The Daily Fitness and Nutrition Journal (ISBN 007741179X) is a handy booklet that guides

students in planning and tracking their fitness programs. It is available as an optional package with new copies of the text.

- The Health and Fitness Pedometer (ISBN 0077411552) allows students to count their daily steps and track their level of physical activity. The pedometer can also be packaged with new copies of the text.

- NutritionCalc Plus (ISBN 0073328642) is a dietary analysis program that allows users to track their nutrient and food group intakes, energy expenditures, and weight control goals. The ESHA database includes thousands of ethnic foods, supplements, fast foods, and convenience foods; users can also add foods to the database. NutritionCalc Plus is available on CD-ROM (Windows only) or in an Internet version.

CHAPTER 1

Introduction to Wellness, Fitness, and Lifestyle Management

LOOKING AHEAD. . .

After reading this chapter, you should be able to:

- Describe the dimensions of wellness
- Identify the major health problems in the United States today, and discuss their causes
- Describe the behaviors that are part of a wellness lifestyle
- Explain the steps in creating a behavior management plan to change a wellness-related behavior
- List some of the available sources of wellness information and explain how to think critically about them

TEST YOUR KNOWLEDGE

1. Which of the following lifestyle factors is the leading preventable cause of death for Americans?
   a. excess alcohol consumption
   b. cigarette smoking
   c. obesity
2. The terms *health* and *wellness* mean the same thing.
   True or false?
3. A person's genetic makeup determines whether he or she will develop certain diseases (such as breast cancer), regardless of that person's health habits.
   True or false?

ANSWERS

1. **b.** Smoking causes about 440,000 deaths per year. Obesity is responsible for more than 100,000 premature deaths, and alcohol is a factor in as many as 85,000 deaths.
2. **False.** Although the words are used interchangeably, they actually have different meanings. The term *health* refers to the overall condition of the body or mind and to the presence or absence of illness or injury. The term *wellness* refers to optimal health and vitality, encompassing all the dimensions of well-being.
3. **False.** In many cases, behavior can tip the balance toward good health even when heredity or environment is a negative factor.

Mc Graw Hill **LearnSmart** GET A BETTER GRADE. TRY LEARNSMART.

A college sophomore sets the following goals for herself:

- To join new social circles and make new friends whenever possible
- To exercise every day
- To clean up trash and plant trees in blighted neighborhoods in her community

These goals may differ, but they have one thing in common. Each contributes, in its own way, to this student's health and well-being. Not satisfied merely to be free of illness, she wants more. She has decided to live actively and fully—not just to be healthy, but to pursue a state of overall wellness.

WELLNESS: NEW HEALTH GOALS

Generations of people have viewed health simply as the absence of disease, and that view largely prevails today. The word **health** typically refers to the overall condition of a person's body or mind and to the presence or absence of illness or injury. **Wellness** is a relatively new concept that expands our idea of health to include our ability to achieve optimal health. Beyond the simple presence or absence of disease, wellness refers to optimal health and vitality—to living life to its fullest. Although we use the terms *health* and *wellness* interchangeably, there are two important differences between them:

- Health—or some aspects of it—can be determined or influenced by factors beyond your control, such as your genes, age, and family history. For example, consider

KEY TERMS

health The overall condition of body or mind and the presence or absence of illness or injury.

wellness Optimal health and vitality, encompassing all the dimensions of well-being.

a man with a strong family history of prostate cancer. These factors place this man at a higher-than-average risk for developing prostate cancer himself.

- Wellness is largely determined by the decisions you make about how you live. That same man can reduce his risk of cancer by eating sensibly, exercising, and having regular screening tests. Even if he develops the disease, he may still rise above its effects to live a rich, meaningful life. This means choosing not only to care for himself physically but also to maintain a positive outlook, keep up his relationships with others, challenge himself intellectually, and nurture other aspects of his life.

Enhanced wellness, therefore, involves making conscious decisions to control **risk factors** that contribute to disease or injury. Age and family history are risk factors you cannot control. Behaviors such as choosing not to smoke, exercising, and eating a healthy diet are well within your control.

The Dimensions of Wellness

Experts have defined six dimensions of wellness:

- Physical
- Emotional
- Intellectual
- Interpersonal
- Spiritual
- Environmental

Each dimension of wellness affects the others. Further, the process of achieving wellness is constant and dynamic (Figure 1.1), involving change and growth. Ignoring any dimension of wellness can have harmful effects on your life. The following sections briefly introduce the dimensions of wellness. Table 1.1 lists some of the specific qualities and behaviors associated with each dimension. Lab 1.1 will help you learn what wellness means to you and where you fall on the wellness continuum.

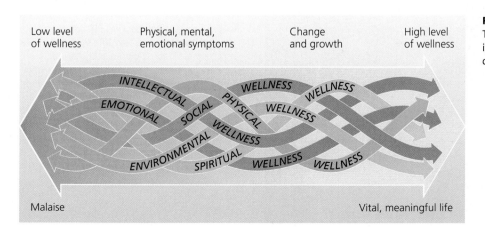

| Low level of wellness | Physical, mental, emotional symptoms | Change and growth | High level of wellness |

Malaise — Vital, meaningful life

FIGURE 1.1 The wellness continuum. The concept of wellness includes vitality in six interrelated dimensions, all of which contribute to overall wellness.

	Table 1.1		Examples of Qualities and Behaviors Associated with the Dimensions of Wellness			
PHYSICAL	EMOTIONAL	INTELLECTUAL	INTERPERSONAL	SPIRITUAL	ENVIRONMENTAL
• Eating well	• Optimism	• Openness to new ideas	• Communication skills	• Capacity for love	• Having abundant, clean natural resources
• Exercising	• Trust	• Capacity to question	• Capacity for intimacy	• Compassion	• Maintaining sustainable development
• Avoiding harmful habits	• Self-esteem	• Ability to think critically	• Ability to establish and maintain satisfying relationships	• Forgiveness	• Recycling whenever possible
• Practicing safer sex	• Self-acceptance	• Motivation to master new skills	• Ability to cultivate a support system of friends and family	• Altruism	• Reducing pollution and waste
• Recognizing symptoms of disease	• Self-confidence	• Sense of humor		• Joy	
• Getting regular checkups	• Ability to understand and accept one's feelings	• Creativity		• Fulfillment	
• Avoiding injuries	• Ability to share feelings with others	• Curiosity		• Caring for others	
		• Lifelong learning		• Sense of meaning and purpose	
				• Sense of belonging to something greater than oneself	

Physical Wellness Your physical wellness includes not just your body's overall condition and the absence of disease, but your fitness level and your ability to care for yourself. The higher your fitness level (which is discussed throughout this book), the higher your level of physical wellness will be. Similarly, as you become more able to care for your own physical needs, you ensure greater physical wellness. To achieve optimum physical wellness, you need to make choices that help you avoid illnesses and injuries. The decisions you make now—and the habits you develop over your lifetime—will largely determine the length and quality of your life.

Emotional Wellness Your emotional wellness reflects your ability to understand and deal with your feelings. Emotional wellness involves attending to your own thoughts and feelings, monitoring your reactions, and identifying obstacles to emotional stability. Achieving this type of wellness means finding solutions to emotional problems, with professional help if necessary.

Intellectual Wellness Those who enjoy intellectual wellness constantly challenge their minds. An active mind is essential to wellness because it detects problems, finds solutions, and directs behavior. People who enjoy intellectual wellness never stop learning; they continue trying to learn new things throughout their lifetime. They seek out and relish new experiences and challenges.

Interpersonal Wellness Your interpersonal (or social) wellness is defined by your ability to develop and maintain satisfying and supportive relationships. Such relationships are essential to physical and emotional health. Social wellness requires participating in and contributing to your community and to society.

Spiritual Wellness To enjoy spiritual wellness is to possess a set of guiding beliefs, principles, or values that give meaning and purpose to your life, especially in difficult times. The spiritually well person focuses on the positive aspects of life and finds spirituality to be an antidote for negative feelings such as cynicism, anger, and pessimism. Organized religions help many people develop spiritual health. Religion, however, is not the only source or form of spiritual wellness. Many people find meaning and purpose in their lives on their own—through nature, art, meditation, or good works—or with their loved ones.

Environmental Wellness Your environmental wellness is defined by the livability of your surroundings. Personal health depends on the health of the planet—from the

risk factor A condition that increases one's chances of disease or injury.

KEY TERM

WELLNESS: NEW HEALTH GOALS   **3**

Wellness Tip

Enhancing one dimension of wellness can have positive effects on others. Joining a meditation group can help you enhance your spiritual well-being, for example, but can also affect the emotional and interpersonal dimensions of wellness by enabling you to meet new people and develop new friendships.

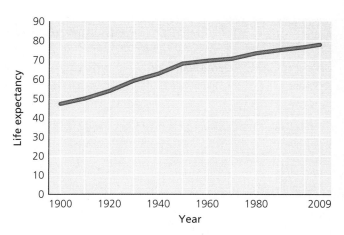

FIGURE 1.2 Life expectancy of Americans from birth, 1900–2009.
SOURCE: National Center for Health Statistics. 2011. Deaths: Preliminary data for 2009. *National Vital Statistics Reports* 59(4).

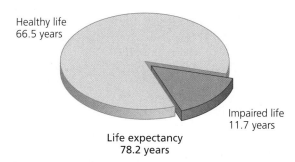

FIGURE 1.3 Quantity of life versus quality of life. Years of healthy life as a proportion of life expectancy in the U.S. population.
SOURCES: National Center for Health Statistics. 2011. Deaths: Preliminary data for 2009. *National Vital Statistics Reports.* 59(4); National Center for Health Statistics. *Healthy People* 2010; Midcourse Review. Hyattsville, Md.: Public Health Service.

safety of the food supply to the degree of violence in society. Your physical environment either supports your wellness or diminishes it. To improve your environmental wellness, you can learn about and protect yourself against hazards in your surroundings and work to make your world a cleaner and safer place.

Other Aspects of Wellness Many experts consider occupational wellness and financial wellness to be additional important dimensions of wellness. *Occupational wellness* refers to the level of happiness and fulfillment you gain through your work. Although high salaries and prestigious titles are nice, they alone generally do not bring about occupational wellness. An occupationally well person truly likes his or her work, feels a connection with others in the workplace, and has opportunities to learn and be challenged. Other aspects of occupational wellness include enjoyable work, job satisfaction, and recognition from managers and colleagues. An ideal job draws on your interests and passions, as well as your vocational or professional skills, and allows you to feel that you are contributing to society in your everyday work.

To achieve occupational wellness, set career goals that reflect your personal values. For example, a career in sales might be a good choice for someone who values financial security, whereas a career in teaching or nursing might be a good choice for someone who values service to others.

Financial wellness refers to your ability to live within your means and manage your money in a way that gives you peace of mind. It includes balancing your income and expenditures, staying out of debt, saving for the future, and understanding your emotions about money. For more on this topic, see the box "Financial Wellness."

New Opportunities for Taking Charge

Wellness is a fairly new concept. A century ago, Americans considered themselves lucky just to survive to adulthood (Figure 1.2). A child born in 1900, for example, could expect to live only about 47 years. Many people died from common **infectious diseases** (such as pneumonia, tuberculosis, or diarrhea) and poor environmental conditions (such as water pollution and poor sanitation).

Since 1900, however, life expectancy has nearly doubled, and as of 2009, the average American's life expectancy was 78.2 years. This increase in life span is due largely to the development of vaccines and antibiotics to fight infections, and to public health measures to improve living conditions. But even though life expectancy has increased, poor health limits most Americans' activities during the last 15% of their lives, resulting in some sort of impaired life (Figure 1.3). Today, a different set of diseases has emerged as our major health threat, and heart disease, cancer, and chronic lower respiratory diseases are now the three leading causes of death for Americans (Table 1.2). Treating such **chronic diseases** is costly and difficult.

KEY TERMS

infectious disease A disease that can spread from person to person; caused by microorganisms such as bacteria and viruses.

chronic disease A disease that develops and continues over a long period of time, such as heart disease or cancer.

Financial Wellness

With the news full of stories of home foreclosures, credit card debt, and personal bankruptcies, it has become painfully clear that many Americans do not know how to manage their finances. You can avoid such stress—and gain financial peace of mind—by developing skills that contribute to financial wellness.

Financial wellness means having a healthy relationship with money. It involves knowing how to manage your money, using self-discipline to live within your means, using credit cards wisely, staying out of debt, meeting your financial obligations, having a long-range financial plan, and saving.

Learn to Budget

Although the word *budget* may conjure up thoughts of deprivation, a budget is really just a way of tracking where your money goes and making sure you're spending it on the things that are most important to you. To start one, list your monthly income and your expenditures. If you aren't sure where you spend your money, track your expenses for a few weeks or a month. Then organize them into categories, such as housing, food, transportation, entertainment, services, personal care, clothes, books and school supplies, health care, credit card and loan payments, and miscellaneous. Use categories that reflect the way you actually spend your money. Knowing where your money goes is the first step in gaining control of it.

Now total your income and expenditures. Are you taking in more than you spend, or vice versa? Are you surprised by your spending patterns? Use this information to set guidelines and goals for yourself. If your expenses exceed your income, identify ways to make some cuts. If you have both a cell phone and a land line, for example, consider whether you can give one up. If you spend money on movies and restaurants, consider less expensive options like having a weekly game night with friends or organizing an occasional potluck.

Be Wary of Credit Cards

College students are prime targets for credit card companies, and most undergraduates have at least one card. In fact, many college students use credit cards to live beyond their means, not just for convenience. According a recent report, half of all students have four or more cards, and the average outstanding balance on undergraduate credit cards is over $3000.

The best way to avoid credit card debt is to have just one card, to use it only when necessary, and to pay off the entire balance every month. Make sure you understand terms like *APR* (annual percentage rate—the interest you're charged on your balance), *credit limit* (the maximum amount you can borrow at any one time), *minimum monthly payment* (the smallest payment your creditor will accept each month), *grace period* (the number of days you have to pay your bill before interest or penalties are charged), and *over-the-limit* and *late fees* (the amount you'll be charged if your payment is late or you go over your credit limit).

Get Out of Debt

If you have credit card debt, stop using your cards and start paying them off. If you can't pay the whole balance, at least try to pay more than the minimum payment each month. It can take a very long time to pay off a loan by making only the minimum payments. For example, to pay off a credit card balance of $2000 at 10% interest with monthly payments of $20 would take 203 months—17 years.

To see for yourself, check out an online credit card calculator like http://www.bankrate.com/calculators/credit-cards/credit-card-payoff-calculator.aspx. And remember: By carrying a balance and incurring finance charges, you are also paying back much more than your initial loan.

Start Saving

The same miracle of compound interest that locks you into years of credit card debt can work to your benefit if you start saving early (for an online compound interest calculator, visit http://www.moneychimp.com/calculator/compound_interest_calculator.htm). Experts recommend "paying yourself first" every month—that is, putting some money into savings before you start paying your bills, depending on what your budget allows. You may want to save for a large purchase, or you may even be looking ahead to retirement. If you work for a company with a 401(k) retirement plan, contribute as much as you can every pay period.

Become Financially Literate

Although modern life requires financial literacy, most Americans have not received any kind of basic financial training. Even before the economic meltdown that began in 2008, the U.S. government had established the Financial Literacy and Education Commission (www.MyMoney.gov) to help Americans develop financial literacy and learn how to save, invest, and manage their money better. The consensus is that developing lifelong financial skills should begin in early adulthood, during the college years, if not earlier.

SOURCES: Federal Deposit Insurance Corporation. 2010. *Money Smart: A Financial Education Program* (http://www.fdic.gov/consumers/consumer/moneysmart/young.html; retrieved June 23, 2011); Plymouth State University. 2011. *Student Monetary Awareness and Responsibility Today!* (http://www.plymouth.edu/finaid/smart; retrieved June 23, 2011); U.S. Financial Literacy and Education Commission. 2010. *Do You Want to Learn How to Save, Manage, and Invest Your Money Better?* (http://www.mymoney.gov; retrieved June 23, 2011).

Table 1.2 Leading Causes of Death in the United States, 2009

RANK	CAUSE OF DEATH	NUMBER OF DEATHS	PERCENTAGE OF TOTAL DEATHS*	DEATH RATE†	LIFESTYLE FACTORS
	All causes	2,436,652	100.0	741.0	
1	Heart disease	598,607	24.5	179.8	D I S A
2	Cancer	568,668	23.3	173.6	D I S A
3	Chronic lower respiratory diseases	137,082	5.6	42.2	■ ■ S ■
4	Stroke	128,603	5.3	38.9	D I S A
5	Unintentional injuries (accidents)	117,176	4.8	37.0	D I S A
6	Alzheimer's disease	78,889	3.2	23.4	
7	Diabetes mellitus	68,504	2.8	20.9	D I S ■
8	Influenza and pneumonia	53,582	2.2	16.2	■ ■ S ■
9	Kidney disease	48,714	2.0	14.8	D I S A
10	Intentional self-harm (suicide)	36,547	1.5	11.7	■ ■ ■ A
11	Septicemia (systemic blood infection)	35,587	1.5	10.9	■ ■ ■ A
12	Chronic liver disease and cirrhosis	30,444	1.2	9.2	■ ■ ■ A
13	Hypertension (high blood pressure)	25,651	1.0	7.7	D I S A
14	Parkinson's disease	20,552	0.8	6.4	
15	Assault (homicide)	16,591	0.6	5.5	■ ■ ■ A
	All other causes	471,455			

Key
D Diet plays a part
I Inactive lifestyle plays a part
S Smoking plays a part
A Excessive alcohol use plays a part

*Percentages may not total 100% due to rounding.

†Age-adjusted death rate per 100,000 persons.

NOTE: Although not among the overall top 15 causes of death, HIV/AIDS is a major killer. In 2009, HIV/AIDS was the twelfth leading cause of death for Americans age 15–24 years and the sixth leading cause of death for those age 25–44 years.

SOURCE: National Center for Health Statistics. 2011. Deaths: Preliminary data for 2009. *National Vital Statistics Report* 59(4).

The good news is that people have some control over whether they develop chronic diseases. People make choices every day that increase or decrease their risks for such diseases. These **lifestyle choices** include behaviors such as smoking, diet, exercise, and alcohol use. As Table 1.3 makes clear, lifestyle factors contribute to many deaths in the United States, and people can influence their own health risks. The need to make good choices is especially true for teens and young adults. For Americans age 15–24, for example, the top three causes of death are accidents, homicide, and suicide (Table 1.4).

The Healthy People Initiative

Wellness is a personal concern, but the U.S. government has financial and humanitarian interests in it, too.

A healthy population is the nation's source of vitality, creativity, and wealth. Poor health drains the nation's resources and raises health care costs for all.

The national Healthy People initiative aims to prevent disease and improve Americans' quality of life. Healthy People reports, published each decade since 1980, set national health goals based on 10-year agendas. The initiative's most recent iteration, *Healthy People 2020*, was developed in 2008–2009 and released to the public in 2010. *Healthy People 2020* envisions "a society in which all people

KEY TERM

lifestyle choice A conscious behavior that can increase or decrease a person's risk of disease or injury; such behaviors include smoking, exercising, eating a healthy diet, and others.

Fitness Tip

In Table 1.2, notice how many causes of death are related to lifestyle. This is an excellent motivator for adopting healthy habits and staying in good condition. Maintaining physical fitness and a healthy diet can lead to a longer life. It's a fact!

VITAL STATISTICS

Table 1.3 — Key Contributors to Death Among Americans

	NUMBER OF DEATHS PER YEAR	PERCENTAGE OF TOTAL DEATHS PER YEAR
Tobacco	440,000	18.1
Obesity*	112,000	4.6
Alcohol consumption	85,000	3.5
Microbial agents	75,000	3.1
Toxic agents	55,000	2.3
Motor vehicles	43,000	1.8
Firearms	29,000	1.2
Sexual behavior	20,000	0.8
Illicit drug use	17,000	0.7

NOTE: The factors listed here are defined as lifestyle and environmental factors that contribute to the leading killers of Americans (health experts often refer to these as the *actual causes of death*). Microbial agents include bacterial and viral infections like influenza and pneumonia; toxic agents include environmental pollutants and chemical agents such as asbestos.

*The number of deaths due to obesity is an area of ongoing controversy and research. Recent estimates have ranged from 112,000 to 365,000.

SOURCES: Centers for Disease Control and Prevention. 2005. *Frequently Asked Questions About Calculating Obesity-Related Risk.* Atlanta, Ga.: Centers for Disease Control and Prevention. Mokdad, A. H., et al. 2005. Correction: Actual causes of death in the United States, 2000. *Journal of the American Medical Association* 293(3): 293–294. Mokdad, A. H., et al. 2004. Actual causes of death in the United States, 2000. *Journal of the American Medical Association* 291(10): 1238–1245.

VITAL STATISTICS

Table 1.4 — Leading Causes of Death Among Americans Age 15–24, 2008

RANK	CAUSE OF DEATH	NUMBER OF DEATHS	PERCENTAGE OF TOTAL DEATHS
1	Accidents:	12,351	40.8
	Motor vehicle	7,648	25.2
	All other accidents	4,703	15.5
2	Homicide	4,820	15.9
3	Suicide	4,341	14.3
4	Cancer	1,659	5.4
5	Heart disease	1,010	3.3
	All causes	30,252	100.0

SOURCE: National Center for Health Statistics. 2011. Deaths: Preliminary data for 2009. *National Vital Statistics Report* 59(4).

live long, healthy lives" and proposes the eventual achievement of the following broad national health objectives:

• ***Eliminate preventable disease, disability, injury, and premature death.*** This objective involves activities such as taking more concrete steps to prevent diseases and injuries among individuals and groups, promoting healthy lifestyle choices, improving the nation's preparedness for emergencies, and strengthening the public health infrastructure.

• ***Achieve health equity, eliminate disparities, and improve the health of all groups.*** This objective involves identifying, measuring, and addressing health differences between individuals or groups that result from a social or economic disadvantage. (See the box "Wellness Issues for Diverse Populations.")

• ***Create social and physical environments that promote good health for all.*** This objective involves the use of health interventions at many different levels (such as anti-smoking campaigns by schools, workplaces, and local agencies), improving the situation of undereducated and poor Americans by providing a broader array of educational and job opportunities, and actively developing healthier living and natural environments for everyone.

• ***Promote healthy development and healthy behaviors across every stage of life.*** This goal involves taking a cradle-to-grave approach to health promotion by encouraging disease prevention and healthy behaviors in Americans of all ages.

In a shift from the past, *Healthy People 2020* emphasizes the importance of health determinants—factors that affect the health of individuals, demographic groups, or entire populations. Health determinants are social (including factors such as ethnicity, education level, and economic status) and environmental (including natural and human-made environments). Thus, one goal is to improve living conditions in ways that reduce the impact of negative health determinants.

Examples of individual health promotion goals from *Healthy People 2020,* along with estimates of how well Americans are tracking toward achieving those goals, appear in Table 1.5.

Behaviors That Contribute to Wellness

A lifestyle based on good choices and healthy behaviors maximizes quality of life. It helps people avoid disease, remain strong and fit, and maintain their physical and mental health as long as they live.

Be Physically Active The human body is designed to work best when it is active. It readily adapts to nearly any level of activity and exertion. **Physical fitness** is a set of physical attributes that allow the body to respond or adapt to the demands and stress of physical effort. The more we ask of our bodies, the stronger and more fit they become.

> **physical fitness** A set of physical attributes that allows the body to respond or adapt to the demands and stress of physical effort.

KEY TERM

Wellness Issues for Diverse Populations

When it comes to striving for wellness, most differences among people are insignificant. We all need to exercise, eat well, and manage stress. We all need to know how to protect ourselves from disease and injuries.

But some of our differences—both as individuals and as members of groups—have important implications for wellness. Some of us, for example, have grown up with eating habits that increase our risk of obesity or heart disease. Some of us have inherited predispositions for certain health problems, such as osteoporosis or high cholesterol levels. These health-related differences among individuals and groups can be biological (determined genetically) or cultural (acquired as patterns of behavior through daily interactions with family, community, and society). Many health conditions are a function of biology and culture combined.

Every person is an individual with her or his own unique genetic endowment as well as unique experiences in life. However, many of these influences are shared with others of similar genetic and cultural backgrounds. Information about group similarities relating to wellness issues can be useful. For example, it can alert people to areas that may be of special concern for them and their families.

Wellness-related differences among groups can be described along several dimensions, including the following:

- **Gender.** Men and women have different life expectancies and different incidences of many diseases, including heart disease, cancer, and osteoporosis. Men have higher rates of death from injuries, suicide, and homicide, whereas women are at greater risk for Alzheimer's disease and depression. Men and women also differ in body composition and certain aspects of physical performance.

- **Race and ethnicity.** A genetic predisposition for a particular health problem can be linked to race or ethnicity as a result of each group's relatively distinct history. Diabetes is more prevalent among individuals of Native American or Latino heritage, for example, and African Americans have higher rates of hypertension. Racial or ethnic groups may also vary in other ways that relate to wellness: traditional diets; patterns of family and interpersonal relationships; and attitudes toward using tobacco, alcohol, and other drugs, to name just a few.

- **Income and education.** Inequalities in income and education underlie many of the health disparities among Americans. People with low incomes (low *socioeconomic status*, or *SES*) and less education have higher rates of injury and many diseases, are more likely to smoke, and have less access to health care. Poverty and low educational attainment are far more important predictors of poor health than any racial or ethnic factor.

Table 1.5	Selected *Healthy People 2020* Objectives		
OBJECTIVE		ESTIMATE OF CURRENT STATUS*	GOAL*
Reduce the proportion of adults who engage in no leisure-time physical activity		36.2	32.6
Increase the proportion of adults who are at a healthy weight		30.8	33.9
Reduce tobacco use (cigarette smoking) among adults		20.6	12.0
Increase the proportion of adults with mental health disorders who receive treatment		58.7	64.6
Reduce the proportion of adults with hypertension		29.9	26.9
Increase the proportion of adults who get sufficient sleep		69.6	70.9
Reduce the proportion of adults who drank excessively in the previous 30 days		28.1	25.3
Increase the proportion of persons who use the Internet to communicate with their health care provider		13	15

*Percentage of adult Americans

SOURCE: U.S. Department of Health and Human Services. 2011. *Healthy People 2010* (http://www.healthypeople.gov; retrieved April 15, 2011).

How Active Are You?

How much of your leisure time do you spend doing nothing? It's easy to figure out: Just keep a simple log (like the one shown here) for a full week. Log the number of minutes of free time you have each day, and list your activities during those times. For our purposes, "free time" means exactly that; it doesn't include time you spend studying.

Day 1: _____   _____
                    (minutes)   (activities)

Day 2: _____   _____
                    (minutes)   (activities)

Day 3: _____   _____
                    (minutes)   (activities)

Day 4: _____   _____
                    (minutes)   (activities)

Day 5: _____   _____
                    (minutes)   (activities)

Day 6: _____   _____
                    (minutes)   (activities)

Day 7: _____   _____
                    (minutes)   (activities)

Based on this information, do you spend less than 30 minutes of your daily free time engaged in some type of physical activity? If so, look at your log and consider switching some of your current leisure-time activities for moderate-intensity exercise (like a brisk walk or a short bike ride).

Remember: you don't need to exercise for 30 minutes at a time to get the benefits of daily activity. You can break your exercise routine into three 10-minute chunks to make exercise fit your schedule and still enjoy all the health benefits of daily activity.

When our bodies are not kept active, however, they deteriorate. Bones lose their density, joints stiffen, muscles become weak, and cellular energy systems degenerate. To be truly well, human beings must be active.

Unfortunately, a **sedentary** lifestyle is common among Americans. According to recent estmates from the Healthy People program, fewer than one-third of adult Americans regularly engage in some sort of moderate physical activity. A recent study by the National Center for Health Statistics (NCHS) found that nearly 40% of adult Americans get no leisure-time activity at all.

The benefits of physical activity are both physical and mental, immediate and long term (Figure 1.4). In the short term, being physically fit makes it easier to do everyday tasks, such as lifting; it provides reserve strength for emergencies; and it helps people look and feel good. In the long term, being physically fit confers protection against chronic diseases and lowers the risk of dying prematurely. (See the box "Does Being Physically Active Make a Difference in How Long You Live?") Physically active people are less likely to develop or die from heart diease, respiratory disease, high blood pressure, cancer,

- Increased endurance, strength, and flexibility
- Healthier muscles, bones, and joints
- Increased energy (calorie) expenditure
- Improved body composition
- More energy
- Improved ability to cope with stress
- Improved mood, higher self-esteem, and a greater sense of well-being
- Improved ability to fall asleep and sleep well

- Reduced risk of dying prematurely from all causes
- Reduced risk of developing and/or dying from heart disease, diabetes, high blood pressure, and colon cancer
- Reduced risk of becoming obese
- Reduced anxiety, tension, and depression
- Reduced risk of falls and fractures
- Reduced spending for health care

FIGURE 1.4   Benefits of regular physical activity.

sedentary   Physically inactive; literally, "sitting."

KEY TERM

THE EVIDENCE FOR EXERCISE

Does Being Physically Active Make a Difference in How Long You Live?

How can we be sure that physical activity and exercise are good for our health? To answer this question, the U.S. Department of Health and Human Services asked a committee to review scientific literature. The committee's mission was to determine if enough evidence exists to warrant the government making physical activity recommendations to the public. The committee's report, the *Physical Activity Guidelines Advisory Committee Report, 2008*, summarizes the scientific evidence for the health benefits of regular physical activity and the risks of sedentary behavior. The report provides the rationale for the federal government's physical activity guidelines.

The committee started by asking whether physical activity actually helps people live longer. The committee investigated the link between physical activity and all-cause mortality—deaths from all causes—by looking at 73 studies dating from 1995 to 2008. The studies included men and women from all age groups (16 to 65 +) and from different racial and ethnic groups.

The data from these studies strongly support an *inverse relation* between physical activity and all-cause mortality; that is, physically active people were less likely to die during a study's follow-up period (ranging from 10 months to 28 years). The review found that active people have about a 30% lower risk of dying compared with inactive people. These inverse associations were found not just for healthy adults but also for older adults (age 65 and older), for people with coronary artery disease and diabetes, for people with impaired mobility, and for people who were overweight or obese. Poor fitness and low physical activity levels were found to be better predictors of premature death than smoking, diabetes, or obesity. Based on the evidence, the committee determined that about 150 minutes (2.5 hours) of physical activity per week is enough to reduce all-cause mortality (see Chapter 2 for more details). It appears that it is the overall volume of energy expended, no matter what kinds of activities are done, that makes a difference in risk of premature death.

The committee also looked at whether there is a *dose-response* relation between physical activity and all-cause mortality—that is, whether more activity reduces death rates even further. Again, the studies showed an inverse relation between these two variables. So, more activity above and beyond 150 minutes per week produces greater benefits. Surprisingly, for inactive people, benefits are seen at levels below 150 minutes per week. In fact, *any* increase in physical activity resulted in reduced risk of death. The committee refers to this as the "some is good; more is better" message. A target of 150 minutes per week is recommended, but any level of activity below the target is encouraged for inactive people.

Looking more closely at this relationship, the committee found that the greatest risk reduction is seen at the lower end of the physical activity spectrum (30 to 90 minutes per week). In fact, sedentary people who become more active have the greatest potential for improving health and reducing the risk of premature death. Additional risk reduction occurs as physical activity increases, but at a slower rate. For example, people who engaged in physical activity 90 minutes per week had a 20% reduction in mortality risk compared with inactive people, and those who were active 150 minutes per week, as noted earlier, had a 30% reduction in risk. But to achieve a 40% reduction in mortality risk, study participants had to be physically active 420 minutes per week (7 hours).

The message from the research is clear: It doesn't matter what activity you choose or even how much time you can devote to it per week, as long as you get moving!

SOURCE: Physical Activity Guidelines Advisory Committee. 2008. *Physical Activity Guidelines Advisory Committee Report, 2008*. Washington, D.C.: U.S. Department of Health and Human Services.

---

osteoporosis, and type 2 diabetes (the most common form of diabetes). As they get older, they may be able to avoid weight gain, muscle and bone loss, fatigue, and other problems associated with aging.

Choose a Healthy Diet In addition to being sedentary, many Americans have a diet that is too high in calories, unhealthy fats, and added sugars and too low in fiber, complex carbohydrates, fruits, and vegetables. Like physical inactivity, this diet is linked to a number of chronic diseases. A healthy diet provides necessary nutrients and

sufficient energy without also providing too much of the dietary substances linked to diseases.

Maintain a Healthy Body Weight Overweight and obesity are associated with a number of disabling and potentially fatal conditions and diseases, including heart disease, cancer, and type 2 diabetes. The Centers for Disease Control and Prevention (CDC) estimates that obesity kills 112,000 Americans each year. Healthy body weight is an important part of wellness—but short-term dieting is not part of fitness or wellness. Maintaining a healthy body

Wellness Tip

If you're overweight, losing as little as 5 pounds can significantly reduce your risk of developing diabetes. To learn more, visit the American Diabetes Association's Web site at http://www.diabetes.org.

Ask Yourself

QUESTIONS FOR CRITICAL THINKING AND REFLECTION

How often do you feel exuberant? Vital? Joyful? What makes you feel that way? Conversely, how often do you feel downhearted, de-energized, or depressed? What makes you feel that way? Have you ever thought about how you might increase experiences of vitality and decrease experiences of discouragement?

weight requires a lifelong commitment to regular exercise, a healthy diet, and effective stress management.

Manage Stress Effectively Many people cope with stress by eating, drinking, or smoking too much. Others don't deal with it at all. In the short term, inappropriate stress management can lead to fatigue, sleep disturbances, and other symptoms. Over longer periods of time, poor stress management can lead to less efficient functioning of the immune system and increased susceptibility to disease. Learning to incorporate effective stress management techniques into daily life is an important part of a fit and well lifestyle.

Avoid Tobacco and Drug Use and Limit Alcohol Consumption Tobacco use is associated with 8 of the top 10 causes of death in the United States; personal tobacco use and second-hand smoke kill about 440,000 Americans each year, more than any other behavioral or environmental factor. With 21% of adult Americans describing themselves as current smokers as of 2009, lung cancer is the most common cause of cancer death among both men and women and one of the leading causes of death overall. On average, the direct health care costs associated with smoking exceed $100 billion per year. If the cost of lost productivity from sickness, disability, and premature death is included, the total is closer to $193 billion.

Excessive alcohol consumption is linked to 6 of the top 10 causes of death and results in about 85,000 deaths a year in the United States. The social, economic, and medical costs of alcohol abuse are estimated at over $185 billion per year. Alcohol or drug intoxication is an especially notable factor in the death and disability of young people, particularly through **unintentional injuries** (such as drownings and car crashes caused by drunken driving) and violence.

Protect Yourself from Disease and Injury The most effective way of dealing with disease and injury is to prevent them. Many of the lifestyle strategies discussed here help protect you against chronic illnesses. In addition, you can take specific steps to avoid infectious diseases, particularly those that are sexually transmitted.

Take Other Steps Toward Wellness Other important behaviors contribute to wellness, including these:

- Developing meaningful relationships
- Planning for successful aging

- Learning about the health care system
- Acting responsibly toward the environment

Labs 1.1 and 1.2 will help you evaluate your behaviors as they relate to wellness.

The Role of Other Factors in Wellness

Heredity, the environment, and adequate health care are other important influences on health and wellness. These factors can interact in ways that raise or lower the quality of a person's life and the risk of developing particular diseases. For example, a sedentary lifestyle combined with a genetic predisposition for diabetes can greatly increase one's risk for developing the disease. If this person also lacks adequate health care, he or she is much more likely to suffer dangerous complications from diabetes.

But in many cases, behavior can tip the balance toward health even if heredity or environment is a negative factor. Breast cancer, for example, can run in families, but it is also associated with overweight and a sedentary lifestyle. A woman with a family history of breast cancer is less likely to die from the disease if she controls her weight, exercises, performs regular breast self-exams, and consults with her physician about mammograms.

REACHING WELLNESS THROUGH LIFESTYLE MANAGEMENT

As you consider this description of behaviors that contribute to wellness—being physically active, choosing a healthy diet, and so on—you may be doing a mental comparison with your own behaviors. If you are like most young adults, you probably have some healthy habits and some habits that place your health at risk. For example, you may be physically active and have a healthy diet but indulge in binge drinking on weekends. You may be careful to wear your seat belt in your car but smoke cigarettes or use chewing tobacco. Moving in the direction of

unintentional injury An injury that occurs without harm being intended.

wellness means cultivating healthy behaviors and working to overcome unhealthy ones. This approach to lifestyle management is called **behavior change.**

As you may already know from experience, changing an unhealthy habit can be harder than it sounds. When you embark on a behavior change plan, it may seem like too much work at first. But as you make progress, you will gain confidence in your ability to take charge of your life. You will also experience the benefits of wellness—more energy, greater vitality, deeper feelings of appreciation and curiosity, and a higher quality of life.

The rest of this chapter outlines a general process for changing unhealthy behaviors that is backed by research and that has worked for many people. You will also find many specific strategies and tips for change. For additional support, work through the activities in the Behavior Change Workbook at the end of the text.

Getting Serious About Your Health

Before you can start changing a wellness-related behavior, you have to know that the behavior is problematic and that you *can* change it. To make good decisions, you need information about relevant topics and issues, including what resources are available to help you change.

Examine Your Current Health Habits Have you considered how your current lifestyle is affecting your health today and how it will affect your health in the future? Do you know which of your current habits enhance your health and which ones may be harmful? Begin your journey toward wellness with self-assessment: Think about your own behavior, complete the self-assessment in Lab 1.2, and talk with friends and family members about what they've noticed about your lifestyle and your health.

> ### Wellness Tip
>
> When it comes to behavior change, you can win big by starting small, so pick a habit that will be easy to fix. Good examples are drinking more water every day or brushing your teeth for 2 minutes, twice a day. Each time you adopt a healthy new behavior, it's a stepping stone toward a bigger goal.

KEY TERMS

behavior change A lifestyle management process that involves cultivating healthy behaviors and working to overcome unhealthy ones.

target behavior An isolated behavior selected as the object of a behavior change program.

Choose a Target Behavior Changing any behavior can be demanding. This is why it's a good idea to start small, by choosing one behavior you want to change—called a **target behavior**—and working on it until you succeed. Your chances of success will be greater if your first goal is simple, such as resisting the urge to snack between classes. As you change one behavior, make your next goal a little more significant, and build on your success over time.

Learn About Your Target Behavior Once you've chosen a target behavior, you need to learn its risks and benefits for you—both now and in the future. Ask these questions:

- How is your target behavior affecting your level of wellness today?
- What diseases or conditions does this behavior place you at risk for?
- What effect would changing your behavior have on your health?

As a starting point, use this text and the resources listed in the For Further Exploration section at the end of

Certain health behaviors are exceptionally difficult to change. Some people can quit smoking on their own; others get help from a smoking cessation program or a nicotine replacement product.

Evaluating Sources of Health Information

Believability of Health Information Sources

Surveys indicate that college students are smart about evaluating health information. They trust the health information they receive from health professionals and educators and are skeptical about popular information sources, such as magazine articles and Web sites.

How smart are you about evaluating health information? Here are some tips.

General Strategies

Whenever you encounter health-related information, take the following steps to make sure it is credible:

● **Go to the original source.** Media reports often simplify the results of medical research. Find out for yourself what a study really reported, and determine whether it was based on good science. What type of study was it? Was it published in a recognized medical journal? Was it an animal study, or did it involve people? Did the study include a large number of people? What did the study's authors actually report?

● **Watch for misleading language.** Reports that tout "breakthroughs" or "dramatic proof" are probably hype. A study may state that a behavior "contributes to" or is "associated with" an outcome, but this does not prove a cause-and-effect relationship.

● **Distinguish between research reports and public health advice.** Do not change your behavior based on the results of a single report or study. If an agency such as the National Cancer Institute urges a behavior change, however, you should follow its advice. Large, publicly funded organizations issue such advice based on many studies, not a single report.

● **Remember that anecdotes are not facts.** A friend may tell you he lost weight on some new diet, but individual success stories do not mean the plan is truly safe or effective. Check with your doctor before making any serious lifestyle changes.

● **Be skeptical.** If a report seems too good to be true, it probably is. Be wary of information contained in advertisements. An ad's goal is to sell a product, even if there is no need for it, and sometimes even if the product has not been proven to be safe or effective.

● **Make choices that are right for you.** Friends and family members can be a great source of ideas and inspiration, but you need to make health-related choices that work best for you.

Internet Resources

Online information sources pose special challenges. When reviewing a health-related Web site, ask these questions:

● **What is the source of the information?** Web sites maintained by government agencies, professional associations, or established academic or medical institutions are likely to present trustworthy information. Many other groups and individuals post accurate information, but it is important to look at the qualifications of the people who are behind the site. (Check the home page or click the "About Us" link.)

● **How often is the site updated?** Look for sites that are updated frequently. Check the "last modified" date of any Web page.

● **Is the site promotional?** Be wary of information from sites that sell specific products, use testimonials as evidence, appear to have a social or political agenda, or ask for money.

● **What do other sources say about a topic?** Be wary of claims and information that appear at only one site or come from a chat room, bulletin board, or blog.

● **Does the site conform to any set of guidelines or criteria for quality and accuracy?** Look for sites that identify themselves as conforming to some code or set of principles, such as those set forth by the Health on the Net Foundation or the American Medical Association. These codes include criteria such as use of information from respected sources and disclosure of the site's sponsors.

---

each chapter; see the box "Evaluating Sources of Health Information" for additional guidelines.

Find Help Have you identified a particularly challenging target behavior or mood—something like alcohol addiction, binge eating, or depression—that interferes with your ability to function or places you at a serious health risk? Help may be needed to change behaviors or conditions that are too deeply rooted or too serious for self-management. Don't be discouraged by the seriousness or extent of the problem; many resources are available to help you solve it. On campus, the student health center or campus counseling center can provide assistance. To locate community resources, consult the yellow pages, your physician, or the Internet.

Building Motivation to Change

Knowledge is necessary for behavior change, but it isn't usually enough to make people act. Millions of people have sedentary lifestyles, for example, even though they know it's bad for their health. This is particularly true of young adults, who may not be motivated to change because they feel healthy in spite of their unhealthy behaviors (see the box "Wellness Matters for College Students"). To succeed at behavior change, you need strong motivation.

Wellness Matters for College Students

If you are like most college students, you probably feel pretty good about your health right now. Most college students are in their late teens or early twenties, lead active lives, have plenty of friends, and look forward to a future filled with opportunity. With all these things going for you, why shouldn't you feel good?

A Closer Look

Although most college-age people look healthy, appearances can be deceiving. Each year, thousands of students lose productive academic time to physical and emotional health problems—some of which can continue to plague them for life.

The following table shows the top 10 health issues affecting students' academic performance, according to the Fall 2010 American College Health Association National College Health Assessment II.

HEALTH ISSUE	STUDENTS AFFECTED (%)
Stress	25.4
Sleep difficulties	17.8
Anxiety	16.4
Cold/flu/sore throat	13.8
Internet use/computer games	11.6
Work	11.4
Concern for a friend/family member	10.1
Depression	10.0
Relationship difficulties	9.6
Extracurricular activities	8.8

Each of these issues is related to one or more of the six dimensions of wellness, and most can be influenced by choices students make daily. Although some troubles—such as the death of a friend—cannot be controlled, other physical and emotional concerns can be minimized by choosing healthy behaviors. For example, there are many ways to manage stress, the top health issue affecting students. By reducing unhealthy choices (such as using alcohol to relax) and by increasing healthy choices (such as using time management techniques), even busy students can reduce the impact of stress on their life.

The survey also estimated that, based on students' reporting of their height and weight, more than 33% of college students are either overweight or obese. Although heredity plays a role in determining one's weight, lifestyle is also a factor in weight and weight management. In many studies over the past few decades, a large percentage of students have reported behaviors such as these:

- Overeating
- Snacking on junk food
- Frequently eating high-fat foods
- Using alcohol and binge drinking

Clearly, eating behaviors are often a matter of choice. Although students may not see (or feel) the effects of their dietary habits today, the long-term health risks are significant. Overweight and obese persons run a higher-than-normal risk of developing diabetes, heart disease, and cancer later in life. We now know with certainty that improving one's eating habits, even a little, can lead to weight loss and improved overall health.

Other Choices, Other Problems

Students commonly make other unhealthy choices. Here are some examples from the Fall 2010 National College Health Assessment II:

- About 50% of students reported that they did not use a contraceptive the last time they had vaginal intercourse.

- About 16% of students had 7 or more drinks the last time they partied.

- Almost 15% of students had smoked cigarettes at least once during the past month.

What choices do you make in these situations? Remember: It's never too late to change. The sooner you trade an unhealthy behavior for a healthy one, the longer you'll be around to enjoy the benefits.

SOURCE: American College Health Association. 2011. *American College Health Association National College Health Assessment II: Reference Group Executive Summary Fall 2010.* Linthicum, Md.: American College Health Association.

Examine the Pros and Cons of Change Health behaviors have short-term and long-term benefits and costs. Consider the benefits and costs of an inactive lifestyle:

- Short-term, such a lifestyle allows you more time to watch TV and hang out with friends, but it leaves you less physically fit and less able to participate in recreational activities.

- Long-term, it increases the risk of heart disease, cancer, stroke, and premature death.

To successfully change your behavior, you must believe that the benefits of change outweigh the costs.

Carefully examine the pros and cons of continuing your current behavior and of changing to a healthier one. Focus on the effects that are most meaningful to you, including those that are tied to your personal identity and values. For example, if you see yourself as an active person who is a good role model for others, then adopting behaviors such as engaging in regular physical activity and getting adequate sleep will support your personal identity.

If you value independence and control over your life, then quitting smoking will be consistent with your values and goals. To complete your analysis, ask friends and family members about the effects of your behavior on them. For example, a younger sister may tell you that your smoking habit influenced her decision to take up smoking.

The short-term benefits of behavior change can be an important motivating force. Although some people are motivated by long-term goals, such as avoiding a disease that may hit them in 30 years, most are more likely to be moved to action by shorter-term, more personal goals. Feeling better, doing better in school, improving at a sport, reducing stress, and increasing self-esteem are common short-term benefits of health behavior change. Many wellness behaviors are associated with immediate improvements in quality of life. For example, surveys of Americans have found that nonsmokers feel healthy and full of energy more days each month than do smokers, and they report fewer days of sadness and troubled sleep. The same is true when physically active people are compared with sedentary people. Over time, these types of differences add up to a substantially higher quality of life for people who engage in healthy behaviors.

Boost Self-Efficacy When you start thinking about changing a health behavior, a big factor in your eventual success is whether you have confidence in yourself and in your ability to change. **Self-efficacy** refers to your belief in your ability to successfully take action and perform a specific task. Strategies for boosting self-efficacy include developing an internal locus of control, using visualization and self-talk, and getting encouragement from supportive people.

LOCUS OF CONTROL Who do you believe is controlling your life? Is it your parents, friends, or school? Is it "fate"? Or is it you? **Locus of control** refers to the figurative "place" a person designates as the source of responsibility for the events in his or her life. People who believe they are in control of their own lives are said to have an *internal locus of control*. Those who believe that factors beyond their control determine the course of their lives are said to have an *external locus of control*.

For lifestyle management, an internal locus of control is an advantage because it reinforces motivation and commitment. An external locus of control can sabotage efforts to change behavior. For example, if you believe that you are destined to die of breast cancer because your mother died from the disease, you may view monthly breast self-exams and regular checkups as a waste of time. In contrast, if you believe that you can take action to reduce your risk of breast cancer in spite of hereditary factors, you will be motivated to follow guidelines for early detection of the disease.

If you find yourself attributing too much influence to outside forces, gather more information about your wellness-related behaviors. List all the ways that making lifestyle changes will improve your health. If you believe

Fitness Tip

Visualization is such a powerful technique that Olympic athletes learn how to harness it for peak performance. It works for average people, too. Set a small fitness goal, then imagine yourself doing it—as clearly and as often as you can. Visualization can help you believe in yourself, and belief can be a step toward success!

you'll succeed, and if you recognize that you are in charge of your life, you're on your way to wellness.

VISUALIZATION AND SELF-TALK One of the best ways to boost your confidence and self-efficacy is to visualize yourself successfully engaging in a new, healthier behavior. Imagine yourself going for an afternoon run 3 days a week or no longer smoking cigarettes. Also visualize yourself enjoying all the short-term and long-term benefits that your lifestyle change will bring. Create a new self-image: What will you and your life be like when you become a regular exerciser or a nonsmoker?

You can also use **self-talk,** the internal dialogue you carry on with yourself, to increase your confidence in your ability to change. Counter any self-defeating patterns of thought with more positive or realistic thoughts: "I am a strong, capable person, and I can maintain my commitment to change." See Chapter 10 for more on self-talk.

ROLE MODELS AND OTHER SUPPORTIVE INDIVIDUALS Social support can make a big difference in your level of motivation and your chances of success. Perhaps you know people who have reached the goal you are striving for; they could be role models or mentors for you, providing information and support for your efforts. Gain strength from their experiences, and tell yourself, "If they can do it, so can I." In addition, find a buddy who wants to make the same changes you do and who can take an active role in your behavior change program. For example, an exercise buddy can provide companionship and encouragement when you might be tempted to skip your workout.

Identify and Overcome Barriers to Change Don't let past failures at behavior change discourage you; they can be a great source of information you can use to boost your chances of future success. Make a list of the problems and challenges you faced in any previous behavior change attempts. To this list, add the short-term costs of behavior

self-efficacy The belief in one's ability to take action and perform a specific task.

locus of control The figurative "place" a person designates as the source of responsibility for the events in his or her life.

self-talk A person's internal dialogue.

KEY TERMS

change that you identified in your analysis of the pros and cons of change. Once you've listed these key barriers to change, develop a practical plan for overcoming each one. For example, if you always smoke when you're with certain friends, decide in advance how you will turn down the next cigarette you are offered.

Enhancing Your Readiness to Change

The transtheoretical, or "stages-of-change," model is an effective approach to lifestyle self-management. According to this model, you move through distinct stages as you work to change your target behavior. It is important to determine what stage you are in now so that you can choose appropriate strategies for progressing through the cycle of change. This approach can help you enhance your readiness and intention to change. Read the following sections to determine what stage you are in for your target behavior. For ideas on changing stages, see the box "Tips for Moving Forward in the Cycle of Behavior Change."

Precontemplation People at this stage do not think they have a problem and do not intend to change their behavior. They may be unaware of the risks associated with their behavior or may deny them. They may have tried unsuccessfully to change in the past and may now think the situation is hopeless. They may also blame other people or external factors for their problems. People in the precontemplation stage believe that there are more reasons or more important reasons not to change than there are reasons to change.

Contemplation People at this stage know they have a problem and intend to take action within 6 months. They acknowledge the benefits of behavior change but are also aware of the costs of changing. To be successful, people must believe that the benefits of change outweigh the costs. People in the contemplation stage wonder about possible courses of action but don't know how to proceed. There may also be specific barriers to change that appear too difficult to overcome.

Preparation People at this stage plan to take action within a month or may already have begun to make small changes in their behavior. They may be engaging in their new, healthier behavior but not yet regularly or consistently. They may have created a plan for change but may be worried about failing.

Action During the action stage, people outwardly modify their behavior and their environment. The action stage requires the greatest commitment of time and energy, and people in this stage are at risk for reverting to old, unhealthy patterns of behavior.

Maintenance People at this stage have maintained their new, healthier lifestyle for at least 6 months. Lapses may have occurred, but people in maintenance have been successful in quickly reestablishing the desired behavior. The maintenance stage can last for months or years.

Termination For some behaviors, a person may reach the sixth and final stage of termination. People at this stage have exited the cycle of change and are no longer tempted to lapse back into their old behavior. They have a new self-image and total self-efficacy with regard to their target behavior.

Dealing with Relapse

People seldom progress through the stages of change in a straightforward, linear way. Rather, they tend to move to a certain stage and then slip back to a previous stage before resuming their forward progress. Research suggests that most people make several attempts before they successfully change a behavior; 4 out of 5 people experience some degree of backsliding. For this reason, the stages of change are best conceptualized as a spiral, in which people cycle back through previous stages but are farther along in the process each time they renew their commitment (Figure 1.5).

If you experience a lapse—a single slip—or a relapse—a return to old habits—don't give up. Relapse can be demoralizing, but it is not the same as failure. Failure means stopping before you reach your goal and never changing your target behavior. During the early stages of

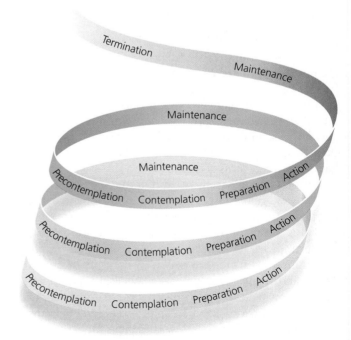

FIGURE 1.5 The stages of change: A spiral model.
SOURCE: Adapted from Prochaska, J. O., C. C. Diclemente, and J. C. Norcross. 1992. In search of how people change. *American Psychologist* 47(9): 1102–1114. Copyright © 1992 by the American Psychological Association. Reprinted by permission.

Tips for Moving Forward in the Cycle of Behavior Change

Precontemplation

● **Raise your awareness.** Research your target behavior and its effects.

● **Be self-aware.** Look at the mechanisms you use to resist change, such as denial or rationalization. Find ways to counteract these mechanisms.

● **Seek social support.** Friends and family members can help you identify target behaviors and understand their impact on the people around you.

● **Identify helpful resources.** These might include exercise classes or stress-management workshops offered by your school.

Contemplation

● **Keep a journal.** A record of your target behavior and the circumstances that elicit the behavior can help you plan a change program.

● **Do a cost-benefit analysis.** Identify the costs and benefits (both current and future) of maintaining your behavior and of changing it. Costs can be monetary, social, emotional, and so on.

● **Identify barriers to change.** Knowing these obstacles can help you overcome them.

● **Engage your emotions.** Watch movies or read books about people with your target behavior. Imagine what your life will be like if you don't change.

● **Create a new self-image.** Imagine what you'll be like after changing your target behavior. Try to think of yourself in new terms right now.

● **Think before you act.** Learn why you engage in the target behavior. Determine what "sets you off," and train yourself not to act reflexively.

Preparation

● **Create a plan.** Include a start date, goals, rewards, and specific steps you will take to change your behavior.

● **Make change a priority.** Create and sign a contract with yourself.

● **Practice visualization and self-talk.** These techniques can help prepare you mentally for challenging situations.

● **Take short steps.** Successfully practicing your new behavior for a short time—even a single day—can boost your confidence and motivation.

Action

● **Monitor your progress.** Keep up with your journal entries.

● **Change your environment.** Make changes that will discourage the target behavior—for example, getting rid of snack foods or not stocking the refrigerator with beer.

● **Find alternatives to your target behavior.** Make a list of things you can do to replace the behavior.

● **Reward yourself.** Rewards should be identified in your change plan. Give yourself lots of praise, and focus on your success.

● **Involve your friends.** Tell them you want to change, and ask for their help.

● **Don't get discouraged.** Real change is difficult.

Maintenance

● **Keep going.** Continue using the positive strategies that worked in earlier stages.

● **Be prepared for lapses.** Don't let slip-ups set you back.

● **Be a role model.** Once you have successfully changed your behavior, you may be able to help someone else do the same thing.

---

the change process, it's a good idea to plan for relapse so you can avoid guilt and self-blame and get back on track quickly. Follow these steps:

1. **Forgive yourself.** A single setback isn't the end of the world, but abandoning your efforts to change could have negative effects on your life.

2. **Give yourself credit for the progress you have already made**. You can use that success as motivation to continue.

3. **Move on.** You can learn from a relapse and use that knowledge to deal with potential setbacks in the future.

If relapses keep occurring or if you can't seem to control them, you may need to return to a previous stage of the behavior change process. If this is necessary, reevaluate your goals and your strategy. A different or less stressful approach may help you avoid setbacks when you try again.

Developing Skills for Change: Creating a Personalized Plan

Once you are committed to making a change, it's time to put together a plan of action. Your key to success is a well-thought-out plan that sets goals, anticipates problems, and includes rewards.

Picking Target Behaviors

When starting out on any behavior change plan, the hardest part can be deciding what behavior you want to change. But it doesn't have to be hard; as mentioned in the chapter, you'll probably have the greatest success if you start small. Use the following list to identify five health-related behaviors that you would like to change. List them in order, starting with the behavior you think would be easiest to change and ending with the most difficult.

1. _____

2. _____

3. _____

4. _____

5. _____

The real challenge of this activity is thinking. Examine your lifestyle thoroughly, and consider the things you do (or don't do) every day that may be having a negative effect on your health or wellness. Don't worry if it takes some time to come up with a list, and don't be surprised if you shuffle the items around a few times. The goal is to come up with a list that is doable and realistic for you.

1. Monitor Your Behavior and Gather Data Keep a record of your target behavior and the circumstances surrounding it. Record this information for at least a week or two. Keep your notes in a health journal or notebook or on your computer (see the sample journal entries in Figure 1.6). Record each occurrence of your behavior, noting the following:

• What the activity was

• When and where it happened

• What you were doing

• How you felt at that time

If your goal is to start an exercise program, track your activities to determine how to make time for workouts. A blank log is provided in Activity 3 in the Behavior Change Workbook at the end of this text.

2. Analyze the Data and Identify Patterns After you have collected data on the behavior, analyze the data to identify patterns. When are you most likely to overeat? What events trigger your appetite? Perhaps you are especially hungry at midmorning or when you put off eating dinner until 9:00 P.M. Perhaps you overindulge in food and drink when you go to a particular restaurant or when you're with certain friends. Note the connections between your feelings and such external cues as time of day, location, situation, and the actions of others around you.

3. Be "SMART" About Setting Goals If your goals are too challenging, you will have trouble making steady progress and will be more likely to give up altogether. If, for example, you are in poor physical condition, it will not make

sense to set a goal of being ready to run a marathon within 2 months. If you set goals you can live with, it will be easier to stick with your behavior change plan and be successful.

Experts suggest that your goals meet the "SMART" criteria. That is, your behavior change goals should be:

• *Specific.* Avoid vague goals like "eat more fruits and vegetables." Instead, state your objectives in specific terms, such as "eat 2 cups of fruit and 3 cups of vegetables every day."

• *Measurable.* Recognize that your progress will be easier to track if your goals are quantifiable, so give your goal a number. You might measure your goal in terms of time (such as "walk briskly for 20 minutes a day"), distance ("run 2 miles, 3 days per week"), or some other amount ("drink 8 glasses of water every day").

• *Attainable.* Set goals that are within your physical limits. For example, if you are a poor swimmer, it might not be possible for you to meet a short-term fitness goal by swimming laps. Walking or biking might be better options.

• *Realistic.* Manage your expectations when you set goals. For example, it may not be possible for a long-time smoker to quit cold turkey. A more realistic approach might be to use nicotine replacement patches or gum for several weeks while getting help from a support group.

• *Time frame–specific.* Give yourself a reasonable amount of time to reach your goal, state the time frame in your behavior change plan, and set your agenda to meet the goal within the given time frame.

Using these criteria, a sedentary person who wants to improve his health and build fitness might set a goal of being able to run 3 miles in 30 minutes, to be achieved within a time frame of 6 months. To work toward that goal, he might set a number of smaller, intermediate goals that are easier to achieve. For example, his list of goals might look like this:

WEEK	FREQUENCY (DAYS/WEEK)	ACTIVITY	DURATION (MINUTES)
1	3	Walk < 1 mile	10–15
2	3	Walk 1 mile	15–20
3	4	Walk 1–2 miles	20–25
4	4	Walk 2–3 miles	25–30
5–7	3–4	Walk/run 1 mile	15–20
~			
21–24	4–5	Run 2–3 miles	25–30

Of course, it may not be possible to meet these goals, but you never know until you try. As you work toward meeting your long-term goal, you may find it necessary to adjust your short-term goals. For example, you may find that you can start running sooner than you thought, or you may be able to run farther than you originally estimated. In such cases, it may be reasonable to make your goals more challenging. Otherwise, you may want to make them easier in order to stay motivated.

For some goals and situations, it may make more sense to focus on something other than your outcome goal. If you are in an early stage of change, for example, your goal may be to learn more about the risks associated with your target behavior or to complete a cost-benefit analysis. If your goal involves a long-term lifestyle change, such as reaching a healthy weight, it is better to focus on developing healthy habits than to target a specific weight loss. Your goal in this case might be exercising for 30 minutes every day, reducing portion sizes, or eliminating late-night snacks.

Your environment contains powerful cues for both positive and negative lifestyle choices. The presence of parks and running/bike paths encourages physical activity, even in an urban setting.

4. Devise a Plan of Action Develop a strategy that will support your efforts to change. Your plan of action should include the following steps:

- *Get what you need.* Identify resources that can help you. For example, you can join a community walking club or sign up for a smoking cessation program. You may also need to buy some new running shoes or nicotine replacement patches. Get the items you need right away; waiting can delay your progress.
- *Modify your environment.* If there are cues in your environment that trigger your target behavior, try to control them. For example, if you normally have alcohol at home, getting rid of it can help prevent you from indulging. If you usually study with a group of friends in an environment that allows smoking, try moving to a nonsmoking area. If you always buy a snack at a certain vending machine, change your route to avoid it.

Date	November 5			Day	M	TU	W	TH	F	SA	SU			
Time of day	M/S	Food eaten	Cals.	H	Where did you eat?	What else were you doing?	How did someone else influence you?	What made you want to eat what you did?	Emotions and feelings?	Thoughts and concerns?
7:30	M	1 C Crispix cereal 1/2 C skim milk coffee, black 1 C orange juice	110 40 — 120	3	home	reading newspaper	alone	I always eat cereal in the morning	a little keyed up & worried	thinking about quiz in class today
10:30	S	1 apple	90	1	hall outside classroom	studying	alone	felt tired & wanted to wake up	tired	worried about next class
12:30	M	1 C chili 1 roll 1 pat butter 1 orange 2 oatmeal cookies 1 soda	290 120 35 60 120 150	2	campus food court	talking	eating w/ friends; we decided to eat at the food court	wanted to be part of group	excited and happy	interested in hearing everyone's plans for the weekend
	M/S = Meal or snack			H = Hunger rating (0–3)						

FIGURE 1.6 Sample health journal entries.

• **Control related habits.** You may have habits that contribute to your target behavior; modifying these habits can help change the behavior. For example, if you usually plop down on the sofa while watching TV, try putting an exercise bike in front of the set so you can burn calories while watching your favorite programs.

• **Reward yourself.** Giving yourself instant, real rewards for good behavior will reinforce your efforts. Plan your rewards; decide in advance what each one will be and how you will earn it. Tie rewards to achieving specific goals or subgoals. For example, you might treat yourself to a movie after a week of avoiding snacks. Make a list of items or events to use as rewards. They should be special to you and preferably unrelated to food or alcohol.

• **Involve the people around you.** Tell family and friends about your plan, and ask them to help. To help them respond appropriately to your needs, create a specific list of dos and don'ts. For example, ask them to support you when you set aside time to exercise or avoid second helpings at dinner.

• **Plan for challenges.** Think about situations and people that might derail your program, and develop ways to cope with them. For example, if you think it will be hard to stick to your usual exercise program during exams, schedule short bouts of physical activity (such as a brisk walk) as stress-reducing study breaks.

5. Make a Personal Contract A serious personal contract—one that commits you to your word—can result in a higher chance of follow-through than a casual, offhand promise. Your contract can help prevent procrastination by specifying important dates and can also serve as a reminder of your personal commitment to change.

Your contract should include a statement of your goal and your commitment to reaching it. The contract should also include details, such as the following:

- The date you will start
- The steps you will take to measure your progress
- The strategies you plan to use to promote change
- The date you expect to reach your final goal

Have someone—preferably someone who will be actively helping you with your program—sign your contract as a witness.

Figure 1.7 shows a sample behavior change contract for someone committing to eating more fruit every day. A blank contract is included as Activity 8 in the Behavior Change Workbook at the end of this text.

Putting Your Plan into Action

The starting date has arrived, and you are ready to put your plan into action. This stage requires commitment, the resolve to stick with the plan no matter what temptations you encounter. Remember all the reasons you have to make the change—and remember that *you* are the boss. Use all

Behavior Change Contract

1. I, __Tammy Lau__, agree to __increase my consumption of fruit from 1 cup per week to 2 cups per day.__

2. I will begin on ___10/5___ and plan to reach my goal of __2 cups of fruit per day__ by __12/7__

3. To reach my final goal, I have devised the following schedule of mini-goals. For each step in my program, I will give myself the reward listed.

I will begin to have ½ cup of fruit with breakfast	10/5	see movie
I will begin to have ½ cup of fruit with lunch	10/26	new cd
I will begin to substitute fruit juice for soda 1 time per day	11/16	concert

   My overall reward for reaching my goal will be __trip to beach__

4. I have gathered and analyzed data on my target behavior and have identified the following strategies for changing my behavior: __Keep the fridge stocked with easy-to-carry fruit. Pack fruit in my backpack every day. Buy lunch at place that serves fruit.__

5. I will use the following tools to monitor my progress toward my final goal: __Chart on fridge door__ __Health journal__

   I sign this contract as an indication of my personal commitment to reach my goal: ___Tammy Lau___ ___9/28___

   I have recruited a helper who will witness my contract and __also increase his consumption of fruit; eat lunch with me twice a week.__
   ___Eric March___ ___9/28___

FIGURE 1.7 A sample behavior change contract.

your strategies to make your plan work. Make sure your environment is change-friendly, and get as much support and encouragement from others as possible. Keep track of your progress in your health journal, and give yourself regular rewards. And don't forget to give yourself a pat on the back—congratulate yourself, notice how much better you look or feel, and feel good about how far you've come and how you've gained control of your behavior.

Staying with It

As you continue with your program, don't be surprised when you run up against obstacles; they're inevitable. In fact, it's a good idea to expect problems and give yourself time to step back, see how you're doing, and make some changes before going on. If your program is grinding to a halt, identify what is blocking your progress. It may come from one of the sources described in the following sections.

Social Influences Take a hard look at the reactions of the people you're counting on, and see if they're really supporting you. If they come up short, connect with others who will be more supportive.

A related trap is trying to get your friends or family members to change *their* behaviors. The decision to make a major behavior change is something people come to only after intensive self-examination. You may be able to influence someone by tactfully providing facts or support, but that's all. Focus on yourself. When you succeed, you may become a role model for others.

Levels of Motivation and Commitment You won't make real progress until an inner drive leads you to the stage of change at which you are ready to make a personal commitment to the goal. If commitment is your problem, you may need to wait until the behavior you're dealing with makes you unhappier or unhealthier; then your desire to change it will be stronger. Or you may find that changing your goal will inspire you to keep going. For more ideas, refer to Activity 9 in the Behavior Change Workbook.

Choice of Techniques and Level of Effort If your plan is not working as well as you thought it would, make changes where you're having the most trouble. If you've lagged on your running schedule, for example, maybe it's because you don't like running. An aerobics class might suit you better. There are many ways to move toward your goal. Or you may not be trying hard enough. You do have to push toward your goal. If it were easy, you wouldn't need a plan.

Stress Barrier If you hit a wall in your program, look at the sources of stress in your life. If the stress is temporary, such as catching a cold or having a term paper due, you may want to wait until it passes before strengthening your efforts. If the stress is ongoing, find healthy ways to manage it (see Chapter 10). You may even want to make stress management your highest priority for behavior change.

Procrastinating, Rationalizing, and Blaming Be alert to games you might be playing with yourself, so you can stop them. Such games include the following:

• *Procrastinating.* If you tell yourself, "It's Friday already; I might as well wait until Monday to start," you're procrastinating. Break your plan into smaller steps that you can accomplish one day at a time.
• *Rationalizing.* If you tell yourself, "I wanted to go swimming today but wouldn't have had time to wash my hair afterward," you're making excuses.
• *Blaming.* If you tell yourself, "I couldn't exercise because Dave was hogging the elliptical trainer," you're blaming others for your own failure to follow through. Blaming is a way of taking your focus off the real problem and denying responsibility for your own actions.

Being Fit and Well for Life

Your first attempts at making behavior changes may never go beyond the contemplation or preparation stage. Those that do may not all succeed. But as you experience some success, you'll start to have more positive feelings about yourself. You may discover new physical activities and sports you enjoy, and you may encounter new situations and meet new people. Perhaps you'll surprise yourself by accomplishing things you didn't think were possible—breaking a long-standing nicotine habit, competing in a race, climbing a mountain, or developing a leaner body. Most of all, you'll discover the feeling of empowerment that comes from taking charge of your health. Being healthy takes effort, but the paybacks in energy and vitality are priceless.

Once you've started, don't stop. Assume that health improvement is forever. Take on the easier problems first, and then use what you learn to tackle more difficult problems later. When you feel challenged, remind yourself that you are creating a lifestyle that minimizes your health risks and maximizes your enjoyment of life. You *can* take charge of your health in a dramatic and meaningful way. *Fit and Well* will show you how.

Ask Yourself

QUESTIONS FOR CRITICAL THINKING AND REFLECTION

Think about the last time you made an unhealthy choice instead of a healthy one. How could you have changed the situation, the people in the situation, or your own thoughts, feelings, or intentions to avoid making that choice? What can you do in similar situations in the future to produce a different outcome?

TIPS FOR TODAY AND THE FUTURE

You are in charge of your health. Many of the decisions you make every day have an impact on the quality of your life, both now and in the future.

RIGHT NOW YOU CAN
■ Go for a 15-minute walk.
■ Have a piece of fruit for a snack.
■ Call a friend and arrange for a time to catch up with each other.
■ Start thinking about whether you have a health behavior you'd like to change. If you do, consider the elements of a behavior change strategy. For example, begin a mental list of the pros and cons of the behavior, or talk to someone who can support you in your attempts to change.

IN THE FUTURE YOU CAN
■ Stay current on health- and wellness-related news and issues.
■ Participate in health awareness and promotion campaigns in your community—for example, support smoking restrictions in local venues.
■ Be a role model for someone else who is working on a health behavior you have successfully changed.

- Wellness is the ability to live life fully, with vitality and meaning. Wellness is dynamic and multidimensional; it incorporates physical, emotional, intellectual, spiritual, interpersonal, and environmental dimensions.

- People today have greater control over and greater responsibility for their health than ever before.

- Behaviors that promote wellness include being physically active, choosing a healthy diet, maintaining a healthy body weight, managing stress effectively, avoiding tobacco and limiting alcohol use, and protecting yourself from disease and injury.

- Although heredity, environment, and health care all play roles in wellness and disease, behavior can mitigate their effects.

- To make lifestyle changes, you need information about yourself, your health habits, and resources available to help you change.

- You can increase your motivation for behavior change by examining the benefits and costs of change, boosting self-efficacy, and identifying and overcoming key barriers to change.

- The stages-of-change model describes six stages that people may move through as they try to change their behavior: precontemplation, contemplation, preparation, action, maintenance, and termination.

- A specific plan for change can be developed by (1) collecting data on your behavior and recording it in a journal; (2) analyzing the recorded data; (3) setting specific goals; (4) devising strategies for modifying the environment, rewarding yourself, and involving others; and (5) making a personal contract.

- To start and maintain a behavior change program, you need commitment, a well-developed and manageable plan, social support, and strong stress-management techniques. It is also important to monitor the progress of your program, revising it as necessary.

FOR FURTHER EXPLORATION

BOOKS

American Medical Association. 2006. *American Medical Association Concise Medical Encyclopedia.* New York: Random House. *Includes more than 3000 entries on health and wellness topics, symptoms, conditions, and treatments.*

Claiborn, J., and C. Pedrick. 2009. *The Habit Change Workbook: How to Break Bad Habits and Form Good Ones.* Oakland, Ca.: New Harbinger Publications. *Provides step-by-step instructions for identifying and overcoming a variety of unhealthy behaviors, such as poor eating habits, reluctance to exercise, and addictive behavior.*

Komaroff, A. L., ed. 2005. *Harvard Medical School Family Health Guide.* New York: Free Press. *Provides consumer-oriented advice for the prevention and treatment of common health concerns.*

Krueger, H., et al. 2007. *The Health Impact of Smoking and Obesity and What to Do About It.* Toronto: University of Toronto Press. *Examines the effects of smoking and sedentary lifestyle, the costs to individuals and society, and strategies for overcoming these behaviors.*

Litin, S. C., ed. 2009. *Mayo Clinic Family Health Book,* 4th ed. New York: HarperCollins Publishers. *A complete health reference for every stage of life, covering thousands of conditions, symptoms, and treatments.*

Murat, B., and G. Stewart. 2009. *Do I Need to See the Doctor? The Home-Treatment Encyclopedia—Written by Medical Doctors—That Lets You Decide,* 2nd ed. New York: John Wiley & Sons. *Fully illustrated, easy-to-read guide to hundreds of common symptoms and ailments, designed to help consumers determine whether they can treat themselves or should seek professional medical attention.*

NEWSLETTERS

Center for Science in the Public Interest Nutrition Action Health Letter
(http://www.cspinet.org/nah/index.htm)
Consumer Reports on Health (800-274-7596;
http://www.consumerreports.org/oh/index.htm)
Harvard Health Publications (877-649-9457;
http://www.health.harvard.edu)
Harvard Men's Health Watch (877-649-9457)
Harvard Women's Health Watch (877-649-9457)
Mayo Clinic Health Letter (800-291-1128)
Tufts University Health & Nutrition Newsletter
(http://www.tuftshealthletter.com)
University of California at Berkeley Wellness Letter
(800-829-9170; http://www.wellnessletter.com)

ORGANIZATIONS, HOTLINES, AND WEB SITES

The Internet addresses listed here were accurate at the time of publication.
Centers for Disease Control and Prevention. Through phone, fax, and the Internet, the CDC provides a wide variety of health information.
http://www.cdc.gov
Federal Trade Commission: Consumer Protection—Health. Includes online brochures about a variety of consumer health topics, including fitness equipment, generic drugs, and fraudulent health claims.
http://www.ftc.gov/bcp/menus/consumer/health.shtm
FirstGov for Consumers: Health. Provides links to online brochures from a variety of government agencies.
http://consumer.gov/ncpw/category/health
Healthfinder. A gateway to online publications, Web sites, support and self-help groups, and agencies and organizations that produce reliable health information.
http://www.healthfinder.gov
Healthy Campus. The American College Health Association's introduction to the Healthy Campus program.
http://www.acha.org/info_resources/hc2010.cfm
Healthy People. Provides information on Healthy People objectives and priority areas.
http://www.healthypeople.gov
MedlinePlus. Provides links to news and reliable information about health from government agencies and professional associations; also includes a health encyclopedia and information on prescription and over-the-counter drugs.
http://www.medlineplus.gov

National Health Information Center (NHIC). Puts consumers in touch with the organizations that are best able to provide answers to health-related questions.

http://www.health.gov/nhic

National Institutes of Health. Provides information about all NIH activities as well as consumer publications, hotline information, and an A-to-Z listing of health issues with links to the appropriate NIH institute.

http://www.nih.gov

National Wellness Institute. Serves professionals and organizations that promote optimal health and wellness.

http://www.nationalwellness.org

National Women's Health Information Center. Provides information and answers to frequently asked questions.

http://www.womenshealth.gov

Office of Minority Health. Promotes improved health among racial and ethnic minority populations.

http://minorityhealth.hhs.gov

Surgeon General. Includes information on activities of the Surgeon General and the text of many key reports on such topics as tobacco use, physical activity, and mental health.

http://www.surgeongeneral.gov

World Health Organization (WHO). Provides information about health topics and issues affecting people around the world.

http://www.who.int

The following are just a few of the many sites that provide consumer-oriented information on a variety of health issues:

CNN Health: http://www.cnn.com/health

FamilyDoctor.Org: http://familydoctor.org/online/famdocen/home.html

InteliHealth: http://www.intelihealth.com

MayoClinic.com: http://www.mayoclinic.com

SELECTED BIBLIOGRAPHY

American Cancer Society. 2011. *Cancer Facts and Figures—2011.* Atlanta: American Cancer Society.

American Heart Association. 2011. *Heart Disease and Stroke Statistics—2011 Update.* Dallas: American Heart Association.

Banks, J., et al. 2006. Disease and disadvantage in the United States and in England. *Journal of the American Medical Association* 295(17): 2037–2045.

Barr, D. A. 2008. *Health Disparities in the United States: Social Class, Race, Ethnicity, and Health.* Baltimore: The Johns Hopkins University Press.

Beckman, M. 2007. Help wanted: In the pursuit of a healthy lifestyle, sheer grit only takes you so far. *Stanford Medicine Magazine* 24(3).

Centers for Disease Control and Prevention. 2008. Racial/Ethnic Disparities in Self-Rated Health Status among Adults with and without Disabilities—United States, 2004–2006. *Morbidity and Mortality Weekly Report* 57(39): 1069–1073.

Centers for Disease Control and Prevention. 2011. *Racial and Ethnic Approaches to Community Health (REACH)* (http://www.cdc.gov/reach; retrieved June 26, 2010).

Finkelstein, E. A., et al. 2008. Do obese persons comprehend their personal health risks? *American Journal of Health Behavior* 32(5): 508–516.

Flegal, K. M., et al. 2005. Excess deaths associated with underweight, overweight, and obesity. *Journal of the American Medical Association* 293(15): 1861–1867.

Flegal, K. M., et al. 2007. Cause-specific excess deaths associated with underweight, overweight, and obesity. *Journal of the American Medical Association* 298(17): 2028–2037.

Flegal, K. M., et al. 2010. Prevalence and Trends in Obesity Among U.S. Adults, 1999–2008. *Journal of the American Medical Association* 303(3): 235–241.

Gorman, B. K., and J. G. Read. 2006. Gender disparities in adult health: An examination of three measures of morbidity. *Journal of Health and Social Behavior* 47(2): 95–110.

Herd, P., et al. 2007. Socioeconomic position and health: The differential effects of education versus income on the onset versus progression of health problems. *Journal of Health and Social Behavior* 48(3): 223–238.

Horneffer-Ginter, K. 2008. Stages of change and possible selves: Two tools for promoting college health. *Journal of American College Health* 56(4): 351–358.

Martin, G., and J. Pear. 2007. *Behaviour Modification: What It Is and How to Do It,* 8th ed. Upper Saddle River, N.J.: Prentice-Hall.

Mokdad, A. H., et al. 2004. Actual causes of death in the United States, 2000. *Journal of the American Medical Association* 291(10): 1238–1245.

Mokdad, A. H., et al. 2005. Correction: Actual causes of death in the United States, 2000. *Journal of the American Medical Association* 293(3): 293–294.

National Center for Health Statistics. 2010. *Health, United States, 2010.* Hyattsville, Md.: National Center for Health Statistics.

National Center for Health Statistics. 2010. Health behaviors of adults: United States, 2005–07. *Vital and Health Statistics* 10(245).

National Center for Health Statistics. 2011. Deaths: Preliminary data for 2009. *National Vital Statistics Report* 59(4).

Nothwehr, F., et al. 2008. Age group differences in diet and physical activity–related behaviors among rural men and women. *Journal of Nutrition, Health and Aging* 12(3): 169–174.

O'Loughlin, J., et al. 2007. Lifestyle risk factors for chronic disease across family origin among adults in multiethnic, low-income, urban neighborhoods. *Ethnicity and Disease* 17(4): 657–663.

Participants at the 6th Global Conference on Health Promotion. The Bangkok Charter for health promotion in a globalized world. Geneva: World Health Organization, August 11, 2005.

Pinkhasov, R. M., et al. 2010. Are men shortchanged on health? Perspective on health care utilization and health risk behavior in men and women in the United States. *International Journal of Clinical Practice* 64(4): 475–487.

Song, J., et al. 2006. Gender differences across race/ethnicity in use of health care among Medicare–aged Americans. *Journal of Women's Health* 15(10): 1205–1213.

U.C. Berkeley. 2010 Update. *Evaluating Web Pages: Techniques to Apply and Questions to Ask* (http://www.lib.berkeley.edu/TeachingLib/Guides/Internet/Evaluate.html; retrieved June 26, 2011).

Walker, B., and C. P. Mouton. 2008. Environmental influences on cardiovascular health. *Journal of the National Medical Association* 100(1): 98–102.

World Health Organization. 2011. *Why Gender and Health?* (http://www.who.int/gender/genderandhealth/en; retrieved June 26, 2011).

Name _____ Section _____ Date _____

LAB 1.1 Your Wellness Profile

Consider how your lifestyle, attitudes, and characteristics relate to each of the six dimensions of wellness. Fill in your strengths for each dimension (examples of strengths are listed with each dimension). Once you've completed your lists, choose what you believe are your five most important strengths, and circle them.

Physical wellness: To maintain overall physical health and engage in appropriate physical activity (e.g., stamina, strength, flexibility, healthy body composition).

_____

_____

_____

Emotional wellness: To have a positive self-concept, deal constructively with your feelings, and develop positive qualities (e.g., optimism, trust, self-confidence, determination).

_____

_____

_____

Intellectual wellness: To pursue and retain knowledge, think critically about issues, make sound decisions, identify problems, and find solutions (e.g., common sense, creativity, curiosity).

_____

_____

_____

Interpersonal/social wellness: To develop and maintain meaningful relationships with a network of friends and family members, and to contribute to your community (e.g., friendly, good-natured, compassionate, supportive, good listener).

_____

_____

_____

Spiritual wellness: To develop a set of beliefs, principles, or values that gives meaning or purpose to your life; to develop faith in something beyond yourself (e.g., religious faith, service to others).

_____

_____

_____

Environmental wellness: To protect yourself from environmental hazards and to minimize the negative impact of your behavior on the environment (e.g., carpooling, recycling).

_____

_____

_____

Next, think about where you fall on the wellness continuum for each of the dimensions of wellness. Indicate your placement for each—physical, emotional, intellectual, interpersonal/social, spiritual, and environmental—by placing Xs on the continuum below.

| Low level of wellness | Physical, psychological, emotional symptoms | Change and growth | High level of wellness |

connect™ http://www.mcgrawhillconnect.com/
FITNESS AND WELLNESS

Based on both your current lifestyle and your goals for the future, what do you think your placement on the wellness continuum will be in 10 years? What new health behaviors will you have to adopt to achieve your goals? Which of your current behaviors will you need to change to maintain or improve your level of wellness in the future?

Does the description of wellness given in this chapter encompass everything you believe is part of wellness for you? Write your own definition of wellness, including any additional dimensions that are important to you. Then rate your level of wellness based on your own definition.

Using Your Results

How did you score? Are you satisfied with your current level of wellness—overall and in each dimension? In which dimension(s) would you most like to increase your level of wellness?

What should you do next? As you consider possible target behaviors for a behavior change program, choose things that will maintain or increase your level of wellness in one of the dimensions you listed as an area of concern. Remember to consider health behaviors such as smoking or eating a high-fat diet that may threaten your level of wellness in the future. Below, list several possible target behaviors and the wellness dimensions that they influence.

For additional guidance in choosing a target behavior, complete the lifestyle self-assessment in Lab 1.2.

LAB 1.2 Lifestyle Evaluation

How does your current lifestyle compare with the lifestyle recommended for wellness? For each question, choose the answer that best describes your behavior. Then add up your score for each section.

	Almost Always	Sometimes	Never

Exercise/Fitness

	Almost Always	Sometimes	Never
1. I engage in moderate exercise, such as brisk walking or swimming, for 20–60 minutes, three to five times a week.	4	1	0
2. I do exercises to develop muscular strength and endurance at least twice a week.	2	1	0
3. I spend some of my leisure time participating in individual, family, or team activities, such as gardening, bowling, or softball.	2	1	0
4. I maintain a healthy body weight, avoiding overweight and underweight.	2	1	0

Exercise/Fitness Score: _____

Nutrition

	Almost Always	Sometimes	Never
1. I eat a variety of foods each day, including seven or more servings of fruits and/or vegetables.	3	1	0
2. I limit the amount of total fat and saturated and trans fat in my diet.	3	1	0
3. I avoid skipping meals.	2	1	0
4. I limit the amount of salt and sugar I eat.	2	1	0

Nutrition Score: _____

Tobacco Use

If you never or no longer use tobacco, enter a score of 10 for this section and go to the next section.

	Almost Always	Sometimes	Never
1. I avoid using tobacco.	2	1	0
2. I smoke only a pipe or cigars, *or* I use smokeless tobacco.	2	1	0

Tobacco Use Score: _____

Alcohol and Drugs

	Almost Always	Sometimes	Never
1. I avoid alcohol, or I drink no more than one (women) or two (men) drinks a day.	4	1	0
2. I avoid using alcohol or other drugs as a way of handling stressful situations or the problems in my life.	2	1	0
3. I am careful not to drink alcohol when taking medications (such as cold or allergy medications) or when pregnant.	2	1	0
4. I read and follow the label directions when using prescribed and over-the-counter drugs.	2	1	0

Alcohol and Drugs Score: _____

Emotional Health

	Almost Always	Sometimes	Never
1. I enjoy being a student, and I have a job or do other work that I enjoy.	2	1	0
2. I find it easy to relax and express my feelings freely.	2	1	0
3. I manage stress well.	2	1	0
4. I have close friends, relatives, or others whom I can talk to about personal matters and call on for help when needed.	2	1	0
5. I participate in group activities (such as community or church organizations) or hobbies that I enjoy	2	1	0

Emotional Health Score: _____

Mc Graw Hill **connect** http://www.mcgrawhillconnect.com/
FITNESS AND WELLNESS

LABORATORY ACTIVITIES

	Almost Always	Sometimes	Never
Safety			
1. I wear a safety belt while riding in a car.	2	1	0
2. I avoid driving while under the influence of alcohol or other drugs.	2	1	0
3. I obey traffic rules and the speed limit when driving.	2	1	0
4. I read and follow instructions on the labels of potentially harmful products or substances, such as household cleaners, poisons, and electrical appliances.	2	1	0
5. I avoid smoking in bed.	2	1	0

Safety Score: _____

Disease Prevention

	Almost Always	Sometimes	Never
1. I know the warning signs of cancer, heart attack, and stroke.	2	1	0
2. I avoid overexposure to the sun and use sunscreen.	2	1	0
3. I get recommended medical screening tests (such as blood pressure and cholesterol checks and Pap tests), immunizations, and booster shots.	2	1	0
4. I practice monthly skin and breast/testicle self-exams.	2	1	0
5. I am not sexually active, *or* I have sex with only one mutually faithful, uninfected partner, *or* I always engage in safer sex (using condoms), and I do not share needles to inject drugs.	2	1	0

Disease Prevention Score: _____

Scores of 9 and 10 Excellent! Your answers show that you are aware of the importance of this area to your health. More important, you are putting your knowledge to work for you by practicing good health habits. As long as you continue to do so, this area should not pose a serious health risk.

Scores of 6 to 8 Your health practices in this area are good, but there is room for improvement.

Scores of 3 to 5 Your health risks are showing.

Scores of 0 to 2 You may be taking serious and unnecessary risks with your health.

Using Your Results

How did you score? In which areas did you score the lowest? Are you satisfied with your scores in each area? In which areas would you most like to improve your scores?

What should you do next? To improve your scores, look closely at any item to which you answered "sometimes" or "never." Identify and list at least three possible targets for a health behavior change program. (If you are aware of other risky health behaviors you currently engage in, but that were not covered by this assessment, you may include those in your list.) For each item on your list, identify your current "stage of change" and one strategy you could adopt to move forward (see pp. 16–21). Possible strategies might be obtaining information about the behavior, completing an analysis of the pros and cons of change, or beginning a written record of your target behavior.

Behavior	Stage	Strategy
1. _____	_____	_____
2. _____	_____	_____
3. _____	_____	_____

SOURCE: Adapted from *Healthstyle: A Self-Test,* developed by the U.S. Public Health Service. The behaviors covered in this test are recommended for most Americans, but some may not apply to people with certain chronic diseases or disabilities or to pregnant women, who may require special advice from their physician.

CHAPTER 2

Stress

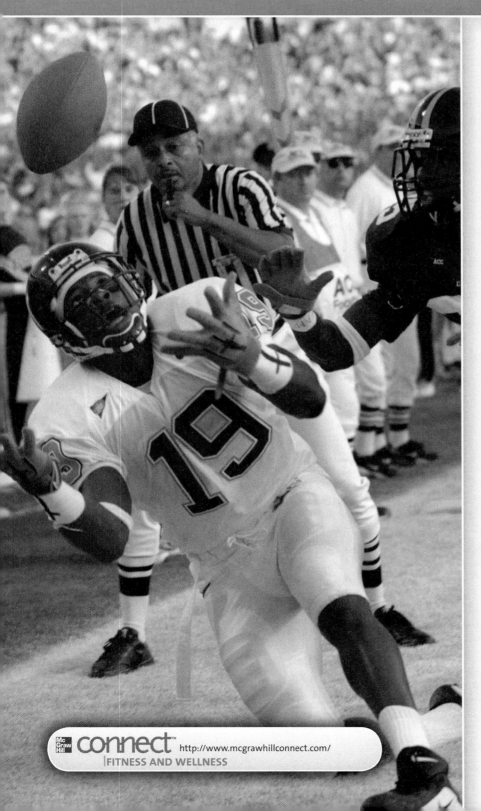

LOOKING AHEAD...

After reading this chapter, you should be able to:

- Explain what stress is and how people react to it—physically, emotionally, and behaviorally
- Describe the relationship between stress and disease
- List common sources of stress
- Describe techniques for preventing and managing stress
- Put together a plan for successfully managing the stress in your life

TEST YOUR KNOWLEDGE

1. Which of the following events can cause stress?
   a. taking out a loan
   b. failing a test
   c. graduating from college

2. Exercise stimulates which of the following?
   a. analgesia (pain relief)
   b. birth of new brain cells
   c. relaxation

3. Which of the following can be a result of chronic stress?
   a. violence
   b. heart attack
   c. stroke

Answers

1. **All three.** Stress-producing factors can be pleasant or unpleasant and can include physical challenges, goal achievement, and events that are perceived as negative.
2. **All three.** Regular exercise is linked to improvements in many dimensions of wellness.
3. **All three.** Chronic—or ongoing— stress can last for years. People who suffer from long-term stress may ultimately become violent toward themselves or others. They also run a greater-than-normal risk for certain ailments, especially cardiovascular disease.

connect http://www.mcgrawhillconnect.com/
FITNESS AND WELLNESS

LearnSmart
GET A BETTER GRADE. TRY LEARNSMART.

Like the term *fitness, stress* is a word many people use without really understanding its precise meaning. Stress is popularly viewed as an uncomfortable response to a negative event, which probably describes *nervous tension* more than the cluster of physical and psychological responses that actually constitute stress. In fact, stress is not limited to negative situations; it is also a response to pleasurable physical challenges and the achievement of personal goals.

Whether stress is experienced as pleasant or unpleasant depends largely on the situation and the individual. Because learning effective responses to stress can enhance psychological health and help prevent a number of serious diseases, stress management can be an important part of daily life.

This chapter explains the physiological and psychological reactions that make up the stress response and describes how these reactions can be risks to good health. The chapter also presents methods of managing stress.

WHAT IS STRESS?

In common usage, the term *stress* refers to two different things: situations that trigger physical and emotional reactions *and* the reactions themselves. This text uses the more precise term **stressor** for a situation that triggers physical and emotional reactions and the term **stress response** for those reactions. A first date and a final exam are examples of stressors; sweaty palms and a pounding heart are symptoms of the stress response. We'll use the term **stress** to describe the general physical and emotional state that accompanies the stress response. So, a person taking a final exam experiences stress.

KEY TERMS

stressor   Any physical or psychological event or condition that produces physical and emotional reactions.

stress response   The physical and emotional reactions to a stressor.

stress   The general physical and emotional state that accompanies the stress response.

autonomic nervous system   The branch of the nervous system that controls basic body processes; consists of the sympathetic and parasympathetic divisions.

parasympathetic division   A division of the autonomic nervous system that moderates the excitatory effect of the sympathetic division, slowing metabolism and restoring energy supplies.

sympathetic division   A division of the autonomic nervous system that reacts to danger or other challenges by almost instantly accelerating body processes.

norepinephrine   A neurotransmitter released by the sympathetic nervous system onto specific tissues to increase their function in the face of increased activity; when released by the brain, causes arousal (increased attention, awareness, and alertness); also called *noradrenaline*.

Physical Responses to Stressors

Imagine a near miss: As you step off the curb, a car speeds toward you. With just a fraction of a second to spare, you leap safely out of harm's way. In that split second of danger and in the moments following it, you experience a predictable series of physical reactions. Your body goes from a relaxed state to one prepared for physical action to cope with a threat to your life.

Two systems in your body are responsible for your physical response to stressors: the nervous system and the endocrine system. Through rapid chemical reactions affecting almost every part of your body, you are primed to act quickly and appropriately in time of danger.

Actions of the Nervous System   The nervous system consists of the brain, spinal cord, and nerves. Part of the nervous system is under voluntary control, as when you tell your arm to reach for a chocolate. The part that is not under conscious supervision—for example, the part that controls the digestion of the chocolate—is the **autonomic nervous system**. In addition to digestion, it controls your heart rate, breathing, blood pressure, and hundreds of other involuntary functions.

The autonomic nervous system consists of two divisions:

- The **parasympathetic division** is in control when you are relaxed. It aids in digesting food, storing energy, and promoting growth.
- The **sympathetic division** is activated during times of arousal, including exercise, and when there is an emergency, such as severe pain, anger, or fear.

Sympathetic nerves use the neurotransmitter **norepinephrine** (or *noradrenaline*) to exert their actions on nearly every organ, sweat gland, blood vessel, and muscle to enable your body to handle an emergency. In general, the sympathetic division commands your body to stop storing energy and to use it in response to a crisis.

Actions of the Endocrine System   During stress, the sympathetic nervous system triggers the **endocrine system**. This system of glands, tissues, and cells helps control body functions by releasing **hormones** and other chemical messengers into the bloodstream to influence metabolism and other body processes. These chemicals act on a variety of targets throughout the body. Along with the nervous system, the endocrine system prepares the body to respond to a stressor.

The Two Systems Together   How do both systems work together in an emergency? Let's go back to your near-collision with a car. Both reflexes and higher cognitive (thinking) areas in your brain quickly make the decision that you are facing a threat, and your body prepares to meet the danger. Chemical messages and actions of sympathetic nerves cause the release of key hormones,

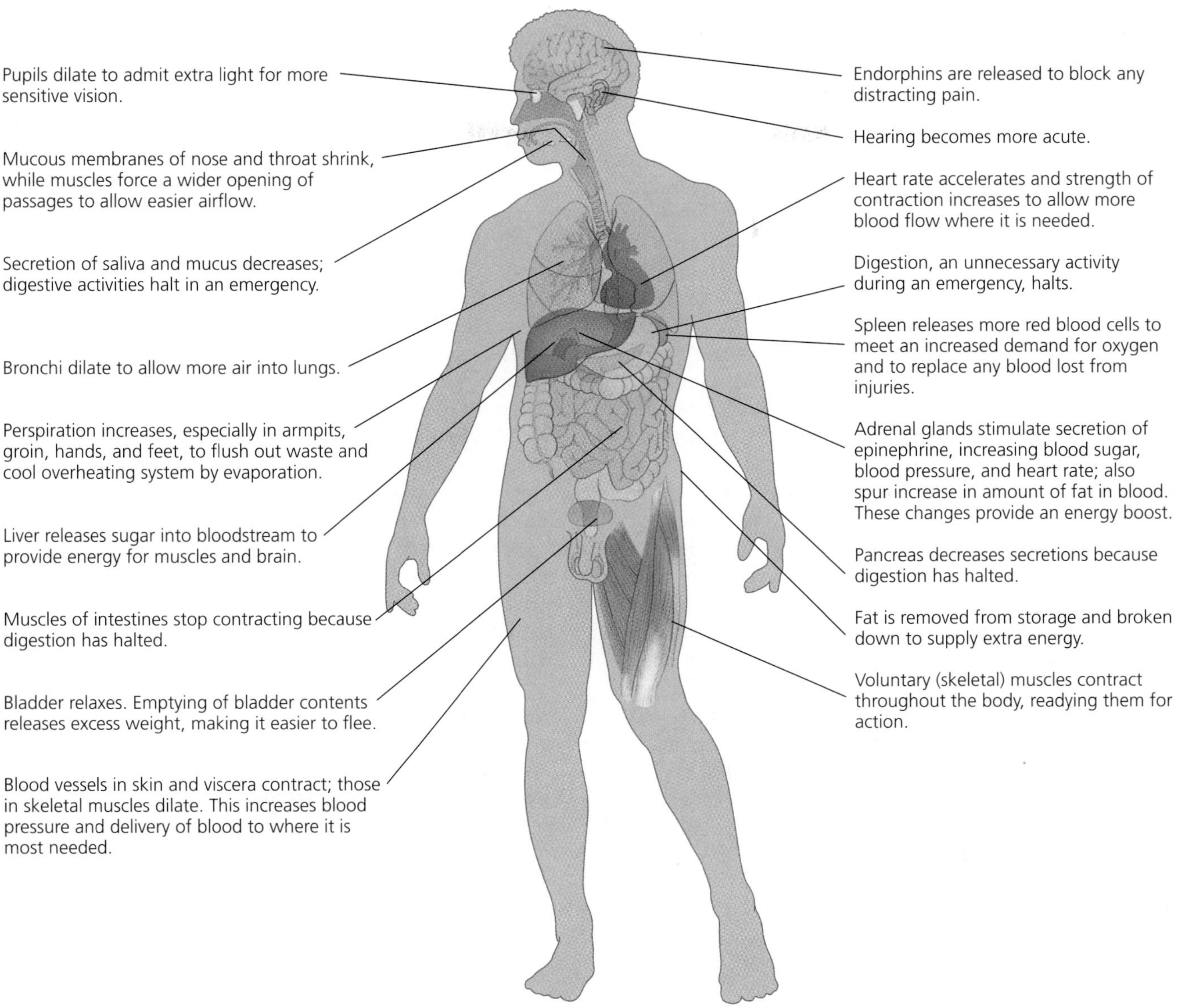

Pupils dilate to admit extra light for more sensitive vision.

Mucous membranes of nose and throat shrink, while muscles force a wider opening of passages to allow easier airflow.

Secretion of saliva and mucus decreases; digestive activities halt in an emergency.

Bronchi dilate to allow more air into lungs.

Perspiration increases, especially in armpits, groin, hands, and feet, to flush out waste and cool overheating system by evaporation.

Liver releases sugar into bloodstream to provide energy for muscles and brain.

Muscles of intestines stop contracting because digestion has halted.

Bladder relaxes. Emptying of bladder contents releases excess weight, making it easier to flee.

Blood vessels in skin and viscera contract; those in skeletal muscles dilate. This increases blood pressure and delivery of blood to where it is most needed.

Endorphins are released to block any distracting pain.

Hearing becomes more acute.

Heart rate accelerates and strength of contraction increases to allow more blood flow where it is needed.

Digestion, an unnecessary activity during an emergency, halts.

Spleen releases more red blood cells to meet an increased demand for oxygen and to replace any blood lost from injuries.

Adrenal glands stimulate secretion of epinephrine, increasing blood sugar, blood pressure, and heart rate; also spur increase in amount of fat in blood. These changes provide an energy boost.

Pancreas decreases secretions because digestion has halted.

Fat is removed from storage and broken down to supply extra energy.

Voluntary (skeletal) muscles contract throughout the body, readying them for action.

FIGURE 10.1 The fight-or-flight reaction.

including **cortisol** and **epinephrine**. These hormones trigger the physiological changes shown in Figure 10.1, including these:

- Heart and respiration rates accelerate to speed oxygen through the body.
- Hearing and vision become more acute.
- The liver releases extra sugar into the bloodstream to boost energy.
- Perspiration increases to cool the skin.
- The brain releases **endorphins**—chemicals that can inhibit or block sensations of pain—in case you are injured.

Taken together, these almost-instantaneous physical changes are called the **fight-or-flight reaction**. They give you the heightened reflexes and strength you need to

KEY TERMS

endocrine system The system of glands, tissues, and cells that secretes hormones into the bloodstream to influence metabolism and other body processes.

hormone A chemical messenger produced in the body and transported in the bloodstream to targeted cells or organs for specific regulation of their activities.

cortisol A steroid hormone secreted by the cortex (outer layer) of the adrenal gland; also called *hydrocortisone*.

epinephrine A hormone secreted by the medulla (inner core) of the adrenal gland that affects the functioning of organs involved in responding to a stressor; also called *adrenaline*.

endorphins Brain secretions that have pain-inhibiting effects.

fight-or-flight reaction A defense reaction that prepares a person for conflict or escape by triggering hormonal, cardiovascular, metabolic, and other changes.

dodge the car or deal with other stressors. Although these physical changes may vary in intensity, the same basic set of physical reactions occurs in response to any type of stressor—positive or negative, physical or psychological.

The Return to Homeostasis Once a stressful situation ends, the parasympathetic division of your autonomic nervous system takes command and halts the stress response. It restores **homeostasis**, a state in which your body maintains blood pressure, heart rate, hormone levels, and other vital functions within a narrow range of normal. Your parasympathetic nervous system calms your body down, slowing a rapid heartbeat, drying sweaty palms, and returning breathing to normal. Gradually, your body resumes its normal "housekeeping" functions, such as digestion and temperature regulation. Damage that may have been sustained during the fight-or-flight reaction is repaired. The day after you narrowly dodge the car, you wake up feeling fine. In this way, your body can grow, repair itself, and build energy reserves. When the next crisis comes, you'll be ready to respond again.

The Fight-or-Flight Reaction in Modern Life The fight-or-flight reaction is a part of our biological heritage, and it's a survival mechanism that has served both humans and animals well. In modern life, however, it is often absurdly inappropriate. Many stressors we face in everyday life—such as an exam, a mess left by a roommate, or a stop light—do not require a physical response. The fight-or-flight reaction prepares the body for physical action regardless of whether such action is a necessary or appropriate response to a particular stressor.

Emotional and Behavioral Responses to Stressors

We all experience a similar set of physical responses to stressors, which make up the fight-or-flight reaction. These responses, however, vary from person to person and from one situation to another. People's perceptions of potential stressors—and their reactions to such stressors—also vary greatly. For example, you may feel confident about taking exams but be nervous about talking to people you

don't know, while your roommate may love challenging social situations but be nervous about taking tests. Many factors, some external and some internal, help explain these differences.

Your cognitive appraisal of a potential stressor strongly influences how you respond to it. Two factors that can reduce the magnitude of the stress response are successful prediction and the perception of control. For instance, receiving course syllabi at the beginning of the term allows you to predict the timing of major deadlines and exams. Having this predictive knowledge also allows you to exert some control over your study plans and can help reduce the stress caused by exams.

Cognitive appraisal is highly individual and strongly related to emotions. The facts of a situation—Who? What? Where? When?—typically are evaluated fairly consistently from person to person. Evaluation with respect to personal outcome, however, varies: What does this mean for me? Can I do anything about it? Will it improve or worsen? If an individual perceives a situation as exceeding her or his ability to cope, the result can be negative emotions and an inappropriate stress response. If, on the other hand, a person perceives a situation as a challenge that is within her or his ability to manage, more positive and appropriate responses are likely. A moderate level of stress, if coped with appropriately, can help promote optimal performance (Figure 10.2).

Effective and Ineffective Responses Common emotional responses to stressors include anxiety, depression, and fear. Although emotional responses are determined in part by inborn personality or temperament, we often can moderate or learn to control them. Coping techniques are discussed later in the chapter.

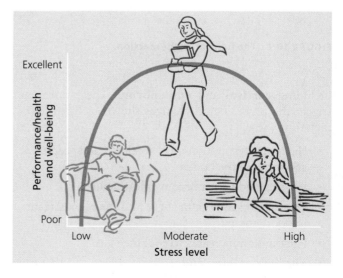

FIGURE 10.2 Stress level, performance, and well-being. A moderate level of stress challenges individuals in a way that promotes optimal performance and well-being. Too little stress, and people are not challenged enough to improve; too much stress, and the challenges become stressors that can impair physical and emotional health.

Wellness Tip

Chronic stress not only harms your health, it can make you age faster. A study of women who were long-term caregivers to very sick children revealed that, over time, the women's bodies lost their ability to create new red blood cells. On average, these women were physically 10 years older than their actual chronological age. This is one reason it pays to learn to manage stress, especially when you're young!

Behavioral responses to stressors—controlled by the **somatic nervous system**, which manages our conscious actions—are entirely under our control. Effective behavioral responses such as talking, laughing, exercising, meditating, learning time-management skills, and becoming more assertive can promote wellness and enable us to function at our best. Ineffective behavioral responses to stressors include overeating, expressing hostility, and using tobacco, alcohol, or other drugs.

Personality and Stress Some people seem to be nervous, irritable, and easily upset by minor annoyances; others are calm and composed even in difficult situations. Scientists remain unsure just why this is or how the brain's complex emotional mechanisms work. But **personality**—the sum of behavioral, cognitive, and emotional tendencies—clearly affects how people perceive and react to stressors. To investigate the links among personality, stress, and wellness, researchers have looked at different clusters of characteristics, or "personality types."

- *Type A.* People with Type A personality are described as ultracompetitive, controlling, impatient, aggressive, and even hostile. Type A people have a higher perceived stress level and more problems coping with stress. They react explosively to stressors and are upset by events that others would consider only annoyances. Studies indicate that certain characteristics of the Type A pattern—anger, cynicism, and hostility—increase the risk of heart disease.

- *Type B.* The Type B personality is relaxed and contemplative. Type B people are less frustrated by daily events and more tolerant of the behavior of others.

- *Type C.* The Type C personality is characterized by anger suppression, difficulty expressing emotions, feelings of hopelessness and despair, and an exaggerated response to minor stressors. This heightened response may impair immune functions.

Studies of Type A and C personalities suggest that expressing your emotions is beneficial but that habitually expressing exaggerated stress responses or hostility is unhealthy.

Researchers have also looked for personality traits that enable people to deal more successfully with stress. One such trait is *hardiness,* a particular form of optimism. People with a hardy personality view potential stressors as challenges and opportunities for growth and learning, rather than as burdens. Hardy people perceive fewer situations as stressful, and their reaction to stressors tends to be less intense. They are committed to their activities, have a sense of inner purpose and an inner locus of control, and feel at least partly in control of their lives.

You probably can't change your basic personality, but you can change your typical behaviors and patterns of

A person's emotional and behavioral responses to stressors depend on many different factors, including personality, gender, and cultural background. Research suggests that women are more likely than men to respond to stressors by seeking social contact and support.

thinking, and you can use positive stress-management techniques like those described later in the chapter.

Gender and Stress Our gender role—the activities, abilities, and behaviors our culture expects of us based on our sex—can affect our experience of stress. Some behavioral responses to stressors, such as crying or openly expressing anger, may be deemed more appropriate for one gender than the other.

Strict adherence to gender roles can limit one's response to stress and can itself become a source of stress. Adherence

homeostasis A state of stability and consistency in a person's physiological functioning.

somatic nervous system The branch of the peripheral nervous system that governs motor functions and sensory information, largely under conscious control.

personality The sum of behavioral, cognitive, and emotional tendencies.

KEY TERMS

Table 10.1	Symptoms of Excess Stress		
PHYSICAL SYMPTOMS	**EMOTIONAL SYMPTOMS**	**BEHAVIORAL SYMPTOMS**
Dry mouth	Anxiety	Crying
Excessive perspiration	Depression	Disrupted eating habits
Frequent illnesses	Edginess	Disrupted sleeping habits
Gastrointestinal problems	Fatigue	Harsh treatment of others
Grinding of teeth	Hypervigilance	Problems communicating
Headaches	Impulsiveness	Sexual problems
High blood pressure	Inability to concentrate	Social isolation
Pounding heart	Irritability	Increased use of tobacco, alcohol, or other drugs
Stiff neck or aching lower back	Trouble remembering things	

? Ask Yourself

QUESTIONS FOR CRITICAL THINKING
AND REFLECTION

Think of the last time you faced a significant stressor. How did you respond? List the physical, emotional, and behavioral reactions you felt. Did these responses help you deal with the stress, or did they interfere with your efforts to handle it?

to traditional gender roles can also affect the perception of a stressor. For example, if a man derives most of his sense of self-worth from his work, retirement may be a more stressful life change for him than for a woman whose self-image is based on several different roles.

Although both men and women experience the fight-or-flight response to stress, women are more likely to respond with a behavioral pattern known as "tend-and-befriend"—nurturing friends and family and seeking social support and social contacts. Rather than becoming aggressive or withdrawing from difficult situations, women are more likely to create or enhance their social networks in ways that reduce stress.

Experience Past experiences can profoundly influence the way you evaluate a potential stressor. Someone who has had a bad experience giving a speech in the past is much more likely to perceive an upcoming speech as stressful than someone who has had positive public speaking experiences. Effective behavioral responses, such as preparing carefully and visualizing success, can help overcome the effects of negative past experiences.

The Stress Experience as a Whole

As Table 10.1 shows, the physical, emotional, and behavioral symptoms of excess negative stress are distinct. But they are also intimately interrelated. The more intense the emotional response, the stronger the physical response.

Effective behavioral responses can lessen stress; ineffective ones only worsen it. Sometimes people have such intense responses to stressors or such ineffective coping techniques that they need professional help to overcome the stress in their lives. More often, however, people can learn to handle stressors on their own.

STRESS AND WELLNESS

According to the American Psychological Association, 43% of adult Americans suffer from stress-related health problems. The role of stress in health is complex, but evidence suggests that stress can increase vulnerability to many ailments. Several theories have been proposed to explain the relationship between stress and disease.

The General Adaptation Syndrome

Biologist Hans Selye was one of the first scientists to develop a comprehensive theory of stress and disease. Based on his work in the 1930s and 1940s, Selye coined the term **general adaptation syndrome (GAS)** to describe what he believed to be a universal and predictable response pattern to all stressors. Some stressors are pleasant, such as attending a party, or unpleasant, such as a bad grade. In the GAS theory, stress triggered by a pleasant stressor is called **eustress**; stress triggered by an unpleasant stressor is called **distress**. The sequence of physical responses associated with GAS (Figure 10.3) is the same for both eustress and distress and occurs in three stages:

- *Alarm.* The alarm stage includes the complex sequence of events brought on by the fight-or-flight reaction. At this stage, the body is more susceptible to disease or injury because it is geared up to deal with a crisis. Someone in this phase may experience headaches, indigestion, anxiety, and disrupted sleeping and eating patterns.

- *Resistance.* With continued stress, the body develops a new level of homeostasis in which it is more

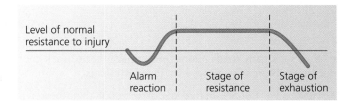

Level of normal
resistance to injury

| Alarm reaction | Stage of resistance | Stage of exhaustion |

FIGURE 10.3 The general adaptation syndrome.
During the alarm stage, a lower resistance to injury is evident. With continued stress, resistance to injury is actually enhanced. With prolonged exposure to repeated stressors, exhaustion sets in, with a return of low resistance levels seen during acute stress.

resistant to disease and injury than normal. In this stage, a person can cope with normal life and added stress.

- *Exhaustion.* The first two stages of GAS require a great deal of energy. If a stressor persists, or if several stressors occur in succession, general exhaustion results. This is not the sort of exhaustion you feel after a long, busy day. Rather, it's a life-threatening type of physiological exhaustion.

Allostatic Load

Although GAS is still viewed as a key conceptual contribution to the understanding of stress, some aspects of it are considered outdated. For example, increased susceptibility to disease after repeated or prolonged stress is now thought to be due to the effects of the stress response itself rather than to a depletion of resources (the exhaustion stage). In particular, long-term overexposure to stress hormones such as cortisol has been linked with health problems. Further, although physical stress reactions promote homeostasis (resistance stage), they also have negative effects on the body.

The long-term wear and tear of the stress response is called the **allostatic load.** A person's allostatic load depends on many factors, including genetics, life experiences, and emotional and behavioral responses to stressors. A high allostatic load may be due to frequent stressors, poor adaptation to common stressors, an inability to shut down the stress response, or imbalances in the

stress responses of different body systems. High allostatic load is linked to heart disease, hypertension, obesity, and reduced brain and immune system functioning. In other words, when your allostatic load exceeds your ability to cope, you are more likely to get sick.

Psychoneuroimmunology

One of the most fruitful areas of current research into the relationship between stress and disease is **psychoneuroimmunology (PNI).** PNI is the study of the interactions among the nervous system, the endocrine system, and the immune system. The underlying premise of PNI is that stress, through the actions of the nervous and endocrine systems, impairs the immune system and thereby affects health.

A complex network of nerve and chemical connections exists between the nervous, endocrine, and immune systems. In general, increased levels of stress hormones are linked to a decreased number of immune system cells, or lymphocytes. Epinephrine appears to promote the release of lymphocytes but at the same time reduces their efficiency. Scientists have identified hormone-like substances called *neuropeptides* that appear to translate emotions into biochemical events, some of which impact the immune system, providing a physical link between emotions and immune function.

Different types of stress may affect immunity in different ways. For example, during acute stress (typically lasting less than 100 minutes), white blood cells move into the skin, where they enhance the immune response. During a stressful sequence of events, such as a personal trauma and the events that follow, however, there are typically no overall significant immune changes. Chronic (ongoing) stressors such as unemployment have negative effects on almost all functional measures of immunity. Chronic stress may cause prolonged secretion of cortisol and may accelerate the course of diseases that involve inflammation, including multiple sclerosis, heart disease, and type 2 diabetes.

Mood, personality, behavior, and immune functioning are intertwined. For example, people who are generally pessimistic may neglect the basics of health care, become

Fitness Tip

Stressed out? Then walk away—literally. Walking is a proven countermeasure against stress, and it contributes to your health in many other ways. A brisk, 10-minute walk may be enough to help you put things in perspective and get back to your normal routine. If not, just keep walking until you feel better. As you walk, try not to think too much about anything specific; the idea is to clear your head!

general adaptation syndrome (GAS) A pattern of stress responses consisting of three stages: alarm, resistance, and exhaustion.

eustress Stress resulting from a pleasant stressor.

distress Stress resulting from an unpleasant stressor.

allostatic load The long-term negative impact of the stress response on the body.

psychoneuroimmunology (PNI) The study of the interactions among the nervous, endocrine, and immune systems.

KEY TERMS

STRESS AND WELLNESS **35**

Overcoming Insomnia

Most people can overcome insomnia by discovering the cause of poor sleep and taking steps to remedy it. Insomnia that lasts for more than 6 months and interferes with daytime functioning requires consultation with a physician. Sleeping pills are not recommended for chronic insomnia because they can be habit-forming; they also lose their effectiveness over time.

If you're bothered by insomnia, try the following:

• Determine how much sleep you need to feel refreshed the next day, and don't sleep longer than that.

• Go to bed at the same time every night, and, more important, get up at the same time every morning, 7 days a week, regardless of how much sleep you got.

• Don't nap more than 30 minutes per day.

• Exercise regularly, but not too close to bedtime. Your metabolism needs at least 6 hours to slow down after exercise.

• Avoid tobacco and caffeine late in the day, and alcohol before bedtime (it causes disturbed, fragmented sleep).

• If you take any medications (prescription or not), ask your doctor or pharmacist if they interfere with sleep.

• Have a light snack before bedtime; you'll sleep better if you're not hungry.

• Use your bed only for sleep. Don't eat, read, study, or watch television in bed.

• Establish a relaxing bedtime routine that helps you unwind and lets your brain know it's time to go to sleep. Read, listen to music, or practice a relaxation technique. Don't lie down in bed until you're sleepy.

• If you don't fall asleep in 15–20 minutes, or if you wake up and can't fall asleep again, get out of bed, leave the room if possible, and do something monotonous until you feel sleepy. Try distracting yourself with imagery instead of counting sheep; imagine yourself on a pleasant vacation or enjoying some beautiful scenery.

• If sleep problems persist, ask your doctor for a referral to a sleep specialist in your area. You may be a candidate for a sleep study—an overnight evaluation of your sleep pattern that can uncover many sleep-related disorders.

? Ask Yourself

QUESTIONS FOR CRITICAL THINKING AND REFLECTION

Have you ever been so stressed that you felt ill in some way? If so, what were your symptoms? How did you handle them? Did the experience affect the way you reacted to other stressful events?

---

passive when ill, and fail to engage in health-promoting behaviors. People who are depressed may reduce physical activity and social interaction, which may in turn affect the immune system and the cognitive appraisal of a stressor. Optimism, successful coping, and positive problem solving, on the other hand, may positively influence immunity.

Links Between Stress and Specific Conditions

Although much remains to be learned, it is clear that people who have unresolved chronic stress in their lives or who handle stressors poorly are at risk for a wide range of health problems. In the short term, the problem might just be a cold, a stiff neck, or a stomachache. Over the long term, the problems can be more severe, such as cardiovascular disease or impairment of the immune system.

Cardiovascular Disease The stress response profoundly affects the cardiovascular system. During the stress response, heart rate increases and blood vessels constrict, causing blood pressure to rise. Chronic high blood pressure is a major cause of *atherosclerosis*, a disease in which the lining of the blood vessels becomes damaged and caked with fatty deposits. These deposits can block arteries, causing heart attacks and strokes (see Chapter 11).

Certain types of emotional responses increase a person's risk of cardiovascular disease. People who exhibit extreme increases in heart rate and blood pressure in response to emotional stressors may face an increased risk of cardiovascular problems.

Altered Immune Function PNI research helps explain how stress affects the immune system. Some of the health problems linked to stress-related changes in immune function include vulnerability to colds and other infections, asthma and allergy attacks, susceptibility to cancer, and flare-ups of chronic diseases such as genital herpes and HIV infection.

Other Health Problems Many other health problems may be caused or worsened by excessive stress, including the following:

• Digestive problems such as stomachaches, diarrhea, constipation, irritable bowel syndrome, and ulcers

• Tension headaches and migraines

- Insomnia and fatigue (see the box "Overcoming Insomnia")
- Injuries, including on-the-job injuries caused by repetitive strain
- Menstrual irregularities, impotence, and pregnancy complications
- Psychological problems, including depression, anxiety, panic attacks, eating disorders, and post-traumatic stress disorder (PTSD), which afflicts people who have suffered or witnessed severe trauma

COMMON SOURCES OF STRESS

Recognizing potential sources of stress is an important step in successfully managing the stress in your life.

Major Life Changes

Any major change in your life that requires adjustment and accommodation can be a source of stress. Early adulthood

Even a joyful occasion can be a source of stress, especially if it involves a major life change.

and the college years are associated with many significant changes, such as moving out of the family home. Even changes typically thought of as positive—such as graduation, job promotion, or marriage—can be stressful.

Clusters of life changes, particularly those that are perceived negatively, may be linked to health problems in some people. Personality and coping skills, however, are important moderating influences. People with a strong support network and a stress-resistant personality are less likely to become ill in response to life changes than people with fewer resources.

Daily Hassles

Although major life changes are undoubtedly stressful, they seldom occur regularly. Researchers have proposed that minor problems—life's daily hassles, such as losing your keys or wallet—can be an even greater source of stress because they occur much more often.

People who perceive hassles negatively are likely to experience a moderate stress response every time they are faced with one. Over time, this can take a significant toll on health. Studies indicate that for some people, daily hassles contribute to a general decrease in overall wellness.

College Stressors

College is a time of major changes and minor hassles. For many students, college means being away from home and family for the first time. Nearly all students share stresses like the following:

- *Academic stress.* Exams, grades, and an endless workload await every college student but can be especially troublesome for young students just out of high school.
- *Interpersonal stress.* Most students are more than just students; they are also friends, children, employees, spouses, parents, and so on. Managing relationships while juggling the rigors of college life can be daunting, especially if some friends or family are less than supportive.
- *Time pressures.* Class schedules, assignments, and deadlines are an inescapable part of college life. But these time pressures can be drastically compounded for students who also have a job and/or family responsibilities.
- *Financial concerns.* The majority of college students need financial aid not just to cover the cost of tuition but to survive from day to day while in school. For many, college life isn't possible without a job, and the pressure to stay afloat financially competes with academic and other stressors.
- *Worries about the future.* As college life comes to an end, students face the reality of life after college. This means thinking about a career, choosing a place to live, and leaving the friends and routines of school behind.

College students face a host of stressors, not the least of which is the pressure to perform academically.

Wellness Tip

If you worry about money, you definitely aren't alone. In the American Psychological Association's 2010 *Stress in America* survey, 76% of Americans cited money as a key source of stress in their lives. If money is a constant cause of worry for you, see the advice on financial wellness in Chapter 1, and get help from a financial planner. It's never too early to have a solid financial plan in place.

Job-Related Stressors

Americans rate their jobs as a key source of stress in their lives. According to the 2010 *Stress in America* survey, 70% of working Americans say their job is a key source of stress in their life. Tight schedules and overtime leave less time for exercising, socializing, and other stress-proofing activities. Worries about job performance, salary, job security, and interactions with others can contribute to stress. High levels of job stress are also common for people who are left out of important decisions relating to their jobs. When workers are given the opportunity to shape their job descriptions and responsibilities, job satisfaction goes up and stress levels go down.

If job-related (or college-related) stress is severe or chronic, the result can be *burnout,* a state of physical, mental, and emotional exhaustion. Burnout occurs most often in highly motivated and driven individuals who come to feel that their work is not recognized or that they are not accomplishing their goals. People in the helping professions—teachers, social workers, caregivers, police officers, and so on—are also prone to burnout. For some people who suffer from burnout, a vacation or leave of absence may be appropriate. For others, a reduced work schedule, better communication with superiors, or a change in job goals may be necessary. Improving time-management skills can also help.

Relationships and Stress

Human beings need social relationships; we cannot thrive as solitary creatures. Simply put, people need people. Even so, our interpersonal relationships—even our deepest, most intimate ones—can be one of the most significant sources of stress in our life.

The first relationships we form outside the family are friendships. With members of either the same or the other sex, friendships give people the opportunity to share themselves and discover others. Friendships are often more stable and longer lasting than intimate partnerships. Friends are often more accepting and less critical than lovers, probably because their expectations are different. Friendships provide people with emotional support and buffer them from stress. Friendships tend to weather conflict and stressful events better than intimate relationships do. During times of stress, in fact, many people initially turn to their friends for comfort, rather than family members or lovers.

Intimate love relationships are among the most profound human experiences. When two people fall in love, their relationship at first is likely to be characterized by high levels of passion and rapidly increasing intimacy. In time, passion decreases as the partners become familiar with each other. The diminishing of passionate love often creates stress between partners (usually affecting one partner more than the other) and can be experienced as a crisis in the relationship. If a quieter, more lasting love fails to emerge, the relationship will likely break up, and each person will search for another who will once again ignite his or her passion.

The key to developing and maintaining any type of friendship or intimate relationship is good communication. Miscommunication creates frustration and distances us from our friends and partners. (For more information, see the section "Communication" later in this chapter.)

Counterproductive Strategies for Coping with Stress

College students develop a variety of habits in response to stress—some of them ineffective and even unhealthy. Here are a few unhealthy coping techniques to avoid:

● **Alcohol.** A few drinks might make you feel at ease, and getting drunk may help you forget the stress in your life—but any relief alcohol provides is temporary. Binge drinking and excessive alcohol consumption are not effective ways to handle stress, and using alcohol to deal with stress puts you at risk for all the short- and long-term problems associated with alcohol abuse.

● **Tobacco.** The nicotine in cigarettes and other tobacco products can make you feel relaxed and may even increase your ability to concentrate. Tobacco, however, is highly addictive, and smoking causes cancer, heart disease, sexual problems, and many other health problems. Tobacco use is the leading preventable cause of death in the United States.

● **Other drugs.** Altering your body chemistry to cope with stress is a strategy with many pitfalls. Caffeine, for example, raises cortisol levels and blood pressure and can disrupt sleep. Marijuana can elicit panic attacks with repeated use,

and some research suggests that it heightens the body's stress response.

● **Binge eating.** Eating can induce relaxation, which reduces stress. Eating as a means of coping with stress, however, may lead to weight gain and to binge eating, a risky behavior associated with eating disorders.

There is one other problem with these methods of fighting stress: None of them addresses the actual cause of the stress in your life. To combat stress in a healthy way, learn some of the stress-management techniques described in this chapter.

Ask Yourself

QUESTIONS FOR CRITICAL THINKING AND REFLECTION

What are the top two or three stressors in your life right now? Are they new to your life—as part of your college experience—or are they stressors you've experienced in the past? Do they include both positive and negative experiences (eustress and distress)?

Other Stressors

Environmental stressors—external conditions or events that cause stress—include loud noises, unpleasant smells, industrial accidents, violence, and natural disasters. (See Appendix A for preparation and coping strategies for large-scale disasters.) Internal stressors are found within ourselves. We put pressure on ourselves to reach personal goals and then evaluate our progress and performance. Physical and emotional states such as illness and exhaustion are also internal stressors.

MANAGING STRESS

What can you do about all this stress? A great deal. By pursuing a wellness lifestyle—being physically active, eating well, getting enough sleep, and so on—and by learning simple ways to identify and moderate individual stressors, you can control the stress in your life. (There are also some stress-management practices you should avoid; see the box "Counterproductive Strategies for Coping with Stress.")

Exercise

Researchers have found that people who exercise regularly react with milder physical stress responses before, during, and after exposure to stressors and that their overall sense of well-being increases as well (see the box "Does Exercise Improve Mental Health?"). Although even light exercise can have a beneficial effect, an integrated fitness program can have a significant impact on stress.

For some people, however, exercise can become just one more stressor in an already-stressful life. People who exercise compulsively risk overtraining, a condition characterized by fatigue, irritability, depression, and diminished athletic performance. An overly strenuous exercise program can even make a person sick by compromising immune function. (For information on creating a safe and effective exercise program, refer to Chapter 7.)

Nutrition

A healthy, balanced diet can help you cope with stress. In addition, eating wisely will enhance your feelings of self-control and self-esteem. Avoiding or limiting caffeine is also important in stress management. Although one or two cups of coffee a day probably won't hurt you, caffeine is a mildly addictive stimulant that leaves some people jittery, irritable, and unable to sleep. Consuming caffeine during stressful situations can raise blood pressure and increase levels of cortisol. (For more on sound nutrition and for advice on evaluating dietary supplements, many of which are marketed for stress, see Chapter 8.)

Does Exercise Improve Mental Health?

THE EVIDENCE FOR EXERCISE

Since 1995, more than 30 major population-based studies (involving 175,000 Americans) have been published on the association between physical activity and mental health. The overall conclusion is that exercise—even modest activity such as taking a daily walk—can help combat a variety of mental health problems. For example, studies found that regular physical activity protects against depression and the onset of major depressive disorder; it can also reduce symptoms of depression in otherwise healthy people. Other studies found that physical activity protects against anxiety and the onset of anxiety disorders (such as specific phobia, social phobia, generalized anxiety, and panic disorder); it also helps reduce symptoms in people affected with anxiety disorders.

Physical activity can enhance feelings of well-being in some people, which may provide some protection against psychological distress. Overall, physically active people are about 25–30% less likely to feel distressed than inactive people. Regardless of the number, age, or health status of the people being studied, those who were active managed stress better than their inactive counterparts.

Researchers have also looked at specific aspects of the activity-stress association. For example, one study found that taking a long walk can be effective at reducing anxiety and blood pressure. Another showed that a brisk walk of as little as 10 minutes' duration can leave people feeling more relaxed and energetic for up to 2 hours. People who took three brisk 45-minute walks each week for 3 months reported that they perceived fewer daily hassles and had a greater sense of general wellness.

The findings are not surprising. The stress response mobilizes energy resources and readies the body for physical emergencies. If you experience stress and do not exert yourself physically, you are not completing the energy cycle. You may not be able to exercise while your daily stressors are occurring, but you can be active later in the day. Such activity allows you to expend the nervous energy you have built up and trains your body to return more readily to homeostasis after stressful situations.

Physical activity also helps you sleep better, and consistently sound sleep is critical to managing stress. According to the National Sleep Foundation, about two-thirds of Americans have trouble sleeping at least a few nights a week, and about 40% say they have difficulty sleeping virtually every night. There are about 70 known sleep disorders, and disordered sleep is associated with a variety of physical and neurological problems, including health problems relating to stress. Although only a few small-scale studies have been done on the relationship between physical activity and sleep, most experts have concluded that regular activity promotes better sleep and provides some protection against sleep interruptions such as insomnia and sleep apnea. Consistent, restful sleep is now regarded as a protective factor in disorders such as depression, anxiety, obesity, and heart disease.

SOURCES: Physical Activity Guidelines Advisory Committee. 2008. *Physical Activity Guidelines Advisory Committee Report, 2008.* Washington, D.C.: U.S. Department of Health and Human Services. National Sleep Foundation. 2011. *2011 Sleep in America Poll: Summary of Findings.* Washington, D.C.: National Sleep Foundation.

Sleep

Most adults need 7–9 hours of sleep every night to stay healthy and perform their best. Getting enough sleep isn't just good for you physically; adequate sleep also improves mood, fosters feelings of competence and self-worth, enhances mental functioning, and supports emotional functioning.

Sleep and Stress Stress hormone levels in the bloodstream vary throughout the day and are related to sleep patterns. Peak concentrations of these hormones occur in the early morning, followed by a slow decline during the day and evening. Concentrations return to peak levels during the final stages of sleep and in the early morning hours.

Even though stress hormones are released during sleep, it is the lack of sleep that has the greatest impact on stress. In someone who is suffering from sleep deprivation (not getting enough sleep over time), mental and physical processes deteriorate steadily. A sleep-deprived person experiences headaches, feels irritable, is unable to concentrate, and is more prone to forgetfulness. Poor-quality sleep has long been associated with stress and depression. A small 2008 study of female college students further associated sleep deprivation with an increased risk of suicide.

Acute sleep deprivation slows the daytime decline in stress hormones, so evening levels are higher than normal. A decrease in total sleep time also causes an increase in the level of stress hormones. Together, these changes may cause an increase in stress hormone levels throughout the day and may contribute to physical and mental exhaustion. Extreme sleep deprivation can lead to hallucinations and other psychotic symptoms, as well as to a significant increase in heart attack risk.

Sleep Disorders According to the National Sleep Foundation's 2011 *Sleep in America Poll,* adults sleep just under 7 hours per night during the week, on average. (Compare this to the recommended 7–9 hours per night.) Many Americans cope with lack of sleep by trying to get extra sleep on the weekends, by napping, and by consuming lots of caffeine during the day. As many as 70 million Americans suffer from chronic sleep disorders—medical conditions that prevent them from sleeping well.

Building Social Support

TAKE CHARGE

Meaningful connections with others can play a key role in stress management and overall wellness. A sense of isolation can lead to chronic stress, which in turn can increase one's susceptibility to temporary illnesses like colds and to chronic illnesses like heart disease. Although the mechanism isn't clear, social isolation can be as significant to mortality rates as factors like smoking, high blood pressure, and obesity.

There is no single best pattern of social support that works for everyone. However, research suggests that having a variety of types of relationships may be important for wellness. Here are some tips for strengthening your social ties:

- **Foster friendships.** Keep in regular contact with your friends. Offer respect, trust, and acceptance, and provide help and support in times of need. Express appreciation for your friends.

- **Keep your family ties strong.** Stay in touch with the family members you feel close to. If your family doesn't function well as a support system for its members, create a second "family" of people with whom you have built meaningful ties.

- **Get involved with a group.** Do volunteer work, take a class, attend a lecture series, or join a religious group. These types of activities can give you a sense of security, a place to talk about your feelings or concerns, and a way to build new friendships. Choose activities that are meaningful to you and that include direct involvement with other people.

- **Build your communication skills.** The more you share your feelings with others, the closer the bonds between you will become. When others are speaking, be a considerate and attentive listener.

SOURCE: Friends Can Be Good Medicine. 1998. As found in the *Mind/Body Newsletter* 7(1): 3–6.

According to the Institute of Medicine, more than 50% of adults suffer from *insomnia*—trouble falling asleep or staying asleep. The most common causes of insomnia are lifestyle factors, such as high caffeine or alcohol intake before bedtime; medical problems, such as a breathing disorder; and stress. About 75% of people who suffer from chronic insomnia report some stressful life event at the onset of their sleeping problems.

Another type of chronic sleep problem, called *sleep apnea,* occurs when a person stops breathing while asleep (Figure 10.4). Apnea can be caused by a number of factors, but it typically results when the soft tissue at the back of the mouth (such as the tongue or soft palate) "collapses" during sleep, blocking the airway. When breathing is interrupted, so is sleep, as the sleeper awakens repeatedly throughout the night to begin breathing again. In most cases, this occurs without the sleeper even being aware of it. However, the disruption to sleep can be significant, and over time acute sleep deprivation can result from apnea. There are several treatments for apnea, including medications, special devices that help keep the airway open during sleep, and surgery.

Social Support

Sharing fears, frustrations, and joys makes life richer and seems to contribute to the well-being of body and mind.

One study of college students living in overcrowded apartments, for example, found that those with a strong social support system were less distressed by their cramped quarters than were the loners who navigated life's challenges on their own. Other studies have shown that married people live longer than single people and have lower death rates from a wide range of conditions. And people infected with HIV remain symptom-free longer if they have a strong social support network. For more on developing and maintaining your social network, see the box "Building Social Support."

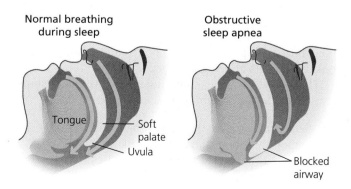

FIGURE 10.4 Sleep apnea.
Sleep apnea occurs when soft tissues surrounding the airway relax, "collapsing" the airway and restricting airflow.

Guidelines for Effective Communication

Getting Started

● When you want to have a serious discussion with your partner, choose an appropriate time and place. Find a private place and a time when you will not be interrupted.

● Face your partner and maintain eye contact. Use nonverbal feedback to show that you are interested and involved in the communication process.

Being an Effective Speaker

● State your concern or issue as clearly as you can.

● Use "I" statements—statements about how *you* feel—rather than statements beginning with "You," which tell another person how you think he or she feels. When you use "I" statements, you are taking responsibility for your feelings. "You" statements are often blaming or accusatory and will probably get a defensive or resentful response. The statement "I feel unloved," for example, sends a clearer, less blaming message than the statement "You don't love me."

● Focus on a specific behavior rather than on the whole person. Be specific about the behavior you like or don't like. Avoid generalizations beginning with "You always" or "You never." Such statements make people feel defensive.

● Make constructive requests. Opening your request with "I would like" keeps the focus on your needs rather than your partner's supposed deficiencies.

● Avoid blaming, accusing, and belittling. Even if you are right, you have little to gain by putting your partner down. Studies have shown that when people feel criticized or attacked, they are less able to think rationally or solve problems constructively.

● Ask for action ahead of time. Tell your partner what you would like to have happen in the future; don't wait for him or her to blow it and then express anger or disappointment.

Being an Effective Listener

● Provide appropriate nonverbal feedback (nodding, smiling, and so on).

● Don't interrupt.

● Develop the skill of reflective listening. Don't judge, evaluate, analyze, or offer solutions (unless asked to do so). Your partner may just need to have you there in order to sort out feelings. By jumping in right away to "fix" the problem, you may be cutting off communication.

● Don't give unsolicited advice. Giving advice implies that you know more about what a person needs to do than he or she does; therefore, it often evokes anger or resentment.

● Clarify your understanding of what your partner is saying by restating it in your own words and asking if your understanding is correct.

● Be sure you are really listening, not off somewhere in your mind rehearsing your reply. Try to tune in to your partner's feelings as well as the words.

● Let your partner know that you value what she or he is saying and want to understand. Respect for the other person is the cornerstone of effective communication.

Communication

Good communication skills can help everyone form and maintain healthy relationships. Communicating in an assertive way that respects the rights of others—as well as your own—can prevent potentially stressful situations from getting out of control. When friends or partners communicate effectively, they can reduce the stresses in their relationship and spend more time focusing on the positive aspects of being together.

Three keys to good communication in relationships are self-disclosure, listening, and feedback.

- *Self-disclosure* involves revealing personal information that we ordinarily wouldn't reveal because of the risk involved. It usually increases feelings of closeness and moves the relationship to a deeper level of intimacy.

- *Listening* is a rare skill. Good listening skills require that we spend more time and energy trying to fully understand another person's "story" and less time judging, evaluating, blaming, advising, analyzing, or trying to control. Empathy, warmth, respect, and genuineness are qualities of skillful listeners. Attentive listening encourages friends or partners to share more and, in turn, to be attentive listeners. To connect with other people and develop real emotional intimacy, listening is essential.

- *Feedback,* a constructive response to another's self-disclosure, is the third key to good communication. Giving positive feedback means acknowledging that the friend's or partner's feelings are valid—no matter how upsetting or troubling—and offering self-disclosure in response. Self-disclosure and feedback can open the door to change, whereas other responses block communication and change.

For tips on improving your skills, see the box "Guidelines for Effective Communication."

Wellness Tip

In a stressful situation, do you ever stop and count to 10? If not, you should. It works! In the few seconds it takes to count to 10, you can calm your mind, get your breathing under control, slow your heart rate, and lower your blood pressure. In effect, that quick 10-count can offset the stress reaction and help you avoid making things worse.

Some people have trouble either telling others what they need or saying no to the needs of others. They may suppress their feelings of anger, frustration, and resentment, and they may end up feeling taken advantage of or suffering in unhealthy relationships. At the other extreme are people who express anger openly and directly by being verbally or physically aggressive or indirectly by making critical, hurtful comments to others. Their abusive behavior pushes other people away, so they also have problems with relationships.

If you typically suppress your feelings, you might want to take an assertiveness training course that can help you identify and change your patterns of communication. If you have trouble controlling your anger, you can benefit from learning anger management strategies; see the box "Dealing with Anger."

Conflict Resolution

Conflict is natural in any relationship, and it can become a key source of stress for friends, coworkers, family members, and intimate partners. No matter how close two people become, they still remain separate individuals with their own needs, desires, past experiences, and ways of seeing the world. Conflict itself isn't dangerous to a relationship; it may simply indicate that the relationship is growing. But if it isn't handled in a constructive way, conflict can damage—and ultimately destroy—a relationship.

Conflict is often accompanied by anger—a natural emotion, but one that can be difficult to handle. When angry, both parties should back off until they calm down and then come back to the issue later and try to resolve it rationally. Negotiation will help dissipate the anger so the conflict can be resolved. Some basic strategies are useful in successfully negotiating with a friend, family member, colleague, or intimate partner:

1. *Clarify the issue.* Take responsibility for thinking through your feelings and discovering what's really bothering you. Agree that one of you will speak first and have the chance to speak fully while the other listens. Then reverse the roles. Try to understand the other person's position fully by repeating what you've heard and asking questions to clarify or elicit more information.

2. *Find out what each person wants.* Ask the other person to express her or his desires. Don't assume you already know what those desires are, and don't try to speak for your friend or partner.

3. *Determine how you both can get what you want.* Brainstorm to generate a variety of options.

4. *Decide how to negotiate.* Work out a plan for change. For example, agree that one of you will do one task and the other will do another task or that one of you will do a task in exchange for something she or he wants.

5. *Solidify the agreements.* Go over the plan verbally and write it down, if necessary, to ensure that you both understand and agree to it.

6. *Review and renegotiate.* Decide on a time frame for trying out the new plan and set a time to discuss how it's working. Make adjustments as needed.

Striving for Spiritual Wellness

Spiritual wellness is associated with greater coping skills and higher levels of overall wellness. It is a very personal wellness component, and there are many ways to develop it. Researchers have linked spiritual wellness to longer life expectancy, reduced risk of disease, faster recovery, and improved emotional health. Although spirituality is difficult to study, and researchers aren't sure how or why spirituality seems to improve health, several explanations have been offered. Lab 10.3 includes exercises designed to help you build spiritual wellness.

Confiding in Yourself Through Writing

Keeping a diary is like confiding in someone else, except that you are confiding in yourself. This form of coping with severe stress may be especially helpful for those who are shy or introverted and find it difficult to open up to others. Although writing about traumatic and stressful events may have a short-term negative effect on mood, over the long term, stress is reduced and positive changes in health occur. A key to promoting health and well-being through journaling is to write about your emotional responses to stressful events. Set aside a special time each day or week to write down your feelings about stressful events in your life.

Time Management

Learning to manage your time can be crucial to coping with everyday stressors. Overcommitment, procrastination, and even boredom are significant stressors for many people. Along with gaining control of nutrition and exercise to maintain a healthy energy balance, time management is an

Dealing with Anger

Anger is a natural response to something we perceive as an injustice, a betrayal, an insult, or some other wrong—whether real or imagined. We may respond physically with faster heart and breathing rates, muscle tension, trembling, a knot in the stomach, or a red face. When anger alerts us that something is wrong, it is a useful emotion that can lead to constructive change. When anger leads to loss of control and to aggression, it causes problems.

According to current popular wisdom, it's healthy to express your feelings, including anger. However, research has shown that people who are overtly hostile are at higher risk for heart disease and heart attacks than calmer people. In addition, expressing anger in thoughtless or out-of-control ways can damage personal and professional relationships.

People who experience rage or explosive anger are particularly at risk for negative repercussions. Some of these people may have *intermittent explosive disorder,* characterized by aggressiveness that is impulsive and out of proportion to the stimulus. Explosive anger renders people temporarily unable to think straight or act in their own best interests. Counseling can help very angry people learn how to manage their anger.

In dealing with anger, it is important to distinguish between a reasonable degree of self-assertiveness and a gratuitous expression of aggression. When you are *assertive,* you stand up for your own rights at the same time that you respect the rights of others. When you are *aggressive,* you violate the rights of others.

Managing Your Own Anger

What are the best ways to handle anger? If you find yourself in a situation where you are getting angry, answer these questions:

- Is the situation important enough to get angry about?
- Are you truly justified in getting angry?
- Is expressing your anger going to make a positive difference?

If the answer to all these questions is yes, then calm, assertive communication may be appropriate. Use "I" statements to express your feelings ("I would like . . .," "I feel . . ."), and listen respectfully to the other person's point of view. Don't attack verbally or make demands; try to negotiate a constructive, mutually satisfying solution.

If you answer no to any of the questions, try to calm yourself. First, reframe the situation by thinking about it differently. Try these strategies:

- Don't take it personally—maybe the driver who cut you off simply didn't see you.
- Look for mitigating factors—maybe the classmate who didn't say hello was preoccupied with money concerns.
- Practice empathy—try to see the situation from the other person's point of view.
- Ask questions—clarify the situation by asking what the other person meant. Avoid defensiveness.
- Focus on the present—don't let this situation trigger thoughts of past incidents that you perceive as similar.

Second, calm your body down.

- Use the old trick of counting to 10 before you respond.
- Concentrate on your breathing, and take long, slow breaths.
- Imagine yourself in a beautiful, peaceful place.
- If needed, take a longer cooling-off period by leaving the situation until your anger has subsided.

Dealing with Other People's Anger

If someone you are with becomes very angry, try these strategies:

- Respond asymmetrically—remain calm. Don't get angry in response.
- Apologize if you think you are to blame. (Don't apologize if you don't think you are to blame.)
- Validate the other person by acknowledging that he or she has some reason to be angry. However, don't accept verbal abuse.
- Focus on the problem and ask what can be done to alleviate the situation.
- If the person cannot be calmed, disengage from the situation, at least temporarily. After a time-out, attempts at rational problem solving may be more successful.

Warning Signs of Violence

Violence is never acceptable. The following behaviors over a period of time suggest the potential for violence:

- A history of making threats and engaging in aggressive behavior
- Drug or alcohol abuse
- Gang membership
- Access to or fascination with weapons
- Feelings of rejection or aloneness; the feeling of constantly being disrespected; victimization by bullies
- Withdrawal from usual activities and friends; poor school performance
- Failure to acknowledge the rights of others

The following are immediate warning signs of violence:

- Daily loss of temper or frequent physical fighting
- Significant vandalism or property damage
- Increased risk-taking behavior; increased drug or alcohol abuse
- Threats or detailed plans to commit acts of violence
- Pleasure in hurting animals
- The presence of weapons

Don't spend time with someone who shows these warning signs of violence. Don't carry a weapon or resort to violence to protect yourself. Ask someone in authority or an experienced professional for help.

important element in a wellness program. Try these strategies for improving your time-management skills:

- **Set priorities.** Divide your tasks into three groups: essential, important, and trivial. Focus on the first two, and ignore the third.

- **Schedule tasks for peak efficiency.** You probably know that you're most productive at certain times of the day (or night). Schedule as many of your tasks for those hours as you can, and stick to your schedule.

- **Set realistic goals and write them down.** Attainable goals spur you on. Impossible goals, by definition, cause frustration and failure. Fully commit yourself to achieving your goals by putting them in writing.

- **Budget enough time.** For each project you undertake, calculate how much time you will need to finish it. Then tack on another 10–15%, or even 25%, as a buffer.

- **Break up long-term goals into short-term ones.** Instead of waiting for large blocks of time, use short amounts of time to start a project or keep it moving.

- **Visualize achieving your goal.** By mentally rehearsing a task, you will be able to do it more smoothly.

- **Keep track of the tasks you put off.** Analyze the reasons you procrastinate. If the task is difficult or unpleasant, look for ways to make it easier or more fun. For example, if you find the readings for one of your classes particularly difficult, choose an especially nice setting for your reading, and then reward yourself each time you complete a section or chapter.

- **Consider doing your least favorite tasks first.** Once you have the most unpleasant ones out of the way, you can work on the tasks you enjoy more.

- **Consolidate tasks when possible.** For example, try walking to the store so that you run your errands and exercise in the same block of time.

- **Identify quick transitional tasks.** Keep a list of 5- to 10-minute tasks you can do while waiting or between other tasks, such as watering your plants, doing the dishes, or checking a homework assignment.

- **Delegate responsibility.** Asking for help when you have too much to do is no cop-out; it's good time management. Just don't delegate the jobs you know you should do yourself.

- **Say no when necessary.** If the demands made on you don't seem reasonable, say no—tactfully, but without guilt or apology.

- **Give yourself a break.** Allow time for play— free, unstructured time when you can ignore

Time-management skills, including careful scheduling with a datebook or computer, can help people cope with busy days.

the clock. Don't consider this a waste of time. Play renews you and enables you to work more efficiently.

- **Avoid your personal "time sinks."** You can probably identify your own time sinks—activities like watching television, surfing the Internet, or talking on the phone that consistently use up more time than you anticipate and put you behind schedule. Some days, it may be best to avoid problematic activities altogether; for example, if you have a big paper due, don't sit down for a 5-minute TV break if it is likely to turn into a 2-hour break. Try a 5-minute walk if you need to clear your head.

- **Stop thinking or talking about what you're going to do, and just do it!** Sometimes the best solution for procrastination is to stop waiting for the right moment and just get started. You will probably find that things are not as bad as you feared, and your momentum will keep you going.

Realistic Self-Talk

Do your patterns of thinking make events seem worse than they truly are? Do negative beliefs about yourself become self-fulfilling prophecies? Substituting realistic self-talk for negative self-talk can help you build and maintain self-esteem and cope better with the challenges in your life. Here are some examples of common types of distorted, negative self-talk, along with suggestions for more accurate and rational responses.

COGNITIVE DISTORTION	NEGATIVE SELF-TALK	REALISTIC SELF-TALK
Focusing on negatives	School is so discouraging—nothing but one hassle after another.	School is pretty challenging and has its difficulties, but there certainly are rewards. It's really a mixture of good and bad.
Expecting the worst	Why would my boss want to meet with me this afternoon if not to fire me?	I wonder why my boss wants to meet with me? I guess I'll just have to wait and see.
Overgeneralizing	[*After getting a poor grade on a paper*] Just as I thought—I'm incompetent at everything.	I'll start working on the next paper earlier. That way, if I run into problems I'll have time to talk to the TA.
Minimizing	I won the speech contest, but none of the other speakers was very good. I wouldn't have done as well against stiffer competition.	It may not have been the best speech I'll ever give, but it was good enough to win the contest.
Blaming others	I wouldn't have eaten so much last night if my friends hadn't insisted on going to that restaurant.	I overdid it last night. Next time I'll make different choices.
Expecting perfection	I should have scored 100% on this test. I can't believe I missed that one problem through a careless mistake.	Too bad I missed one problem through carelessness, but overall I did very well on this test. Next time I'll be more careful.

SOURCE: Based on W. Schafer. 1999. *Stress Management for Wellness*, 4th ed. Copyright © 2000 Wadsworth, a part of Cengage Learning, Inc. Reproduced by permission. www.cengage.com/permissions.

For more help with time management, complete Activity 10 in the Behavior Change Workbook.

Cognitive Techniques

Certain thought patterns and ways of thinking, including ideas, beliefs, and perceptions, can contribute to stress and have a negative impact on health. But other habits of mind, if practiced with patience and consistency, can help break unhealthy thought patterns. Below are some suggestions for changing destructive thinking:

- Monitor your self-talk and try to minimize hostile, critical, suspicious, and self-deprecating thoughts (see the box "Realistic Self-Talk").

- Modify your expectations. They often restrict experience and lead to disappointment. Try to accept life as it comes.

- Live in the present. Clear your mind of old debris and fears so you can enjoy life as it is now.

- Go with the flow. Accept what you can't change, forgive others for their faults, and be flexible.

Cultivating your sense of humor is another key cognitive stress-management technique. Even a fleeting smile produces changes in your autonomic nervous system that can lift your spirits. Hearty laughter triggers the release of endorphins, and after a good laugh, your muscles go slack and your pulse and blood pressure dip below normal; you are relaxed.

Relaxation Techniques

The **relaxation response** is a physiological state characterized by a feeling of warmth and quiet mental alertness. This state is the opposite of the fight-or-flight response. When you induce the relaxation response by using a relaxation technique, your heart rate, breathing, and metabolism slow down. Blood pressure and oxygen consumption decrease. At the same time, blood flow to the brain and skin increases, and brain waves shift from an alert beta rhythm to a relaxed alpha rhythm.

The techniques described in this section are among the most popular techniques and the easiest to learn; also, see

Solving Problems

Got a problem that's stressing you out? Solve it! Problem solving is a skill—one that requires practice and patience, but one that can pay off in a more balanced, less stressful life. Think of a problem that's bugging you right now, and take the following steps to solve it:

1. Define the problem in a sentence or two. Write it down.
2. List the problem's cause. There may be more than one.
3. List some potential solutions. Don't stop with one or the most obvious one. Write down several options.
4. For each solution, list the potential positive and negative consequences. Be thorough.
5. Choose the solution you think will work best, or will have the fewest negative consequences.
6. List the steps you'll need to take to carry out your solution.
7. Get started with the list of steps you just made. Don't delay unless you have to.
8. As you work on solving the problem, pause occasionally and reevaluate. Revise your approach, if necessary.

If you can't seem to solve a problem on your own, get help. Talk to someone who knows you well, or get help from a counselor, and work through these steps again. Any problem can be solved, but some may just be too big to handle on your own.

the box "Relaxing Through Meditation." All these techniques take practice, so it may be several weeks before the benefits become noticeable in everyday life.

Progressive Relaxation In this simple relaxation technique, you tense and then relax the muscles of the body one group at a time. Also known as deep muscle relaxation, this technique addresses the muscle tension that occurs when the body is experiencing stress. Consciously relaxing tensed muscles sends a message to other body systems to reduce the stress response.

To practice progressive relaxation, begin by inhaling as you contract your right fist. Then exhale as you release your fist. Repeat. Contract and relax your right bicep. Repeat. Do the same using your left arm. Then, working from forehead to feet, contract and relax other muscles. Repeat each contraction at least once, inhaling as you tense and exhaling as you relax. To speed up the process, tense and relax more muscles at one time—for example, both arms simultaneously. With practice, you'll be able to relax quickly just by clenching and releasing only your fists.

Visualization Also known as imagery, visualization is so effective in enhancing sports performance that it has become part of the curriculum at training camps for U.S. Olympic athletes. This same technique can be used to induce relaxation, to help change habits, and to improve performance on an exam, on stage, or on a playing field.

To practice visualization, imagine yourself floating on a cloud, sitting on a mountaintop, or lying in a meadow. Try to identify all the perceptible qualities of the environment—sight, sound, temperature, smell, and so on. Your body will respond as if your imagery were real.

An alternative is to close your eyes and imagine a deep purple light filling your body. Then change the color to a soothing gold. As the color lightens, so should your distress. Imagery can also enhance performance: Visualize yourself succeeding at a task that worries you.

Deep Breathing Your breathing pattern is closely tied to your stress level. Deep, slow breathing is associated with relaxation. Rapid, shallow, often irregular breathing occurs during the stress response. With practice, you can learn to slow and quiet your breathing pattern, thereby

Fitness Tip

Activities like yoga and tai chi are well known for their relaxing, meditative aspects. But they're great workouts, too. If you're looking for a way to improve your flexibility and muscle tone while exercising in a quiet, pressure-free environment, check out a local yoga or tai chi class. Be sure the class is led by a qualified professional.

relaxation response A physiological state characterized by a feeling of warmth and quiet mental alertness.

KEY TERM

Relaxing Through Meditation

connect
ACTIVITY
DO IT ONLINE

Techniques for managing stress by inducing the relaxation response have been developed in many cultures over the centuries. One such technique is yoga, described in Chapter 5. Another technique that has become popular in the United States is meditation.

At its most basic level, meditation, or self-reflective thought, involves quieting or emptying the mind to achieve deep relaxation. Some practitioners of meditation view it on a deeper level as a means of focusing concentration, increasing self-awareness, and bringing enlightenment to their lives. Meditation has been integrated into the practices of several religions—Buddhism, Hinduism, Confucianism, Taoism—but it is not a religion itself, nor does its practice require any special knowledge, belief, or background.

There are many styles of meditation, based on different ways of quieting the mind. Here is a simple, practical technique for eliciting the relaxation response using one style:

1. Pick a word, a phrase, or an object to focus on. You can choose a word or phrase that has a deep meaning for you, but any word or phrase will work. Some meditators prefer to focus on their breathing.

2. Sit comfortably in a quiet place. Close your eyes if you're not focusing on an object.

3. Relax your muscles.

4. Breathe slowly and naturally. If you're using a focus word or phrase, silently repeat it each time you exhale. If you're using an object, focus on it as you breathe.

5. Keep your attitude passive. Disregard thoughts that drift in.

6. Continue for 10–20 minutes once or twice a day.

7. After you've finished, sit quietly for a few minutes with your eyes closed, then open. Then stand up.

Allow relaxation to occur at its own pace; don't force it. Don't be surprised if you can't tune your mind out for more than a few seconds at a time. It's nothing to get angry about. The more you ignore the intrusions, the easier it will become. If you want to time your session, peek at a watch or clock occasionally, but don't set a jarring alarm.

Although you'll feel refreshed even after the first session, it may take a month or more to get noticeable results. Be patient. Eventually, the relaxation response becomes so natural that it occurs spontaneously or on demand when you sit quietly for a few moments.

also quieting your mind and relaxing your body. Try one of the breathing techniques described in the box "Breathing for Relaxation" for on-the-spot tension relief, as well as for long-term stress reduction.

Listening to Music Music can relax us. It influences pulse, blood pressure, and the electrical activity of muscles. Listening to soothing, lyrical music can lessen depression, anxiety, and stress levels. To experience the stress-management benefits of music, set aside a period of at least 15 minutes to listen quietly. Choose music you enjoy and selections that make you feel relaxed.

Other Stress-Management Techniques

Techniques such as biofeedback, hypnosis and self-hypnosis, and massage require a partner or professional training or assistance. As with the relaxation techniques presented, all take practice, and it may be several weeks before the benefits are noticeable.

Biofeedback helps people reduce their response to stress by enabling them to become more aware of their level of physiological arousal. In biofeedback, some measure of stress—perspiration, heart rate, skin temperature, or muscle tension—is electronically monitored, and feedback is given using sound (a tone or music), light, or a meter or dial. With practice, people begin to exercise conscious control over their physiological stress responses. The point of biofeedback training is to develop the ability

to transfer the skill to daily life without the use of electronic equipment.

GETTING HELP

You can use the principles of behavioral self-management described in Chapter 1 to create a stress-management program tailored specifically to your needs. The starting point of a successful program is to listen to your body. When you learn to recognize the stress response and the emotions and thoughts that accompany it, you'll be in a position to begin handling stress. Labs 10.1 and 10.2 can guide you in identifying and finding ways to cope with stress-inducing situations.

If you feel you need guidance beyond the information in this text, excellent self-help guides can be found in bookstores or the library; helpful Web sites are listed in For Further Exploration at the end of the chapter. Some people also find it helpful to express their feelings in a journal. Grappling with a painful experience in this way provides an emotional release and can help you develop more constructive ways of dealing with similar situations in the future.

Peer Counseling and Support Groups

If you still feel overwhelmed despite efforts to manage your stress, you may want to seek outside help. Peer counseling, often available through the student health

Breathing for Relaxation

Controlled breathing can do more than just help you relax. It can also help control pain, anxiety, and other conditions that lead to or are related to stress. There are many methods of controlled breathing. Two of the most popular are belly breathing and tension-release breathing.

Belly Breathing

1. Lie on your back and relax.
2. Place one hand on your chest and the other on your abdomen. Your hands will help you gauge your breathing.
3. Take in a slow, deep breath through your nose and into your belly. Your abdomen should rise significantly (check with your hand); your chest should rise only slightly. Focus on filling your abdomen with air.

4. Exhale through your mouth, gently pushing out the air from your abdomen.

Tension-Release Breathing

1. Lie down or sit in a chair and get comfortable.
2. Take a slow, deep breath into your abdomen. Inhale through your nose. Try to visualize the air moving to every part of your body. As you breathe in, say to yourself, "Breathe in relaxation."
3. Exhale through your mouth. Visualize tension leaving your body. Say to yourself, "Breathe out tension."

These techniques have many variations. For example, sit in a chair and raise your arms, shoulders, and chin as you inhale; lower them as you exhale. Or slowly count to 4 as you inhale, then again as you exhale.

Many yoga experts suggest breathing rhythmically, in time with your own heartbeat. Relax and listen closely for the sensation of your heart beating, or monitor your pulse while you breathe. As you inhale, count to 4 or 8 in time with your heartbeat, then repeat the count as you exhale. Breathing in time with soothing music can work well, too.

Experts suggest inhaling through the nose and exhaling through the mouth. Breathe slowly, deeply, and gently. To focus on breathing gently, imagine a candle burning a few inches in front of you. Try to exhale softly enough to make the candle's flame flicker, not hard enough to blow it out.

Practice is important, too. Perform your chosen breathing exercise two or more times daily, for 5–10 minutes per session.

Many people seek help from professional therapists when dealing with stress-related problems.

center or counseling center, is usually staffed by volunteer students with special training that emphasizes maintaining confidentiality. Peer counselors can steer those seeking help to appropriate campus and community resources or just offer sympathetic listening.

Support groups are typically organized around a particular issue or problem: All group members might be entering a new school, reentering school after an interruption, struggling with single parenting, experiencing eating disorders, or coping with particular kinds of trauma. Simply voicing concerns that others share can relieve stress.

Professional Help

Psychotherapy, especially a short-term course of sessions, can also be tremendously helpful in dealing with stress-related problems. Not all therapists are right for all people, so it's a good idea to shop around for a compatible psychotherapist with reasonable fees. (See the box "Choosing and Evaluating Mental Health Professionals.")

Is It Stress or Something More Serious?

Most of us have periods of feeling down when we become pessimistic, anxious, less energetic, and less able to enjoy life. Such feelings and thoughts can be normal responses to the ordinary challenges of life. Symptoms that may indicate a more serious problem include the following:

- Depression, anxiety, or other emotional problems begin to interfere seriously with school or work performance or in getting along with others.

Choosing and Evaluating Mental Health Professionals

College students are usually in a good position to find convenient, affordable mental health care. Larger schools typically have health services that employ psychiatrists and psychologists as well as counseling centers staffed by professionals and peer counselors. Resources in the community may include a school of medicine, a hospital, and a variety of professionals who work independently. It's a good idea to get recommendations from physicians, friends who have been in therapy, or community agencies, rather than to pick a counselor or therapist at random.

Financial considerations are also important. Find out the cost of different services and what your health insurance will cover. If you're not adequately covered by a health plan, don't let that stop you from getting help; investigate low-cost alternatives on campus and in your community. The cost of treatment is linked to how many therapy sessions will be needed, which in turn depends on the type of therapy and the nature of the problem. Psychological therapies focusing on specific problems may require eight or ten sessions at weekly intervals. Therapies aiming for psychological awareness and personality change can last months or years.

Deciding whether a therapist is right for you requires meeting the therapist in person. Before or during your first meeting, find out about the therapist's background and training:

- Does she or he have a degree from an appropriate professional school and a state license to practice?

- Has she or he had experience treating people with problems similar to yours?

- How much will therapy cost?

You have a right to know the answers to these questions and should not hesitate to ask them. After your initial meeting, evaluate your impressions:

- Does the therapist seem like a warm, intelligent person who would be able to help you and is interested in doing so?

- Are you comfortable with the personality, values, and beliefs of the therapist?

- Is the therapist willing to talk about the techniques he or she will use? Do these techniques make sense to you?

If you answer yes to these questions, this therapist may be satisfactory for you. If you feel uncomfortable—and if you are not in need of emergency care—it's worthwhile to set up one-time consultations with one or two others before you make up your mind. Take the time to find someone who feels right for you.

Later in your treatment, evaluate your progress:

- Are you being helped by the treatment?

- If you are displeased, is it because you aren't making progress or because therapy is raising difficult, painful issues you don't want to deal with?

- Can you express dissatisfaction to your therapist? Such feedback can improve your treatment.

If you're convinced your therapy isn't working or is harmful, thank your therapist for her or his efforts and find another.

- Suicide is attempted or is seriously considered.
- Symptoms such as hallucinations, delusions, incoherent speech, or loss of memory occur.
- Alcohol or drugs are used to the extent that they impair normal functioning, finding or taking drugs occupies much of the week, or reducing the dosage leads to psychological or physical withdrawal symptoms.

Depression is of particular concern because severe depression is linked to suicide, one of the leading causes of death among college students. In some cases, depression, like severe stress, is a clear-cut reaction to a specific event, such as losing a loved one or failing in school or work. In other cases, no trigger event is obvious. Symptoms of depression include the following:

- Negative self-concept
- Pervasive feelings of sadness and hopelessness

- Loss of pleasure in usual activities
- Poor appetite and weight loss
- Insomnia or disturbed sleep
- Restlessness or fatigue
- Thoughts of worthlessness and guilt
- Trouble concentrating or making decisions
- Thoughts of death or suicide

Not all of these symptoms are present in everyone who is depressed, but most experience a loss of interest or pleasure in their usual activities. Warning signs of suicide include expressing the wish to be dead, revealing contemplated suicide methods, increasing social withdrawal and isolation, and exhibiting a sudden, inexplicable lightening of mood (which can indicate the person has finally decided to commit suicide).

If you are severely depressed or know someone who is, expert help from a mental health professional is essential. Most communities and many colleges have hotlines and/or health services and counseling centers that can provide help. The National Suicide Prevention Lifeline can be reached at 1-800-273-TALK. Treatments for depression and many other psychological disorders are highly effective.

KEY TERM

depression A mood disorder characterized by loss of interest, sadness, hopelessness, loss of appetite, disturbed sleep, and other physical symptoms.

What percentage of your daily stress is time related? How effective are your time-management skills? Identify one thing you can start doing right now to manage your time better, and describe how you can apply it to one aspect of your daily routine.

TIPS FOR TODAY AND THE FUTURE

For the stress you can't avoid, develop a range of stress-management techniques and strategies.

RIGHT NOW YOU CAN

- Practice deep breathing for 5–10 minutes.
- Visualize a relaxing, peaceful place and imagine yourself experiencing it as vividly as possible. Stay there as long as you can.
- Do some stretching exercises.
- Get out your datebook and schedule what you'll be doing the rest of today and tomorrow. Pencil in a short walk and a conversation with a friend.

IN THE FUTURE YOU CAN

- Take a class or workshop, such as one in assertiveness training or time management, that can help you overcome a source of stress.
- Find a way to build relaxing time into every day. Just 15 minutes of meditation, stretching, or deep breathing can induce the relaxation response.

SUMMARY

- Stress is the collective physiological and emotional response to any stressor. Physiological responses to stressors are the same for everyone.

- The autonomic nervous system and the endocrine system are responsible for the body's physical response to stressors. The sympathetic nervous system mobilizes the body and activates key hormones of the endocrine system, causing the fight-or-flight reaction. The parasympathetic system returns the body to homeostasis.

- Behavioral responses to stress are controlled by the somatic nervous system and fall under a person's conscious control.

- The general adaptation syndrome model and research in psychoneuroimmunology contribute to our understanding of the links between stress and disease. People who have many stressors in their lives or who handle stress poorly are at risk for cardiovascular disease, impairment of the immune system, and many other problems.

- Potential sources of stress include major life changes, daily hassles, college- and job-related stressors, and interpersonal and social stressors.

- Positive ways of managing stress include regular exercise, good nutrition, support from other people, clear communication, spiritual wellness, effective time management, cognitive techniques, and relaxation techniques.

- If a personal program for stress management doesn't work, peer counseling, support groups, and psychotherapy are available.

FOR FURTHER EXPLORATION

BOOKS

Greenberg, J. 2010. *Comprehensive Stress Management,* 12th ed. New York: McGraw-Hill. *Provides a clear explanation of the physical, psychological, sociological, and spiritual aspects of stress and offers numerous stress-management techniques.*

Kabat-Zinn, J. 2006. *Coming to Our Senses: Healing Ourselves and the World Through Mindfulness.* New York: Hyperion. *Explores the connections among mindfulness, health, and physical and spiritual well-being.*

Pennebaker, J. W. 2004. *Writing to Heal: A Guided Journal for Recovering from Trauma and Emotional Upheaval.* Oakland, Calif.: New Harbinger Press. *Provides information about using journaling to cope with stress.*

Seaward, B. L. 2009. *Managing Stress: Principles and Strategies for Health and Well-Being,* 6th ed. Boston: Jones and Bartlett. *A comprehensive textbook for college students.*

ORGANIZATIONS AND WEB SITES

American Headache Society. Provides information for consumers and clinicians about different types of headaches, their causes, and their treatment.
http://www.americanheadachesociety.org/

The American Institute of Stress. A resource of in-depth information on stress, its causes, and its treatments.
http://www.stress.org

American Psychiatric Association: Healthy Minds, Healthy Lives. Provides information on mental wellness especially for college students.
http://www.healthyminds.org

American Psychological Association. Provides information on stress management and psychological disorders.
http://www.apa.org
http://apa.org/helpcenter

Association for Applied Psychophysiology and Biofeedback. Provides information about biofeedback and referrals to certified biofeedback practitioners.
http://www.aapb.org

Benson-Henry Institute for Mind Body Medicine. Provides information about stress-management and relaxation techniques.
http://www.massgeneral.org/bhi

National Institute of Mental Health (NIMH). Publishes informative brochures about stress and stress management as well as other aspects of mental health.
http://www.nimh.nih.gov

National Sleep Foundation. Provides information about sleep and how to overcome sleep problems such as insomnia, apnea, and jet lag.
http://www.sleepfoundation.org

Q Are there any relaxation techniques I can use in response to an immediate stressor?

A Yes. Try the deep breathing techniques described in the chapter, and try some of the following to see which work best for you:

- Do a full-body stretch while standing or sitting. Stretch your arms out to the sides and then reach them as far as possible over your head. Rotate your body from the waist. Bend over as far as is comfortable for you.
- Do a partial session of progressive muscle relaxation. Tense and then relax some of the muscles in your body. Focus on the muscles that are stiff or tense. Shake out your arms and legs.
- Take a short, brisk walk (3–5 minutes). Breathe deeply.
- Engage in realistic self-talk about the stressor. Mentally rehearse dealing successfully with the stressor. As an alternative, focus your mind on some other activity.
- Briefly reflect on something personally meaningful. In one study of college students, researchers found that self-reflection on important personal values prior to a stressful task reduces the hormonal response to the stressor.

Q Can stress cause headaches?

A Stress is one possible cause of the most common type of headache, the tension headache. About 90% of headaches are tension headaches, characterized by a dull, steady pain, usually on both sides of the head. It may feel as though a band of pressure is tightening around the head, and the pain may extend to the neck and shoulders. Acute tension headaches may last from hours to days, while chronic tension headaches may occur almost every day for months or even years. Stress, poor posture, and immobility are leading causes of tension headaches. There is no cure, but the pain can be relieved with over-the-counter painkillers; many people also try such therapies as massage, relaxation, hot or cold showers, and rest. Stress is also one possible trigger of migraine headaches, which are typically characterized by throbbing pain (often on one side of the head), heightened sensitivity to light and noise, visual disturbances such as flashing lights, nausea, and fatigue.

If your headaches are frequent, keep a journal with details about the events surrounding each one. Are your tension headaches associated with late nights, academic deadlines, or long periods spent sitting at a computer? Are migraines associated with certain foods, stress, fatigue, specific sounds or odors, or (in women) menstruation? If you can identify the stressors or other factors that are consistently associated with your headaches, you can begin to gain more control over the situation. If you suffer persistent tension or migraine headaches, consult your physician.

For more Common Questions Answered about stress, visit the Online Learning Center at www.mhhe.com/fahey.

SELECTED BIBLIOGRAPHY

American College Health Association. 2010. *American College Health Association–National College Health Assessment II Reference Group Executive Summary, Spring 2010*. Linthicum, Md.: American College Health Association.

American Psychological Association. 2010. *How Does Stress Affect Us?* (http://www.apa.org/helpcenter/stress-effects.aspx; retrieved March 20, 2011).

American Psychological Association. 2010. *Learning to Deal with Stress* (http://www.apa.org/helpcenter/stress-learning.aspx; retrieved March 20, 2011).

American Psychological Association. 2010. *Mind/Body Health: Stress* (http://www.apa.org/helpcenter/stress.aspx; retrieved March 20, 2011).

American Psychological Association. 2010. *Stress in America 2010*. Washington, D.C.: American Psychological Association.

Caldwell, K., et al. 2010. Developing mindfulness in college students through movement-based courses: Effects on self-regulatory self-efficacy, mood, stress, and sleep quality. *Journal of American College Health* 58(5): 433–442.

Centers for Disease Control and Prevention. 2010. *Coping with a Disaster or Traumatic Event: Information for Individuals and Families* (http://emergency.cdc.gov/mentalhealth/general.asp; retrieved March 20, 2011).

Cohen, S., W. J. Doyle, and A. Baum. 2006. Socioeconomic status is associated with stress hormones. *Psychosomatic Medicine* 68(3): 414–420.

Freedman, N. 2010. Treatment of obstructive sleep apnea syndrome. *Clinics in Chest Medicine* 31(2): 187–201.

Hefner, J., and D. Eisenberg. 2009. Social support and mental health among college students. *American Journal of Orthopsychiatry* 79(4): 491–499.

Hook, J. N., et al. 2010. Empirically supported religious and spiritual therapies. *Journal of Clinical Psychology* 66(1): 46–72.

Institute of Medicine Committee on Sleep Medicine and Research. 2006. *Sleep Disorders and Sleep Deprivation: An Unmet Public Health Problem*, ed. H. R. Colton and B. M. Altevogt. Washington, D.C.: National Academies Press.

Mayo Foundation for Medical Education and Research. 2008. *Stress: Win Control over the Stress in Your Life* (http://www.mayoclinic.com/health/stress/SR00001; retrieved March 20, 2011).

National Sleep Foundation. 2011. *2011 Sleep in America Poll*. Washington, D.C.: National Sleep Foundation.

Nordboe, D. J., et al. 2007. Immediate behavioral health response to the Virginia Tech shootings. *Disaster Medicine and Public Health Preparedness* 1(Suppl. 1.): S31–S32.

Roddenberry, A., and K. Renk. 2010. Locus of control and self-efficacy: Potential mediators of stress, illness, and utilization of health services in college students. *Child Psychiatry and Human Development* 41(4): 353–370.

Telles, S., et al. 2009. Effect of a yoga practice session and a yoga theory session on state anxiety. *Perceptual and Motor Skills* 109(3): 924–930.

The New York Times. 2010 Update. *Times Topics: School Shootings* (http://topics.nytimes.com/top/reference/timestopics/subjects/s/school_shootings/index.html; retrieved March 20, 2011).

Torpy, J. M. 2008. Chronic stress and the heart. *Journal of the American Medical Association* 298(14): 1722.

U.S. Department of Health and Human Services, National Institutes of Health. 2009. *Stress* (http://www.nlm.nih.gov/medlineplus/stress.html; retrieved March 20, 2011).

LAB 10.1 Identifying Your Stress Level and Key Stressors

How Stressed Are You?

To help determine how much stress you experience on a daily basis, answer the following questions.
How many of the symptoms of excess stress in the list below do you experience frequently? _____

Symptoms of Excess Stress

Physical Symptoms	*Emotional Symptoms*	*Behavioral Symptoms*
Dry mouth	Anxiety	Crying
Excessive perspiration	Depression	Disrupted eating habits
Frequent illnesses	Edginess	Disrupted sleeping habits
Gastrointestinal problems	Fatigue	Harsh treatment of others
Grinding of teeth	Hypervigilance	Increased use of tobacco,
Headaches	Impulsiveness	alcohol, or other drugs
High blood pressure	Inability to concentrate	Problems communicating
Pounding heart	Irritability	Sexual problems
Stiff neck or aching lower back	Trouble remembering things	Social isolation

Yes	No	
_____	_____	1. Are you easily startled or irritated?
_____	_____	2. Are you increasingly forgetful?
_____	_____	3. Do you have trouble falling or staying asleep?
_____	_____	4. Do you continually worry about events in your future?
_____	_____	5. Do you feel as if you are constantly under pressure to produce?
_____	_____	6. Do you frequently use tobacco, alcohol, or other drugs to help you relax?
_____	_____	7. Do you often feel as if you have less energy than you need to finish the day?
_____	_____	8. Do you have recurrent stomachaches or headaches?
_____	_____	9. Is it difficult for you to find satisfaction in simple life pleasures?
_____	_____	10. Are you often disappointed in yourself and others?
_____	_____	11. Are you overly concerned with being liked or accepted by others?
_____	_____	12. Have you lost interest in intimacy or sex?
_____	_____	13. Are you concerned that you do not have enough money?

Experiencing some stress-related symptoms or answering yes to a few questions is normal. However, if you experience a large number of stress symptoms or you answered yes to a majority of the questions, you may be experiencing a high level of stress. Take time out to develop effective stress-management techniques. Many coping strategies that can aid you in dealing with college stressors are described in this chapter. Additionally, your school's counseling center can provide valuable support.

connect http://www.mcgrawhillconnect.com/
FITNESS AND WELLNESS

Weekly Stress Log

Now that you are familiar with the signals of stress, complete the weekly stress log to map patterns in your stress levels and identify sources of stress. Enter a score for each hour of each day according to the ratings listed below.

	A.M.							P.M.												Average
	6	7	8	9	10	11	12	1	2	3	4	5	6	7	8	9	10	11	12	*Average*
Monday																				
Tuesday																				
Wednesday																				
Thursday																				
Friday																				
Saturday																				
Sunday																				
Average																				

Ratings: 1 = No anxiety; general feeling of well-being
2 = Mild anxiety; no interference with activity
3 = Moderate anxiety; specific signal(s) of stress present
4 = High anxiety; interference with activity
5 = Very high anxiety and panic reactions; general inability to engage in activity

To identify daily or weekly patterns in your stress level, average your stress rating for each hour and each day. For example, if your scores for 6:00 A.M. are 3, 3, 4, 3, and 4, with blanks for Saturday and Sunday, your 6:00 A.M. rating would be 17 ÷ 5, or 3.4 (moderate to high anxiety). Then calculate an average weekly stress score by averaging your daily average stress scores. Your weekly average will give you a sense of your overall level of stress.

Using Your Results

How did you score? How high are your daily and weekly stress scores?

Are you satisfied with your stress rating? If not, set a specific goal:

What should you do next? Enter the results of this lab in the Preprogram Assessment column in Appendix C. If you've set a goal for improvement, begin by using your log to look for patterns and significant time periods in order to identify key stressors in your life. Below, list any stressors that caused you a significant amount of discomfort this week; these can be people, places, events, or recurring thoughts or worries. For each, enter one strategy that would help you deal more successfully with the stressor. Examples of strategies might include practicing an oral presentation in front of a friend or engaging in positive self-talk.

Next, begin to put your strategies into action. In addition, complete Lab 10.2 to help you incorporate lifestyle stress-management techniques into your daily routine.

Name _____ Section _____ Date _____

LAB 10.2 Stress-Management Techniques

Part I Lifestyle Stress Management

For each of the areas listed in the table below, describe your current lifestyle as it relates to stress management. For example, do you have enough social support? How are your exercise and nutrition habits? Is time management a problem for you? For each area, list two ways that you could change your current habits to help you manage your stress. Sample strategies might include calling a friend before a challenging class, taking a short walk before lunch, and buying and using a datebook to track your time.

	Current lifestyle	Lifestyle change #1	Lifestyle change #2
Social support system			
Exercise habits			
Nutrition habits			
Time-management techniques			
Self-talk patterns			
Sleep habits			

Mc Graw Hill **connect** http://www.mcgrawhillconnect.com/
FITNESS AND WELLNESS

Part II Relaxation Techniques

Choose two relaxation techniques described in this chapter (progressive relaxation, visualization, deep breathing, meditation, listening to music). If a recording is available for progressive relaxation or visualization, these techniques can be performed by your entire class as a group.

List the techniques you tried.

1. _____

2. _____

How did you feel before you tried these techniques?

_____

_____

_____

What did you think or how did you feel during each of the techniques you tried?

1. _____

_____

_____

2. _____

_____

_____

How did you feel after you tried these techniques?

_____

_____

_____

LAB 10.3 Developing Spiritual Wellness

To develop spiritual wellness, it is important to take time out to think about what gives meaning and purpose to your life and what actions you can take to support the spiritual dimension of your life.

Look Inward

This week, spend some quiet time alone with your thoughts and feelings. Slow the pace of your day, remove your watch, turn your phone off, and focus on your immediate experience. Try one of the following activities or develop another that is meaningful to you and that contributes to your sense of spiritual well-being.

- *Spend time in nature.* Experience continuity with the natural world by spending solitary time in a natural setting. Watch the sky (day or night), a sunrise, or a sunset; listen to waves on a shore or wind in the trees; feel the breeze on your face or raindrops on your skin; smell the grass, brush, trees, or flowers. Open all your senses to the beauty of nature.
- *Experience art, architecture, or music.* Spend time with a work of art or architecture or a piece of music. Choose one that will awaken your senses, engage your emotions, and challenge your understanding. Take a break and then repeat the experience to see how your responses change the second time.
- *Express your creativity.* Set aside time for a favorite activity, one that allows you to express your creative side. Sing, draw, paint, play a musical instrument, sculpt, build, dance, cook, garden—choose an activity in which you will be so engaged that you will lose track of time. Strive for feelings of joy and exhilaration.
- *Engage in a personal spiritual practice.* Pray, meditate, do yoga, chant. Choose a spiritual practice that is familiar to you or try one that is new. Tune out the outside world and turn your attention inward, focusing on the experience.

In the space below, describe the personal spiritual activity you tried and how it made you feel—both during the activity and after.

Reach Out

Spiritual wellness can be a bond among people and can promote values such as altruism, forgiveness, and compassion. Try one of the following spiritual activities that involve reaching out to others.

- *Share writings that inspire you.* Find two writings that inspire, guide, and comfort you—passages from sacred works, poems, quotations from literature, songs. Share them with someone else by reading them aloud and explaining what they mean to you.
- *Practice kindness.* Spend a day practicing small acts of personal kindness for people you know as well as for strangers. Compliment a friend, send a card, let someone go ahead of you in line, pick up litter, do someone else's chores, help someone with packages, say please and thank you, smile.
- *Perform community service.* Foster a sense of community by becoming a volunteer. Find a local nonprofit group and offer your time and talent. Mentor a youth, work at a food bank, support a literacy project, help build low-cost housing, visit seniors in a nursing home. You can also work on national or international issues by writing letters to your elected representatives and other officials.

In the space below, describe the spiritual activity you performed and how it made you feel—during the activity and after. Include details about the writings you chose or the acts of kindness or community service you performed.

Keep a Journal

One strategy for continuing on the path toward spiritual wellness is to keep a journal. Use a journal to record your thoughts, feelings, and experiences; to jot down quotes that engage you; to sketch pictures and write poetry about what is meaningful to you. Begin your spiritual journal today.

CHAPTER 3

Nutrition

LOOKING AHEAD...

After reading this chapter, you should be able to:

- List the essential nutrients and describe the functions they perform in the body
- Describe the guidelines that have been developed to help people choose a healthy diet, avoid nutritional deficiencies, and reduce their risk of diet-related chronic diseases
- Describe nutritional guidelines for vegetarians and for special population groups
- Explain how to use food labels and other consumer tools to make informed choices about foods
- Put together a personal nutrition plan based on affordable foods that you enjoy and that will promote wellness, today and in the future

TEST YOUR KNOWLEDGE

1. It is recommended that all adults consume 1–2 servings each of fruits and vegetables every day. True or false?

2. Candy is the leading source of added sugars in the American diet. True or false?

3. Which of the following is not a whole grain?
   a. brown rice
   b. wheat flour
   c. popcorn

Answers

1. **False.** For someone consuming 2000 calories per day, a minimum of 9 servings per day—4 of fruits and 5 of vegetables—is recommended. This is the equivalent of 4 1/2 cups per day.

2. **False.** Regular (nondiet) sodas are the leading source of added sugars. Together with energy drinks and sports drinks, they account for 36% of the added sugars in the American diet, and added sugars contribute an average of 16% of the total calories in American diets. Each 12-ounce soda supplies about 10 teaspoons of sugar, or nearly 10% of the calories in a 2000-calorie diet.

3. **b.** Unless labeled "whole wheat," wheat flour is processed to remove the bran and germ and is not a whole grain.

McGraw Hill **connect**™ http://www.mcgrawhillconnect.com
|FITNESS AND WELLNESS

McGraw Hill **LearnSmart**
GET A BETTER GRADE. TRY LEARNSMART.
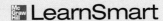

n your lifetime, you will spend about 6 years eating—about 70,000 meals and 60 tons of food. What you eat affects your energy level, well-being, and overall health. Your nutritional habits help determine your risk of major chronic diseases, including heart disease, cancer, stroke, and diabetes. Choosing foods that provide the nutrients you need while limiting the substances linked to disease should be an important part of your daily life.

Choosing a healthy diet is a two-part process. First, you have to know which nutrients you need and in what amounts. Second, you have to translate those requirements into a diet consisting of foods you like that are both available and affordable. Once you know what constitutes a healthy diet for you, you can adjust your current diet to bring it into line with your goals.

This chapter explains the basic principles of **nutrition.** It introduces the six classes of essential nutrients, explaining their role in the functioning of the body. It also provides guidelines that you can use to design a healthy eating plan. Finally, it offers practical tools and advice to help you apply the guidelines to your life.

NUTRITIONAL REQUIREMENTS: COMPONENTS OF A HEALTHY DIET

You probably think about your diet in terms of the foods you like to eat. More important for your health, though, are the nutrients contained in those foods. Your body requires proteins, fats, carbohydrates, vitamins, minerals, and water—about 45 **essential nutrients.** In this context, the word *essential* means that you must get these substances from food because your body is unable to manufacture them, or at least not fast enough to meet your physiological needs. The six classes of nutrients, along with their functions and major sources, are listed in Table 8.1

The body needs some essential nutrients in relatively large amounts; these **macronutrients** include protein, fat, carbohydrate, and water. **Micronutrients,** such as vitamins and minerals, are required in much smaller amounts. Your body obtains nutrients through the process of **digestion,** which breaks down food into compounds that the gastrointestinal tract can absorb and the body can use (Figure 8.1, p. 226). A diet that provides enough essential nutrients is vital because they provide energy, help build and maintain body tissues, and help regulate body functions.

Calories

The energy in foods is expressed as **kilocalories.** One kilocalorie represents the amount of heat it takes to raise the temperature of one liter of water 1°C. A person needs about 2000 kilocalories a day to meet his or her energy needs. In common usage, people refer to kilocalories as *calories,* which is a much smaller energy unit: 1 kilocalorie contains 1000 calories. This text uses the familiar word *calorie* to stand for the larger energy unit; you'll also find *calorie* used on food labels.

Of the six classes of essential nutrients, three supply energy:

- Fat = 9 calories per gram
- Protein = 4 calories per gram
- Carbohydrate = 4 calories per gram

Alcohol, though not an essential nutrient, also supplies energy, providing 7 calories per gram. (One gram equals a little less than 0.04 ounce.) The high caloric content of fat is one reason experts often advise against high fat consumption; most of us do not need the extra calories to meet energy needs. Regardless of their source, calories consumed in excess of energy needs can be converted to fat and stored in the body.

Table 8.1	The Six Classes of Essential Nutrients	
NUTRIENT	**FUNCTION**	**MAJOR SOURCES**
Proteins products, (4 calories/gram)	Form important parts of muscles, bone, blood, enzymes, some hormones, and cell membranes; repair tissue; regulate water and acid-base balance; help in growth; supply energy	Meat, fish, poultry, eggs, milk legumes, nuts
Carbohydrates (4 calories/gram)	Supply energy to cells in brain, nervous system, and blood; supply energy to muscles during exercise	Grains (breads and cereals), fruits, vegetables, milk
Fats (9 calories/gram)	Supply energy; insulate, support, and cushion organs; provide medium for absorption of fat-soluble vitamins	Animal foods, grains, nuts, seeds, fish, vegetables
Vitamins	Promote (initiate or speed up) specific chemical reactions within cells	Abundant in fruits, vegetables, and grains; also found in meat and dairy products
Minerals	Help regulate body functions; aid in growth and maintenance of body tissues; act as catalysts for release of energy	Found in most food groups
Water	Makes up 50–60% of body weight; provides medium for chemical reactions; transports chemicals; regulates temperature; removes waste products	Fruits, vegetables, liquids

Tracking Your Junk Food Intake

How much junk food do you eat on any given day? Let's find out. Write down all the different kinds of junk food you eat during the day today:

_____

_____

_____

_____

_____

_____

Now, write down your reason for eating each of those items:

_____

_____

_____

_____

_____

_____

_____

Whether you eat junk for pleasure or to help cope with stress, it pays to be mindful of your eating habits. Consider your reasons for eating junk food, and try to catch yourself the next time you're tempted to reach for some. If you're able to stop yourself, you can make healthier choices.

Fitness Tip

A pound of body fat is equal to 3500 calories. If you eat 100 calories more than you expend every day, you will gain more than 10 pounds in a year.

Just meeting energy needs is not enough. Our bodies need enough of the essential nutrients to grow and function properly. Practically all foods contain combinations of nutrients, although foods are commonly classified according to their predominant nutrients. For example, spaghetti is considered a carbohydrate food, although it contains small amounts of other nutrients. The following sections discuss the functions and sources of each class of nutrients.

Proteins—The Basis of Body Structure

Proteins form important parts of the body's main structural components: muscles and bones. Proteins also form

KEY TERMS

nutrition The science of food and how the body uses it in health and disease.

essential nutrients Substances the body must get from foods because it cannot manufacture them at all or fast enough to meet its needs. These nutrients include proteins, fats, carbohydrates, vitamins, minerals, and water.

macronutrient An essential nutrient required by the body in relatively large amounts.

micronutrient An essential nutrient required by the body in minute amounts.

digestion The process of breaking down foods into compounds the gastrointestinal tract can absorb and the body can use.

kilocalorie A measure of energy content in food; 1 kilocalorie represents the amount of heat needed to raise the temperature of 1 liter of water 1°C; commonly referred to as *calorie*.

protein An essential nutrient that forms important parts of the body's main structures (muscles and bones) as well as blood, enzymes, hormones, and cell membranes; also provides energy.

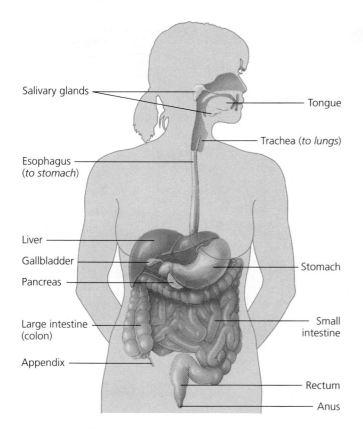

Salivary glands
Tongue
Trachea (*to lungs*)
Esophagus
(*to stomach*)
Liver
Gallbladder
Pancreas
Stomach
Large intestine
(colon)
Small
intestine
Appendix
Rectum
Anus

FIGURE 8.1   The digestive system.
Food is partially broken down by being chewed and mixed with saliva
in the mouth. After traveling to the stomach via the esophagus,
food is broken down further by stomach acids and other secretions.
As food moves through the digestive tract, it is mixed by muscular
contractions and broken down by chemicals. Most absorption of
nutrients occurs in the small intestine, aided by secretions from
the pancreas, gallbladder, and intestinal lining. The large intestine
reabsorbs excess water; the remaining solid wastes are collected in
the rectum and excreted through the anus.

important parts of blood, enzymes, cell membranes, and
some hormones. As mentioned earlier, proteins also provide energy (4 calories per gram) for the body.

Amino Acids   The building blocks of proteins are called
amino acids. Twenty common amino acids are found in
food. Nine of these are essential (or indispensable). The
other 11 amino acids can be produced by the body as
long as the necessary components are supplied by foods.

Complete and Incomplete Proteins   Individual protein sources are considered "complete" if they supply
all the essential amino acids in adequate amounts and
"incomplete" if they do not. Meat, fish, poultry, eggs, milk,
cheese, and soy provide complete proteins. Incomplete
proteins, which come from plant sources such as nuts
and **legumes** (dried beans and peas), are good sources
of most essential amino acids but are usually low in one
or two.

Certain combinations of vegetable proteins, such as
wheat and peanuts in a peanut butter sandwich, allow

Table 8.2	Protein Content of Common Food Items

ITEM	PROTEIN (GRAMS)
3 ounces lean meat, poultry, or fish	20–25
⅓ cup tofu	20–25
1 cup dried beans	15–20
1 cup milk, yogurt	8–12
1½ ounces cheese	8–12
1 serving of cereals, grains, nuts, vegetables	2–4

each vegetable protein to make up for the amino acids
missing in the other protein. The combination yields a
complete protein. It was once believed that vegetarians had
to "complement" their proteins at each meal in order to
receive the benefit of a complete protein. It is now known,
however, that proteins consumed throughout the course
of the day can complement each other to form a pool of
amino acids the body can draw from to produce proteins.
Vegetarians should include a variety of vegetable protein
sources in their diets to make sure they get all the essential amino acids in adequate amounts. (Healthy vegetarian
diets are discussed later in the chapter.)

Recommended Protein Intake   Adequate daily intake
of protein for adults is 0.8 gram per kilogram (0.36 gram
per pound) of body weight, corresponding to 50 grams of
protein per day for someone who weighs 140 pounds and
65 grams of protein for someone who weighs 180 pounds.
Table 8.2 lists some popular food items and the amount
of protein each provides.

Most Americans meet or exceed the protein intake
needed for adequate nutrition. If you consume more
protein than your body needs, the extra protein is synthesized into fat for energy storage or burned for energy
requirements. A little extra protein is not harmful, but it
can contribute fat to the diet because protein-rich foods
are often fat-rich, as well.

A fairly broad range of protein intakes is associated
with good health, and the Food and Nutrition Board of
the Institute of Medicine recommends that the amount of
protein adults eat should fall within the range of 10–35%
of total daily calories, depending on the individual's age.
The average American diet includes about 15–16% of
total daily calories as protein.

Wellness Tip

Research shows that some protein-rich foods can give
you a quick mental boost, which can be helpful before
an exam.

Fats—Essential in Small Amounts

Fats, also known as *lipids,* are the most concentrated source of energy, at 9 calories per gram. The fats stored in your body represent usable energy, help insulate your body, and support and cushion your organs. Fats in the diet help your body absorb fat-soluble vitamins, and they add flavor and texture to foods. Fats are the major fuel for the body during rest and light activity.

Two fats—linoleic acid and alpha-linolenic acid—are essential components of the diet. They are used to make compounds that are key regulators of such body functions as the maintenance of blood pressure and the progress of a healthy pregnancy.

Types and Sources of Fats Most of the fats in foods are fairly similar in composition, generally including a molecule of glycerol (an alcohol) with three fatty acid chains attached to it. The resulting structure is called a *triglyceride.* Animal fat, for example, is primarily made of triglycerides. Within a triglyceride, differences in the fatty acid structure result in different types of fats. Depending on this structure, a fat may be unsaturated, monounsaturated, polyunsaturated, or saturated. (The essential fatty acids—linoleic and alpha-linolenic acids—are both polyunsaturated.) The different types of fatty acids have different characteristics and different effects on your health.

Food fats are often composed of both saturated and unsaturated fatty acids; the dominant type of fatty acid determines the fat's characteristics. Food fats containing large amounts of saturated fatty acids are usually solid at room temperature; they are generally found naturally in animal products. The leading sources of saturated fat in the American diet are red meats (hamburger, steak, roasts), whole milk, cheese, hot dogs, and lunch meats. Food fats containing large amounts of monounsaturated and polyunsaturated fatty acids usually come from plant sources and are liquid at room temperature. Olive, canola, safflower, and peanut oils contain mostly monounsaturated fatty acids. Corn, soybean, and cottonseed oils contain mostly polyunsaturated fatty acids.

Hydrogenation There are notable exceptions to these generalizations. When unsaturated vegetable oils undergo the process of **hydrogenation,** a mixture of saturated and unsaturated fatty acids is produced, creating a more solid fat from a liquid oil. Hydrogenation also changes some unsaturated fatty acids into **trans fatty acids (trans fats),** unsaturated fatty acids with an atypical shape that affects their behavior in the body. Food manufacturers use hydrogenation to increase the stability of an oil so it can be reused for deep frying, to improve the texture of certain foods (to make pastries and pie crusts flakier, for example), and to extend the shelf life of foods made with oil. Hydrogenation is also used to transform liquid vegetable oils into margarine or shortening.

Many baked and fried foods are prepared with hydrogenated vegetable oils, which means they can be relatively high in saturated and trans fatty acids. Leading sources of trans fats in the American diet are deep-fried fast foods such as french fries and fried chicken (typically fried in vegetable shortening rather than oil), baked and snack foods, and stick margarine.

In general, the more solid a hydrogenated oil is, the more saturated and trans fats it contains. For example, stick margarines typically contain more saturated and trans fats than do tub or squeeze margarines. Small amounts of trans fatty acids are also found naturally in meat and milk.

Hydrogenated vegetable oils are not the only plant fats that contain saturated fats. Palm and coconut oils,

---

amino acids The building blocks of proteins.

legumes Vegetables such as dried beans and peas that are high in fiber and are also important sources of protein.

hydrogenation A process by which hydrogens are added to unsaturated fats, increasing the degree of saturation and turning liquid oils into solid fats. Hydrogenation produces a mixture of saturated fatty acids and standard and trans forms of unsaturated fatty acids.

trans fatty acid (trans fat) A type of unsaturated fatty acid produced during the process of hydrogenation; trans fats have an atypical shape that affects their chemical activity.

although derived from plants, are also highly saturated. Yet fish oils, derived from an animal source, are rich in polyunsaturated fats.

Fats and Health Different types of fats have very different effects on health. Many studies have examined the effects of dietary fat intake on blood **cholesterol** levels and the risk of heart disease. However, the results of a recent analysis concluded that dietary saturated fat is not associated with an increased risk of certain forms of heart disease, and that the benefits of diets low in saturated fat may come from the higher amounts of polyunsaturated fats that these diets provide.

Saturated and trans fatty acids raise blood levels of **low-density lipoprotein (LDL),** or "bad" cholesterol, thereby increasing a person's risk of heart disease. Unsaturated fatty acids lower LDL. Monounsaturated fatty acids, such as those found in olive and canola oils, may also increase levels of **high-density lipoprotein (HDL),** or "good" cholesterol, providing even greater benefits for heart health. In large amounts, trans fatty acids may lower HDL. Saturated fats impair the ability of HDLs to prevent inflammation of the blood vessels, a key factor in vascular disease. Saturated fats also reduce the blood vessels' ability to react normally to stress. Thus, to reduce the risk of heart disease, it is important to choose unsaturated fats instead of saturated and trans fats. (See Chapter 11 for more on cholesterol.)

Most Americans consume 4–5 times as much saturated fat as trans fat (8–10% versus 2% of total daily calories). However, health experts are particularly concerned about trans fats because of their double-negative effect on heart health—they not only raise LDL but also lower HDL—and because there is less public awareness of trans fats, although awareness is growing. Since 2006, federal law has required food labels to include trans fat content, and numerous states and cities have banned the use of trans fats in restaurant food. Consumers can also check for the presence of trans fats by examining a food's ingredient list for partially hydrogenated oil or vegetable shortening.

For heart health, it's important to limit your consumption of both saturated and trans fats. The best way to reduce saturated fat in your diet is to eat less meat and full-fat dairy products (whole milk, cream, butter, cheese, ice cream). To lower trans fats, eat fewer deep-fried foods and baked goods made with hydrogenated vegetable oils (such as many kinds of crackers and cookies), use liquid oils for cooking, and favor tub or squeeze margarines over stick margarines. Remember: The softer or more liquid a fat is, the less saturated and trans fat it is likely to contain.

Although saturated and trans fats pose health hazards, other fats can be beneficial. When used in place of saturated fats, monounsaturated fatty acids—as found in avocados, most nuts, and olive, canola, peanut, and safflower oils—improve cholesterol levels and may help protect against some cancers.

Omega-3 fatty acids, a form of polyunsaturated fat found primarily in fish, may be even more healthful. Omega-3s and the compounds the body makes from them have a number of heart-healthy effects: They reduce the tendency of blood to clot, inhibit inflammation and abnormal heart rhythms, and reduce blood pressure and the risk of heart attack and stroke in some people. Because of these benefits, nutritionists recommend that Americans increase the proportion of omega-3s in their diet by eating fish two or more times a week. Salmon, tuna, trout, mackerel, herring, sardines, and anchovies are all good sources of omega-3s. Lesser amounts are found in plant foods, including dark green leafy vegetables; walnuts; flaxseeds; and canola, walnut, and flaxseed oils.

Most of the polyunsaturated fats currently consumed by Americans are *omega-6* fatty acids, primarily from corn oil and soybean oil. The American Heart Association (AHA) recommends consuming at least 5–10% of energy from omega-6 fatty acids as part of a low-saturated-fat and low-cholesterol diet to reduce the risk of coronary heart disease.

In addition to its effects on heart disease risk, dietary fat can affect health in other ways. Diets high in fatty red meat are associated with an increased risk of certain forms of cancer, especially colon cancer. A high-fat diet can also make weight management more difficult. Because fat is a concentrated source of calories, a high-fat diet is often a high-calorie diet that can lead to weight gain.

Although more research is needed on the precise effects of different types and amounts of fat on overall health, a great deal of evidence points to the fact that most people benefit from lowering their overall fat intake to recommended levels and choosing unsaturated fats instead of saturated and trans fats. The types of fatty acids and their effects on health are summarized in Table 8.3.

Recommended Fat Intake To meet the body's need for essential fats, adult men need about 17 grams per day of linoleic acid and 1.6 grams per day of alpha-linolenic acid. Women need 12 grams of linoleic acid and 1.1 grams of alpha-linolenic acid. It takes only 3–4 teaspoons (15–20 grams) of vegetable oil per day incorporated into your diet to supply the essential fats. Most Americans get enough essential fats. Limiting unhealthy fats is a much greater health concern.

Limits for total fat, saturated fat, and trans fat intake have been set by a number of government and research organizations. The Institute of Medicine's Food and Nutrition Board has released recommendations for the balance of energy sources in a healthful diet. These recommendations—called Acceptable Macronutrient Distribution Ranges (AMDRs)—are based on ensuring adequate intake of essential nutrients while reducing the risk of chronic diseases. As with protein, a range of levels of fat intake is associated with good health. The AMDR for total fat is 20–35% of total calories. Although more difficult for consumers to monitor, AMDRs have also been set for omega-6 fatty acids (5–10%) and omega-3 fatty acids (0.6–1.2%) as part of total fat intake.

Table 8.3 — Types of Fatty Acids and Their Possible Effects on Health

	TYPE OF FATTY ACID	FOUND IN[a]	POSSIBLE EFFECTS ON HEALTH
Keep Intake Low	SATURATED	• Animal fats (especially fatty meats and poultry fat and skin) • Butter, cheese, and other high-fat dairy products • Palm and coconut oils	• Raises total cholesterol and LDL cholesterol • May increase risk of heart disease • May increase risk of colon and prostate cancers
	TRANS	• Deep-fried fast foods • Stick margarines, shortening • Packaged cookies and crackers • Processed snacks and sweets	• Raises total cholesterol and LDL cholesterol • Lowers HDL cholesterol • May increase risk of heart disease and breast cancer
	MONOUNSATURATED	• Olive, canola, and safflower oils • Avocados, olives • Peanut butter (without added fat) • Many nuts, including almonds, cashews, pecans, and pistachios	• Lowers total cholesterol and LDL cholesterol • May reduce blood pressure and lower triglycerides (a risk factor for heart disease) • May reduce risk of heart disease, stroke, and some cancers
Choose Moderate Amounts	**POLYUNSATURATED (two groups)[b]**		
	Omega-3	• Fatty fish, including salmon, white albacore tuna, mackerel, anchovies, and sardines • Lesser amounts in walnut, flaxseed, canola, and soybean oils; tofu; walnuts; flaxseeds; and dark green leafy vegetables	• Reduces blood clotting and inflammation and inhibits abnormal heart rhythms • Lowers triglycerides • May lower blood pressure in some people • May reduce the risk of fatal heart attack, stroke, and some cancers
	Omega-6	• Corn, soybean, and cottonseed oils (often used in margarine, mayonnaise, and salad dressings)	• Lowers total cholesterol and LDL cholesterol • May lower HDL cholesterol • May reduce risk of heart disease • May slightly increase risk of cancer if omega-6 intake is high and omega-3 is low

[a] Food fats contain a combination of types of fatty acids in various proportions. For example, canola oil is composed mainly of monounsaturated fatty acids (62%) but also contains polyunsaturated (32%) and saturated (6%) fatty acids. Food fats are categorized here according to their predominant fatty acid.

[b] The essential fatty acids are polyunsaturated: Linoleic acid is an omega-6 fatty acid and alpha-linolenic acid is an omega-3 fatty acid.

Because any amount of saturated and trans fat increases the risk of heart disease, the Food and Nutrition Board recommends that saturated and trans fat intake be kept as low as possible; most fat in a healthy diet should be unsaturated.

For advice on setting individual intake goals, see the box "Setting Intake Goals for Protein, Fat, and Carbohydrate." To determine how close you are to meeting your personal intake goals for fat, keep a running total over the course of the day. For prepared foods, food labels list the number of grams of fat, protein, and carbohydrate. Nutrition information is also available in many grocery stores, in published nutrition guides, and online (see For Further Exploration at the end of the chapter). By checking these resources, you can keep track of the total grams of fat, protein, and carbohydrate you eat and assess your current diet.

In reducing fat intake to recommended levels, the emphasis should be on lowering saturated and trans fats (see Table 8.3). You can still eat high-fat foods, but it makes sense to limit the size of your portions and to balance your intake with low-fat foods. For example, peanut butter is high in fat, with 8 grams (72 calories) of fat in each 90-calorie tablespoon. Two tablespoons of peanut butter eaten on whole-wheat bread and served with a banana, carrot sticks, and a glass of nonfat milk make a nutritious lunch—high in protein and carbohydrate, relatively low in total and saturated fat (500 calories, 18 grams of total fat, 4 grams of saturated fat). By comparison, four tablespoons of peanut butter on high-fat crackers with potato chips, cookies, and whole milk is a less healthy combination (1000 calories, 62 grams of total fat, 15 grams of saturated fat). So although it's important to evaluate individual food items for their fat content, it is more important to look at them in the context of your overall diet.

KEY TERMS

cholesterol   A waxy substance found in the blood and cells and needed for synthesis of cell membranes, vitamin D, and hormones.

low-density lipoprotein (LDL)   Blood fat that transports cholesterol to organs and tissues; excess amounts result in the accumulation of fatty deposits on artery walls.

high-density lipoprotein (HDL)   Blood fat that helps transport cholesterol out of the arteries, thereby protecting against heart disease.

Setting Intake Goals for Protein, Fat, and Carbohydrate

The Food and Nutrition Board has established goals to help ensure adequate intake of the essential amino acids, fatty acids, and carbohydrate. The daily goals for adequate intake for adults follow:

	MEN	WOMEN
Protein	56 grams	46 grams
Fat: Linoleic acid	17 grams	12 grams
Alpha-linoleic acid	1.6 grams	1.1 grams
Carbohydrate	130 grams	130 grams

Protein intake goals can be calculated more specifically by multiplying your body weight in kilograms by 0.8 or your body weight in pounds by 0.36. (Refer to the Nutrition Resources section at the end of the chapter for information for specific age groups and life stages.)

To meet your daily energy needs, you need to consume more than the minimally adequate amounts of the energy-providing nutrients listed above, which alone supply only about 800–900 calories.

The Food and Nutrition Board provides additional guidance in the form of Acceptable Macronutrient Distribution Ranges (AMDRs). These ranges can help you balance your intake of energy-providing nutrients in ways that ensure adequate intake and reduce the risk of chronic disease.

The AMDRs for protein, total fat, and carbohydrate are as follows:

Protein	10–35% of total daily calories
Total fat	20–35% of total daily calories
Carbohydrate	45–65% of total daily calories

To set individual goals, begin by estimating your total daily energy (calorie) needs. If your weight is stable, your current energy intake is the number of calories you need to maintain your weight at your current activity level. Next, select percentage goals for protein, fat, and carbohydrate. You can allocate your total daily calories among the three classes of macronutrients to suit your preferences; just make sure that the three percentages you select total 100% and that you meet the minimum intake goals listed. Two samples reflecting different total energy intake and nutrient intake goals are shown in the table below.

To translate your percentage goals into daily intake goals expressed in calories and grams, multiply the appropriate percentages by total calorie intake, and then divide the results by the corresponding calories per gram. For example, a fat limit of 35% applied to a 2200-calorie diet would be calculated as follows: 0.35 x 2200 = 770 calories of total fat; 770 ÷ 9 calories per gram = 86 grams of total fat. (Remember that fat has 9 calories per gram and that protein and carbohydrate have 4 calories per gram.)

Two Sample Macronutrient Distributions

		SAMPLE 1		SAMPLE 2	
NUTRIENT	AMDR	INDIVIDUAL GOALS	AMOUNTS FOR A 1600-CALORIE DIET	INDIVIDUAL GOALS	AMOUNTS FOR A 2800-CALORIE DIET
PROTEIN	10–35%	15%	240 calories = 60 grams	30%	840 calories = 210 grams
FAT	20–35%	30%	480 calories = 53 grams	25%	700 calories = 78 grams
CARBOHYDRATE	45–65%	55%	880 calories = 220 grams	45%	1260 calories = 315 grams

SOURCE: Food and Nutrition Board, Institute of Medicine, National Academies. 2002. *Dietary Reference Intakes: Applications in Dietary Planning.* Washington, D.C.: National Academies Press. © 2003 by the National Academy of Sciences. Reprinted with permission from the National Academies Press, Washington, D.C.

Carbohydrates—An Ideal Source of Energy

Carbohydrates ("carbs") are needed in the diet primarily to supply energy to body cells. Some cells, such as those in the brain and other parts of the nervous system and in the blood, use only carbohydrates for fuel. During high-intensity exercise, muscles also get most of their energy from carbohydrates.

Simple and Complex Carbohydrates Carbohydrates are classified into two groups: simple and complex. *Simple carbohydrates* include sucrose (table sugar), fructose (fruit sugar, honey), maltose (malt sugar), and lactose (milk sugar). Simple carbohydrates provide much of

the sweetness in foods. They are found naturally in fruits and milk and are added to soft drinks, fruit drinks, candy, and sweet desserts. There is no evidence that any type of simple carbohydrate is more nutritious than others.

Complex carbohydrates include starches and most types of dietary fiber. Starches are found in a variety of plants, especially grains (wheat, rye, rice, oats, barley, and millet), legumes (dried beans, peas, and lentils), and tubers (potatoes and yams). Most other vegetables contain a mix of complex and simple carbohydrates. Fiber, which is discussed later in this chapter, is found in fruits, vegetables, and grains.

During digestion, your body breaks down carbohydrates into simple sugar molecules, such as **glucose**, for absorption. Once glucose is in the bloodstream, the

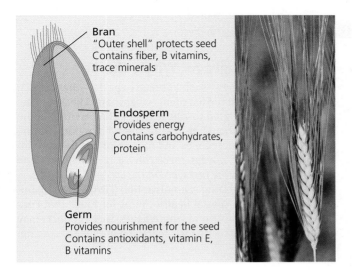

Bran
"Outer shell" protects seed
Contains fiber, B vitamins,
trace minerals

Endosperm
Provides energy
Contains carbohydrates,
protein

Germ
Provides nourishment for the seed
Contains antioxidants, vitamin E,
B vitamins

FIGURE 8.2   The parts of a whole grain kernel.

pancreas releases the hormone insulin, which allows cells to take up glucose and use it for energy. The liver and muscles also take up glucose and store it in the form of a starch called **glycogen**. The muscles use glucose from glycogen as fuel during endurance events or long workouts.

Refined Carbohydrates Versus Whole Grains Complex carbohydrates can be further divided between refined, or processed, carbohydrates and unrefined carbohydrates, or whole grains. Before they are processed, all grains are **whole grains**, consisting of an inner layer of germ, a middle layer called the endosperm, and an outer layer of bran (Figure 8.2). During processing, the germ and bran are often removed, leaving just the starchy endosperm. The refinement of whole grains transforms whole-wheat flour into white flour, brown rice into white rice, and so on.

Refined carbohydrates usually retain all the calories of their unrefined counterparts, but they tend to be much lower in fiber, vitamins, minerals, and other beneficial compounds. Refined grain products are often enriched or fortified with vitamins and minerals, but many of the nutrients lost in processing are not replaced.

Unrefined carbohydrates tend to take longer to chew and digest than refined ones; they also enter the bloodstream more slowly. This slower digestive pace tends to make people feel full sooner and for a longer period. Also, a slower rise in blood glucose levels following consumption of complex carbohydrates may help in the

management of diabetes. Whole grains are also high in dietary fiber (discussed later).

Consumption of whole grains has been linked to a reduced risk of heart disease, diabetes, high blood pressure, stroke, and certain forms of cancer. For all these reasons, whole grains are recommended over those that have been refined. This does not mean you should never eat refined carbohydrates such as white bread or white rice; it simply means that whole-wheat bread, brown rice, and other whole grains are healthier choices. See the box "Choosing More Whole-Grain Foods" for tips on increasing your intake of whole grains.

Glycemic Index and Glycemic Response Insulin and glucose levels rise following a meal or snack containing any type of carbohydrate. Some foods cause a quick and dramatic rise in glucose and insulin levels, while others have a slower, more moderate effect. A food that has a rapid effect on blood glucose levels is said to have a high **glycemic index**. The glycemic index of a food indicates the type of carbohydrate in that food. High-glycemic-index foods do not, as some popular diets claim, directly cause weight gain beyond the calories they contain.

Attempting to base food choices on glycemic index is a difficult task. Unrefined complex carbohydrates and high-fiber foods generally tend to have a lower glycemic index, but patterns are less clear for other types of foods. The fat content of a food also affects its glycemic index; the higher in fat a food is, the lower its effect on glucose levels. Ripeness, storage time, processing, and food preparation are other factors that can affect a food's glycemic index. The body's response to carbohydrates also depends on other factors, such as what other foods are consumed at the same time, as well as the individual's fitness status.

For people with particular health concerns, such as diabetes, glycemic index may be an important consideration in choosing foods. Still, it should not be the sole criterion for food choices. Carbohydrate choices (low versus high glycemic index) that replace dietary saturated fat may also be an important factor in determining the effects of diet on the risk of cardiovascular disease. Some unrefined grains, fruits, vegetables, and legumes are rich in nutrients, have a relatively low energy density, and have a

---

Wellness Tip

Certain carbohydrate-rich foods, such as a bagel or a plain baked potato, can have a temporary calming effect on some people during stressful situations.

---

carbohydrate   An essential nutrient; sugars, starches, and dietary fiber are all carbohydrates.

glucose   A simple sugar that is the body's basic fuel.

glycogen   A starch stored in the liver and muscles.

whole grain   The entire edible portion of a grain (such as wheat, rice, or oats), including the germ, endosperm, and bran; processing removes parts of the grain, often leaving just the endosperm.

glycemic index   A measure of how a particular food affects blood glucose levels.

KEY TERMS

Choosing More Whole-Grain Foods

What Are Whole Grains?

The first step in increasing your intake of whole grains is to correctly identify them. The following are whole grains:

- whole wheat
- whole rye
- whole oats
- oatmeal
- whole-grain corn
- popcorn
- brown rice
- whole-grain barley

Other choices include bulgur (cracked wheat), millet, kasha (roasted buckwheat kernels), quinoa, wheat and rye berries, amaranth, wild rice, graham flour, whole-grain kamut, whole-grain spelt, and whole-grain triticale.

Wheat flour, unbleached flour, enriched flour, and degerminated corn meal are not whole grains. Wheat germ and wheat bran are also not whole grains, but they are the constituents of wheat typically left out when wheat is processed and so are healthier choices than regular wheat flour, which typically contains just the grain's endosperm.

Checking Packages for Whole Grains

To find packaged foods—such as bread or pasta—that are rich in whole grains, read the list of ingredients and check for special health claims related to whole grains. The *first* item in the list of ingredients should be one of the whole grains in the preceding list. Product names and food color can be misleading. *When in doubt, always check the list of ingredients and make sure "whole" is the first word in the list.*

The U.S. Food and Drug Administration (FDA) allows manufacturers to include special health claims for foods that contain 51% or more whole-grain ingredients. Such products may contain a statement such as the following on their packaging:

- "Rich in whole grain"
- "Made with 100% whole grain"
- "Diets rich in whole-grain foods may help reduce the risk of heart disease and certain cancers."

However, many whole-grain products will not carry such claims. This is one more reason to check the ingredient list to make sure you're buying a product made from one or more whole grains.

---

low to moderate glycemic index. Your best bet, therefore, is to choose a variety of vegetables daily and limit refined grains as well as foods that are high in added sugars but low in other nutrients.

Recommended Carbohydrate Intake On average, Americans consume 200–300 grams of carbohydrate per day, well above the 130 grams needed to meet the body's requirement for essential carbohydrate. A range of intakes is associated with good health, and experts recommend that adults consume 45–65% of total daily calories as carbohydrate. (That's about 225–325 grams of carbohydrate for someone who consumes 2000 calories per day.) The focus should be on consuming a variety of foods rich in complex carbohydrates, especially whole grains.

Athletes in training can especially benefit from high-carbohydrate diets (60–70% of total daily calories), which enhance the amount of carbohydrates stored in their muscles as glycogen and therefore provide more carbohydrate fuel for use during endurance events or long workouts. Carbohydrates consumed during prolonged athletic events (often in the form of sports beverages) can help fuel muscles and extend the availability of the glycogen stored in muscles. Caution is in order, however, because overconsumption of carbohydrates can lead to feelings of fatigue and underconsumption of other nutrients.

Although the Food and Nutrition Board set an AMDR for added sugars of 25% or less of total daily calories,

many health experts recommend an even lower intake. (Recall that sugars are a form of carbohydrate.) World Health Organization guidelines suggest a limit of 10% of total daily calories from added sugars. Limits set by the U.S. Department of Agriculture (USDA) are even lower, with a maximum of about 8 teaspoons (32 grams) suggested for someone consuming 2000 calories per day. Foods high in added sugar are generally high in calories and low in nutrients and fiber, thus providing "empty" calories.

To reduce your intake of added sugars, limit soft drinks, candy, desserts, and sweetened fruit drinks. The simple carbohydrates in your diet shoulde come mainly from fruits, which are excellent sources of vitamins and minerals, and from low-fat or fat-free milk and other dairy products, which are high in protein and calcium.

Fiber—A Closer Look

Fiber is the term given to nondigestible carbohydrates provided by plants. Instead of being digested, like starch, fiber moves through the intestinal tract and provides bulk for feces in the large intestine, which in turn facilitates elimination. In the large intestine, some types of fiber are broken down by bacteria into acids and gases, which explains why eating too much fiber-rich food can lead to intestinal gas. Even though humans don't digest fiber, it is necessary for good health.

Fruits, vegetables, and whole grains are excellent sources of carbohydrates and fiber.

Types of Dietary Fiber The Food and Nutrition Board has defined two types of fiber:

- **Dietary fiber** is the nondigestible carbohydrates (and the noncarbohydrate substance lignin) that are present naturally in plants such as grains, legumes, and vegetables.
- **Functional fiber** is any nondigestible carbohydrate that has been either isolated from natural sources or synthesized in a lab and then added to a food product or supplement.
- **Total fiber** is the sum of dietary and functional fiber in a person's diet.

Fibers have different properties that lead to different physiological effects in the body. **Soluble (viscous) fiber** such as that found in oat bran or legumes can delay stomach emptying, slow the movement of glucose into the blood after eating, and reduce absorption of cholesterol. **Insoluble fiber**, such as that found in wheat bran or psyllium seed, increases fecal bulk and helps prevent constipation, hemorrhoids, and other digestive disorders.

A high-fiber diet can help reduce the risk of type 2 diabetes, heart disease, and pulmonary disease, as well as improve gastrointestinal health and aid in weight management. Some studies have linked high-fiber diets with a reduced risk of colon and rectal cancer. Other studies have suggested that other characteristics of diets rich in fruits, vegetables, and whole grains may be responsible for this reduction in risk.

Sources of Fiber All plant foods contain some dietary fiber. Fruits, legumes, oats (especially oat bran), and barley all contain the viscous types of fiber that help lower blood glucose and cholesterol levels. Wheat (especially wheat bran), cereals, grains, and vegetables are all good sources of cellulose and other fibers that help prevent

Wellness Tip

To avoid intestinal discomfort, add fiber to your diet slowly so you can build a tolerance to it.

constipation. Psyllium, which is often added to cereals or used in fiber supplements and laxatives, improves intestinal health and also helps control glucose and cholesterol levels. The processing of packaged foods can remove fiber, so it's important to depend on fresh fruits and vegetables and foods made from whole grains as your main sources of fiber.

Recommended Fiber Intake To reduce the risk of chronic disease and maintain intestinal health, the Food and Nutrition Board recommends a daily fiber intake of 38 grams for adult men and 25 grams for adult women. Americans currently consume about half this amount. Fiber should come from foods, not supplements, which should be used only under medical supervision.

Vitamins—Organic Micronutrients

Vitamins are organic (carbon-containing) substances required in small amounts to regulate various processes within living cells (Table 8.4). Humans need 13 vitamins; of these, four are fat-soluble (A, D, E, and K), and nine are water-soluble (C and the B-complex vitamins thiamin, riboflavin, niacin, vitamin B-6, folate, vitamin B-12, biotin, and pantothenic acid).

Solubility affects how a vitamin is absorbed, transported, and stored in the body. The water-soluble vitamins are absorbed directly into the bloodstream, where they travel freely. Excess water-soluble vitamins are removed by the kidneys and excreted in urine. Fat-soluble vitamins require a more complex absorptive process. They are usually carried in the blood by special proteins and are stored in the liver and in fat tissues rather than excreted.

dietary fiber Nondigestible carbohydrates and lignin that are intact in plants.

functional fiber Nondigestible carbohydrates either isolated from natural sources or synthesized; these may be added to foods and dietary supplements.

total fiber The total amount of dietary fiber and functional fiber in the diet.

soluble (viscous) fiber Fiber that dissolves in water or is broken down by bacteria in the large intestine.

insoluble fiber Fiber that does not dissolve in water and is not broken down by bacteria in the large intestine.

vitamins Carbon-containing substances needed in small amounts to help promote and regulate chemical reactions and processes in the body.

KEY TERMS

Table 8.4 Facts About Vitamins

VITAMIN	IMPORTANT DIETARY SOURCES	MAJOR FUNCTIONS	SIGNS OF PROLONGED DEFICIENCY	TOXIC EFFECTS OF MEGADOSES
FAT-SOLUBLE				
Vitamin A	Liver, milk, butter, cheese, fortified margarine; carrots, spinach, and other orange and deep green vegetables and fruits	Maintenance of vision, skin, linings of the nose, mouth, digestive and urinary tracts, immune function	Night blindness; dry, scaling skin; increased susceptibility to infection; loss of appetite; anemia; kidney stones	Liver damage, miscarriage and birth defects, headache, vomiting and diarrhea, vertigo, double vision, bone abnormalities
Vitamin D	Fortified milk and margarine, fish oils, butter, egg yolks (sunlight on skin also produces vitamin D)	Development and maintenance of bones and teeth; promotion of calcium absorption	Rickets (bone deformities) in children; bone softening, loss, fractures in adults	Kidney damage, calcium deposits in soft tissues, depression, death
Vitamin E	Vegetable oils, whole grains, nuts and seeds, green leafy vegetables, asparagus, peaches	Protection and maintenance of cellular membranes	Red blood cell breakage and anemia, weakness, neurological problems, muscle cramps	Relatively nontoxic, but may cause excess bleeding or formation of blood clots
Vitamin K	Green leafy vegetables; smaller amounts widespread in other foods	Production of factors essential for blood clotting and bone metabolism	Hemorrhaging	None reported
WATER-SOLUBLE				
Biotin	Cereals, yeast, egg yolks, soy flour, liver; widespread in foods	Synthesis of fat, glycogen, and amino acids	Rash, nausea, vomiting, weight loss, depression, fatigue, hair loss	None reported
Folate	Green leafy vegetables, yeast, oranges, whole grains, legumes, liver	Amino acid metabolism, synthesis of RNA and DNA, new cell synthesis	Anemia, weakness, fatigue, irritability, shortness of breath, swollen tongue	Masking of vitamin B-12 deficiency
Niacin	Eggs, poultry, fish, milk, whole grains, nuts, enriched breads and cereals, meats, legumes	Conversion of carbohydrates, fats, and proteins into usable forms of energy	Pellagra (symptoms include diarrhea, dermatitis, inflammation of mucous membranes, dementia)	Flushing of skin, nausea, vomiting, diarrhea, liver dysfunction, glucose intolerance
Pantothenic acid	Animal foods, whole grains, broccoli, potatoes; widespread in foods	Metabolism of fats, carbohydrates, and proteins	Fatigue, numbness and tingling of hands and feet, gastrointestinal disturbances	None reported
Riboflavin	Dairy products, enriched breads and cereals, lean meats, poultry, fish, green vegetables	Energy metabolism; maintenance of skin, mucous membranes, nervous system structures	Cracks at corners of mouth, sore throat, skin rash, hypersensitivity to light, purple tongue	None reported
Thiamin	Whole-grain and enriched breads and cereals, organ meats, lean pork, nuts, legumes	Conversion of carbohydrates into usable forms of energy; maintenance of appetite and nervous system function	Beriberi (symptoms include muscle wasting, mental confusion, anorexia, enlarged heart, nerve changes)	None reported
Vitamin B-6	Eggs, poultry, fish, whole grains, nuts, soybeans, liver, kidney, pork	Metabolism of amino acids and glycogen	Anemia, convulsions, cracks at corners of mouth, dermatitis, nausea, confusion	Neurological abnormalities and damage
Vitamin B-12	Meat, fish, poultry, fortified cereals	Synthesis of blood cells; other metabolic reactions	Anemia, fatigue, nervous system damage, sore tongue	None reported
Vitamin C	Peppers, broccoli, brussels sprouts, spinach, citrus fruits, strawberries, tomatoes, potatoes, cabbage, other fruits and vegetables	Maintenance and repair, of connective tissue, bones, teeth, cartilage; promotion of healing; aid in iron absorption	Scurvy, anemia, reduced resistance to infection, loosened teeth, joint pain, poor wound healing, hair loss, poor iron absorption	Urinary stones in some people, acid stomach from ingesting supplements in pill form, nausea, diarrhea, headache, fatigue

SOURCES: Food and Nutrition Board, Institute of Medicine. 2006. *Dietary Reference Intakes: The Essential Guide to Nutrient Requirements.* Washington, D.C.: National Academies Press. The complete Dietary Reference Intake reports are available from the National Academies Press (http://www.nap.edu). Shils, M. E., et al., eds. 2005. *Modern Nutrition in Health and Disease,* 10th ed. Baltimore: Lippincott Williams and Wilkins.

Vitamin and mineral supplements are popular, but they are not usually necessary for healthy people who eat a balanced diet.

Functions of Vitamins Many vitamins help chemical reactions take place. They provide no energy to the body directly but help unleash the energy stored in carbohydrates, proteins, and fats. Other vitamins are critical in the production of red blood cells and the maintenance of the nervous, skeletal, and immune systems. Some vitamins act as **antioxidants**, which help preserve the health of cells. Key vitamin antioxidants include vitamin E, vitamin C, and the vitamin A precursor beta-carotene. (Antioxidants are described later in the chapter.)

Sources of Vitamins The human body does not manufacture most of the vitamins it requires and must obtain them from foods. Vitamins are abundant in fruits, vegetables, and grains. In addition, many processed foods, such as flour and breakfast cereals, contain added vitamins. A few vitamins are made in certain parts of the body: The skin makes vitamin D when it is exposed to sunlight, and intestinal bacteria make vitamin K. Nonetheless, you still need to get vitamin D and vitamin K from foods (see Table 8.4).

Vitamin Deficiencies and Excesses If your diet lacks a particular vitamin, characteristic symptoms of deficiency can develop (see Table 8.4). For example, vitamin A deficiency can cause blindness, and vitamin B-12 deficiency can cause anemia. Vitamin deficiency diseases are most often seen in developing countries; they are relatively rare in the United States because vitamins are readily available from our food supply. However, intakes below recommended levels can have adverse effects on health even if they are not low enough to cause a deficiency disease. For example, low intake of folate increases a woman's chance of giving birth to a baby with a neural tube defect (a congenital malformation of the central nervous system). Low intake of folate and vitamins B-6 and B-12 has been linked to increased heart disease risk. A great deal of recent research has focused on vitamin D, suggesting that vitamin D supplementation can reduce the risk of cardiovascular disease and linking low vitamin D levels to an increased risk of several cancers. As important as vitamins are, however, many Americans consume less-than-recommended amounts of some vitamins.

Extra vitamins in the diet can be harmful, especially when taken as supplements. Megadoses of fat-soluble vitamins are particularly dangerous because the excess is stored in the body rather than excreted, increasing the risk of toxicity. Even when supplements are not taken in excess, relying on them for an adequate intake of vitamins can be problematic. There are many substances in foods other than vitamins and minerals, and some of these compounds may have important health effects. Later, this chapter discusses specific recommendations for vitamin intake and when a supplement is advisable. For now, keep in mind that it's best to get most of your vitamins from foods rather than supplements.

The vitamins and minerals in foods can be easily lost or destroyed during storage or cooking. To retain their value, eat or process vegetables immediately after buying them. If you can't do this, store them in a cool place, covered to retain moisture—either in the refrigerator (for a few days) or in the freezer (for a longer term). To reduce nutrient losses during food preparation, minimize the amount of water used and the total cooking time. Develop a taste for a crunchier texture in cooked vegetables. Baking, steaming, broiling, grilling, and microwaving are all good methods of preparing vegetables.

Minerals—Inorganic Micronutrients

Minerals are inorganic (non-carbon-containing) elements you need in relatively small amounts to help regulate body functions, aid in the growth and maintenance of body tissues, and help release energy (Table 8.5). There are about 17 essential minerals. The major minerals, those that the body needs in amounts exceeding 100 milligrams per day, include calcium, phosphorus, magnesium, sodium, potassium, and chloride. The essential trace minerals, which you need in minute amounts, include copper, fluoride, iodine, iron, selenium, and zinc.

Characteristic symptoms develop if an essential mineral is consumed in a quantity too small or too large for good health. The minerals commonly lacking in the American diet are iron, calcium, magnesium, and potassium. Iron-deficiency **anemia** is a problem in some

antioxidant A substance that protects against the breakdown of food or body constituents by free radicals; antioxidants' actions include binding oxygen, donating electrons to free radicals, and repairing damage to molecules.

minerals Inorganic compounds needed in relatively small amounts for the regulation, growth, and maintenance of body tissues and functions.

anemia A deficiency in the oxygen-carrying material in the red blood cells.

KEY TERMS

Table 8.5 — Facts About Selected Minerals

MINERAL	IMPORTANT DIETARY SOURCES	MAJOR FUNCTIONS	SIGNS OF PROLONGED DEFICIENCY	TOXIC EFFECTS OF MEGADOSES
Calcium	Milk and milk products, tofu, fortified orange juice and bread, green leafy vegetables, bones in fish	Formation of bones and teeth; control of nerve impulses, muscle contraction, blood clotting	Stunted growth in children, bone mineral loss in adults; urinary stones	Kidney stones, calcium deposits in soft tissues, inhibition of mineral absorption, constipation
Fluoride	Fluoridated water, tea, marine fish eaten with bones	Maintenance of tooth and bone structure	Higher frequency of tooth decay	Increased bone density, mottling of teeth, impaired kidney function
Iodine	Iodized salt, seafood, processed foods	Essential part of thyroid hormones, regulation of body metabolism	Goiter (enlarged thyroid), cretinism (birth defect)	Depression of thyroid activity, hyperthyroidism in susceptible people
Iron	Meat and poultry, fortified grain products, dark green vegetables, dried fruit	Component of hemoglobin, myoglobin, and enzymes	Iron-deficiency anemia, weakness, impaired immune function, gastrointestinal distress	Nausea, diarrhea, liver and kidney damage, joint pains, sterility, disruption of cardiac function, death
Magnesium	Widespread in foods and water (except soft water); especially found in grains, legumes, nuts, seeds, green vegetables, milk	Transmission of nerve impulses, energy transfer, activation of many enzymes	Neurological disturbances, cardiovascular problems, kidney disorders, nausea, growth failure in children	Nausea, vomiting, diarrhea, central nervous system depression, coma; death in people with impaired kidney function
Phosphorus	Present in nearly all foods, especially milk, cereal, peas, eggs, meat	Bone growth and maintenance, energy transfer in cells	Impaired growth, weakness, kidney disorders, cardiorespiratory and nervous system dysfunction	Drop in blood calcium levels, calcium deposits in soft tissues, bone loss
Potassium	Meats, milk, fruits, vegetables, grains, legumes	Nerve function and body water balance	Muscular weakness, nausea, drowsiness, paralysis, confusion, disruption of cardiac rhythm	Cardiac arrest
Selenium	Seafood, meat, eggs, whole grains	Defense against oxidative stress; regulation of thyroid hormone action	Muscle pain and weakness, heart disorders	Hair and nail loss, nausea and vomiting, weakness, irritability
Sodium	Salt, soy sauce, fast food, processed foods, especially lunch meats, canned soups and vegetables, salty snacks, processed cheese	Body water balance, acid-base balance, nerve function	Muscle weakness, loss of appetite, nausea, vomiting; deficiency rarely seen	Edema, hypertension in sensitive people
Zinc	Whole grains, meat, eggs, liver, seafood (especially oysters)	Synthesis of proteins, RNA, and DNA; wound healing; immune response; ability to taste	Growth failure, loss of appetite, impaired taste acuity, skin rash, impaired immune function, poor wound healing	Vomiting, impaired immune function, decline in blood HDL levels, impaired copper absorption

SOURCES: Food and Nutrition Board, Institute of Medicine. 2006. *Dietary Reference Intakes: The Essential Guide to Nutrient Requirements.* Washington, D.C.: National Academies Press. The complete Dietary Reference Intake reports are available from the National Academies Press (http://www.nap.edu). Shils, M. E., et al., eds. 2005. *Modern Nutrition in Health and Disease,* 10th ed. Baltimore: Lippincott Williams and Wilkins.

age groups, and researchers fear poor calcium intakes in childhood are sowing the seeds for future **osteoporosis**, especially in women. See the box "Eating for Healthy Bones" to learn more.

Water—Vital but Often Ignored

Water is the major component in both foods and the human body: You are composed of about 50–60% water. Your need for other nutrients, in terms of weight, is much less than your need for water. You can live up to 50 days without food but only a few days without water.

Water is distributed all over the body, among lean and other tissues and in blood and other body fluids. Water is used in the digestion and absorption of food and is the medium in which most chemical reactions take place within the body. Some water-based fluids, such as blood, transport substances around the body; other fluids serve as lubricants or cushions. Water also helps regulate body temperature.

Eating for Healthy Bones

TAKE CHARGE

Osteoporosis is a condition in which the bones become dangerously thin and fragile over time. An estimated 10 million Americans over age 50 have osteoporosis, and another 34 million are at risk. Women account for about 80% of osteoporosis cases.

Most bone mass is built by age 18. After bone density peaks between ages 25 and 35, bone mass is lost over time. To prevent osteoporosis, the best strategy is to build as much bone as possible during your youth and do everything you can to maintain it as you age. Up to 50% of bone loss is determined by controllable lifestyle factors such as diet and exercise. Key nutrients for bone health include the following:

- **Calcium.** Getting enough calcium is important throughout life to build and maintain bone mass. Milk, yogurt, and calcium-fortified orange juice, bread, and cereals are all good sources.

- **Vitamin D.** Vitamin D is necessary for bones to absorb calcium; a daily intake of 600 IU is recommended for individuals age 1–70. Vitamin D can be obtained from foods and is manufactured by the skin when exposed to sunlight. Candidates for vitamin D supplements include people who don't eat many foods rich in vitamin D; those who don't expose their face, arms, and hands to the sun (without sunscreen) for 5–15 minutes a few times each week; and people who live north of an imaginary line drawn across the United States from Boston to the Oregon-California border (where the sun is weaker).

- **Vitamin K.** Vitamin K promotes the synthesis of proteins that help keep bones strong. Broccoli and leafy green vegetables are rich in vitamin K.

- **Other nutrients.** Other nutrients that may play an important role in bone health include vitamin C, magnesium, potassium, phosphorus, fluoride, manganese, zinc, copper, and boron.

Several dietary substances may have a *negative* effect on bone health, especially if consumed in excess. These include alcohol, sodium, caffeine, and retinol (a form of vitamin A). Drinking lots of soda, which often replaces milk in the diet, has been shown to increase the risk of bone fracture in teenage girls.

The effect of protein intake on bone mass depends on other nutrients: Protein helps build bone as long as calcium and vitamin D intake are adequate. But if intake of calcium and vitamin D is low, high protein intake can lead to bone loss.

Weight-bearing aerobic exercise helps maintain bone mass throughout life, and strength training improves bone density, muscle mass, strength, and balance. Drinking alcohol only in moderation, refraining from smoking, and managing depression and stress are also important for maintaining strong bones. For people who develop osteoporosis, a variety of medications are available to treat the condition.

Water is contained in almost all foods, particularly in liquids, fruits, and vegetables. The foods and fluids you consume provide 80–90% of your daily water intake; the remainder is generated through metabolism. You lose water each day in urine, feces, and sweat and through evaporation from your lungs.

Most people can maintain a healthy water balance by consuming beverages at meals and drinking fluids in response to thirst. The Food and Nutrition Board has set levels of adequate water intake to maintain hydration. All fluids, including those containing caffeine, can count toward your total daily fluid intake. Under these guidelines, men need to consume about 3.7 total liters of water, with 3.0 liters (about 13 cups) coming from beverages; women need 2.7 total liters, with 2.2 liters (about 9 cups) coming from beverages. About 20% of daily water intake comes from food. (See Table 1 in the Nutrition Resources section at the end of the chapter for recommendations for specific age groups.) If you exercise vigorously or live in a hot climate, you need to consume additional fluids to maintain a balance between water consumed and water lost. Severe dehydration causes weakness and can lead to death.

Other Substances in Food

Many substances in food are not essential nutrients but may influence health.

Antioxidants When the body uses oxygen or breaks down certain fats or proteins as a normal part of metabolism, it gives rise to substances called **free radicals.** Environmental factors such as cigarette smoke, exhaust fumes, radiation, excessive sunlight, certain drugs, and stress can increase free radical production. A free radical is a

---

Fitness Tip

Drink plenty of water before, during, and after workouts, especially when the weather is warm. Proper hydration helps you avoid cramps and heat-related problems such as heat stroke.

KEY TERMS

osteoporosis A condition in which the bones become extremely thin and brittle and break easily; due largely to insufficient calcium intake.

free radical An electron-seeking compound that can react with fats, proteins, and DNA, damaging cell membranes and mutating genes in its search for electrons; produced through chemical reactions in the body and by exposure to environmental factors such as sunlight and tobacco smoke.

Ask Yourself

Experts say that two of the most important factors in a healthy diet are eating the "right" kinds of carbohydrates and eating the "right" kinds of fats. Based on what you've read so far in this chapter, which are the "right" carbohydrates and the "right" fats? How would you say your own diet stacks up when it comes to carbs and fats?

chemically unstable molecule that reacts with fats, proteins, and DNA, damaging cell membranes and mutating genes. Free radicals have been implicated in aging, cancer, cardiovascular disease, and other degenerative diseases like arthritis.

Antioxidants found in foods can help protect the body by blocking the formation and action of free radicals and repairing the damage they cause. Some antioxidants, such as vitamin C, vitamin E, and selenium, are also essential nutrients. Others—such as carotenoids, found in yellow, orange, and dark green leafy vegetables—are not. Researchers recently identified the top antioxidant-containing foods and beverages as blackberries, walnuts, strawberries, artichokes, cranberries, brewed coffee, raspberries, pecans, blueberries, cloves, grape juice, unsweetened baking chocolate, sour cherries, and red wine. Also high in antioxidants are brussels sprouts, kale, cauliflower, and pomegranates.

Phytochemicals Antioxidants fall into the broader category of **phytochemicals**, substances found in plant foods that may help prevent chronic disease. In the past 30 years, researchers have identified and studied hundreds of different compounds found in foods, and many findings are promising. For example, certain substances found in soy foods may help lower cholesterol levels. Sulforaphane, a compound isolated from broccoli and other **cruciferous vegetables**, may render some carcinogenic compounds harmless. Allyl sulfides, a group of chemicals found in garlic and onions, appear to boost the activity of cancer-fighting immune cells. Carotenoids found in green vegetables may help preserve eyesight with age. Further research on phytochemicals may extend the role of nutrition to the prevention and treatment of many chronic diseases.

To increase your intake of phytochemicals, eat a variety of fruits, vegetables, and grains rather than relying on supplements. Like many vitamins and minerals, isolated phytochemicals may be harmful if taken in high doses. In many cases, their health benefits may be the result of chemical substances working in combination. The role of phytochemicals in disease prevention is discussed further in Chapters 11 and 12.

NUTRITIONAL GUIDELINES: PLANNING YOUR DIET

Various tools have been created by scientific and government groups to help people design healthy diets:

- The **Dietary Reference Intakes (DRIs)** are standards for nutrient intake designed to prevent nutritional deficiencies and reduce the risk of chronic diseases.

- The **Dietary Guidelines for Americans** were established to promote health and reduce the risk of major chronic diseases through diet and physical activity.

- **MyPlate** (formerly MyPyramid) provides daily food intake patterns that meet the DRIs and are consistent with the Dietary Guidelines for Americans.

Dietary Reference Intakes (DRIs)

The Food and Nutrition Board establishes dietary standards, or recommended intake levels, for Americans of all ages. The current set of standards, called Dietary Reference Intakes (DRIs), was introduced in 1997. The DRIs are frequently reviewed and are updated as substantial new nutrition-related information becomes available. The DRIs present different categories of nutrients in easy-to-read table format. The DRIs have a broad focus, being based on research that looks not just at the prevention of nutrient deficiencies but also at the role of nutrients in promoting health and preventing chronic diseases such as cancer, osteoporosis, and heart disease.

The DRIs include standards for both recommended intakes and maximum safe intakes. The recommended intake of each nutrient is expressed as either a *Recommended Dietary Allowance (RDA)* or as *Adequate Intake (AI)*. An AI is set when there is not enough information available to set an RDA value; regardless of the type of standard used, however, the DRI represents the best available estimate of intake for optimal health. The Estimated Average Requirement (EAR) is the average daily nutrient intake level estimated to meet the requirement of half the healthy individuals in a particular life stage and gender group. The *Tolerable Upper Intake Level (UL)* is the maximum daily intake that is unlikely to cause health problems in a healthy person. For example, the RDA for calcium for an 18-year-old female is 1300 milligrams (mg) per day; the UL is 3000 milligrams per day.

Because of a lack of data, ULs have not been set for all nutrients. This does not mean that people can tolerate long-term intakes of these vitamins and minerals above recommended levels. Like all chemical agents, nutrients can produce adverse effects if intakes are excessive. There is no established benefit from consuming nutrients at levels above the RDA or AI. The DRIs can be found in the Nutrition Resources section at the end of the chapter.

Daily Values Because the DRIs are too cumbersome to use as a basis for food labels, the FDA developed another set of dietary standards, the **Daily Values.** The Daily Values are based on several different sets of guidelines and include standards for fat, cholesterol, carbohydrate, dietary fiber, and selected vitamins and minerals. The Daily Values represent appropriate intake levels for a 2000-calorie diet. The percent Daily Value shown on a food label shows how well that food contributes to your recommended daily intake. Food labels are described in detail later in the chapter.

Should You Take Supplements? The aim of the DRIs is to guide you in meeting your nutritional needs primarily with food, rather than with vitamin and mineral supplements. Supplements lack potentially beneficial phytochemicals and fiber that are found only in whole foods. Most Americans can get the vitamins and minerals they need by eating a varied, nutritionally balanced diet.

The question of whether to take supplements is a serious one. Some vitamins and minerals are dangerous when ingested in excess, as described previously in Tables 8.4 and 8.5. Large doses of particular nutrients can also cause health problems by affecting the absorption of other vitamins and minerals. For all these reasons, you should think carefully about whether to take high-dose supplements; consider consulting a physician or registered dietitian.

Over the past two decades, high-dose supplement use has been promoted as a way to prevent or delay the onset of many diseases, including heart disease and several forms of cancer. These claims remain controversial, however, and a growing body of research shows that vitamin or mineral supplements have no significant impact on the risk of developing such illnesses. For example, a 2008 study conducted as part of the Women's Health Initiative showed no differences in the levels of heart disease, cancer, or overall mortality between postmenopausal women who took multivitamin supplements and those who did not. A similar study of adult men indicated that taking vitamins C and E did not reduce the risk of heart disease or certain cancers. According to the experts behind these and other studies, the research provides further proof that a balanced diet of whole foods—not high-dose supplementation—is the best way to promote health and prevent disease.

In setting the DRIs, the Food and Nutrition Board recommended supplements of particular nutrients for the following groups:

- Women who are capable of becoming pregnant should take 400 micrograms (µg) per day of folic

acid (the synthetic form of the vitamin folate) from fortified foods and/or supplements in addition to folate from a varied diet. Research indicates that this level of folate intake will reduce the risk of neural tube defects. Enriched breads, flours, corn meals, rice, noodles, and other grain products are fortified with folic acid. Folate is found naturally in green leafy vegetables, legumes, oranges, and strawberries.

- People over age 50 should eat foods fortified with vitamin B-12, take B-12 supplements, or both to meet the majority of the DRI of 2.4 micrograms of B-12 daily. Up to 30% of people over 50 may have problems absorbing protein-bound B-12 in foods.

- Because of the oxidative stress caused by smoking, smokers should get 35 milligrams *more* vitamin C per day than the RDA set for their age and sex. However, supplements are not usually needed because this extra vitamin C can easily be found in foods. For example, an 8-ounce glass of orange juice has about 100 mg of vitamin C.

Supplements may also be recommended in other cases. Women with heavy menstrual flows may need extra iron. Older people, people with dark skin, and people exposed to little sunlight may need extra vitamin D. Some vegetarians may need supplemental calcium, iron, zinc, and vitamin B-12, depending on their food choices. Other people may benefit from supplementation based on their lifestyle physical condition, medicines, or dietary habits.

Before deciding whether to take a vitamin or mineral supplement, consider whether you already eat a fortified breakfast cereal every day. Many breakfast cereals contain almost as many nutrients as a multivitamin pill. If you

KEY TERMS

phytochemical A naturally occurring substance found in plant foods that may help prevent and treat chronic diseases such as heart disease and cancer; *phyto* means "plant."

cruciferous vegetables Vegetables of the cabbage family, including cabbage, broccoli, brussels sprouts, kale, and cauliflower; the flower petals of these plants form the shape of a cross, hence the name.

Dietary Reference Intakes (DRIs) An umbrella term for four types of nutrient standards: Adequate Intake (AI), Estimated Average Requirement (EAR), and Recommended Dietary Allowance (RDA) are levels of intake considered adequate to prevent nutrient deficiencies and reduce the risk of chronic disease; Tolerable Upper Intake Level (UL) is the maximum daily intake that is unlikely to cause health problems.

Dietary Guidelines for Americans General principles of good nutrition intended to help prevent certain diet-related diseases.

MyPlate A food-group plan that provides practical advice to ensure a balanced intake of the essential nutrients.

Daily Values A simplified version of the RDAs used on food labels; also included are values for nutrients with no established RDA.

Wellness Tip

If you take a supplement, *never* take more than the recommended dosage unless your doctor tells you to.

Food choices and portion control are key factors in weight management.

elect to take a supplement, choose one that contains 50–100% of the Daily Value for vitamins and minerals. Avoid supplements containing large doses of nutrients that may be harmful.

Dietary Guidelines for Americans

To provide general guidance for choosing a healthy diet, the USDA and the U.S. Department of Health and Human Services (DHHS) jointly issue the Dietary Guidelines for Americans, updating and revising the guidelines every 5 years. The guidelines are intended for all Americans aged 2 and older. Following these guidelines promotes health and reduces the risk of chronic diseases, including heart disease, cancer, diabetes, stroke, osteoporosis, and obesity. Each of the recommendations is supported by an extensive review of scientific and medical evidence.

The 2010 Dietary Guidelines highlight four areas. First, because the majority of Americans are overweight or obese, the guidelines focus on ways to balance calorie consumption and calorie expenditure to manage weight. Second, because Americans also tend to consume too many calories without getting enough of certain nutrients, the guidelines focus on foods to reduce in the diet (the second highlighted area) and foods to increase in the diet (the third highlighted area). Finally, the guidelines focus on ways to incorporate the recommendations into overall healthy eating patterns. Specific recommendations for putting the Dietary Guidelines into practice are provided in MyPlate (discussed in the next section).

Balancing Calories to Manage Weight Calorie balance—the balance between calories consumed and calories expended—is the key to weight management. Current high rates of overweight and obesity can be attributed at least in part to people consuming more calories in foods and beverages than they expend in physical activity.

The guidelines recognize that many aspects of American life promote obesity, leading to an "obesogenic food environment." Factors contributing to this environment include an increase in the number of fast-food restaurants in communities, an increase in meals eaten outside the home, increased portion sizes, sedentary work and home environments, limited availability of safe outdoor walking and recreational spaces, and increased dependence on transportation and technological advances that lead to lower calorie expenditure on everyday tasks.

Still, managing body weight means that individuals need to control total calorie intake, and for people who are overweight or obese, this means consuming fewer calories from foods and beverages. The guidelines encourage people to become more conscious of what, when, why, and how much they eat; to deliberately make better choices; and to seek ways to be more physically active. Several specific behaviors and practices can help people manage their calorie balance and maintain a healthy weight. Recommendations include:

- Know what calorie level is appropriate for you at your current level of activity, and be aware of how many calories you are consuming.

- Cook at home more and eat out less, and when you do eat out, eat smaller portions and lower-calorie options.

- Limit screen time, whether watching television, playing games, or using a computer, and don't eat when watching TV.

Foods and Food Components to Reduce In addition to overall calories, Americans tend to consume certain foods and food components in excess—in particular, sodium, solid fats, added sugars, and refined grains. These foods often replace needed nutrients in the diet. Key recommendations include:

- Reduce daily sodium intake to less than 2300 mg, and further reduce intake to 1500 mg if you are 51 or older, are African American, or have hypertension, diabetes, or chronic kidney disease. The 1500 mg recommendation applies to about half the U.S. population, including children, and the majority of adults. The average intake of sodium for all Americans is estimated at 3400 mg; for boys and men between the ages of 12 and 50, it is estimated at more than 4000 mg. High sodium intake is associated with high blood pressure. Most salt in the diet comes from salt added during food processing.

- Limit intake of saturated fat, trans fat, and dietary cholesterol. Consume less than 10% of calories from saturated fats by replacing them with monounsaturated and polyunsaturated fats. Keep trans fatty acid consumption as low as possible, especially by limiting foods that contain synthetic sources of trans fats, such as partially hydrogenated oils. (See the

Nutrient	Recommended Daily Intake* 2000 calories	Orange Juice 168 calories % Daily	Nutrient value	Low-Fat (1%) Milk 150 calories % Daily	Nutrient value	Regular Cola 152 calories % Daily	Nutrient value	Bottled Iced Tea 150 calories % Daily	Nutrient value
Carbohydrate	300 g	14%	40.5 g	6%	18 g	13%	38 g	13%	37.5 g
Added sugars	32 g					119%	38 g +	108%	34.5 g +
Fat	65 g			6%	3.9 g				
Protein	55 g			22%	12 g				
Calcium	1000 mg	3%	33 mg	45%	450 mg	1%	11 mg		
Potassium	4700 mg	15%	710 mg	12%	570 mg	<1%	4 mg		
Vitamin A	700 µg	4%	30 µg	31%	216 µg				
Vitamin C	75 mg	193%	145.5 mg +	5%	3.6 mg				
Vitamin D	5 µg			74%	3.7 µg				
Folate	400 µg	40%	160 µg	5%	20 µg				

Bars show percentage of recommended daily intake or limit

[bar] + = Greater than 100% of recommended

*Recommended intakes and limits appropriate for a 20-year-old woman consuming 2000 calories per day.

FIGURE 8.3 Nutrient density of 12-ounce portions of selected beverages.
Color bars represent percentage of recommended daily intake or limit for each nutrient.

box "Reducing the Saturated and Trans Fats in Your Diet" for more information.) Consume less than 300 mg per day of dietary cholesterol.

- Reduce the intake of calories from solid fats and added sugars. Together, solid fats and added sugars contribute about 35% of the calories consumed by Americans, without contributing many nutrients. Most people should consume no more than 5–15% of daily calories from foods in these categories. Suggestions include limiting the amount of solid fats and added sugars when cooking and eating; consuming smaller and fewer portions of foods and beverages with these components, such as desserts and sodas; and eating the most nutrient-dense forms of foods in all food groups. Sodas, energy drinks, and sports drinks are the biggest source of added sugars in the American diet. The differences in nutrients between soda and other beverages are shown in Figure 8.3.

- Limit the consumption of foods that contain refined grains, especially refined grain foods that contain solid fats, added sugars, and sodium.

Wellness Tip

About a dozen major American cities, and the entire state of California, have enacted laws restricting the use of trans fats in commercially prepared foods.

- If alcohol is consumed, it should be consumed in moderation.

Foods and Nutrients to Increase In general, Americans don't eat a wide enough variety of nutrient-dense foods to obtain all the nutrients they need for optimal health. Recommendations include:

- Eat more fruits and vegetables, and eat a variety of vegetables, especially dark green, red, and orange vegetables and beans and peas. These foods are major sources of many nutrients that are underconsumed by many Americans, and they are relatively low in calories (unless prepared with added fats and sugars).

- Consume at least half of all grains as whole grains, which are a source of important nutrients such as iron, B vitamins, and dietary fiber.

- Increase intake of fat-free and low-fat milk and milk products, such as milk, yogurt, cheese, and fortified soy beverages. These foods are important sources of calcium, potassium, magnesium, vitamin D, and vitamin A. Milk and yogurt are preferable to cheese, which has more solid fat and more calories.

- Choose a variety of protein foods, including seafood, lean meat and poultry, eggs, beans and peas, soy products, and unsalted nuts and seeds. Increase the amount and variety of seafood, and reduce protein foods that are high in solid fats and calories. In addition to protein, these foods provide B vitamins,

TAKE CHARGE

Reducing the Saturated and Trans Fats in Your Diet

Your overall goal is to limit total fat intake to no more than 35% of total calories. Favor unsaturated fats over saturated and trans fats. Here are some steps that can help reduce these types of fat in your diet:

• Be moderate in your consumption of foods high in fat, including fast foods, commercially prepared baked goods and desserts, deep-fried food, meat, poultry, nuts and seeds, and regular dairy products.

• When you eat high-fat foods, limit your portion sizes, and balance your intake with other foods that are low in fat.

• Choose lean cuts of meat, and trim any visible fat from meat before and after cooking. Remove skin from poultry before or after cooking.

• Drink fat-free or low-fat milk instead of whole milk, and use lower-fat milk when cooking or baking. Substitute plain low-fat yogurt, low-fat cottage cheese, or buttermilk for sour cream.

• Use vegetable oil instead of butter or margarine. Use tub or squeeze margarine instead of stick margarine. Look for margarines that are free of trans fats. Minimize intake of coconut or palm oil.

• Season vegetables, seafood, and meats with herbs and spices rather than with creamy sauces, butter, or margarine.

• Use olive oil and lemon juice on salad, or use a yogurt-based salad dressing instead of mayonnaise or sour cream dressings.

• Steam, boil, bake, or microwave vegetables, or stir-fry them in a small amount of vegetable oil.

• Roast, bake, or broil meat, poultry, or fish so that fat drains away as the food cooks.

• Use a nonstick pan for cooking so that added fat will be unnecessary; use a vegetable spray for frying.

• Substitute egg whites for whole eggs when baking; limit the number of egg yolks when scrambling eggs.

• Choose fruits as desserts most often.

• Eat a low-fat vegetarian main dish at least once a week.

---

vitamin E, zinc, and magnesium. Seafood provides a range of nutrients, notably omega-3 fatty acids, which are associated with reduced risk of heart disease. (Seafood consumption is discussed in more detail later in the chapter.)

• Replace solid fats with oils where possible. Oils should not be added to the diet in addition to solid fats; instead, they should replace them.

• Because most Americans do not get enough potassium, dietary fiber, calcium, or vitamin D in their diet, they should consume more foods that contain these nutrients.

  • Potassium, which can help lower blood pressure, is found in many fruits, vegetables, and milk products. Recommended intake is 4700 mg per day.

  • Dietary fiber is found in beans and peas, other vegetables, fruits, nuts, and whole grains. Recommended daily intake for fiber is 25 g for women and 38 g for men; the current average daily intake is only about 15 g.

  • Calcium plays several important roles in health, including bone health. Low intake of calcium is a concern in children 9 and older, adolescent girls, adult women, and all adults age 51 and older. The chief sources of calcium in the diet are milk and milk products.

  • Vitamin D also has an important role in bone health. Chief sources are fortified foods, especially milk and yogurt.

• Other nutrients are a concern for certain special population groups, such as folic acid for women who may become pregnant.

Building Healthy Eating Patterns There are many different ways to incorporate the recommendations of the 2010 Dietary Guidelines into healthy eating patterns that (1) meet nutrient needs; (2) stay within calorie limits; (3) accommodate cultural, ethnic, traditional, and personal preferences; and (4) consider food cost and availability. In other words, people can eat healthfully in many different ways. Currently, howevere, there is a large discrepancy between the guidelines and the actual American diet.

Three eating plans that show how to put the Dietary Guidelines recommendations into action are the USDA Food Pattern (MyPlate), vegetarian adaptations of the USDA Food Pattern, and the DASH Eating Plan. (MyPlate and vegetarian diets are discussed later in the chapter, and the DASH Eating Plan is explained in the Nutrition Resources section at the end of this chapter.) A general principle in all these diets is that people should eat nutrient-dense foods—foods with little or no solid fats and added sugars. Another principle is that people should get their nutrients from foods rather than from supplements, although dietary supplements or fortification may be helpful in certain situations.

Helping Americans Make Healthy Choices A final area covered by the 2010 Dietary Guidelines for Americans is the environment in which people make their food choices.

To make healthy choices, individuals need *opportunities* to obtain healthy foods and engage in physical activity. Significant numbers of Americans—notably, members of racial and ethnic minorities, people with disabilities, and people with lower incomes—lack access to affordable, nutritious foods and/or opportunities for safe physical activity in their neighborhoods. The guidelines recognize the problem of *food security* in the United States—the ability to acquire adequate food to meet nutritional needs. Nearly 15% of the population is not able to obtain sufficient food to meet basic nutritional needs, and as noted above, many more Americans have diets that provide adequate calories but are deficient in essential nutrients.

The Dietary Guidelines propose the Social Ecological Model as a way to understand and address these complex problems. This model considers the interaction among individual factors (such as gender, income, and race/ethnicity), environmental settings (such as schools, workplaces, and restaurants), various sectors of influence (such as health care systems, agriculture, and media), and social and cultural norms and values (such as assumptions regarding body weight, types of foods consumed, and amount of physical activity incorporated into one's free time). All these factors play a role in a person's food and physical activity choices—and ultimately, in the person's health risks and outcomes.

The guidelines call on all elements of society, ranging from educators to communities to government policy makers, to implement strategies aimed at improving the food and activity environment in the United States. Examples of such strategies are expanding access to grocery stores, farmers markets, and other sources of healthy food; ensuring that meals and snacks served in schools are consistent with the Dietary Guidelines; encouraging physical activity in schools; developing policies to limit food and beverage marketing to children; supporting sustainable agricultural practices; and providing nutrition assistance programs. Such measures have the potential to improve the health of current and future generations by making healthy physical activity and eating choices the norm.

USDA's MyPlate

To help consumers put the Dietary Guidelines for Americans into practice, the USDA also issues the food guidance system known as MyPlate (called MyPyramid until 2011). MyPlate is designed for individuals to take advantage of the customization made possible by the Internet (Figure 8.4).

Key Messages of MyPlate MyPlate was developed to remind consumers to make healthy food choices and to be active every day. Key messages include the following:

- *Personalization* is an important element of the MyPlate program and the ChooseMyPlate.gov site, which includes individualized recommendations, interactive assessments of food intake and physical

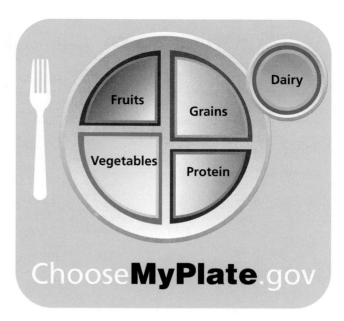

FIGURE 8.4   USDA's MyPlate.
The USDA food guidance system, called MyPlate, can be personalized based on an individual's sex, age, and activity level; visit www .ChooseMyPlate.gov to obtain a food plan appropriate for you.
SOURCE: U.S. Department of Agriculture. 2011. *MyPlate* (http://www .choosemyplate.gov; retrieved August 6, 2011).

activity, weight-management tools, and tips for success.

- *Daily physical activity* is important for maintaining a healthy weight and reducing the risk of chronic disease.

- *Moderation* of food intake is represented by advice to use smaller plates and to carefully watch portion sizes.

- *Proportionality* is represented by the different sizes of the food groups on the plate. The serving sizes provide a general guide for how much food a person should choose from each group.

- *Variety* is represented by the five food groups. Foods from all groups are needed daily for good health.

- *Gradual improvement* is a good strategy; people can benefit from taking small steps to improve their diet and activity habits each day.

The MyPlate chart in Figure 8.5 shows the food intake patterns recommended for different levels of calorie intake. Table 8.6 provides guidance for determining an appropriate calorie intake for weight maintenance. Use the table to identify an energy intake that is about right for you, and then refer to the appropriate column in Figure 8.5. You can also get a personalized version of MyPlate recommendations by visiting ChooseMyPlate.gov. Each food group is described briefly in the following sections. Many Americans have trouble identifying serving sizes, so recommended daily intakes from each group are given in terms of cups and ounces; see the box "Judging Portion Sizes" for additional advice.

Daily Amount of Food from Each Group
Food group amounts shown in cups (c) or ounce-equivalents (oz-eq)

Calorie level of pattern	1600	1800	2000	2200	2400	2600	2800	3000
Fruits	1.5 c	1.5 c	2 c	2 c	2 c	2 c	2.5 c	2.5 c
Vegetables	2 c	2.5 c	2.5 c	3 c	3 c	3.5 c	3.5 c	4 c
Dark-green	1.5 c/wk	1.5 c/wk	1.5 c/wk	2 c/wk	2 c/wk	2.5 c/wk	2.5 c/wk	2.5 c/wk
Red and orange	4 c/wk	5.5 c/wk	5.5 c/wk	6 c/wk	6 c/wk	7 c/wk	7 c/wk	7.5 c/wk
Beans and peas (legumes)	1 c/wk	1.5 c/wk	1.5 c/wk	2 c/wk	2 c/wk	2.5 c/wk	2.5 c/wk	3 c/wk
Starchy	4 c/wk	5 c/wk	5 c/wk	6 c/wk	6 c/wk	7 c/wk	7 c/wk	8 c/wk
Other	3.5 c/wk	4 c/wk	4 c/wk	5 c/wk	5 c/wk	5.5 c/wk	5.5 c/wk	7 c/wk
Grains	5 oz-eq	6 oz-eq	6 oz-eq	7 oz-eq	8 oz-eq	9 oz-eq	10 oz-eq	10 oz-eq
Whole grains	3 oz-eq	3 oz-eq	3 oz-eq	3.5 oz-eq	4 oz-eq	4.5 oz-eq	5 oz-eq	5 oz-eq
Enriched grains	2 oz-eq	3 oz-eq	3 oz-eq	3.5 oz-eq	4 oz-eq	4.5 oz-eq	5 oz-eq	5 oz-eq
Protein foods	5 oz-eq	5 oz-eq	5.5 oz-eq	6 oz-eq	6.5 oz-eq	6.5 oz-eq	7 oz-eq	7 oz-eq
Seafood	8 oz/wk	8 oz/wk	8 oz/wk	9 oz/wk	10 oz/wk	10 oz/wk	11 oz/wk	11 oz/wk
Meat poultry, eggs	24 oz/wk	24 oz/wk	26 oz/wk	29 oz/wk	31 oz/wk	31 oz/wk	34 oz/wk	34 oz/wk
Nuts, seeds, soy products	4 oz/wk	4 oz/wk	4 oz/wk	4 oz/wk	5 oz/wk	5 oz/wk	5 oz/wk	5 oz/wk
Dairy	3 c	3 c	3 c	3 c	3 c	3 c	3 c	3 c
Oils	22 g	24 g	27 g	29 g	31 g	34 g	36 g	44 g
Maximum SoFAS limit, calories (% of calories)	121 (8%)	161 (9%)	258 (13%)	266 (12%)	330 (14%)	362 (14%)	395 (14%)	459 (15%)

FIGURE 8.5 MyPlate food intake patterns.
To determine an appropriate amount of food from each group, find the column with your approximate daily energy intake. That column lists the daily recommended intake from each food group. Visit ChooseMyPlate.gov for a personalized intake plan and for intakes for other calorie levels.
SOURCE: U.S. Department of Health and Human Services and U.S. Department of Agriculture. 2011. *Dietary Guidelines for Americans, 2010, Appendix 7. USDA Food Patterns* (http://www.cnpp.usda.gov/Publications/DietaryGuidelines/2010/PolicyDoc/PolicyDoc.pdf; retrieved August 7, 2011).

Whole and Refined Grains Foods from this group are usually low in fat and rich in complex carbohydrates, dietary fiber (if grains are unrefined), and many vitamins and minerals. A 2000-calorie diet should include 6 ounce-equivalents each day. The following count as 1 ounce-equivalent:

- 1 slice of bread
- 1 small (2½-inch diameter) muffin
- 1 cup ready-to-eat cereal flakes
- ½ cup cooked cereal, rice, grains, or pasta
- 1 6-inch tortilla

Choose foods that are typically made with little fat or added sugar (bread, rice, pasta) over those that are high in fat and added sugar (croissants, chips, cookies, doughnuts). The key message is to make at least half your grains whole grains.

Vegetables Vegetables contain carbohydrates, dietary fiber, and many other nutrients, and they are naturally low in fat. A 2000-calorie diet should include 2½ cups of

Judging Portion Sizes

Studies have shown that most people underestimate the size of their food portions, in many cases by as much as 50%. If you need to retrain your eye, try using measuring cups and spoons and an inexpensive kitchen scale when you eat at home. With a little practice, you'll learn the difference between 3 and 8 ounces of chicken or meat, and what a half-cup of rice really looks like. For quick estimates, use the following equivalents:

- 1 teaspoon of margarine = one dice

- 1 ½ ounce of cheese = your thumb, four dice stacked together

- 3 ounces of chicken or meat = a deck of cards

- ½ cup of cooked rice, pasta, or potato = ½ baseball

- 1 cup of cereal flakes = a fist

- 2 tablespoons of peanut butter = a ping-pong ball

- 1 medium potato = a computer mouse

- 1–2-ounce muffin or roll = a plum or large egg

- 2-ounce bagel = a hockey puck or yo-yo

- 1 medium fruit (apple or orange) = a baseball

- ¼ cup nuts = a golf ball

- Small cookie or cracker = a poker chip

vegetables daily. Each of the following counts as 1/2 cup or equivalent of vegetables:

- ½ cup raw or cooked vegetables
- 1 cup raw leafy salad greens
- ½ cup vegetable juice

Because vegetables vary in the nutrients they provide, MyPlate recommends servings from five different sub-groups within the vegetables group. Choose vegetables from several subgroups each day. (For clarity, Figure 8.5 shows servings from the subgroups in terms of weekly consumption.) The key message is to fill half your plate with fruits and vegetables.

Fruits Fruits are rich in carbohydrates, dietary fiber, and many vitamins, especially vitamin C. A 2000-calorie diet should include 2 cups of fruits daily. Each of the following counts as ½ cup or equivalent of fruit:

- ½ cup fresh, canned, or frozen fruit
- ½ cup fruit juice (100% juice)
- ½ large (3½" diameter) whole fruit
- ¼ cup dried fruit

Choose whole fruits often; they are higher in fiber and often lower in calories than fruit juices. Fruit *juices* typically contain more nutrients and less added sugar than fruit *drinks*. Choose canned fruits packed in 100% fruit juice or water rather than in syrup. Again, MyPlate's key message for consumers is to fill half your plate with fruits and vegetables.

Dairy This group includes all milk and milk products, as well as lactose-free and lactose-reduced products. Those consuming 2000 calories per day should include 3 cups of milk or the equivalent daily. Each of the following counts as the equivalent of 1 cup:

- 1 cup milk or yogurt
- ½ cup ricotta cheese
- 1½ ounces natural cheese
- 2 ounces processed cheese

Cottage cheese is lower in calcium than most other cheeses; ½ cup is equivalent to ¼ cup milk. Ice cream is also lower in calcium and higher in sugar and fat than many other dairy products; one scoop counts as ⅓ cup milk. MyPlate's key message for consumers is to switch to fat-free or low-fat (1%) milk and dairy products.

Protein Foods (Meat and Beans) This group includes meat, poultry, fish, dried beans and peas, eggs, nuts, and seeds. A 2000-calorie diet should include 5½ ounce-equivalents daily. Each of the following counts as equivalent to 1 ounce:

- 1 ounce cooked lean meat, poultry, or fish
- ¼ cup cooked dry beans (legumes) or tofu
- 1 egg
- 1 tablespoon peanut butter
- ½ ounce nuts or seeds

Choose lean meats and skinless poultry, and watch your serving sizes carefully. Choose at least one serving of plant proteins, such as black beans, lentils, or tofu, every day.

Oils Oils and soft margarines include vegetable oils and soft vegetable oil table spreads that have no trans fats. These are major sources of vitamin E and unsaturated fatty

Table 8.6	USDA Daily Calorie Intake Levels		

AGE (YEARS)	SEDENTARY*	MODERATELY ACTIVE**	ACTIVE+
FEMALE			
2–3	1000	1000–1200	1000–1400
4–8	1200–1400	1400–1600	1400–1800
9–13	1400–1600	1600–2000	1800–2200
14–18	1800	2000	2400
19–25	2000	2200	2400
26–30	1800	2000	2400
31–50	1800	2000	2200
51 +	1600	1800	2000–2200
MALE			
2–3	1000–1200	1000–1400	1000–1400
4–8	1200–1400	1400–1600	1600–2000
9–13	1600–2000	1800–2200	2000–2600
14–18	2000–2400	2400–2800	2800–3200
19–20	2600	2800	3000
21–25	2400	2800	3000
26–30	2400	2600	3000
31–35	2400	2600	3000
36–40	2400	2600	2800
41–45	2200	2600	2800
46–50	2200	2400	2800
51–55	2200	2400	2800
56 +	2000–2200	2200–2400	2400–2600

*A lifestyle that includes only the light physical activity associated with typical day-to-day life.

**A lifestyle that includes physical activity equivalent to walking about 1.5–3 miles per day at 3–4 miles per hour (30–60 minutes a day of moderate physical activity), in addition to the light physical activity associated with typical day-to-day life.

+A lifestyle that includes physical activity equivalent to walking more than 3 miles per day at 3–4 miles per hour (60 or more minutes a day of moderate physical activity), in addition to the light physical activity associated with typical day-to-day life.

SOURCE: U.S. Department of Health and Human Services and U.S. Department of Agriculture. 2011. *Dietary Guidelines for Americans, 2010, Appendix 6. Estimated Calorie Needs per Day by Age, Gender, and Physical Activity Level* (http://www.cnpp.usda.gov/Publications /DietaryGuidelines/2010/PolicyDoc/PolicyDoc.pdf; retrieved August 7, 2011).

acids, including the essential fatty acids. A 2000-calorie diet should include 6 teaspoons of oils per day. One teaspoon is the equivalent of the following:

- 1 teaspoon vegetable oil or soft margarine
- 1 tablespoon salad dressing or light mayonnaise

Foods that are mostly oils include nuts, olives, avocados, and some fish. The following portions include about 1 teaspoon of oil: 4 large olives, ½ medium avocado, 2 tablespoons peanut butter, and 1 ounce roasted nuts.

Food labels can help you identify the type and amount of fat in various foods.

Solid Fats and Added Sugars If you consistently choose nutrient-dense foods that are fat-free or low-fat and that contain no added sugars, you can also have a small amount of additional calories in the form of solid fats and added sugars (SoFAS). Figure 8.5 shows the maximum number of SoFAS calories allowed at each calorie level in MyPlate.

People who are trying to lose weight may choose not to use SoFAS calories. For those wanting to maintain weight, these calories may be used to increase the amount of food from a food group; to consume foods that are not in the lowest-fat form or that contain added sugars; to add oil, fat, or sugars to foods; or to consume alcohol.

The current American diet includes higher levels of sugar intake and more calories per day from sugar than recommended. For teenagers age 14–18, sodas and energy and sports drinks are the top source of calories in the diet, accounting for 226 calories per beverage; teens typically drink more than one such beverage daily. In particular, experts advise consumers to be wary of products containing high-fructose corn syrup. Although this sweetener is not harmful in itself, it is high in calories and very low in nutritional value. High-fructose corn syrup is found in many products, especially soft drinks and processed foods. Research has linked high consumption of high-fructose corn syrup with obesity, diabetes, and other health problems.

Physical Activity Like the Dietary Guidelines and other plans, MyPlate encourages physical activity for improving health, preventing chronic diseases, and managing weight. The physical activity recommendations in MyPlate are very similar to those found in the Dietary Guidelines (described earlier in this chapter); if you meet the Department of Health and Human Services' guidelines of 150 minutes per week of moderate physical activity, you will meet the recommendations found in MyPlate.

Other Food-Group Plans

A variety of experts have proposed other food-group plans. Some of these address perceived shortcomings in the USDA plans, and some have adapted the old MyPyramid plans to special populations. Two alternative food plans appear in the Nutrition Resources section at the end

Fitness Tip

Consumption of red meats, sweets, eggs, and butter is greatly reduced or eliminated entirely in most forms of the Mediterranean diet.

of the chapter: the DASH eating plan and the Harvard Healthy Eating Pyramid. The USDA Center for Nutrition Policy and Promotion (www.usda.gov/cnpp) has more on alternative food plans for special populations such as young children, older adults, and people choosing particular ethnic diets. MyPlate is available in Spanish, and there are special adaptations of MyPlate for children and for women who are pregnant or breastfeeding.

Another food plan that has received attention in recent years is the Mediterranean diet, which emphasizes vegetables, fruits, and whole grains; daily servings of beans, legumes, and nuts; moderate consumption of fish, poultry, and dairy products; and the use of olive oil over other types of fat, especially saturated fat. The Mediterranean diet has been associated with lower rates of heart disease and cancer, and recent studies have found a link between the diet and a greatly reduced risk of Parkinson's disease and Alzheimer's disease.

The Vegetarian Alternative

Vegetarians choose a diet with one essential difference from the diets described previously—they eliminate or restrict foods of animal origin (meat, poultry, fish, eggs, milk). Many people choose such diets for health reasons; vegetarian diets tend to be lower in saturated fat, cholesterol, and animal protein and higher in complex carbohydrates, dietary fiber, folate, vitamins C and E, carotenoids, and phytochemicals. Some people adopt a vegetarian diet out of concern for the environment, for financial considerations, or for reasons related to ethics or religion.

Types of Vegetarian Diets There are various vegetarian styles. The wider the variety of the diet eaten, the easier it is to meet nutritional needs.

- *Vegans* eat only plant foods.
- *Lacto-vegetarians* eat plant foods and dairy products.
- *Lacto-ovo-vegetarians* eat plant foods, dairy products, and eggs.

Others can be categorized as partial vegetarians, semi-vegetarians, or pescovegetarians. These people eat plant foods, dairy products, eggs, and usually a small selection of poultry, fish, and other seafood. Many other people choose vegetarian meals frequently but are not strictly vegetarian. Including some animal protein (such as dairy products) in a mostly vegetarian diet makes meal planning easier, but it is not necessary.

A Food Plan for Vegetarians MyPlate can be adapted for use by vegetarians with only a few key modifications. For the meat and beans group, vegetarians can focus on the nonmeat choices of dry beans and peas, nuts, seeds, eggs, and soy foods like tofu. Vegans and other vegetarians who do not eat or drink any dairy products must find other rich sources of calcium (see the following list). Fruits, vegetables, and whole grains are healthy choices for people following all types of vegetarian diets.

A healthy vegetarian diet emphasizes a wide variety of plant foods. Although plant proteins are generally of a lower quality than animal proteins, choosing a variety of plant foods will supply all of the essential amino acids. Choosing minimally processed and unrefined foods will maximize nutrient value and provide ample dietary fiber. Daily consumption of a variety of plant foods in amounts that meet total energy needs can provide all needed nutrients except vitamin B-12 and possibly vitamin D. Strategies for getting these and other nutrients include the following:

- *Vitamin B-12* is found naturally only in animal foods. If dairy products and eggs are limited or avoided, B-12

Variety is the key to maintaining a healthy, balanced vegetarian diet.

vegetarian Someone who follows a diet that restricts or eliminates foods of animal origin.

can be found in fortified foods such as ready-to-eat cereals, soy beverages, meat substitutes, special yeast products, and supplements.

- *Vitamin D* can be obtained by spending 5–15 minutes a day in the sun, by consuming vitamin D–fortified products like ready-to-eat cereals and soy or rice milk, or by taking a supplement.
- *Calcium* is found in legumes, tofu processed with calcium, dark-green leafy vegetables, nuts, tortillas made from lime-processed corn, fortified orange juice, soy milk, bread, and other foods.
- *Iron* is found in whole grains, fortified bread and breakfast cereals, dried fruits, leafy green vegetables, nuts and seeds, legumes, and soy foods. The iron in plant foods is more difficult for the body to absorb than the iron from animal sources. Eating or drinking a good source of vitamin C with most meals is helpful because vitamin C improves iron absorption.
- *Zinc* is found in whole grains, nuts, legumes, and soy foods.

If you are a vegetarian, remember that it's especially important to eat as wide a variety of foods as possible to ensure that all your nutritional needs are satisfied. Consulting with a registered dietitian will make your planning easier. Vegetarian diets for children, teens, and pregnant and lactating women warrant professional guidance.

Dietary Challenges for Various Population Groups

MyPlate and the Dietary Guidelines for Americans provide a basis that nearly everyone can use to create a healthy diet. However, different population groups should be aware of special dietary challenges.

Children and Teenagers The best approach for parents with young children is to provide a variety of foods. For example, parents can add vegetables to casseroles and fruit to cereal, or they can offer fruit and vegetable juices or homemade yogurt or fruit shakes instead of sugary drinks. Allowing children to help prepare meals is another good way to encourage good eating habits.

Women Women tend to need fewer calories than men, so they may need to focus more on nutrient-dense foods to make sure they are getting enough of all the essential nutrients. Two nutrients of special concern to women are calcium and iron. Low calcium intake may be linked to the development of osteoporosis in later life. Nonfat and low-fat dairy products and fortified cereal, bread, and orange juice are good sources of calcium.

Ask Yourself

QUESTIONS FOR CRITICAL THINKING AND REFLECTION

What factors influence your food choices—convenience, cost, availability, habit? Do you ever consider nutritional content or nutritional recommendations like those found in MyPlate? If not, how big a change would it be for you to think of nutritional content first when choosing food? Is it something you could do easily?

Menstruating women have higher iron requirements than other groups, and a lack of iron in the diet can lead to iron-deficiency anemia. Lean red meat, leafy green vegetables, and fortified breakfast cereals are good sources of iron. As discussed earlier, all women capable of becoming pregnant should also get enough folate or folic acid from fortified foods and/or supplements.

Good nutrition is essential to a healthy pregnancy. Nutritional counseling can help a woman create a plan for healthy eating before and during pregnancy. Diet is especially important for any woman with special nutritional needs or an eating disorder, or who is overweight or obese. Physicians commonly prescribe prenatal vitamin supplements to pregnant women. The U.S. Public Health Service recommends that all women of childbearing age get 400 µg of folic acid from fortified foods and/or supplements each day to reduce the risk of neural tube defects that can arise in the fetus.

College Students Foods that are convenient for college students are not always the healthiest choices. However, it is possible to make healthy eating both convenient and affordable. See the tips in the box "Eating Strategies for College Students."

Older Adults As people age, they tend to become less active, so they require fewer calories to maintain their weight. At the same time, the absorption of nutrients tends to be lower in older adults because of age-related changes in the digestive tract. As discussed earlier, foods fortified with vitamin B-12 and/or B-12 supplements are recommended for people over age 50. Because constipation is a common problem, consuming foods high in dietary fiber and drinking enough fluids are important goals.

Athletes Key dietary concerns for athletes are meeting increased energy and fluid requirements for training and making healthy food choices throughout the day. For more on this topic, see the box "Do Athletes Need a Different Diet?"

People with Special Health Concerns Many Americans have special health concerns that affect their dietary needs. For example, women who are pregnant or breastfeeding

Eating Strategies for College Students

In General

● Eat a colorful, varied diet. The more colorful your diet is, the more varied and rich in fruits and vegetables it will be. Fruits and vegetables are typically inexpensive, delicious, nutritious, and low in fat and calories.

● Eat breakfast. You'll have more energy in the morning and be less likely to grab an unhealthy snack later on.

● Choose healthy snacks—fruits, vegetables, whole grains, and cereals.

● Drink nonfat milk, water, mineral water, or 100% fruit juice more often than soft drinks or sweetened beverages.

● Pay attention to portion sizes.

● Combine physical activity with healthy eating.

Eating in the Dining Hall

● Choose a meal plan that includes breakfast.

● Decide what you want to eat before you get in line, and stick to your choices.

● Build your meals around whole grains and vegetables. Ask for small servings of meat and high-fat main dishes.

● Choose leaner poultry, fish, or bean dishes rather than high-fat meats and fried entrees.

● Ask that gravies and sauces be served on the side; limit your intake.

● Choose broth-based or vegetable soups rather than cream soups.

● At the salad bar, load up on leafy greens, beans, and fresh vegetables. Avoid mayonnaise-coated salads, bacon, croutons, and high-fat dressings. Put dressing on the side; dip your fork into it rather than pouring it over the salad.

● Choose fruit for dessert rather than cookies or cakes.

Eating in Fast-Food Restaurants

● Most fast-food chains can provide a brochure with the nutritional content of their menu items. Ask for it, or check the restaurant's Web site for nutritional information. Order small single burgers with no cheese instead of double burgers with many toppings. If possible, get them broiled instead of fried.

● Ask for items to be prepared without mayonnaise, tartar sauce, sour cream, or other high-fat sauces. Ketchup, mustard, and fat-free mayonnaise or sour cream are better choices and are available at many fast-food restaurants.

● Choose whole-grain buns or bread for sandwiches.

● Choose chicken items made from chicken breast, not processed chicken.

● Order vegetable pizzas without extra cheese.

● If you order french fries or onion rings, get the smallest size and/or share them with a friend. Better yet, get a salad or a fruit cup instead.

Eating on the Run

● When you need to eat in a hurry, remember that you can carry healthy foods in your backpack or a small insulated lunch sack (with a frozen gel pack to keep fresh food from spoiling).

● Carry items that are small and convenient but nutritious, such as fresh fruits or vegetables, whole-wheat buns or muffins, snack-size cereal boxes, and water.

TAKE CHARGE

Do Athletes Need a Different Diet?

If you exercise vigorously and frequently, or if you are an athlete in training, you likely have increased energy and fluid requirements. Research supports the following recommendations for athletes:

- **Energy intake:** Someone engaged in a vigorous training program may have energy needs as high as 6000 calories per day—far greater than the energy needs of a moderately active person. For athletes, the Academy of Nutrition and Dietetics (formerly the American Dietetic Association) recommends a diet with 60–65% of calories coming from carbohydrates, 10–15% from protein, and no more than 30% from fat.

Athletes who need to maintain low body weight and fat (such as gymnasts, skaters, and wrestlers) need to get enough calories and nutrients while avoiding unhealthy eating patterns such as bulimia. The combination of low body fat, high physical activity, disordered eating habits—and, in women, amenorrhea—is associated with osteoporosis, stress fractures, and other injuries. If keeping your weight and body fat low for athletic reasons is important to you, seek dietary advice from a qualified dietician and make sure your physician is aware of your eating habits.

- **Carbohydrates:** Endurance athletes involved in competitive events lasting longer than 90 minutes may benefit from increasing carbohydrate intake to 65–70% of their total calories. Specifically, the American College of Sports Medicine (ACSM) recommends that athletes consume 2.7–4.5 grams per pound of body weight daily, depending on their weight, sport, and other nutritional needs. This increase should come in the form of complex carbohydrates.

High carbohydrate intake builds and maintains glycogen stores in the muscles, resulting in greater endurance and delayed fatigue during competitive events. The ACSM recommends that before exercise an active adult or athlete eat a meal or snack that is relatively high in carbohydrates, moderate in protein, and low in fat and fiber. Eating carbohydrates 30 minutes, 2 hours, and 4 hours after exercise can help replenish glycogen stores in the liver and muscles.

- **Fat:** The ACSM recommends that all athletes get 20–35% of calories from fat in their diets. This is in line with the daily intake suggested by the Food and Nutrition Board. Reducing fat intake to less than 20% of daily calories can negatively affect performance and be harmful to health.

- **Protein:** For endurance and strength-trained athletes, the ACSM recommends eating 0.5–0.8 gram of protein per pound of body weight each day, which is considerably higher than the standard DRI of 0.36 gram per pound. This level of protein is easily obtainable from foods; in fact, most Americans eat more protein than they need every day. A balanced, moderate-protein diet can provide the protein most athletes need.

There is no evidence that consuming supplements containing vitamins, minerals, protein, or specific amino acids builds muscle or improves sports performance. Strength and muscle are built with exercise, not extra protein, and carbohydrates provide the fuel needed for muscle-building exercise.

- **Fluids:** If you exercise heavily or live in a hot climate, you should drink extra fluids to maximize performance and prevent heat illness. For a strenuous endurance event, prepare yourself the day before by drinking plenty of fluids. The ACSM recommends drinking 2–3 milliliters of fluid per pound of body weight about 4 hours before the event. During the event, take in enough fluids to compensate for fluid loss due to sweating; the amount required depends on the individual and his or her sweat rate. Afterward, drink enough to replace lost fluids—about 16–24 ounces for every pound of weight lost.

Water is a good choice for fluid replacement for events lasting 60–90 minutes. For longer workouts or events, a sports drink can be a good choice. These contain water, electrolytes, and carbohydrates and can provide some extra energy as well as replace electrolytes like sodium lost in sweat.

SOURCE: American College of Sports Medicine. 2009. *American College of Sports Medicine Position Stand: Nutrition and Athletic Performance* (http://www.acsm-msse.org/pt/pt-core/template-journal/msse/media/0309nutrition.pdf; retrived April 23, 2011).

require extra calories, vitamins, and minerals. People with diabetes benefit from a well-balanced diet that is low in simple sugars, high in complex carbohydrates, and relatively rich in monounsaturated fats. People with high blood pressure need to limit their sodium consumption and control their weight. If you have a health problem or concern that may require a special diet, discuss your situation with a physician or registered dietitian.

Using Food Labels

The "Nutrition Facts" section of a food label designed to help consumers make food choices based on the nutrients that are most important to good health. In addition to listing nutrient content by weight, the label puts the information in the context of a daily diet of 2000 calories that includes no more than 65 grams of fat (approximately 30% of total calories). For example, if a serving of a particular product has 13 grams of fat, the label will show that the serving represents 20% of the daily fat allowance. If your daily diet contains fewer or more than 2000 calories, you need to adjust these calculations accordingly.

Food labels contain uniform serving sizes. This means that if you look at different brands of salad dressing, for example, you can compare calories and fat content based on the serving amount. (Food label serving sizes may be larger or smaller than USDA serving size equivalents, however.) Regulations also require that foods meet strict definitions if their packaging includes the terms *light, low-fat,* or *high-fiber* (see below). Health claims such as "good source of dietary fiber" or "low in saturated fat" on packages are signals that those products can wisely be included in your diet. Overall, the food label is an important tool to help you choose a diet that conforms to My-Plate and the Dietary Guidelines.

Selected Nutrient Claims and What They Mean

- **Healthy** A food that is low in fat, is low in saturated fat, has no more than 360–480 mg of sodium and 60 mg of cholesterol, *and* provides 10% or more of the Daily Value for vitamin A, vitamin C, protein, calcium, iron, or dietary fiber.

- **Light or lite** 33% fewer calories or 50% less fat than a similar product.

- **Reduced or fewer** At least 25% less of a nutrient than a similar product; can be applied to fat ("reduced fat"), saturated fat, cholesterol, sodium, and calories.

- **Extra or added** 10% or more of the Daily Value per serving when compared to what a similar product has.

- **Good source** 10–19% of the Daily Value for a particular nutrient per serving.

- **High, rich in, or excellent source of** 20% or more of the Daily Value for a particular nutrient per serving.

- **Low calorie** 40 calories or less per serving.

- **High fiber** 5 g or more of fiber per serving.

- **Good source of fiber** 2.5–4.9 g of fiber per serving.

- **Fat-free** Less than 0.5 g of fat per serving.

- **Low-fat** 3 g of fat or less per serving.

- **Saturated fat-free** Less than 0.5 g of saturated fat and 0.5 g of trans fatty acids per serving.

- **Low saturated fat** 1 g or less of saturated fat per serving and no more than 15% of total calories.

- **Cholesterol-free** Less than 2 mg of cholesterol and 2 g or less of saturated fat per serving.

- **Low cholesterol** 20 mg or less of cholesterol and 2 g or less of saturated fat per serving.

- **Low sodium** 140 mg or less of sodium per serving.

- **Very low sodium** 35 mg or less of sodium per serving.

- **Lean** Cooked seafood, meat, or poultry with less than 10 g of fat, 4.5 g or less of saturated fat, and less than 95 mg of cholesterol per serving.

- **Extra lean** Cooked seafood, meat, or poultry with less than 5 g of fat, 2 g of saturated fat, and 95 mg of cholesterol per serving.

NOTE: The FDA has not yet defined nutrient claims relating to carbohydrates, so foods labeled low- or reduced-carbohydrate do not conform to any approved standard.

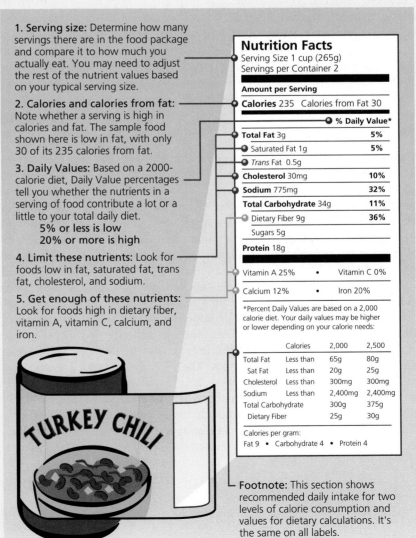

1. **Serving size:** Determine how many servings there are in the food package and compare it to how much you actually eat. You may need to adjust the rest of the nutrient values based on your typical serving size.

2. **Calories and calories from fat:** Note whether a serving is high in calories and fat. The sample food shown here is low in fat, with only 30 of its 235 calories from fat.

3. **Daily Values:** Based on a 2000-calorie diet, Daily Value percentages tell you whether the nutrients in a serving of food contribute a lot or a little to your total daily diet.
   5% or less is low
   20% or more is high

4. **Limit these nutrients:** Look for foods low in fat, saturated fat, trans fat, cholesterol, and sodium.

5. **Get enough of these nutrients:** Look for foods high in dietary fiber, vitamin A, vitamin C, calcium, and iron.

Nutrition Facts
Serving Size 1 cup (265g)
Servings per Container 2

Amount per Serving

Calories 235   Calories from Fat 30

% Daily Value*

Total Fat 3g	**5%**
Saturated Fat 1g	**5%**
Trans Fat 0.5g	
Cholesterol 30mg	**10%**
Sodium 775mg	**32%**
Total Carbohydrate 34g	**11%**
Dietary Fiber 9g	**36%**
Sugars 5g	
Protein 18g	

Vitamin A 25%	•	Vitamin C 0%
Calcium 12%	•	Iron 20%

*Percent Daily Values are based on a 2,000 calorie diet. Your daily values may be higher or lower depending on your calorie needs:

		Calories	2,000	2,500
Total Fat	Less than		65g	80g
Sat Fat	Less than		20g	25g
Cholesterol	Less than		300mg	300mg
Sodium	Less than		2,400mg	2,400mg
Total Carbohydrate			300g	375g
Dietary Fiber			25g	30g

Calories per gram:
Fat 9 • Carbohydrate 4 • Protein 4

Footnote: This section shows recommended daily intake for two levels of calorie consumption and values for dietary calculations. It's the same on all labels.

NUTRITIONAL PLANNING: MAKING INFORMED CHOICES ABOUT FOOD

Knowing about nutrition is a good start to making sound choices about food. It also helps if you can interpret food labels, understand food additives, and avoid foodborne illnesses.

Food Labels

All processed foods regulated by either the FDA or the USDA include standardized nutrition information on their labels. Every food label shows serving sizes and the amount of fat, saturated fat, trans fat, cholesterol, protein, dietary fiber, sugars, total carbohydrate, and sodium in each serving. To make intelligent choices about food, learn to read and understand food labels (see the box "Using Food Labels").

Food labels are not required on fresh meat, poultry, fish, fruits, and vegetables (many of these products are not packaged). You can get information on the nutrient content of these items from basic nutrition books, registered dietitians, nutrient analysis computer software, the Web, and the companies that produce or distribute these foods. Also, supermarkets often have posters or pamphlets listing the nutrient contents of these foods. In Lab 8.3, you compare foods using the information on their labels.

Dietary Supplements

Dietary supplements include vitamins, minerals, amino acids, herbs, enzymes, and other compounds. Although dietary supplements are often thought of as safe and natural, they contain powerful bioactive chemicals that have the potential for harm. About one-quarter of all pharmaceutical drugs are derived from botanical sources, and even essential vitamins and minerals can have toxic effects if consumed in excess.

In the United States, supplements are not legally considered drugs and are not regulated the way drugs are. Before they are approved by the FDA and put on the market, drugs undergo clinical studies to determine safety, effectiveness, side effects and risks, possible interactions with other substances, and appropriate dosages. The FDA does not authorize or test dietary supplements, and manufacturers are not required to demonstrate either safety or effectiveness before they are marketed. Although dosage guidelines exist for some of the compounds in dietary supplements, dosages for many are not well established.

Many ingredients in dietary supplements are classified by the FDA as "generally recognized as safe," but some have been found to be dangerous on their own or to interact with prescription or over-the-counter drugs in dangerous ways. Garlic supplements, for example, can cause bleeding if taken with anticoagulant (blood-thinning) medications. Some supplements can have side effects. St. John's wort, for example, increases the skin's sensitivity to sunlight and may decrease the effectiveness of oral contraceptives, drugs used to treat HIV infection, and many other medications.

There are also key differences in the way drugs and supplements are manufactured: FDA-approved medications are standardized for potency, and quality control and proof of purity are required. Dietary supplement manufacture is not as closely regulated, and there is no guarantee that a product contains a given ingredient at all, let alone in the appropriate amount. The potency of herbal supplements can vary widely due to differences in growing and harvesting conditions, preparation methods, and storage. Contamination and misidentification of plant compounds are also potential problems.

In an effort to provide consumers with more reliable and consistent information about supplements, the FDA has developed labeling regulations. Labels similar to those found on foods are now required for dietary supplements; for more information, see the box "Using Dietary Supplement Labels."

Food Additives

Today, some 2800 substances are intentionally added to foods to maintain or improve nutritional quality, to maintain freshness, to help in processing or preparation, or to alter taste or appearance. Additives make up less than 1% of our food. The most widely used are sugar, salt, and corn syrup; these three, plus citric acid, baking soda, vegetable colors, mustard, and pepper, account for 98% by weight of all food additives used in the United States.

Food additives pose no significant health hazard to most people because the levels used are well below any that could produce toxic effects. Two additives of potential concern for some people are sulfites, used to keep vegetables from turning brown, and monosodium glutamate (MSG), used as a flavor enhancer. Sulfites can cause severe reactions in some people, and the FDA strictly limits their use and requires clear labeling on any food containing sulfites. MSG may cause some people to experience episodes of sweating and increased blood pressure. If you have any sensitivity to an additive, check food labels when you shop and ask questions when you eat out.

Foodborne Illness

Many people worry about additives or pesticide residues in their food, but a greater threat comes from microorganisms that cause foodborne illnesses. Raw or

KEY TERM

pathogen A microorganism that causes disease.

Using Dietary Supplement Labels

Since 1999, specific types of information have been required on the labels of dietary supplements. In addition to basic information about the product, labels include a "Supplement Facts" panel, modeled after the "Nutrition Facts" panel used on food labels (see the figure). Under the Dietary Supplement Health and Education Act (DSHEA) and food labeling laws, supplement labels can make three types of health-related claims:

- *Nutrient-content claims,* such as "high in calcium," "excellent source of vitamin C," or "high potency." The claims "high in" and "excellent source of" mean the same as they do on food labels. A "high potency" single-ingredient supplement must contain 100% of its Daily Value; a "high potency" multi-ingredient product must contain 100% or more of the Daily Value of at least two-thirds of the nutrients present for which Daily Values have been established.

- *Health claims,* if they have been authorized by the FDA or another authoritative scientific body. The association between adequate calcium intake and lower risk of osteoporosis is an example of an approved health claim. The FDA also allows so-called *qualified health claims* for situations in which there is emerging but as yet inconclusive evidence for a particular claim. Such claims must include qualifying language such as "scientific evidence suggests but does not prove" the claim.

- *Structure-function claims,* such as "antioxidants maintain cellular integrity" or "this product enhances energy levels." Because these claims are not reviewed by the FDA, they must carry a disclaimer (see the sample label).

Tips for Choosing and Using Dietary Supplements

- Check with your physician before taking a supplement. Many are not meant for children, older people, women who are pregnant or breastfeeding, people with chronic illnesses or upcoming surgery, or people taking prescription or over-the-counter medications.

- Follow the cautions, instructions for use, and dosage given on the label.

- Look for the USP verification mark on the label, indicating that the product meets minimum safety and purity standards developed under the Dietary Supplement Verification Program by the United States Pharmacopeia (USP). The USP mark means that the product (1) contains the ingredients stated on the label, (2) has the declared amount and strength of ingredients, (3) will dissolve effectively, (4) has been screened for harmful contaminants, and (5) has been manufactured using safe, sanitary, and well-controlled procedures. The National Nutritional Foods Association has a self-regulatory testing program for its members; other, smaller associations and labs, including ConsumerLab.com, also test and rate dietary supplements.

- Choose brands made by nationally known food and drug manufacturers or " house brands" from large retail chains. Due to their size and visibility, such sources are likely to have high manufacturing standards.

- If you experience side effects, stop using the product and contact your physician. Report any serious reactions to the FDA's MedWatch monitoring program (1-800-FDA-1088 or online at http://www.fda.gov/Safety/MedWatch/default.htm).

For More Information About Dietary Supplements

ConsumerLab.Com: http://www.consumerlab.com

Food and Drug Administration: http://www.fda.gov/Food/DietarySupplements/default.htm

National Institutes of Health, Office of Dietary Supplements: http://ods.od.nih.gov

Natural Products Association: http://www.npainfo.org

U.S. Department of Agriculture: http://fnic.nal.usda.gov/nal_display/index.php?info_center=4&tax_level=1&tax_subject=274

U.S. Pharmacopeia: http://www.usp.org/USPVerified/DietarySupplements

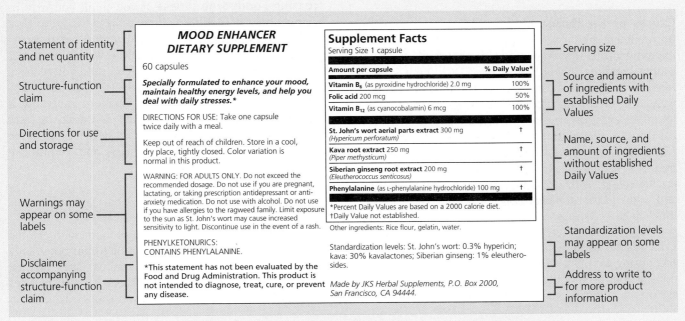

Statement of identity and net quantity	**MOOD ENHANCER DIETARY SUPPLEMENT** 60 capsules
Structure-function claim	***Specially formulated to enhance your mood, maintain healthy energy levels, and help you deal with daily stresses.*** *
Directions for use and storage	DIRECTIONS FOR USE: Take one capsule twice daily with a meal. Keep out of reach of children. Store in a cool, dry place, tightly closed. Color variation is normal in this product.
Warnings may appear on some labels	WARNING: FOR ADULTS ONLY. Do not exceed the recommended dosage. Do not use if you are pregnant, lactating, or taking prescription antidepressant or anti-anxiety medication. Do not use with alcohol. Do not use if you have allergies to the ragweed family. Limit exposure to the sun as St. John's wort may cause increased sensitivity to light. Discontinue use in the event of a rash. PHENYLKETONURICS: CONTAINS PHENYLALANINE.
Disclaimer accompanying structure-function claim	*This statement has not been evaluated by the Food and Drug Administration. This product is not intended to diagnose, treat, cure, or prevent any disease.

Supplement Facts
Serving Size 1 capsule

Amount per capsule	% Daily Value*
Vitamin B6 (as pyroxidine hydrochloride) 2.0 mg	100%
Folic acid 200 mcg	50%
Vitamin B12 (as cyanocobalamin) 6 mcg	100%
St. John's wort aerial parts extract 300 mg (*Hypericum perforatum*)	†
Kava root extract 250 mg (*Piper methysticum*)	†
Siberian ginseng root extract 200 mg (*Eleutherococcus senticosus*)	†
Phenylalanine (as L-phenylalanine hydrochloride) 100 mg	†

*Percent Daily Values are based on a 2000 calorie diet.
†Daily Value not established.

Other ingredients: Rice flour, gelatin, water.

Standardization levels: St. John's wort: 0.3% hypericin; kava: 30% kavalactones; Siberian ginseng: 1% eleutherosides.

Made by JKS Herbal Supplements, P.O. Box 2000, San Francisco, CA 94444.

Labels:
- Serving size
- Source and amount of ingredients with established Daily Values
- Name, source, and amount of ingredients without established Daily Values
- Standardization levels may appear on some labels
- Address to write to for more product information

Careful food handling greatly reduces the risk of foodborne illness.

Wellness Tip

To get produce as clean as possible, rub it with a soft brush while holding it under running water.

undercooked animal products, such as chicken, hamburger, and oysters, pose the greatest risk, although in recent years contaminated fruits and vegetables have been catching up.

The CDC estimates that 48 million illnesses, 128,000 hospitalizations, and 3000 deaths occur each year in the United States due to foodborne contaminants. Symptoms include diarrhea, vomiting, fever, pain, headache, and weakness. Although the effects of foodborne illness are usually not serious, some groups, such as children, pregnant women, and elderly people, are more at risk for severe complications such as rheumatic diseases, seizures, blood poisoning, and death.

Causes of Foodborne Illnesses Most cases of foodborne illness are caused by **pathogens**, disease-causing microorganisms that contaminate food, usually from improper handling. According to the CDC, about 90% of foodborne illnesses, hospitalizations, and deaths in 2010 were due to seven pathogens: *Salmonella* (most often found in eggs, on vegetables, and on poultry); norovirus (most often found in salad ingredients and shellfish); *Campylobacter jejuni* (most often found in meat and poultry); *Toxoplasma* (most often found in meat); *Escherichia coli (E. coli)* O157:H7 (most often found in meat and water); *Listeria monocytogenes* (most often found in lunch meats, sausages, and hot dogs); and *Clostridium perfringens* (most often found in meat and gravy). Salmonella was the leading cause of hospitalizations and deaths, accounting for 28% of deaths and 35% of hospitalizations. About 60% of illness, but a much smaller percentage of severe illness, was caused by norovirus.

Although pathogens are usually destroyed during cooking, the U.S. government is taking steps to bring down levels of contamination by improving national testing and surveillance. Raw meat and poultry products are now sold with safe-handling and -cooking instructions, and all packaged, unpasteurized fresh fruit and vegetable juices carry warnings about potential contamination. Although foodborne illness outbreaks associated with food-processing plants make headlines, most cases of illness trace back to poor food handling in the home or in restaurants. The 2010 Dietary Guidelines for Americans encourages people to follow four basic food safety principles:

- **Clean** hands, food contact surfaces, and vegetables and fruits.
- **Separate** raw, cooked, and read-to-eat foods while shopping, storing, and preparing foods.
- **Cook** foods to a safe temperature.
- **Chill** (refrigerate) perishable foods promptly.

The Dietary Guidelines also advise people to avoid certain high-risk foods, including raw (unpasteurized) milk, cheeses, and juices; raw or undercooked animal foods, such as seafood, meat, poultry, and eggs; and raw sprouts. These precautions are especially important for pregnant women, young children, older adults, and people with weakened immune systems or certain chronic diseases. For more information on food safety, see the box "Safe Food Handling."

Treating Foodborne Illness If you think you may be having a bout of foodborne illness, drink plenty of clear fluids to prevent dehydration, and rest to speed recovery. To prevent further contamination, wash your hands often and always before handling food until you recover. A fever higher than 102°F, blood in the stool, or dehydration deserves a physician's evaluation, especially if the symptoms persist for more than 2–3 days. In cases of suspected botulism—characterized by symptoms such as double vision, paralysis, dizziness, and vomiting—consult a physician immediately.

Irradiated Foods

Food irradiation is the treatment of foods with gamma rays, X-rays, or high-voltage electrons to kill potentially harmful pathogens, including bacteria, parasites, insects, and fungi that cause foodborne illness. It also reduces spoilage and extends shelf life. Even though irradiation

Safe Food Handling

Shopping

- Don't buy food in containers that leak, bulge, or are severely dented. Refrigerated foods should be cold, and frozen foods should be solid.

- Check the food label for an expiration date and for safe-handling instructions.

- Place meat, poultry, and seafood in plastic bags, and separate foods in your grocery cart.

- Select cold and frozen food last to ensure that they stay refrigerated until just before checkout.

Storing Food

- Store raw meat, poultry, fish, and shellfish in containers in the refrigerator so that the juices don't drip onto other foods. Keep these items away from other foods, surfaces, utensils, and serving dishes to prevent cross-contamination.

- Store eggs in the coldest part of the refrigerator, not in the door, and use them within 3–5 weeks.

- Keep hot foods hot (140°F or above) and cold foods cold (40°F or below); harmful bacteria can grow rapidly between these two temperatures. Refrigerate foods within 2 hours of purchase or preparation and within 1 hour if the air temperature is above 90°F. Freeze foods at or below 0°F. Use or freeze fresh meats within 3–5 days and fresh poultry, fish, and ground meat within 1–2 days. Use refrigerated leftovers within 3–4 days.

Preparing Food

- Thoroughly wash your hands with warm soapy water for 20 seconds before and after handling food, especially raw meat, fish, shellfish, poultry, or eggs.

- Make sure counters, cutting boards, dishes, utensils, and other equipment are thoroughly cleaned with hot soapy water before and after use. Wash dishcloths and kitchen towels frequently.

- Use separate cutting boards for meat, poultry, and seafood and for foods that will be eaten raw, such as fruits and vegetables. Replace cutting boards once they become worn or develop hard-to-clean grooves.

- Thoroughly rinse and scrub fruits and vegetables with a brush (but not with soap or detergent), or peel off the skin.

- Don't eat raw animal products, including raw eggs in homemade hollandaise sauce, eggnog, or cookie dough.

- Thaw frozen food in the refrigerator, in cold water, or in the microwave, not on the kitchen counter. Cook foods immediately after thawing.

Cooking

- Cook foods thoroughly, especially beef, poultry, fish, pork, and eggs; cooking kills most microorganisms. Use a food thermometer to ensure that foods are cooked to a safe temperature. Hamburgers should be cooked to 160°F. Turn or stir microwaved food to make sure it is heated evenly throughout.

- Cook stuffing separately from poultry; or wash poultry thoroughly, stuff immediately before cooking, and transfer the stuffing to a clean bowl immediately after cooking. The temperature of cooked stuffing should reach 165°F.

- Cook eggs until they're firm, and fully cook foods containing eggs.

- To protect against *Listeria*, reheat ready-to-eat foods like hot dogs and cold cuts until steaming hot.

- Because of possible contamination with *E. coli* 0157:H7 and *Salmonella*, avoid raw sprouts.

According to the USDA, "When in doubt, throw it out." Even if a food looks and smells fine, it may not be safe. If you aren't sure that a food has been prepared, served, and stored safely, don't eat it. For more information, see the USDA's *Kitchen Companion: Your Safe Food Handbook* at http://www.fsis.usda.gov/PDF/Kitchen_Companion.pdf.

TAKE CHARGE

has been generally endorsed by agencies such as the World Health Organization, the CDC, and the American Medical Association, few irradiated foods are currently on the market due to consumer resistance and skepticism. Studies haven't conclusively identified any harmful effects of food irradiation, and newer methods of irradiation involving electricity and X-rays do not require the use of any radioactive materials. Studies indicate that

when consumers are given information about the process of irradiation and the benefits of irradiated foods, most want to purchase them.

> **food irradiation** The treatment of foods with gamma rays, X-rays, or high-voltage electrons to kill potentially harmful pathogens and increase shelf life.
>
> KEY TERM

All primary irradiated foods (meat, vegetables, and so on) are labeled with the flowerlike radura symbol and a brief information label; spices and foods that are merely ingredients do not have to be labeled. It is important to remember that although irradiation kills most pathogens, it does not completely sterilize foods. Proper handling of irradiated foods is still critical for preventing foodborne illness.

Environmental Contaminants and Organic Foods

Contaminants are present in the food-growing environment. Environmental contaminants include various minerals, antibiotics, hormones, pesticides, and industrial chemicals. Safety regulations attempt to keep our exposure to contaminants at safe levels, but monitoring is difficult, and many substances (such as pesticides) persist in the environment long after being banned from use.

Organic Foods Some people who are concerned about pesticides and other environmental contaminants choose to buy foods that are **organic.** To be certified as organic, foods must meet strict production, processing, handling, and labeling criteria. Organic crops must meet limits on pesticide residues. For meat, milk, eggs, and other animal products to be certified organic, animals must be given organic feed and access to the outdoors and may not be given antibiotics or growth hormones. The use of genetic engineering, ionizing radiation, and sewage sludge is prohibited. Products can be labeled "100% organic" if they contain all organic ingredients and "organic" if they contain at least 95% organic ingredients; all such products may carry the USDA organic seal. A product with at least 70% organic ingredients can be labeled "made with organic ingredients" but cannot use the USDA seal.

Organic foods, however, are not necessarily free of chemicals. They may be contaminated with pesticides used on neighboring lands or on foods transported in the same train or truck. However, they tend to have lower levels of pesticide residues than conventionally grown crops. Some experts recommend that consumers who want to buy organic fruits and vegetables spend their money on those that carry lower pesticide residues than their conventional counterparts (the "dirty dozen"): apples, bell peppers, celery, cherries, imported grapes, nectarines, peaches, pears, potatoes, red raspberries, spinach, and strawberries. Experts also recommend buying organic

 KEY TERM

> **organic** A designation applied to foods grown and produced according to strict guidelines limiting the use of pesticides, nonorganic ingredients, hormones, antibiotics, genetic engineering, irradiation, and other practices.

Ask Yourself

QUESTIONS FOR CRITICAL THINKING AND REFLECTION

Have you ever taken a dietary supplement, such as St. John's wort for mild depression or echinacea or zinc for a cold? If so, who or what influenced your decision to use this product? Did you do any research before taking it? Did you read the label on the package? Do you think the product had the desired effect?

beef, poultry, eggs, dairy products, and baby food. Fruits and vegetables that carry little pesticide residue whether grown conventionally or organically include asparagus, avocadoes, bananas, broccoli, cauliflower, corn, kiwi, mangoes, onions, papaya, pineapples, and peas. All foods are subject to strict pesticide limits; the debate about the health effects of small amounts of residue is ongoing.

Whether organic foods are better for your health cannot be said for certain, but organic farming is better for the environment. It helps maintain biodiversity of crops and replenish the Earth's resources. It is less likely to degrade soil, contaminate water, or expose farm workers to toxic chemicals. As multinational food companies get into the organic food business, however, consumers who want to support environmentally friendly farming methods should look for foods that are not only organic but also locally grown.

Guidelines for Fish Consumption A specific area of concern has been possible mercury contamination in fish. Overall, fish and shellfish are healthy sources of protein, omega-3 fats, and other nutrients. Prudent choices can minimize the risk of any possible negative health effects. High mercury concentrations are most likely to be found in predator fish—large fish that eat smaller fish. Mercury can cause brain damage to fetuses and young children. According to FDA and Environmental Protection Agency (EPA) guidelines, women who are or who may become pregnant and nursing mothers should follow these guidelines to minimize their exposure to mercury:

- Do not eat shark, swordfish, king mackerel, or tilefish.
- Eat up to 12 ounces a week of a variety of fish and shellfish that are lower in mercury, such as shrimp, canned light tuna, salmon, pollock, and catfish. Limit consumption of albacore tuna to 6 ounces per week.
- Check advisories about the safety of recreationally caught fish from local lakes, rivers, and coastal areas. If no information is available, limit consumption to 6 ounces per week.

The same FDA/EPA guidelines apply to children, although they should consume smaller servings.

Ethnic Foods

There is no one ethnic diet that clearly surpasses all others in providing people with healthful foods. Every diet has its advantages and disadvantages, and within each cuisine, some foods are better choices. The dietary guidelines described in this chapter can be applied to any ethnic cuisine. For additional guidance, refer to the table below.

	Choose More Often	Choose Less Often
CHINESE	Dishes that are steamed, poached (jum), boiled (chu), roasted (kow), barbecued (shu), or lightly stir-fried Hoisin sauce, oyster sauce, wine sauce, plum sauce, velvet sauce, or hot mustard Fresh fish and seafood, skinless chicken, tofu Mixed vegetables, Chinese greens Steamed rice, steamed spring rolls, soft noodles	Fried wontons or egg rolls Crab rangoon Crispy (Peking) duck or chicken Sweet-and-sour dishes made with breaded and deep-fried meat, poultry, or fish Fried or crispy noodles Fried rice
FRENCH	Dishes prepared au vapeur (steamed), en brochette (skewered and broiled), or grillé (grilled) Fresh fish, shrimp, scallops, mussels, or skinless chicken, without sauces Clear soups	Dishes prepared á la créme (in cream sauce), au gratin or gratinée (baked with cream and cheese), or en croûte (in pastry crust) Drawn butter, hollandaise sauce, and remoulade (mayonnaise-based sauce)
GREEK	Dishes that are stewed, broiled, or grilled, including shish kabobs (souvlaki) Dolmas (grape leaves) stuffed with rice Tzatziki (yogurt, cucumbers, and garlic) Tabouli (bulgur-based salad) Pita bread, especially whole wheat	Moussaka, saganaki (fried cheese) Vegetable pies such as spanakopita and tyropita Baba ghanoush (eggplant and olive oil) Deep-fried falafel (chickpea patties) Gyros stuffed with ground meat Baklava
INDIAN	Dishes prepared masala (curry), tandoori (roasted in a clay oven), or tikke (pan roasted); kabobs Raita (yogurt and cucumber salad) and other yogurt-based dishes and sauces Dal (lentils), pullao or pilau (basmati rice) Chapati (baked bread)	Ghee (clarified butter) Korma (meat in cream sauce) Samosas, pakoras (fried dishes) Molee and other coconut milk-based dishes Poori, bhatura, or paratha (fried breads)
ITALIAN	Pasta primavera or pasta, polenta, risotto, or gnocchi withmarinara, red or white wine, white or red clam, or light mushroom sauce Dishes that are grilled or prepared cacciatore (tomato-based sauce), marsala (broth and wine sauce), or piccata (lemon sauce) Cioppino (seafood stew) Vegetable soup, minestrone or fagioli (beans)	Antipasto (cheese, smoked meats) Dishes that are prepared alfredo, frito (fried), crema (creamed), alla panna (with cream), or carbonara Veal scaloppini Chicken, veal, or eggplant parmigiana Italian sausage, salami, and prosciutto Buttered garlic bread Cannoli
JAPANESE	Dishes prepared nabemono (boiled), shabu-shabu (in boiling broth), mushimono (steamed), nimono (simmered), yaki (broiled), or yakimono (grilled) Sushi or domburi (mixed rice dish) Steamed rice or soba (buckwheat), udon (wheat), or rice noodles	Tempura (battered and fried) Agemono (deep fried) Katsu (fried pork cutlet) Sukiyaki Fried tofu
MEXICAN	Soft corn or wheat tortillas Burritos, fajitas, enchiladas, soft tacos, and tamales filled with beans, vegetables, or lean meats Refried beans, nonfat or low-fat; rice and beans Ceviche (fish marinated in lime juice) Salsa, enchilada sauce, and picante sauce Gazpacho, menudo, or black bean soup Fruit or flan for dessert	Crispy, fried tortillas Dishes that are fried, such as chile rellenos, chimichangas, flautas, and tostadas Nachos and cheese, chili con queso, and other dishes made with cheese or cheese sauce Guacamole, sour cream, and extra cheese Refried beans made with lard Fried ice cream
THAI	Dishes that are barbecued, sauteed, broiled, boiled, steamed, braised, or marinated Sáte (skewered and grilled meats) Fish sauce, basil sauce, chili or hot sauces Bean thread noodles, Thai salad	Coconut milk soup Peanut sauce or dishes topped with nuts Mee-krob (crispy noodles) Red, green, and yellow curries, which typically contain coconut milk

Some experts have also expressed concern about the presence of toxins in farmed fish, especially farmed salmon. Although no federal guidelines have been set, some researchers suggest that consumers limit themselves to 8 ounces of farmed salmon per month. Fish should be labeled with its country of origin and whether it is wild or farmed; most canned salmon is wild.

A PERSONAL PLAN: APPLYING NUTRITIONAL PRINCIPLES

Based on your particular nutrition and health status, there probably is an ideal diet for you, but no single type of diet provides optimal health for everyone. Many cultural dietary patterns can meet people's nutritional requirements (see the box "Ethnic Foods"). Customize your food plan based on your age, gender, weight, activity level, medical risk factors, and personal tastes.

Assessing and Changing Your Diet

The first step in planning a healthy diet is to examine what you currently eat. Labs 8.1 and 8.2 help you analyze your current diet and compare it with optimal dietary goals. (This analysis can be completed using a nutritional analysis software program or one of several Web sites.)

To put your plan into action, use the behavioral self-management techniques and tips described in Chapter 1. If you identify several changes you want to make, focus on one at a time. You might start, for example, by substituting nonfat or low-fat milk for whole milk. When you become used to that, you can try substituting whole-wheat bread for white bread. The information on eating behavior in Lab 8.1 will help you identify and change unhealthy patterns of eating.

Staying Committed to a Healthy Diet

Beyond knowledge and information, you also need support in difficult situations. Keeping to your plan is easiest when you choose and prepare your own food at home. Advance planning is the key: mapping out meals and shopping appropriately, cooking in advance when possible, and preparing enough food for leftovers. A tight budget does not necessarily make it more difficult to eat

Ask yourself

QUESTIONS FOR CRITICAL THINKING AND REFLECTION

What is the least healthy food you eat every day (either during meals or as a snack)? Identify at least one substitute that would be healthier but just as satisfying.

TIPS FOR TODAY AND THE FUTURE

Opportunities to improve your diet present themselves every day, and small changes add up.

RIGHT NOW YOU CAN
- Substitute a healthy snack for an unhealthy one.
- Drink a glass of water and put a bottle of water in your backpack for tomorrow.
- Plan to make healthy selections when you eat out, such as steamed vegetables instead of french fries or salmon instead of steak.

IN THE FUTURE YOU CAN
- Visit the MyPlate Web site at www.choosemyplate.gov and use the online tools to create a personalized nutrition plan and begin tracking your eating habits.
- Learn to cook healthier meals. There are hundreds of free Web sites and low-cost cookbooks that provide recipes for healthy dishes.

healthy meals. It makes good health sense and good budget sense to use only small amounts of meat and to have a few meatless meals each week.

In restaurants, sticking to food plan goals becomes somewhat more difficult. Portion sizes in restaurants tend to be larger than MyPlate serving size equivalents, but by remaining focused on your goals, you can eat only part of your meal and take the rest home for a meal later in the week. Don't hesitate to ask questions when you're eating in a restaurant. Most restaurant personnel are glad to explain how menu selections are prepared and to make small adjustments, such as serving salad dressings and sauces on the side so they can be avoided or used sparingly.

Strategies like these are helpful, but small changes cannot change a fundamentally high-fat, high-calorie meal into a moderate, healthful one. Often, the best advice is to bypass a large steak with potatoes au gratin for a flavorful but low-fat entree. Many of the selections offered in ethnic restaurants are healthy choices (refer to the box on ethnic foods for suggestions).

SUMMARY

- The six classes of nutrients are carbohydrates, proteins, fats, vitamins, minerals, and water.

- The nutrients essential to humans are released into the body through digestion. Nutrients in foods provide energy, measured in kilocalories (commonly called calories), build and maintain body tissues, and regulate body functions.

- Protein, an important component of body tissue, is composed of amino acids; nine are essential to good health. Foods from animal sources provide complete proteins. Plants provide incomplete proteins.

- Fats, a major source of energy, also insulate the body and cushion the organs. Just 3–4 teaspoons of vegetable oil per day supply the essential fats. For most people, dietary fat intake should be 20–35% of total calories, and unsaturated fats should be favored over saturated and trans fats.

- Carbohydrates provide energy to the brain, nervous system, and blood and to muscles during high-intensity exercise. Naturally occurring simple carbohydrates and unrefined complex carbohydrates should be favored over added sugars and refined carbohydrates.

- Fiber includes plant substances that are impossible for the human body to digest. It helps reduce cholesterol levels and promotes the passage of wastes through the intestines.

- The 13 essential vitamins are organic substances that promote specific chemical and cell processes and act as antioxidants. The 17 known essential minerals are inorganic substances that regulate body functions, aid in growth and tissue maintenance, and help in the release of energy from food. Deficiencies in vitamins and minerals can cause severe symptoms over time, but excess doses are also dangerous.

- Water aids in digestion and food absorption, allows chemical reactions to take place, serves as a lubricant or cushion, and helps regulate body temperature.

- Foods contain other substances, such as phytochemicals, that may not be essential nutrients but that may protect against chronic diseases.

- The Dietary Reference Intakes, Dietary Guidelines for Americans, and MyPlate food guidance system provide standards and recommendations for getting all essential nutrients from a varied, balanced diet and for eating in ways that protect against chronic disease.

- The Dietary Guidelines for Americans advise us to balance calorie intake and calorie expenditure to manage weight; reduce consumption of sodium, solid fats, added sugars, and refined grains; increase consumption of fruits, vegetables, and whole grains; and follow a healthy eating pattern.

- Choosing foods from each group in MyPlate every day helps ensure the appropriate amounts of necessary nutrients.

- A vegetarian diet requires special planning but can meet all human nutritional needs.

- Different population groups, such as college students and athletes, face special dietary challenges and should plan their diets to meet their particular needs.

- Consumers can get help applying nutritional principles by reading the standardized labels that appear on all packaged foods and on dietary supplements.

- Although nutritional basics are well established, no single diet provides wellness for everyone. Individuals should focus on their particular needs and adapt general dietary principles to meet them.

FOR FURTHER EXPLORATION

BOOKS

Byrd-Bredbenner, C., et al. 2009. *Wardlaw's Perspectives in Nutrition,* 8th ed. New York: McGraw-Hill. *An easy-to-understand review of major concepts in nutrition.*

Duyff, R. L. 2006. *ADA Complete Food and Nutrition Guide,* 3rd ed. Hoboken, N.J.: Wiley. *An excellent review of current nutrition information.*

Insel, P., D. Ross, K. McMahon, and M. Bernstein. 2011. *Nutrition,* 4th ed. Sudbury, Mass.: Jones & Bartlett. *An introductory nutrition textbook covering a variety of key topics.*

Nestle, M. 2007. *What to Eat.* New York: North Point Press. *A nutritionist examines the marketing of food and explains how to interpret food-related information while shopping.*

Selkowitz, A. 2005. *The College Student's Guide to Eating Well on Campus,* revised ed. Bethesda, Md.: Tulip Hill Press. *Provides practical advice for students, including how to make healthy choices when eating in a dorm or restaurant and how to stock a first pantry.*

Warshaw, H. 2008. *Eat Out Eat Right: The Guide to Healthier Restaurant Eating.* 3rd ed. Agate Surrey. *A registered dietitian provides realistic, informative guidelines for restaurant eating to enable diners to make healthy menu choices from a wide variety of foods and cuisines.*

NEWSLETTERS

Environmental Nutrition (800-424-7887;
   http://www.environmentalnutrition.com)
Nutrition Action Health Letter (202-332-9110;
   http://www.cspinet.org/nah/index.htm)
Tufts University Health & Nutrition Letter (800-274-7581;
   http://www.tuftshealthletter.com)

ORGANIZATIONS, HOTLINES, AND WEB SITES

Academy of Nutrition and Dietetics. Provides a wide variety of educational materials on nutrition.
   http://www.eatright.org
American Heart Association: Delicious Decisions. Provides basic information about nutrition, tips for shopping and eating out, and heart-healthy recipes.
   http://www.deliciousdecisions.org
FDA: Food. Offers information and interactive tools about topics such as food labeling, food additives, dietary supplements, and foodborne illness.
   http://www.fda.gov/food/default.htm
Food Safety Hotlines. Provide information on the safe purchase, handling, cooking, and storage of food.
   800-535-4555 (USDA)
   888-SAFEFOOD (FDA)

Q Which should I eat— butter or margarine?

A Both butter and margarine are concentrated sources of fat, containing about 11 grams of fat and 100 calories per tablespoon. Butter is higher in saturated fat, which raises levels of artery-clogging LDL ("bad" cholesterol). Each tablespoon of butter has about 8 grams of saturated fat; margarine has about 2. Butter also contains cholesterol, which margarine does not.

Margarine, on the other hand, contains trans fat, which not only raises LDL but lowers HDL ("good" cholesterol). A tablespoon of stick margarine contains about 2 grams of trans fat. Butter contains a small amount of trans fat as well. Although butter has a combined total of saturated and trans fats that is twice that of stick margarine, the trans fat in stick margarine may be worse for you. Clearly, you should avoid both butter and stick margarine. To solve this dilemma, remember that softer is better. The softer or more liquid a margarine or spread is, the less hydrogenated it is and the less trans fat it contains. Tub and squeeze margarines contain less trans fat than stick margarines; some margarines are modified to be low-trans or trans-fat-free and are labeled as such. Vegetable oils are an even better choice for cooking and for table use (such as olive oil for dipping bread) because most are low in saturated fat and completely free of trans fats.

Q MyPlate recommends such large amounts of vegetables and fruit.

How can I possibly eat that many servings without gaining weight?

A First, consider your typical portion sizes; you may be closer to meeting the recommendations than you think. Many people consume large servings of foods and underestimate the size of their portions. For example, a large banana may contain the equivalent of a cup of fruit, or half the recommended daily total for someone consuming 2000–2600 calories per day. Likewise, a medium baked potato (3-inch diameter) or an ear of corn (8-inch length) counts as a cup of vegetables. Use a measuring cup or a food scale for a few days to train your eye to accurately estimate food portion sizes. The ChooseMyPlate .gov Web site includes charts of portion-size equivalents for each food group.

If an analysis of your diet indicates that you need to increase your overall intake of fruits and vegetables, look for healthy substitutions. If you are like most Americans, you are consuming more than the recommended number of calories from added sugars and solid fats; trim some of these calories to make room for additional servings of fruits and vegetables. Your beverage choices may be a good place to start. Do you routinely consume regular sodas, sweetened energy or fruit drinks, or whole milk? One regular 12-ounce soda contains the equivalent of about 150 calories of added sugars; an 8-ounce glass of whole milk provides about 75 calories as discretionary fats. Substituting water or low-fat milk would free up calories for additional servings of fruits and vegetables. A half-cup of carrots, tomatoes,

apples, or melon has only about 25 calories; you could consume 6 cups of these foods for the calories in one can of regular soda. Substituting lower-fat condiments for such full-fat items as butter, mayonnaise, and salad dressing is another good way to trim calories to make room for additional servings of nutrient-rich fruits and vegetables.

Also consider your portion sizes and/or the frequency with which you consume foods high in discretionary calories: You may not need to eliminate a favorite food—instead, just cut back. For example, cut your consumption of fast-food fries from four times a week to once a week, or reduce the size of your ice cream dessert from a cup to half a cup. Treats should be consumed infrequently, and in small amounts.

For additional help on improving food choices to meet dietary recommendations, visit the ChooseMyPlate.gov Web site and the family-friendly chart of "Go, Slow, and Whoa" foods at the site for the National Heart, Lung, and Blood Institute (www.nhlbi.nih.gov/health /public/heart/ obesity/wecan/downloads /gswtips.pdf).

Q What exactly are genetically modified foods? Are they safe? How can I recognize them on the shelf, and how can I know when I'm eating them?

A Genetic engineering involves altering the characteristics of a plant, animal, or microorganism by adding, rearranging, or replacing genes in its

---

Fruits and Veggies Matter. Hosted by a partnership of the CDC, DHHS, and National Cancer Institute; promotes the consumption of fruits and vegetables every day.
    http://www.fruitsandveggiesmatter.gov
Gateways to Government Nutrition Information. Provides access to government resources relating to food safety, including consumer advice and information on specific pathogens.
    http://www.foodsafety.gov
    http://www.nutrition.gov

Harvard School of Public Health: Nutrition Source. Provides advice on interpreting news on nutrition; an overview of the Healthy Eating Pyramid, an alternative to the basic USDA pyramid; and suggestions for building a healthy diet.
    http://www.hsph.harvard.edu/nutritionsource
International Food Information Council. Provides information on food safety and nutrition for consumers, journalists, and educators.
    http://www.ific.org

DNA; the result is a genetically modified (GM) organism. New DNA may come from related species of organisms or from entirely different types of organisms. Many GM crops are already grown in the United States: About 75% of the current U.S. soybean crop has been genetically modified to be resistant to an herbicide used to kill weeds, and about a third of the U.S. corn crop carries genes for herbicide resistance or to produce a protein lethal to a destructive type of caterpillar. Products made with GM organisms include juice, soda, nuts, tuna, frozen pizza, spaghetti sauce, canola oil, chips, salad dressing, and soup.

The potential benefits of GM foods cited by supporters include improved yields overall and in difficult growing conditions, increased disease resistance, improved nutritional content, lower prices, and less use of pesticides. Critics of biotechnology argue that unexpected effects may occur: Gene manipulation could elevate levels of naturally occurring toxins or allergens, permanently change the gene pool and reduce biodiversity, and produce pesticide-resistant insects through the transfer of genes. In 2000, a form of GM corn approved for use only in animal feed was found to have commingled with other varieties of corn and to have been used in human foods; this mistake sparked fears of allergic reactions and led to recalls. Opposition to GM foods is particularly strong in Europe; in many developing nations that face food shortages, responses to GM crops have tended to be more positive.

In April 2000, the National Academy of Sciences released a report stating that there is no proof that GM food on the market is unsafe but that changes are needed to better coordinate regulation of GM foods and to assess potential problems.

Labeling has been another major concern. Surveys indicate that the majority of Americans want to know if their foods contain GM organisms. However, under current rules, the FDA requires special labeling only when a food's composition is changed significantly or when a known allergen is introduced. For example, soybeans that contain a gene from a peanut would have to be labeled because peanuts are a common allergen. The only foods guaranteed not to contain GM ingredients are those certified as organic.

Q How can I tell if I'm allergic to a food?

A A true food allergy is a reaction of the body's immune system to a food or food ingredient, usually a protein. This immune reaction can occur within minutes of ingesting the food, resulting in symptoms such as hives, diarrhea, difficulty breathing, or swelling of the lips or tongue. The most severe response is a systemic reaction called anaphylaxis, which involves a potentially life-threatening drop in blood pressure. Food allergies affect only about 1.5% of the adult population and 4% of children. Between 1997 and 2007, the food allergy rate among American children increased 18%. People with food allergies, especially children, are more likely to have asthma or other allergic conditions.

Just eight foods account for more than 90% of the food allergies in the United States: cow's milk, eggs, peanuts, tree nuts (walnuts, cashews, and so on), soy, wheat, fish, and shellfish. Food manufacturers are now required to state the presence of these eight allergens in plain language in the list of ingredients on food labels.

Many people who believe they have food allergies may actually suffer from a food intolerance, a much more common source of adverse food reactions that typically involves problems with metabolism rather than with the immune system. The body may not be able to adequately digest a food or the body may react to a particular food compound. Food intolerances have been attributed to lactose (milk sugar), gluten (a protein in some grains), tartrazine (yellow food coloring), sulfite (a food additive), MSG, and the sweetener aspartame. Although symptoms of a food intolerance may be similar to those of a food allergy, they are typically more localized and not life-threatening. Many people with food intolerance can safely and comfortably consume small amounts of the food that affects them.

If you suspect you have a food allergy or intolerance, a good first step is to keep a food diary. Note everything you eat or drink, any symptoms you develop, and how long after eating the symptoms appear. Then make an appointment with your physician to go over your diary and determine if any additional tests are needed. People at risk for severe allergic reactions must diligently avoid trigger foods and carry medications to treat anaphylaxis.

For more Common Questions Answered about nutrition, visit the Online Learning Center at www.mhhe.com/fahey.

MedlinePlus: Nutrition. Provides links to information from government agencies and major medical associations on a variety of nutrition topics.
http://www.nlm.nih.gov/medlineplus/nutrition.html
MyPlate. Provides personalized dietary plans and interactive food and activity tracking tools.
http://www.choosemyplate.gov

National Academies' Food and Nutrition Board. Provides information about the Dietary Reference Intakes and related guidelines.
http://www.iom.edu/CMS/3788.aspx
National Institutes of Health: Osteoporosis and Related Bone Diseases' National Resource Center. Provides information about osteoporosis prevention and treatment; includes a special section on men and osteoporosis.
http://www.osteo.org

National Osteoporosis Foundation. Provides information on the causes, prevention, detection, and treatment of osteoporosis.

http://www.nof.org

USDA Center for Nutrition Policy and Promotion. Includes information on the Dietary Guidelines and the Food Guide Pyramid.

http://www.cnpp.usda.gov

USDA Food and Nutrition Information Center. Provides a variety of materials relating to the Dietary Guidelines, food labels, Food Guide Pyramid, MyPlate, and many other topics.

http://www.nal.usda.gov/fnic

Vegetarian Resource Group. Provides information and links for vegetarians and people interested in learning more about vegetarian diets.

http://www.vrg.org

You can find nutrient breakdowns of individual food items at the following sites:

Nutrition Analysis Tool, University of Illinois, Urbana/Champaign
http://www.nat.uiuc.edu

USDA Nutrient Data Laboratory
http://www.ars.usda.gov/ba/bhnrc/ndl

See also the resources listed in Chapters 9, 11, and 12.

SELECTED BIBLIOGRAPHY

A guide to the best and worst drinks. 2006. *Consumer Reports on Health,* July, 8–9.

American Heart Association. 2010. *Diet and Lifestyle Recommendations* (http://www.americanheart.org/presenter.jhtml?identifier=851; retrieved September 15, 2010).

American Heart Association. 2010. *Fish, Levels of Mercury and Omega-3 Fatty Acids* (http://www.americanheart.org/presenter.jhtml?identifier=3013797; retrieved September 15, 2010).

American Heart Association. 2010. Trans Fats (http://www.americanheart.org/presenter.jhtml?identifier=3045792; retrieved September 15, 2010).

Bleich, S. N., et al. 2009. Increasing consumption of sugar-sweetened beverages among U.S. adults: 1988–1994 to 1999–2004. *American Journal of Clinical Nutrition* 89(1): 372–381.

Centers for Disease Control and Prevention. 2009. Application of lower sodium intake recommendations to adults—United States, 1999–2006. *Morbidity and Mortality Weekly Report* 58(11): 281–283.

Centers for Disease Control and Prevention. 2009. *Listeriosis* (http://www.cdc.gov/nczved/divisions/dfbmd/diseases/listeriosis; retrieved September 15, 2010).

Centers for Disease Control and Prevention. 2010. *Foodborne Illness* (http://www.cdc.gov/ncidod/dbmd/diseaseinfo/foodborneinfections_g.htm; retrieved September 15, 2010).

Council for Responsible Nutrition. 2009. *Dietary Supplements: Safe, Regulated and Beneficial* (http://www.crnusa.org/pdfs/CRN_FACT_DSSafe RegulatedBeneficial_09.pdf; retrieved September 15, 2010).

Food and Agriculture Organization of the United Nations. 2009. 1.02 billion people hungry (http://www.fao.org/news/story/en/item/20568/icode: retrieved September 15, 2010).

Food and Nutrition Board, Institute of Medicine. 2005. *Dietary Reference Intakes for Energy, Carbohydrate, Fiber, Fat, Fatty Acids, Cholesterol, Protein, and Amino Acids.* Washington, D.C.: National Academy Press.

Food and Nutrition Board, Institute of Medicine. 2005. *Dietary Reference Intakes for Water, Potassium, Sodium, Chloride, and Sulfate.* Washington, D.C.: National Academy Press.

Grisenbeck, J. S., et al. 2010. Maternal characteristics associated with the dietary intake of nitrates, nitrites, and nitrosamines in women of childbearing age: A cross-sectional study. *Environmental Health* 9(1): 10.

Harris, W. S., et al. 2009. Omega-6 fatty acids and risk for cardiovascular disease: A science advisory from the American Heart Association Nutrition Subcommittee of the Council on Nutrition, Physical Activity, and Metabolism; Council on Cardiovascular Nursing; and Council on Epidemiology and Prevention. *Circulation* 119(6): 902–907

Harvard School of Public Health, Department of Nutrition. 2010. *The Nutrition Source: Knowledge for Healthy Eating* (http://www.hsph.harvard.edu/nutritionsource; retrieved September 15, 2010).

Hasler, C. M., et al. 2009. Position of the American Dietetic Association: Functional foods. *Journal of the American Dietetic Association* 109(4): 735–736.

Johnson, R. K., et al. 2009. Dietary sugars intake and cardiovascular health: A scientific statement from the American Heart Association. *Circulation* 120(11): 1011–1020.

Lichtenstein, A. H., et al. 2006. Diet and Lifestyle Recommendations, Revision 2006. A Scientific Statement from the American Heart Association Nutrition Committee. *Circulation* 114(1): 82–96.

Liebman, B. 2006. Whole Grains: The Inside Story. *Nutrition Action Health Letter* 33(4): 1–5.

Maki, K. C., et al. 2010. Whole-grain ready-to-eat oat cereal, as part of a dietary program for weight loss, reduces low-density lipoprotein cholesterol in adults with overweight and obesity more than a dietary program including low-fiber control foods. *Journal of the American Dietetic Association* 110(2): 205–214.

Mayo Clinic. 2010. *Food Pyramids: Explore These Healthy Diet Options* (http://www.mayoclinic.com/health/healthy-diet/NU00190; retrieved September 15, 2010).

Mosaffarian, D., et al. 2006. Trans fatty acids and cardiovascular disease. *New England Journal of Medicine* 354(15): 1601–1613.

Nicholls, S. J., et al. 2006. Consumption of saturated fat impairs the antiinflammatory properties of high-density lipoproteins and endothelial function. *Journal of the American College of Cardiology* 48(4): 715–720.

Siri-Tarino, P. W., et al. 2010. Meta-analysis of prospective cohort studies evaluating the association of saturated fat with cardiovascular disease. *American Journal of Clinical Nutrition* 91(3): 535–546.

Trump, D. L., et al. 2010. Vitamin D: Considerations in the continued development as an agent for cancer prevention and therapy. *Cancer Journal* 16(1): 1–9.

Tucker, K. L. 2009. Osteoporosis prevention and nutrition. *Current Osteoporosis Reports* 7(4): 111–117.

U.S. Department of Agriculture and Centers for Disease Control and Prevention. 2010. *What We Eat in America* (http://www.ars.usda.gov/Services/docs.htm?docid=15044; retrieved September 15, 2010).

U.S. Department of Health and Human Services and U.S. Department of Agriculture. 2010. *Dietary Guidelines for Americans 2010* (http://www.cnpp.usda.gov/DGAs2010-PolicyDocument.htm; retrieved April 1, 2011).

U.S. Food and Drug Administration. 2009. *Food Allergies* (http://www.fda.gov/Food/FoodSafety/FoodAllergens/default.htm; retrieved September 15, 2010).

Varraso R, et al. 2010. Prospective study of dietary fiber and risk of chronic obstructive pulmonary disease among U.S. women and men. *American Journal of Epidemiology* (Published online Feb. 19).

Wang, Y. C., et al. 2008. Increasing caloric contribution from sugar-sweetened beverages and 100% fruit juices among U.S. children and adolescents, 1988–2004. *Pediatrics* 121(6): e1604–e1614.

Nutrition Resources

Table 1 — Dietary Reference Intakes (DRIs): Recommended Levels for Individual Intake

Life Stage	Group	BIOTIN (µg/day)[a]	CHOLINE (mg/day)[a]	FOLATE (µg/day)[b]	NIACIN (mg/day)[c]	PANTOTHENIC ACID (mg/day)	RIBOFLAVIN (mg/day)	THIAMIN (mg/day)	VITAMIN A (µg/day)[d]	VITAMIN B-6 (mg/day)	VITAMIN B-12 (µg/day)	VITAMIN C (mg/day)[e]	VITAMIN D (IU/day)[f]	VITAMIN E (mg/day)[g]
Infants	0–6 months	5	125	65	2	1.7	0.3	0.2	400	0.1	0.4	40	400	4
	7–12 months	6	150	80	4	1.8	0.4	0.3	500	0.3	0.5	50	400	5
Children	1–3 years	8	200	150	6	2	0.5	0.5	300	0.5	0.9	15	600	6
	4–8 years	12	250	200	8	3	0.6	0.6	400	0.6	1.2	25	600	7
Males	9–13 years	20	375	300	12	4	0.9	0.9	600	1.0	1.8	45	600	11
	14–18 years	25	550	400	16	5	1.3	1.2	900	1.3	2.4	75	600	15
	19–30 years	30	550	400	16	5	1.3	1.2	900	1.3	2.4	90	600	15
	31–50 years	30	550	400	16	5	1.3	1.2	900	1.3	2.4	90	600	15
	51–70 years	30	550	400	16	5	1.3	1.2	900	1.7	2.4[h]	90	600	15
	>70 years	30	550	400	16	5	1.3	1.2	900	1.7	2.4[h]	90	800	15
Females	9–13 years	20	375	300	12	4	0.9	0.9	600	1.0	1.8	45	600	11
	14–18 years	25	400	400[i]	14	5	1.0	1.0	700	1.2	2.4	65	600	15
	19–30 years	30	425	400[i]	14	5	1.1	1.1	700	1.3	2.4	75	600	15
	31–50 years	30	425	400[i]	14	5	1.1	1.1	700	1.3	2.4	75	600	15
	51–70 years	30	425	400[i]	14	5	1.1	1.1	700	1.5	2.4[h]	75	600	15
	>70 years	30	425	400	14	5	1.1	1.1	700	1.5	2.4[h]	75	600	15
Pregnancy	≤18 years	30	450	600[j]	18	6	1.4	1.4	750	1.9	2.6	80	600	15
	19–30 years	30	450	600[j]	18	6	1.4	1.4	770	1.9	2.6	85	600	15
	31–50 years	30	450	600[j]	18	6	1.4	1.4	770	1.9	2.6	85	600	15
Lactation	≤18 years	35	550	500	17	7	1.6	1.4	1200	2.0	2.8	115	600	19
	19–30 years	35	550	500	17	7	1.6	1.4	1300	2.0	2.8	120	600	19
	31–50 years	35	550	500	17	7	1.6	1.4	1300	2.0	2.8	120	600	19
Tolerable Upper Intake Levels for Adults (19–70)		3500	1000[k]	35[k]				3000	100		2000	50	4000[k]	

NOTE: The table includes values for the type of DRI standard—Adequate Intake (AI) or Recommended Dietary Allowance (RDA)—that has been established for that particular nutrient and life stage; RDAs are shown in **bold** type. The final row of the table shows the Tolerable Upper Intake Levels (ULs) for adults; refer to the full DRI report for information on other ages and life stages. A UL is the maximum level of daily nutrient intake that is likely to pose no risk of adverse effects. There is insufficient data to set ULs for all nutrients, but this does not mean that there is no potential for adverse effects; source of intake should be from food only to prevent high levels of intake of nutrients without established ULs. In healthy individuals, there is no established benefit from nutrient intakes above the RDA or AI.

[a] Although AIs have been set for choline, there are few data to assess whether a dietary supply of choline is needed at all stages of the life cycle, and it may be that the choline requirement can be met by endogenous synthesis at some of these stages.

[b] As dietary folate equivalents (DFE): 1 DFE = 1 µg food folate = 0.6 µg folate from fortified food or as a supplement consumed with food = 0.5 µg of a supplement taken on an empty stomach.

[c] As niacin equivalents (NE): 1 mg niacin = 60 mg tryptophan.

Table 1 Dietary Reference Intakes (DRIs): Recommended Levels for Individual Intake (continued)

Life Stage	Group	VITAMIN K (µg/day)	CALCIUM (mg/day)	CHROMIUM (µg/day)	COPPER (µg/day)	FLUORIDE (mg/day)	IODINE (mg/day)	IRON (mg/day)[i]	MAGNESIUM (mg/day)	MANGANESE (mg/day)	MOLYBDENUM (µg/day)	PHOSPHORUS (mg/day)	SELENIUM (µg/day)	ZINC (mg/day)[m]
Infants	0–6 months	2.0	200	0.2	200	0.01	110	0.27	30	0.003	2	100	15	2
	7–12 months	2.5	260	5.5	220	0.5	130	11	75	0.6	3	275	20	3
Children	1–3 years	30	700	11	340	0.7	90	7	80	1.2	17	460	20	3
	4–8 years	55	1000	15	440	1	90	10	130	1.5	22	500	30	5
Males	9–13 years	60	1300	25	700	2	120	8	240	1.9	34	1250	40	8
	14–18 years	75	1300	35	890	3	150	11	410	2.2	43	1250	55	11
	19–30 years	120	1000	35	900	4	150	8	400	2.3	45	700	55	11
	31–50 years	120	1000	35	900	4	150	8	420	2.3	45	700	55	11
	51–70 years	120	1000	30	900	4	150	8	420	2.3	45	700	55	11
	>70 years	120	1200	30	900	4	150	8	420	2.3	45	700	55	11
Females	9–13 years	60	1300	21	700	2	120	8	240	1.6	34	1250	40	8
	14–18 years	75	1300	24	890	3	150	15	360	1.6	43	1250	55	9
	19–30 years	90	1000	25	900	3	150	18	310	1.8	45	700	55	8
	31–50 years	90	1000	25	900	3	150	18	320	1.8	45	700	55	8
	51–70 years	90	1200	20	900	3	150	8	320	1.8	45	700	55	8
	>70 years	90	1200	20	900	3	150	8	320	1.8	45	700	55	8
Pregnancy	≤18 years	75	3000	29	1000	3	220	27	400	2.0	50	1250	60	13
	19–30 years	90	2500	30	1000	3	220	27	350	2.0	50	700	60	11
	31–50 years	90	2500	30	1000	3	220	27	360	2.0	50	700	60	11
Lactation	≤18 years	75	3000	44	1300	3	290	10	360	2.6	50	1250	70	14
	19–30 years	90	2500	45	1300	3	290	9	310	2.6	50	700	70	12
	31–50 years	90	2500	45	1300	3	290	9	320	2.6	50	700	70	12
Tolerable Upper Intake Levels for Adults (19–70)			2500		10,000	10	1100	45	350[k]	11	2000	4000	400	40

[a] As retinol activity equivalents (RAEs). 1 RAE = 1 µg retinol, 12 µg β-carotene, or 24 µg α-carotene or β-cryptoxanthin. Preformed vitamin A (retinol) is abundant in animal-derived foods; provitamin A carotenoids are abundant in some dark yellow, orange, red, and deep-green fruits and vegetables. For preformed vitamin A and for provitamin A carotenoids in supplements, IRE = 1 RAE; for provitamin A carotenoids in foods, divide the REs by 2 to obtain RAEs. The UL applies only to preformed vitamin A.

[e] Individuals who smoke require an additional 35 mg/day of vitamin C over that needed by nonsmokers; nonsmokers regularly exposed to tobacco smoke should ensure they meet the RDA for vitamin C.

[f] IU = International Unit.

[g] As α-tocopherol. Includes naturally occurring RRR-α-tocopherol and the 2R-stereoisomeric forms from supplements; does not include the 2S-stereoisomeric forms from supplements.

[h] Because 10–30% of older people may malabsorb food-bound B-12, those over age 50 should meet their RDA mainly with supplements or foods fortified with B-12.

[i] In view of evidence linking folate intake with neural tube defects in the fetus it is recommended that all women capable of becoming pregnant consume 400 µg of folate from supplements or fortified foods in addition to consuming folate from a varied diet.

[j] It is assumed that women will continue consuming 400 µg from supplements or fortified food until their pregnancy is confirmed and they enter prenatal care, which ordinarily occurs after the end of the periconceptional period—the critical time for formation of the neural tube.

[k] The UL applies only to intake from supplements, fortified foods, and/or pharmacological agents and not to intake from foods.

[l] Because the absorption of iron from plant foods is low compared to that from animal foods, the RDA for strict vegetarians is approximately 1.8 times higher than the values established for omnivores (14 mg/day for adult male vegetarians; 33 mg/day for premenopausal female vegetarians). Oral contraceptives (OCs) reduce menstrual blood losses, so women taking them need less daily iron; the RDA for premenopausal women taking OCs is 10.9 mg/day. For more on iron requirements for other special situations, refer to *Dietary Reference Intakes for Vitamin A, Vitamin K, Arsenic, Boron, Chromium, Copper, Iodine, Iron, Manganese, Molybdenum, Nickel, Silicon, Vanadium, and Zinc* (visit http://www.nap.edu for the complete report).

[m] Zinc absorption is lower for those consuming vegetarian diets, so the zinc requirement for vegetarians is approximately twofold greater than for those consuming a nonvegetarian diet.

Table 1 Dietary Reference Intakes (DRIs): Recommended Levels for Individual Intake (continued)

Life Stage	Group	POTASSIUM (g/day)	SODIUM (g/day)	CHLORIDE (g/day)	CARBOHYDRATE RDA/AI (g/day)	AMDR[n] (%)	TOTAL FIBER RDA/AI (g/day)	TOTAL FAT AMDR[o] (%)	LINOLEIC ACID RDA/AI (g/day)	AMDR[o] (%)	ALPHA-LINOLENIC ACID RDA/AI (g/day)	AMDR[o] (%)	PROTEIN[n] RDA/AI (g/day)	AMDR[o] (%)	WATER[p] (L/day)
Infants	0–6 months	0.4	0.12	0.18	60	ND[q]	ND	r	4.4	ND[q]	0.5	ND[q]	9.1	ND[q]	0.7
	7–12 months	0.7	0.37	0.57	95	ND[q]	ND	r	4.6	ND[q]	0.5	ND[q]	13.5	ND[q]	0.8
Children	1–3 years	3.0	1.0	1.5	130	45–65	19	30–40	7	5–10	0.7	0.6–1.2	13	5–20	1.3
	4–8 years	3.8	1.2	1.9	130	45–65	25	25–35	10	5–10	0.9	0.6–1.2	19	10–30	1.7
Males	9–13 years	4.5	1.5	2.3	130	45–65	31	25–35	12	5–10	1.2	0.6–1.2	34	10–30	2.4
	14–18 years	4.7	1.5	2.3	130	45–65	38	25–35	16	5–10	1.6	0.6–1.2	52	10–30	3.3
	19–30 years	4.7	1.5	2.3	130	45–65	38	20–35	17	5–10	1.6	0.6–1.2	56	10–35	3.7
	31–50 years	4.7	1.5	2.3	130	45–65	38	20–35	17	5–10	1.6	0.6–1.2	56	10–35	3.7
	51–70 years	4.7	1.3	2.0	130	45–65	30	20–35	14	5–10	1.6	0.6–1.2	56	10–35	3.7
	>70 years	4.7	1.2	1.8	130	45–65	30	20–35	14	5–10	1.6	0.6–1.2	56	10–35	3.7
Females	9–13 years	4.5	1.5	2.3	130	45–65	26	25–35	10	5–10	1.0	0.6–1.2	34	10–30	2.1
	14–18 years	4.7	1.5	2.3	130	45–65	26	25–35	11	5–10	1.1	0.6–1.2	46	10–30	2.3
	19–30 years	4.7	1.5	2.3	130	45–65	25	20–35	12	5–10	1.1	0.6–1.2	46	10–35	2.7
	31–50 years	4.7	1.5	2.3	130	45–65	25	20–35	12	5–10	1.1	0.6–1.2	46	10–35	2.7
	51–70 years	4.7	1.3	2.0	130	45–65	21	20–35	11	5–10	1.1	0.6–1.2	46	10–35	2.7
	>70 years	4.7	1.2	1.8	130	45–65	21	20–35	11	5–10	1.1	0.6–1.2	46	10–35	2.7
Pregnancy	≤18 years	4.7	1.5	2.3	175	45–65	28	20–35	13	5–10	1.4	0.6–1.2	71	10–35	3.0
	19–30 years	4.7	1.5	2.3	175	45–65	28	20–35	13	5–10	1.4	0.6–1.2	71	10–35	3.0
	31–50 years	4.7	1.5	2.3	175	45–65	28	20–35	13	5–10	1.4	0.6–1.2	71	10–35	3.0
Lactation	≤18 years	5.1	1.5	2.3	210	45–65	29	20–35	13	5–10	1.3	0.6–1.2	71	10–35	3.8
	19–30 years	5.1	1.5	2.3	210	45–65	29	20–35	13	5–10	1.3	0.6–1.2	71	10–35	3.8
	31–50 years	5.1	1.5	2.3	210	45–65	29	20–35	13	5–10	1.3	0.6–1.2	71	10–35	3.8
Tolerable Upper Intake Level for Adults (19–70)			2.3	3.6											

[n] Daily protein recommendations are based on body weight for reference body weights. To calculate for a specific body weight, use the following values: 1.5 g/kg for infants, 1.1 g/kg for 1–3 years, 0.95 g/kg for 4–13 years, 0.85 g/kg for 14–18 years, 0.8 g/kg for adults, and 1.1 g/kg for pregnant (using prepregnancy weight) and lactating women.

[o] Acceptable Macronutrient Distribution Range (AMDR), expressed as a percent of total daily calories, is the range of intake for a particular energy source that is associated with reduced risk of chronic disease while providing intakes of essential nutrients. If an individual consumes in excess of the AMDR, there is a potential for increasing the risk of chronic diseases and/or insufficient intakes of essential nutrients.

[p] Total water intake from fluids and food.

[q] Not determinable due to lack of data of adverse effects in this age group and concern with regard to lack of ability to handle excess amounts. Source of intake should be from food only to prevent high levels of intake.

[r] For infants, Adequate Intake of total fat is 31 grams/day (0–6 months) and 30 grams per day (7–12 months) from breast milk and, for infants 7–12 months, complementary food and beverages.

SOURCE: Food and Nutrition Board, Institute of Medicine, National Academies. 2004. *Dietary Reference Intakes Tables*. Washington, D.C.: National Academics Press. *Dietary Reference Intakes Applications in Dietary Planning*. Copyright © 2004 by the National Academy of Sciences. Reprinted with permission from the National Academies Press, Washington, D.C.

*Reprinted with permission from *Dietary Reference Intakes Applications in Dietary Planning*. Copyright © 2004 by the National Academy of Sciences. Reprinted with permission from the National Academy Press (http://www.nap.edu).

Nutrition Resources

Number of servings per day (or per week, as noted)

Food groups	1600 calories	2000 calories	2600 calories	3100 calories	Serving sizes and notes
Grains	6	6–8	10–11	12–13	1 slice bread, 1 oz dry cereal, 1/2 cup cooked rice, pasta, or cereal; choose whole grains
Vegetables	3–4	4–5	5–6	6	1 cup raw leafy vegetables, 1/2 cup cooked vegetables, 1/2 cup vegetable juice
Fruits	4	4–5	5–6	6	1/2 cup fruit juice, 1 medium fruit, 1/4 cup dried fruit, 1/2 cup fresh, frozen, or canned fruit
Low-fat or fat-free dairy foods	2–3	2–3	3	3–4	1 cup milk; 1 cup yogurt, 1 1/2 oz cheese; choose fat-free or low-fat types
Meat, poultry, fish	3–6	6 or less	6	6–9	1 oz cooked meats, poultry, or fish: select only lean; trim away visible fats; broil, roast, or boil instead of frying; remove skin from poultry
Nuts, seeds, legumes	3 servings per week	4–5 servings per week	1	1	1/3 cup or 1 1/2 oz nuts, 2 Tbsp or 1/2 oz seeds, 1/2 cup cooked dry beans/peas, 2 Tbsp peanut butter
Fats and oils	2	2–3	3	4	1 tsp soft margarine, 1 Tbsp low-fat mayonnaise, 2 Tbsp light salad dressing, 1 tsp vegetable oil; DASH has 27% of calories as fat (low in saturated fat)
Sweets	0	5 servings/ week or less	2	2	1 Tbsp sugar, 1 Tbsp jelly or jam, 1/2 cup sorbet, 1 cup lemonade; sweets should be low in fat

FIGURE 1   The DASH Eating Plan.

SOURCE: National Institutes of Health, National Heart, Lung, and Blood Institute. 2006. *Your Guide to Lowering Your Blood Pressure with DASH: How Do I Make the Dash?* (http://www.nhlbi.nih.gov/health/public/heart/hbp/dash/how_make_dash html; retrieved April 30, 2009).

FIGURE 2   Healthy Eating Pyramid. The Healthy Eating Pyramid is an alternative food-group plan developed by researchers at the Harvard School of Public Health. This pyramid reflects many major research studies that have looked at the relationship between diet and long-term health. The Healthy Eating Pyramid differentiates between the various dietary sources of fat, protein, and carbohydrates, and it emphasizes whole grains, vegetable oils, fruits and vegetables, nuts, and dried peas and beans.

SOURCE: Reprinted by permission of Simon & Schuster Inc., from *Eat, Drink, and Be Healthy: The Harvard Medical School Guide to Healthy Eating* by Walter C. Willett, M.D. Copyright © 2001, 2005 by President and Fellows of Harvard College. All rights reserved.

Red Meat and Butter *USE SPARINGLY*

White Rice, White Bread, Potatoes, Pasta, and Sweets *USE SPARINGLY*

Dairy or Calcium Supplement

Alcohol *IN MODERATION UNLESS CONTRAINDICATED*

Fish, Poultry, and Eggs *0–2 SERVINGS*

Multiple Vitamins *FOR MOST*

Nuts and Legumes *1–3 SERVINGS*

Fruit *2–3 SERVINGS*

Vegetables *IN ABUNDANCE*

Whole-Grain Foods *AT MOST MEALS*

Plant Oils (olive, canola, soy, corn, sunflower, peanut, and other vegetable oils) *AT MOST MEALS*

Daily exercise and weight control

Name _____ Section _____ Date _____

LAB 8.1 Your Daily Diet Versus MyPlate

Make three photocopies of the worksheet in this lab and use them to keep track of everything you eat for 3 consecutive days. Break down each food item into its component parts, and list them separately in the column labeled "Food." Then enter the portion size you consumed in the correct food-group column. For example, a turkey sandwich might be listed as follows: whole-wheat bread, 2 oz-equiv of whole grains; turkey, 2 oz-equiv of meat/beans; tomato, $\frac{1}{3}$ cup other vegetables; romaine lettuce, $\frac{1}{4}$ cup dark green vegetables; 1 tablespoon mayonnaise dressing, 1 teaspoon oils. It can be challenging to track values for added sugars and oils and fats, but use food labels to be as accurate as you can. ChooseMyPlate.gov has additional guidelines for counting discretionary calories.

For vegetables, enter your portion sizes in both the "Total" column and the column corresponding to the correct subgroup; for example, the spinach in a spinach salad would be entered under "Dark Green" and carrots would be entered under "Orange." For the purpose of this 3-day activity, you will compare only your total vegetable consumption against MyPlate guidelines; as described in the chapter, vegetable subgroup recommendations are based on weekly consumption. However, it is important to note which vegetable subgroups are represented in your diet; over a 3-day period, you should consume several servings from each of the subgroups.

Date: _____

Food	Grains (oz-eq)		Vegetable (cups)						Fruits (cups)	Milk (cups)	Meat/ Beans (oz-eq)	Oils (tsp)	Discretionary Calories	
	Whole	Other	Total	Dark Green	Orange	Legume	Starchy	Other					Solid Fats (g)	Added Sugars (g/tsp)
Daily Total														

Mc Graw Hill connect™ http://www.mcgrawhillconnect.com/
FITNESS AND WELLNESS

Next, average your daily intake totals for the 3 days and enter them in the chart below. For example, if your three daily totals for the fruit group were 1 cup, 1½ cups, and 2 cups, your average daily intake would be 1½ cups. Fill in the recommended intake totals that apply to you from Figure 8.5 and Table 8.6.

MyPlate Food Group	Recommended Daily Amounts or Limits	Your Actual Average Daily Intake
Grains (total)	oz-eq	oz-eq
Whole grains	oz-eq	oz-eq
Other grains	oz-eq	oz-eq
Vegetables (total)	cups	cups
Fruits	cups	cups
Milk	cups	cups
Meat and beans	oz-eq	oz-eq
Oils	tsp	tsp
Solid fats	g	g
Added sugars	g/tsp	g/tsp

Using Your Results

How did you score? How close is your diet to that recommended by MyPlate? Are you surprised by the amount of food you are consuming from each food group or from added sugars and solid fats?

What should you do next? If the results of the assessment indicate that you could boost your level of wellness by improving your diet, set realistic goals for change. Do you need to increase or decrease your consumption of any food groups? List any areas of concern below, along with a goal for change and strategies for achieving the goal you've set. If you see that you are falling short in one food group, such as fruits or vegetables, but have many foods that are rich in discretionary calories from solid fats and added sugars, you might try decreasing those items in favor of an apple, a bunch of grapes, or some baby carrots. Think carefully about the reasons behind your food choices. For example, if you eat doughnuts for breakfast every morning because you feel rushed, make a list of ways to save time to allow for a healthier breakfast.

Problem: _____
Goal: _____
Strategies for change: _____
_____
_____

Problem: _____
Goal: _____
Strategies for change: _____
_____
_____

Problem: _____
Goal: _____
Strategies for change: _____
_____
_____

Enter the results of this lab in the Preprogram Assessment column in Appendix C. If you've set goals and identified strategies for change, begin putting your plan into action. After several weeks of your program, complete this lab again and enter the results in the Postprogram Assessment column of Appendix C. How do the results compare?

Name _____ Section _____ Date _____

LAB 8.2 Dietary Analysis

You can complete this activity using either a nutrition analysis software program or information about the nutrient content of foods available online; see the For Further Exploration section and page A–1 for recommended Web sites. (This lab asks you to analyze 1 day's diet. For a more complete and accurate assessment of your diet, analyze the results from several different days, including a weekday and a weekend day.)

| DATE _____ | | | | | | | | | | DAY: M | Tu | W | Th | F | Sa | Su |

Food	Amount	Calories	Protein (g)	Carbohydrate (g)	Dietary fiber (g)	Fat, total (g)	Saturated fat (g)	Cholesterol (mg)	Sodium (mg)	Vitamin A (RE)	Vitamin C (mg)	Calcium (mg)	Iron (mg)
Recommended totals*			10–35%	45–65%	25–38 g	20–35%	<10%	≤300 mg	≤2300 mg	RE	mg	mg	mg
Actual totals**		cal	g / %	g / %	g	g / %	g / %	mg	mg	RE	mg	mg	mg

*Fill in the appropriate DRI values for vitamin A, vitamin C, calcium, and iron from Table 1 in the Nutrition Resources section.

**Total the values in each column. Protein and carbohydrate provide 4 calories per gram; fat provides 9 calories per gram. For example, if you consume a total of 270 grams of carbohydrates and 2000 calories, your percentage of total calories from carbohydrates would be (270 g × 4 cal/g) ÷ 2000 cal = 54%. Do not include data for alcoholic beverages in your calculations. Percentages may not total 100% due to rounding.

Using Your Results

How did you score? How close is your diet to that recommended in this chapter? Are you surprised by any of the results of this assessment?

What should you do next? Enter the results of this lab in the Preprogram Assessment column in Appendix C. If your daily diet meets all the recommended intakes, congratulations—and keep up the good work. If the results of the assessment pinpoint areas of concern, then work with your food record on the previous page to determine what changes you could make to meet all the guidelines. Make changes, additions, and deletions until it conforms to all or most of the guidelines. Or, if you prefer, start from scratch to create a day's diet that meets the guidelines. Use the chart below to experiment and record your final, healthy sample diet for 1 day. Then put what you learned from this exercise into practice in your daily life. After several weeks of your program, complete this lab again and enter the results in the Postprogram Assessment column of Appendix C. How do the results compare?

DATE														DAY: M Tu W Th F Sa Su

Food	Amount	Calories	Protein (g)	Carbohydrate (g)	Dietary fiber (g)	Fat, total (g)	Saturated fat (g)	Cholesterol (mg)	Sodium (mg)	Vitamin A (RE)	Vitamin C (mg)	Calcium (mg)	Iron (mg)
Recommended totals			10–35%	45–65%	25–38 g	20–38%	< 10%	≤300 mg	≤2300 mg	RE	mg	mg	mg
Actual totals		cal	g / %	g / % g		g / %	g / %	mg	mg	RE	mg	mg	mg

Name _____ Section _____ Date _____

LAB 8.3 Informed Food Choices

Part I Using Food Labels

Choose three food items to evaluate. You might want to select three similar items, such as regular, low-fat, and nonfat salad dressing, or three very different items. Record the information from their food labels in the table below.

Food Items			
Serving size			
Total calories	cal	cal	cal
Total fat—grams	g	g	g
—% Daily Value	%	%	%
Saturated fat—grams	g	g	g
—% Daily Value	%	%	%
Trans fat—grams	g	g	g
Cholesterol—milligrams	mg	mg	mg
—% Daily Value	%	%	%
Sodium—milligrams	mg	mg	mg
—% Daily Value	%	%	%
Carbohydrates (total)—gram	g	g	g
—% Daily Value	%	%	%
Dietary fiber—grams	g	g	g
—% Daily Value	%	%	%
Sugars—grams	g	g	g
Protein—grams	g	g	g
Vitamin A—% Daily Value	%	%	%
Vitamin C—% Daily Value	%	%	%
Calcium—% Daily Value	%	%	%
Iron—% Daily Value	%	%	%

How do the items you chose compare? You can do a quick nutrient check by totaling the Daily Value percentages for nutrients you should limit (total fat, cholesterol, sodium) and the nutrients you should favor (dietary fiber, vitamin A, vitamin C, calcium, iron) for each food. Which food has the largest percent Daily Value sum for nutrients to limit? For nutrients to favor?

Food Items			
Calories	cal	cal	cal
% Daily Value total for nutrients to limit (total fat, cholesterol, sodium)	%	%	%
% Daily Value total for nutrients to favor (fiber, vitamin A, vitamin C, calcium, iron)	%	%	%

Part II Evaluating Fast Food

Use the nutritional information available from fast-food restaurants to complete the chart on this page for the last fast-food meal you ate. Add up your totals for the meal. Compare the values for fat, protein, carbohydrate, cholesterol, and sodium content for each food item and for the meal as a whole with the levels suggested by the Dietary Guidelines for Americans. Calculate the percent of total calories derived from fat, saturated fat, protein, and carbohydrate using the formulas given.

To get fast-food nutritional information, ask for a nutrition information brochure when you visit the restaurant, or visit restaurant Web sites: Arby's (http://www.arbysrestaurant.com), Burger King (http://www.burgerking.com), Domino's Pizza (http://www.dominos.com), Jack in the Box (http://www.jackinthebox.com), KFC (http://www.kfc.com), McDonald's (http://www.mcdonalds.com), Subway (http://www.subway.com), Taco Bell (http://www.tacobell.com), Wendy's (http://www.wendys.com).

If you haven't recently been to a fast-food restaurant, fill in the chart for any sample meal you might eat.

FOOD ITEMS

	Dietary Guidelines							Total**
Serving size (g)		g	g	g	g	g	g	g
Calories		cal	cal	cal	cal	cal	cal	cal
Total fat—grams		g	g	g	g	g	g	g
—% calories*	20–35%	%	%	%	%	%	%	%
Saturated fat—grams		g	g	g	g	g	g	g
—% calories*	<10%	%	%	%	%	%	%	%
Protein—grams		g	g	g	g	g	g	g
—% calories*	10–35%	%	%	%	%	%	%	%
Carbohydrate—grams		g	g	g	g	g	g	g
—% calories*	45–65%	%	%	%	%	%	%	%
Cholesterol†	100 mg	mg	mg	mg	mg	mg	mg	mg
Sodium†	800 mg	mg	mg	mg	mg	mg	mg	mg

*To calculate the percent of total calories from each food energy source (fat, carbohydrate, protein), use the following formula:

$$\frac{(\text{number of grams of energy source}) \times (\text{number of calories per gram of energy source})}{(\text{total calories in serving of food item})}$$

(*Note:* Fat and saturated fat provide 9 calories per gram; protein and carbohydrate provide 4 calories per gram.) For example, the percent of total calories from protein in a 150-calorie dish containing 10 grams of protein is

$$\frac{(10 \text{ grams of protein}) \times (4 \text{ calories per gram})}{(150 \text{ calories})} = \frac{40}{150} - 0.27, \text{ or } 27\% \text{ of total calories from protein}$$

**For the Total column, add up the total grams of fat, carbohydrate, and protein contained in your sample meal and calculate the percentages based on the total calories in the meal. (Percentages may not total 100% due to rounding.) For cholesterol and sodium values, add up the total number of milligrams.

†Recommended daily limits of cholesterol and sodium are divided by 3 here to give an approximate recommended limit for a single meal.

SOURCE: Insel, P. M., and W. T. Roth. 2010. Wellness Worksheet 66. *Core Concepts in Health,* 11th ed. Copyright © 2010 The McGraw-Hill Companies, Inc. Reprinted with permission.

Weight Management

LOOKING AHEAD...

After reading this chapter, you should be able to

- Discuss different methods for assessing body weight and body composition

- Explain the health risks associated with overweight and obesity

- Explain factors that may contribute to a weight problem, including genetic, physiological, lifestyle, and psychosocial factors

- Describe lifestyle factors that contribute to weight gain and loss, including the roles of diet, exercise, and emotions

- Identify and describe the symptoms of eating disorders and the health risks associated with them

- Design a personal plan for successfully managing body weight

TEST YOUR KNOWLEDGE

1. About what percentage of American adults are overweight?
   a. 15%
   b. 35%
   c. 69%

2. Genetic factors explain most cases of obesity.
   True or false?

3. The consumption of low-calorie sweeteners has helped Americans control their weight.
   True or false?

4. Approximately how many female high school and college students have either anorexia or bulimia?
   a. 0%
   b. 1%
   c. 2%

5. Which of the following is the most significant risk factor for type 2 diabetes (the most common type of diabetes)?
   a. Smoking
   b. Low-fiber diet
   c. Overweight or obesity

ANSWERS

1. **C.** About 69% of American adults are overweight, including 35.7% who are obese.

2. **FALSE.** Genetic factors may increase an individual's tendency to gain weight, but lifestyle is the key contributing factor.

3. **FALSE.** Ever since the introduction of low-calorie sweeteners, both total calorie and sugar intake have increased, as has the proportion of Americans who are overweight.

4. **C.** About 2–4% of female students suffer from bulimia or anorexia, and many more occasionally engage in behaviors associated with these eating disorders.

5. **C.** All are risk factors for diabetes, but overweight or obesity is the most significant. It's estimated that 90% of cases of type 2 diabetes could be prevented if people adopted healthy lifestyle behaviors.

A chieving and maintaining a healthy body weight is a public health priority and a serious challenge for many Americans. By the standards developed by the National Institutes of Health (NIH), 68.8% of American adults are overweight, including 35.7% who are obese (Table 14.1 and Figure 14.1). Of adult men, an estimated 35.5% are obese, and of adult women, an estimated 35.8%. One study predicted that at current rates, 42% of Americans will be obese by 2050. And while millions struggle to lose weight, others fall into dangerous eating patterns such as binge eating or self-starvation.

Although not completely understood, managing body weight is not a mysterious process. It's basically a matter of balancing the calories you take in with calories you expend in daily activities—in other words, eating a moderate diet and being physically active. Unfortunately this reality is not as exciting as fad diets or "scientific breakthroughs" that promise rapid weight loss without effort. Many people fail in their efforts at weight management because they focus on short-term weight loss rather than permanent changes in lifestyle. To manage your weight successfully, you must coordinate many aspects of your life—including nutrition, physical activity, and stress control—over the long term.

Table 14.1	Weight of Americans Aged 20 and Older, 2009–2010	
GROUP	PERCENT OVERWEIGHT*	PERCENT OBESE
Both sexes	68.8	35.7
All races, male	74.1	35.5
All races, female	64.5	35.8
White, male	74.0	36.2
White, female	59.5	32.2
African American, male	69.9	38.8
African American, female	82.1	58.5
Latino, male	81.7	37.0
Latino, female	75.7	41.4

*Includes obesity

SOURCE: Flegal, K. M., et al. 2012. Prevalence of Obesity and Trends in the Distribution of Body Mass Index among U.S. Adults, 1999–2010. *Journal of the American Medical Association* 307(5): published online January 17.

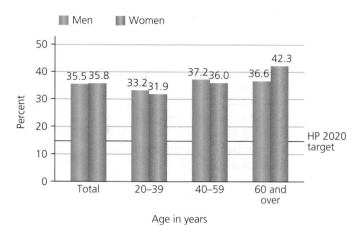

FIGURE 14.1 Prevalence of obesity in American adults, by sex and age, 2009–2010. *Healthy People 2020* sets a target obesity prevalence of 15% for all adults.

This chapter explores the factors that contribute to the development of overweight and to eating disorders. It also takes a closer look at weight management through lifestyle behaviors and suggests specific strategies for reaching and maintaining a healthy weight.

BASIC CONCEPTS OF WEIGHT MANAGEMENT

If you are like most people, you are concerned about your weight. But how do you decide if you are overweight? At what point does being overweight present a health risk? And how thin is too thin?

What Is Body Composition, and Why Is It Important?

The human body can be divided into fat-free mass and body fat. Fat-free mass is composed of all the body's nonfat tissues: bone, water, muscle, connective tissue, organ tissues, and teeth.

A certain amount of body fat is necessary for the body to function. Fat is incorporated into the nerves, brain, heart, lungs, liver, mammary glands, and other body organs and tissues. It is the main source of stored energy in the body; it also cushions body organs and helps regulate body temperature. This **essential fat** makes up about 3–5% of total body weight in men and about 8–12% in women. The percentage is higher in women due to fat deposits in the breasts, uterus, and other sex-specific sites.

Most of the fat in the body is stored in fat cells, or **adipose tissue,** located under the skin (**subcutaneous fat**) and around major organs (**visceral** or *intra-abdominal* **fat**). People have a genetically determined number of fat cells, but these cells can increase or decrease in size depending on how much fat is being

stored. The amount of stored fat depends on several factors, including age, sex, metabolism, diet, and activity level. The primary source of excess body fat is excess calories consumed in the diet—that is, calories consumed in excess of calories expended in metabolism, physical activity, and exercise.

A pound of body fat is equal to 3500 calories. If you take in 100 calories per day in excess of the calories you expend, you will gain 10 pounds in a year. Excess stored body fat is associated with increased risk of chronic diseases like arthritis, diabetes, and cardiovascular disease.

Overweight and Obesity Defined

Commonly used methods of assessing and classifying body composition are described later in this chapter. Some methods are based on body weight and others on body fat. Methods based on body weight are less accurate than those based on body fat, but they are commonly used because body weight is easier to measure than body fat.

In the past, many people relied on height/weight tables (which were based on insurance company mortality statistics) to determine whether they were at a healthy weight. Such tables can be very inaccurate for some people. Because muscle tissue is denser and heavier than fat, a fit person can easily weigh more that the recommended weight on a height/weight table, and an unfit person may weigh less.

When looking at body composition, the most important consideration is the proportion of the body's total weight that

essential fat Fat incorporated in various tissues of the body; critical for normal body functioning.

adipose tissue Connective tissue in which fat is stored.

subcutaneous fat Fat located under the skin.

visceral fat Fat located around major organs; also called *intra-abdominal fat.*

TERMS

is fat—the **percent body fat.** For example, two women may both be 5 feet, 5 inches tall and weigh 130 pounds. But one woman may have only 15% of her body weight as fat, whereas the other woman could have 34% body fat. Although neither woman is overweight by most standards, the second woman is overfat. Too much body fat can have a negative effect on health and well-being. Just as the amount of body fat is important, so is its distribution in your body. Visceral fat is more harmful to health than subcutaneous fat.

Overweight is usually defined as total body weight above the recommended range for good health, as determined by large-scale population surveys. **Obesity** is defined as a more serious degree of overweight that carries multiple health risks. Both terms are used to identify weight ranges that are associated with increased likelihood of certain diseases and health problems. Cutoff points for defining overweight and obesity vary with the method used to measure and evaluate body weight and percent body fat.

QUICK STATS

In 1970, **15%** of adult Americans were obese. In 2010, more than **35%** were obese.

—National Center for Health Statistics

Energy Balance

The key to achieving and maintaining a healthy body weight and keeping a healthy ratio of fat to fat-free mass across the lifespan is energy balance (Figure 14.2). You take in energy (calories) from the food you eat. Your body uses energy (calories) to maintain vital body functions (resting metabolism), to digest food, and to fuel physical activity. When energy in equals energy out, you maintain your current weight. To change your weight and body composition, you must tip the energy balance equation in a particular direction. If you take in more calories daily than your body burns (a *positive* energy balance), the excess calories will be stored as fat and you will gain weight over time. If you eat fewer calories than you burn each day (a *negative* energy balance), you will lose some of the stored fat and probably lose weight.

If we look at the energy balance equation today as expressed for the general American population, the equation is tipped heavily toward the energy-in side. The 2010 Dietary Guidelines for Americans attribute this calorie imbalance in part to the obesogenic environment in which many Americans currently live. Our environment is rich in large portion sizes; high-fat, high-calorie foods; and palatable, easily available, and inexpensive foods. Unfortunately the energy-out side of the equation has not compensated for increased energy intake; instead we've decreased work-related physical activity, decreased activity associated with daily living, and increased time spent in sedentary pastimes like TV watching and computer use.

The good news, however, is that you control both parts of the energy balance equation. Specific strategies for altering energy balance are discussed later in the chapter.

Evaluating Body Weight and Body Composition

Several methods can be used to measure and evaluate body weight and percent body fat, some of them simple and inexpensive. These assessments can give you information about the health risks associated with your current body weight and body composition. They can also help you establish reasonable goals and set a starting point for current and future decisions about weight loss and weight gain.

Body Mass Index Body mass index (BMI) is a measure of body weight that is useful for estimating a person's weight status and for classifying the health risks of body weight if more sophisticated methods aren't available. BMI is based on the concept that weight should be proportional to height. Easy to calculate and rate, BMI is a fairly accurate measure of

ENERGY IN
Food calories

ENERGY OUT
Physical activity 20–30%
Food digestion ±10%
Resting metabolism 65–70%

FIGUR E 14.2 The energy balance equation.

percent body fat The percentage of total body weight that is composed of fat.

overweight Body weight above the recommended range for good health.

obesity Severe overweight, characterized by an excessive accumulation of body fat; may also be defined in terms of some measure of total body weight.

body mass index (BMI) A measure of relative body weight that takes height into account and is highly correlated with more direct measures of body fat; calculated by dividing total body weight (in kilograms) by the square of height (in meters).

	<18.5 Underweight		18.5–24.9 Normal						25–29.9 Overweight					30–34.9 Obesity (Class I)					35–39.9 Obesity (Class II)					≥40 Extreme obesity
BMI	17	18	19	20	21	22	23	24	25	26	27	28	29	30	31	32	33	34	35	36	37	38	39	40
Height												Body Weight (pounds)												
4' 10"	81	86	91	96	101	105	110	115	120	124	129	134	139	144	148	153	158	163	168	172	177	182	187	192
4' 11"	84	89	94	99	104	109	114	119	124	129	134	139	144	149	154	159	163	168	173	178	183	188	193	198
5'	87	92	97	102	108	113	118	123	128	133	138	143	149	154	159	164	169	174	179	184	190	195	200	205
5' 1"	90	95	101	106	111	117	122	127	132	138	143	148	154	159	164	169	175	180	185	191	196	201	207	212
5' 2"	93	98	104	109	115	120	126	131	137	142	148	153	159	164	170	175	181	186	191	197	202	208	213	219
5' 3"	96	102	107	113	119	124	130	136	141	147	153	158	164	169	175	181	186	192	198	203	209	215	220	226
5' 4"	99	105	111	117	122	128	134	140	146	152	157	163	169	175	181	187	192	198	204	210	216	222	227	233
5' 5"	102	108	114	120	126	132	138	144	150	156	162	168	174	180	186	192	198	204	210	216	222	229	235	241
5' 6"	105	112	118	124	130	136	143	149	155	161	167	174	180	186	192	198	205	211	217	223	229	236	242	248
5' 7"	109	115	121	128	134	141	147	153	160	166	173	179	185	192	198	204	211	217	224	230	236	243	249	256
5' 8"	112	118	125	132	138	145	151	158	165	171	178	184	191	197	204	211	217	224	230	237	244	250	257	263
5' 9"	115	122	129	136	142	149	156	163	169	176	183	190	197	203	210	217	224	230	237	244	251	258	264	271
5' 10"	119	126	133	139	146	153	160	167	174	181	188	195	202	209	216	223	230	237	244	251	258	265	272	279
5' 11"	122	129	136	143	151	158	165	172	179	187	194	201	208	215	222	230	237	244	251	258	265	273	280	287
6'	125	133	140	148	155	162	170	177	184	192	199	207	214	221	229	236	243	251	258	266	273	280	288	295
6' 1"	129	137	144	152	159	167	174	182	190	197	205	212	220	228	235	243	250	258	265	273	281	288	296	303
6' 2"	132	140	148	156	164	171	179	187	195	203	210	218	226	234	242	249	257	265	273	281	288	296	304	312
6' 3"	136	144	152	160	168	176	184	192	200	208	216	224	232	240	248	256	264	272	280	288	296	304	312	320
6' 4"	140	148	156	164	173	181	189	197	206	214	222	230	238	247	255	263	271	280	288	296	304	312	321	329

FIGURE 14.3 Body mass index (BMI). To determine your BMI, find your height in the left column. Move across the appropriate row until you find the weight closest to your own. The number at the top of the column is the BMI at that height and weight.

SOURCE: Ratings from National Heart, Lung, and Blood Institute. 1998. *Clinical Guidelines on the Identification, Evaluation, and Treatment of Overweight and Obesity in Adults: The Evidence Report.* Bethesda, Md.: National Institutes of Health

the health risks of body weight for most average (nonathletic) people. BMI is correlated with body fat, but it does not directly measure body fat.

CALCULATING YOUR BMI BMI is calculated by dividing your body weight (expressed in kilograms or pounds) by the square of your height (expressed in meters or inches). You can look up your BMI in the chart in Figure 14.3, or you can use the following formula to calculate it more precisely:

$$BMI = \frac{\text{weight in kg}}{(\text{height in meters})^2}$$

OR

$$\frac{\text{weight in pounds}}{(\text{height in inches})^2} \times 703 \text{ (conversion factor)}$$

Body weight status is categorized as underweight, healthy weight, overweight, or obese in comparison with what is considered healthy for a given height. Under standards issued by the National Institutes of Health and adopted by the Dietary Guidelines for Americans, a BMI between 18.5 and 24.9 is considered healthy, a BMI of 25 or above is classified as overweight, and a BMI of 30 or above is classified as obese. A person with a BMI below 18.5 is classified as underweight, although low BMI values may be healthy in some cases if they are not the result of smoking, an eating disorder, or an underlying disease. A BMI of 17.5 or less is sometimes used as a diagnostic criterion for the eating disorder anorexia nervosa.

THE DRAWBACKS OF BMI BMI is a valuable tool for assessing weight, but it is not such a good tool for determining body composition. Like height–weight tables, it does not distinguish between fat weight and fat-free weight. It can also be inaccurate for some groups, including short people (under 5 feet tall), muscular athletes, and older adults with little muscle mass due to inactivity or an underlying disease. People in these groups should use one of the methods described in the next section for estimating percent body fat to assess whether their weight and body composition are healthy. BMI is also not particularly useful for tracking changes in body composition—gains in muscle mass and losses of fat. Women are likely to have more body fat for a given BMI than men.

Body Composition Analysis

The most accurate and direct way to evaluate body composition is to determine percent body fat, and there are several methods to do so. However, specific guidelines for healthy body fat ranges have not been established. On average, women have about 10–12% more body fat than men. A healthy body fat range for men is usually considered to be about 12–20%, and for women, about 20–30%. Men with more than 25% body fat are considered obese, as are women with more than 33% body fat. No matter which method of body composition analysis is used, the measurements must be performed by someone with appropriate training to ensure accuracy.

SKINFOLD MEASUREMENT Skinfold measurement is a simple and practical way to assess body composition based on amount of subcutaneous fat. A practitioner measures the thickness of skinfolds at several different sites on the body with special calipers, and the measurements are plugged into formulas that calculate body fat percentages. The accuracy of this method is highly dependent on the expertise of the practitioner.

BIOELECTRICAL IMPEDANCE ANALYSIS (BIA)
In this method, electrodes are attached to the body, and a harmless electrical current is transmitted from electrode to electrode. The electrical conduction through the body favors the path of the fat-free tissues over the fat tissues, so the amount of resistance to the current is related to the amount of fat-free tissue in the body. A computer then calculates fat percentages from measurements of the resistance to the current.

HYDROSTATIC WEIGHING AND THE BOD POD
In hydrostatic (underwater) weighing, a person is submerged and weighed under water. Percent body fat can be calculated from body density. Muscle has a higher density and fat a lower density than water, so people with more fat tend to float and weigh less under water, while lean people tend to sink and weigh more under water.

A specialized body composition analysis device called the Bod Pod uses air instead of water. A person sits in a chamber, and computerized pressure sensors determine the amount of air displaced by the person's body to determine percentage of body fat.

SCANNING PROCEDURES High-tech scanning procedures are very accurate means of assessing body composition, but they require expensive equipment. These procedures include computed tomography (CT), magnetic resonance imaging (MRI), dual-energy X-ray absorptiometry (DEXA), and dual-photon absorptiometry. Other procedures include infrared reactance (Futrex 1100) and total body electrical conductivity (TOBEC). These techniques are generally offered only at medical or research facilities.

> To ensure accuracy, body composition measurements must be performed by **someone with appropriate training**.

Body Fat Distribution As noted earlier, the location of fat on your body also has implications for health, with abdominal fat posing a greater risk than fat located in other places. Abdominal fat appears to be an independent risk factor regardless of BMI.

Two of the simplest methods for measuring body fat distribution are waist circumference measurement and waist-to-hip ratio calculation. In the first method, you measure your waist circumference using a tape measure placed around your abdomen at the top of your hip bone. A waist circumference of ≥40 inches (102cm) for men or ≥35 in (88 cm) for women is associated with an increased risk for chronic disease for most adults. In the second method, you divide your waist circumference by your hip circumference (measured around the widest part of the buttocks). A waist-to-hip ratio above 0.94 for young men and above 0.82 for young women is associated with an increased risk of heart disease and diabetes. More research is needed to determine the precise degree of risk associated with specific values for these two assessments of body fat distribution.

EXCESS BODY FAT AND WELLNESS

The amount and distribution of fat in the body can have profound effects on health. Obesity doubles mortality rates and can reduce life expectancy by 10–20 years. In fact, if the current trends in overweight and obesity (and their related health problems) continue, some experts predict that the average American's life expectancy will soon decline by 5 years.

Obese people have an increased risk of death from all causes compared with people of normal weight. Obesity is associated with diabetes, cardiovascular diseases, many kinds of cancer, impaired immune function, gallbladder and kidney diseases,

Skinfold measurements are a simple and inexpensive way to determine body fat levels. This method requires a caliper designed for this purpose and a practitioner trained in its use.

skin problems, impotence, sleep and breathing disorders, back pain, arthritis, and other bone and joint disorders. Obesity is also associated with complications of pregnancy, menstrual irregularities, urine leakage (stress incontinence), increased surgical risk, and psychological disorders and problems (such as depression, low self-esteem, and body dissatisfaction).

There is debate over the health risks for people who are overweight but not obese (BMI of 25 to 29), particularly for people who are overweight and physically active. These risks depend in part on an individual's overall health and other risk factors, such as high blood pressure, unhealthy cholesterol levels, body fat distribution, tobacco use, and level of physical activity. The Nurses' Health Study, in which Harvard researchers have followed more than 120,000 women since 1976, has found that even mildly to moderately overweight women have an 80% increased risk of developing coronary heart disease (CHD) compared to leaner women.

This conclusion was supported by a 10-year study that ended in 2006 after following a half-million Americans in their fifties. Researchers concluded that subjects who were even slightly overweight were up to 40% more likely to die within the next decade, compared to age-matched people who had a desirable weight. But it is also important to realize that small weight losses—5% to 10% of total body weight—can lead to significant health improvements.

Diabetes

About 26 million Americans have one of the two major types of **diabetes mellitus,** a disease that disrupts normal metabolism. About 5–10% of people with diabetes have a form known as type 1 diabetes, a disease that usually begins in childhood or adolescence and is not related to obesity. The remaining 90–95% of people with diabetes have type 2 diabetes, a disease that is strongly associated with excess body fat. The prevalence of type 2 diabetes has been rising dramatically in parallel with the increase in prevalence of obesity. In 2010 almost 2 million new cases of diabetes were diagnosed in adults over the age of 20.

Diabetes involves the production of the hormone insulin by the pancreas. In normal metabolism, the pancreas secretes insulin, which stimulates cells to take up blood sugar (glucose) to produce energy (Figure 14.4; see also page T2-5 of the color transparency insert "Touring the Cardiorespiratory

---

TERMS

diabetes mellitus   A disease that disrupts normal metabolism, interfering with cells' ability to take in glucose for energy production.

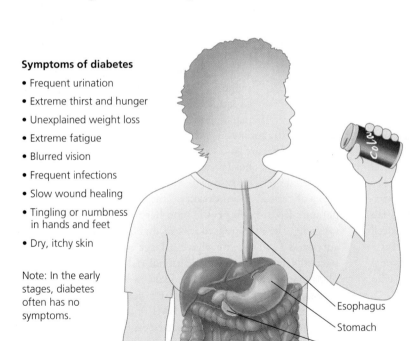

Symptoms of diabetes

- Frequent urination
- Extreme thirst and hunger
- Unexplained weight loss
- Extreme fatigue
- Blurred vision
- Frequent infections
- Slow wound healing
- Tingling or numbness in hands and feet
- Dry, itchy skin

Note: In the early stages, diabetes often has no symptoms.

Esophagus
Stomach
Pancreas
Small intestine

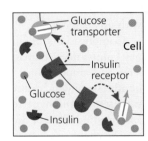

Normal
Insulin binds to receptors on the surface of a cell and signals special transporters in the cell to transport glucose inside.

Glucose transporter
Cell
Insulin receptor
Glucose
Insulin

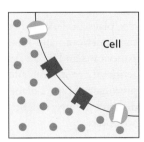

Type 1 diabetes
The pancreas produces little or no insulin. Thus, no signal is sent instructing the cell to transport glucose, and glucose builds up in the bloodstream.

Cell

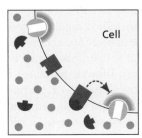

Type 2 diabetes
The pancreas produces too little insulin and/or the body's cells are resistant to it. Some insulin binds to receptors on the cell's surface, but the signal to transport glucose is blocked. Glucose builds up in the bloodstream.

Cell

FIGURE 14.4   Diabetes mellitus. During digestion, carbohydrates are broken down in the small intestine into glucose, a simple sugar that enters the bloodstream. The presence of glucose signals the pancreas to release insulin, a hormone that helps cells take up glucose; once inside a cell, glucose can be converted to energy. In diabetes, this process is disrupted, resulting in a buildup of glucose in the bloodstream.

System" in Chapter 15). In diabetes, this process is disrupted, causing a buildup of glucose in the bloodstream. In type 1 diabetes, the body's immune system, triggered by a viral infection or some other environmental factor, destroys the insulin-producing cells in the pancreas. Little or no insulin is produced, so daily doses of insulin are required. In type 2 diabetes, the pancreas doesn't produce enough insulin, or body cells are resistant to insulin (called *insulin resistance*), or both. This condition can develop slowly, and about 25% of type 2 diabetics are unaware of their condition. About one-third of people with type 2 diabetes must take insulin; others may take medications that increase insulin production or stimulate the cells to take up glucose.

A third type of diabetes, called *gestational diabetes*, occurs in about 7% of women during pregnancy. The condition usually disappears after pregnancy, but about half of women who experience it eventually develop type 2 diabetes. *Prediabetes* is a condition in which blood sugar levels are higher than normal but not high enough for a diagnosis of full-blown diabetes. About 57 million Americans have prediabetes, and most will develop type 2 diabetes unless they adopt preventive lifestyle measures. The warning signs of diabetes include frequent urination, extreme hunger or thirst, unexplained weight loss, extreme fatigue, blurred vision, frequent infections, tingling or numbness in the hands or feet, and generalized itching with no rash.

Complications of diabetes include kidney failure; nerve damage; circulation problems and amputations; retinal damage and blindness; and increased rates of heart attack, stroke, and hypertension. Diabetes is currently the seventh leading cause of death in the United States

The major risk factors for diabetes are age, obesity, physical inactivity, a family history of diabetes, and lifestyle. Ethnicity also plays a role, with Native Americans, Alaska Natives, African Americans, and Hispanics having higher rates than Asian Americans and white Americans. Excess body fat reduces cell sensitivity to insulin, and insulin resistance is almost always a precursor of type 2 diabetes. Nearly 90% of people with type 2 diabetes are overweight when diagnosed, including 55% who are obese.

It is estimated that 90% of cases of type 2 diabetes could be prevented if people adopted healthy lifestyle behaviors, including regular physical activity, a moderate diet to control body fat, and modest weight loss. Even a small amount of weight loss can be beneficial. For people with prediabetes, lifestyle measures are more effective than medication for delaying or preventing the development of diabetes. Exercise (endurance and/or strength training) makes cells more sensitive to insulin and helps stabilize blood glucose levels; it also helps keep body fat at healthy levels. Regular exercise and a healthy diet are often sufficient to control type 2 diabetes. There is no cure for diabetes, but it can be successfully managed by keeping blood sugar levels within safe limits through diet, exercise, and, if necessary, medication.

Obesity is one of the six major controllable risk factors for heart disease. Excess body fat is strongly associated with hypertension, unhealthy cholesterol and triglyceride levels, and impaired heart function. Many overweight and obese people—especially those who are sedentary and eat a poor diet—also suffer from a group of symptoms called *metabolic syndrome*. Symptoms include insulin resistance, high blood pressure, high blood glucose, unhealthy cholesterol levels, chronic inflammation, and abdominal fat. Metabolic syndrome increases the risk of heart disease, more so in men than in women (see Chapter 15 for more about metabolic syndrome).

Obesity is also a risk factor for certain types of cancer, including colon and rectal cancer, breast cancer, prostate cancer, and ovarian cancer (see Chapter 16).

QUICK STATS

More than **one-third** of children and adolescents in the United States are overweight or obese.

—CDC, 2012

Body Fat Distribution and Health

As noted earlier, the distribution of body fat (that is, the locations of fat on the body) is an important indicator of health. Men and postmenopausal women tend to store fat in the upper regions of their bodies, particularly in the abdominal area, as visceral fat. People with this pattern of fat distribution, called *android obesity*, are said to be apple-shaped. Premenopausal women usually store fat in the hips, buttocks, and thighs, as subcutaneous fat. People with this pattern, called *gynoid obesity*, are said to be pear-shaped.

Abdominal obesity increases the risk of high blood pressure, diabetes, early-onset heart disease, stroke, certain types of cancer, and mortality. This risk is independent of a person's BMI. Even people who have a BMI in the normal range may be at increased risk of diabetes, high blood pressure, and CVD if they have a large waist circumference, particularly if they have additional risk factors. For example, a man with a BMI of 27, a waist circumference above 40 inches, and diabetes is at greater risk for health problems than another man who has a BMI of 27 but has a smaller waist and no other risk factors. Abdominal obesity (as measured by waist circumference) is a primary component of metabolic syndrome and a forewarning of diabetes and heart disease.

The reason for the increased risk associated with abdominal obesity appears to be that visceral fat is more easily mobilized and sent into the bloodstream, increasing disease-related blood fat levels. Visceral fat contains many biologically active substances such as inflammatory chemicals and growth factors, which can adhere to the lining of blood vessels, cause insulin resistance, and have a negative influence on cardiovascular

Overweight men tend to have an apple shape (android obesity). Overweight women tend to have a pear shape (gynoid obesity).

health. Subcutaneous fat tends to be soft and flabby (whereas visceral fat is hard) and is not metabolically active the way visceral fat is.

Body Image

The collective picture of the body as seen through the mind's eye, **body image** consists of perceptions, images, thoughts, attitudes, and emotions. A negative body image is characterized by dissatisfaction with the body in general or some part of the body in particular. Recent surveys indicate that the majority of Americans, many of whom are not actually overweight, are unhappy with their body weight or with some aspect of their appearance. People may be dissatisfied with their bodies for a variety of reasons, including sociocultural forces and factors that are specific to life stages. For example, the ideal female body size in Western society has become progressively thinner while actual female body size continues to increase, along with the frequency of unhealthy attitudes and behaviors surrounding food and body weight.

Losing weight or getting cosmetic surgery does not necessarily improve body image. However, improvements in body image may occur in the absence of changes in weight or appearance. Many experts now believe that body image issues must be dealt with as part of treating obesity and eating disorders. Body image and eating disorders are discussed in detail later in this chapter.

Problems Associated with Very Low Levels of Body Fat

Health experts have generally viewed very low levels of body fat—less than 8–12% for women and 3–5% for men—as a threat to wellness. Extreme leanness has been linked with reproductive, circulatory, and immune system disorders. Extremely lean people may experience muscle wasting and fatigue; they are also more likely to suffer from dangerous eating disorders.

In physically active women and girls, particularly those involved in sports where weight and appearance are important (ballet, gymnastics, skating, and distance running, for example), a condition called the **female athlete triad** may develop (Figure 14.5). The triad consists of three interrelated disorders: abnormal eating patterns (and excessive exercising), followed by **amenorrhea** (absence of menstruation), followed by decreased bone density (premature osteoporosis). Prolonged amenorrhea can cause bone density to erode to a point that a woman in her twenties will have the bone density of a woman in her sixties. Left untreated, the triad can lead to decreased physical performance, increased incidence of bone fractures, disturbances of heart rhythm and metabolism, and even death.

What Is the Right Weight for You?

To answer the question of what you should weigh, let your lifestyle be your guide. Don't focus on a particular weight as your goal. Instead focus on living a lifestyle that includes

---

Ask Yourself

QUESTIONS FOR CRITICAL THINKING AND REFLECTION

Calculate your BMI using the formula given in this chapter; then compare it with the BMIs of some classmates. Do the results surprise you? How well do you think BMI reflects body composition? Why do you think it is such a commonly used measure?

TERMS

body image The mental representation a person holds about his or her body at any given time, consisting of perceptions, images, thoughts, attitudes, and emotions about the body.

female athlete triad A condition consisting of three interrelated disorders: abnormal eating patterns (and excessive exercising) followed by lack of menstrual periods (amenorrhea) and decreased bone density (premature osteoporosis).

amenorrhea The absence of menstruation.

WELLNESS ON CAMPUS
The Freshman 15: Fact or Myth?

According to popular belief, college students typically gain 15 pounds in their first year at school—the infamous "freshman 15." Is this the fate of all college students, or is it a myth that adds stress for body-conscious young adults?

Research indicates that the truth lies somewhere between these two scenarios. While many people do gain weight in the first year at college, the weight gain tends to be less than 5 pounds. A 2011 study found that freshmen gain between 2.5 and 3.5 pounds, on average, during their first year. This is only half a pound more than is gained by individuals of the same age who are not attending college. Reasons for the weight gain include newfound food independence, changes in eating habits, stress, and social comparison and the influence of roommates and friends.

Although 5 pounds may not seem like a lot of weight, it still can pose a health risk or contribute to lower self-esteem. Changes in body composition—specifically, increased body fat—can begin a troublesome pattern for students. Even if they don't have a spike in weight during their first year, college-educated individuals tend to experience a moderate but steady weight gain during and after college.

More importantly, whether the weight gain is 5 pounds, 15 pounds, or even more, freshman weight gain is avoidable! In addition to the healthy eating strategies for college students described in Chapter 12, try following these tips and guidelines for avoiding freshman weight gain:

- Listen to your hunger cues.
- Watch portion sizes, and avoid second and third servings.
- Follow a daily schedule for your meals and snack times.
- Don't skip meals—especially breakfast.
- Plan ahead so you have healthy snacks in your room.
- Eat when you are hungry—not for emotional reasons.
- If you cook, try to shop at a regular grocery store and not a campus convenience store.
- Avoid late-night eating.
- Be more physically active: walk to and from class, use the campus fitness facility, and consider taking a sports class for credit (tennis, dance, aerobics, weight training).

SOURCES: Zagorsky, J. L., and P. K. Smith. 2011. The freshman 15: critical time for obesity intervention or media myth? *Social Science Quarterly*, 92(5): 1389–1407; Smith-Jackson, T., and J. J. Reed. 2012. Freshman women and the "Freshman 15": perspectives on prevalence and causes of college weight gain. *Journal of American College Health*, 60(1): 14–20; Yakusheva, O., K. Kapinos, and M. Weiss. 2011. Peer effects and the freshman 15: evidence from a natural experiment. *Economics & Human Biology* 9(2):119–132.

---

eating moderate amounts of healthful foods, getting plenty of exercise, thinking positively, and learning to cope with stress. Then let the pounds fall where they may. For most people, the result will be close to the recommended weight ranges discussed earlier. For some, their weight will be somewhat higher than societal standards—but right for them. By letting a healthy lifestyle determine your weight, you can avoid developing unhealthy patterns of eating and a negative body image.

Because overweight and obesity are risk factors for chronic disease, people who are currently overweight should make preventing additional weight gain and managing risk factors for disease their important priorities (Table 14.2). Obese adults should strive to change their calorie balance to promote weight loss by making changes to their diet and level of physical activity.

FACTORS CONTRIBUTING TO EXCESS BODY FAT

Body weight and body composition may be determined by multiple factors that may vary with each individual. These factors can be grouped into genetic, physiological, lifestyle, and psychosocial factors.

Genetic Factors

Nutrigenomics is the study of how nutrients and genes interact and how genetic variations can cause people to respond differently to nutrients in food. Estimates of the genetic contribution to obesity vary widely, from about 25% to 40% of an

Excess exercise and disordered eating

Decreased bone density

Absent or infrequent menstruation

FIGURE 14.5 Female athlete triad Some girls and women striving for unrealistic thinness develop a condition called the female athlete triad. Disordered eating combined with intense exercise can suppress the hormones that control the menstrual cycle, and absence of menstrual periods can lead to osteoporosis.

Table 14.2 — Body Mass Index (BMI) Classification and Disease Risk

CLASSIFICATION	BMI (kg/m²)	OBESITY CLASS	DISEASE RISK RELATIVE TO NORMAL WEIGHT AND WAIST CIRCUMFERENCE[a]	
			MEN ≤ 40 in. (102 cm) WOMEN ≤ 35 in. (88 cm)	> 40 in. (102 cm) > 35 in. (88 cm)
Underweight[b]	<18.5		—	—
Normal[c]	18.5–24.9		—	—
Overweight	25.0–29.9		Increased	High
Obesity	30.0–34.9	I	High	Very high
	35.0–39.9	II	Very high	Very high
Extreme obesity	≥ 40.0	III	Extremely high	Extremely high

[a]Disease risk for type 2 diabetes, hypertension, and cardiovascular disease. The waist circumference cutoff points for increased risk are 40 inches (102 cm) for men and 35 inches (88 cm) for women.
[b]Research suggests that a low BMI can be healthy in some cases, as long as it is not the result of smoking, an eating disorder, or an underlying disease process. A BMI of 17.5 or less is sometimes used as a diagnostic criterion for the eating disorder anorexia nervosa.
[c]Increased waist circumference can also be a marker for increased risk, even in people of normal weight.

SOURCE: Adapted from National Heart, Lung, and Blood Institute. 1998. *Clinical Guidelines on the Identification, Evaluation, and Treatment of Overweight and Obesity in Adults: The Evidence Report*. Bethesda, MD: National Institutes of Health.

individual's body fat. Scientists have so far identified more than 600 genes associated with obesity. Genes influence body size and shape, body fat distribution, and metabolic rate. Genetic factors also affect the ease with which weight is gained as a result of overeating and where on the body extra weight is added.

If both parents are obese, their children have an 80% risk of being obese; children with only one obese parent face a 50% risk of becoming obese. In studies that compared adoptees and their biological parents, the weights of the adoptees were found to be more like those of the biological parents than those of the adoptive parents, again indicating a strong genetic link.

Hereditary influences, however, must be balanced against the contribution of environmental factors. Not all children of obese parents become obese, and normal-weight parents may have overweight children. Environmental factors like diet and exercise are probably responsible for such differences. Thus the *tendency* to develop obesity may be inherited, but the expression of this tendency is affected by environmental influences.

The message you should get from this research is that genes are not destiny. It is true that some people have a harder time losing weight and maintaining weight loss than others. However, with increased exercise and attention to diet, even those with a genetic tendency toward obesity can maintain a healthy body weight. And regardless of genetic factors, lifestyle choices remain the cornerstone of successful weight management.

Physiological Factors

Metabolism is a key physiological factor in the regulation of body fat and body weight; hormones and fat cell types also play a role.

> **QUICK STATS**
>
> An obese teenager has a **70%** risk of becoming an obese adult.
>
> —U.S. Dept. of Health and Human Services, 2010

Metabolism Metabolism is the sum of all the vital processes by which food energy and nutrients are made available to and used by the body. The largest component of metabolism, **resting metabolic rate (RMR),** is the energy required to maintain vital body functions, including respiration, heart rate, body temperature, and blood pressure, while the body is at rest. As shown in Figure 14.2, RMR accounts for about 65–70% of daily energy expenditure. The energy required to digest food accounts for as much as 10% of daily energy expenditure. The remaining 20–30% is expended during physical activity.

Both genetics and behavior affect metabolic rate. Men, who have a higher proportion of muscle mass than women, have a higher RMR because muscle tissue is more metabolically active than fat. Also, some individuals inherit a higher or lower RMR than others. A higher RMR means that a person burns more calories while at rest and can therefore take in more calories without gaining weight.

Weight loss or gain also affects metabolic rate. When a person loses weight, both RMR and the energy required to perform physical tasks decrease. The reverse occurs when weight is gained. One of the reasons why exercise is so important during a weight loss program is that exercise, especially resistance training, helps maintain muscle mass and metabolic rate.

> **TERMS**
>
> **resting metabolic rate (RMR)** The energy required to maintain vital body functions, including respiration, heart rate, body temperature, and blood pressure, while the body is at rest.

Hormones   Hormones clearly play a role in the accumulation of body fat, especially for females. Hormonal changes at puberty, during pregnancy, and at menopause contribute to the amount and location of fat accumulation. For example, during puberty, hormones cause the development of secondary sex characteristics, including larger breasts, wider hips, and a fat layer under the skin.

One hormone thought to be linked to obesity is *leptin*. Secreted by the body's fat cells, leptin is carried to the brain, where it appears to let the brain know how big or small the body's fat stores are. With this information, the brain can regulate appetite and metabolic rate accordingly. Several other hormones, such as ghrelin, may be involved in the regulation of appetite. Researchers hope to use these hormones to develop treatments for obesity based on appetite control; however, as most of us will admit, hunger is often *not* the primary reason we overeat. Cases of obesity based solely or primarily on hormone abnormalities do exist, but they are rare.

Fat Cells   The amount of fat (adipose tissue) the body can store is a function of the number and size of fat (adipose) cells. These fat cells are like little compartments that can inflate to hold body fat; when existing fat cells are filled, the body makes more, thereby increasing its ability to store fat.

Some people are born with an above-average number of fat cells and thus have the potential for storing more energy as body fat. Overeating at critical times, such as in childhood, can cause the body to create more fat cells. If a person loses weight, fat cell content is depleted, but it is unclear whether the number of fat cells can be decreased.

Further, it appears that all fat cells are not created equal. As mentioned earlier, visceral fat, located in the abdomen, is more metabolically active than subcutaneous fat and poses more health risks.

Lifestyle Factors

Although genetic and physiological factors may increase the risk for excess body fat, they are not sufficient to explain the increasingly high rate of obesity seen in the United States. The gene pool has not changed dramatically in the past 60 years, but the rate of obesity among Americans has more than doubled (see the box "Overweight and Obesity among U.S. Ethnic Populations"). Clearly other factors are at work—particularly lifestyle factors such as increased eating and decreased physical activity.

Eating   Americans have access to plenty of calorie-dense foods, and many have eating habits that contribute to weight gain. Most overweight adults admit to eating more than they should of high-fat, high-sugar, high-calorie foods. Americans eat out more frequently now than in the past and rely more heavily on fast food and packaged convenience foods. Restaurant and convenience food portion sizes tend to be large, and the foods themselves are likely to be high in fat, sugar, and calories and low in nutrients. Many people underestimate the actual number of calories they eat.

Research indicates that when more food is available, people eat more. Many of the extra calories consumed by Americans come from carbohydrates, such as refined sugars, fats, and full-fat milk and milk products. The popularity of sugar-free soft drinks does not appear to be helping people lose weight, though it is not yet clear why this may be the case. Compared to people who don't drink soda, people who drink more than one soda per day, either regular or diet, are more likely to be obese, develop metabolic syndrome, and have high blood pressure.

Physical Activity   Activity levels among Americans are declining, beginning in childhood and continuing throughout life. Many schools have cut back on physical education classes and recess. Most adults drive to work, sit all day, and then relax in front of the TV at night. Incidence of overweight is consistently linked to excessive screen time—whether time spent watching TV, playing video games, or using computers. Fewer than 5% of American adults participate in daily physical activity for at least 30 minutes.

An "Obesogenic" Environment   The 2010 Dietary Guidelines for Americans focused attention on the "obesogenic" environment in which most Americans live. This environment promotes overconsumption of calories while at the same time discouraging physical activity. Food and activity choices are influenced by the communities in which individuals live, their socioeconomic status, religion and culture, and geographic location. People living in areas with limited access to healthy foods and opportunities for physical activity do not have the same options for choosing a healthy lifestyle as do people living in more enriched environments.

Psychosocial Factors

Many people have learned to use food as a means of coping with stress and negative emotions. Eating can provide a powerful distraction from difficult feelings—loneliness, anger, boredom, anxiety, shame, sadness, inadequacy. It can be used to combat low moods, low energy levels, and low self-esteem (see the box "What Triggers Your Eating?"). When food and eating become the primary means of regulating emotions, binge eating or other disturbed eating patterns can develop.

Obesity is strongly associated with socioeconomic status. The prevalence of obesity in women and children tends to go down as income level goes up, though it stays the same in men. These differences may reflect the greater sensitivity and concern for a slim physical appearance among upper-income women, as well as greater access to

The prevalence of overweight and obesity is growing among all population groups in the United States. However, rates and trends vary by ethnic group and by other population characteristics.

• Certain groups, including African Americans, Latinos, and American Indians and Alaska Natives, have higher-than-average rates of obesity. Asian Americans have a low rate of obesity.

• The process of acculturation into mainstream culture in the United States boosts body weight. The longer a foreign-born person lives in the United States, the more likely she or he is to become obese. BMI among immigrants begins to climb after about 10 years of U.S. residence, and after 15 years, it approaches the national average.

• Cultural factors that influence dietary and exercise behaviors appear to play a role in the development of obesity. There are also cultural differences in acceptance of larger body size and in body image perception. For example, one study found that African Americans were more likely to think they were thinner than they really were and whites were more likely to think they were fatter than they really were.

• The health consequences of obesity affect ethnic populations in different ways. At a given level of BMI, Latinos are significantly more likely to have type 2 diabetes than whites. Obesity in African Americans is associated with increased risk of developing hypertension at a younger age and in a more severe form.

• For Asian Americans or people of Asian descent, waist circumference is a better indicator of relative disease risk than BMI, and disease risk goes up at a lower level of

BMI than for individuals of other groups. For Asian populations, WHO guidelines have a lower BMI cutoff for defining overweight (BMI 23).

• The prevalence of obesity differs among racial and ethnic groups in the United States in children as young as age 4. Obesity is twice as common in young American Indian/Native Alaskan children as it is in white and Asian children, and obesity prevalence is higher in Hispanic and black children than it is in whites and Asians.

• Fast-food restaurants are more prevalent in low-income areas compared with middle- to higher-income area and in areas with higher concentrations of ethnic minority groups in comparison with Caucasians. Higher BMIs may be associated with living in areas with increased expo-

sure to fast food, although there is some debate about this.

SOURCES: Anderson, S. E., and R. C. Whitaker. 2009. Prevalence of obesity among US preschool children in different racial and ethnic groups. *Archives of Pediatrics and Adolescent Medicine*, 163(4): 344–348; Fleischhacker, S. E., et al. 2011. A systematic review of fast food access studies. *Obesity Reviews*, 12(5): e460–471; Ogden, C. L., et al. 2010. Obesity and socioeconomic status in adults: United States, 2005–2008. NCHIS Data Brief, 50: 1–8. (http://www.ncbi.nlm.nih.gov /pubmed/21211165); Kumanyika, S., and S. Grier. 2006. Targeting interventions for ethnic minority and low-income populations. *The Future of Children* 16(1): 187–207, 578–584; Goel, M. S., et al. 2004. Obesity among U.S. immigrant subgroups by duration of residence. *Journal of the American Medical Association* 292(23): 2860–2867.

connect
ACTIVITY
DO IT ONLINE

Ask Yourself

QUESTIONS FOR CRITICAL THINKING AND REFLECTION

How do you view your own body composition? Where do you think you've gotten your ideas about how your body should look and perform? In light of what you've read in this chapter, do the ideals and images promoted in our culture seem reasonable? Do they seem healthy?

information about nutrition, to low-fat and low-calorie foods, and to opportunities for physical activity. It may also reflect the greater acceptance of obesity among certain ethnic groups, as well as different cultural values related to food choices.

In some families and cultures, food is used as a symbol of love and caring. It is an integral part of social gatherings and celebrations. In such cases, it may be difficult to change established eating patterns because they are linked to cultural and family values.

ADOPTING A HEALTHY LIFESTYLE FOR SUCCESSFUL WEIGHT MANAGEMENT

When all the research has been assessed, it is clear that most weight problems are lifestyle problems. Despite the growing prevalence of obesity in children and adolescents, many young adults get away with very unhealthy eating and exercise habits and don't develop a weight problem. But as the rapid growth of adolescence slows and family and career obligations increase, maintaining a healthy weight becomes a greater challenge. Slow weight gain—just one or two pounds per year—is a major cause of overweight and obesity, so weight management is important for everyone, not just for people who are currently overweight. A good time to develop a lifestyle for successful weight management is during early adulthood, when healthy behavior patterns have a better chance of taking a firm hold.

Permanent weight loss is not something you should start and stop. You need to adopt healthy behaviors that you can maintain throughout life, including eating habits, level of physical activity, an ability to think positively and manage your emotions effectively, and the coping strategies you use to deal with the stresses and challenges in your life.

Diet and Eating Habits

In contrast to dieting, which involves some form of food restriction, the term *diet* refers to your daily food choices. Everyone has a diet, but not everyone is dieting. You need to develop a diet that you enjoy and that enables you to maintain a healthy body composition. Use MyPlate or the DASH Eating Plan as the basis for a healthy diet (see Chapter 12). For weight management, pay special attention to total calories, portion sizes, energy density, fat and carbohydrate intake, and eating habits.

Total Calories   MyPlate suggests approximate daily energy needs based on gender, age, and activity level. However, energy balance may be a more important consideration for weight management than total calories consumed (refer back to Figure 14.2). To maintain your current weight, the total number of calories you eat must equal the number you burn. To lose weight, you must decrease your calorie intake and/or increase the number of calories you burn; to gain weight, the reverse is true. (One pound of body fat represents 3500 calories.)

The best approach for weight loss is combining an increase in physical activity with moderate calorie restriction. Don't go on a crash diet. To maintain weight loss, you may need to maintain some degree of the calorie restriction you used to lose the weight. Therefore, you need to adopt a level of food intake that provides all the essential nutrients that you can live with over the long term. For most people, maintaining weight loss is more difficult than losing the weight in the first place.

> One pound of body fat represents **3500 calories**.

Portion Sizes   Overconsumption of total calories is closely tied to portion sizes. Many Americans are unaware that the portions of packaged foods and of foods served at restaurants have increased in size, and most of us significantly underestimate the amount of food we eat. Studies have found that the larger the meal, the more calories people tend to eat. People also commonly eat much more of the foods that they perceive as being healthy, and in the process consume far more calories than they need. Portion size is associated with body weight, so limiting portion sizes is critical for maintaining a healthy body weight. For many people, concentrating on portion sizes is easier than counting calories.

Energy (Calorie) Density   Experts also recommend that you pay attention to *energy density*—the number of calories per ounce or gram of weight in a food. Ice cream, potato chips, croissants, crackers, and cakes and cookies are examples of foods high in energy density. Studies suggest that it isn't consumption of a certain amount of fat or calories in food that reduces hunger and leads to feelings of fullness and satisfaction; rather, it is consumption of a certain weight of food. Foods that are low in energy density have more volume and bulk—that is, they are relatively heavy but have few calories (see Table 14.3). For example, for the same 100 calories, you could eat 21 baby carrots or 4 pretzel twists; you are more likely to feel full after eating the serving of carrots because it weighs 10 times as much as the serving of pretzels (10 ounces versus 1 ounce).

As you decrease foods high in energy density, increase foods high in nutrient density—foods that are low in calories and high in nutrients. For example, fresh fruits and vegetables, with their high water and fiber content, are low in calories and high in nutrients, as are whole-grain foods. Fresh fruits contain fewer calories and more fiber than fruit juices or drinks. Strategies

Table 14.3	Examples of Foods Low in Energy Density	
FOOD	**AMOUNT**	**CALORIES**
Carrot, raw	1 medium	25
Popcorn, air popped	2 cups	62
Apple	1 medium	72
Vegetable soup	1 cup	72
Plain instant oatmeal	½ cup	80
Fresh blueberries	1 cup	80
Corn on the cob (plain)	1 ear	80
Cantaloupe	½ melon	95
Light (fat-free) yogurt with fruit	6 oz.	100
Unsweetened applesauce	1 cup	100
Pear	1 medium	100
Corn flakes	1 cup	101
Sweet potato, baked	1 medium	120

Hunger isn't the only reason people eat. Efforts to maintain a healthy body weight can be sabotaged by eating related to other factors, including emotions, environment, and patterns of thinking. This quiz is designed to provide you with a score for five factors that describe many people's eating habits. This information will put you in a better position to manage your eating behavior and control your weight. Circle the number that indicates to what degree each situation is likely to make you start eating.

	Very Unlikely								Very Likely	

Social

1. Arguing or having a conflict with someone
2. Being with others when they are eating
3. Being urged to eat by someone else
4. Feeling inadequate around others

1	2	3	4	5	6	7	8	9	10
1	2	3	4	5	6	7	8	9	10
1	2	3	4	5	6	7	8	9	10
1	2	3	4	5	6	7	8	9	10

Emotional

5. Feeling bad, such as being anxious or depressed
6. Feeling good, happy, or relaxed
7. Feeling bored or having time on my hands
8. Feeling stressed or excited

1	2	3	4	5	6	7	8	9	10
1	2	3	4	5	6	7	8	9	10
1	2	3	4	5	6	7	8	9	10
1	2	3	4	5	6	7	8	9	10

Situational

9. Seeing an advertisement for food or eating
10. Passing by a bakery, cookie shop, or other enticement to eat
11. Being involved in a party, celebration, or special occasion
12. Eating out

1	2	3	4	5	6	7	8	9	10
1	2	3	4	5	6	7	8	9	10
1	2	3	4	5	6	7	8	9	10
1	2	3	4	5	6	7	8	9	10

Thinking

13. Making excuses to myself about why it's OK to eat
14. Berating myself for being fat or unable to control my eating
15. Worrying about others or about difficulties I'm having
16. Thinking about how things should or shouldn't be

1	2	3	4	5	6	7	8	9	10
1	2	3	4	5	6	7	8	9	10
1	2	3	4	5	6	7	8	9	10
1	2	3	4	5	6	7	8	9	10

Physiological

17. Experiencing pain or physical discomfort
18. Experiencing trembling, headache, or light-headedness associated with not eating or too much caffeine
19. Experiencing fatigue or feeling overtired
20. Experiencing hunger pangs or urges to eat, even though I've eaten recently

1	2	3	4	5	6	7	8	9	10
1	2	3	4	5	6	7	8	9	10
1	2	3	4	5	6	7	8	9	10
1	2	3	4	5	6	7	8	9	10

Scoring

Total your scores for each category, and enter them below. Then rank the scores by marking the highest score 1, next highest score 2, and so on. Focus on the highest-ranked categories first, but any score above 24 is high and indicates that you need to work on that category.

Category	Total Score	Rank Order
Social (items 1–4)	_____	_____
Emotional (items 5–8)	_____	_____
Situational (items 9–12)	_____	_____
Thinking (items 13–16)	_____	_____
Physiological (items 17–20)	_____	_____

What Your Score Means

Social   A high score here means you are very susceptible to the influence of others. Work on better ways to communicate more assertively, handle conflict, and manage anger. Challenge your beliefs about the need to be polite and the obligations you feel you must fulfill.

Emotional   A high score here means you need to develop effective ways to cope with emotions. Work on developing skills in stress management, time management, and communication. Practicing positive but realistic self-talk can help you handle small daily upsets.

Situational   A high score here means you are especially susceptible to external influences. Try to avoid external cues and respond differently to those you cannot avoid. Control your environment by changing the way you buy, store, cook, and serve food. Anticipate potential problems, and have a plan for handling them.

Thinking   A high score here means that the way you think—how you talk to yourself, the beliefs you hold, your memories, and your expectations—has a powerful influence on your eating habits. Try to be less self-critical, less perfectionistic, and more flexible in your ideas about the way things ought to be. Recognize when you're making excuses or rationalizations that allow you to eat.

Physiological   A high score here means that the way you eat, what you eat, or medications you are taking may be affecting your eating behavior. You may be eating to reduce physical arousal or deal with physical discomfort. Try eating three meals a day, supplemented with regular snacks if needed. Avoid too much caffeine. If any medication you're taking produces adverse physical reactions, switch to an alternative, if possible. If your medications may be affecting your hormone levels, discuss possible alternatives with your physician.

SOURCE: "What Triggers Your Eating?" Adapted from Nash, J.D. 1997. *The New Maximize Your Body Potential*. Boulder, CO: Bull Publishing. Reprinted by permission.

CRITICAL CONSUMER
Evaluating Fat and Sugar Substitutes

Foods made with fat and sugar substitutes are often promoted for weight loss. But what are fat and sugar substitutes? And can they really contribute to weight management?

Fat Substitutes

A variety of substances are used to replace fats in processed foods and other products. Some contribute calories, protein, fiber, or other nutrients; others do not. Fat replacers fall into three general categories:

• *Carbohydrate-based fat replacers* are often found in dairy and meat products, baked goods, salad dressings, and many other prepared foods. Oatrim, Z-trim, and Nu-trim are made from types of dietary fiber that may actually lower cholesterol levels. Carbohydrate-based fat replacers contribute 0–4 calories per gram.

• *Protein-based fat replacers* are typically made from milk, egg whites, soy, or whey; trade names include Simplesse, Dairy-lo, and Supro. They are used in cheese, sour cream, mayonnaise, margarine spreads, frozen desserts, salad dressings, and baked goods. Protein-based fat replacers typically contribute 1–4 calories per gram.

• *Fat-based fat replacers.* Some of these compounds are not absorbed well by the body and so provide fewer calories per gram (5 calories compared with the standard 9 for fats); others are impossible for the body to digest and so contribute no calories at all. Olestra, marketed under the trade name Olean and used in fried snack foods, is an example of the latter type of compound.

ACTIVITY
DO IT ONLINE

Nonnutritive Sweeteners and Sugar Alcohols

Sugar substitutes are often referred to as nonnutritive sweeteners because they provide no calories or essential nutrients. The FDA has approved five types of nonnutritive sweeteners for use in the United States: acesulfame-K (Sunett, Sweet One), aspartame (NutraSweet, Equal, NatraTaste), saccharin (Sweet 'N Low), sucralose (Splenda), and neotame. They are used in beverages, desserts, baked goods, yogurt, chewing gum, and products such as toothpaste, mouthwash, and cough syrup. Another sweetener, stevia, is an extract of a South American shrub.

Sugar alcohols are made by altering the chemical form of sugars extracted from fruits and other plant sources; the best known of these sorbitol. Sugar alcohols provide 0.2–2.5 calories per gram, compared to 4 calories per gram in standard sugar. They have typically been used to sweeten sugar-free candies but are now being added to many sweet foods that are promoted as low-carbohydrate products, often combined with other sweeteners.

Fat and Sugar Substitutes in Weight Management

Whether fat and sugar substitutes help you achieve and maintain a healthy weight depends on your overall eating and activity habits. The increase in the availability of fat-free and sugar-free foods in the United States has *not* been associated with a drop in calorie consumption. Reduced-fat foods often contain extra sugar to improve the taste and texture lost when fat is removed, so such foods may be as high or even higher in total calories than their fattier counterparts. If you consume low-fat, no-sugar-added ice cream instead of regular ice cream, you may save calories.

Finally, many of the foods containing fat and sugar substitutes are low-nutrient snack foods. Fruits, vegetables, and whole grains are healthier snack choices.

---

for lowering the energy density of your diet while at the same time increasing its nutrient density include the following:

• Eat fruit with breakfast and for dessert.

• Add extra vegetables to sandwiches, casseroles, stir-fry dishes, pizza, pasta dishes, and fajitas.

• Start meals with a bowl of broth-based soup; include a green salad or fruit salad.

• Snack on fresh fruits and vegetables rather than crackers, chips, or other energy-dense snack foods.

Limit serving sizes of energy-dense foods such as butter, mayonnaise, cheese, chocolate, fatty meats, croissants, and snack foods that are fried, are high in added sugars (including reduced-fat products), or contain trans fats.

It is also important to watch out for processed foods, which can be high in fat and sodium. Even processed foods labeled "fat-free" or "reduced fat" may be high in calories; such products

may contain sugar and fat substitutes (see the box "Evaluating Fat and Sugar Substitutes"). Stick to the calorie and nutrient recommendations offered by the Dietary Guidelines for Americans, MyPlate, or the DASH Eating Plan (see Chapter 12).

Eating Habits Equally important to weight management is the habit of eating regular meals daily, including breakfast and snacks. Skipping meals leads to excessive hunger, feelings of deprivation, and increased vulnerability to binge eating or unhealthy snacking. In addition to establishing a regular pattern of eating, set some rules to govern your food choices. Rules for breakfast might be these, for example: Choose a high-fiber cereal that is low in added sugar with fat-free milk on most days; save pancakes and waffles for special occasions unless they are whole-grain. For effective weight management, it is better to consume the majority of calories during the day when your activity levels are higher rather than in the evening.

If you gaze into the mirror and wish you could change the way your body looks, consider getting some exercise—not to reshape your contours but to firm up your body image and enhance your self-esteem. Adults who participate in exercise programs not only improve their fitness but also benefit psychologically in mood, self-concept, and reduced anxiety. People who exercise regularly often gain a sense of mastery and competence that enhances their self-esteem and body image. In addition, exercise contributes to a more toned look, which many adults prefer.

Research suggests that physically active people are more comfortable with their bodies and with their body image than sedentary people are. For example, employees asked to complete a 36-session stretching program to prevent muscle strains at work improved not only in measurements of flexibility but also in perception of their bodies and overall sense of self-worth.

Similar results have been found in middle-aged people at risk for heart disease randomly assigned to one of four groups: diet, diet plus exercise, exercise, and no intervention. The greater the participation of individuals was in the exercise component of the program, the higher were their scores in perceived competence, self-esteem, and coping.

Decreeing some foods off-limits generally sets up a rule to be broken. A more sensible principle is "everything in moderation." If a particular food becomes troublesome, place it off-limits until you gain control over it. The ultimate goal is to eat in moderation; no foods need to be entirely off-limits, though some should be eaten judiciously.

Physical Activity and Exercise

Regular physical activity is another important lifestyle factor in weight management (see Chapter 13). Physical activity and exercise burn calories and keep the metabolism geared to using food for energy instead of storing it as fat. Exercise has a positive effect on metabolism. When people exercise, they slightly increase the number of calories their bodies burn at rest (resting metabolic rate). They also increase their muscle mass, which is associated with a higher metabolic rate. The exercise itself also burns calories, raising total energy expenditure. The higher the energy expenditure, the more the person can eat without gaining weight.

Making significant cuts in food intake to lose weight is a difficult strategy to maintain; increasing your physical activity is a better approach. Regular physical activity protects against weight gain, is essential for maintaining weight loss, and improves quality of life (see the box "Exercise, Body Image, and Self-Esteem"). The sooner you establish good habits, the better. The key to success is making exercise an integral part of the lifestyle you can enjoy now and in the future.

> For weight management, it's **better to have the majority of calories during the day** rather than in the evening.

Thinking and Emotions

The way you think about yourself and your world influences, and is influenced by, how you feel and how you act. In fact, research on people who have a weight problem indicates that low self-esteem and the negative emotions that accompany it are significant problems. Often people with low self-esteem mentally compare the actual self to an internally held picture of an "ideal self," an image based on perfectionistic goals and beliefs about how they and others should be. The more these two pictures differ, the larger the impact on self-esteem and the more likely the presence of negative emotions.

Besides the internal picture we carry of ourselves, all of us carry on an internal dialogue about events happening to us and around us. This *self-talk* can be self-deprecating or positively motivating, depending on our beliefs and attitudes. Having realistic beliefs and goals, and practicing positive self-talk and problem solving, support a healthy lifestyle.

Ask Yourself

?

QUESTIONS FOR CRITICAL THINKING AND REFLECTION

Have you ever used food as an escape when you were stressed out or distraught? Were you aware of what you were doing at the time? How can you avoid using food as a coping mechanism in the future?

TAKE CHARGE
Lifestyle Strategies for Successful Weight Management

Food Choices

- Follow the recommendations in MyPlate for eating a moderate, varied diet. Focus on making good choices from each food group.

- Favor foods with a high nutrient density.

- Check food labels for serving sizes, calories, and nutrient levels. Watch for hidden calories.

- Drink fewer calories in the form of sugar-sweetened beverages such as soda, fruit drinks, sports drinks, alcohol, and specialty coffees and teas.

- For problem foods, try eating small amounts under controlled conditions. Go out for a scoop of ice cream, for example, rather than buying half a gallon for your freezer.

Planning and Serving

- Keep a log of what you eat. Individuals who keep a log are more successful in weight loss programs.

- Eat regular meals and snacks daily, *including breakfast,* to distribute calories throughout your day.

- Consume the majority of your daily calories during the day, not in the evening.

- Pay special attention to portion sizes. Use measuring cups and spoons and a food scale until you become familiar with appropriate portion sizes.

- When you eat, just eat—don't do anything else, such as reading, using the computer, or watching TV.

- Avoid late-night eating—a behavior specifically associated with weight gain among college students.

- Eat slowly and stop before you are stuffed. It takes time for your brain to get the message that your stomach is full. Take small bites and chew food thoroughly and enjoy your food.

Special Occasions

- When you eat out, choose a restaurant where you can make healthy food choices. If portion sizes are large, take half your food home for a meal later in the week.

- Focus on the occasion and the people, not the food.

- If you cook a large meal for friends, send leftovers home with your guests or freeze them for later.

Physical Activity and Stress Management

- Increase your level of daily physical activity.

- Begin a formal exercise program that includes cardiorespiratory endurance exercise, strength training, and stretching.

- Develop techniques for handling stress that don't involve food. (See Chapter 2 for more about stress management.)

- Develop strategies for coping with nonhunger cues to eat, such as boredom, sleepiness, or anxiety. Try calling a friend, taking a shower, or going for a short walk.

- Tell family members and friends that you're changing your eating and exercise habits. Ask them to be supportive.

For more tips, visit the Let's Move website (www.letsmove.gov).

Coping Strategies

Appropriate coping strategies help you deal with the stresses of life; they are also an important lifestyle factor in weight management. Many people use eating as a way to cope; others may cope by turning to drugs, alcohol, smoking, or gambling. Those who overeat might use food to alleviate loneliness or to serve as a pickup for fatigue, as an antidote to boredom, or as a distraction from problems. Some people even overeat to punish themselves for real or imagined transgressions.

Those who recognize that they are misusing food in such ways can analyze their eating habits with fresh eyes. They can consciously attempt to find new coping strategies and begin to use food appropriately—to fuel life's activities, to foster growth, and to bring pleasure, but *not* as a way to manage stress. For a summary of the components of weight management through healthy lifestyle choices, see the box "Lifestyle Strategies for Successful Weight Management."

APPROACHES TO OVERCOMING A WEIGHT PROBLEM

Americans spend approximately $62 billion on weight loss efforts every year, including diet plans, diet products, and health club memberships. If you are overweight, you may already be creating a plan to lose weight and keep it off. You have many options.

Doing It Yourself

If you need to lose weight, focus on adopting the healthy lifestyle described throughout this book. The right weight for you will naturally evolve, and you won't have to diet. Combine modest cuts in energy intake with exercise, and avoid very low-calorie diets. (In general, a low-calorie diet should provide 1200–1500 calories per day.) By producing a negative energy balance of 250–1000 calories per day, you will produce the recommended weight loss of 0.5–2.0 pounds per week.

Don't try to lose weight more rapidly. Most low-calorie diets cause a rapid loss of body water at first. When this phase passes, weight loss declines. As a result, dieters are often misled into believing that their efforts are not working. They then give up, not realizing that smaller, mostly fat, losses later in the diet are actually better than the initial larger, mostly fluid losses. Reasonable weight loss is 8–10% of body weight over six months.

For many Americans, maintaining weight loss is a bigger challenge than losing weight. Most weight lost during a period of dieting is regained. When planning a weight management program, it is extremely important to include strategies that you can maintain over the long term, both for food choices and for physical activity. Weight management is a lifelong project. A registered dietitian or nutritionist can recommend an appropriate plan for you when you want to lose weight on your own. For more tips, refer to the "Behavior Change Strategy" section at the end of the chapter.

Diet Books

Many people who try to lose weight by themselves fall prey to one or more of the dozens of diet books on the market. Although some contain useful advice and motivational tips, most make empty promises. Accept books that advocate a balanced approach to diet plus exercise and sound nutritional advice, but reject any book that

- Advocates an unbalanced way of eating, such as a high-carbohydrate-only diet or a low-carbohydrate, high-protein diet, or that promotes a single food, such as cabbage or grapefruit.
- Claims to be based on a "scientific breakthrough" or to have the "secret to success."

- Uses gimmicks, such as matching eating to blood type, hyping insulin resistance as the single cause of obesity, or combining foods in special ways to achieve weight loss.
- Promises quick weight loss or limits food choices.

Many diets can cause weight loss if the diet is maintained; however, the real difficulty is finding a safe and healthy pattern of food choices and physical activity that results in long-term maintenance of a healthy body weight and reduced risk of chronic disease (see the box "Is Any Diet Best for Weight Loss?").

Dietary Supplements and Diet Aids

The number of dietary supplements and other weight loss aids on the market has also increased in recent years. Promoted in advertisements, magazines, direct mail campaigns, infomercials, and websites, these products typically promise a quick and easy path to weight loss. Most of these products are marketed as dietary supplements and so are subject to fewer regulations than over-the-counter (OTC) medications. According to the Federal Trade Commission, more than half of advertisements for weight loss products make representations that were likely to be false. And although the FTC will order companies to stop making baseless and bogus product claims when monitors become aware of them, consumers are urged to critically evaluate any product that sounds too good to be true.

The following sections describe some commonly marketed OTC products for weight loss.

Formula Drinks and Food Bars Canned diet drinks, powders used to make shakes, and diet food bars and snacks are designed to achieve weight loss by substituting for some or all of a person's daily food intake. However, most people find it difficult to use these products for long periods, and muscle loss and other serious health problems may result if they are used as the sole source of nutrition for an extended period. Use of such products sometimes results in rapid short-term weight loss, but the weight is typically regained because users don't learn to change their eating and lifestyle behaviors.

Herbal Supplements Most herbal weight loss products work by increasing urination (causing water loss); by stimulating the central nervous system (causing the body's activities to speed up or increasing metabolism); or by affecting levels of brain chemicals (causing appetite suppression). As described in Chapter 12, herbs are marketed as dietary supplements, so there is little information about effectiveness, proper dosage, drug interactions, or side effects. In addition, labels may not accurately reflect the ingredients and dosages present, and safe manufacturing practices are not guaranteed. Weight loss occurs only while the product is being taken.

> **QUICK STATS**
>
> A 16-ounce whole-milk latte has **265 calories**; beverages have a huge impact on calorie intake.
>
> —CDC, 2011

CRITICAL CONSUMER
Is Any Diet Best for Weight Loss?

Many popular weight loss plans promote specific food choices and macronutrient combinations. Research findings have been mixed, but two points are clear: total calorie intake matters, and the best diet is probably the one you can stick with.

Low-Carbohydrate Diets

Some low-carb diets advocate fewer than 10% of total calories from carbohydrates, compared to the 45–65% recommended by the Food and Nutrition Board. Some suggest daily carbohydrate intake below the 130 grams needed to provide essential carbohydrates in the diet. Low-carb diets that advocate switching to "healthy carbs" are better for you than the more extreme versions.

Low-Fat Diets

Many experts advocate diets that are relatively low in fat, high in carbohydrates, and moderate in protein. If you try a low-fat diet, high-carb diet, you still need to pay attention to the quality of the carbohydrates you consume, focusing on whole grains, and your total calorie intake. A low-fat diet is not a license to consume excess calories, even in low-fat foods.

High-Protein Diets

High-protein diets advocate high protein intake, moderate fat intake, and low carbohydrate intakes. These diets can be low in fiber, whole grains, vegetables, and fruits and so may lack some essential nutrients. Diets high in protein and saturated fat have been linked to an increased risk of heart disease, high blood pressure, and cancer. One study found that following a diet with a normal protein-to-carbohydrate ratio (1 gram of protein to 2 grams of carbohydrate) promoted more improvements in body fat, waist circumference, and waist-to-hip ratio than following either a low-protein diet (1 gram of protein to 4 grams of carbohydrate) or a high-protein diet (1 gram of protein to 1 gram of carbohydrate) and was probably superior in reducing long-term chronic disease risk.

How Do Different Diets Measure Up?

A study comparing weight loss among adults assigned to one of four reduced-calorie diets differing in percentages of protein, carbohydrate, and fat found that weight loss at two years was similar for all four diets (about 9 pounds). Weight loss was strongly associated with attendance at group sessions. Other studies have also found little difference in weight loss among popular reduced-calorie diets; most resulted in modest weight loss and reduced heart disease risk factors. The more closely people adhered to each diet, the more weight they lost.

Adding exercise helps people lose weight and improve disease risk factors. A study found that when overweight and obese people added exercise and weight loss to the DASH Eating Plan, they experienced greater reductions in blood pressure and greater improvements in insulin sensitivity and lipid levels than those who follow the DASH diet alone or regular diet plans.

Energy Balance Counts: The National Weight Control Registry

Future research may determine that certain macronutrient patterns are somewhat more helpful for disease reduction in people with particular risk profiles. In terms of weight loss, however, such differences among diets are likely overshadowed by the importance of total calorie intake and physical activity. Important lessons about energy balance can be drawn from the National Weight Control Registry—an ongoing study of people who have lost significant amounts of weight and kept it off. The average participant in the registry has lost 71 pounds and kept the weight off for more than five years. Nearly all participants use a combination of diet and exercise to manage their weight. This study illustrates that to lose weight and keep it off, you must decrease daily calorie intake and/or increase daily physical activity—and continue to do so over your lifetime.

SOURCES: Campbell, D. D., and K. A. Meckling. 2012. Effect of the protein: carbohydrate ratio in hypenergetic diets on metabolic syndrome risk factors in exercising overweight and obese women. *British Journal of Nutrition,* Jan 16: 1–14; Sacks, F. M., et al. 2009. Comparison of weight loss diets with different compositions of fat, protein, and carbohydrates. *The New England Journal of Medicine* 360: 859–873; Blumenthal, J. A., et al. 2010. Effects of the dietary approaches to stop hypertension diet alone and in combination with exercise and caloric restriction on insulin sensitivity and lipids. *Hypertension* 55(5): 1199–1205; Hill, J., and R. Wing. 2003. The National Weight Control Registry. *Permanente Journal* 7(3): 34–37.

ACTIVITY
DO IT ONLINE

The FDA has banned the sale of ephedra (*ma huang* in Chinese medicine), stating that it presented a significant and unreasonable risk to human health. Ephedrine, the active ingredient in ephedra, is structurally similar to amphetamine and was widely used in weight loss supplements. It may suppress appetite, but adverse effects have included elevated blood pressure, panic attacks, seizures, insomnia, and increased risk of heart attack or stroke, particularly when combined with another stimulant such as caffeine. The FDA banned the synthetic stimulant phenylpropanolamine for similar reasons. Other herbal stimulants still on the market are described in Table 14.4.

Other Supplements　　Fiber is another common ingredient in OTC diet aids, promoted for appetite control. Many diet aids contain only 3 or fewer grams of fiber, which does

Table 14.4	Ingredients Commonly Found in Weight Loss Products		
COMMON NAME	**USE/CLAIM**	**EVIDENCE/EFFICACY**	**SAFETY ISSUES**
Bitter orange extract (*Citrus aurantium*)	CNS stimulant	Limited evidence	Highly concentrated extracts may increase blood pressure; should not be used by people with cardiac problems
Caffeine	CNS stimulant; increases fat metabolism	Amplifies effects of ephedra	Generally considered safe; caution advised in caffeine-sensitive individuals
Garcinia cambogia	May interfere with fat metabolism or suppress appetite	Inconclusive evidence	Short-term use (<12 weeks) generally considered safe when used as directed
Green tea extract	Diuretic; increases metabolism	Limited evidence	Generally considered safe
Guarana	CNS stimulant; diuretic	Few clinical trials	Same as for caffeine; overdose can cause painful urination, abdominal spasms, and vomiting
Senna, cascara, aloe, buckthorn berries	Stimulant, laxative	Not effective for weight loss	Chronic use decreases muscle tone in large intestine, causes electrolyte imbalances, and leads to dependence on laxatives
Tea, kola, dandelion, bucho, uva-ursi, damiana, juniper	Diuretic	Not effective for weight loss	Chronic use can cause possible electrolyte imbalance in some people
Yerba mate	Stimulant, laxative, diuretic	Limited evidence	Long-term use as a beverage may increase risk of oral cancer

SOURCES: WebMD 2011. *Over-the-Counter and Herbal Remedies for Weight Loss* (http://www.webmd.com/diet/guide/herbal-remedies); Leslie, K. K. 2003. Herbal weight loss products: effective and appropriate? *Today's Dietitian* 5(8).

not contribute much toward the recommended daily intake of 25–38 grams. Other popular dietary supplements include conjugated linoleic acid, carnitine, chromium, pyruvate, calcium, B vitamins, chitosan, and a number of products labeled "fat absorbers," "fat blockers," and "starch blockers." Research has not found these products to be effective, and many have potentially adverse side effects.

Weight Loss Programs

Weight loss programs come in a variety of types, including noncommercial support organizations, commercial programs, websites, and clinical programs. All weight loss programs should encourage healthy behaviors that help you lose weight and that you can stick with every day. According to the NIH, safe and effective weight loss programs should include

- Healthy eating plans that reduce calories but do not exclude specific foods or food groups.
- Tips on ways to increase moderate-intensity physical activity.
- Tips on healthy habits that also keep your cultural needs in mind, such as lower-fat versions of your favorite foods.
- Slow and steady weight loss. Depending on your starting weight, experts recommend losing weight at a rate of ½ to 2 pounds per week.

- A recommendation for medical evaluation and care if you have health problems, are taking medication, or are planning to follow a special formula diet that requires monitoring by a doctor.
- A plan to keep the weight off after you have lost it.

Noncommercial Weight Loss Programs Noncommercial programs such as TOPS (Take Off Pounds Sensibly) and Overeaters Anonymous (OA) mainly provide group support. They do not advocate any particular diet but do recommend seeking professional advice for creating an individualized plan. Like Alcoholics Anonymous, OA is a 12-step program with a spiritual orientation that promotes abstinence from compulsive overeating. These types of programs are generally free. Your physician or a registered dietitian can also provide information and support for weight loss.

Commercial Weight Loss Programs Commercial weight loss programs typically provide group support, nutrition education, physical activity recommendations, and behavior modification advice. Some also make available packaged foods to assist in following dietary advice.

In addition to the features of a safe and effective program outlined earlier, commercial weight loss programs should provide information about all fees and costs, including those of supplements and prepackaged foods, as

Weight Watchers is one of the best-known commercial weight loss programs. Actor Jennifer Hudson lost 80 pounds and became a spokesperson for the program.

well as data on risks and expected outcomes of participating in the program. They should also have a registered dietitian on staff along with qualified counselors and health professionals.

A strong commitment and a plan for maintenance are especially important because only about 10–15% of program participants maintain their weight loss—the rest gain back all or more than they had lost. One study found that important predictors of weight loss and maintenance of weight loss in commercial programs include an increased intake of vegetables, fruit, and low-fat dairy products; decreased intake of sweets; and regular exercise. A strong predictor of weight gain was frequent television viewing.

Online Weight Loss Programs   Online diet websites have millions of subscribers worldwide. Most weight loss websites combine self-help with group support through chat rooms, bulletin boards, and e-newsletters. Many sites offer online self-assessment for diet and physical activity habits as well as a meal plan; some provide access to a staff professional for individualized help. Many are free, but some charge a weekly or monthly fee.

Research suggests that this type of program provides an alternative to in-person diet counseling and can lead to weight loss for some people. Studies found that people who logged onto Internet programs more frequently tended to lose more weight; weekly online contact proved most successful for weight loss. The criteria used to evaluate commercial programs can also be applied to Internet-based programs. In addition, make sure the program offers member-to-member support and access to staff professionals.

> **All prescription weight loss medications have potential side effects,** ranging from diarrhea to elevated blood pressure.

Clinical Weight Loss Programs   Medically supervised clinical programs are usually located in a hospital or other medical setting. Designed to help those who are severely obese, these programs typically involve a closely monitored very low-calorie diet. The cost of a clinical program is usually high, but insurance may cover part of the fee for those with obesity-related health problems.

Prescription Drugs

For a medicine to cause weight loss, it must reduce energy consumption, increase energy expenditure, and/or interfere with energy absorption. The medications most often prescribed for weight loss are appetite suppressants that reduce feelings of hunger or increase feelings of fullness. Appetite suppressants usually work by increasing levels of catecholamine or serotonin—two brain chemicals that affect mood and appetite.

All prescription weight loss drugs have potential side effects. Reported side effects include sleeplessness, nervousness, and euphoria, as well as increases in blood pressure and heart rate. Headaches, constipation or diarrhea, dry mouth, and insomnia are other side effects. If you are taking a prescription medication, discuss any concerns about side effects with your physician.

Most appetite suppressants are approved by the FDA only for short-term use. Some however, are approved for longer-term use, including sibutramine and orlistat (Xenical). Sibutramine's safety and efficacy record is good, but regular monitoring of blood pressure is required during therapy. Another type of weight loss drug works by blocking fat absorption in the intestines. Orlistat (Xenical) prevents about 30% of the fat in food from being digested. Similar to the fat substitute olestra, orlistat reduces the absorption of fat-soluble vitamins and antioxidants. Therefore, taking a vitamin supplement is highly recommended for people taking orlistat. Side effects include diarrhea, cramping, and other gastrointestinal problems if users do not follow a low-fat diet. Alli is an FDA-approved, lower-dose version of orlistat that is sold over the counter.

These medications work best in conjunction with behavior modification. Studies have generally found that appetite suppressants produce modest weight loss—about 5–22 pounds above the loss expected with nondrug obesity treatments. Individuals respond very differently, however, and some experience more weight loss than others. Unfortunately weight loss tends to level off or reverse after 4–6 months on a medication, and many people regain the weight they've lost when they stop taking the drug.

Prescription weight loss drugs are not for people who want to lose only a few pounds. The latest federal guidelines advise people to try lifestyle modification for at least six months before trying drug therapy. Prescription drugs are recommended only in certain cases: for people who have been unable to lose weight with nondrug options and who have a BMI over 30 (or over 27 if two or more additional risk factors such as diabetes and high blood pressure are present). For severely obese people who have been unable to lose weight by other methods, prescription drugs may provide a good option.

Surgery

It is estimated that 5.7% of adult Americans have a BMI greater than 40, qualifying them as extremely or "morbidly" obese. The number of severely obese people has nearly doubled in the last two decades. Extreme obesity is a serious medical condition that is often complicated by other health problems such as diabetes, heart disease, arthritis, and sleep disorders. Surgical intervention may be necessary as a treatment of last resort. According to the NIH, weight loss (bariatric) surgery is recommended for patients with a BMI greater than 40, or greater than 35 with obesity-related illnesses.

Due to the increasing prevalence of severe obesity, surgical treatment of obesity is growing worldwide. Obesity-related health conditions, as well as risk of premature death, generally improve after surgical weight loss. However, as with any surgery, gastric surgery is not without risks, including death. In the short term, the risks of gastric bypass surgery can include excessive bleeding, infection, reaction to anesthesia, blood clots, breathing problems, and leaks in the gastrointestinal system. Long-term complications can include bowel obstruction, diarrhea, nausea, vomiting, gallstones, and malnutrition. Bariatric surgery modifies the gastrointestinal tract by changing either the size of the stomach or how the intestine drains, thereby reducing food intake. Three common surgeries are the Roux-en-Y gastric bypass, the vertical sleeve gastrectomy, and the adjustable gastric banding procedure.

The *Roux-en-Y gastric bypass* surgery separates the stomach into two pouches. The smaller pouch is attached to the small intestine, and the larger one is bypassed. The procedure restricts food intake and reduces calorie absorption.

The **vertical sleeve gastrectomy** surgery removes approximately 80–85% of the stomach, leaving a new, smaller stomach shaped like a banana or garden hose. Like the bypass surgery, the procedure restricts food intake and causes the person to feel full after eating a small amount of food.

In the **adjustable gastric banding** procedure, commonly called the *Lap-Band*, an adjustable band is placed around the stomach to create a smaller stomach pouch. The band, which is filled with saline solution and can be tightened or loosened by adding or removing saline, ties off a portion of the stomach, restricting food intake. Results from the Lap-Band procedure may not be as significant as results from bypass surgery, in which part of the digestive system is rerouted. However, the Lap-Band procedure is often considered safer because it is less invasive, and patients generally have fewer complications. In mildly to moderately obese (BMI 30–35) adults, gastric banding surgery has been found to be more effective in reducing weight and improving quality of life than nonsurgical methods.

Liposuction Another procedure, *liposuction*, has become popular for removing localized fat deposits beneath the skin. This cosmetic procedure does not improve health the way weight loss does and involves considerable pain and discomfort.

> ## QUICK STATS
> **Most bariatric surgery patients can expect to lose 50% or more of their excess weight within two years of the procedure.**
> —Mayo Clinic, 2011

BODY IMAGE

As described earlier in the chapter, body image consists of perceptions, images, thoughts, attitudes, and emotions. Developing a positive body image is an important aspect of psychological wellness and an important component of successful weight management.

Severe Body Image Problems

Poor body image can cause significant psychological distress. A person can become preoccupied with a perceived defect in appearance, thereby damaging self-esteem and interfering with relationships. Adolescents and adults who have a negative body image are more likely to diet restrictively, eat compulsively, or develop some other form of disordered eating.

When one's dissatisfaction with his or her own body image becomes extreme, the condition is called *body dysmorphic disorder (BDD)*. BDD affects about 2% of Americans, males and females in equal numbers; BDD usually begins before age 18 but can begin in adulthood. Sufferers are overly

> ## Ask Yourself ?
> ### QUESTIONS FOR CRITICAL THINKING AND REFLECTION
> Why do you think people continue to buy into fad diets and weight loss gimmicks, even though they are constantly reminded that the key to weight management is lifestyle change? Have you ever tried a fad diet or weight loss supplement? If so, what were your reasons for trying it? What were the results?

concerned with physical appearance, often focusing on slight flaws that are not obvious to others. Low self-esteem is common. Individuals with BDD may spend hours every day thinking about their flaws and looking at themselves in mirrors; they may desire and seek repeated cosmetic surgeries. BDD is related to obsessive-compulsive disorder and can lead to depression, social phobia, and suicide if left untreated. An individual with BDD needs to get professional evaluation and treatment. Medication and therapy can help people with BDD.

In some cases, body image may bear little resemblance to fact. A person suffering from the eating disorder anorexia nervosa typically has a severely distorted body image—she believes herself to be fat even when she has become emaciated (see the next section for more about anorexia). Distorted body image is also a hallmark of *muscle dysmorphia*, a disorder experienced by some bodybuilders and other active people who see themselves as small and out of shape despite being very muscular. Those who suffer from muscle dysmorphia may let obsessive exercise—particularly muscle-building exercise, such as weight training—interfere with their work and relationships. They may also use steroids and other potentially dangerous muscle-building drugs.

Acceptance and Change

There are limits to the changes that can be made to body weight and body shape, both of which are influenced by heredity. The changes that can and should be made are lifestyle changes, as described throughout this chapter.

Knowing when you've reached the limits of healthy change—and learning to accept those limits—is crucial for overall wellness. Women in particular tend to measure self-worth in terms of their appearance. When they don't measure up to an unrealistic cultural ideal, they see themselves as defective, and their self-esteem falls. The result can be negative body image, disordered eating, or even a diagnosable eating disorder. Women who view their bodies positively tend to be more intuitive eaters, relying on internal hunger and fullness cues to regulate what and how much they eat. They think more about how their bodies feel and function than how they appear to others.

> Knowing when you've **reached the limits of healthy change,** and accepting those limits, are crucial for overall wellness.

A balanced, realistic attitude toward weight management is part of overall wellness. Many healthy people do not fit society's image of ideal body size and shape.

Weight management needs to take place in a positive and realistic atmosphere. For an obese person, losing as few as 10 pounds can improve blood glucose control, reduce blood pressure and improve mood. The hazards of excessive dieting and overconcern about body weight need to be countered by a change in attitude. A reasonable weight must take into account a person's weight history, social circumstances, metabolic profile, and psychological well-being.

EATING DISORDERS

Problems with body weight and weight control are not limited to excessive body fat. A growing number of people, especially adolescent girls and young women, experience **eating disorders**—psychological disorders characterized by severe disturbances in body image, eating patterns, and eating-related behaviors. The major eating disorders are anorexia nervosa, bulimia nervosa, and binge-eating disorder. In the United States, almost 10 million females and 1 million males suffer from anorexia and bulimia, and millions more suffer from binge eating disorder. Many more people have abnormal eating habits and attitudes about food that disrupt their lives, even though these habits do not meet the criteria for a major eating disorder.

Many factors are probably involved in the development of an eating disorder. Although widely differing explanations

eating disorder A serious disturbance in eating patterns or eating-related behavior, characterized by a negative body image and concerns about body weight or body fat. **TERMS**

Ask Yourself

QUESTIONS FOR CRITICAL THINKING AND REFLECTION

Describe your own body image in the fewest words possible. What satisfies you most and least about your body? Do you think your self-image is in line with the way others see you?

have been proposed, they share one central feature: a dissatisfaction with body image and body weight. Such dissatisfaction is created by distorted thinking, including perfectionistic beliefs, unreasonable demands for self-control, and excessive self-criticism. Dissatisfaction with body weight leads to dysfunctional attitudes about eating, such as fear of fat and preoccupation with food, and problematic eating behaviors, including excessive dieting, constant calorie counting, and frequent weighing.

Heredity and the interaction of genes with environment appear to play an important role in the development of eating disorders. But as with other conditions, only the tendency to develop an eating disorder is explained by heredity; the expression of this tendency is affected by other factors. The home environment is one factor: families in which there is hostility, abuse, or lack of cohesion provide fertile ground for the development of an eating disorder. A rigid or overprotective parent can also increase the risk. Cultural messages, as well as family, friends, and peers, shape attitudes toward the self and others. Comparing oneself negatively with others can damage self-esteem and increase vulnerability. Young people who see themselves as lacking control over their lives are also at high risk for eating disorders. About 90% of eating disorders begin during adolescence. In recent years, however, cases of eating disorders have increased among children as young as 8.

Certain turning points in life, such as leaving home for college, often trigger an eating disorder. How a person copes with such stresses can influence risk, particularly in individuals who have few stress management skills. An eating disorder may become a means of coping: the abnormal eating behavior reduces anxiety by producing numbness and alleviating emotional pain. Restrictive dieting is another possible trigger for the development of eating disorders.

Anorexia Nervosa

A person with **anorexia nervosa** does not eat enough food to maintain a reasonable body weight. Anorexia affects 0.6% of Americans, only one-third of whom are receiving treatment. Although it can occur earlier or later, anorexia typically develops during puberty and the late teenage years, with an average age of onset of about 19 years.

Characteristics of Anorexia Nervosa   People with anorexia have an intense fear of gaining weight or becoming fat. Their body image is so distorted that even when emaciated they think they are fat. People with anorexia may engage in compulsive behaviors or rituals that help keep them from eating, though some may also binge and **purge.** They often use vigorous and prolonged exercise to reduce body weight as well. Although they may express a great interest in food, even taking over the cooking responsibilities for the rest of the family, their own diet becomes more and more restricted. People with anorexia often hide or hoard food without eating it.

People with anorexia are typically introverted, emotionally reserved, and socially insecure. They are often model

Exercise is a healthy practice, but people with eating disorders sometimes exercise compulsively, building their lives around their workouts. Compulsive exercise can lead to injuries, low body fat, and other health problems.

children who rarely complain and are anxious to please others and win their approval. Although school performance is typically above average, they are often critical of themselves and not satisfied with their accomplishments. For people with anorexia nervosa, their entire sense of self-esteem may be tied up in their evaluation of their body shape and weight.

Health Risks of Anorexia Nervosa   Because of extreme weight loss, females with anorexia often stop menstruating,

TERMS

anorexia nervosa   An eating disorder characterized by a refusal to maintain body weight at a minimally healthy level and an intense fear of gaining weight or becoming fat; self-starvation.

purging   The use of vomiting, laxatives, excessive exercise, restrictive dieting, enemas, diuretics, or diet pills to compensate for food that has been eaten and that the person fears will produce weight gain.

become intolerant of cold, and develop low blood pressure and heart rate. They develop dry skin that is often covered by fine body hair like that of a newborn. Their hands and feet may swell and take on a blue tinge.

Anorexia nervosa has been linked to a variety of medical complications, including disorders of the cardiovascular, gastrointestinal, endocrine, and skeletal systems. When body fat is virtually gone and muscles are severely wasted, the body turns to its own organs in a desperate search for protein. Death can occur from heart failure caused by electrolyte imbalances. About 1 in 10 women with anorexia dies of starvation, cardiac arrest, or other medical complications—the highest death rate for any psychiatric disorder. Depression is also a serious risk: about half the fatalities related to anorexia are suicides.

Bulimia Nervosa

A person suffering from **bulimia nervosa** engages in recurrent episodes of binge eating followed by purging. Bulimia is often difficult to recognize because sufferers conceal their eating habits and usually maintain a normal weight, although they may experience weight fluctuations of 10–15 pounds. Although bulimia usually begins in adolescence or young adulthood, it has begun to emerge at increasingly younger (11–12 years) and older (40–60 years) ages; the average age of onset is about 20 years.

Characteristics of Bulimia Nervosa   During a binge, a bulimic person may rapidly consume thousands of calories. This is followed by an attempt to get rid of the food by purging, usually by vomiting or using laxatives or diuretics. During a binge, bulimics feel as though they have lost control and cannot stop or limit how much they eat. Some binge and purge only occasionally; others do so many times every day.

People with bulimia may appear to eat normally, but they are rarely comfortable around food. Binges usually occur in secret and can become nightmarish—uncontrollably raiding the kitchen for food, going from one grocery store to another to buy food, or stealing food. During the binge, food acts as an anesthetic, blocking out feelings. Afterward, bulimics feel physically drained and emotionally spent. They usually feel deeply ashamed and disgusted with both themselves and their behavior and terrified that they will gain weight from the binge.

Major life changes such as leaving for college, getting married, having a baby, or losing a job can trigger a binge-purge cycle. At such times, stress is high and the person may have no good outlet for emotional conflict or tension. As with anorexia, bulimia sufferers are often insecure and depend on others for approval and self-esteem. They may hide difficult emotions such as anger and disappointment from themselves and others. Binge eating and purging become a way of dealing with feelings.

Health Risks of Bulimia Nervosa   The binge-purge cycle of bulimia places a tremendous strain on the body and can have serious health effects. Contact with vomited stomach acids erodes tooth enamel. Bulimic people often develop tooth decay because they binge on foods that are high in simple sugars. Repeated vomiting or the use of laxatives, in combination with deficient calorie intake, can damage the liver and kidneys and cause cardiac arrhythmia. Chronic hoarseness and esophageal tearing with bleeding may also result from vomiting. More rarely, binge eating can lead to rupture of the stomach. Although many bulimic women maintain normal weight, even a small weight loss to lower-than-normal weight can cause menstrual problems. And although less often associated with suicide or premature death than anorexia, bulimia is associated with increased depression, excessive preoccupation with food and body image, and sometimes disturbances in cognitive functioning.

Binge-Eating Disorder

Binge-eating disorder (BED) affects almost 3% of American adults. It is characterized by uncontrollable eating, usually followed by feelings of guilt and shame about weight gain. Common eating patterns are eating more rapidly than normal, eating until uncomfortably full, eating when not hungry, and preferring to eat alone. Binge eaters may eat large amounts of food throughout the day, with no planned mealtimes. Many people with binge-eating disorder mistakenly see rigid dieting as the only solution to their problem. However, rigid dieting usually causes feelings of deprivation and a return to overeating.

Compulsive overeaters rarely eat because of hunger. Instead food is used as a means of coping with stress, conflict, and other difficult emotions or to provide solace and entertainment. People who do not have the resources to deal effectively with stress may be more vulnerable to binge-eating disorder. Inappropriate overeating often begins during childhood. In some families, eating may be used as an activity to fill otherwise empty time. Parents may reward children with food for good

---

TERMS

bulimia nervosa   An eating disorder characterized by recurrent episodes of binge eating and purging—overeating and then using compensatory behaviors such as vomiting, laxatives, and excessive exercise to prevent weight gain.

binge-eating disorder   An eating disorder characterized by binge eating and a lack of control over eating behavior in general.

Ask Yourself   ?

QUESTIONS FOR CRITICAL THINKING AND REFLECTION

Do you know someone you suspect may suffer from an eating disorder? Does the advice in this chapter seem helpful to you? Do you think you could follow it? Why or why not? Have you ever experienced disordered eating patterns yourself? If so, can you identify the reasons for them?

Secrecy and denial are two hallmarks of eating disorders, so it can be hard to know if someone has anorexia or bulimia. Signs that someone may have anorexia include sudden weight loss, excessive dieting or exercise, guilt or preoccupation with food or eating, frequent weighing, fear of becoming fat despite being thin, and baggy or layered clothes to conceal weight loss. Signs that someone may have bulimia include excessive eating without weight gain, secretiveness about food (stealing, hiding, or hoarding food), self-induced vomiting (bathroom visits during or after a meal), swollen glands or puffy face, erosion of tooth enamel, and use of laxatives, diuretics, or diet pills to control weight.

- If you decide to approach a friend with your concerns, here are some tips to follow:

- Find out about treatment resources in your community (see the "For More Information" section for suggestions). You may want to consult a professional at your school clinic or counseling center about the best way to approach the situation.

- Arrange to speak with your friend in a private place, and allow enough time to talk.

- Express your concerns, with specific observations of your friend's behavior. Expect him or her to deny or minimize the problem and possibly to become angry with you. Stay calm and nonjudgmental, and continue to express your concern.

- Avoid giving simplistic advice about eating habits. Listen if your friend wants to talk, and offer your support and understanding. Give your friend the information you found about where he or she can get help, and offer to go along.

- If the situation is an emergency—if your friend has fainted, for example, or attempted suicide—call 911 for help immediately.

- If you are upset about the situation, consider talking to someone yourself. The professionals at the clinic or counseling center are there to help you. Remember, you are not to blame for another person's eating disorder.

behavior or withhold food as a means of punishment, thereby creating distorted feelings about the use of food.

Binge eaters are almost always obese, so they face all the health risks associated with obesity. In addition, binge eaters may have higher rates of depression and anxiety. To overcome binge eating, a person must learn to put food and eating into proper perspective and develop other ways of coping with stress and painful emotions.

Borderline Disordered Eating

Eating habits and body image run along a continuum from healthy to seriously disordered. Where an individual falls along that continuum can change depending on life stresses, illnesses, and many other factors. People with borderline disordered eating have some symptoms of eating disorders but do not meet the full diagnostic criteria for anorexia, bulimia, or binge-eating disorder. Behaviors such as excessive dieting, occasional bingeing or purging, or the inability to control eating turn food into the enemy and create havoc in the lives of millions of Americans.

How do you know if you have disordered eating habits? When thoughts about food and weight dominate your life, you have a problem. If you're convinced that your worth as a person hinges on how you look and how much you weigh, it's time to get help. Other danger signs include frequent feelings of guilt after a meal or snack, any use of vomiting or laxatives

QUICK STATS

Only about **34%** of people with anorexia, **43%** of those with bulimia, and **44%** of those with binge-eating disorders receive treatment.

—National Institutes of Mental Health Statistics

after meals, or overexercising or severely restricting your food intake to compensate for what you've already eaten.

If you suspect you have an eating problem, don't go it alone or delay getting help because disordered eating habits can develop into a full-blown eating disorder. Check with your student health or counseling center—nearly all colleges have counselors and medical personnel who can help you or refer you to a specialist if needed. If you are concerned about the eating habits of a family member or friend, refer to the suggestions in the box "If Someone You Know Has an Eating Disorder . . .".

Treating Eating Disorders

The treatment of eating disorders must address both problematic eating behaviors and the misuse of food to manage stress and emotions. Anorexia nervosa treatment first involves averting a medical crisis by restoring adequate body weight; then the psychological aspects of the disorder can be addressed. The treatment of bulimia nervosa or binge-eating disorder involves first stabilizing the eating patterns, then identifying and changing the patterns of thinking that led to disordered eating, and then improving coping skills. Concurrent problems, such as depression, anxiety, and other mental disorders may be present and must also be addressed. A 2012 study found that body dysmorphic disorder, involving an abnormal preoccupation with perceived defects in one or more body parts, was present in almost half of the patients with eating disorders.

Treatment of eating disorders usually involves a combination of psychotherapy and medical management. The therapy may be done individually or in a group; sessions involving the entire family may be recommended. A support or self-help group can be a useful adjunct to such treatment. Medical professionals, including physicians, dentists, gynecologists, and registered dietitians, can evaluate and manage the physical damage caused by the disorder. If a patient is severely depressed or emaciated, hospitalization may be necessary.

connect™

Connect to Your Choices

Have you ever thought about how you came to have the body weight and body composition you have? Many factors can influence our weight management choices, some not as obvious as others. Do you have easy access to high-calorie, high-fat snacks in your dorm or dining hall? Does your school provide transportation around campus, making it less appealing to walk to class? Does your TV or computer lure you into hours of sedentary entertainment?

What are the external factors that influence your choices about weight management? What are your inner motivations and core values, and how do they affect your choices? Based on what you learned in this chapter, will you make some different choices in the future? If so, what will they be?

Go online to Connect to complete this activity: www.mcgraw-hillconnect.com

TIPS FOR TODAY AND THE FUTURE

Many approaches work, but the simplest formula for weight management is moderate food intake coupled with regular exercise.

RIGHT NOW YOU CAN:

- Assess your weight management needs. Do you need to gain weight, lose weight, or stay at your current weight?
- List five things you can do to add more physical activity (not exercise) to your daily routine.
- Identify the foods you regularly eat that may be sabotaging your ability to manage your weight.

IN THE FUTURE YOU CAN:

- Make an honest assessment of your current body image. Is it accurate and fair, or is it unduly negative and unhealthy? If your body image presents a problem, consider getting professional advice on how to view yourself realistically.
- Keep track of your energy needs to determine whether your energy balance equation is correct. Use this information as part of your long-term weight management efforts.

SUMMARY

- Body composition is the relative amounts of fat-free mass and fat in the body. *Overweight* and *obesity* refer to body weight or the percentage of body fat that exceeds what is associated with good health.

- The key to weight management is maintaining a balance of calories in (food) and calories out (resting metabolism, food digestion, and physical activity).

- Standards for assessing body weight and body composition include body mass index (BMI) and percent body fat.

- Too much or too little body fat is linked to health problems; the distribution of body fat can also be a significant risk factor for many kinds of health problems.

- An inaccurate or negative body image is common and can lead to psychological distress.

- Genetic factors help determine a person's weight, but the influence of heredity can be overcome with attention to lifestyle factors.

- Physiological factors involved in the regulation of body weight and body fat include metabolic rate, hormonal influences, and the size and number of fat cells.

- Nutritional guidelines for weight management include consuming a moderate number of calories; limiting portion sizes, energy density, and the intake of fat, simple sugars, refined carbohydrates, and protein to recommended levels; and developing an eating schedule and rules for food choices.

- Activity guidelines for weight management emphasize daily physical activity and regular sessions of cardiorespiratory endurance exercise and strength training.

- Weight management requires developing positive self-talk and self-esteem, realistic weight and body composition goals, and a repertoire of appropriate techniques for handling stress and other emotional and physical challenges.

- People can be successful at long-term weight loss on their own by combining diet and exercise.

- Diet books, OTC diet aids and supplements, and formal weight loss programs should be assessed for safety and efficacy.

- Professional help is needed in cases of severe obesity; medical treatments include prescription drugs, surgery, and psychological therapy.

- Dissatisfaction with weight and shape are common to all eating disorders. Anorexia nervosa is characterized by self-starvation, distorted body image, and an intense fear of gaining weight. Bulimia nervosa is characterized by recurrent episodes of uncontrolled binge eating and frequent purging. Binge-eating disorder involves binge eating without regular use of compensatory purging.

FOR MORE INFORMATION

BOOKS

American Heart Association. 2011. *American Heart Association No-Fad Diet, 2nd Edition: A Personal Plan for Healthy Weight Loss.* New York: Clarkson Potter. *Provides guidelines for successful weight management.*

Costin, C., and G. S. Grabb. 2011. *8 Keys to Recovery from an Eating Disorder: Effective Strategies from Therapeutic Practice and Personal Experience.* New York: Norton. *A motivating description of the recovery process, written by two therapists who interweave their personal narratives with clinical strategies.*

Dillon, E. 2009. *Issues That Concern You: Obesity.* New York: Greenhaven Press. *A collection of perspectives on the causes of obesity, its management, and its impact on individuals and society.*

Fulda, J. 2008. *Half-Assed: A Weight-Loss Memoir.* Berkeley, CA: Seal Press. *A funny, inspiring memoir detailing how the author lost half her body weight, 186 pounds, while struggling with issues of identity, self-acceptance, and change.*

Gaesser, G. A., and K. Kratina. 2006. *It's the Calories, Not the Carbs.* Victoria, BC: Trafford. *Provides a detailed look at the facts behind successful weight loss by shunning fad diets and practicing sound energy balance.*

Mayo Clinic. 2012. *Mayo Clinic's Essential Diabetes Book,* 2nd ed. Rochester, MN: Mayo Clinic. *A user-friendly guide to diabetes.*

Samuelson, D. A., and A. D. Salzburg. 2011. *The Weight Loss Surgery Workbook: Deciding on Bariatric Surgery, Preparing for the Procedure, and Changing Habits for Post-Surgery Success.* Oakland, CA: New Harbinger Publications. *A step-by-step workbook that guides patients through the process of weight loss surgery; written by a psychologist and a physician.*

ORGANIZATIONS, HOTLINES, AND WEBSITES

American Diabetes Association. Provides information, a free newsletter, and referrals to local support groups; the website includes an online diabetes risk assessment.

http://www.diabetes.org

Calorie Control Council. This site includes a variety of interactive calculators, including an Exercise Calculator that estimates the calories burned from various forms of physical activity.

http://www.caloriecontrol.org

Centers for Disease Control and Prevention: Obesity. The home page for accessing all the CDC's information about overweight and obesity, their health risks, statistics, and diet and exercise.

http://www.cdc.gov/obesity/index.html

FDA Center for Food Safety and Applied Nutrition: Dietary Supplements. Provides background facts and information on the current regulatory status of dietary supplements, including compounds marketed for weight loss.

http://www.fda.gov/Food/DietarySupplements/default.htm

National Heart, Lung, and Blood Institute (NHLBI): Aim for a Healthy Weight. Provides information and tips on diet and physical activity, as well as a BMI calculator.

http://www.nhlbi.nih.gov/health/public/heart/obesity/lose_wt

National Institute of Diabetes and Digestive and Kidney Diseases (NIDDK): Weight-Control Information Network. Provides information and referrals for problems related to obesity, weight control, and nutritional disorders.

http://win.niddk.nih.gov

RESOURCES FOR PEOPLE CONCERNED ABOUT EATING DISORDERS

Eating Disorder Referral and Information Center

http://www.edreferral.com

Eating Disorders Coalition for Research, Policy and Action

http://www.something-fishy.org

MedlinePlus: Eating Disorders

http://www.nlm.nih.gov/medlineplus/eatingdisorders.html

National Association of Anorexia Nervosa and Associated Eating Disorders

630-577-1330 (help line)

http://www.anad.org

National Eating Disorders Association

800-931-2237

http://www.nationaleatingdisorders.org

National Institute of Mental Health: Eating Disorders

http://www.nimh.nih.gov/health/topics/eating-disorders/index.shtml

See also the listings in Chapters 12 and 13.

SELECTED BIBLIOGRAPHY

American Academy of Child and Adolescent Psychiatry. 2011. *Obesity in Children and Teens* (http://www.aacap.org/cs/root/facts_for_families/obesity _in_children_and_teens).

American Diabetes Association. 2011. *Diabetes Statistics* (http://www.diabetes .org/diabetes-basics/diabetes-statistics/).

Anderson, S. E., and R. C. Whitaker. 2009. Prevalence of obesity among US preschool children in different racial and ethnic groups. *Archives of Pediatrics and Adolescent Medicine,* 163(4): 344–348.

Campbell, I. C., J. Miller, R. Uher, and U. Schmidt. 2011. Eating disorders, gene–environment interactions, and epigenetics. *Neuroscience & Biobehavioral Reviews,* 35(3): 784–793.

Canfi, A., et al. 2011. Effect of changes in the intake of weight of specific food groups on successful body weight loss during a multi-dietary strategy intervention trial. *Journal of the American College of Nutrition,* 30(6): 491–501.

Centers for Disease Control and Prevention. 2011. *National Diabetes Fact Sheet: General Information and National Estimates on Diabetes and Prediabetes in the United States, 2011.* Atlanta: U.S. Department of Health and Human Services, Centers for Disease Control and Prevention.

Centers for Disease Control and Prevention. 2011. *Rethink Your Drink. Healthy Weight: It's Not a Diet, It's a Lifestyle* (http://www.cdc.gov/healthyweight /healthy_eating/drinks.html).

Centers for Disease Control and Prevention. 2012. *Genomics and Health: Genes and Obesity* (http://www.cdc.gov/genomics/resources/diseases/obesity /obesedit.htm).

Champagne, C. M., et al. 2011. Dietary intakes associated with successful weight loss and maintenance during the Weight Loss Maintenance trial. *Journal of the American Dietetic Association,* 111(12): 1826–1835.

Dingemans, A. E., Y. R. van Rood, I. de Groot, and E. F. van Furth. 2012. Body dysmorphic disorder in patients with an eating disorder: prevalence and characteristics. *International Journal of Eating Disorders,* 45(4): 562–569.

Drewnowski, A., and P. Eichelsdoerfer. 2010. Can low-income Americans afford a healthy diet? *Nutrition Today* 44(6): 246–249.

Federal Trade Commission. 2011. *Facts for Consumers: Dietary Supplements* (http://www.ftc.gov/bcp/edu/pubs/consumer/health/hea11.shtm).

Federal Trade Commission. 2011. *Facts for Consumers: Weighing the Evidence in Diet Ads* (http://www.ftc.gov/bcp/edu/pubs/consumer/health/hea03.shtm).

Flegal, K., et al. 2012. Prevalence of obesity and trends in the distribution of body mass index among U.S. adults, 1999–2010. *Journal of the American Medical Association,* 307(5): published online January 17.

Fleischhacker, S. E., et al. 2011. A systematic review of fast food access studies. *Obesity Reviews,* 12(5): e460–471.

Hill, A., et al. 2010. Infectious disease modeling of social contagion in networks. *PLoS Computational Biology,* November.

Hudson, J. I., E. Hiripi, H. G. Pope, and R. C. Kessler. 2007. The prevalence and correlates of eating disorders in the National Comorbidity Survey Replication. *Biological Psychiatry*, 61:348–358.

Karlamangla, A. S., et al. 2010. Socioeconomic and ethnic disparities in cardiovascular risk in the United States, 2001–2006. *Annals of Epidemiology* 20(8): 617–628.

Mata, J., et al. 2010. When weight management lasts: lower perceived rule complexity increases adherence. *Appetite* 54(1): 37–43.

Mayo Clinic. 2011. *Gastric Bypass Surgery* (http://www.mayoclinic.com/health /g.astric-bypass/MY00825/DSECTION=results).

Medscape. 2008. *Gastric Bypass Surgery May Be Effective for Weight Loss in Most Patients* (http://www.medscape.org/viewarticle/580560).

Ogden, C. L., et. 2010. Obesity and socioeconomic status in adults: United States, 2005–2008. *NCHIS Data Brief* 50: 1–8. (http://www.ncbi.nlm.nih .gov/pubmed/21211165).

Ogden, C. L., et al. 2010. Prevalence of high body mass index in US children and adolescents, 2007–2008. *Journal of the American Medical Association* 303(3): 242–249.

Ogden, C. L., and M. D. Carroll. 2011. *Prevalence of Overweight, Obesity, and Extreme Obesity among Adults: United States, Trends 1960–1962 through 2007–2008* (http://www.cdc.gov/nchs/data/hestat/obesity_adult_07 _08/obesity_adult_07_08.htm).

Ogden, C. L., et al. 2012. Prevalence of obesity in the United States, 2009–2010. NCHS Data Brief, No. 82 (http://www.cdc.gov/nchs/data/databriefs /db82.pdf).

Olshansky, S. J., et al. 2005. A potential decline in life expectancy in the United States in the 21st century. *New England Journal of Medicine* 352(11): 1138–1145.

Sax, H. C. 2011. Selecting the "best" weight loss procedure: more may be better. *Archives of Surgery* 146(2): 155.

Schmidt, M. E., et al. 2012. Systematic review of effective strategies for reducing screen time among young children. *Obesity*, 5 January, epub ahead of print (http:// www.nature.com/oby/journal/vaop/ncurrent/full/oby2011348a.html).

Slevec, J. H., and M. Tiggerman. 2011. Predictors of body dissatisfaction and disordered eating in middle-aged women. *Clinical Psychology Review*, 31(4): 515–524.

Tsai, A. G., and T. A. Wadden. 2005. Systematic review: an evaluation of major commercial weight loss programs in the United States. *Annals of Internal Medicine* 142(1): 56–66.

Urquhart, C. S., and T. V. Mihalynuk. 2011. Disordered eating in women: implications for the obesity pandemic. *Canadian Journal of Dietetic Practice and Research* 72(1): e115–125.

U.S. Department of Agriculture and U.S. Department of Health and Human Services. 2011. *Dietary Guidelines for Americans, 2010.* 7th ed. Washington, DC: U.S. Government Printing Office.

U.S. Department of Health and Human Services. 2012. *Healthy People 2020: Nutrition and Weight Status* (http://healthypeople.gov/2020/ topicsobjectives2020/overview.aspx?topicid=29).

Wang, Y., and M. A. Beydoun. 2007. The obesity epidemic in the United States—gender, age, socioeconomic, racial/ethnic and geographical characteristics: a systematic review and meta-regression analysis. *Epidemiologic Reviews* 29: 6–28.

The behavior management plan described in Chapter 1 provides an excellent framework for a weight management program. Following are some suggestions about specific ways you can adapt that general plan to controlling your weight.

Motivation and Commitment

Make sure you are motivated and committed before you begin. Failure at weight loss is a frustrating experience that can make it more difficult to lose weight in the future. Think about why you want to lose weight. Make a list of your reasons for wanting to lose weight, and post it in a prominent place.

Setting Goals

Choose a reasonable weight you think you would like to reach over the long term, and be willing to renegotiate it as you get further along. Break down your long-term weight and behavioral goals into a series of short-term action-oriented goals.

Creating a Negative Energy Balance

When your weight is constant, you are burning approximately the same number of calories as you are taking in. To tip the energy balance toward weight loss, you must consume fewer calories, or burn more calories through physical activity, or both. To generate a negative energy balance, it's usually best to begin by increasing activity level rather than decreasing your calorie consumption.

Physical Activity

Consider how you can increase your energy output simply by increasing routine physical activity, such as walking or taking the stairs. (Chapter 13 lists activities that use about 150 calories.) If you are not already involved in a regular exercise routine aimed at increasing endurance and building or maintaining muscle mass, seek help from someone who is competent to help you plan and start an appropriate exercise routine. If you are already doing regular physical exercise, evaluate your program according to the guidelines in Chapter 13.

Diet and Eating Habits

If you can't generate a large enough negative energy balance solely by increasing

physical activity, you may want to supplement exercise with modest cuts in your calorie intake. Your goal is to make small changes in your diet that you can maintain for a lifetime. Focus on cutting your intake of saturated and trans fats and added sugars and on eating a variety of nutritious foods in moderation. Don't skip meals, fast, or go on a very low-calorie diet or a diet that is unbalanced.

Making changes in eating habits is another important strategy for weight management. Refer to the box "Lifestyle Strategies for Successful Weight Management" for suggestions.

Self-Monitoring

Keep a record of your weight and behavior change progress. Try keeping a record of everything you eat. Write down what you plan to eat, in what quantity, *before* you eat. You'll find that just having to record something that is not OK to eat is likely to stop you from eating it. Also, keep track of your daily activities and your formal exercise program so you can monitor increases in physical activity.

Putting Your Plan into Action

- Examine the environmental cues that trigger poor eating and exercise habits, and devise strategies for dealing

with them. Anticipate problem situations, and plan ways to handle them more effectively.

- Create new environmental cues that will support your new healthy behaviors. Move fruits and vegetables to the front of the refrigerator.

- Get others to help. Talk to friends and family members about what they can do to support your efforts. Find a buddy to join you in your exercise program.

- Give yourself lots of praise and rewards. Focus attention to your accomplishments and achievements and congratulate yourself. Plan special nonfood treats for yourself, such as a walk or a movie. Reward yourself often and for anything that counts toward success.

- If you slip, don't waste time on self-criticism. Think positively instead of getting into a cycle of guilt and self-blame.

- Don't get discouraged. Be aware that although weight loss is bound to slow down after the first loss of body fluid, the weight loss at this slower rate is more permanent than earlier, more dramatic, losses.

- Remember that weight management is a lifelong project. You need to adopt reasonable goals and strategies that you can maintain over the long term.

Cardiovascular Health

After reading this chapter, you should be able to

- List the major components of the cardiovascular system and describe how blood is pumped and circulated throughout the body

- Describe the controllable and uncontrollable risk factors associated with cardiovascular disease

- Discuss the major forms of cardiovascular disease and how they develop

- List the steps you can take to lower your personal risk of developing cardiovascular disease

TEST YOUR KNOWLEDGE

1. Reducing the amount of cholesterol you eat is the most important dietary change you can make to improve your blood cholesterol levels.
   True or false?

2. Women are about as likely to die of cardiovascular disease as they are to die of breast cancer.
   True or false?

3. On average, how much earlier does heart disease develop in people who don't exercise regularly than in people who do?
   a. 6 months
   b. 2 years
   c. 6 years

4. Healthy teenagers have no signs of cardiovascular disease.
   True or false?

5. Which of the following foods would be a good choice for promoting heart health?
   a. Whole grains
   b. Salmon
   c. Bananas

ANSWERS

1. **FALSE.** Limiting your intake of saturated and trans fats, which promote the production of cholesterol by the liver, is the key dietary change for improving blood cholesterol levels; dietary cholesterol has much less effect on blood cholesterol.

2. **FALSE.** Nearly 1 in 3 American women die of cardiovascular disease; about 1 in 30 die from breast cancer.

3. **C.** Both aerobic exercise and strength training significantly improve cardiovascular health.

4. **FALSE.** Autopsy studies of young trauma victims show that narrowing of the arteries that supply the heart with blood begins in adolescence in many people.

5. **ALL THREE.** Whole grains (such as whole wheat), foods with omega-3 fatty acids (salmon), and foods high in potassium and low in sodium (bananas) all improve cardiovascular health.

Cardiovascular disease (CVD) affects more than 81 million Americans and is the leading cause of death in the United States, claiming one life every 38 seconds—nearly 2300 Americans every day. Heart attacks and strokes are the number-one and number-three causes of death, respectively, making them the most common life-threatening manifestations of CVD. Though we typically think of CVD as affecting primarily men and older adults, heart attack is the number-one killer of American women, and over 18% of CVD-related deaths occur in people under age 65.

CVD results largely from our way of life. Too many Americans eat an unhealthy diet, are overweight and sedentary, smoke, manage stress ineffectively, have uncontrolled high blood pressure or high cholesterol level, and don't know the signs of CVD. Not all the risk factors for CVD

are controllable—for example, family history of CVD increases your risk. But many key risk factors can be treated or modified, and you can reduce your overall risk of developing CVD.

This chapter introduces the workings of the cardiovascular system, explains CVD and its risks, and shows you how to keep your heart healthy for life.

THE CARDIOVASCULAR SYSTEM

The **cardiovascular system** consists of the heart and blood vessels. Together they move blood throughout the body (see page T2-2 of the color transparency insert "Touring the Cardiorespiratory System"). When the lungs are included, the system is known as the *cardiorespiratory* or *cardiopulmonary system*.

The Heart

The heart is a four-chambered, fist-sized muscle located just beneath the sternum (breastbone). It pumps deoxygenated (oxygen-poor) blood to the lungs and delivers oxygenated (oxygen-rich) blood to the rest of the body.

Blood actually travels through two separate circulatory systems. The right side of the heart pumps blood to the lungs in what is called **pulmonary circulation,** and the left side pumps blood through the rest of the body in the **systemic circulation.** The path of blood flow through the heart and cardiorespiratory system is illustrated on page T2-3 of the color transparency insert "Touring the Cardiorespiratory System." Refer to that illustration as you trace these steps:

1. Oxygen-poor blood travels through large vessels, the **venae cavae,** into the heart's right upper chamber, the right **atrium.**

2. After the right atrium fills, it contracts and pumps blood into the heart's right lower chamber, the right **ventricle.**

3. When the right ventricle is full, it contracts and pumps blood through the pulmonary artery into the lungs.

4. In the lungs, blood picks up oxygen and discards carbon dioxide.

5. The oxygenated blood flows from the lungs through the pulmonary veins into the heart's left atrium.

6. After the left atrium fills, it contracts and pumps blood into the left ventricle.

7. When the left ventricle is full, it pumps blood through the **aorta**—the body's largest artery—for distribution to the rest of the body's blood vessels.

Each heartbeat consists of two basic parts: diastole and systole. During **diastole,** the atria and ventricles relax and begin to fill with blood. At the end of diastole, the atria contract (atrial systole), which pumps blood into the ventricles. The atria then begin to relax. During **systole,** the ventricles contract (ventricular systole) to pump blood out of the heart.

Blood pressure, the force exerted by blood on the walls of the blood vessels, is created by the pumping action of the heart and the resistance of the blood vessels. This is an important concept because high blood pressure is treated by medicines that work on contraction as well as on the overall resistance of the blood vessels. Blood pressure is greater during systole than during diastole.

The heartbeat—the sequence of contractions of the heart's four chambers—is controlled by nerve impulses. These signals originate in a bundle of specialized cells in the right

QUICK STATS

Approximately **47 percent of adults** aged 18 and over have some form of CVD.
—CDC, 2012

Monitoring blood pressure is a key strategy for the prevention of CVD. Blood pressure can be measured by a health care professional during a health care visit or at home with a home blood pressure monitor.

TERMS

cardiovascular disease (CVD) The collective term for various diseases of the heart and blood vessels.

cardiovascular system The system that circulates blood through the body; consists of the heart and blood vessels.

pulmonary circulation The part of the circulatory system controlled by the right side of the heart: the circulation of blood between the heart and the lungs.

systemic circulation The part of the circulatory system controlled by the left side of the heart: the circulation of blood between the heart and the rest of the body.

vena cava Either of two large veins through which blood is returned to the right atrium of the heart (plural, *venae cavae*).

atrium Either of the two upper chambers of the heart in which blood collects before passing to the ventricles (plural, *atria*).

ventricle Either of the two lower chambers of the heart that pump blood to the lungs and other parts of the body.

aorta The large artery that receives blood from the left ventricle and distributes it to the body.

diastole The relaxation phase of the heart.

systole The contraction phase of the heart.

blood pressure The force exerted by the blood on the walls of the blood vessels, created by the pumping of the heart and the resistance of the blood vessels.

atrium called the *sinoatrial node* or *pacemaker.* This pacemaker produces a steady heart rate that can be speeded up or slowed down by a number of factors, including the brain's response to stimuli such as stress or the tissues' need for more oxygen.

The Blood Vessels

Blood vessels are classified by size and function. **Veins** carry blood to the heart. **Arteries** carry blood away from the heart. Veins have thin walls, but arteries have thick elastic walls that enable them to expand and relax with the volume of blood being pumped through them.

After leaving the heart, the aorta branches into smaller and smaller vessels. The smallest arteries branch still further into **capillaries**—tiny vessels with walls only one cell thick. The capillaries deliver oxygen- and nutrient-rich blood to the tissues and pick up oxygen-poor, carbon dioxide–laden blood. From the capillaries, this blood empties into small veins (*venules*) and then into larger veins that return it to the heart to repeat the cycle.

Blood pumped through the heart does not reach the cells of the heart, so the organ has its own network of arteries, veins, and capillaries. Two large vessels, the right and left **coronary arteries,** branch off the aorta and supply the heart muscle with oxygenated blood. (The coronary arteries are shown on page T2-3 of the color transparency insert "Touring the Cardiorespiratory System.") Blockage of a coronary artery is the leading cause of heart attacks.

RISK FACTORS FOR CARDIOVASCULAR DISEASE

Researchers have identified a variety of factors associated with an increased risk of developing CVD. They are grouped into two categories: major risk factors and contributing risk factors. Some risk factors are linked to controllable aspects of lifestyle and can therefore be changed. Others are beyond our control.

Major Risk Factors That Can Be Changed

The American Heart Association (AHA) has identified six major risk factors for CVD that can be changed: tobacco use, high blood pressure, unhealthy blood cholesterol levels, phys-ical inactivity, overweight and obesity, and diabetes. Most Americans, including young adults, have at least one major risk factor for CVD.

Tobacco Use Nearly one in five deaths is attributable to smoking. In 2010 an estimated 19.3 percent of American adults smoked, including 20.1 percent of those aged 18–24. Smoking remains the number-one preventable cause of CVD in the United States. People who smoke a pack of cigarettes a day have twice the risk of heart attack as nonsmokers; smoking two or more packs a day triples the risk. When smokers have heart attacks, they are two to three times more likely than nonsmokers to die from them. Cigarette smoking also doubles the risk of stroke.

Smoking harms the cardiovascular system in the following ways:

- It damages the lining of arteries.
- It reduces the level of high-density lipoproteins (HDL), or "good" cholesterol.
- It raises the levels of triglycerides and low-density lipoproteins (LDL), or "bad" cholesterol.
- Nicotine increases blood pressure and heart rate.
- The carbon monoxide in cigarette smoke displaces oxygen in the blood, reducing the amount of oxygen available to the body.
- Smoking causes **platelets** to stick together in the bloodstream, leading to clotting.
- Smoking speeds the development of fatty deposits in the arteries.

You don't have to smoke to be affected. The risk of developing heart disease increases up to 30% among those exposed to environmental tobacco smoke (ETS) at home or at work. Researchers estimate that about 46,000 nonsmokers die from heart disease each year as a result of exposure to ETS. (See Chapter 11 for more information about smoking.)

High Blood Pressure High blood pressure, or **hypertension,** is a risk factor for many forms of cardiovascular disease, including heart attacks and strokes, and is itself the most prevalent form of CVD.

Ask Yourself

QUESTIONS FOR CRITICAL THINKING AND REFLECTION

How often do you think about the health of your heart? Are there certain situations that make you aware of your heart rate, or make you wonder how strong your heart is?

TERMS

vein A vessel that carries blood to the heart.

artery A vessel that carries blood away from the heart.

capillary A small blood vessel that exchanges oxygen and nutrients between the blood and the tissues.

coronary artery One of the system of arteries branching from the aorta that provides blood to the heart muscle.

platelets Cells in the blood that are necessary for the formation of blood clots.

hypertension Sustained abnormally high blood pressure.

Smoking is a major risk factor for cardiovascular disease, doubling the risk for both heart attack and stroke.

Blood pressure, the force exerted by the blood on the vessel walls, is created by the pumping action of the heart and the resistance of the arteries. High blood pressure occurs when too much force is exerted against the walls of the arteries. Many factors affect blood pressure, such as exercise or excitement. Short periods of high blood pressure are normal, but chronic high blood pressure is a health risk.

Health care professionals measure blood pressure with a stethoscope and an instrument called a *sphygmomanometer*. At home you can track your own blood pressure by using an electronic blood pressure monitor. Blood pressure is expressed as two numbers—for example, 120 over 80—and measured in millimeters of mercury (mm Hg). The first number is the *systolic* blood pressure; the second is the *diastolic* blood pressure. A normal blood pressure reading for a healthy adult is below 120 systolic and below 80 diastolic, and CVD risk increases when blood pressure rises above that level. High blood pressure in adults is defined as equal to or greater than 140 over 90 (Table 15.1).

In about 90% of people with high blood pressure, the cause is unknown. This type of high blood pressure is called *primary* (or *essential*) *hypertension* and is probably due to a mixture of genetic and environmental factors, including obesity, stress, excessive alcohol intake, inactivity, and a high-fat, high-salt diet. In the remaining 10% of people, the condition is caused by an underlying illness and is referred to as *secondary hypertension*.

CAUSES High blood pressure results from an increased output of blood by the heart or from increased resistance to blood flow in the arteries. The latter condition can be caused by constriction of smooth muscle surrounding the arteries or by **atherosclerosis,** a disease process that causes arteries to become clogged and narrowed. (Atherosclerosis is discussed in detail later in this chapter.) Atherosclerosis also scars and hardens arteries, making them less elastic and further increasing blood pressure. When a person has high blood pressure, the heart must work harder than normal to force blood through the narrowed and stiffened arteries, straining both the heart and the arteries. Eventually the strained heart weakens and tends to enlarge, which can weaken it even more.

HEALTH RISKS High blood pressure is often called a silent killer because it usually has no symptoms. A person may have high blood pressure for years without realizing it. But during that time, it damages vital organs and increases the risk of heart attack, congestive heart failure, stroke, kidney failure, and blindness.

Recent research has shed new light on the importance of lowering blood pressure to improve cardiovascular health. The risk of death from heart attack or stroke begin to rise when blood pressure is above 115 over 75, well below the traditional 140 over 90 cutoff for a diagnosis of hypertension. People with blood pressure in the prehypertension range are at increased risk of heart attack and stroke as well as at significant risk of developing full-blown hypertension.

PREVALENCE Hypertension is common. About 30% of adults have hypertension, and 37% have prehypertension (defined as systolic pressure of 120–139 and/or diastolic pressure of 80–89). The incidence of high blood pressure increases with age, but it can occur among children and young adults, and women sometimes develop hypertension during pregnancy (blood pressure usually returns to normal following pregnancy). High blood pressure is two to three times more common in women taking oral contraceptives, especially in obese and older women; this risk increases with the duration of use. The rate of hypertension is highest in African Americans (41%). Among African Americans, compared with other groups, the disorder is often more

> **QUICK STATS**
>
> **33%** of Americans have high blood pressure; **20%** of them aren't aware of their condition.
>
> —CDC, 2010

TERMS

atherosclerosis A form of CVD in which the inner layers of artery walls are made thick and irregular by plaque deposits; arteries become narrow, and blood supply is reduced.

Table 15.1 Blood Pressure Classification for Healthy Adults

CATEGORY[a]	SYSTOLIC (mm Hg)		DIASTOLIC (mm Hg)
Normal[b]	below 120	and	below 80
Prehypertension	120–139	or	80–89
Hypertension[c]			
Stage 1	140–159	or	90–99
Stage 2	160 and above	or	100 and above

[a]When systolic and diastolic pressure fall into different categories, the higher category should be used to classify blood pressure status.

[b]The risk of death from heart attack and stroke begins to rise when blood pressure is above 115/75.

[c]Based on the average of two or more readings taken at different physician visits. In people older than 50, systolic blood pressure greater than 140 is a much more significant CVD risk factor than diastolic blood pressure.

SOURCE: *The Seventh Report of the Joint National Committee on Prevention, Detection, Evaluation, and Treatment of High Blood Pressure.* 2003. Bethesda, MD: National Heart, Lung, and Blood Institute. National Institutes of Health (NIH Publication No. 03-5233).

severe, more resistant to treatment, and more likely to be fatal at an early age.

TREATMENT Primary hypertension cannot be cured, but it can be controlled. Because hypertension has no early warning signs, it's crucial to have your blood pressure tested at least once every two years (more often if you have other CVD risk factors). In fact, experts now advise that anyone with hypertension or prehypertension monitor their own blood pressure several times each week. Self-monitoring is easy to do with a low-cost digital home blood pressure monitor. It is also important to follow your physician's advice about lifestyle changes and medication.

Lifestyle changes are recommended for everyone with prehypertension and hypertension. These changes include weight reduction, regular exercise, a healthy diet, and moderation of alcohol use. The DASH diet (see Chapter 12) is recommended specifically for people with high blood pressure. It emphasizes fruits, vegetables, and whole grains and increasing potassium and fiber intake. Even small increases in fruit and vegetable intake can create measurable drops in blood pressure.

Sodium restriction is also helpful for most people with hypertension. The 2010 Dietary Guidelines for Americans recommend restricting sodium consumption to less than 2,300 mg per day and to less than 1500 mg per day for people with hypertension, African Americans, and middle-aged and older adults.

Both sodium and chloride, the two consituents of table salt, have been shown to increase the risk of hypertension. Over the short term, dietary salt restriction has relatively modest effects on blood pressure; but over the course of several decades, the reduction may be far more significant, in part because salt restriction minimizes the normal rise in blood pressure associated with aging. In addition, certain groups appear to have more dramatic decreases in blood pressure as a result of salt restriction. These more salt-sensitive groups include older adults, African-Americans, obese individuals, people with metabolic syndrome, and those with chronic kidney disease. High dietary salt intake over many years probably plays a greater role in the development of hypertension in these groups.

Since approximately 80% of dietary salt in the American diet comes from the salt added in food and drink processing, the easiest way to achieve populationwide reduction is by lowering the amount of salt added by food processors. Reductions in supplemental salt in restaurant food have also been suggested.

A recent study demonstrated that reducing salt in the American diet would significantly reduce the number of new cases of coronary heart disease, stroke, and heart attack in the United States. The benefits of reduced salt intake were estimated to be similar to the benefits of populationwide reductions in tobacco use, obesity, and cholesterol levels.

Adequate potassium intake is also important. The recommended intake is 4.7 grams per day, which should be obtained through food. Supplements should be taken only when recommended by a physician because excessive levels of potassium can be lethal.

For people whose blood pressure isn't adequately controlled with lifestyle changes, medication is prescribed. Because many different types of antihypertensive drugs are available, physicians are usually able to find one that lowers blood pressure effectively with few side effects.

High Cholesterol *Cholesterol* is a fatty, waxlike substance that circulates through the bloodstream. It is an important component of cell membranes, sex hormones, vitamin D, the fluid that coats the lungs, and the protective sheaths around nerves. Adequate cholesterol is essential for the proper functioning of the body. Excess cholesterol, however, can clog arteries and increase the risk of CVD. There are two sources of cholesterol: your liver manufactures it, and you get it from the foods you eat.

GOOD VERSUS BAD CHOLESTEROL Cholesterol is carried in the blood in protein-and-lipid packages called **lipoproteins** (Figure 15.1). Two types of lipoproteins influence an individual's risk of heart disease:

• **Low-density lipoproteins (LDLs)** shuttle cholesterol from the liver to the organs and tissues that require it. LDL is known as "bad" cholesterol because if there is more than the

TERMS

lipoproteins Protein-and-lipid substances in the blood that carry fats and cholesterol; classified according to size, density, and chemical composition.

low-density lipoprotein (LDL) A lipoprotein containing a moderate amount of protein and a large amount of cholesterol, which tends to become deposited on artery walls and increase the risk of heart disease; "bad" cholesterol.

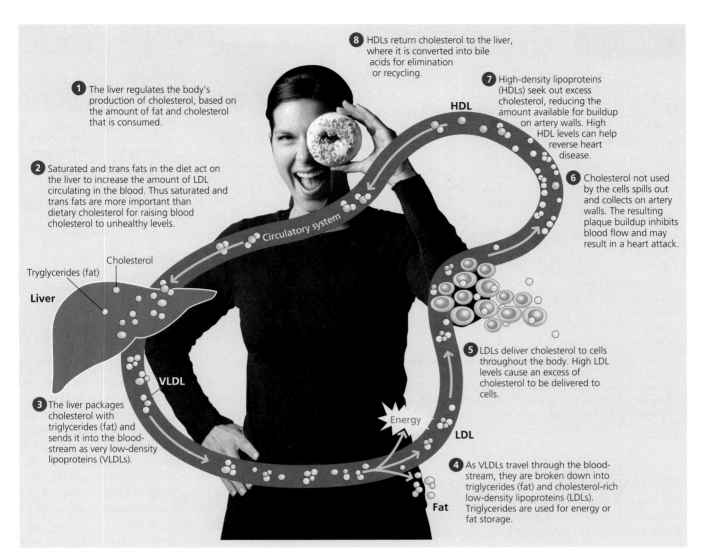

1 The liver regulates the body's production of cholesterol, based on the amount of fat and cholesterol that is consumed.

2 Saturated and trans fats in the diet act on the liver to increase the amount of LDL circulating in the blood. Thus saturated and trans fats are more important than dietary cholesterol for raising blood cholesterol to unhealthy levels.

Tryglycerides (fat)

Cholesterol

Liver

3 The liver packages cholesterol with triglycerides (fat) and sends it into the bloodstream as very low-density lipoproteins (VLDLs).

VLDL

Circulatory system

8 HDLs return cholesterol to the liver, where it is converted into bile acids for elimination or recycling.

HDL

7 High-density lipoproteins (HDLs) seek out excess cholesterol, reducing the amount available for buildup on artery walls. High HDL levels can help reverse heart disease.

6 Cholesterol not used by the cells spills out and collects on artery walls. The resulting plaque buildup inhibits blood flow and may result in a heart attack.

5 LDLs deliver cholesterol to cells throughout the body. High LDL levels cause an excess of cholesterol to be delivered to cells.

Energy

LDL

4 As VLDLs travel through the bloodstream, they are broken down into triglycerides (fat) and cholesterol-rich low-density lipoproteins (LDLs). Triglycerides are used for energy or fat storage.

Fat

FIGURE 15.1   Cholesterol in the body.

body can use, the excess is deposited in the blood vessels. LDL that accumulates and becomes trapped in artery walls may be oxidized by free radicals, speeding inflammation and damage to artery walls and increasing the likelihood of a blockage. If coronary arteries are blocked, the result may be a heart attack; if an artery carrying blood to the brain is blocked, a stroke may occur.

• **High-density lipoproteins (HDLs),** or "good" cholesterol, shuttle unused cholesterol back to the liver for recycling. By removing cholesterol from blood vessels, HDL helps protect against atherosclerosis.

high-density lipoprotein (HDL)   A lipoprotein containing relatively little cholesterol that helps transport cholesterol out of the arteries and thus protects against heart diseases; "good" cholesterol.   **TERMS**

RECOMMENDED BLOOD CHOLESTEROL LEVELS   The risk for cardiovascular disease increases with higher blood cholesterol levels, especially LDL (Table 15.2). The National Cholesterol Education Program (NCEP) recommends lipoprotein testing at least once every five years for all adults, beginning at age 20. The recommended test measures total cholesterol, LDL cholesterol, HDL cholesterol, and triglycerides (another blood fat). In general, high LDL, total cholesterol, and triglyceride levels, combined with low HDL levels, are associated with a higher risk for CVD. You can reduce this risk by lowering LDL, total cholesterol, and triglycerides. Raising HDL is important because a high HDL level seems to offer protection from CVD even in cases where total cholesterol is high. This appears to be especially true for women.

As shown in Table 15.2, LDL levels below 100 mg/dl (milligrams per deciliter) and total cholesterol levels below 200 mg/dl are desirable. An estimated 102 million American adults have total cholesterol levels of 200 mg/dl or higher

Table 15.2 — Cholesterol Guidelines

TOTAL CHOLESTEROL (mg/dl)

Less than 200	Desirable
200–239	Borderline high
240 or more	High

LDL CHOLESTEROL (mg/dl)

Less than 100	Optimal
100–129	Near optimal/above optimal
130–159	Borderline high
160–189	High
190 or more	Very high

HDL CHOLESTEROL (mg/dl)

Less than 40	Low (undesirable)
60 or more	High (desirable)

TRIGLYCERIDES (mg/dl)

Less than 150	Normal
150–199	Borderline high
200–499	High
500 or more	Very high

SOURCE: Expert Panel on Detection, Evaluation, and Treatment of High Blood Cholesterol in Adults. 2001. Executive Summary of the Third Report of the National Cholesterol Education Program (NCEP) Expert Panel on Detection, Evaluation, and Treatment of High Blood Cholesterol in Adults (Adult Treatment Panel III). *Journal of the American Medical Association* 285(19).

Table 15.3 — Prevalence of High Cholesterol in Adult Americans

	TOTAL CHOLESTEROL ≥ 200 mg/dl	TOTAL CHOLESTEROL ≥ 240 mg/dl
Both sexes	44.4%	15.0%
Males	41.8%	13.5%
Females	46.3%	16.2%
White males	41.2%	13.7%
White females	47.0%	16.9%
Black males	37.0%	9.7%
Black females	41.2%	13.3%
Mexican American males	50.1%	16.9%
Mexican American females	46.5%	14.0%

SOURCE: American Heart Association. 2012. *Heart Disease and Stroke Statistics, 2012 Update.* Dallas: American Heart Association.

(Table 15.3). Even though these tables define an optimal level, research now shows that levels of cholestrol as low as 60mg/dl have even better outcomes. Increasing data show that in certain populations, the lower the cholestrol levels, the better.

The CVD risk associated with elevated cholesterol levels also depends on other factors. For example, an above-optimal level of LDL would be of more concern for someone who also smokes and has high blood pressure than for someone without these additional CVD risk factors, and it is especially a concern for diabetics. For this reason, optimal levels (LDL <70mg/dl) for patients who have diabetes or have had a previous heart attack are much lower than those for people without these risk factors.

BENEFITS OF CONTROLLING CHOLESTEROL

People can cut their heart attack risk by about 2% for every 1% that they reduce their total blood cholesterol levels. People who lower their total cholesterol from 250 to 200 mg/dl, for example, reduce their risk of heart attack by 40%. Studies indicate that lowering LDL and raising HDL levels not only reduces the likelihood that arteries will become clogged but may also reverse deposits on artery walls.

Your primary goal should be to reduce your LDL to healthy levels. Important dietary changes for reducing LDL levels include increasing fiber intake and substituting unsat-

> Exercise is thought to be **the closest thing we have to a magic bullet** against heart disease.

urated for saturated and trans fats. Decreasing saturated and trans fats is particularly important because they promote the production of cholesterol by the liver. Exercising regularly and eating more fruits, vegetables, fish, and whole grains also help. Many experts believe that cholesterol-lowering foods may be most effective when eaten in combination, rather than separately. You can raise your HDL levels by exercising regularly, losing weight if you are overweight, quitting smoking, and altering the amount and type of fat you consume.

In recent years, a group of medications called statins have been shown to reduce total cholestrol levels and LDL. Statins dramatically reduce the risk of CVD in individuals with high cholesterol levels. These medications may also decrease CVD risk even in those without high cholesterol levels.

See Chapter 12 for detailed information about nutrition and guidelines for heart-healthy eating.

Physical Inactivity An estimated 40–60 million Americans are so sedentary that they are at high risk for developing CVD. Exercise is thought to be the closest thing we have to a magic bullet against heart disease. It lowers CVD risk by helping to decrease blood pressure and resting heart rate, increase HDL levels, maintain desirable weight, improve the condition of blood vessels, and prevent or control diabetes. One study found that women who accumulated at least three hours of brisk walking each week cut their risk of heart attack and stroke by more than 50%.

See Chapter 13 for detailed explanations of the benefits of physical activity and for help in creating your own exercise plan.

Obesity　As your weight increases, your risk of CVD increases. Death from CVD is two to three times more likely in obese people (BMI ≥ 30) than it is in lean people (BMI 18.5–24.9), and for every 5-unit increase in BMI, a person's risk of death from coronary heart disease increases by 30%. BMI at age 18 predicts mortality due to CVD—the higher your BMI at age 18, the more likely you are to eventually die from CVD. Maintaining a healthy weight is also important. Researchers found that middle-aged women who had gained 22 pounds or more since age 18 had a significantly higher risk of subsequent death from CVD than those who maintained their weight over time.

As explained in Chapter 14, excess body fat is strongly associated with hypertension, high cholesterol levels, insulin resistance, diabetes, physical inactivity, and increasing age. It is also associated with endothelial cell dysfunction and increased inflammatory markers (discussed later in this chapter). **Endothelial cells** line the inside of arteries, including the coronary arteries, and they help regulate blood flow to the heart and keep platelets and other cells from sticking to artery walls. When the endothelial cells are healthy, the coronary arteries dilate (widen) when the heart needs more blood; but when the cells are dysfunctional, the coronary arteries instead constrict, limiting blood flow to the heart. With excess weight, there is also more blood to pump and the heart has to work harder. This causes chronically elevated pressures within the heart chambers that can lead to ventricular **hypertrophy** (enlargement). Eventually the heart muscle can start to fail.

Physical activity and fitness have a strong positive influence on cardiovascular health in those who are overweight and obese. People who are obese but have at least moderate cardiorespiratory fitness may have lower rates of cardiovascular disease than their normal-weight but unfit peers. For someone who is overweight, even modest weight

> **QUICK STATS**
>
> **65% of people with diabetes die from CVD.**
> —American Heart Association, 2012

reduction—5–10% of body weight—can reduce CVD risk.

Diabetes　As described in Chapter 14, *diabetes* is a disorder characterized by elevated blood glucose levels due to an insufficient supply or inadequate action of insulin. Diabetes doubles the risk of CVD for men and triples the risk for women. The most common cause of death in adults with diabetes is CVD, and they usually die at younger ages than people without diabetes. There is an estimated loss of 5–10 years of life in those with diabetes.

People with diabetes have higher rates of other CVD risk factors, including hypertension, obesity, and unhealthy blood lipid levels (typically, high triglyceride levels and low HDL levels). The elevated blood glucose and insulin levels that occur in diabetes can damage the endothelial cells that line the arteries, making them more vulnerable to atherosclerosis. Diabetics also often have platelet and blood coagulation abnormalities that increase the risk of heart attack and stroke. People with prediabetes also face a significantly increased risk of CVD.

The number of people with diabetes (25.8 million) and prediabetes (79 million) continues to climb and is closely linked to obesity. It is estimated that for every kilogram (2.2 pounds) increase in weight, the risk of diabetes increases by approximately 9%. The largest increase in prevalence of type 2 diabetes over the past decade has been among people aged 30–39, and there has also been an alarming increase among children and adolescents. Children who are diagnosed with diabetes typically develop complications in their twenties or thirties.

Complications of diabetes affect mainly the arteries. When the larger arteries are affected, all forms of CVD may result, including heart attacks, strokes, and peripheral vascular disease. Having diabetes is considered to be a heart disease risk equivalent, meaning that your CVD morbidity and mortality risk is the same as if you already had coronary artery disease (CAD). Diabetics who have CAD fare even worse: they have accelerated atherosclerosis and benefit less from common forms of treatment than nondiabetics.

Routine screening for diabetes is not currently recommended unless a person has symptoms of diabetes or other CVD risk factors. In people with prediabetes, a healthy diet and exercise are more effective than medication at preventing diabetes. For people with diabetes, a healthy diet, exercise, and careful control of glucose levels are recommended to reduce the chances of developing complications. Even people

Overweight and obesity are major risk factors for cardiovascular disease, but physical activity, including walking, can lower that risk. Modest weight loss can also reduce CVD risk.

> **TERMS**
>
> **endothelial cells**　Cells lining the inside of arteries.
>
> **hypertrophy**　Abnormal enlargement of an organ.

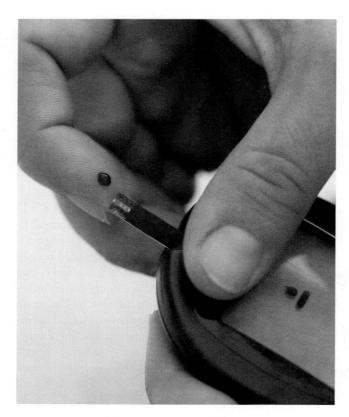

Blood glucose monitoring is important in managing diabetes and its associated risks.

difficult to identify any potential independent benefit of lowering triglyceride levels.

A full lipid profile should include testing and evaluation of triglyceride levels (see Table 15.2). For people with borderline high triglyceride levels, increased physical activity, reduced intake of added sugars, and weight reduction can help bring levels down into the healthy range. For people with high triglyceride levels, drug therapy may be recommended. Being moderate in the use of alcohol and quitting smoking are also important.

Insulin Resistance and Metabolic Syndrome When you consume carbohydrates, your blood glucose level increases. This stimulates the pancreas to secrete insulin, which allows body cells to pick up glucose to use for energy (see Chapter 14). The function of insulin is to maintain proper glucose levels in the body, which it does by affecting the uptake of glucose from the blood by muscle and fat tissue and by limiting the liver's production of glucose. As people gain weight and become less active, their muscles, fat, and liver become less sensitive to the effect of insulin—a condition known as *insulin resistance* (or prediabetes). As the body becomes increasingly insulin resistant, the pancreas must secrete more and more insulin (hyperinsulinemia) to keep glucose levels within a normal range. Eventually even high levels of insulin may become insufficient, and blood glucose levels start to rise (hyperglycemia), resulting in type 2 diabetes.

Those who have insulin resistance tend to have several other related risk factors. This cluster of abnormalities is called *metabolic syndrome* or *insulin resistance syndrome* (Table 15.4). Metabolic syndrome significantly increases the risk of CVD—more so in women than in men. It is estimated that about 34% of the adult U.S. population has metabolic syndrome.

To reduce your risk of metabolic syndrome, choose a healthy diet and get plenty of exercise. Regular physical activity increases your body's sensitivity to insulin, improves cholesterol levels, and decreases blood pressure. Reducing calorie intake to prevent weight gain or losing weight if needed also reduces insulin resistance. The amount and type of carbohydrate intake is also important: diets high in simple carbohydrates, such as white sugar and white flour (high-glycemic-index foods) can raise levels of glucose and triglycerides while lowering HDL, thus contributing to metabolic syndrome and CVD. This is particularly true for people who are already sedentary and overweight. For people prone to insulin resistance, eating more unsaturated fats, protein,

whose diabetes is under control face a high risk of CVD, so control of other risk factors is critical.

Contributing Risk Factors That Can Be Changed

Other CVD risk factors that can be changed include triglyceride levels and psychological and social factors.

High Triglyceride Levels Like cholesterol, **triglycerides** are blood fats that are obtained from food and manufactured by the body. High triglyceride levels are a reliable predictor of heart disease, especially if associated with other risk factors, such as low HDL levels, obesity, and diabetes. Factors contributing to elevated triglyceride levels include excess body fat, physical inactivity, cigarette smoking, type 2 diabetes, excessive alcohol intake, very high-carbohydrate diets, and certain diseases and medications.

Much of the picture regarding triglycerides remains unclear. Studies have yet to show whether lowering triglyceride levels will actually decrease heart disease. Elevated triglyceride levels are most often seen in people with other lipid abnormalities. Further, the lifestyle modifications that help lower cholesterol also help decrease triglycerides, making it

> **QUICK STATS**
>
> ## 2.9 million
> **American teenagers have metabolic syndrome.**
> —American Heart Association, 2010

---

triglyceride A type of blood fat that can be a predictor of heart disease.   **TERMS**

Table 15.4	Defining Characteristics of Metabolic Syndrome*

Abdominal obesity (waist circumference)	
Men	>40 in (>102 cm)
Women	>35 in (>88 cm)
Triglycerides	≥150 mg/dl
HDL cholesterol	
Men	<40 mg/dl or drug-treated
Women	<50 mg/dl or drug-treated
Blood pressure	≥130/≥85 mmHg or drug-treated
Fasting glucose	≥100 mg/dl or drug-treated

*A person is diagnosed with metabolic syndrome if she or he has three or more of the risk factors listed here.

SOURCE: Adapted with permission of the American Heart Association from Table 2. Grundy, S. M., et al. 2005. Diagnosis and management of the metabolic syndrome: an American Heart Association/National Heart, Lung, and Blood Institute scientific statement. *Circulation* 112: 2735.

vegetables, and fiber while limiting added sugars and starches may be beneficial.

Psychological and Social Factors

Many of the psychological and social factors that influence other areas of wellness are also important risk factors for CVD. The cardiovascular system is affected by both sudden, acute episodes of mental stress and the more chronic underlying emotions of anger, anxiety, and depression.

STRESS Excessive stress can strain the heart and blood vessels over time and contribute to CVD. When you experience stress, stress hormones activate the sympathetic nervous system. As described in Chapter 2, the sympathetic nervous system causes the fight-or-flight response; this response increases heart rate and blood pressure so that more blood is distributed to the heart and other muscles in anticipation of physical activity. Blood glucose concentrations and cholesterol also increase to provide a source of energy, and the platelets become activated so they will be more likely to clot in case of injury. If you are healthy, you can tolerate the cardiovascular responses that take place during stress; but if you already have CVD, stress can lead to adverse outcomes such as abnormal heart rhythms (arrhythmias) and heart attacks.

Because avoiding all stress is impossible, having healthy mechanisms to cope with it is your best defense. Instead of adopting unhealthy habits such as smoking or overeating, use healthier coping strategies such as exercising, getting enough sleep, and talking to others.

CHRONIC HOSTILITY AND ANGER Certain traits in the hard-driving Type A personality—hostility, cynicism, and anger—are associated with increased risk of heart disease. Men prone to anger have two to three times the heart attack risk of calmer men and are much more likely to develop

CVD at young ages. In a 10-year study of young adults aged 18–30 years, those with high hostility levels were more than twice as likely to develop coronary artery calcification (a marker of early atherosclerosis) as those with low hostility levels. See the box "Anger, Hostility, and Heart Disease" for more information.

SUPPRESSING PSYCHOLOGICAL DISTRESS Consistently suppressing anger and other negative emotions may also be hazardous to a healthy heart. People who hide psychological distress appear to have higher rates of heart disease than people who experience similar distress but share it with others. People with such Type D personalities tend to be pessimistic, negative, and unhappy and to suppress these feelings. This Type D trait may have physical effects, or it may lead to social isolation and poor communication with physicians.

DEPRESSION Depression appears to increase the risk of CVD in healthy people, and it definitely increases the risk of adverse cardiac events in those who already have heart disease. You do not need to have a major depressive disorder to be affected: for each depressive symptom you have, the risk seems to increase in a linear fashion (see Chapter 3 for symptoms of depression).

Depression is common in people with CHD, and patients who are depressed tend to have worse outcomes than those who are not. Up to one-third of patients experience major depression within one year of having a heart attack, and those who are depressed after having a heart attack are more likely

A strong social support network is a major antidote to stress and can help promote and support a healthy lifestyle, such as opportunities for exercise and relaxation.

People with a quick temper, a persistently hostile outlook, and a cynical, mistrusting attitude toward life are more likely to develop heart disease than those with a calmer, more trusting attitude. People who are angry frequently and for long periods experience the stress response much more often than more relaxed individuals. Over the long term, the effects of stress may damage arteries and promote CVD.

Are You Too Hostile?

To help answer that question, Duke University researcher Redford Williams, M.D., has devised a short self-test. It's not a scientific evaluation, but it offers a rough measure of hostility. Are the following statements true or false for you?

1. I often get annoyed at checkout cashiers or the people in front of me when I'm waiting in line.
2. I usually keep an eye on the people I work or live with to make sure they do what they should.
3. I often wonder how homeless people can have so little respect for themselves.
4. I believe that most people will take advantage of you if you let them.
5. The habits of friends or family members often annoy me.
6. When I'm stuck in traffic, I often start breathing faster and my heart pounds.
7. When I'm annoyed with people, I really want to let them know it.
8. If someone does me wrong, I want to get even.
9. I'd like to have the last word in any argument.

10. At least once a week, I have the urge to yell at or even hit someone.

According to Williams, five or more "true" statements suggest that you're excessively hostile and should consider taking steps to mellow out.

Managing Your Anger

Begin by monitoring your angry responses and looking for triggers—people or situations that typically make you angry. Familiarize yourself with the patterns of thinking that lead to angry or hostile feelings, and then try to head them off before they develop into full-blown anger. If you feel your anger starting to build, try reasoning with yourself by asking the following questions:

1. *Is this really important enough to get angry about?*
2. *Am I really justified in getting angry?*
3. *Is getting angry going to make a real and positive difference in this situation?*

If you answer yes to all three questions, then calm but assertive communication may be an appropriate response. If your anger isn't reasonable, try distracting yourself or removing yourself from the situation. Exercise, humor, social support, and other stress management techniques can also help (see Chapter 3 for additional anger management tips). Your heart—and the people around you—will benefit from your calmer, more positive outlook.

SOURCE: Virginia Williams and Redford Williams. 1999. *Lifeskills: 8 Simple Ways to Build Stronger Relationships, Communicate More Clearly, and Improve Your Health,* New York: Times Books. Reprinted by permission.

---

to have another heart attack or die of a cardiac cause. Even in those with CHD who have not had a recent cardiac event, up to 20% have depression, and this number may be even higher in women. Major depressive disorder at the time of treatment for coronary artery disease is associated with both short- and long-term complications, including subsequent heart attack and death.

The relationship between depression and CHD is complex and not fully understood. Depressed people may be more likely to smoke or be sedentary. They may not consistently take prescribed medications, and they may not cope well with having an illness or undergoing a medical procedure. Depression also causes physiological changes; for example, it elevates basal levels of stress hormones, which induce a variety of stress-related responses.

ANXIETY There is evidence to suggest that chronic anxiety and anxiety disorders (such as phobias and panic disorder) are associated with up to a threefold increased risk of coronary heart disease, heart attack, and sudden cardiac death. There is also some evidence that, similar to people with depression, people with anxiety are more likely to have a subsequent adverse cardiac event after having a heart attack. At the same time, people with anxiety and depression often have medically unexplained chest pain, meaning that no obvious coronary artery disease can be found. This can create difficulties in diagnosis and disease management, but it is important to always seek medical attention if you experience unexplained chest pain.

SOCIAL ISOLATION Social isolation and low social support (living alone, or having few friends or family members) are associated with an increased incidence of CHD and poorer outcomes after the first diagnosis of CHD. Elderly men and women who report less emotional support from others before they have a heart attack are almost three times more likely to die in the first six months after the heart attack. A strong social support network is a major antidote to stress. Friends and family members can also promote and support a healthy lifestyle.

LOW SOCIOECONOMIC STATUS Low socioeconomic status and low educational attainment are also associated with an increased risk of CVD. These associations are probably due to a variety of factors, including lifestyle and access to health care.

Alcohol and Drugs Although moderate drinking (defined as no more than one or two drinks per day for men and no more than one drink per day for women) may have health benefits for some people, drinking too much alcohol raises blood pressure and can increase the risk of stroke and heart failure.

Stimulant drugs, particularly cocaine and methamphetamines, can also cause serious cardiac problems, including heart attack, stroke, and sudden cardiac death. For example, cocaine stimulates the nervous system, promotes platelet aggregation, and can cause spasms in the coronary arteries. Injection drug use can cause heart infections and stroke. See Chapters 9 and 10 for more information about the use of alcohol and drugs.

> In general, men face **a greater risk of heart attack, hypertension, and stroke** than women.

Major Risk Factors That Can't Be Changed

A number of major risk factors for CVD cannot be changed. These include family history of CVD (heredity), aging, male gender, and ethnicity.

Heredity Multiple genes contribute to the development of CVD and its associated risk factors, such as high cholesterol, hypertension, diabetes, and obesity. Having a favorable set of genes decreases your risk of developing CVD; having an unfavorable set of genes increases your risk. Risk, however, may be modified by lifestyle factors such as whether you smoke, exercise, or eat a healthy diet.

Because of the genetic complexity of CVD, genetic screening is usually recommended for only a few specific conditions (for example, certain inherited cholesterol disorders); but you can learn more about your personal risk just by assessing your family history. If you have a first-degree relative (parent, sibling, child) who developed CAD before the age of 65, for example, you can have up to a two-fold increased risk of developing CAD yourself.

Don't forget the role of lifestyle factors, however. Coronary artery disease is usually the result of the interaction of several unfavorable genetic and lifestyle factors, and people with the greatest number of genetic and lifestyle risk factors will face the highest risks. People with favorable genes may not develop CAD despite having an unhealthy lifestyle, and people with many healthy habits may still develop CAD because they have an unfavorable genetic makeup. People who inherit a tendency for CVD are not destined to develop it. They may, however, have to work harder than other people to prevent CVD.

Aging About 70% of all heart attack victims are age 65 or older, and about 75% who suffer fatal heart attacks are over 65. For people over 55, the incidence of stroke more than doubles in each successive decade. However, even people in their thirties and forties, especially men, can have heart attacks.

Gender Although CVD is the leading killer of both men and women in the United States, men face a greater risk of heart attack than women, especially earlier in life. Until age 55, men also have a greater risk of hypertension. The incidence of stroke is higher for males than females until age 65. Estrogen production, which is highest during the childbearing years, may protect premenopausal women against CVD. By age 75 this gender gap nearly disappears.

Risk factors for CVD are similar for men and women (age, family history, smoking, hypertension, high cholesterol, and diabetes) but there are gender differences. HDL appears to be an even more powerful predictor of CAD risk in women than in men. Also, women with diabetes have a greater risk of having CVD events like heart attack and stroke than men with diabetes.

Women who have heart attacks are more likely than men to die within a year. One reason is that because women develop heart disease at older ages, they are more likely to have other health problems that complicate treatment. There also may be biological or psychosocial risk factors contributing to women's mortality.

Ethnicity Rates of heart disease vary among ethnic groups in the United States, with African Americans having much higher rates of hypertension, heart disease, and stroke than other groups (see the box "Ethnicity and CVD"). Figure 15.2 compares rates of CVD among non-Hispanic whites, blacks, and Mexican Americans in the United States. Puerto Rican Americans, Cuban Americans, and Mexican Americans are also more likely to suffer from high blood pressure and angina (a warning sign of blocked coronary arteries) than non-Hispanic white Americans. Asian Americans historically have had far lower rates of CVD than white Americans.

Inflammation and C-Reactive Protein Inflammation plays a key role in the development of CVD. When an artery is

Although cardiovascular disease is the leading cause of death for all Americans, there is a higher prevalence of CVD in adult African Americans, and a higher prevalence of many associated risk factors in Mexican Americans, than in whites and Asian Americans. The reasons for these disparities likely include both genetic and environmental factors.

African Americans are at substantially higher risk of death from CVD than other groups. The rate of hypertension among African Americans is among the highest of any group in the world. Blacks tend to develop hypertension at an earlier age than whites, and their average blood pressures are much higher. African Americans have a higher risk of stroke, have strokes at younger ages, and if they survive, have more significant stroke-related disabilities. Some experts recommend that blacks be treated with antihypertensive drugs when blood pressure reaches 130/80 rather than the typical 140/90 cutoff for hypertension.

A number of genetic and biological factors may contribute to CVD in African Americans. They may be more sensitive to dietary sodium, leading to greater blood pressure elevation in response to a given amount of sodium. African Americans may also experience less dilation of blood vessels in response to stress, an attribute that also raises blood pressure.

Heredity also plays a large role in the tendency to develop diabetes, another important CVD risk factor that is more common in blacks than whites. However, Latinos are even more likely to develop diabetes and insulin resistance, and at a younger age, than African Americans. There is variation within the Latino population, however: a higher prevalence of diabetes occurs among Mexican Americans and Puerto Ricans and a relatively lower prevalence among Cuban Americans.

Another factor that likely contributes to the high incidence of CVD among ethnic minority groups is low income, which usually means reduced access to health care. Also associated with low income is low educational attainment, which often means

less information about preventive health measures, such as diet and stress management. People with low incomes tend to smoke more, use more salt, and exercise less than those with higher incomes.

Discrimination may also play a role in CVD. Physicians and hospitals may treat the medical problems of ethnic minorities differently than those of whites. Discrimination, low income, and other forms of deprivation may also increase stress, which is linked with hypertension and CVD. Lack of access to care, such as insurance coverage and availability of high-tech cardiac equipment in hospitals that serve minorities, may also play a role.

All Americans are advised to have their blood pressure checked regularly, exercise, eat a healthy diet, manage stress, and avoid smoking. These general preventive strategies may be particularly helpful for ethnic minorities. Tailoring your lifestyle to your particular ethnic risk may also be helpful in some cases. Discuss your particular risk profile with your physician to help identify the lifestyle changes most appropriate for you.

connect
ACTIVITY
DO IT ONLINE

---

injured by smoking, cholesterol, hypertension, or other factors, the body's response is to produce inflammation. A substance called *C-reactive protein (CRP)* is released into the bloodstream during the inflammatory response, and high levels of CRP indicate a substantially elevated risk of heart attack and stroke. CRP may also harm the coronary arteries themselves.

The CDC and the American Heart Association recommend that it is reasonable to test for CRP levels in people at intermediate risk for CVD because people in this risk category with high CRP levels may benefit from additional testing or treatment. (This guideline assumes that people at high risk for CVD are already receiving treatment.)

Lifestyle changes and certain drugs can reduce CRP levels. Statin drugs, widely prescribed to lower cholesterol, also decrease inflammation and reduce CRP levels. Patients who receive intensive statin treatment fare better than patients who receive less aggressive treatment that primarily targets LDL levels. The reduction in risk from decreased CRP levels is independent of changes in LDL levels.

The benefits of statins were confirmed in 2008, when findings were released from a study involving 18,000 patients in 26 countries. Volunteers who took statins reduced their risk of CVD by about 50% even if they had normal cholesterol levels. The patients had undergone a simple blood test that checked for inflammation by measuring levels of CRP; because statins lower CRP regardless of cholesterol levels, researchers concluded that CRP levels and inflammation are important markers of CVD risk.

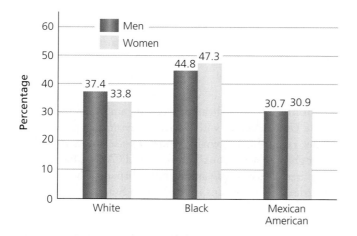

VITAL STATISTICS

FIGURE 15.2   Percentage of adult Americans with cardiovascular disease.

SOURCE: American Heart Association. 2012. *Heart Disease and Stroke Statistics—2012 Update*. Dallas: American Heart Association.

Possible Risk Factors Currently Being Studied

In recent years other possible risk factors for cardiovascular disease have been identified. These range from levels of various amino acids in the blood to infectious agents and even the season of the year. All of these risk factors are currently under study.

Homocysteine   Elevated levels of homocysteine, an amino acid circulating in the blood, are associated with an increased risk of CVD. Homocysteine appears to damage the lining of blood vessels, resulting in inflammation and the development of fatty deposits in artery walls. These changes can lead to the formation of clots and blockages in arteries, which in turn can cause heart attacks and strokes. High homocysteine levels are also associated with cognitive impairment, such as memory loss.

Infectious Agents   Several infectious agents have been identified as possible culprits in the development of CVD. *Chlamydia pneumoniae*, a common cause of flulike respiratory infections, has been found in sections of clogged, damaged arteries but not in sections of healthy arteries. This effect may be secondary to the inflammation that many of these infectious agents produce in the body. It does not appear that antibiotic treatment for *C. pneumoniae* reduces risk, but further research is needed. Other infectious agents may also play a role in CVD.

Lipoprotein(a)   A high level of a specific type of LDL called lipoprotein(a), or Lp(a), may be a risk factor for CHD, especially when associated with high LDL or low HDL levels. Lp(a) is thought to contribute to CVD by promoting clots and delivering cholesterol to a site of vascular injury. Lp(a) levels have a strong genetic component and are difficult to treat. Lp(a) levels tend to increase with age and vary by race, with higher levels found in African Americans than in whites. About 25% of the U.S. population has elevated lipoprotein(a) levels.

LDL Particle Size   LDL particles differ in size and density, and concentrations of different particles vary among individuals. LDL cholesterol profiles can be divided into three general types: People with pattern A have mostly large, buoyant LDL particles; people with pattern B have mostly small, dense LDL particles; and people with pattern C have a mixture of particle types. Small, dense LDL particles pose a greater CVD risk than large particles; thus people with LDL pattern B are at greatest risk for CVD. Exercise, a low-fat diet, and certain lipid-lowering drugs may help lower CVD risk in people with pattern B. In a recent study of men who walked or jogged 12–20 miles per week, total cholesterol and LDL levels were often unchanged, but the LDL particles became larger and less dense.

Blood Viscosity and Iron   High blood viscosity (thickness) may increase the risk of CVD, as may excess iron stores, especially for men and postmenopausal women (iron stores are usually lower in younger women because of menstrual blood loss). Regular blood donation, which reduces iron stores and blood viscosity, is associated with lower CVD risk in men. Drinking five or more glasses of water a day may also reduce risk by reducing blood viscosity. On the flip side, high consumption of heme iron—found in meat, fish, and poultry—is associated with an increased risk of heart attack. Men and postmenopausal women should consult a physician before taking iron supplements.

Uric Acid   Recent research suggests a link between high blood levels of uric acid and CVD mortality, particularly among postmenopausal women and African Americans. Uric acid may raise CVD risk by increasing inflammation and platelet aggregation or by influencing the development of hypertension. High uric acid levels also cause gout (a type of arthritis), kidney stones, and certain forms of kidney disease. Medications to lower uric acid levels are available, but it is not yet known if they are useful in preventing CVD.

Time of Day and Time of Year   More heart attacks and sudden cardiac deaths occur between 6:00 a.m. and noon than during other times of the day. This trend may be explained by the natural increase in adrenaline and cortisol levels that occurs

> ## Ask Yourself
>
> ### QUESTIONS FOR CRITICAL THINKING AND REFLECTION
>
> What risk factors do you have for cardiovascular disease? Which ones are factors you have control over, and which are factors you can't change? If you have risk factors you cannot change (such as a family history of CVD), were you aware that you can make lifestyle adjustments to reduce your risk? Do you think you will make them?

More heart attacks occur in winter than in summer, and more heart attacks occur in the morning than other times of the day. Several different explanations have been proposed for both phenomena.

in the morning and by an increase in the sympathetic nervous system activity at the beginning of the day. Blood pressure is often lowest during sleep and highest in the morning, and endothelial function may be impaired in the early morning.

There is also a seasonal pattern of heart attacks, with up to 50% more occurring in winter months than in summer months. Heart attacks that occur in winter also tend to be more often fatal than those that occur during summer. Possible explanations include low temperatures, which can constrict blood vessels; bursts of exertion, such as snow shoveling; increased rates of smoking; increased stress and depression, including seasonal affective disorder (see Chapter 3); holiday-related episodes of high-fat eating and binge drinking; and physiological factors, including levels of cholesterol and C-reactive protein, which appear to rise in winter. People who have symptoms of heart trouble may also be more reluctant to seek help during the holidays.

MAJOR FORMS OF CARDIOVASCULAR DISEASE

Although deaths from CVD have declined drastically over the past 60 years, it remains the leading cause of death in America. According to the CDC, heart diseases killed nearly 616,000 Americans in 2008. Figure 15.3 shows the death rates among various ethnic groups due to heart disease in 2008, the most recent year for which data are available.

The main forms of CVD are atherosclerosis, coronary artery disease and heart attack, stroke, peripheral arterial disease (PAD), congestive heart failure, congenital heart disease, rheumatic heart disease, and heart valve problems. Many forms are interrelated and have elements in common; we

treat them separately here for the sake of clarity. Hypertension, which is both a major risk factor and a form of CVD, was described earlier in the chapter.

Atherosclerosis

Atherosclerosis is a form of arteriosclerosis, or thickening and hardening of the arteries. In atherosclerosis, arteries become narrowed by deposits of fat, cholesterol, and other substances (see page T2-4 of the color transparency insert "Touring the Cardiorespiratory System"). The process begins when the endothelial cells (cells that line the arteries) become damaged, most likely through a combination of factors such as smoking, high blood pressure, high insulin or glucose levels, and deposits of oxidized LDL particles. The body's response to this damage results in inflammation and changes in the artery lining that create a magnet for LDL, platelets, and other cells. These cells build up and cause a bulge in the wall of the artery. As these deposits, called **plaques,** accumulate in artery walls, the arteries lose their elasticity and their ability to expand and contract, restricting blood flow. Once narrowed by a plaque, an artery is vulnerable to blockage by blood clots. The risk of life-threatening clots and heart attacks increases if the fibrous cap covering a plaque ruptures.

If the heart, brain, or other organs are deprived of blood and the oxygen it carries, the effects of atherosclerosis can be deadly. Coronary arteries, which supply the heart with blood, are particularly susceptible to plaque buildup, a condition called **coronary heart disease (CHD)** or *coronary artery disease (CAD)*. The blockage of a coronary artery causes a heart attack, and blockage of a cerebral artery (leading to the brain) causes a stroke. Blockage of an artery in a limb causes *peripheral arterial disease*, a condition that causes pain and sometimes amputation of the affected limb.

The main risk factors for atherosclerosis are cigarette smoking, physical inactivity, high blood cholesterol levels, high blood pressure, and diabetes. Atherosclerosis often begins in childhood: autopsy studies of young trauma victims have revealed atherosclerosis of the coronary arteries in adolescents.

Coronary Artery Disease and Heart Attack

The most common form of heart disease is coronary artery disease caused by atherosclerosis. When one of the coronary arteries becomes blocked, the result is a **heart attack,** or

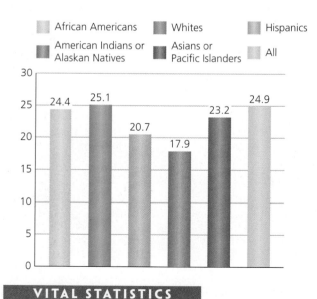

VITAL STATISTICS

FIGURE 15.3 Percentage of deaths due to heart disease, by ethnic group.

SOURCE: Miniño, A. M., et al. 2011. Deaths: final data for 2008. *National Vital Statistics Reports* 59(10). Hyattsville, MD: National Center for Health Statistics.

plaque A deposit of fatty (and other) substances on the inner wall of an artery.

coronary heart disease (CHD) Heart disease caused by atherosclerosis in the arteries that supply blood to the heart muscle; also called *coronary artery disease.*

heart attack Damage to, or death of, heart muscle, resulting from a failure of the coronary arteries to deliver enough blood to the heart; also known as *myocardial infarction (MI).*

TERMS

Table 15.5	Deaths from Acute Myocardial Infarction, 2007	
AGE		**DEATHS**
Birth–24		79
25–44		2,802
45–64		27,302
65 and older		102,781

SOURCE: National Center for Health Statistics. 2010. Deaths: final data for 2007. *National Vital Statistics Reports* 58(19): 1–73. Hyattsville, MD: National Center for Health Statistics.

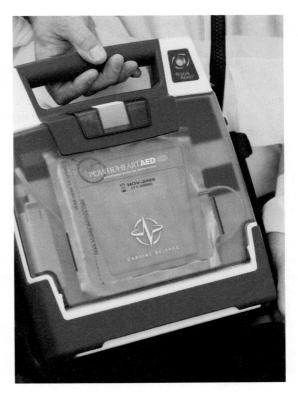

Automated external defibrillators can save the lives of individuals experiencing sudden cardiac arrest. AEDs are becoming more common in public places.

myocardial infarction (MI). During a heart attack, the heart muscle (the myocardium) is damaged, and part of it may die from lack of blood. Although a heart attack may come without warning, it usually results from a chronic disease process.

Myocardial infarctions are a significant cause of death in the United States, especially among people aged 65 and older (Table 15.5). The average age for a first heart attack is 66 for men and 70 for women.

Heart attack symptoms may include the following:

- Chest pain or pressure.
- Arm, neck, or jaw pain.
- Difficulty breathing.
- Excessive sweating.
- Nausea and vomiting.
- Loss of consciousness.

Most people having a heart attack suffer chest pain, but about one-third of heart attack victims do not. Women, ethnic minorities, older adults, and people with diabetes are the most likely groups to experience heart attacks without chest pain.

Women presenting are likely to report non-chest-pain symptoms, which may obscure the diagnosis of heart disease. These "nontypical" symptoms include fatigue, weakness, shortness of breath, nausea, vomiting, and pain in the abdomen, neck, jaw, and back. Women are also more likely to have pain at rest, during sleep, or with mental stress. A woman who experiences these symptoms should be persistent in seeking accurate diagnosis and appropriate treatment. The American Heart Association estimates that 785,000 people have a first heart attack each year; 470,000 people have a recurrent attack. An estimated 195,000 people suffer a symptomless or "silent" heart attack each year.

Angina Arteries narrowed by disease may still be open enough to deliver blood to the heart. At times, however—during stress or exertion, for example—the heart needs more oxygen than can flow through narrowed arteries. When the need for oxygen exceeds the supply, chest pain, called **angina pectoris,** may occur.

Angina pain is usually felt as an extreme tightness in the chest and heavy pressure behind the breastbone or in the shoulder,

neck, arm, hand, or back. This pain is usually relieved by rest or medicine called nitroglycerin. This pain, although not actually a heart attack, is a warning that the load on the heart must be reduced. The symptoms of angina are often very difficult to distinguish from a heart attack. Any severe chest pain that lasts more than a few minutes should be considered life-threatening, and emergency medical help should be sought immediately.

Angina may be controlled in a number of ways (with drugs and surgical or nonsurgical procedures), but its course is unpredictable. Over a period ranging from hours to years, the narrowing may go on to full blockage and a heart attack.

Arrhythmias and Sudden Cardiac Death The pumping of the heart is controlled by electrical impulses from the sinus node that maintain a regular heartbeat of 60–100 beats per minute. If this electrical conduction system is disrupted, the heart may beat too quickly, too slowly, or in an irregular fashion—a condition known as an **arrhythmia.** Arrhythmias can cause symptoms ranging from imperceptible to severe and even fatal.

---

angina pectoris   Pain in the chest, and often in the left arm and shoulder, caused by the heart muscle not receiving enough blood. The pain is usually brought on by exercise or stress.

arrhythmia   A change in the heartbeat's normal pattern.

TERMS

Sudden cardiac death, also called *cardiac arrest,* is most often caused by an arrhythmia called *ventricular fibrillation,* a kind of quivering of the ventricle that makes it ineffective in pumping blood. If ventricular fibrillation continues for more than a few minutes, it is generally fatal. Cardiac defibrillation, in which an electrical shock is delivered to the heart, can be effective in jolting the heart into a more efficient rhythm. Emergency personnel typically carry defibrillators, and automated external defibrillators (AEDs) are becoming increasingly available in public places for use by the general public. AEDs monitor the heart's rhythm and, if appropriate, deliver an electrical shock. (Training in the use of AEDs is available from organizations such as the American Red Cross and the American Heart Association.) Sudden cardiac death most often occurs in people with coronary heart disease. Serious arrhythmias frequently develop during or after a heart attack and are often the actual cause of death in cases of a fatal myocardial infarction.

Other potential causes of arrhythmia include congenital heart abnormalities, infections, drug use, abnormal concentrations of electrolytes, chest trauma, and congestive heart failure. Some arrhythmias cause no problems and resolve without treatment; more serious arrhythmias are usually treated with medication or a surgically implanted pacemaker or defibrillator that delivers electrical stimulation to the heart to create a more normal rhythm.

Helping a Heart Attack Victim Most deaths from heart attacks occur within two hours of the first symptoms. Unfortunately half of all heart attack victims wait more than two hours before getting help. If you or someone you are with has any of the warning signs of heart attack listed in the box "What to Do in Case of a Heart Attack, Stroke, or Cardiac Arrest," take immediate action. Get help even if the person denies there is something wrong. Many experts also suggest that the heart attack victim chew and swallow one adult aspirin tablet (325 mg) as soon as possible after symptoms begin. Aspirin has an immediate anticlotting effect.

If the victim loses consciousness, a qualified person should immediately start administering emergency **cardiopulmonary resuscitation (CPR).** Damage to the heart muscle increases with time. If the person receives emergency care quickly enough, a clot-dissolving agent or emergency surgical procedure can be used to break up the clot in the coronary artery.

Detecting and Treating Heart Disease Physicians have an expanding array of tools to evaluate the condition of the heart and its arteries. Currently the most common initial screening tool for CAD is the stress, or exercise, test. During an exercise stress test, a patient runs or walks on a treadmill or pedals a stationary cycle while being monitored for abnormalities with an **electrocardiogram (ECG or EKG).** Certain characteristic changes in the heart's electrical activity while under stress can reveal particular heart problems, such as restricted blood flow. Exercise testing can also be performed in conjunction with imaging techniques

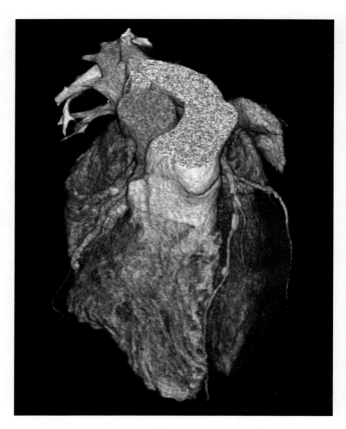

This coronary angiogram shows a patient with diffuse coronary calcifications. The coronary arteries and the calcifications along the arteries have been color enhanced.

such as nuclear medicine or echocardiography that provide pictures of the heart, which can help pinpoint abnormal areas of the heart.

Other tests for evaluating CHD include the following:

• *Electron-beam computed tomography (EBCT)* uses a sweeping electron beam to produce computerized cross-sectional images of calcium in the arteries, which is a marker for atherosclerosis.

• *Echocardiography* utilizes sound waves to examine the heart's pumping function and valves.

• *Multi-slice computed tomography (MSCT)* is another type of CT that produces thinly sliced images of the heart, allowing physicians to see very small structures such as the coronary arteries.

TERMS

sudden cardiac death   A nontraumatic, unexpected death from sudden cardiac arrest, most often due to arrhythmia; in most instances, victims have underlying heart disease.

cardiopulmonary resuscitation (CPR)   A technique involving mouth-to-mouth breathing and/or chest compressions to keep oxygen flowing to the brain.

electrocardiogram (ECG or EKG)   A test to detect cardiac abnormalities by evaluating the electrical activity in the heart.

What to Do in Case of a Heart Attack, Stroke, or Cardiac Arrest

Warning Signs of Heart Attack

Some heart attacks are sudden and intense—the "movie heart attack," where no one doubts what's happening. But most heart attacks start slowly with mild pain or discomfort. Often people affected aren't sure what's wrong and wait too long before getting help. Here are signs that can mean a heart attack is happening:

- **Chest discomfort.** Heart attacks often involve discomfort in the chest that lasts more than a few minutes, or that goes away and comes back. It can feel like uncomfortable pressure, squeezing, fullness, or pain.

- **Discomfort in other areas of the upper body.** Symptoms can include pain or discomfort in one or both arms, the back, neck, jaw, or stomach.

- **Shortness of breath.** May occur with or without chest discomfort.

- **Other signs:** These may include breaking out in a cold sweat, nausea, vomiting, or lightheadedness.

Not all the signs occur in every heart attack. As with men, women's most common heart attack symptom is chest pain or discomfort, but women are somewhat more likely than men to experience some of the other symptoms, particularly shortness of beath, nausea/vomiting, and back or jaw pain.

If you or someone you're with has chest discomfort, especially with one or more of the other signs, don't wait longer than a few minutes (no more than five) before calling for help.

Calling 911 is almost always the fastest way to get lifesaving treatment. Emergency medical services staff can begin treatment when they arrive—up to an hour sooner than if someone gets to the hospital by car. The staff are also trained to revive someone whose heart has stopped. Patients with chest pain who arrive by ambulance usually receive faster treatment at the hospital, too. Today medications and treatments are available that weren't available in the past, but they must be given relatively quickly after the heart attack to be effective.

If you can't access emergency medical services (EMS), have someone drive you to the hospital right away. If you're the one having symptoms, don't drive yourself unless you have absolutely no other option.

Warning Signs of Stroke

- Sudden numbness or weakness of the face, arm, or leg, especially on one side of the body.

- Sudden confusion or trouble speaking or understanding.

- Sudden trouble seeing in one or both eyes.

- Sudden trouble walking, dizziness, or loss of balance or coordination.

- Sudden severe headache with no known cause.

If you or someone with you has one or more of these signs, don't delay! Immediately call 911 or the emergency medical services (EMS) number so an ambulance (ideally with advanced life support) can be sent for you. Also, check the time so you'll know when the first symptoms appeared. It's very important to take immediate action. If given within three hours of the start of symptoms, a clot-busting drug called tissue plasminogen activator (tPA) can reduce long-term disability for the most common type of stroke. tPA is the only FDA-approved medication for the treatment of stroke within three hours of symptom onset.

Signs of Cardiac Arrest

Cardiac arrest strikes immediately and without warning. Here are the signs:

- Sudden loss of responsiveness.

- No response to tapping on the shoulders.

- No normal breathing. The victim does not take a normal breath when you tilt the head up and check for at least five seconds.

If these signs of cardiac arrest are present, tell someone to call 911 and to get an automated external defibrillator (AED) if one is available before you begin CPR. Use the AED as soon as it arrives.

SOURCE: Adapted from American Heart Association. 2005. *Heart Attack, Stroke, and Cardiac Arrest Warning Signs.* http://www.heart.org/HEARTORG /General/Heart-Attack-Stroke-and-Cardiac-Arrest-Signs_UCM_303977 _SubHomePage.jsp. Copyright © 2007 American Heart Association. Reprinted with permission.

connect ACTIVITY DO IT ONLINE

- **Magnetic resonance imaging (MRI)** uses powerful magnets to look inside the body and generate pictures of the heart and blood vessels.

- *Nuclear myocardial perfusion imaging* injects radiotracers such as thallium-201 into the bloodstream. The radiotracers' location and density in the heart can be imaged and quantified, which allows physicians to determine the blood flow to various areas of the heart and identify possible coronary artery disease.

- *Positron emission tomography (PET)* involves the use of positron-emitting isotopes to image and quantify regional blood flow in the heart and identify coronary artery disease. PET scans can also measure the metabolism of cells in the

> **magnetic resonance imaging (MRI)** A computerized imaging technique that uses a strong magnetic field to create detailed pictures of body structures.
>
> **TERMS**

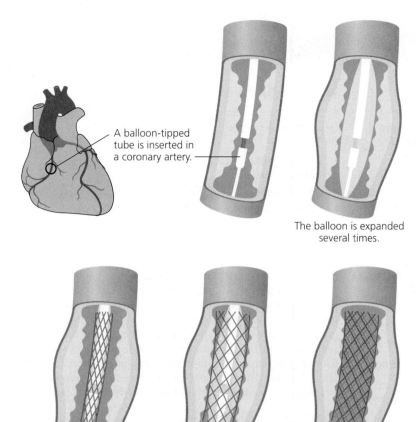

A balloon-tipped tube is inserted in a coronary artery.

The balloon is expanded several times.

Stent insertion.

Stent expansion.

The stent remains in the coronary artery.

FIGURE 15.4   Balloon angioplasty and stenting.

heart and therefore determine which parts of the heart are no longer alive.

If symptoms or noninvasive tests suggest coronary artery disease, the next step is usually a coronary **angiogram,** performed in a cardiac catheterization lab. In this test, a catheter (a small plastic tube) is threaded into an artery, usually in the groin, and advanced through the aorta to the coronary arteries. The catheter is then placed into the opening of the coronary artery and a special dye is injected. The dye can be seen moving through the arteries via X-ray, and any narrowings or blockages can be identified. If a problem is found, it is commonly treated with a metal stent or **balloon angioplasty,** which is performed by specially trained cardiologists (Figure 15.4). This technique involves feeding a balloon-tipped catheter into the artery. The balloon is advanced to the site of the narrowing and then inflated, flattening the fatty plaque and widening the arterial opening.

Balloon angioplasty is generally followed by placement of a *stent*—a small metal tube that helps keep the artery open. Repeat clogging of the artery (*restenosis*) can occur, but the introduction of stents coated with medication, which is slowly released over a few months, significantly decreases the chance of restenosis.

Other treatments, ranging from medication to major surgery, are also available. Along with a low-fat diet, regular exercise, and smoking cessation, one frequent recommendation for people at intermediate to high risk for CVD is to take a low-dose aspirin tablet every day. Aspirin helps prevent platelets in the blood from sticking to arterial plaques and forming clots, and it also reduces inflammation. Low-dose aspirin therapy appears to help prevent first heart attacks in men, second heart attacks in men and women, and strokes in women over age 65.

Prescription drugs can help control heart rate, dilate arteries, lower blood pressure, and reduce the strain on the heart—improving both the quality and length of life in heart patients. In patients with coronary artery disease, cholesterol-lowering statins are effective in preventing heart attacks; statins also have beneficial anti-inflammatory effects.

In **coronary bypass surgery,** surgeons remove a healthy blood vessel—usually a vein from the patient's leg—and graft it from the aorta to one or more coronary arteries to bypass a blockage.

Stroke

For brain cells to function as they should, they must have a continuous supply of oxygen-rich blood. If brain cells are deprived of blood for more than a few minutes, they die. A **stroke,** also called a *cerebrovascular accident (CVA),* occurs when the blood supply to the brain is cut off. One study found that about 2 million brain cells die per minute and the brain ages about 3.5 years each hour during a stroke.

In the past, not much could be done for stroke victims. Today, however, prompt treatment can greatly decrease the risk of permanent disability. Everyone should know the warning signs of a stroke and seek immediate medical help, just as they would at the first sign of a heart attack.

Types of Strokes   There are two major types of strokes (Figure 15.5), which are described in the following sections.

TERMS

angiogram   A picture of the arterial system taken after injecting a dye that is opaque to X-rays.

balloon angioplasty   A technique in which a catheter with a deflated balloon on the tip is inserted into an artery; the balloon is then inflated at the point of obstruction in the artery, pressing the plaque against the artery wall to improve blood supply.

coronary bypass surgery   Surgery in which a blood vessel is grafted from the aorta to a point below an obstruction in a coronary artery, improving the blood supply to the heart.

stroke   Impeded blood supply to some part of the brain resulting in the destruction of brain cells; also called a *cerebrovascular accident.*

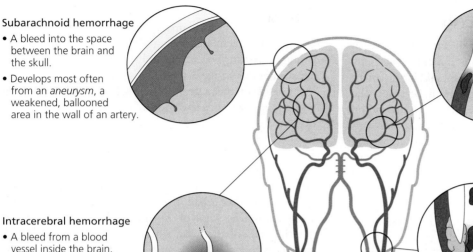

HEMORRHAGIC STROKE

- 13% of strokes.
- Caused by ruptured blood vessels followed by blood leaking into tissue.
- Usually more serious than ischemic stroke.

Subarachnoid hemorrhage
- A bleed into the space between the brain and the skull.
- Develops most often from an *aneurysm*, a weakened, ballooned area in the wall of an artery.

Intracerebral hemorrhage
- A bleed from a blood vessel inside the brain.
- Often caused by high blood pressure and the damage it does to arteries.

ISCHEMIC STROKE

- 87% of strokes.
- Caused by blockages in brain blood vessels; potentially treatable with clot-busting drugs.
- Brain tissue dies when blood flow is blocked.

Embolic stroke
- Caused by *emboli*, blood clots that travel from elsewhere in the body to the brain blood vessels.
- 25% of embolic strokes are related to atrial fibrillation.

Thrombotic stroke
- Caused by *thrombi*, blood clots that form where an artery has been narrowed by atherosclerosis.
- Most often develops when part of a thrombus breaks away and causes a blockage in a downstream artery.

FIGURE 15.5 Types of stroke.

SOURCE: Excerpted from *Harvard Health Letter,* April 2000. © 2000 Harvard University. Reprinted with permission. For more information visit http://www.health.harvard.edu.

ISCHEMIC STROKE An **ischemic stroke** is caused by a blockage in a blood vessel. There are two types of ischemic strokes:

- A *thrombotic stroke* is caused by a **thrombus,** which is a blood clot that forms in a cerebral or carotid artery that has been narrowed or damaged by atherosclerosis.

- An *embolic stroke* is caused by an **embolus,** which is a wandering blood clot that is carried in the bloodstream and may become wedged in a cerebral artery. Many embolic strokes are linked to a type of abnormal heart rhythm called *atrial fibrillation.* When this arrhythmia occurs, blood may pool in the left atrium and form a clot that travels to the brain.

Ischemic strokes, which account for 87% of all strokes, are potentially treatable with clot-busting drugs, so immediate medical help is critical to improving the victim's chances of recovery.

HEMORRHAGIC STROKE A **hemorrhagic stroke** occurs when a blood vessel in the brain bursts, spilling blood into the surrounding tissue. Cells normally nourished by the vessel are deprived of blood and cannot function. In addition, accumulated blood from the burst vessel may put pressure on surrounding brain tissue, causing damage and even death. There are two types of hemorrhagic strokes:

QUICK STATS

795,000
Americans suffer strokes each year.
—American Heart Association, 2011

- In an *intracerebral hemorrhage,* a blood vessel ruptures within the brain. About 10% of strokes are caused by intracerebral hemorrhages.

- In a *subarachnoid hemorrhage,* a blood vessel on the brain's surface ruptures and bleeds into the space between the brain and the skull. About 3% of strokes are of this type.

Hemorrhages can be caused by head injuries or the bursting of a malformed blood vessel or **aneurysm,** which is a blood-filled pocket that bulges out from a weak spot in the artery wall. Aneurysms in the brain may remain

ischemic stroke Impeded blood supply to the brain caused by the obstruction of a blood vessel by a clot.

thrombus A blood clot in a blood vessel that usually remains at the point of its formation.

embolus A blood clot that breaks off from its place of origin in a blood vessel and travels through the bloodstream.

hemorrhagic stroke Impeded blood supply to the brain caused by the rupture of a blood vessel.

aneurysm A sac formed by a distention or dilation of the artery wall.

stable and never break. But when they do, the result is a stroke. Aneurysms may be caused or worsened by hypertension.

The Effects of a Stroke The interruption of the blood supply to any area of the brain prevents the nerve cells there from functioning—in some cases causing death. Stroke survivors usually have some lasting disability. Which parts of the body are affected depends on the area of the brain that has been damaged. Brain cells control sensation and most of our body movements, and a stroke may cause paralysis, walking disability, speech impairment, memory loss, or changes in behavior. The severity of the stroke and how long the effects last depend on which brain cells have been injured, how widespread the damage is, how effectively the body can restore the blood supply, and how rapidly other areas of the brain can take over the functions of the damaged areas. Early treatment can significantly reduce the severity of disability resulting from a stroke.

Detecting and Treating Stroke Death rates from stroke have declined significantly over the past decades—from nearly 90% in 1950 to about 19% today. Effective treatment requires the prompt recognition of symptoms and correct diagnosis of the type of stroke.

A quick way to recognize a stroke is to ask the person to do four simple things:

1. Ask the person to smile. If her smile droops on one side, or if she is unable to move or open one side of her mouth, she may be having a stroke.

2. Ask the person to hold his arms or legs out. If the person cannot move one arm/leg or hold one arm/leg still, it may be a sign of a stroke.

3. Ask the person to repeat a simple, short sentence, such as "Take me out to the ball game." If she has trouble speaking or cannot speak, a stroke is possible.

4. Ask the person whether he has any decreased sensation, numbness, or abnormal tingling in his legs, arms, or other body parts.

If someone has difficulty performing any of these four tests, follow the steps described in the box "What to Do in Case of a Heart Attack, Stroke, or Cardiac Arrest."

Many people have strokes without knowing it. These "silent strokes" do not cause any noticeable symptoms while they are occurring. Although they may be mild, silent strokes leave their victims at a higher risk for subsequent and more serious strokes. They also contribute to loss of mental and cognitive skills. In 2008 a study of MRI scans of 2000 elderly people revealed that 11% of the subjects had brain damage from one or more strokes but did not realize they had ever had a stroke.

Some stroke victims have a **transient ischemic attack (TIA),** or "ministroke," days, weeks, or months before they have a full-blown stroke. A TIA produces temporary stroke-like symptoms, such as weakness or numbness in an arm or a leg, speech difficulty, or dizziness. These symptoms are brief, often lasting just a few minutes, and do not cause permanent damage. TIAs should be taken as warning signs of a stroke,

however, and anyone with a suspected TIA should get immediate medical attention.

Strokes should be treated with the same urgency as heart attacks. A person with stroke symptoms should be rushed to the hospital. A **computed tomography (CT)** scan, which uses a computer to construct an image of the brain from X-rays, can assess brain damage and determine the type of stroke. Newer techniques using MRI and ultrasound are becoming increasingly available and should improve the speed and accuracy of stroke diagnosis.

If tests reveal that a stroke is caused by a blood clot—and if help is sought within a few hours of the onset of symptoms—the person can be treated with the same kind of clot-dissolving drugs that are used to treat coronary artery blockages. If the clot is dissolved quickly enough, brain damage is minimized and symptoms may disappear. The longer the brain goes without blood, the greater the risk of permanent damage.

People who have had TIAs or who are at high risk for stroke due to narrowing of the carotid arteries (large arteries on either side of the neck, which carry blood to the head) may undergo a surgical procedure called *carotid endarterectomy*, in which plaque is removed. There is also a nonsurgical procedure, similar to coronary angioplasty and stenting, for patients who are at increased risk of surgical complications.

If tests reveal that a stroke was caused by a cerebral hemorrhage, drugs may be prescribed to lower the blood pressure, which will usually be high. Careful diagnosis is crucial, because administering clot-dissolving drugs to a person suffering a hemorrhagic stroke could cause more bleeding and potentially more brain damage.

If detection and treatment of stroke come too late, rehabilitation is the only treatment. Although damaged or destroyed brain tissue does not normally regenerate, nerve cells in the brain can make new pathways, and some functions can be taken over by other parts of the brain. Some spontaneous recovery starts immediately after a stroke and continues for a few months.

Rehabilitation consists of physical therapy, which helps strengthen muscles and improve balance and coordination; speech and language therapy, which helps those whose speech has been damaged; and occupational therapy, which helps improve hand–eye coordination and everyday living skills. Some people recover completely in a matter of days or weeks, but most stroke victims who survive must adapt to some disability.

Peripheral Arterial Disease

Peripheral arterial disease (PAD) refers to atherosclerosis in the leg or arm arteries, which can eventually limit or completely obstruct blood flow. The same process that occurs in the heart

transient ischemic attack (TIA) A small stroke; usually a temporary interruption of blood supply to the brain, causing numbness or difficulty with speech.

computed tomography (CT) The use of computerized X-ray images to create a cross-sectional depiction (scan) of tissue density.

TERMS

arteries can occur in any artery of the body. In fact, patients with PAD frequently also have coronary artery disease and cerebrovascular disease, and they have an increased risk of death from CVD. PAD affects 8 to 12 million people in the United States.

The risk factors associated with coronary atherosclerosis, such as smoking, diabetes, hypertension, and high cholesterol, also contribute to atherosclerosis in the peripheral circulation. The risk of PAD is significantly increased in people with diabetes and people who smoke. The likelihood of needing an amputation is increased in those who continue to smoke, and PAD in people with diabetes tends to be extensive and severe. Patient with diabetes and PAD also have a more difficult time fighting infections or healing ulcerations that form in the leg or foot.

Symptoms of PAD include claudication and rest pain. *Claudication* is aching or fatigue in the affected leg with exertion, particularly walking, which resolves with rest. Claudication occurs when leg muscles do not get adequate blood and oxygen supply. *Rest pain* occurs when the limb artery is unable to supply adequate blood and oxygen even when the body is not physically active. This occurs when the artery is significantly narrowed or completely blocked. If blood flow is not restored quickly, cells and tissues die; in severe cases, amputation may be needed. PAD is the leading cause of amputation in people over age 50.

> The same disease process that occurs in the heart arteries **can occur in any artery of the body.**

Congestive Heart Failure

A number of conditions—high blood pressure, heart attack, atherosclerosis, alcoholism, illicit drug use, heart valve disease, viral infections, rheumatic fever, birth defects—can damage the heart's pumping mechanism. When the heart cannot maintain its regular pumping rate and force, fluid begins to back up. When extra fluid seeps through capillary walls, edema (swelling) results, usually in the legs and ankles, but sometimes in other parts of the body as well. Fluid can collect in the lungs and interfere with breathing, particularly when a person is lying down. This condition is called **pulmonary edema,** and the entire process is known as **congestive heart failure.** About 5 million Americans suffer from heart failure.

Congestive heart failure can be controlled. Treatment includes reducing the workload on the heart, modifying salt intake, and using drugs that help the body eliminate excess fluid. Drugs used to treat congestive heart failure improve the pumping action of the heart, lower blood pressure so the heart doesn't have to work as hard, and help the body eliminate excess salt and water. When medical therapy is ineffective, heart transplant or mechanical ventricular assist devices are solutions for some patients with severe heart failure, but the need greatly exceeds the number of donor hearts available.

The risk of heart failure increases with age, and being overweight is a significant independent risk factor. Experts fear that the incidence of heart failure will increase dramatically over the next few decades as our population ages and becomes increasingly obese.

Other Forms of Heart Disease

Other, less common, forms of heart disease include congenital heart disease, rheumatic heart disease, and heart valve disorders.

Congenital Heart Defects About 36,000 children born each year in the United States have a defect or malformation of the heart or major blood vessels. These conditions are collectively referred to as **congenital heart defects,** and they cause about 3600 deaths a year. Most of the common congenital defects can now be accurately diagnosed and treated with medication or surgery. Early recognition of heart disease in a newborn is important in saving lives. The most common congenital defects are holes in the wall that divides the chambers of the heart. Such defects cause the heart to produce a distinctive sound, making diagnosis relatively simple. Another common defect is *coarctation of the aorta*—a narrowing, or constriction, of the aorta. Heart failure may result unless the constricted area is repaired by surgery.

Hypertrophic cardiomyopathy (HCM) occurs in 1 out of every 600 people in the United States and is the most common cause of sudden death among athletes younger than age 35. It causes the heart muscle to become hypertrophic (enlarged), primarily in the septum, which is the area between the two ventricles. People with hypertrophic cardiomyopathy are at high risk for sudden death, mainly due to serious arrhythmias. Hypertrophic cardiomyopathy may be identified by a **murmur** and diagnosed using echocardiography. Possible treatments include medication and a pacemaker or an internal defibrillator. If the hypertrophy is mainly in the septum, some of the septum can be surgically removed or a nonsurgical procedure can be done to kill off the extra muscle.

TERMS

peripheral arterial disease (PAD) Atherosclerosis in the arteries in the legs (or less commonly, the arms) that can impede blood flow and lead to pain, infection, and loss of the affected limb.

pulmonary edema The accumulation of fluid in the lungs.

congestive heart failure A condition resulting from the heart's inability to pump enough blood to keep up with the body's metabolic needs: blood backs up in the veins leading to the heart, causing an accumulation of fluid in various parts of the body.

congenital heart defect A defect or malformation of the heart or its major blood vessels, present at birth.

hypertrophic cardiomyopathy (HCM) An inherited condition in which there is an enlargement of the heart muscle, especially the muscle between the two ventricles.

murmur An abnormal heart sound indicating turbulent blood flow through a valve or hole in the heart.

Rheumatic Heart Disease   **Rheumatic fever,** a consequence of certain types of untreated streptococcal throat infections, is a leading cause of heart trouble worldwide. Rheumatic fever can permanently damage the heart muscle and heart valves, a condition called *rheumatic heart disease (RHD)*. Many of the approximately 100,000 operations on heart valves performed annually are related to RHD, and about 3,300 Americans die each year from RHD. The incidence of rheumatic fever has declined significantly in the United States since the introduction of antibiotics.

Symptoms of strep throat include the sudden onset of a sore throat, painful swallowing, fever, swollen glands, headache, nausea, and vomiting. Careful laboratory diagnosis is important because strep throat is treated with antibiotics, which are not useful in the treatment of far more common viral sore throats. If left untreated, up to 3% of strep infections progress into rheumatic fever. Rheumatic fever affects primarily children between the ages of 5 and 15.

Heart Valve Disorders   Age, previous heart attacks, congenital defects, and certain types of infections can cause abnormalities in the valves between the chambers of the heart. Heart valve problems generally fall into two categories—the valve fails to open fully, or it fails to close completely. In either case, blood flow through the heart is impaired.

Treatment for heart valve disorders depends on their location and severity. Serious problems may be treated with surgery to repair or replace a valve. People with certain types of heart valve defects are advised to take antibiotics prior to some types of dental and surgical procedures in order to prevent bacteria, which may be dislodged into the bloodstream during the procedure, from infecting the defective valve.

The most common heart valve disorder is **mitral valve prolapse (MVP),** which occurs in about 3% of the population. MVP is characterized by a billowing of the mitral valve, which separates the left ventricle and left atrium, during ventricular contraction. In some cases, blood leaks from the ventricle into the atrium. Most people with MVP have no symptoms: they have the same ability to exercise and live as long as people without MVP. The condition is often diagnosed during a routine medical exam when an extra heart sound (a click) or murmur is heard. The diagnosis can be confirmed with echocardiography.

QUICK STATS

Only **19%** of Americans with hypertension follow the DASH diet.

—American Heart Association, 2010

Ask Yourself

QUESTIONS FOR CRITICAL THINKING AND REFLECTION

Has anyone you know ever had a heart attack? If so, was the onset gradual or sudden? Were appropriate steps taken to help the person (for example, did anyone call 911, give CPR, or use an AED)? Do you feel comfortable dealing with a cardiac emergency? If not, what can you do to improve your readiness?

PROTECTING YOURSELF AGAINST CARDIOVASCULAR DISEASE

There are several important steps you can take now to lower your risk of developing CVD (Figure 15.6). CVD can begin very early in life. For example, fatty streaks (very early atherosclerosis) can be seen on the aorta in children younger than age 10. Also, young adults with relatively low cholesterol levels go on to live substantially longer than those with higher levels. Reducing CVD risk factors when you are young can pay off with many extra years of life and health (see the box "Are You at Risk for CVD?").

Eat Heart-Healthy

For most Americans, eating a heart-healthy diet involves many of the changes suggested in the Dietary Guidelines for Americans. See Chapter 12 for a detailed discussion of nutrition and dietary guidelines. The following aspects of nutrition apply directly to heart health:

- *Decrease fat and cholesterol intake.*
- *Eat a high-fiber diet.*
- *Reduce sodium intake and increase potassium intake.*
- *Avoid excessive alcohol consumption.*
- *Eat foods rich in omega-3 fatty acids.*

In addition to these familiar guidelines, a few specifics pertain to heart health:

- *Plant stanols and sterols.* Plant stanols and sterols, found in some types of trans-fat–free margarines and other products, reduce the absorption of cholesterol in the body and help lower LDL levels. For people with high LDL levels that do not respond to changes in fat intake, the NCEP suggests an intake of 2 grams per day of plant stanols or sterols.

- *Folic acid, vitamin B-6, and vitamin B-12.* These vitamins lower homocysteine levels, and folic acid has also been found to reduce the risk of hypertension.

- *Calcium.* Diets rich in calcium may help prevent hypertension and possibly stroke by reducing insulin resistance and platelet aggregation. Good sources of calcium are low-fat and fat-free dairy products.

TERMS

rheumatic fever   A disease, mainly of children, characterized by fever, inflammation, and pain in the joints. It often damages the heart valves and muscle, a condition called rheumatic heart disease.

mitral valve prolapse (MVP)   A condition in which the mitral valve billows out during ventricular contraction, allowing leakage of blood from the left ventricle into the left atrium.

Do More

- Eat a diet rich in fruits, vegetables, whole grains, and low-fat or fat-free dairy products. Eat five to nine servings of fruits and vegetables each day.

- Eat several servings of high-fiber foods each day.

- Eat two or more servings of fish per week; try a few servings of nuts and soy foods each week.

- Choose unsaturated fats rather than saturated and trans fats.

- Be physically active; do both aerobic exercise and strength training on a regular basis.

- Achieve and maintain a healthy weight.

- Develop effective strategies for handling stress and anger. Nurture old friendships and family ties, and make new friends; pay attention to your spiritual side.

- Obtain recommended screening tests and follow your physician's recommendations.

Do Less

- Don't use tobacco in any form: cigarettes, spit tobacco, cigars and pipes, bidis and clove cigarettes.

- Limit consumption of fats, especially trans fats and saturated fats.

- Limit consumption of salt to no more than 1500 mg of sodium per day.

- Avoid exposure to environmental tobacco smoke.

- Avoid excessive alcohol consumption— no more than one drink per day for women and two drinks per day for men.

- Limit consumption of cholesterol, added sugars, and refined carbohydrates.

- Avoid excess stress, anger, and hostility.

FIGURE 15.6 **Strategies for reducing your risk of cardiovascular disease.**

- *Soy protein.* Although soy itself doesn't seem to have much effect on cholesterol, replacing some animal proteins with soy protein (such as tofu) may help lower LDL cholesterol.

- *Healthy carbohydrates.* Healthy carbohydrate choices include whole grains, fruits, and nonstarchy vegetables. Healthy carbohydrates are important for people with insulin resistance, prediabetes, or diabetes.

- *Total calories.* Some studies have found that reducing energy intake can improve cholesterol and triglyceride levels as much as reducing fat intake does. Reduced calorie intake also helps control body weight—an extremely important risk factor for CVD.

Most experts recommend against taking nutritional supplements (especially extra folic acid and B vitamins) as a way to prevent heart disease. In fact, a 10-year-long study revealed that vitamin C and E supplements provided no protection against heart disease in men. In some of the study's subjects, vitamin E supplementation was associated with an increased risk of stroke. An estimated 12% of Americans take vitamin C and E supplements, and many people do so because of a long-standing yet unproven theory that these antioxidants protect against heart disease. There is some evidence that vitamin D deficiency may increase the risk of heart disease, especially in men, but experts do not currently advise taking vitamin D supplements to prevent CVD. If you are concerned about your heart health and think you may not be getting the nutrition you need, ask your physician or a registered dietician for advice.

A diet plan that reflects many of the recommendations described here was released as part of a study called Dietary Approaches to Stop Hypertension, or DASH. The DASH study found that a diet low in fat and high in fruits, vegetables, and low-fat dairy products reduces blood pressure. It also follows the recommendations for lowering the risk of heart disease, cancer, and osteoporosis. See Chapter 12 for details about the DASH diet plan, including specific serving information for people with different caloric needs.

Exercise Regularly

You can significantly reduce your risk of CVD with a moderate amount of physical activity. Follow the guidelines for physical activity and exercise described in Chapter 13. In addition to aerobic exercise for building and maintaining cardiovascular health, strength training helps reduce body fat and improves lipid levels and glucose metabolism.

The more exercise you get, the less likely you are to develop or die from CVD. Compared to sedentary individuals, people who engage in regular, moderate physical activity lower their risk of CVD by 20% or more. People who get regular, vigorous exercise reduce their risk of CVD by 30% or more. This positive benefit applies regardless of gender, age, race, or ethnicity.

The type of exercise performed is less important than the amount of energy expended during the activity. The greater the energy expenditure, the greater the health benefits. Exercise affects heart health via many mechanisms: it helps people lose weight and improve body composition. Weight loss can improve heart health by reducing the amount of stress on the heart. Changing body composition to a more positive ratio of fat to fat-free mass boosts resting metabolic rate. Exercise can also prevent metabolic syndrome and reverse many of its negative effects on the body. Exercise directly strengthens the heart muscle itself, and it improves the balance of fats in the blood by boosting HDL and reducing LDL and triglyceride levels.

One of the clearest positive effects of exercise is on hypertension. Many studies, involving thousands of people, have

Your chances of suffering an early heart attack or stroke depend on a variety of factors, many of which are under your control. You can significantly affect your future health and quality of life if you adopt healthy behaviors when you are young. To help identify your risk factors, circle the response for each risk category that best describes you:

1. Gender and age:

   0 Female age 55 or younger, or male age 45 or younger

   2 Female age 55 or older, or male age 45 or older

2. Heredity:

   0 Neither parent suffered a heart attack or stroke before age 60

   3 One parent suffered a heart attack or stroke before age 60

   7 Both parents suffered a heart attack or stroke before age 60

3. Smoking:

   0 Never smoked

   3 Quit more than two years ago, and lifetime smoking is less than five pack-years*

   6 Quit less than two years ago, and/or lifetime smoking is greater than five pack-years*

   8 Smoke less than half a pack per day

   13 Smoke more than half a pack per day

   15 Smoke more than one pack per day

4. Environmental tobacco smoke:

   0 Do not live or work with smokers

   2 Exposed to ETS at work

   3 Live with a smoker

   4 Both live and work with smokers

5. Blood pressure— if available, average your last three readings:

   0 120/80 or below

   1 121/81–130/85

   3 Don't know

   5 131/86–150/90

   9 151/91–170/100

   13 Above 170/100

6. Total cholesterol (mg/dl):

   0 Lower than 190

   1 190–210

   2 Don't know

   3 211–240

   4 241–270

   5 271–300

   6 Over 300

7. HDL cholesterol (mg/dl):

   0 Over 60

   1 55–60

   2 Don't know

   3 45–54

   5 35–44

   7 25–34

   12 Lower than 25

8. Exercise:

   0 Exercise three times a week

   1 Exercise once or twice a week

   2 Occasional exercise less than once a week

   7 Rarely exercise

9. Diabetes:

   0 No personal or family history

   2 One parent with diabetes

   6 Two parents with diabetes

   9 Non–insulin-dependent diabetes

   13 Insulin-dependent diabetes

10. Body mass index (using the formula provided in Chapter 14):

    0 <23.0

    1 23.0–24.9

    2 25.0–28.9

    3 29.0–34.9

    5 35.0–39.9

    7 ≥40

11. Stress:

    0 Relaxed most of the time

    1 Occasional stress and anger

    2 Frequently stressed and angry

    3 Usually stressed and angry

Scoring

Total your risk factor points. Refer to the following below to get an approximate rating of your risk of suffering an early heart attack or stroke.

Score	Estimated Risk
Less than 20	Low risk
20–29	Moderate risk
30–45	High risk
Over 45	Extremely high risk

*Pack-years can be calculated by multiplying the number of packs you smoked per day by the number of years you smoked. For example, if you smoked a pack and a half a day for five years, you would have smoked the equivalent of $1.5 \times 5 = 7.5$ pack-years.

shown that physical activity reduces both systolic and diastolic blood pressure. These studies showed that people who did regular aerobic exercise lowered their resting blood pressure by 2–4% on average. Lowered blood pressure itself reduces the risk of other kinds of cardiovascular disease.

Avoid Tobacco

The number-one risk factor for CVD that you can control is smoking. If you smoke, quit. If you don't, don't start. If you live or work with people who smoke, encourage them to quit—for their sake and yours. Exposure to environmental tobacco smoke raises your risk of CVD, and there is no safe level of exposure. If you find yourself breathing in smoke, take steps to prevent or stop the exposure. See Chapter 11 for detailed information about the effects of smoking and strategies for quitting.

Know and Manage Your Blood Pressure

If you have no CVD risk factors, have your blood pressure measured by a trained professional at least once every two years. Yearly tests are recommended if you have risk factors. If your blood pressure is high, follow your physician's advice on how to lower it. For those with hypertension that is not readily controlled with lifestyle changes, an array of antihypertension medications are available.

Know and Manage Your Cholesterol Levels

All people aged 20 and over should have their cholesterol checked at least once every five years. The NCEP recommends a fasting lipoprotein profile that measures total cholesterol, HDL, LDL, and triglyceride levels. Once you know your baseline numbers, you and your physician can develop an LDL goal and lifestyle plan.

Develop Effective Ways to Handle Stress and Anger

To reduce the psychological and social risk factors for CVD, develop effective strategies for handling the stress in

your life. Shore up your social support network, and try some of the techniques described in Chapter 2 for managing stress.

TIPS FOR TODAY AND THE FUTURE

Because cardiovascular disease is a long-term process that can begin when you're young, it's important to develop heart-healthy habits early in life.

RIGHT NOW YOU CAN:
- Make an appointment to have your blood pressure and cholesterol levels checked.
- List the key stressors in your life, and decide what to do about the ones that bother you most.
- Plan to replace one high-fat item in your diet with one that is high in fiber. For example, replace a doughnut with a bowl of whole-grain cereal.

IN THE FUTURE YOU CAN:
- Track your eating habits for one week, then compare them to the DASH eating plan. Make adjustments to bring your diet closer to the DASH recommendations.
- Sign up for a class in cardiopulmonary resuscitation (CPR). A CPR certification equips you with valuable lifesaving skills you can use to help someone who is choking, having a heart attack, or experiencing cardiac arrest.

connect™

Connect to Your Choices

Have you ever thought about where you get your behaviors and habits related to the health of your heart and cardiovascular system? Many factors can influence our behaviors and habits, some not as obvious as others. When you were growing up, did your family avoid risk-increasing behaviors like smoking and being physically inactive? Currently do you live on a campus or in a community where smoking is discouraged and physical activity is encouraged? Does your health clinic offer programs to help smokers quit or to promote and facilitate physical activity? Does your clinic offer free blood pressure and cholesterol checks?

What are the external factors that influence your choices about heart health–related behaviors and choices? What are your inner motivations and core values, and how do they affect your choices? Based on what you learned in this chapter, will you make some different choices in the future? If so, what will they be?

Go online to Connect to complete this activity: www.mcgraw-hillconnect.com

Ask Yourself

QUESTIONS FOR CRITICAL THINKING AND REFLECTION

Do you know what your blood pressure and cholesterol levels are? If not, is there a reason you don't know? Is something preventing you from getting this information about yourself? How can you motivate yourself to have these easy but important health checks?

- The cardiovascular system circulates blood throughout the body. The heart pumps blood to the lungs via the pulmonary artery and to the body via the aorta.

- The exchange of nutrients and waste products takes place between the capillaries and the tissues.

- The six major risk factors for CVD that can be changed or controlled are smoking, high blood pressure, unhealthy cholesterol levels, inactivity, overweight and obesity, and diabetes.

- Effects of smoking include lower HDL levels, increased blood pressure and heart rate, accelerated plaque formation, and increased risk of blood clots.

- Hypertension occurs when blood pressure exceeds normal levels most of the time. It weakens the heart, scars and hardens arteries, and can damage the eyes and kidneys.

- High LDL and low HDL cholesterol levels contribute to clogged arteries and increase the risk of CVD.

- Physical inactivity, obesity, and diabetes are interrelated and are associated with high blood pressure and unhealthy cholesterol levels.

- Contributing risk factors that can be changed include high triglyceride levels and psychological and social factors.

- Risk factors for CVD that can't be changed include being over 65, being male, being African American, and having a family history of CVD.

- Atherosclerosis is a progressive hardening and narrowing of arteries that can lead to restricted blood flow and even complete blockage.

- Heart attacks are usually the result of a long-term disease process. Warning signs of a heart attack include chest discomfort, shortness of breath, nausea, and sweating.

- A stroke occurs when the blood supply to the brain is cut off by a blood clot or hemorrhage. A transient ischemic attack (TIA) may be a warning sign of an impending stroke.

- Congestive heart failure occurs when the heart's pumping action becomes less efficient and fluid collects in the lungs or in other parts of the body.

- Dietary changes that can protect against CVD include decreasing your intake of fat, especially saturated and trans fats, and cholesterol, and increasing your intake of fiber by eating more fruits, vegetables, and whole grains.

- CVD risk can also be reduced by exercising regularly, avoiding tobacco and environmental tobacco smoke, knowing and managing your blood pressure and cholesterol levels, and developing effective ways of handling stress and anger.

FOR MORE INFORMATION

BOOKS

Freeman, M. W., and C. E. Junge. 2005. *Harvard Medical School Guide to Lowering Your Cholesterol*. New York: McGraw-Hill. *Information*

about cholesterol, including lifestyle changes and medication for improving cholesterol levels.

Heller, M. 2005. *The DASH Diet Action Plan, Based on the National Institutes of Health Research: Dietary Approaches to Stop Hypertension*. Northbrook, IL: Amidon Press. *Provides background information and guidelines for adopting the DASH diet; also includes meal plans to suit differing caloric needs and recipes.*

Lipsky, M. S., et al. 2008. *American Medical Association Guide to Preventing and Treating Heart Disease*. New York: Wiley. *A team of doctors provides advice for heart health to consumers.*

Mostyn, B. 2007. *Pocket Guide to Low Sodium Foods*, 2nd ed. Olympia, WA: InData Publishing. *Lists thousands of low-sodium products that can be purchased in supermarkets, as well as low-sodium choices available in many restaurants.*

ORGANIZATIONS, HOTLINES, AND WEBSITES

American Heart Association. Provides information about hundreds of topics relating to cardiovascular disease; the AHA's website links to several sites focusing on specific heart-related topics.

http://www.heart.org (general information)

Dietary Approaches to Stop Hypertension (DASH). Provides information about the design, diets, and results of the DASH study, including tips on how to follow the DASH diet at home.

http://www.nhlbi.nih.gov/health/public/heart/hbp/dash

The Human Heart: An On-Line Exploration. An online museum exhibit containing information about the structure and function of the heart, how to monitor your heart's health, and how to maintain a healthy heart.

http://www.fi.edu/learn/heart/index.html

MedlinePlus: Blood, Heart, and Circulation Topics. Provides links to reliable sources of information on many topics relating to cardiovascular health.

http://www.nlm.nih.gov/medlineplus/bloodheartandcirculation
.html

National Cholesterol Education Program (NCEP): Cholesterol Counts for Everyone. Provides information about cholesterol for people with heart disease and people who want to avoid it.

http://www.nhlbi.nih.gov/about/ncep/index.htm

National Heart, Lung, and Blood Institute. Provides information about and interactive applications for a variety of topics relating to cardiovascular health and disease, including cholesterol, smoking, obesity, hypertension, and the DASH diet.

http:// http://www.nhlbi.nih.gov/

National Stroke Association. Provides information and referrals for stroke victims and their families as well as a stroke risk assessment.

http://www.stroke.org

See also the listings for Chapters 2, 3, and 12–14.

SELECTED BIBLIOGRAPHY

Albert, C. M., et al. 2008. Effect of folic acid and B vitamins on risk of cardiovascular events and total mortality among women at high risk for cardiovascular disease: a randomized trial. *Journal of the American Medical Association* 299(17): 2027–2036.

American Cancer Society. 2010. *Cancer Facts and Figures, 2010.* Atlanta, GA: American Cancer Society.

American Heart Association. 2012. *Heart Disease and Stroke Statistics—2012 Update.* Dallas: American Heart Association.

Berger, J. S., et al. 2006. Aspirin for the primary prevention of cardiovascular events in women and men: a sex-specific meta-analysis of randomized controlled trials. *Journal of the American Medical Association* 295(3): 306–313.

Bibbins-Doming, K., et al. 2010. Projected Effect of Dietary Salt Reductions on Future Cardiovascular Disease. *New England Journal of Medicine* 362(7): 590–599.

Bonaa, K. H., et al. 2006. Homocysteine lowering and cardiovascular events after acute myocardial infarction. *New England Journal of Medicine* 354(15): 1578–1588.

Centers for Disease Control and Prevention. 2008. Awareness of stroke warning symptoms—13 states and the District of Columbia, 2005. *Morbidity and Mortality Weekly Report* 57(18): 481–485.

Centers for Disease Control and Prevention. 2009. Application of lower sodium intake recommendations to adults—United States, 1999–2006. *Morbidity and Mortality Weekly Report* 58(11): 281–283.

Centers for Disease Control and Prevention. 2011. Vital signs: current cigarette smoking among adults aged ≥18 years—United States, 2005–2010. *Morbidity and Mortality Weekly Report* (60)35: 1207–1212.

de Torbal, A., et al. 2006. Incidence of recognized and unrecognized myocardial infarction in men and women aged 55 and older: the Rotterdam Study. *European Heart Journal* 27(6): 729–736.

Elliott, P., et al. 2006. Association between protein intake and blood pressure: the INTERMAP study. *Archives of Internal Medicine* 166(1): 79–87.

Giovannucci, E., et al. 2008. 25-hydroxyvitamin D and risk of myocardial infarction in men: a prospective study. *Archives of Internal Medicine* 168(11): 1174–1180.

Gommans, J., et al. 2009. Preventing strokes: the assessment and management of people with transient ischemic attack. *New Zealand Medical Journal* 122(1293): 50–60.

Gurfinkel, E. P., et al. 2007. Invasive vs. non-invasive treatment in acute coronary syndromes and prior bypass surgery. *International Journal of Cardiology* 119(1): 65–72.

Harvard Medical School. 2008. The status of statins. *Harvard Women's Health Watch* 15(6): 1–3.

Jenkins, D. J., et al. 2006. Assessment of the longer-term effects of a dietary portfolio of cholesterol-lowering foods in hypercholesterolemia. *American Journal of Clinical Nutrition* 83(3): 582–591.

Kidambi, S., et al. 2009. Hypertension, insulin resistance, and aldosterone: sex-specific relationships. *Journal of Clinical Hypertension* 11(3): 130–137.

Marshall, D. A., et al. 2009. Achievement of heart health characteristics through participation in an intensive lifestyle change program (Coronary Artery Disease Reversal Study). *Journal of Cardiopulmonary Rehabilitation and Prevention* 29(2): 84–94.

Mirmiran, P., et al. 2009. Fruit and vegetable consumption and risk factors for cardiovascular disease. *Metabolism* 58(4): 460–468.

Müller, D., et al. 2006. How sudden is sudden cardiac death? *Circulation* 114(11): 1146–1150.

National Center for Health Statistics. 2012. Deaths: final data for 2008. *National Vital Statistics Reports* 58(19): 1–73.

Nita, C., et al. 2008. Hypertensive waist: first step of the screening for metabolic syndrome. *Metabolic Syndrome and Related Disorders* 7(2): 105–110.

Ostrom, M. P., et al. 2008. Mortality incidence and the severity of coronary atherosclerosis assessed by computed tomography angiography. *Journal of the American College of Cardiology* 52(16): 1335–1343.

Pickering, T. G., et al. 2008. Call to action on use and reimbursement for home blood pressure monitoring: a joint scientific statement from the American Heart Association, American Society of Hypertension, and Preventive Cardiovascular Nurses Association. *Hypertension* 52(1): 10–29.

Raggi, P., et al. 2008. Coronary artery calcium to predict all-cause mortality in elderly men and women. *Journal of the American College of Cardiology* 52(1): 17–23.

Refsum, H., et al. 2006. The Hordaland Homocysteine Study: A community-based study of homocysteine, its determinants, and associations with disease. *Journal of Nutrition* 136(6 Suppl.): 1731S–1740S.

Rho, R. W., and R. L. Page. 2007. The automated external defibrillator. *Journal of Cardiovascular Electrophysiology* 18: 1–4.

Ridker, P. M., et al. 2008. Rosuvastatin to prevent vascular events in men and women with elevated C-reactive protein. *New England Journal of Medicine* 359(21): 2195–2207.

Schiller, J.S., et al. 2012. Summary health statistics for U.S. adults: National Health Interview Survey, 2010. National Center for Health Statistics. *Vital Health Stat* 10(252).

Sesso, H. D., et al. 2008. Vitamins E and C in the prevention of cardiovascular disease in men: Physician's Health Study II randomized controlled trial. *Journal of the American Medical Association* 300(18): 2123–2133.

Sui, X., et al. 2007. Cardiorespiratory fitness and the risk of nonfatal cardiovascular disease in women and men with hypertension. *American Journal of Hypertension* 20(6): 608–615.

Tufts University. 2006. Pendulum swings on estrogen and women's heart health risk. *Health & Nutrition Newsletter* 24(3): 1–2.

University of California, Berkeley. 2008. Heart tests: low- to high-tech. *University of California, Berkeley, Wellness Letter*, August 5.

Wang, X., et al. 2007. Efficacy of folic acid supplementation in stroke prevention: a meta-analysis. *Lancet* 369(9576): 1876–1882.

BEHAVIOR CHANGE STRATEGY
Reducing the Saturated and Trans Fats in Your Diet

The American Heart Association recommends that no more than 7% of the calories in your diet come from saturated fats and no more than 1% from trans fats. Similarly, the report of the 2010 Dietary Guidelines Advisory Committee recommends that Americans limit saturated fat intake to no more than 7% of daily calories and that they avoid trans fat from industrial sources completely and consume only small amounts (less than 0.5% of calories) of trans fat from natural sources. Foods high in saturated fat include red meat, poultry skin, full-fat dairy products, coconut and palm oils, and hydrogenated vegetable oils. Hydrogenated fats, products made with them, and deep-fried fast food are high in trans fats. Although food manufacturers are phasing out trans fats, it's important to read labels to see how much trans fat a product contains. If a product contains less than 0.5% trans fat, the manufacturer is allowed to list trans fat content as 0%.

Monitor Your Current Diet

To see how your diet measures up, keep track of everything you eat for three days in your health journal. Information about the calorie and saturated fat and trans fat content of foods is available on many food labels, in books, and on the Internet.

At the end of the monitoring period, write in the calories and grams of saturated and trans fat for the foods you've eaten. Determine the percentage of daily calories as fat that you consumed for each day: multiply grams of saturated and trans fats by 9 (fat has 9 calories per gram) and then divide by total calories. For example, if you consumed 30 grams of saturated and trans fats and 2100 calories on a particular day, then your saturated and trans fat consumption as a percentage of total calories would be calculated as $30 \times 9 = 270$ calories of fat $\div 2100$ total calories $= 0.13$, or 13%. If you have trouble obtaining all the data you need to do the calculations, you can still estimate whether your diet is high in saturated and trans fats by seeing how many servings of foods high in unhealthy fats you typically consume on a daily basis.

Making Healthy Changes

To reduce your intake of unhealthy fats, you may want to set a limit on the number of servings of foods high in saturated and trans fats that you have each day. Or you may want to set a more precise goal and then continue to monitor your daily consumption. The 7% limit set by the American Heart Association corresponds to 12 grams of saturated fats in a 1600-calorie diet, 17 grams in a 2200-calorie diet, and 22 grams in a 2800-calorie diet.

To plan healthy changes, take a close look at your food record. Do you choose many foods high in saturated fats? Do you limit your portion sizes to those recommended by MyPlate? Try making healthy substitutions. Instead of a grilled cheese sandwich, try turkey, or substitute a plain baked potato for french fries. If you frequently eat in fast-food restaurants, try finding an appealing alternative—and recruit some friends to join you.

When you choose foods that are rich in saturated fats, *watch your portion sizes carefully*. Choose cuts of meat that have the least amount of visible fat, and trim off what you see. And try to balance your choices throughout the day. For example, if your lunch includes a hamburger and fries, choose a vegetarian pasta dish for dinner. Plan your diet around a variety of whole grains, vegetables, legumes, and fruits, which are nearly always low in fats and high in nutrients. See Chapter 12 for more details about a heart-healthy diet and for a list of alternatives to some popular foods.

CHAPTER 6

Principles of Physical Fitness

LOOKING AHEAD...

After reading this chapter, you should be able to:

- Describe how much physical activity is recommended for developing health and fitness
- Identify the components of physical fitness and the way each component affects wellness
- Explain the goal of physical training and the basic principles of training
- Describe the principles involved in designing a well-rounded exercise program
- List the steps that can be taken to make an exercise program safe, effective, and successful

TEST YOUR KNOWLEDGE

1. To improve your health, you must exercise vigorously for at least 30 minutes straight, 5 or more days per week. True or false?

2. Which of the following activities uses about 150 calories?
   a. washing a car for 45–60 minutes
   b. shooting a basketball for 30 minutes
   c. jumping rope for 15 minutes

3. Regular exercise can make a person smarter. True or false?

Answers

1. **False.** Experts recommend 150 minutes of moderate-intensity physical activity per week, but activity can be done in short bouts—10-minute sessions, for example—spread out over the course of the day.

2. **All three.** The more intense an activity is, the more calories it burns in a given amount of time. This is one reason that people who exercise vigorously can get the same benefits in less time than people who exercise longer at a moderate intensity.

3. **True.** Regular exercise (even moderate-intensity exercise) benefits the human brain and nervous system in a variety of ways. For example, exercise improves cognitive function—that is, the brain's ability to learn, remember, think, and reason.

Mc Graw Hill **connect** http://www.mcgrawhillconnect.com/
FITNESS AND WELLNESS

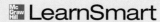

Mc Graw Hill **LearnSmart**
GET A BETTER GRADE. TRY LEARNSMART.

A ny list of the benefits of physical activity is impressive. Although people vary greatly in physical fitness and performance ability, the benefits of regular physical activity are available to everyone.

This chapter provides an overview of physical fitness. It explains how both lifestyle physical activity and more formal exercise programs contribute to wellness. It also describes the components of fitness, the basic principles of physical training, and the essential elements of a well-rounded exercise program. Chapters 3–6 provide an in-depth look at each of the elements of a fitness program; Chapter 7 puts these elements together in a complete, personalized program.

PHYSICAL ACTIVITY AND EXERCISE FOR HEALTH AND FITNESS

Despite the many benefits of an active lifestyle, levels of physical activity remain low for all populations of Americans (Figure 2.1). However, there is some good news. In August 2010, the Centers for Disease Control and Prevention (CDC) reported the following statistics about the physical activity levels of adult Americans:

- About 33% participate in some leisure-time physical activity, 35% engage in leisure-time physical activity on a regular basis, and 28% participate in vigorous leisure-time physical activity lasting at least 10 minutes three or more times per week.
- The percentage of people reporting no leisure-time physical activity decreased by nearly 6% between 1988 and 2009. Physical activity levels decline with age; are higher in men than in women; and are lower in Hispanics, American Indians, and blacks than in whites. Approximately 25% of Americans participate in no leisure-time physical activity—a level that has remained steady for a decade.

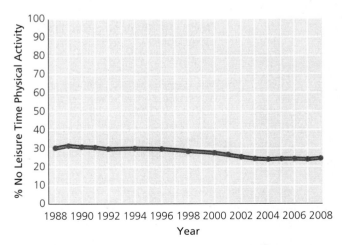

FIGURE 2.1 Percentage of adult Americans reporting no leisure-time physical activity.
SOURCE: Centers for Disease Control and Prevention. 2010. *Physical Activity Statistics* (http://www.cdc.gov/nccdphp/dnpa/physical/stats/leisure_time.htm; retrieved June 26, 2011).

- People with higher levels of education exercise vigorously more often than people with less education. For example, 78% of high school dropouts never exercise vigorously, compared with 39% of college graduates.
- People living in large urban areas are less active than those living in smaller communities, and those living in the South and Northeast were less active than people living in other areas of the country.

Possible barriers to increased activity include lack of time and resources, social and environmental influences, and—most important—lack of motivation and commitment (see Lab 2.2 for more on barriers). Some people also fear injury. Although physical activity carries some risks, the risks from inactivity are far greater. Increased physical activity may be the single most important lifestyle behavior for promoting health and well-being.

Physical Activity on a Continuum

Physical activity is movement carried out by the skeletal muscles that requires energy. Different types of physical activity can vary by ease or intensity. Standing up or walking down a hallway require little energy or effort. More intense, sustained activities, such as cycling five miles or running in a race, require considerably more.

Exercise refers to planned, structured, repetitive movement intended specifically to improve or maintain physical fitness. As discussed in Chapter 1, physical fitness is a set of physical attributes that allows the body to respond or adapt to the demands and stress of physical effort—to perform moderate to vigorous levels of physical activity without becoming overly tired. Levels of fitness depend on such physiological factors as the heart's ability to pump blood and the energy-generating capacity of the cells. These factors depend on genetics—a person's inborn potential for physical fitness—and behavior—getting enough physical activity to stress the body and cause long-term physiological changes.

Physical activity is essential to health and confers wide-ranging health benefits, but exercise is necessary to significantly improve physical fitness. This important distinction between physical activity, which improves health and wellness, and exercise, which improves fitness, is a key concept in understanding the guidelines discussed in this section.

Increasing Physical Activity to Improve Health and Wellness In 2010, the U.S. Surgeon General issued *The Surgeon General's Vision for a Healthy and Fit Nation*, following up the U.S. Department of Health and Human Services' landmark 2008 report, titled *Physical Activity Guidelines for Americans*, which made specific recommendations for promoting exercise and health. (You can read these reports at www.surgeongeneral.gov/library /obesityvision/obesityvision2010.pdf and www.health .gov/paguidelines.) Also, in 2011 the ACSM released its

Is Exercise Good for Your Brain?

Some scientists are now calling exercise the new "brain food." A variety of studies show that even moderate physical activity can improve brain health and function and may delay the decline in cognitive function that occurs for many people as they age. Recent evidence shows that regular physical activity has the following positive effects on the brain:

- Exercise improves cognitive function—the brain's ability to learn, remember, think, and reason.

- Exercise can help overcome the negative effects of a poor diet on brain health.

- Exercise promotes the creation of new nerve cells (neurons) throughout the nervous system. By promoting this process (called *neurogenesis*), exercise provides protection against injury and degenerative conditions that destroy neurons.

- Exercise enhances the nervous system's *plasticity*—its ability to change and adapt. In the brain, spinal cord, and nerves, this can mean developing new pathways for transmitting sensory information or motor commands.

- Exercise appears to have a protective effect on the brain as people age, helping to delay or even prevent the onset of neurodegenerative disorders such as Alzheimer's disease.

Although most people consider brain health to be a concern for the elderly, it is vital to wellness throughout life. For this reason, many studies on exercise and brain health include children as well as older adults. Targeted research has also focused on the impact of exercise on people with disorders such as cerebral palsy, multiple sclerosis, and developmental disabilities. Generally speaking, these studies all reach a similar conclusion: Exercise enhances brain health, at least to some degree, in people of all ages and a wide range of health statuses.

Along with the brain's physical health, mental health is enhanced by exercise. Even modest activity, such as taking a daily walk, can help combat a variety of mental health disorders.

It's hard to understate the impact of physical and mental disorders related to brain health. According to the Alzheimer's Association, 5.3 million Americans currently suffer from Alzheimer's disease, and the number is increasing at a rate of 70 people per second. People with depression, anxiety, or other mental disorders are more likely to suffer from chronic physical conditions. Taken together, these and other brain-related disorders cost untold millions of dollars in health care costs and lost productivity, as well as thousands of years of productive lifetime lost.

So, for the sake of your brain—as well as your muscles, bones, and heart—start creating your exercise program soon. You'll be healthier, and you may even feel a little smarter.

SOURCES: Garber, C. E., et al. 2011. Quantity and quality of exercise for developing and maintaining cardiorespiratory, musculoskeletal, and neuromotor fitness in apparently healthy adults: guidance for prescribing exercise. *Medicine and Science in Sports and Exercise* 43(7): 1334–1359; Physical Activity Guidelines Advisory Committee. 2008. *Physical Activity Guidelines Advisory Committee Report, 2008.* Washington, D.C.: U.S. Department of Health and Human Services; Stranahan, A. M., and M. P. Mattson. 2011. Bidirectional metabolic regulation of neurocognitive function. *Neurobiology of Learning and Memory* January (epub); Ploughman, M. 2008. Exercise is brain food: The effects of physical activity on cognitive function. *Developmental Neurorehabilitation* 11(3): 236–240; van Praag, H. 2009. Exercise and the brain: Something to chew on. *Trends in Neurosciences* 32(5): 283–290.

---

exercise guidelines for healthy adults titled, "Quantity and quality of exercise for developing and maintaining cardiorespiratory, musculoskeletal, and neuromotor fitness in apparently healthy adults: guidance for prescribing exercise." These reports stress the importance of regular physical activity and emphasize that some physical activity is better than none. They also present evidence that regular activity promotes health and prevents premature death and a variety of diseases (see the box "Is Exercise Good for Your Brain?"). The guidelines follow previous recommendations from the Surgeon General (issued in 1996), the Department of Health and Human Services (2005 and 2008), and the American College of Sports Medicine and American Heart Association (2007). *Physical Activity Guidelines for Americans* and the Surgeon General's recommendations include the following key guidelines for adults:

- For substantial health benefits, adults should do at least 150 minutes (2 and a half hours) a week of moderate-intensity aerobic physical activity, or 75 minutes (1 hour and 15 minutes) a week of vigorous-intensity aerobic physical activity, or an equivalent combination of moderate- and

physical activity Body movement carried out by the skeletal muscles that requires energy.

exercise Planned, structured, repetitive movement intended to improve or maintain physical fitness.

KEY TERMS

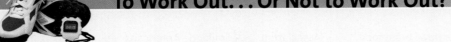

To Work Out... Or Not to Work Out?

What reasons do you have for not exercising—or not exercising more? Forget about superficial excuses such as "I couldn't run today because a SpongeBob marathon was on." Focus on *real* reasons that consistently interfere with your ability to be physically active. List the top three reasons, in order of significance:

Reason #1: _____

Reason #2: _____

Reason #3: _____

Now, focus on a real solution to each of the three problems. What can you do to prevent these issues from interfering with your ability to exercise in the future? Don't worry about one-time solutions; think about real, permanent solutions that will make these reasons for not exercising go away. List the solutions in the same order as the reasons you listed above:

Solution #1: _____

Solution #2: _____

Solution #3: _____

Think of this as more than just a list. Think of it as a commitment to resolve issues that keep you from meeting your fitness goals. That's the challenging part: Apply your solutions and stay active!

vigorous-intensity aerobic activity. Activity should preferably be spread throughout the week.

- For additional and more extensive health benefits, adults should increase their aerobic physical activity to 300 minutes (5 hours) a week of moderate-intensity activity, or 150 minutes a week of vigorous-intensity activity, or an equivalent combination of moderate- and vigorous-intensity activity. Adults can enjoy additional health benefits by engaging in physical activity beyond this amount.

- Adults should also do muscle-strengthening activities that are moderate or high intensity and involve all major muscle groups on two or more days a week, as these activities provide additional health benefits.

- Everyone should avoid inactivity. Adults, teenagers, and children should spend less time in front of a television or computer screen because it decreases metabolic health and contributes to a sedentary lifestyle and increases the risk of obesity.

The reports state that physical activity benefits people of all ages and of all racial and ethnic groups, including people with disabilities. The reports emphasize that the benefits of activity outweigh the dangers.

These levels of physical activity promote health and wellness by lowering the risk of high blood pressure, stroke, heart disease, type 2 diabetes, colon cancer, and osteoporosis and by reducing feelings of mild to moderate depression and anxiety.

What exactly is moderate physical activity? Activities such as brisk walking, dancing, swimming, cycling, and yard work can all count toward the daily total. A moderate amount of activity uses about 150 calories of energy

and causes a noticeable increase in heart rate, such as would occur with a brisk walk. Examples of activities that use about 150 calories are shown in Figure 2.2. You

Common Activities	Duration (min.)	
Washing and waxing a car	45–60	**Less Vigorous, More Time**
Washing windows or floors	45–60	
Gardening	30–45	
Wheeling self in wheelchair	30–40	
Pushing a stroller 1½ miles	30	
Raking leaves	30	
Walking 2 miles	30 (15 min/mile)	
Shoveling snow	15	
Stairwalking	15	
Sporting Activities		
Playing volleyball	45–60	
Playing touch football	45	
Walking 1¾ miles	35 (20 min/mile)	
Basketball (shooting baskets)	30	
Bicycling 5 miles	30	
Dancing fast (social)	30	
Water aerobics	30	
Swimming laps	20	
Basketball (playing game)	15–20	
Bicycling 4 miles	15	
Jumping rope	15	
Running 1½ miles	15 (10 min/mile)	**More Vigorous, Less Time**

FIGURE 2.2 Examples of moderate-intensity physical activity. Each example uses about 150 calories.
SOURCE: National Heart, Lung, and Blood Institute. 2010. *Why Is Exercise Important?* (www.nhlbi.nih.gov/health/public/heart/obesity/lose_wt/physical .htm; retrieved June 26, 2011).

Classifying Activity Levels

Assessing your physical activity level is easier if you know how to classify different kinds of activities. Fitness experts categorize activities into the following three levels:

- *Light activity* includes the routine tasks associated with typical day-to-day life, such as vacuuming, walking slowly, shopping, or stretching. You probably perform dozens of light activities every day without even thinking about it. You can gain significant health benefits by turning light activities into moderate activities—by walking briskly instead of slowly, for example.

- *Moderate activity*, such as walking at 3–4 miles per hour, causes your breathing and heart rate to accelerate but still allows for comfortable conversation. It is sometimes described as activity that can be performed comfortably for about 45 minutes. Examples of moderate physical activity include brisk walking, social dancing, and cycling moderately on level terrain.

- *Vigorous activity* elevates your heart and breathing rates considerably and has other physical effects that improve your fitness level. Examples include jogging, hiking uphill, swimming laps, and playing most competitive sports.

can burn the same number of calories by doing a lower-intensity activity for a longer time or a higher-intensity activity for a shorter time. College-age people are more likely to participate in physical activities they enjoy, such as dancing.

In contrast to moderate-intensity activity, *vigorous* physical activity causes rapid breathing and a substantial increase in heart rate, as exemplified by jogging. Physical activity and exercise recommendations for promoting general health, fitness, and weight management are shown in Table 2.1. Examples of light, moderate, and vigorous activities are given in the box "Classifying Activity Levels."

The daily total of physical activity can be accumulated in multiple bouts of 10 or more minutes per day—for example, two 10-minute bike rides to and from class and

Fitness Tip

To make your workouts more effective, find an exercise buddy. You can help each other set goals, stay on track, keep time, and count reps. Exercising with a friend makes working out more enjoyable, too.

Table 2.1	Physical Activity and Exercise Recommendations for Promoting General Health, Fitness, and Weight Management
GOAL	RECOMMENDATION
General health	Perform moderate-intensity aerobic physical activity for at least 150 minutes per week or 75 minutes of vigorous-intensity physical activity per week. Examples of moderate-intensity physical activity include brisk walking, water aerobics, tennis (doubles), dancing, and cycling less than 10 miles per hour. Examples of vigorous-intensity physical activity include jogging, power-walking, tennis (singles), jumping rope, hiking uphill, and cycling faster than 10 miles per hour. Also, be more active in your daily life: Walk instead of driving, take the stairs instead of the elevator, and watch less television.
Increased health benefits	Exercise at moderate intensity for 300 minutes per week or at vigorous intensity for 150 minutes per week.
Achieve or maintain weight loss	Exercise moderately for 60–90 minutes per day on most days of the week.
Muscle strength and endurance	Perform 1 or more sets of resistance exercises that work the major muscle groups for 8–12 repetitions (10–15 reps for older adults) on at least 2 nonconsecutive days per week. Examples include weight training and exercises that use body weight as resistance (such as core stabilizing exercises, pull-ups, push-ups, lunges, and squats).
Flexibility	Perform range-of-motion (stretching) exercises at least 2 days per week. Hold each stretch for 10–30 seconds.
Neuromuscular training	Older adults should do balance training 2–3 days per week. Examples include yoga, tai chi, and balance exercises (standing on one foot, step-ups, and walking lunges). These exercises are probably beneficial for young and middle-aged adults, as well.

SOURCES: Garber, C. E., et al. 2011. Quantity and quality of exercise for developing and maintaining cardiorespiratory, musculoskeletal, and neuromotor fitness in apparently health adults: Guidance for prescribing exercise. *Medicine and Science in Sports and Exercise* 43(7): 1334–1359; Physical Activity Guidelines Advisory Committee. 2008. *Physical Activity Guidelines Advisory Committee Report, 2008.* Washington, D.C.: U.S. Department of Health and Human Services; U.S. Department of Health and Human Services. 2010. *The Surgeon General's Vision for a Healthy and Fit Nation.* Rockville, Md: U.S. Department of Health and Human Services, Office of the Surgeon General.

a brisk 10-minute walk to the store. In this lifestyle approach to physical activity, people can choose activities that they find enjoyable and that fit into their daily routine; everyday tasks at school, work, and home can be structured to contribute to the daily activity total. If all Americans who are currently sedentary were to increase their lifestyle physical activity to 30 minutes per day, there would be an enormous benefit to public health and to individual well-being.

Increasing Physical Activity to Manage Weight
Because two-thirds of Americans are overweight, the U.S. Department of Health and Human Services has also published physical activity guidelines focusing on weight management. These guidelines recognize that for people who need to prevent weight gain, lose weight, or maintain weight loss, 150 minutes per week of physical activity may not be enough. Instead, they recommend up to 90 minutes of physical activity per day.

Exercising to Improve Physical Fitness As mentioned earlier, moderate physical activity confers significant health and wellness benefits, especially for those who are currently sedentary and become moderately active. However, people can obtain even greater health and wellness benefits by increasing the duration and intensity of physical activity. With increased activity, they will see more improvements in quality of life and greater reductions in disease and mortality risk.

More vigorous activity, as in a structured, systematic exercise program, is also needed to improve physical fitness; moderate physical activity alone is not enough. Physical fitness requires more intense movement that poses a substantially greater challenge to the body. The American College of Sports Medicine issued guidelines in 2006 and again in 2011 for creating a formal exercise program that will develop physical fitness. These guidelines are described in detail later in the chapter.

How Much Physical Activity Is Enough?

Some experts feel that people get most of the health benefits of physical activity simply by becoming more active over the course of the day; the amount of activity needed depends on an individual's health status and goals. Other experts feel that leisure-time physical activity is not enough; they argue that people should exercise long enough and intensely enough to improve the body's capacity for exercise—that is, to improve physical fitness. There is probably some truth in both of these positions.

Regular physical activity, regardless of the intensity, makes you healthier and can help protect you from many chronic diseases. Although you get many of the health benefits of exercise simply by being more active, you obtain even more benefits when you are physically fit. In addition to long-term health benefits, fitness also contributes significantly to quality of life. Fitness can give you

Wellness Tip

Do you set aside blocks of time every day for studying? If so, your schedule probably makes it easier to get your work done. The same is true of exercising, so make it a part of your daily routine, like studying.

freedom to move your body the way you want. Fit people have more energy and better body control. They can enjoy a more active lifestyle than their more sedentary counterparts. Even if you don't like sports, you need physical energy and stamina in your daily life and for many nonsport leisure activities such as visiting museums, playing with children, gardening, and so on.

Where does this leave you? Most experts agree that some physical activity is better than none, but that more—as long as it does not result in injury—is better than some. To set a personal goal for physical activity and exercise, consider your current activity level, your health status, and your overall goals. At the very least, strive to become more active and do 30 minutes of moderate-intensity activity at least 5 days per week. Choose to be active whenever you can. If weight management is a concern for you, begin by achieving the goal of 30 minutes of activity per day and then try to raise your activity level further, to 60–90 minutes per day or more. For even better health and well-being, participate in a structured exercise program that develops physical fitness. Any increase in physical activity will contribute to your health and well-being, now and in the future.

HEALTH-RELATED COMPONENTS OF PHYSICAL FITNESS

Some components of fitness are related to specific activities, and others relate to general health. **Health-related fitness** includes the following components:

- Cardiorespiratory endurance
- Muscular strength

Ask Yourself

QUESTIONS FOR CRITICAL THINKING AND REFLECTION

Does your current lifestyle include enough physical activity—30 minutes of moderate-intensity activity 5 or more days a week—to support health and wellness? Does your lifestyle go beyond this level to include enough vigorous physical activity and exercise to build physical fitness? What changes could you make in your lifestyle to develop physical fitness?

Fitness Tip

Very few activities build all the health-related components of fitness at the same time. This is why variety is important. Create a routine that lets you build one or two fitness components every day. Variety also keeps your workouts enjoyable.

- Muscular endurance
- Flexibility
- Body composition

Health-related fitness helps you withstand physical challenges and protects you from diseases.

Cardiorespiratory Endurance

Cardiorespiratory endurance is the ability to perform prolonged, large-muscle, dynamic exercise at moderate to high levels of intensity. It depends on such factors as the ability of the lungs to deliver oxygen from the environment to the bloodstream, the capacity of the heart to pump blood, the ability of the nervous system and blood vessels to regulate blood flow, and the capability of the cells' chemical systems to use oxygen and process fuels for exercise.

Cardiorespiratory endurance is a key component of health-related fitness.

When cardiorespiratory fitness is low, the heart has to work hard during normal daily activities and may not be able to work hard enough to sustain high-intensity physical activity in an emergency. As cardiorespiratory fitness improves, related physical functions also improve. For example:

- The heart pumps more blood per heartbeat.
- Resting heart rate slows.
- Blood volume increases.
- Blood supply to tissues improves.
- The body can cool itself better.
- Resting blood pressure decreases.
- Metabolism in skeletal muscle is enhanced, which improves fuel use.
- Resistance and aerobic training increases the level of antioxidant chemicals in the body and lowers oxidative stress.

A healthy heart can better withstand the strains of everyday life, the stress of occasional emergencies, and the wear and tear of time.

Endurance training also improves the functioning of the body's chemical systems, particularly in the muscles and liver. These changes enhance the body's ability to derive energy from food, allow the body to perform more exercise with less effort, increase sensitivity to insulin, and prevent type 2 diabetes.

Cardiorespiratory endurance is a central component of health-related fitness because heart and lung function is so essential to overall good health. A person can't live very long or very well without a healthy heart. Poor cardiorespiratory fitness is linked with heart disease, type 2 diabetes, colon cancer, stroke, depression, and anxiety. A moderate level of cardiorespiratory fitness can help compensate for certain health risks, including excess body fat: People who are lean but have low cardiorespiratory fitness have been found to have higher death rates than people with higher levels of body fat who are otherwise fit.

You can develop cardiorespiratory endurance through activities that involve continuous, rhythmic movements of large-muscle groups, such as the legs. Such activities include walking, jogging, cycling, and group aerobics.

Muscular Strength

Muscular strength is the amount of force a muscle can produce with a single maximum effort. It depends on

---

health-related fitness   Physical capacities that contribute to health: cardiorespiratory endurance, muscular strength, muscular endurance, flexibility, and body composition.

cardiorespiratory endurance   The ability of the body to perform prolonged, large-muscle, dynamic exercise at moderate to high levels of intensity.

muscular strength   The amount of force a muscle can produce with a single maximum effort.

KEY TERMS

such factors as the size of muscle cells and the ability of nerves to activate muscle cells. Strong muscles are important for everyday activities, such as climbing stairs, as well as for emergency situations. They help keep the skeleton in proper alignment, preventing back and leg pain and providing the support necessary for good posture. Muscular strength has obvious importance in recreational activities. Strong people can hit a tennis ball harder, kick a soccer ball farther, and ride a bicycle uphill more easily.

Muscle tissue is an important element of overall body composition. Greater muscle mass means a higher rate of **metabolism** and faster energy use. Greater muscle mass reduces markers of oxidative stress and maintains mitochondria (the "powerhouses" of the cell), both of which are important for metabolic health and longevity. Training to build muscular strength can also help people manage stress and boost their self-confidence.

Maintaining strength and muscle mass is vital for healthy aging. Older people tend to experience a decrease in both number and size of muscle cells, a condition called *sarcopenia*. Many of the remaining muscle cells become slower, and some become nonfunctional because they lose their attachment to the nervous system. Strength training (also known as *resistance training* or *weight training)* increases antioxidant enzymes and lowers oxidative stress. It also helps maintain muscle mass and function and possibly helps decrease the risk of osteoporosis (bone loss) in older people, which greatly enhances their quality of life and prevents life-threatening injuries.

Muscular Endurance

Muscular endurance is the ability to resist fatigue and sustain a given level of muscle tension—that is, to hold a muscle contraction for a long time or to contract a muscle over and over again. It depends on such factors as the size of muscle cells, the ability of muscles to store fuel, and the blood supply to muscles.

Muscular endurance is important for good posture and for injury prevention. For example, if abdominal and back muscles cannot support the spine correctly when sitting or standing for long periods, the chances of low-back pain and back injury are increased. Good muscular endurance in the trunk muscles is more important than muscular strength for preventing back pain. Muscular endurance helps people cope with daily physical demands and enhances performance in sports and work.

Flexibility

Flexibility is the ability to move the joints through their full range of motion. It depends on joint structure, the length and elasticity of connective tissue, and nervous system activity. Flexible, pain-free joints are important for good health and well-being. Inactivity causes the joints to become stiffer with age. Stiffness, in turn, often causes

people to assume unnatural body postures that can stress joints and muscles. Stretching exercises can help ensure a healthy range of motion for all major joints.

Body Composition

Body composition refers to the proportion of fat and **fat-free mass** (muscle, bone, and water) in the body. Healthy body composition involves a high proportion of fat-free mass and an acceptably low level of body fat, adjusted for age and gender. A person with excessive body fat—especially excess fat in the abdomen—is more likely to experience health problems, including heart disease, insulin resistance, high blood pressure, stroke, joint problems, type 2 diabetes, gallbladder disease, blood vessel inflammation, some types of cancer, back pain, and premature death.

The best way to lose fat is through a lifestyle that includes a sensible diet and exercise. The best way to add muscle mass is through strength training. Large changes in body composition are not necessary to improve health; even a small increase in physical activity and a small decrease in body fat can lead to substantial health improvements.

Skill (Neuromuscular)-Related Components of Fitness

In addition to the five health-related components of physical fitness, the ability to perform a particular sport or activity may depend on **skill (neuromuscular)-related fitness** components such as the following:

- *Speed*—the ability to perform a movement in a short period of time
- *Power*—the ability to exert force rapidly, based on a combination of strength and speed
- *Agility*—the ability to change the position of the body quickly and accurately
- *Balance*—the ability to maintain equilibrium while moving or while stationary
- *Coordination*—the ability to perform motor tasks accurately and smoothly using body movements and the senses
- *Reaction and movement time*—the ability to respond and react quickly to a stimulus

Skill-related fitness tends to be sport-specific and is best developed through practice. For example, the speed, coordination, and agility needed to play basketball can be developed by playing basketball. These activities are particularly important for older adults for preventing life-threatening falls. Participating in sports is fun, can help you build fitness, and contributes to other areas of wellness. Young adults often find it easier to exercise regularly when they participate in sports and activities they enjoy, such as dancing, tennis, snowboarding, or basketball.

Elite athletes demonstrate sport-specific skills such as speed, power, agility, coordination, and reaction time.

Older adults can develop balance by practicing exercises such as yoga and tai chi.

PRINCIPLES OF PHYSICAL TRAINING: ADAPTATION TO STRESS

The human body is very adaptable. The greater the demands made on it, the more it adjusts to meet those demands. Over time, immediate, short-term adjustments translate into long-term changes and improvements. When breathing and

Ask Yourself

QUESTIONS FOR CRITICAL THINKING AND REFLECTION

When you think about exercise, do you think of only one or two of the five components of health-related fitness, such as muscular strength or body composition? If so, where do you think your ideas come from? What role do the media play in shaping your ideas about fitness?

Wellness Tip

The words "over time" are key to realizing the benefits of physical activity. If you get in the habit of being active, you'll notice the benefits over time. After a few workouts, you'll breathe with less effort and recover faster, feel stronger and more flexible. In a few weeks your clothes will fit differently, and you'll notice changes in the mirror. Practice patience and watch the rewards pile up!

heart rate increase during exercise, for example, the heart gradually develops the ability to pump more blood with each beat. Then, during exercise, it doesn't have to beat as fast to meet the cells' demands for oxygen. The goal of **physical training** is to produce these long-term changes and improvements in the body's functioning. Although people differ in the maximum levels of physical fitness and performance they can achieve through training, the wellness benefits of exercise are available to everyone (see the box "Fitness and Disability").

Particular types and amounts of exercise are most effective in developing the various components of fitness. To put together an effective exercise program, you should first understand the basic principles of physical training, including the following:

- Specificity
- Progressive overload
- Reversibility
- Individual differences

All of these rest on the larger principle of adaptation.

KEY TERMS

metabolism The sum of all the vital processes by which food energy and nutrients are made available to and used by the body.

muscular endurance The ability of a muscle to remain contracted or to contract repeatedly for a long period of time.

flexibility The ability to move joints through their full range of motion.

body composition The proportion of fat and fat-free mass (muscle, bone, and water) in the body.

fat-free mass The nonfat component of the human body, consisting of skeletal muscle, bone, and water.

skill (neuromuscular)-related fitness Physical capacities that contribute to performance in a sport or an activity: speed, power, agility, balance, coordination, and reaction time; neuromuscular fitness refers to specific fitness related to maintaining performance levels of balance, agility, coordination, and gait.

physical training The performance of different types of activities that cause the body to adapt and improve its level of fitness.

Fitness and Disability

Physical fitness and athletic achievement are not limited to the able-bodied. People with disabilities can also attain high levels of fitness and performance, as shown by the elite athletes who compete in the Paralympics. The premier event for athletes with disabilities, the Paralympics are held in the same year and city as the Olympics. The performance of these skilled athletes makes it clear that people with disabilities can be active, healthy, and extraordinarily fit. Just like able-bodied athletes, athletes with disabilities strive for excellence and can serve as role models.

According to the U.S. Census Bureau, about 54 million Americans have some type of chronic disability. Some disabilities are the result of injury, such as spinal cord injuries sustained in car crashes or war. Other disabilities result from illness, such as the blindness that sometimes occurs as a complication of diabetes or the joint stiffness that accompanies arthritis. And some disabilities are present at birth, as in the case of congenital limb deformities or cerebral palsy.

Exercise and physical activity are as important for people with disabilities as for able-bodied individuals—if not *more* important. Being active helps prevent secondary conditions that may result from prolonged inactivity, such as circulatory or muscular problems. Currently, about 19% of people with disabilities engage in regular moderate-intensity activity.

People with disabilities don't have to be elite athletes to participate in sports and lead an active life. Some health clubs, fitness centers, city recreation centers, and universities offer activities and events geared for people of all ages and types of disabilities. They may have modified aerobics classes, special weight training machines, classes involving mild exercise in warm water, and other activities adapted for people with disabilities. Popular sports and recreational activities include adapted horseback riding, golf, swimming, and skiing. Competitive sports are also available— for example, there are wheelchair versions of billiards, tennis, weight lifting, hockey, and basketball, as well as sports for people with hearing, visual, or mental impairments. For those who prefer to get their exercise at home, special videos are available geared to individuals who use wheelchairs or who have arthritis, hearing impairments, metabolic diseases, or many other disabilities.

If you have a disability and want to be more active, check with your physician about what's appropriate for you. Call your local community center, university, YMCA/YWCA, hospital, independent living center, or fitness center to locate facilities. Look for a facility with experienced personnel and appropriate adaptive equipment. For specialized videos, check with hospitals and health associations that are geared to specific disabilities, such as the Arthritis Foundation.

Specificity—Adapting to Type of Training

To develop a particular fitness component, you must perform exercises designed specifically for that component. This is the principle of **specificity**. Weight training, for example, develops muscular strength but is less effective for developing cardiorespiratory endurance or flexibility. Specificity also applies to the skill-related fitness components (to improve at tennis, you must practice tennis) and to the different parts of the body (to develop stronger arms, you must exercise your arms). A well-rounded exercise program includes exercises geared to each component of fitness, to different parts of the body, and to specific activities or sports.

Progressive Overload—Adapting to the Amount of Training and the FITT Principle

The body adapts to the demands of exercise by improving its functioning. When the amount of exercise (also called *overload* or *stress*) is increased progressively, fitness continues to improve. This is the principle of **progressive overload**.

The amount of overload is important. Too little exercise will have no effect on fitness (although it may improve health); too much may cause injury and problems with the body's immune or endocrine (hormone) systems. The point at which exercise becomes excessive is highly individual; it occurs at a much higher level in an Olympic athlete than in a sedentary person. For every type of exercise, there is a training threshold at which fitness benefits begin to occur, a zone within which maximum fitness benefits occur, and an upper limit of safe training.

The amount of exercise needed depends on the individual's current level of fitness, the person's genetically determined capacity to adapt to training, his or her fitness goals, and the component being developed. A novice, for example, might experience fitness benefits from jogging a mile in 10 minutes, but this level of exercise would cause no physical adaptations in a trained distance runner. Beginners should start at the lower end of the fitness benefit zone; fitter individuals will make more rapid gains by exercising at the higher end of the fitness benefit zone. Progression is critical because fitness increases only if the volume and intensity of workouts increase. Exercising at the same intensity every training session will maintain fitness but will not increase it, because the training stress is below the threshold required to produce adaptation.

The amount of overload needed to maintain or improve a particular level of fitness for a particular fitness component is determined through four dimensions, represented by the acronym FITT:

- *Frequency*—how often
- *Intensity*—how hard
- *Time*—how long (duration)
- *Type*—mode of activity

Chapters 3, 4, and 5 show you how to apply the FITT principle to exercise programs for cardiorespiratory endurance, muscular strength and endurance, and flexibility, respectively.

Progressive overload is important because fitness increases only when the volume and intensity of exercise increase. The body adapts to overload by becoming more fit.

Frequency Developing fitness requires regular exercise. Optimum exercise frequency, expressed in number of days per week, varies with the component being developed and the individual's fitness goals. For most people, a frequency of 3–5 days per week for cardiorespiratory endurance exercise and 2 or more days per week for resistance and flexibility training is appropriate for a general fitness program.

An important consideration in determining appropriate exercise frequency is recovery time, which is also highly individual and depends on factors such as training experience, age, and intensity of training. For example, 24 hours of rest between highly intense workouts involving heavy weights or track sprints is not enough recovery time for safe and effective training. Intense workouts need to be spaced out during the week to allow for sufficient recovery time. On the other hand, you can exercise every day if your program consists of moderate-intensity walking or cycling. Learn to "listen to your body" to get enough rest between workouts. Chapters 3–5 provide more detailed information about training techniques and recovery periods for workouts focused on different fitness components.

Intensity Fitness benefits occur when a person exercises harder than his or her normal level of activity. The appropriate exercise intensity varies with each fitness component. To develop cardiorespiratory endurance, for example, you must raise your heart rate above normal. To develop muscular strength, you must lift a heavier weight than normal. To develop flexibility, you must stretch muscles beyond their normal length.

Time (Duration) Fitness benefits occur when you exercise for an extended period of time. For cardiorespiratory endurance exercise, 20–60 minutes is recommended. Exercise can take place in a single session or in several sessions of 10 or more minutes. The greater the intensity of exercise, the less time needed to obtain fitness benefits. For high-intensity exercise, such as running, 20–30 minutes is appropriate. For moderate-intensity exercise, such as walking, 45–60 minutes may be needed. High-intensity exercise poses a greater risk of injury than low-intensity exercise, so if you are a nonathletic adult, it's best to first emphasize low- to moderate-intensity activity of longer duration.

To build muscular strength, muscular endurance, and flexibility, similar amounts of time are advisable, but these exercises are more commonly organized in terms of a

specificity The training principle that the body adapts to the particular type and amount of stress placed on it.

progressive overload The training principle that placing increasing amounts of stress on the body causes adaptations that improve fitness.

KEY TERMS

specific number of repetitions of particular exercises. For resistance training, for example, a recommended program includes one or more sets of 8–12 repetitions of 8–10 different exercises that work the major muscle groups. Older adults should do 10–15 repetitions per set.

Type (Mode of Activity) The type of exercise in which you should engage varies with each fitness component and with your personal fitness goals. To develop cardiorespiratory endurance, you need to engage in continuous activities involving large-muscle groups—walking, jogging, cycling, or swimming, for example. Resistance exercises develop muscular strength and endurance, while stretching exercises build flexibility. The frequency, intensity, and time of the exercise will be different for each type of activity. (See pp. 41–44 for more on choosing appropriate activities for your fitness program.)

Reversibility—Adapting to a Reduction in Training

Fitness is a reversible adaptation. The body adjusts to lower levels of physical activity the same way it adjusts to higher levels. This is the principle of **reversibility**. When a person stops exercising, up to 50% of fitness improvements are lost within 2 months. However, not all fitness levels reverse at the same rate. Strength fitness is very resilient, so a person can maintain strength fitness by doing resistance exercise as infrequently as once a week. On the other hand, cardiovascular and cellular fitness reverse themselves more quickly—sometimes within just a few days or weeks. If you must temporarily curtail your training, you can maintain your fitness improvements by keeping the intensity of your workouts constant while reducing their frequency or duration.

Individual Differences—Limits on Adaptability

Anyone watching the Olympics can see that, from a physical standpoint, we are not all created equal. There are large individual differences in our ability to improve fitness, achieve a desirable body composition, and learn and perform sports skills. Some people are able to run longer distances, or lift more weight, or kick a soccer ball more skillfully than others will ever be able to, no matter how much they train. People respond to training at different rates, so a program that works for one person may not be right for another person.

There are limits on the adaptability—the potential for improvement—of any human body. The body's ability to transport and use oxygen, for example, can be improved by only about 5–30% through training. An endurance athlete must therefore inherit a large metabolic capacity in order to reach competitive performance levels. In the past few years, scientists have identified specific genes

Fitness Tip

At the gym, it can be intimidating to find yourself surrounded by people who seem to be in better shape than you are. But remember: They got in shape by focusing on themselves, not by worrying about what other people thought about them. You can avoid feeling intimidated by doing the same thing. Focus on *you*, and let others worry about themselves.

Ask Yourself

QUESTIONS FOR CRITICAL THINKING AND REFLECTION

Many people who play sports have had the experience of realizing that they are not as physically gifted as a teammate or that they are never going to be in the Olympics. What can you say to encourage someone who is discouraged by this realization? What benefits of physical activity, exercise, and sports might you point out?

that influence body fat, strength, and endurance. For example, they have identified more than 800 genes associated with endurance performance, and 100 of those determine individual differences in exercise capacity. However, physical training improves fitness regardless of heredity. For the average person, the body's adaptability is enough to achieve reasonable fitness goals.

DESIGNING YOUR OWN EXERCISE PROGRAM

Physical training works best when you have a plan. A plan helps you make gradual but steady progress toward your goals. Once you've determined that exercise is safe for you, planning for physical fitness consists of assessing how fit you are now, determining where you want to be, and choosing the right activities to help you get there.

Getting Medical Clearance

People of any age who are not at high risk for serious health problems can safely exercise at a moderate intensity (60% or less of maximum heart rate) without a prior medical evaluation (see Chapter 3 for a discussion of maximum heart rate). Likewise, if you are male and under 40 or female and under 50 and in good health, exercise is probably safe for you. If you do not fit into these age groups, or if you have health problems—especially high blood pressure, heart disease, muscle or joint problems,

Are You Healthy Enough for Exercise?

Heart disease and diabetes aren't the only reasons to get a doctor's approval before starting an exercise program. If you are severely overweight, have a family history of some chronic disease, or have just never exercised before, it could be advisable to talk to your doctor before becoming physically active.

Think about your current health status and your family history. If you think of any issues that might interfere with being physically active—or that might make exercise dangerous for you—list them below:

_____

_____

_____

_____

_____

If you write down anything, even *one* thing, make an appointment to see your doctor as soon as possible. Ask your doctor for an overall health evaluation, review your family history, and make sure the doctor knows you want to start being physically active on a regular basis. Then address the specific issues you listed above.

If your physician offers any specific advice, follow it. But if you can be physically active, even with some restrictions, make a commitment and get started on your exercise plan. And see your doctor regularly to make sure physical activity is working for you.

---

or obesity—see your physician before starting a vigorous exercise program. The Canadian Society for Exercise Physiology has developed the Physical Activity Readiness Questionnaire (PAR-Q) to help evaluate exercise safety; it is included in Lab 2.1. Completing it should alert you to any potential problems you may have. If a physician isn't sure whether exercise is safe for you, she or he may recommend an **exercise stress test** or a **graded exercise test (GXT)** to see whether you show symptoms of heart disease during exercise. For most people, however, it's far safer to exercise than to remain sedentary. For more information, see the box "Exercise and Cardiac Risk."

Assessing Yourself

The first step in creating a successful fitness program is to assess your current level of physical activity and fitness for each of the five health-related fitness components. The results of the assessment tests will help you set specific fitness goals and plan your fitness program. Lab 2.3 gives you the opportunity to assess your current overall level of activity and determine if it is appropriate. Assessment tests in Chapters 3–6 will help you evaluate your cardiorespiratory endurance, muscular strength, muscular endurance, flexibility, and body composition.

Setting Goals

The ultimate general goal of every health-related fitness program is the same—wellness that lasts a lifetime.

Whatever your specific goals, they must be important enough to you to keep you motivated. Most sports psychologists believe that setting and achieving goals is the most effective way to stay motivated about exercise. (Refer to Chapter 1 for more on goal setting, as well as Common Questions Answered at the end of this chapter.) After you complete the assessment tests in Chapters 3–6, you will be able to set goals directly related to each fitness component, such as working toward a 3-mile jog or doing 20 push-ups. First, though, think carefully about your overall goals, and be clear about why you are starting a program.

Choosing Activities for a Balanced Program

An ideal fitness program combines a physically active lifestyle with a systematic exercise program to develop and maintain physical fitness. This overall program is

KEY TERMS

reversibility   The training principle that fitness improvements are lost when demands on the body are lowered.

exercise stress test   A test usually administered on a treadmill or cycle ergometer that involves analysis of the changes in electrical activity in the heart from an electrocardiogram (EKG or ECG) taken during exercise; used to determine if any heart disease is present and to assess current fitness level.

graded exercise test (GXT)   An exercise test that starts at an easy intensity and progresses to maximum capacity.

Exercise and Cardiac Risk

IN FOCUS

Participating in exercise and sports is usually a wonderful experience that improves wellness in both the short and long term. In rare instances, however, vigorous exertion is associated with sudden death. It may seem difficult to understand that although regular exercise protects people from heart disease, it also increases the risk of sudden death.

Congenital heart defects (heart abnormalities present at birth) are the most common cause of exercise-related sudden death in people under 35. In nearly all other cases, coronary artery disease is responsible. In this condition, fat and other substances build up in the arteries that supply blood to the heart. Death can result if an artery becomes blocked or if the heart's rhythm and pumping action are disrupted. Exercise, particularly intense exercise, may trigger a heart attack in someone with underlying heart disease.

A study of jogging deaths in Rhode Island found that there was one death per 396,000 hours of jogging, or about one death per 7620 joggers per year—an extremely low risk for each individual jogger. Another study of men involved in a variety of physical activities found one death per 1.51 million hours of exercise. This 12-year study of more than 21,000 men found that those who didn't exercise vigorously were 74 times more likely to die suddenly from cardiac arrest during or shortly after exercise. It is also important to note that people are much safer exercising than engaging in many other common activities, including driving a car.

Although quite small, the risk does exist and may lead some people to wonder why exercise is considered such an important part of a wellness lifestyle. Exercise causes many positive changes in the body—in healthy people as well as those with heart disease—that more than make up for the slightly increased short-term risk of sudden death. Training slows or reverses the fatty buildup in arteries, helps protect people from deadly heart rhythm abnormalities, and enhances blood sugar regulation. People who exercise regularly have an overall risk of sudden death only about two-thirds that of nonexercisers. Active people who stop exercising can expect their heart attack risk to increase by 300%.

Obviously, someone with underlying coronary artery disease is at greater risk than someone who is free from the condition. However, many cases of heart disease go undiagnosed. The riskiest scenario may involve the middle-aged or older individual who suddenly begins participating in a vigorous sport or activity after being sedentary for a long time. This finding provides strong evidence for the recommendation that people increase their level of physical activity gradually and engage in regular, rather than sporadic, activity. Fortunately, the risk of heart-related

sudden death in middle-aged and older adults is least in people who exercise approximately 150 minutes per week—the activity level recommended by the U.S. Department of Health and Human Services.

SOURCES: Fahey, T. D., and G. D. Swanson. 2008. A model for defining the optimal amount of exercise contributing to health and avoiding sudden cardiac death. *Medicina Sportiva* 12(4): 124–128; Albert, C. M., et al. 2000. Trigger of sudden death from cardiac causes by vigorous exertion. *New England Journal of Medicine* 343(19): 1355–1361.

shown in the physical activity pyramid in Figure 2.3. If you are currently sedentary, your goal should be to focus on activities at the bottom of the pyramid and gradually increase the amount of moderate-intensity physical activity in your daily life. Appropriate activities include walking briskly, climbing stairs, doing yard work, and washing your car. You don't have to exercise vigorously, but you should experience a moderate increase in your heart and breathing rates. As described earlier, your activity time can be broken up into small blocks over the course of a day.

The next two levels of the pyramid illustrate parts of a formal exercise program. The principles of this program are consistent with those of the American College of Sports Medicine (ACSM), the professional organization for people involved in sports medicine and exercise science. The ACSM has established guidelines for creating an exercise program that will develop physical fitness (Table 2.2). A balanced program includes activities to develop all the health-related components of fitness:

• *Cardiorespiratory endurance* is developed by continuous rhythmic movements of large-muscle groups in activities such as walking, jogging, cycling, swimming, and aerobic dance and other forms of group exercise. Choose activities that you enjoy and that are convenient. Other popular choices are in-line skating, dancing, and backpacking. Start-and-stop activities such as tennis, racquetball, and soccer can also develop cardiorespiratory endurance if your skill level is sufficient to enable periods of continuous play. Training for cardiorespiratory endurance is discussed in Chapter 3.

Sedentary Activities
Do infrequently

Watching television, surfing the Internet, talking on the telephone

Strength Training
2–3 nonconsecutive days per week (all major muscle groups)

Bicep curls, push-ups, abdominal curls, bench press, calf raises

Flexibility Training
At least 2–3 days per week, ideally 5–7 days per week (all major joints)

Calf stretch, side lunge, step stretch, hurdler stretch

Cardiorespiratory Endurance Exercise
3–5 days per week (20–60 minutes per day)

Walking, jogging, bicycling, swimming, aerobic dancing, in-line skating, cross-country skiing, dancing, basketball

Moderate-Intensity Physical Activity
150 minutes per week; for weight loss or prevention of weight regain following weight loss, 60–90 minutes per day

Walking to the store or bank, washing windows or your car, climbing stairs, working in your yard, walking your dog, cleaning your room

FIGURE 2.3   Physical activity pyramid.

Table 2.2	ACSM Exercise Recommendations for Fitness Development in Healthy Adults
EXERCISE TO DEVELOP AND MAINTAIN CARDIORESPIRATORY ENDURANCE AND BODY COMPOSITION	
Frequency of training	3–5 days per week.
Intensity of training	55/65–90% of maximum heart rate or 40/50–85% of heart rate reserve or maximum oxygen uptake reserve.* The lower-intensity values (55–64% of maximum heart rate and 40–49% of heart rate reserve) are most applicable to unfit individuals. For average individuals, intensities of 70–85% of maximum heart rate or 60–80% of heart rate reserve are appropriate.
Time (duration) of training	20–60 total minutes per day of continuous or intermittent (in sessions lasting 10 or more minutes) aerobic activity. Duration depends on the intensity of activity; thus, low-intensity activity should be conducted over a longer period of time (30 minutes or more). Low to moderate-intensity activity of longer duration is recommended for nonathletic adults.
Type (mode) of activity	Any activity that uses large-muscle groups, can be maintained continuously, and is rhythmic and aerobic in nature—for example, walking-hiking, running-jogging, bicycling, cross-country skiing, aerobic dancing and other forms of group exercise, rope skipping, rowing, stair climbing, swimming, skating, and endurance game activities.
EXERCISE TO DEVELOP AND MAINTAIN MUSCULAR STRENGTH AND ENDURANCE, FLEXIBILITY, AND BODY COMPOSITION	
Resistance training	One set of 8–10 exercises that condition the major muscle groups, performed at least 2 days per week. Most people should complete 8–12 repetitions of each exercise to the point of fatigue; practicing other repetition ranges (for example, 3–5 or 12–15) also builds strength and endurance; for older and frailer people (approximately 50–60 and older), 10–15 repetitions with a lighter weight may be more appropriate. Multiple-set regimens will provide greater benefits if time allows. Any mode of exercise that is comfortable throughout the full range of motion is appropriate (for example, free weights, elastic bands, or machines).
Flexibility training	Static stretches, performed for the major muscle groups at least 2–3 days per week, ideally 5–7 days per week. Stretch to the point of tightness, holding each stretch for 10–30 seconds; perform 2–4 repetitions of each stretch.

*Instructions for calculating target heart rate intensity for cardiorespiratory endurance exercise are presented in Chapter 3.

SOURCE: Adapted from American College of Sports Medicine. 2009. *ACSM's Guidelines for Exercise Testing and Prescription*, 8th ed. Philadelphia: Lippincott Williams and Wilkins; Garber, C. E., et al. 2011. Quantity and quality of exercise for developing and maintaining cardiorespiratory, musculoskeletal, and neuromotor fitness in apparently healthy adults: guidance for prescribing exercise. *Medicine and Science in Sports and Exercise* 43(7): 1334–1359.

	Lifestyle physical activity	Moderate exercise program	Vigorous exercise program
Description	Moderate physical activity (150 minutes per week; muscle-strengthening exercises 2 or more days per week)	Cardiorespiratory endurance exercise (20–60 minutes, 3–5 days per week); strength training (2–3 nonconsecutive days per week); and stretching exercises (2 or more days per week)	Cardiorespiratory endurance exercise (20–60 minutes, 3–5 days per week); interval training; strength training (3–4 nonconsecutive days per week); and stretching exercises (5–7 days per week)
Sample activities or program	• Walking to and from work, 15 minutes each way • Cycling to and from class, 10 minutes each way • Doing yard work for 30 minutes • Dancing (fast) for 30 minutes • Playing basketball for 20 minutes • Muscle exercises such as push-ups, squats, or back exercises	• Jogging for 30 minutes, 3 days per week • Weight training, 1 set of 8 exercises, 2 days per week • Stretching exercises, 3 days per week	• Running for 45 minutes, 3 days per week • Intervals, running 400 m at high effort, 4 sets, 2 days per week • Weight training, 3 sets of 10 exercises, 3 days per week • Stretching exercises, 6 days per week
Health and fitness benefits	Better blood cholesterol levels, reduced body fat, better control of blood pressure, improved metabolic health, and enhanced glucose metabolism; improved quality of life; reduced risk of some chronic diseases Greater amounts of activity can help prevent weight gain and promote weight loss	All the benefits of lifestyle physical activity, plus improved physical fitness (increased cardiorespiratory endurance, muscular strength and endurance, and flexibility) and even greater improvements in health and quality of life and reductions in chronic disease risk	All the benefits of lifestyle physical activity and a moderate exercise program, with greater increases in fitness and somewhat greater reductions in chronic disease risk Participating in a vigorous exercise program may increase risk of injury and overtraining

FIGURE 2.4 Health and fitness benefits of different amounts of physical activity and exercise.

• *Muscular strength and endurance* can be developed through resistance training—training with weights or performing calisthenic exercises such as push-ups and curl-ups. Training for muscular strength and endurance is discussed in Chapter 4.

• *Flexibility* is developed by stretching the major muscle groups regularly and with proper technique. Flexibility is discussed in Chapter 5.

• *Healthy body composition* can be developed through a sensible diet and a program of regular exercise. Cardiorespiratory endurance exercise is best for reducing body fat; resistance training builds muscle mass, which, to a small extent, helps increase metabolism. Body composition is discussed in Chapter 6.

Chapter 7 contains guidelines to help you choose activities and put together a complete exercise program that will suit your goals and preferences. (Refer to Figure 2.4 for a summary of the health and fitness benefits of different levels of physical activity.)

What about the tip of the activity pyramid? Although sedentary activities are often unavoidable—attending class, studying, working in an office, and so on—many people choose inactivity over activity during their leisure time. Change sedentary patterns by becoming more active whenever you can. Move more and sit less.

Guidelines for Training

The following guidelines will make your exercise program more effective and successful.

Train the Way You Want Your Body to Change
Stress your body so it adapts in the desired manner. To have a more muscular build, lift weights. To be more flexible, do stretching exercises. To improve performance in a particular sport, practice that sport or its movements.

Train Regularly Consistency is the key to improving fitness. Fitness improvements are lost if too much time passes between exercise sessions.

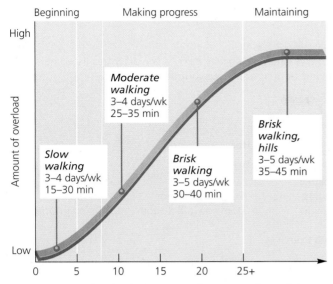

FIGURE 2.5 Progression of an exercise program.
This figure shows how the amount of overload is increased gradually over time in a sample walking program. Regardless of the activity chosen, it is important that an exercise program begin slowly and progress gradually. Once you achieve the desired level of fitness, you can maintain it by exercising 3–5 days a week.
SOURCE: Progression data from American College of Sports Medicine. 2009. *ACSM's Guidelines for Exercise Testing and Prescription,* 8th ed. Philadelphia: Lippincott Williams and Wilkins.

Start Slowly, and Get in Shape Gradually

As Figure 2.5 shows, an exercise program can be divided into three phases:

- *Beginning phase.* The body adjusts to the new type and level of activity.
- *Progress phase.* Fitness increases.
- *Maintenance phase.* The targeted level of fitness is sustained over the long term.

When beginning a program, start slowly to give your body time to adapt to the stress of exercise. Choose activities carefully according to your fitness status. If you have been sedentary or are overweight, try an activity such as walking or swimming that won't jar the body or strain the joints.

As you progress, increase duration and frequency before increasing intensity. If you train too much or too intensely, you are more likely to suffer injuries or become **overtrained**, a condition characterized by lack of energy, aching muscles and joints, and decreased physical performance. Injuries and overtraining slow down an exercise program and impede motivation. The goal is not to get in shape as quickly as possible but to gradually become and then remain physically fit.

Warm Up Before Exercise

Warming up can decrease your chances of injury by helping your body gradually progress from rest to activity. A good warm-up can increase muscle temperature, reduce joint stiffness, bathe the joint surfaces in lubricating fluid, and increase blood flow to the muscles, including the heart. Some studies suggest that warming up may also enhance muscle metabolism and mentally prepare you for a workout.

A warm-up should include low-intensity, whole-body movements similar to those used in the activity that will follow. For example, runners may walk and jog slowly prior to running at full speed. A tennis player might hit forehands and backhands at a low intensity before playing a vigorous set of tennis. A warm-up is not the same as a stretching workout. For safety and effectiveness, it is best to stretch *after* an endurance or strength training workout, when muscles are warm—and not as part of a warm-up. (Appropriate and effective warm-ups are discussed in greater detail in Chapters 3–5.)

Cool Down After Exercise

During exercise, as much as 90% of circulating blood is directed to the muscles and skin, up from as little as 20% during rest. If you suddenly stop moving after exercise, the amount of blood returning to your heart and brain may be insufficient, and you may experience dizziness, a drop in blood pressure, or other problems. Cooling down at the end of a workout helps safely restore circulation to its normal resting condition. So, after you exercise, cool down before you sit or lie down or jump into the shower. Cool down by continuing to move at a slow pace—walking for 5–10 minutes, for example, as your heart and breathing rate and blood pressure slowly return to normal. At the end of the cool-down period, do stretching exercises while your muscles are still warm. Cool down longer after intense exercise sessions.

Exercise Safely

Physical activity can cause injury or even death if you don't consider safety. For example, you should always:

- Wear a helmet when biking, skiing, or rock climbing.
- Wear eye protection when playing racquetball or squash.

Wellness Tip

Moderation is important, especially if you're just starting to get physically active. Work at a pace that's comfortable and enjoyable, with a goal of making gradual improvements. This will help you get into the habit of being active, and will help you avoid burnout.

overtraining A condition caused by training too much or too intensely, characterized by lack of energy, decreased physical performance, and aching muscles and joints.

KEY TERM

Vary Your Activities

Do you have a hard time thinking of new activities to try? Check the boxes next to the activities listed here that interest you. Then look for resources and facilities on your campus or in your community.

TAKE CHARGE

Outdoor Exercises

❏ Walking   ❏ In-line skating   ❏ Hiking
❏ Running   ❏ Skateboarding   ❏ Backpacking
❏ Cycling   ❏ Rowing   ❏ Ice skating
❏ Swimming   ❏ Horseback riding   ❏ Fly fishing

Sports and Games

❏ Basketball   ❏ Softball   ❏ Bowling
❏ Tennis   ❏ Water skiing   ❏ Surfing
❏ Volleyball   ❏ Windsurfing   ❏ Dancing
❏ Golf   ❏ Badminton   ❏ Snow skiing
❏ Soccer   ❏ Ultimate Frisbee   ❏ Gymnastics

Exercises You Can Do at Home and Work

❏ Desk exercises   ❏ Yard work   ❏ Painting walls
❏ Calisthenics   ❏ Sweeping   ❏ Walking the dog
❏ Gardening   ❏ Exploring on foot   ❏ Shopping
❏ Housework   ❏ Doing a walk-a-thon   ❏ Doing errands

Health Club Exercises

❏ Weight training   ❏ Ski machine   ❏ Elliptical trainer
❏ Circuit training   ❏ Supine bike   ❏ Medicine ball
❏ Group exercise   ❏ Rowing machine   ❏ Rope skipping
❏ Treadmill   ❏ Plyometrics   ❏ Punching bag
❏ Stationary bike   ❏ Water aerobics   ❏ Racquetball

- Wear bright clothing when exercising on a public street.
- Walk or run with a partner on a deserted track or in a park.
- Give vehicles plenty of leeway, even when you have the right of way.
- In the weight room, be aware of people exercising near you, and use spotters when appropriate.

Overloading your muscles and joints can lead to serious injury, so train within your capacity. Use high-quality equipment and keep it in good repair. Report broken gym equipment to the health club manager. (See Appendix A for more information on personal safety.)

Listen to Your Body and Get Adequate Rest Rest can be as important as exercise for improving fitness. Fitness reflects an adaptation to the stress of exercise. Building fitness involves a series of exercise stresses, recuperation, and adaptation leading to improved fitness, followed by further stresses. Build rest into your training program, and don't exercise if it doesn't feel right. Sometimes you need a few days of rest to recover enough to train with the intensity required for improving fitness. Getting enough sleep is an important part of the recovery process. On the other hand, you can't train sporadically, either. If you listen to your body and it always tells you to rest, you won't make any progress.

Cycle the Volume and Intensity of Your Workouts To add enjoyment and variety to your program and to further improve fitness, don't train at the same intensity during every workout. Train intensely on some days and

train lightly on others. Proper management of workout intensity is a key to improving physical fitness. Use cycle training, also known as *periodization,* to provide enough recovery for intense training: By training lightly one workout, you can train harder the next. However, take care to increase the volume and intensity of your program gradually—never more than 10% per week.

Vary Your Activities Change your exercise program from time to time to keep things fresh and help develop a higher degree of fitness. The body adapts quickly to an exercise stress, such as walking, cycling, or swimming. Gains in fitness in a particular activity become more difficult with time. Varying the exercises in your program allows you to adapt to many types of exercise and develops fitness in a variety of activities (see the box "Vary Your Activities"). Changing activities may also help reduce your risk of injury.

Train with a Partner Training partners can motivate and encourage each other through rough spots and help each other develop proper exercise techniques. Training with a partner can make exercising seem easier and more fun. It can also help you keep motivated and on track. A commitment to a friend is a powerful motivator. If you can afford it, you may benefit from a personal trainer who can give you instruction in exercise techniques and help provide motivation.

Train Your Mind Becoming fit requires commitment, discipline, and patience. These qualities come from understanding the importance of exercise and having clear and reachable goals. Use the lifestyle management

Digital Workout Aids

When you're just starting to get physically active, you can wind up with a lot of questions. How many miles did I walk? How many sit-ups did I do? How many minutes did I run? When your mind is completely focused on just *doing* an activity, it's easy to lose count of time, distance, and reps. But it's important to keep track of these things: Move too little and you won't see any progress; move too much and you run the risk of injury or burnout. Either outcome is bad news for your exercise program.

Luckily, we live in a digital age, and the fitness industry is providing an ever-growing array of tools that can track your progress for you. If you like to walk or run, digital pedometers can track your distance and the number of steps you take. Advanced trackers can even record any hills you encounter during your workout. If calisthenics are your choice, there are gaming systems and smartphone apps that work for specific exercises to count reps, assess your form, and challenge you to push yourself harder.

You can track more than just your exercise habits with digital assistance. Electronic devices and smart programs are available to help with many aspects of wellness, including the following:

- Dietary habits
- Calories consumed and burned
- Stress management
- Meditation and spirituality
- Heart rate and respiration
- Menstrual cycles
- Family medical history
- Journaling

And that's just to name a few. We'll introduce a variety of these digital devices and apps in later chapters, in the new "Wellness in the Digital Age" feature box like this one. You may find one or more digital apps (many of which are free) that appeal to you and can help you make progress toward your own fitness and wellness goals.

---

techniques discussed in Chapter 1 to keep your program on track.

Fuel Your Activity Appropriately Good nutrition, including rehydration and resynthesis of liver and muscle carbohydrate stores, is part of optimal recuperation from exercise. Consume enough calories to support your exercise program without gaining body fat. Many studies show that consuming carbohydrates and protein before or after exercise promotes restoration of stored fuels and helps heal injured tissues so that you can exercise intensely again shortly. Nutrition for exercise is discussed in greater detail in Chapters 3 and 8.

Have Fun You are more likely to stick with an exercise program if it's fun. Choose a variety of activities that you enjoy. Some people like to play competitive sports, such as tennis, golf, or volleyball. Competition can boost motivation, but remember: Sports are competitive, whereas training for fitness is not. Other people like more solitary activities, such as jogging, walking, or swimming. Still others like high-skill individual sports, such as skiing, surfing, or skateboarding. Many activities can help you get fit, so choose the ones you enjoy. You can also boost your enjoyment and build your social support network by exercising with friends and family.

Track Your Progress Monitoring the progress of your program can help keep you motivated and on track. Depending on the activities you've included in your program, you may track different measures of your program—minutes of jogging, miles of cycling, laps of swimming, number of push-ups, amount of weight lifted, and so on. If your program focuses on increasing daily physical activity, consider using an inexpensive pedometer to monitor the number of steps you take each day. (See Lab 2.3 for more information on setting goals and monitoring activity with a pedometer; see the box "Digital Workout Aids" for an introduction to products and apps that can help you track your progress.) Specific examples of program monitoring can be found in the labs for Chapters 3–5.

Keep Your Exercise Program in Perspective As important as physical fitness is, it is only part of a well-rounded life. You need time for work and school, family and friends, relaxation and hobbies. Some people become overinvolved in exercise and neglect other parts of their lives. They think of themselves as runners, dancers,

Ask Yourself

QUESTIONS FOR CRITICAL THINKING
AND REFLECTION

If you were to start planning a program, what would be your three most important long-term goals? What would you set as short-term goals? What rewards would be meaningful to you?

swimmers, or triathletes rather than as people who participate in those activities. Balance and moderation are the key ingredients of a fit and well life.

TIPS FOR TODAY AND THE FUTURE

Physical activity and exercise offer benefits in nearly every area of wellness. Even a low to moderate level of activity provides valuable health benefits. The important thing is to get moving!

RIGHT NOW YOU CAN

- Look at your calendar for the rest of the week and write in some physical activity—such as walking, running, biking, skating, swimming, hiking, or playing Frisbee—on as many days as you can. Schedule the activity for a specific time and stick to it.
- Call a friend and invite her or him to start planning a regular exercise program with you.

IN THE FUTURE YOU CAN

- Schedule a session with a qualified personal trainer who can evaluate your current fitness level and help you set personalized fitness goals.
- Create seasonal workout programs for the spring, summer, fall, and winter. Develop programs that are varied but consistent with your overall fitness goals.

SUMMARY

- Moderate daily physical activity contributes substantially to good health. Even without a formal, vigorous exercise program, you can get many of the same health benefits by becoming more physically active.

- If you are already active, you benefit even more by increasing the intensity or duration of your activities.

- The five components of physical fitness most important for health are cardiorespiratory endurance, muscular strength, muscular endurance, flexibility, and body composition.

- Physical training is the process of producing long-term improvements in the body's functioning through exercise.

All training is based on the fact that the body adapts to physical stress.

- According to the principle of specificity, bodies change specifically in response to the type of training received.

- Bodies also adapt to progressive overload. When you progressively increase the frequency, intensity, and time (duration) of the right type of exercise, you become increasingly fit.

- Bodies adjust to lower levels of activity by losing fitness, a principle known as reversibility. To counter the effects of reversibility, it's important to keep training at the same intensity, even if you have to reduce the number or length of sessions.

- According to the principle of individual differences, people vary in the maximum level of fitness they can achieve and in the rate of change they can expect from an exercise program.

- When designing an exercise program, determine if medical clearance is needed, assess your current level of fitness, set realistic goals, and choose activities that develop all the components of fitness.

- Train regularly, get in shape gradually, warm up and cool down, maintain a structured but flexible program, exercise safely, consider training with a partner or personal trainer, train your mind, have fun, and keep exercise in perspective.

FOR FURTHER EXPLORATION

BOOKS

American College of Sports Medicine. 2009. *ACSM's Guidelines for Exercise Testing and Prescription,* 8th ed. Philadelphia: Lippincott Williams and Wilkins. *Includes the ACSM guidelines for safety of exercising, a basic discussion of exercise physiology, and information about fitness testing and prescription.*

Earle, R. W., and T. R. Baechle, eds. 2008. *NSCA's Essentials of Personal Training,* 3rd ed. Champaign, Ill.: Human Kinetics. *Comprehensive discussions of fitness testing, exercise and disease, nutrition and physical performance, and exercise prescription.*

Marcus, B. H., and L. A. Forsyth. 2009. *Motivating People to Be Physically Active,* 2nd ed. Champaign, Ill.: Human Kinetics. *Describes methods for helping people increase physical activity levels.*

Page, P. 2011. *Pilates Illustrated.* Champaign, Ill.: Human Kinetics. *A guide to improving muscle fitness, while improving posture, flexibility, and balance.*

JOURNALS

ACSM Health and Fitness Journal (401 West Michigan Street, Indianapolis, In. 46202; http://journals.lww.com/acsm-healthfitness/pages/default.aspx)

Physician and Sportsmedicine (1235 Westlakes Drive, Suite 220, Berwyn, Pa. 19312; https://physsportsmed.com)

Q I have asthma. Is it OK for me to start an exercise program?

A Probably, but you should see your doctor before you start exercising, especially if you have been sedentary up to this point. Your personal physician can advise you on the type of exercise program that is best for you, given the severity of your condition, and how to avoid suffering exercise-related asthma attacks.

Q What should my fitness goals be?

A Begin by thinking about your general overall goals—the benefits you want to obtain by increasing your activity level and/or beginning a formal exercise program. Examples of long-term goals include reducing your risk of chronic diseases, increasing your energy level, and maintaining a healthy body weight.

To help shape your fitness program, you need to set specific, short-term goals based on measurable factors. These specific goals should be an extension of your overall goals—the specific changes to your current activity and exercise habits needed to achieve your general goals. In setting short-term goals, be sure to use the SMART criteria described in Chapter 1. As noted there, your goals should be **S**pecific, **M**easurable, **A**ttainable, **R**ealistic, and **T**ime frame–specific (SMART).

You need information about your current levels of physical activity and physical fitness in order to set appropriate goals. The labs in this chapter will help you determine your physical activity level—for example, how many minutes per day you engage in moderate or vigorous activity or how many daily steps you take. Using this information, you can set goals for lifestyle physical activity to help you meet your overall goals. For example, if your general long-term goals are to reduce the risk of chronic disease and prevent weight gain, the Dietary Guidelines recommend 60 minutes of moderate physical activity daily.

If you currently engage in 30 minutes of moderate activity daily, then your behavior change goal would be to add 30 minutes of daily physical activity (or an equivalent number of additional daily steps—about 3500–4000); your time frame for the change might be 8–12 weeks.

Labs in Chapters 3–6 provide opportunities to assess your fitness status for all the health-related components of fitness. The results of these assessments can guide you in setting specific fitness goals. For instance, if the labs in Chapter 4 indicate that you have good muscular strength and endurance in your lower body but poor strength and endurance in your upper body, then setting a specific goal for improving upper-body muscle fitness would be an appropriate goal—increasing the number of push-ups you can do from 22 to 30, for example. Chapters 3–6 include additional advice for setting appropriate goals.

Once you start your behavior change program, you may discover that your goals aren't quite appropriate; perhaps you were overly optimistic, or maybe you set the bar too low. There are limits to the amount of fitness you can achieve, but within the limits of your genes, health status, and motivation, you can make significant improvements in fitness. Adjust your goals as needed.

Q How can I fit a workout into my day?

A Good time management is an important skill in creating and maintaining an exercise program. Choose a regular time to exercise, preferably the same time every day. Don't tell yourself you'll exercise "sometime during the day when you have free time." That free time may never come. Schedule your workout, and make it a priority. Include alternative plans in your program to account for circumstances like bad weather or vacations.

Q Where can I get help and advice about exercise?

A One of the best places to get help is an exercise class. If you join a health club or fitness center, follow the guidelines in the box "Choosing a Fitness Center." There, expert instructors can help you learn the basics of training and answer your questions. Make sure the instructor is certified by a recognized professional organization and/or has formal training in exercise physiology. Read articles by credible experts in fitness magazines (such as *Fitness Rx for Women* and *Fitness Rx for Men*). Many of these magazines include articles by leading experts in exercise science written at a layperson's level.

A qualified personal trainer can also help you get started in an exercise program or a new form of training. Make sure this person has proper qualifications, such as certification by the ACSM, National Strength and Conditioning Association (NSCA), or International Sports Sciences Association (ISSA). Don't seek out a person for advice simply because he or she looks fit. UCLA researchers found that 60% of the personal trainers in their study couldn't pass a basic exam on training methods, exercise physiology, or biomechanics. Trainers who performed best had college degrees in exercise physiology, physical education, or physical therapy. So choose your trainer carefully and don't get caught up with fads or appearances.

Q Should I follow my exercise program if I'm sick?

A If you have a mild head cold or feel one coming on, it is probably OK to exercise moderately. Just begin slowly and see how you feel. However, if you have symptoms of a more serious illness—fever, swollen glands, nausea, extreme tiredness, muscle aches—wait until you have recovered fully before resuming your exercise program. Continuing to exercise while suffering from an illness more serious than a cold can compromise your recovery and may even be dangerous.

*For more **Common Questions Answered** about fitness, visit the Online Learning Center at www.mhhe.com/fahey.*

Choosing a Fitness Center

Fitness centers can provide you with many benefits—motivation and companionship are among the most important. A fitness center may also offer expert instruction and supervision as well as access to better equipment than you could afford on your own. All fitness centers, however, are not of the same overall quality, and every fitness center is not for every person. If you're thinking of joining a fitness center, here are some guidelines to help you choose a club that's right for you.

Convenience

• Look for an established facility that's within 10–15 minutes of your home or work. If it's farther away, your chances of sticking to an exercise regimen start to diminish.

• Visit the facility at the time you would normally exercise. Is there adequate parking? Will you have easy access to equipment and classes at that time?

• What child care services are available, and how are they supervised?

Atmosphere

• Look around to see if there are other members who are your age and at about your fitness level. Some clubs cater to a certain age group or lifestyle, such as hard-core bodybuilders.

• Observe how the members dress. Will you fit in, or will you be uncomfortable?

• Observe the staff. Are they easy to identify? Are they friendly, professional, and helpful?

• Check to see that the facility is clean, including showers and lockers. Make sure the facility is climate controlled, well ventilated, and well lit.

Safety

• Find out if the facility offers some type of preactivity screening as well as basic fitness testing that includes cardiovascular screening.

• Determine if personnel are trained in CPR and if there is emergency equipment such as automated external defibrillators (AEDs) on the premises. An AED can help someone who has a cardiac arrest.

• Ask if at least one staff member on each shift is trained in first aid.

Trained Personnel

• Determine if the personal trainers and fitness instructors are certified by a recognized professional association such as the American College of Sports Medicine (ACSM), Aerobics and Fitness Association of America (AFAA), National Strength and Conditioning Association (NSCA), or International Sports Sciences Association (ISSA). All personal trainers are not equal; more than 100 organizations certify trainers, and few of these require much formal training.

• Find out if the club has a trained exercise physiologist on staff, such as someone with a degree in exercise physiology, kinesiology, or exercise science. If the facility offers nutritional counseling, it should employ someone who is a registered dietitian (RD) or has similar formal training.

• Ask how much experience the instructors have. Ideally, trainers should have both academic preparation and practical experience.

Cost

• Buy only what you need and can afford. If you want to use only workout equipment, you may not need a club that has racquetball courts and saunas.

• Check the contract. Choose the one that covers the shortest period of time possible, especially if it's your first fitness club experience. Don't feel pressured to sign a long-term contract.

• Make sure the contract permits you to extend your membership if you have a prolonged illness or go on vacation. Some clubs have exchange agreements that allow you to train in other cities while on vacation or business.

• Try out the club. Ask for a free trial workout, or a 1-day pass, or an inexpensive 1- or 2-week trial membership.

• Find out whether there is an extra charge for the particular services you want. Get any special offers in writing.

Effectiveness

• Tour the facility. Does it offer what the brochure says it does? Does it offer the activities and equipment you want?

• Check the equipment. A good club will have treadmills, bikes, stair-climbers, resistance machines, and weights. Make sure these machines are up to date and well maintained.

• Find out if new members get a formal orientation and instruction on how to safely use the equipment. Will a staff member help you develop a program that is appropriate for your current fitness level and goals?

• Make sure the facility is certified. Look for the displayed names American College of Sports Medicine (ACSM), American Council on Exercise (ACE), Aerobics and Fitness Association of America (AFAA), or International Health, Racquet, and Sports club Association (IHRSA).

ORGANIZATIONS, HOTLINES, AND WEB SITES

American Alliance for Health, Physical Education, Recreation, and Dance (AAHPERD). A professional organization dedicated to promoting quality health and physical education programs.

http://www.aahperd.org

American College of Sports Medicine (ACSM). The principal professional organization for sports medicine and exercise science. Provides brochures, publications, and audio- and videotapes.

http://www.acsm.org

American Council on Exercise (ACE). Promotes exercise and fitness; the Web site features fact sheets on many consumer topics, including choosing shoes, cross-training, and steroids.

http://www.acefitness.org

American Heart Association: Start! Walking for a Healthier Lifestyle. Provides practical advice for people of all fitness levels plus an online fitness diary.

http://startwalkingnow.org

CDC Physical Activity Information. Provides information on the benefits of physical activity and suggestions for incorporating moderate physical activity into daily life.

http://www.cdc.gov/physicalactivity

Disabled Sports USA. Provides sports and recreation services to people with physical or mobility disorders.

http://www.dsusa.org

International Health, Racquet, and Sportsclub Association (IHRSA): Health Clubs. Provides guidelines for choosing a health or fitness facility and links to clubs that belong to IHRSA.

http://www.healthclubs.com

International Sports Sciences Association (ISSA). Trains and certifies personal trainers.

http://www.issaonline.com

MedlinePlus: Exercise and Physical Fitness. Provides links to news and reliable information about fitness and exercise from government agencies and professional associations.

http://www.nlm.nih.gov/medlineplus/exerciseandphysicalfitness
.html

President's Council on Fitness, Sports and Nutrition. Provides information on programs and publications, including fitness guides and fact sheets.

http://www.fitness.gov
http://www.presidentschallenge.org

Shape Up America! A nonprofit organization that provides information and resources on exercise, nutrition, and weight loss.

http://www.shapeup.org

SmallStep.Gov. Provides resources for increasing activity and improving diet through small changes in daily habits.

http://www.smallstep.gov

SELECTED BIBLIOGRAPHY

Alzheimer's Association. 2011. *Generation Alzheimer's: The Defining Disease of the Baby Boomers.* Chicago: Alzheimer's Association.

American College of Sports Medicine. 1998. The recommended quantity and quality of exercise for developing and maintaining cardiorespiratory and muscular fitness, and flexibility in healthy adults. ACSM position paper. *Medicine and Science in Sports and Exercise* 30(6): 975–991.

American College of Sports Medicine. 2007. *ACSM's Health/Fitness Facility Standards and Guidelines,* 3rd ed. Champaign, Ill.: Human Kinetics.

American College of Sports Medicine. 2009. *ACSM's Guidelines for Exercise Testing and Prescription,* 8th ed. Philadelphia: Lippincott Williams and Wilkins.

American College of Sports Medicine. 2009. *ACSM's Resource Manual for Guidelines for Exercise Testing and Prescription,* 6th ed. Philadelphia: Lippincott Williams and Wilkins.

American Heart Association. 2007. Resistance exercise in individuals with and without cardiovascular disease, 2007 update: A scientific statement from the American Heart Association Council on Clinical Cardiology and Council on Nutrition, Physical Activity, and Metabolism. *Circulation* 116(5): 572–584.

Ascensao, A., et al. 2011. Mitochondria as a target for exercise-induced cardioprotection. *Current Drug Targets* 12(6): 860–871.

Bouchard, C., et al. 2007. *Physical Activity and Health.* Champaign, Ill.: Human Kinetics.

Centers for Disease Control and Prevention. 2008. Prevalence of self-reported physically active adults—United States, 2007. *Morbidity and Mortality Weekly Report* 57(48): 1297–1300.

Dietary Guidelines Advisory Committee. 2011. *Report of the Dietary Guidelines Advisory Committee on the Dietary Guidelines for Americans, 2010, to the Secretary of Agriculture and the Secretary of Health and Human Services.* Washington, D.C.: U.S. Department of Agriculture, Agricultural Research Service.

Cooper, K. H. 2010. The benefits of exercise in promoting long and healthy lives—my observations. *Methodist DeBakey Cardiovascular Journal* 6(4): 10–12.

Courneya, K. S., and C. M. Friedenreich. 2011. Physical activity and cancer: an introduction. *Recent Results Cancer Research* 186: 1–10.

Donnelly, J. E., et al. 2009. Appropriate physical activity intervention strategies for weight loss and prevention of weight regain for adults (ACSM position stand). *Medicine and Science in Sports and Exercise.* 41(2): 459–471.

Duke University Medical Health News. 2010. Exercise! The anti-aging weapon. 4 new studies affirm the multiple benefits of exercise—at any age, even starting in midlife. *Duke Medical Health News* 16(5): 5–6.

Garber, C. E., et al. 2011. Quantity and quality of exercise for developing and maintaining cardiorespiratory, musculoskeletal, and neuromotor fitness in apparently healthy adults: Guidance for prescribing exercise. *Medicine and Science in Sports and Exercise* 43(7): 1334–1359.

Haskell, W. L., et al. 2007. Physical activity and public health: Updated recommendation for adults from the American College of Sports Medicine and the American Heart Association. *Medicine and Science in Sports and Exercise* 39(8): 1423–1434.

Hobson, K. 2010. How exercise can boost longevity. *US News World Report* 147(2): 30.

Hughes, E., et al. 2010. Surveillance for Certain Health Behaviors Among States and Selected Local Areas — United States, 2008. *Morbidity and Mortality Weekly Report* 597(ss1044): 1203–1205.

Keller, P., et al. 2011. A transcriptional map of the impact of endurance exercise training on skeletal muscle phenotype. *Journal of Applied Physiology* 110(1): 46–59.

Kushi, L. H., et al. 2006. American Cancer Society guidelines on nutrition and physical activity for cancer prevention: Reducing the risk of cancer with healthy food choices and physical activity. *Cancer Journal for Clinicians* 56(5): 254–281.

Lanza, I. R., and K. S. Nair. 2010. Mitochondrial function as a determinant of life span. *Pflugers Archives* 459(2): 277–289.

Masley, S., et al. 2009. Aerobic exercise enhances cognitive flexibility. *Journal Clinical Psychology in Medical Settings* 16(2): 186–193.

Muscari, A., et al. 2010. Chronic endurance exercise training prevents aging-related cognitive decline in healthy older adults: a randomized controlled trial. *International Journal of Geriatric Psychiatry* 25(10): 1055–1064.

National Center for Health Statistics. 2010. *Summary Health Statistics for U.S. Adults: National Health Interview Survey, 2009.* Series 10 (249). Hyattsville, Md.: National Center for Health Statistics.

Nelson, M. E., et al. 2007. Physical activity and public health in older adults: Recommendation from the American College of Sports Medicine and the American Heart Association. *Medicine and Science in Sports and Exercise* 39(8): 1435–1445.

Physical Activity Guidelines Advisory Committee. 2008. *Physical Activity Guidelines Advisory Committee Report, 2008.* Washington, D.C.: U.S. Department of Health and Human Services.

Rhyu, I. J., et al. 2010. Effects of aerobic exercise training on cognitive function and cortical vascularity in monkeys. *Neuroscience* 167(4): 1239–1248.

Richardson, C. R., et al. 2008. A meta-analysis of pedometer-based walking interventions and weight loss. *Annals of Family Medicine* 6(1): 69–77.

Sailors, M. H., et al. 2010. Exposing college students to exercise: the Training Interventions and Genetics of Exercise Response (TIGER) study. *Journal American College of Health* 59(1): 13–20.

Smith, J. K. 2010. Exercise and cardiovascular disease. *Cardiovascular Hematologic Disorders Drug Targets* 10(4): 269–272.

Stranahan, A. M., and M. P. Mattson. 2011. Bidirectional metabolic regulation of neurocognitive function. *Neurobiology Learning Memory.* Published online January 11, 2011.

Tarnopolsky, M. A. 2009. Mitochondrial DNA shifting in older adults following resistance exercise training. *Applied Physiology, Nutrition, and Metabolism* 34(3): 348–354.

Teixeira-Lemos, E., et al. 2011. Regular physical exercise training assists in preventing type 2 diabetes development: focus on its antioxidant and anti-inflammatory properties. *Cardiovascular Diabetology* 10(1): 12.

U.S. Department of Health and Human Services. 1996. *Physical Activity and Health: A Report of the Surgeon General.* Atlanta: U.S. Department of Health and Human Services.

U.S. Department of Health and Human Services. 2008. *Physical Activity Guidelines for Americans.* Washington, D.C.: U.S. Department of Health and Human Services.

U.S. Department of Health and Human Services. 2010. *The Surgeon General's Vision for a Healthy and Fit Nation.* Rockville, Md.: U.S. Department of Health and Human Services, Office of the Surgeon General.

World Health Organization. 2010. *World Health Statistics 2010.* Geneva: World Health Organization.

Name _____ Section _____ Date _____

Physical Activity Readiness
Questionnaire - PAR-Q
(revised 2002)

LAB 2.1 Safety of Exercise Participation

PAR-Q & YOU

(A Questionnaire for People Aged 15 to 69)

Regular physical activity is fun and healthy, and increasingly more people are starting to become more active every day. Being more active is very safe for most people. However, some people should check with their doctor before they start becoming much more physically active.

If you are planning to become much more physically active than you are now, start by answering the seven questions in the box below. If you are between the ages of 15 and 69, the PAR-Q will tell you if you should check with your doctor before you start. If you are over 69 years of age, and you are not used to being very active, check with your doctor.

Common sense is your best guide when you answer these questions. Please read the questions carefully and answer each one honestly: check YES or NO.

YES	NO		
☐	☐	1.	Has your doctor ever said that you have a heart condition <u>and</u> that you should only do physical activity recommended by a doctor?
☐	☐	2.	Do you feel pain in your chest when you do physical activity?
☐	☐	3.	In the past month, have you had chest pain when you were not doing physical activity?
☐	☐	4.	Do you lose your balance because of dizziness or do you ever lose consciousness?
☐	☐	5.	Do you have a bone or joint problem (for example, back, knee or hip) that could be made worse by a change in your physical activity?
☐	☐	6.	Is your doctor currently prescribing drugs (for example, water pills) for your blood pressure or heart condition?
☐	☐	7.	Do you know of <u>any other reason</u> why you should not do physical activity?

If

you

answered

YES to one or more questions

Talk with your doctor by phone or in person BEFORE you start becoming much more physically active or BEFORE you have a fitness appraisal. Tell your doctor about the PAR-Q and which questions you answered YES.

- You may be able to do any activity you want — as long as you start slowly and build up gradually. Or, you may need to restrict your activities to those which are safe for you. Talk with your doctor about the kinds of activities you wish to participate in and follow his/her advice.
- Find out which community programs are safe and helpful for you.

NO to all questions

If you answered NO honestly to <u>all</u> PAR-Q questions, you can be reasonably sure that you can:

- start becoming much more physically active — begin slowly and build up gradually. This is the safest and easiest way to go.
- take part in a fitness appraisal — this is an excellent way to determine your basic fitness so that you can plan the best way for you to live actively. It is also highly recommended that you have your blood pressure evaluated. If your reading is over 144/94, talk with your doctor before you start becoming much more physically active.

→

DELAY BECOMING MUCH MORE ACTIVE:
- if you are not feeling well because of a temporary illness such as a cold or a fever — wait until you feel better; or
- if you are or may be pregnant — talk to your doctor before you start becoming more active.

PLEASE NOTE: If your health changes so that you then answer YES to any of the above questions, tell your fitness or health professional. Ask whether you should change your physical activity plan.

<u>Informed Use of the PAR-Q</u>: The Canadian Society for Exercise Physiology, Health Canada, and their agents assume no liability for persons who undertake physical activity, and if in doubt after completing this questionnaire, consult your doctor prior to physical activity.

No changes permitted. You are encouraged to photocopy the PAR-Q but only if you use the entire form.

NOTE: If the PAR-Q is being given to a person before he or she participates in a physical activity program or a fitness appraisal, this section may be used for legal or administrative purposes.

"I have read, understood and completed this questionnaire. Any questions I had were answered to my full satisfaction."

NAME _____

SIGNATURE _____ DATE _____

SIGNATURE OF PARENT _____ WITNESS _____
or GUARDIAN (for participants under the age of majority)

Note: This physical activity clearance is valid for a maximum of 12 months from the date it is completed and becomes invalid if your condition changes so that you would answer YES to any of the seven questions.

 © Canadian Society for Exercise Physiology   Supported by:  Health   Santé
Canada   Canada

Physical Activity Readiness Questionnaire (PAR-Q) © 2002. Reprinted with permission from the Canadian Society for Exercise Physiology. http://www.csep.ca/forms.asp.

 http://www.mcgrawhillconnect.com/
FITNESS AND WELLNESS

General Health Profile

To help further assess the safety of exercise for you, complete as much of this health profile as possible.

General Information

Age: _____   Total cholesterol: _____   Blood pressure: _____ / _____

Height: _____   HDL: _____   Triglycerides: _____

Weight: _____   LDL: _____   Blood glucose: _____

Are you currently trying to _____ gain or _____ lose weight? (check one if appropriate)

Medical Conditions/Treatments

Check any of the following that apply to you, and add any other conditions that might affect your ability to exercise safely.

_____ heart disease   _____ depression, anxiety, or other   _____ other injury to joint problem: _____

_____ lung disease   psychological disorder   _____ substance abuse problem

_____ diabetes   _____ eating disorder   _____ other: _____

_____ allegies   _____ back pain   _____ other: _____

_____ asthma   _____ arthritis   _____ other: _____

_____ Do you have a family history of cardiovascular disease (CVD) (a parent, sibling, or child who had a heart attack or stroke before age 55 for men or 65 for women)?

List any medications or supplements you are taking or any medical treatments you are undergoing. Include the name of the substance or treatment and its purpose. Include both prescription and over-the-counter drugs and supplements.

_____   _____

_____   _____

Lifestyle Information

Check any of the following that is true for you, and fill in the requested information.

_____ I usually eat high-fat foods (fatty meats, cheese, fried foods, butter, full-fat dairy products) every day.

_____ I consume fewer than 5 servings of fruits and vegetables on most days.

_____ I smoke cigarettes or use other tobacco products. If true, describe your use of tobacco (type and frequency): _____

_____ I regularly drink alcohol. If true, describe your typical weekly consumption pattern: _____

_____ I often feel as if I need more sleep. (I need about _____ hours per day; I get about _____ hours per day.)

_____ I feel as though stress has adversely affected my level of wellness during the past year.

Describe your current activity pattern. What types of moderate physical activity do you engage in on a daily basis? Are you involved in a formal exercise program, or do you regularly participate in sports or recreational activities?

_____

_____

Using Your Results

How did you score? Did the PAR-Q indicate that exercise is likely to be safe for you? Is there anything in your health profile that you think may affect your ability to exercise safely? Have you had any problems with exercise in the past?

What should you do next? If the assessments in this lab indicate that you should see your physician before beginning an exercise program, or if you have any questions about the safety of exercise for you, make an appointment to talk with your health care provider to address your concerns.

Name _____ Section _____ Date _____

LAB 2.2 Overcoming Barriers to Being Active

Barriers to Being Active Quiz

Directions: Listed below are reasons that people give to describe why they do not get as much physical activity as they think they should. Please read each statement and indicate how likely you are to say each of the following statements.

How likely are you to say this?	Very likely	Somewhat likely	Somewhat unlikely	Very unlikely
1. My day is so busy now, I just don't think I can make the time to include physical activity in my regular schedule.	3	2	1	0
2. None of my family members or friends like to do anything active, so I don't have a chance to exercise.	3	2	1	0
3. I'm just too tired after work to get any exercise.	3	2	1	0
4. I've been thinking about getting more exercise, but I just can't seem to get started.	3	2	1	0
5. I'm getting older so exercise can be risky.	3	2	1	0
6. I don't get enough exercise because I have never learned the skills for any sport.	3	2	1	0
7. I don't have access to jogging trails, swimming pools, bike paths, etc.	3	2	1	0
8. Physical activity takes too much time away from other commitments—like work, family, etc.	3	2	1	0
9. I'm embarrassed about how I will look when I exercise with others.	3	2	1	0
10. I don't get enough sleep as it is. I just couldn't get up early or stay up late to get some exercise.	3	2	1	0
11. It's easier for me to find excuses not to exercise than to go out and do something.	3	2	1	0
12. I know of too many people who have hurt themselves by overdoing it with exercise.	3	2	1	0
13. I really can't see learning a new sport at my age.	3	2	1	0
14. It's just too expensive. You have to take a class or join a club or buy the right equipment.	3	2	1	0
15. My free times during the day are too short to include exercise.	3	2	1	0
16. My usual social activities with family or friends do not include physical activity.	3	2	1	0
17. I'm too tired during the week and I need the weekend to catch up on my rest.	3	2	1	0

connect http://www.mcgrawhillconnect.com/
FITNESS AND WELLNESS

How likely are you to say this?	Very likely	Somewhat likely	Somewhat unlikely	Very unlikely
18. I want to get more exercise, but I just can't seem to make myself stick to anything.	3	2	1	0
19. I'm afraid I might injure myself or have a heart attack.	3	2	1	0
20. I'm not good enough at any physical activity to make it fun.	3	2	1	0
21. If we had exercise facilities and showers at work, then I would be more likely to exercise.	3	2	1	0

Scoring

- Enter the circled numbers in the spaces provided, putting the number for statement 1 on line 1, statement 2 on line 2, and so on.
- Add the three scores on each line. Your barriers to physical activity fall into one or more of seven categories: lack of time, social influences, lack of energy, lack of willpower, fear of injury, lack of skill, and lack of resources. A score of 5 or above in any category shows that this is an important barrier for you to overcome.

$$\overline{}_{1} + \overline{}_{8} + \overline{}_{15} = \overline{}_{\text{Lack of time}}$$

$$\overline{}_{2} + \overline{}_{9} + \overline{}_{16} = \overline{}_{\text{Social influences}}$$

$$\overline{}_{3} + \overline{}_{10} + \overline{}_{17} = \overline{}_{\text{Lack of energy}}$$

$$\overline{}_{4} + \overline{}_{11} + \overline{}_{18} = \overline{}_{\text{Lack of willpower}}$$

$$\overline{}_{5} + \overline{}_{12} + \overline{}_{19} = \overline{}_{\text{Fear of injury}}$$

$$\overline{}_{6} + \overline{}_{13} + \overline{}_{20} = \overline{}_{\text{Lack of skill}}$$

$$\overline{}_{7} + \overline{}_{14} + \overline{}_{21} = \overline{}_{\text{Lack of resources}}$$

Using Your Results

How did you score? How many key barriers did you identify? Are they what you expected?

What should you do next? For your key barriers, try the strategies listed on the following pages and/or develop additional strategies that work for you. Check off any strategy that you try.

Suggestions for Overcoming Physical Activity Barriers

Lack of Time

_____ Identify available time slots. Monitor your daily activities for 1 week. Identify at least three 30-minute time slots you could use for physical activity.

_____ Add physical activity to your daily routine. For example, walk or ride your bike to work or shopping, organize social activities around physical activity, walk the dog, exercise while you watch TV, park farther from your destination, etc.

_____ Make time for physical activity. For example, walk, jog, or swim during your lunch hour, or take fitness breaks instead of coffee breaks.

_____ Select activities requiring minimal time, such as walking, jogging, or stair climbing.

_____ Other: _____

Social Influences

_____ Explain your interest in physical activity to friends and family. Ask them to support your efforts.

_____ Invite friends and family members to exercise with you. Plan social activities involving exercise.

_____ Develop new friendships with physically active people. Join a group, such as the YMCA or a hiking club.

_____ Other: _____

Lack of Energy

_____ Schedule physical activity for times in the day or week when you feel energetic.

_____ Convince yourself that if you give it a chance, exercise will increase your energy level. Then try it.

_____ Other: _____

Lack of Willpower

_____ Plan ahead. Make physical activity a regular part of your daily or weekly schedule and write it on your calendar.

_____ Invite a friend to exercise with you on a regular basis and write it on _both_ your calendars.

_____ Join an exercise group or class.

_____ Other: _____

Fear of Injury

_____ Learn how to warm up and cool down to prevent injury.

_____ Learn how to exercise appropriately considering your age, fitness level, skill level, and health status.

_____ Choose activities involving minimal risk.

_____ Other: _____

Lack of Skill

_____ Select activities requiring no new skills, such as walking, jogging, or stair climbing.

_____ Exercise with friends who are at the same skill level as you are.

_____ Find a friend who is willing to teach you some new skills.

_____ Take a class to develop new skills.

_____ Other: _____

Lack of Resources

_____ Select activities that require minimal facilities or equipment, such as walking, jogging, jumping rope, or calisthenics.

_____ Identify inexpensive, convenient resources available in your community (community education programs, park and recreation programs, worksite programs, etc.).

_____ Other: _____

Are any of the following additional barriers important for you? If so, try some of the strategies listed here or invent your own.

Weather Conditions

_____ Develop a set of regular activities that are always available regardless of weather (indoor cycling, aerobic dance, indoor swimming, calisthenics, stair climbing, rope skipping, mall walking, dancing, gymnasium games, etc.).

_____ Look on outdoor activities that depend on weather conditions (cross-country skiing, outdoor swimming, outdoor tennis, etc.) as "bonuses"—extra activities possible when weather and circumstances permit.

_____ Other: _____

Travel

_____ Put a jump rope in your suitcase and jump rope.

_____ Walk the halls and climb the stairs in hotels.

_____ Stay in places with swimming pools or exercise facilities.

_____ Join the YMCA or YWCA (ask about reciprocal membership agreements).

_____ Visit the local shopping mall and walk for half an hour or more.

_____ Bring a personal music player loaded with your favorite workout music.

_____ Other: _____

Family Obligations

_____ Trade babysitting time with a friend, neighbor, or family member who also has small children.

_____ Exercise *with* the kids—go for a walk together, play tag or other running games, or get an aerobic dance or exercise DVD for kids (there are several on the market) and exercise together. You can spend time together and still get your exercise.

_____ Hire a babysitter and look at the cost as a worthwhile investment in your physical and mental health.

_____ Jump rope, do calisthenics, ride a stationary bicycle, or use other home gymnasium equipment while the kids watch TV or when they are sleeping.

_____ Try to exercise when the kids are not around (e.g., during school hours or their nap time).

_____ Other: _____

Retirement Years

_____ Look on your retirement as an opportunity to become more active instead of less. Spend more time gardening, walking the dog, and playing with your grandchildren. Children with short legs and grandparents with slower gaits are often great walking partners.

_____ Learn a new skill you've always been interested in, such as ballroom dancing, square dancing, or swimming.

_____ Now that you have the time, make regular physical activity a part of every day. Go for a walk every morning or every evening before dinner. Treat yourself to an exercycle and ride every day during a favorite TV show.

_____ Other: _____

SOURCE: Adapted from CDC Division of Nutrition and Physical Activity. 1999. *Promoting Physical Activity: A Guide for Community Action.* Champaign, Ill.: Human Kinetics.

LAB 2.3 Using a Pedometer to Track Physical Activity

How physically active are you? Would you be more motivated to increase daily physical activity if you had an easy way to monitor your level of activity? If so, consider wearing a pedometer to track the number of steps you take each day—a rough but easily obtainable reflection of daily physical activity.

Determine Your Baseline

Wear the pedometer for a week to obtain a baseline average daily number of steps.

	M	T	W	Th	F	Sa	Su	Average
Steps								

Set Goals

Set an appropriate goal for increasing steps. The goal of 10,000 steps per day is widely recommended, but your personal goal should reflect your baseline level of steps. For example, if your current daily steps are far below 10,000, a goal of walking 2000 additional steps each day might be appropriate. If you are already close to 10,000 steps per day, choose a higher goal. Also consider the following guidelines from health experts:

- To reduce the risk of chronic disease, aim to accumulate at least 150 minutes of moderate physical activity per week.

- To help manage body weight and prevent gradual, unhealthy weight gain, engage in 60 minutes of moderate to vigorous-intensity activity on most days of the week.

- To sustain weight loss, engage daily in at least 60–90 minutes of moderate-intensity physical activity.

To help gauge how close you are to meeting these time-based physical activity goals, you might walk for 10–15 minutes while wearing your pedometer to determine how many steps correspond with the time-based goals.

Once you have set your overall goal, break it down into several steps. For example, if your goal is to increase daily steps by 2000, set mini-goals of increasing daily steps by 500, allowing 2 weeks to reach each mini-goal. Smaller goals are easier to achieve and can help keep you motivated and on track. Having several interim goals also gives you the opportunity to reward yourself more frequently. Note your goals below:

Mini-goal 1: _____   Target date: _____   Reward: _____
Mini-goal 2: _____   Target date: _____   Reward: _____
Mini-goal 3: _____   Target date: _____   Reward: _____
Overall goal: _____   Target date: _____   Reward: _____

Develop Strategies for Increasing Steps

What can you do to become more active? The possibilities include walking when you do errands, getting off one stop from your destination on public transportation, parking an extra block or two away from your destination, and doing at least one chore every day that requires physical activity. If weather or neighborhood safety is an issue, look for alternative locations to walk. For example, find an indoor gym or shopping mall or even a long hallway. Check out locations that are near or on the way to your campus, workplace, or residence. If you think walking indoors will be dull, walk with friends or family members or wear headphones (if safe) and listen to music or audiobooks.

Are there any days of the week for which your baseline steps are particularly low and/or it will be especially difficult because of your schedule to increase your number of steps? Be sure to develop specific strategies for difficult situations.

Below, list at least five strategies for increasing daily steps:

_____   _____

_____   _____

_____   _____

Track Your Progress

Based on the goals you set, fill in your goal portion of the progress chart with your target average daily steps for each week. Then wear your pedometer every day and note your total daily steps. Track your progress toward each mini-goal and your final goal. Every few weeks, stop and evaluate your progress. If needed, adjust your plan and develop additional strategies for increasing steps. In addition to the chart in this worksheet, you might also want to graph your daily steps to provide a visual reminder of how you are progressing toward your goals. Make as many copies of this chart as you need.

Week	Goal	M	Tu	W	Th	F	Sa	Su	Average
1									
2									
3									
4									

Progress Checkup

How close are you to meeting your goal? How do you feel about your program and your progress?

If needed, describe changes to your plan and additional strategies for increasing steps:

Week	Goal	M	Tu	W	Th	F	Sa	Su	Average
5									
6									
7									
8									

Progress Checkup

How close are you to meeting your goal? How do you feel about your program and your progress?

If needed, describe changes to your plan and additional strategies for increasing steps:

Week	Goal	M	Tu	W	Th	F	Sa	Su	Average
9									
10									
11									
12									

Progress Checkup

How close are you to meeting your goal? How do you feel about your program and your progress?

If needed, describe changes to your plan and additional strategies for increasing steps in the space below.

Cardiorespiratory Endurance

LOOKING AHEAD...

After reading this chapter, you should be able to:

- Describe how the body produces the energy it needs for exercise
- List the major effects and benefits of cardiorespiratory endurance exercise
- Explain how cardiorespiratory endurance is measured and assessed
- Describe how frequency, intensity, time (duration), and type of exercise affect the development of cardiorespiratory endurance
- Explain the best ways to prevent and treat common exercise injuries

TEST YOUR KNOWLEDGE

1. Compared to sedentary people, those who engage in regular moderate endurance exercise are likely to
   a. have fewer colds.
   b. be less anxious and depressed.
   c. fall asleep more quickly and sleep better.
   d. be more alert and creative.

2. About how much blood does the heart pump each minute during aerobic exercise?
   a. 5 quarts
   b. 10 quarts
   c. 20 quarts

3. During an effective 30-minute cardiorespiratory endurance workout, you should lose 1–2 pounds. True or false?

Answers

1. **All four.** Endurance exercise has many immediate benefits that affect all the dimensions of wellness and improve overall quality of life.

2. **c.** During exercise, cardiac output increases to 20 or more quarts per minute, compared to about 5 quarts per minute at rest.

3. **False.** Any weight loss during an exercise session is due to fluid loss that needs to be replaced to prevent dehydration and enhance performance. It is best to drink enough during exercise to match fluid lost as sweat; weigh yourself before and after a workout to make sure you are drinking enough.

McGraw Hill **connect**™ http://www.mcgrawhillconnect.com
FITNESS AND WELLNESS

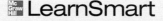

McGraw Hill **LearnSmart**

GET A BETTER GRADE. TRY LEARNSMART.

ardiorespiratory endurance—the ability of the body to perform prolonged, large-muscle, dynamic exercise at moderate to high levels of intensity—is a key health-related component of fitness. As explained in Chapter 2, a healthy cardiorespiratory system is essential to high levels of fitness and wellness.

This chapter reviews the short- and long-term effects and benefits of cardiorespiratory endurance exercise. It then describes several tests that are commonly used to assess cardiorespiratory fitness. Finally, it provides guidelines for creating your own cardiorespiratory endurance training program—one that is geared to your current level of fitness and built around activities you enjoy.

BASIC PHYSIOLOGY OF CARDIORESPIRATORY ENDURANCE EXERCISE

A basic understanding of the body processes involved in cardiorespiratory endurance exercise can help you design a safe and effective fitness program.

The Cardiorespiratory System

The **cardiorespiratory system** consists of the heart, the blood vessels, and the respiratory system. (See page T3-2 of the color transparency insert "Touring the Cardiorespiratory System" in this chapter.) The cardiorespiratory system circulates blood through the body, transporting oxygen, nutrients, and other key substances to the organs and tissues that need them. It also carries away waste products so they can be used or expelled.

The Heart The heart is a four-chambered, fist-sized muscle located just beneath the sternum (breastbone) (Figure 3.1). It pumps deoxygenated (oxygen-poor) blood to the lungs and delivers oxygenated (oxygen-rich) blood to the rest of the body. Blood actually travels through two separate circulatory systems: The right side of the heart pumps blood to the lungs in what is called **pulmonary circulation**, and the left side pumps blood through the rest of the body in **systemic circulation**.

The path of blood flow through the heart and cardiorespiratory system is illustrated on page T3-3 of the color transparency insert "Touring the Cardiorespiratory System" in this chapter. Refer to that illustration as you trace these steps:

1. Waste-laden, oxygen-poor blood travels through large vessels, called **venae cavae**, into the heart's right upper chamber, or **atrium.**

2. After the right atrium fills, it contracts and pumps blood into the heart's right lower chamber, or **ventricle.**

3. When the right ventricle is full, it contracts and pumps blood through the pulmonary artery into the lungs.

4. In the lungs, blood picks up oxygen and discards carbon dioxide.

5. The cleaned, oxygenated blood flows from the lungs through the pulmonary veins into the heart's left atrium.

6. After the left atrium fills, it contracts and pumps blood into the left ventricle.

7. When the left ventricle is full, it pumps blood through the **aorta**—the body's largest artery—for distribution to the rest of the body's blood vessels.

The period of the heart's contraction is called **systole**; the period of relaxation is called **diastole**. During systole, the atria contract first, pumping blood into the ventricles. A fraction of a second later, the ventricles contract, pumping blood to the lungs and the body. During diastole, blood flows into the heart.

Blood pressure, the force exerted by blood on the walls of the blood vessels, is created by the pumping action of the heart. Blood pressure is greater during systole than during diastole. A person weighing 150 pounds has about 5 quarts of blood, which are circulated about once every minute.

The heartbeat—the split-second sequence of contractions of the heart's four chambers—is controlled by nerve impulses. These signals originate in a bundle of specialized cells in the right atrium called the *pacemaker,* or *sinoatrial (SA) node.* Unless it is speeded up or slowed down by the brain in response to such stimuli as danger or the tissues' need for more oxygen, the heart produces nerve impulses at a steady rate.

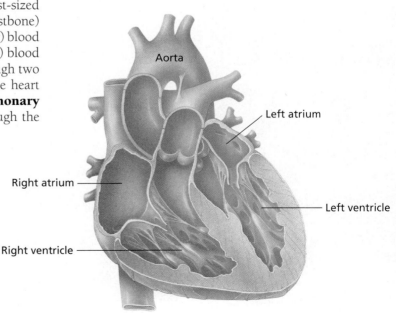

Aorta

Left atrium

Right atrium

Left ventricle

Right ventricle

FIGURE 3.1 **Chambers of the heart.**

Wellness Tip

Aerobic exercise reduces blood pressure. Regular physical activity, regardless of intensity, helps you maintain a healthy blood pressure.

The Blood Vessels Blood vessels are classified by size and function. **Veins** carry blood to the heart. **Arteries** carry it away from the heart. Veins have thin walls, but arteries have thick elastic walls that enable them to expand and relax with the volume of blood being pumped through them.

After leaving the heart, the aorta branches into smaller and smaller vessels. The smallest arteries branch still further into **capillaries,** tiny vessels only one cell thick. The capillaries deliver oxygen and nutrient-rich blood to the tissues and pick up oxygen-poor, waste-laden blood. From the capillaries, this blood empties into small veins (*venules*) and then into larger veins that return it to the heart to repeat the cycle.

Blood pumped through the heart doesn't reach the heart's own cells, so the organ has its own network of blood vessels. Two large vessels, the right and left **coronary arteries,** branch off the aorta and supply the heart muscle with oxygenated blood. The coronary arteries are shown on page T3-3 of the color transparency insert "Touring the Cardiorespiratory System" in this chapter.

The Respiratory System The **respiratory system** supplies oxygen to the body, carries off carbon dioxide—a waste product of body processes—and helps regulate acid produced during metabolism. Air passes in and out of the lungs as a result of pressure changes brought about by the contraction and relaxation of the diaphragm and rib muscles. As air is inhaled, it passes through the nasal passages, throat, larynx, trachea (windpipe), and bronchi into the lungs. The lungs consist of many branching tubes that end in tiny, thin-walled air sacs called **alveoli.**

Carbon dioxide and oxygen are exchanged between alveoli and capillaries in the lungs. Carbon dioxide passes from blood cells into the alveoli, where it is carried up and out of the lungs (exhaled). Oxygen from inhaled air is passed from the alveoli into blood cells; these oxygen-rich blood cells then return to the heart and are pumped throughout the body. Oxygen is an important component of the body's energy-producing system, so the cardiorespiratory system's ability to pick up and deliver oxygen is critical for the functioning of the body.

The Cardiorespiratory System at Rest and During Exercise At rest and during light activity, the cardiorespiratory system functions at a fairly steady pace. Your heart beats at a rate of about 50–90 beats per minute, and you take about 12–20 breaths per minute. A typical resting blood pressure in a healthy adult, measured in millimeters of mercury, is 120 systolic and 80 diastolic (120/80).

During exercise, the demands on the cardiorespiratory system increase. Body cells, particularly working muscles, need to obtain more oxygen and fuel and to eliminate more waste products. To meet these demands, your body makes the following changes:

- Heart rate increases, up to 170–210 beats per minute during intense exercise.
- The heart's **stroke volume** increases, meaning that the heart pumps out more blood with each beat.
- The heart pumps and circulates more blood per minute as a result of the faster heart rate and greater

KEY TERMS

cardiorespiratory system The system that circulates blood through the body; consists of the heart, blood vessels, and respiratory system.

pulmonary circulation The part of the circulatory system that moves blood between the heart and lungs; controlled by the right side of the heart.

systemic circulation The part of the circulatory system that moves blood between the heart and the rest of the body; controlled by the left side of the heart.

venae cavae The large veins through which blood is returned to the right atrium of the heart.

atrium One of the two upper chambers of the heart in which blood collects before passing to the ventricles (pl. *atria*).

ventricle One of the two lower chambers of the heart, from which blood flows through arteries to the lungs and other parts of the body.

aorta The body's largest artery; receives blood from the left ventricle and distributes it to the body.

systole Contraction of the heart.

diastole Relaxation of the heart.

blood pressure The force exerted by the blood on the walls of the blood vessels; created by the pumping action of the heart.

veins Vessels that carry blood to the heart.

arteries Vessels that carry blood away from the heart.

capillaries Very small blood vessels that distribute blood to all parts of the body.

coronary arteries A pair of large blood vessels that branch off the aorta and supply the heart muscle with oxygenated blood.

respiratory system The lungs, air passages, and breathing muscles; supplies oxygen to the body and removes carbon dioxide.

alveoli Tiny air sacs in the lungs that allow the exchange of oxygen and carbon dioxide between the lungs and blood.

stroke volume The amount of blood the heart pumps with each beat.

stroke volume. During exercise, this **cardiac output** increases to 20 or more quarts per minute, compared to about 5 quarts per minute at rest.

- Blood flow changes, so as much as 85–90% of the blood may be delivered to working muscles. At rest, about 15–20% of blood is distributed to the skeletal muscles.
- Systolic blood pressure increases, while diastolic blood pressure holds steady or declines slightly. A typical exercise blood pressure might be 175/65.
- To oxygenate this increased blood flow, you take deeper breaths and breathe faster, up to 40–60 breaths per minute.

All of these changes are controlled and coordinated by special centers in the brain, which use the nervous system and chemical messengers to control the process.

Energy Production

Metabolism is the sum of all the chemical processes necessary to maintain the body. Energy is required to fuel vital body functions—to build and break down tissue, contract muscles, conduct nerve impulses, regulate body temperature, and so on.

The rate at which your body uses energy—its **metabolic rate**—depends on your level of activity. At rest, you have a low metabolic rate; if you begin to walk, your metabolic rate increases. If you jog, your metabolic rate may increase more than 800% above its resting level. Olympic-caliber distance runners can increase their metabolic rate by 2000% or more.

Energy from Food The body converts chemical energy from food into substances that cells can use as fuel. These fuels can be used immediately or stored for later use. The body's ability to store fuel is critical, because if all the energy from food were released immediately, much of it would be wasted.

The three classes of energy-containing nutrients in food are carbohydrates, fats, and proteins. During digestion, most carbohydrates are broken down into the simple sugar **glucose**. Some glucose remains circulating in the blood ("blood sugar"), where it can be used as a quick source of fuel to produce energy. Glucose may also be converted to **glycogen** and stored in the liver, muscles, and kidneys. If glycogen stores are full and the body's immediate need for energy is met, the remaining glucose is converted to fat and stored in the body's fatty tissues. Excess energy from dietary fat is also stored as body fat. Protein in the diet is used primarily to build new tissue, but it can be broken down for energy or incorporated into fat stores. Glucose, glycogen, and fat are important fuels for the production of energy in the cells; protein is a significant energy source only when other fuels are lacking. (See Chapter 8 for more on the roles of carbohydrate, fat, and protein in the body.)

ATP: The Energy "Currency" of Cells The basic form of energy used by cells is **adenosine triphosphate,** or ATP. When a cell needs energy, it breaks down ATP, a process that releases energy in the only form the cell can use directly. Cells store a small amount of ATP; when they need more, they create it through chemical reactions that utilize the body's stored fuels—glucose, glycogen, and fat. When you exercise, your cells need to produce more energy. Consequently, your body mobilizes its stores of fuel to increase ATP production.

Exercise and the Three Energy Systems

The muscles in your body use three energy systems to create ATP and fuel cellular activity. These systems use different fuels and chemical processes and perform different, specific functions during exercise (Table 3.1).

Table 3.1	Characteristics of the Body's Energy Systems		
	ENERGY SYSTEM*		
	IMMEDIATE	NONOXIDATIVE	OXIDATIVE
DURATION OF ACTIVITY FOR WHICH SYSTEM PREDOMINATES	0–10 seconds	10 seconds–2 minutes	>2 minutes
INTENSITY OF ACTIVITY FOR WHICH SYSTEM PREDOMINATES	High	High	Low to moderately high
RATE OF ATP PRODUCTION	Immediate, very rapid	Rapid	Slower, but prolonged
FUEL	Adenosine triphosphate (ATP), creatine phosphate (CP)	Muscle stores of glucose and glycogen	Body stores of glycogen, glucose, fat, and protein
OXYGEN USED?	No	No	Yes
SAMPLE ACTIVITIES	Weight lifting, picking up a bag of groceries	400-meter run, running up several flights of stairs	1500-meter run, 30-minute walk, standing in line for a long time

*For most activities, all three systems contribute to energy production; the duration and intensity of the activity determine which system predominates.

SOURCE: Adapted from Brooks, G. A., et al. 2005. *Exercise Physiology: Human Bioenergetics and Its Applications,* 4th ed. New York: McGraw-Hill. Copyright © 2005 The McGraw-Hill Companies. Reproduced with permission of The McGraw-Hill Companies.

The Immediate Energy System The **immediate ("explosive") energy system** provides energy rapidly but for only a short period of time. It is used to fuel activities that last for about 10 or fewer seconds—examples in sports include weight lifting and shot-putting; examples in daily life include rising from a chair or picking up a bag of groceries. The components of this energy system include existing cellular ATP stores and creatine phosphate (CP), a chemical that cells can use to make ATP. CP levels are depleted rapidly during exercise, so the maximum capacity of this energy system is reached within a few seconds. Cells must then switch to the other energy systems to restore levels of ATP and CP. (Without adequate ATP, muscles will stiffen and become unusable.)

The Nonoxidative Energy System The **nonoxidative (anaerobic) energy system** is used at the start of an exercise session and for high-intensity activities lasting for about 10 seconds to 2 minutes, such as the 400-meter run. During daily activities, this system may be called on to help you run to catch a bus or dash up several flights of stairs. The nonoxidative energy system creates ATP by breaking down glucose and glycogen. This system doesn't require oxygen, which is why it is sometimes referred to as the **anaerobic** system. This system's capacity to produce energy is limited, but it can generate a great deal of ATP in a short period of time. For this reason, it is the most important energy system for very intense exercise.

There are two key limitations to the nonoxidative energy system. First, the body's supply of glucose and glycogen is limited. If these are depleted, a person may experience fatigue and dizziness, and judgment may be impaired. (The brain and nervous system rely on carbohydrates as fuel.) Second, increases in hydrogen and potassium ions (which are thought to interfere with metabolism and muscle contraction) cause fatigue. During heavy exercise, such as sprinting, large increases in hydrogen and potassium ions cause muscles to fatigue rapidly.

The anaerobic energy system also creates metabolic acids. Fortunately, exercise training increases the body's ability to cope with metabolic acid. Improved fitness allows you to exercise at higher intensities before the abrupt buildup of metabolic acids—a point that scientists call the *lactate threshold*. One metabolic acid, called **lactic acid** (lactate), is often linked to fatigue during intense exercise. However, lactic acid is an important fuel at rest and during exercise.

The Oxidative Energy System The **oxidative (aerobic) energy system** is used during any physical activity that lasts longer than about 2 minutes, such as distance running, swimming, hiking, or even standing in line. The oxidative system requires oxygen to generate ATP, which is why it is considered an **aerobic** system. The oxidative system cannot produce energy as quickly as the other two systems, but it can supply energy for much longer periods of time. It provides energy during most daily activities.

In the oxidative energy system, ATP production takes place in cellular structures called **mitochondria**. Because mitochondria can use carbohydrates (glucose and glycogen) or fats to produce ATP, the body's stores of fuel for this system are much greater than those for the other two energy systems. The actual fuel used depends on the intensity and duration of exercise and on the fitness status of the individual. Carbohydrates are favored during more intense exercise (over 65% of maximum capacity); fats are used for mild, low-intensity activities. During a prolonged exercise session, carbohydrates are the predominant fuel at the start of the workout, but fat utilization increases over time. Fit individuals use a greater proportion of fat as fuel because increased fitness allows people to do activities at lower intensities. This is an important adaptation because glycogen depletion is one of the limiting factors for the oxidative energy system. Thus, by being able to use more fat as fuel, a fit individual can exercise for a longer time before glycogen is depleted and muscles become fatigued.

Oxygen is another limiting factor. The oxygen requirement of this energy system is proportional to the intensity of exercise. As intensity increases, so does oxygen

---

KEY TERMS

cardiac output   The amount of blood pumped by the heart each minute; a function of heart rate and stroke volume.

metabolic rate   The rate at which the body uses energy.

glucose   A simple sugar that circulates in the blood and can be used by cells to fuel adenosine triphosphate (ATP) production.

glycogen   A complex carbohydrate stored principally in the liver and skeletal muscles; the major fuel source during most forms of intense exercise. Glycogen is the storage form of glucose.

adenosine triphosphate (ATP)   The energy source for cellular processes.

immediate ("explosive") energy system   The system that supplies energy to muscle cells through the breakdown of cellular stores of ATP and creatine phosphate (CP).

nonoxidative (anaerobic) energy system   The system that supplies energy to muscle cells through the breakdown of muscle stores of glucose and glycogen; also called the *anaerobic system* or the *lactic acid system* because chemical reactions take place without oxygen and produce lactic acid.

anaerobic   Occurring in the absence of oxygen.

lactic acid   A metabolic acid resulting from the metabolism of glucose and glycogen.

oxidative (aerobic) energy system   The system that supplies energy to cells through the breakdown of glucose, glycogen, and fats; also called the *aerobic system* because its chemical reactions require oxygen.

aerobic   Dependent on the presence of oxygen.

mitochondria   Cell structures that convert the energy in food to a form the body can use.

consumption. The body's ability to increase oxygen use is limited; this limit is referred to as **maximal oxygen consumption**, or $\dot{V}O_{2max}$. $\dot{V}O_{2max}$ determines how intensely a person can perform endurance exercise and for how long, and it is considered the best overall measure of the capacity of the cardiorespiratory system. (The assessment tests described later in the chapter are designed to help you evaluate your $\dot{V}O_{2max}$.)

The Energy Systems in Combination Your body typically uses all three energy systems when you exercise. The intensity and duration of the activity determine which system predominates. For example, when you play tennis, you use the immediate energy system when hitting the ball, but you replenish cellular energy stores by using the nonoxidative and oxidative systems. When cycling, the oxidative system predominates. However, if you must suddenly exercise intensely—by riding up a steep hill, for example—the other systems become important because the oxidative system is unable to supply ATP fast enough to sustain high-intensity effort.

Physical Fitness and Energy Production Physically fit people can increase their metabolic rate substantially, generating the energy needed for powerful or sustained exercise. People who are not fit cannot respond to exercise in the same way. Their bodies are less capable of delivering oxygen and fuel to exercising muscles, they can't burn as many calories during or after exercise, and they are less able to cope with lactic acid and other substances produced during intense physical activity that contribute to fatigue. Because of this, they become fatigued more rapidly; their legs hurt and they breathe heavily walking up a flight of stairs, for example. Regular physical training can substantially improve the body's ability to produce energy and meet the challenges of increased physical activity.

Wellness Tip

Feeling tired? Try taking a brisk walk instead of a nap. The more physically active you are, the more energetic you'll feel over the long run.

Ask Yourself

QUESTIONS FOR CRITICAL THINKING AND REFLECTION

When you think about the types of physical activity you engage in during your typical day or week, which ones use the immediate energy system? The nonoxidative energy system? The oxidative energy system? How can you increase activities that use the oxidative energy system?

In designing an exercise program, focus on the energy system most important to your goals. Because improving the functioning of the cardiorespiratory system is critical to overall wellness, endurance exercise that utilizes the oxidative energy system—activities performed at moderate to high intensities for a prolonged duration—is a key component of any health-related fitness program.

BENEFITS OF CARDIORESPIRATORY ENDURANCE EXERCISE

Cardiorespiratory endurance exercise helps the body become more efficient and better able to cope with physical challenges. It also lowers risk for many chronic diseases.

Improved Cardiorespiratory Functioning

Earlier, this chapter described some of the major changes that occur in the cardiorespiratory system when you exercise, such as increases in cardiac output and blood

Exercise offers both long-term health benefits and immediate pleasures. Many popular sports and activities develop cardiorespiratory endurance.

Immediate effects

Increased levels of neurotransmitters; constant or slightly increased blood flow to the brain.

Increased heart rate and stroke volume (amount of blood pumped per beat).

Increased pulmonary ventilation (amount of air breathed into the body per minute). More air is taken into the lungs with each breath and breathing rate increases.

Reduced blood flow to the stomach, intestines, liver, and kidneys, resulting in less activity in the digestive tract and less urine output.

Increased energy (ATP) production.

Increased blood flow to the skin and increased sweating to help maintain a safe body temperature.

Increased systolic blood pressure; increased blood flow and oxygen transport to working skeletal muscles and the heart; increased oxygen consumption. As exercise intensity increases, blood levels of lactic acid increase.

Long-term effects

Improved self-image, cognitive functioning, and ability to manage stress; enhanced learning, memory, energy level, and sleep; decreased depression, anxiety, and risk for stroke.

Increased heart size and resting stroke volume; lower resting heart rate. Risk of heart disease and heart attack reduced significantly.

Improved ability to extract oxygen from air during exercise. Reduced risk of colds and upper respiratory tract infections.

Increased sweat rate and earlier onset of sweating, helping to cool the body.

Decreased body fat.

Reduced risk of colon cancer and certain other forms of cancer.

Increased number and size of mitochondria in muscle cells; increased amount of stored glycogen; improved ability to use lactic acid and fats as fuel. All of these changes allow for greater energy production and power output. Insulin sensitivity remains constant or improves, helping to prevent type 2 diabetes. Fat-free mass may also increase somewhat.

Increased density and breaking strength of bones, ligaments, and tendons; reduced risk for low-back pain, injuries, and osteoporosis.

Increased blood volume and capillary density; higher levels of high-density lipoproteins (HDL) and lower levels of triglycerides; lower resting blood pressure; increased ability of blood vessels to secrete nitric oxide; and reduced platelet stickiness (a factor in coronary artery disease).

FIGURE 3.2   Immediate and long-term effects of regular cardiorespiratory endurance exercise.
When endurance exercise is performed regularly, short-term changes in the body develop into more permanent adaptations; these include improved ability to exercise, reduced risk of many chronic diseases, and improved psychological and emotional well-being.

pressure, breathing rate, and blood flow to the skeletal muscles. In the short term, all these changes help the body respond to the challenge of exercise. When performed regularly, endurance exercise also leads to permanent adaptations in the cardiorespiratory system (Figure 3.2). These improvements reduce the effort required to perform everyday tasks and make the body better able to respond to physical challenges. This, in a nutshell, is what it means to be physically fit.

Endurance exercise enhances the heart's health by:

- Maintaining or increasing the heart's own blood and oxygen supply.

- Improving the heart muscle's function, so it pumps more blood per beat. This improved function keeps the heart rate lower both at rest and during exercise. The resting heart rate of a fit person is often

10–20 beats per minute lower than that of an unfit person. This translates into as many as 10 million fewer beats in the course of a year.

- Strengthening the heart's contractions.

- Increasing the heart's cavity size (in young adults).

- Increasing blood volume so the heart pushes more blood into the circulatory system during each contraction (larger stroke volume).

- Reducing blood pressure.

maximal oxygen consumption ($\dot{V}O_{2max}$) The highest rate of oxygen consumption an individual is capable of during maximum physical effort, reflecting the body's ability to transport and use oxygen; measured in milliliters of oxygen used per minute per kilogram of body weight.

KEY TERM

Benefits of Exercise for Older Adults

Research has shown that most aspects of physiological functioning peak when people are about 30 years old, then decline at a rate of about 0.5–1.0% per year. This decline in physical capacity is characterized by a decrease in maximal oxygen consumption, cardiac output, muscular strength, fat-free mass, joint mobility, and other factors. However, regular exercise can substantially alter the rate of decline in functional status, and it is associated with both longevity and improved quality of life.

Regular endurance exercise can improve maximal oxygen consumption in older adults by up to 15–30%—the same degree of improvement seen in younger adults. In fact, studies have shown that Masters athletes in their seventies have $\dot{V}O_{2max}$ values equivalent to those of sedentary 20-year-olds. At any age, endurance training can improve cardiorespiratory functioning, cellular metabolism, body composition, and psychological and emotional well-being. Older adults who exercise regularly have better balance and greater

bone density and are less likely than their sedentary peers to suffer injuries as a result of falls. Regular endurance training also substantially reduces the risk of many chronic and disabling diseases, including heart disease, cancer, diabetes, osteoporosis, and dementia.

Other forms of exercise training are also beneficial for older adults. Resistance training is a safe and effective way to build strength and fat-free mass and can help people remain independent as they age. Lifting weights has also been shown to boost spirits in older people, perhaps because improvements in strength appear quickly and are easily applied to everyday tasks such as climbing stairs and carrying groceries. Flexibility exercises can improve the range of motion in joints and also help people maintain functional independence as they age.

It's never too late to start exercising. Even in people over 80, beginning an exercise program can improve physical functioning and quality of life. Most older adults can participate in moderate walking and strengthening and stretching

exercises, and modified programs can be created for people with chronic conditions and other special health concerns. The wellness benefits of exercise are available to people of all ages and levels of ability.

Improved Cellular Metabolism

Regular endurance exercise improves the body's metabolism, down to the cellular level, enhancing your ability to produce and use energy efficiently. Cardiorespiratory training improves metabolism by doing the following:

- Increasing the number of capillaries in the muscles. Additional capillaries supply the muscles with more fuel and oxygen and more quickly eliminate waste products. Greater capillary density also helps heal injuries and reduce muscle aches.

- Training muscles to make the most of oxygen and fuel so they work more efficiently.

- Increasing the size of and number of mitochondria in muscle cells, increasing cells' energy capacity.

- Preventing glycogen depletion and increasing the muscles' ability to use lactate and fat as fuels.

Regular exercise may also help protect cells from chemical damage caused by agents called *free radicals.* (See Chapter 8 for details on free radicals and special enzymes the body uses to fight them.)

Fitness programs that best develop metabolic efficiency include both long-duration, moderately intense endurance exercise and brief periods of more intense effort. For example, climbing a small hill while jogging or

cycling introduces the kind of intense exercise that leads to more efficient use of lactate and fats.

Reduced Risk of Chronic Disease

Regular endurance exercise lowers your risk of many chronic, disabling diseases. It can also help people with those diseases improve their health (see the box "Benefits of Exercise for Older Adults"). The most significant health benefits occur when someone who is sedentary becomes moderately active.

Cardiovascular Diseases Sedentary living is a key contributor to cardiovascular disease (CVD). CVD is a general category that encompasses several diseases of the heart and blood vessels, including coronary heart disease (which can cause heart attacks), stroke, and high blood pressure (see the box "Why Is It Important to Combine Aerobic Exercise with Strength Training?"). Sedentary people are significantly more likely to die of CVD than are fit individuals.

Cardiorespiratory endurance exercise lowers your risk of CVD by doing the following:

- Promoting a healthy balance of fats in the blood. High concentrations of blood fats such as cholesterol and triglycerides are linked to CVD. Exercise raises levels

Why Is It Important to Combine Aerobic Exercise with Strength Training?

connect ACTIVITY DO IT ONLINE

For a variety of reasons, many people choose to focus on only one aspect of physical wellness or fitness. For example, many women concentrate on cardiorespiratory and flexibility exercises but ignore weight training for fear of developing bulky muscles. Many men, conversely, focus exclusively on resistance training in the hope of developing large, strong muscles. They often avoid cardio or flexibility workouts, fearing such exercises will result in loss of hard-earned muscle mass. The fact remains, however, that it is best to include activities that develop all components of health-related fitness.

Emphasizing one aspect of fitness at the expense of others may be a special concern for weight trainers who don't do enough cardiorespiratory conditioning. Although exercise experts universally agree that resistance training is beneficial for a variety of reasons (as detailed in Chapter 4), it also has a downside.

A number of studies conducted around the world have tracked the impact of weight-training exercises on the cardiovascular system, to determine whether resistance training is helpful or harmful to the heart and blood vessels. These studies have shown that strength training poses short- and long-term risks to cardiovascular health and especially to arterial health. Aside from the risk of injury, lifting weights has been shown to have the following adverse effects on the cardiovascular system:

• Weight training promotes short-term stiffness of the blood vessels, which could promote hypertension (high blood pressure) over time and increase the load on the heart.

• Lifting weights (especially heavy weights) causes extreme short-term boosts in blood pressure; a Canadian study revealed that blood pressure can reach 480/350 mm Hg during heavy lifting. Over the long term, sharp elevations in blood pressure can damage arteries, even if each pressure increase lasts only a few seconds.

• Weight training places stress on the endothelial cells that line blood vessels. Because these cells secrete nitric oxide (a chemical messenger involved in a variety of bodily functions), this stress can contribute to a wide range of negative effects, from erectile dysfunction to heart disease.

A variety of studies have shown that the best way to offset cardiovascular stress caused by strength training is to do cardiorespiratory endurance exercise (such as brisk walking or using an elliptical machine) immediately after a weight-training session. Ground-breaking Japanese research showed that following resistance training with aerobic exercise prevents the stiffening of blood vessels and its associated damage. In this 8-week study, participants did aerobics before lifting weights, after lifting weights, or not at all. The group that did aerobics after weight training saw the greatest positive impact on arterial health; participants who did aerobics before lifting weights did not see any improvement in the health of their blood vessels.

Strength training also promotes endurance fitness by improving nervous control of the muscles, increasing type IIa motor units (muscle fibers have a blend of strength and endurance capacity), and increasing tendon stiffness. These changes increase muscle strength and the rate of force development, enhance the economy of movement, and increase the speed that blood cells travel through the muscles.

The bottom line of all this research? Resistance training and cardiorespiratory exercise are both good for you, if you do them in the right order. So, when you plan your workouts, be sure to do 15–60 minutes of aerobic exercise after each weight-training session.

SOURCES: Aagaard, P., and J. L. Andersen. 2010. Effects of strength training on endurance capacity in top-level endurance athletes. *Scandinavian Journal Medicine Science Sports.* 20(supplement 2): 39–47; Okamoto, T., M. Masuhara, and K. Ikuta. 2006. Effects of eccentric and concentric resistance training on arterial stiffness. *Journal of Human Hypertension* 20(5): 348–354; Okamoto, T., M. Masuhara, and K. Ikuta. 2007. Combined aerobic and resistance training and vascular function: Effect of aerobic exercise before and after resistance training. *Journal of Applied Physiology* 103(5): 1655–1661; Physical Activity Guidelines Advisory Committee. 2008. *Physical Activity Guidelines Advisory Committee Report, 2008.* Washington, D.C.: U.S. Department of Health and Human Services.

of "good cholesterol" (high-density lipoproteins, or HDL) and may lower levels of "bad cholesterol" (low-density lipoproteins, or LDL).

• Reducing high blood pressure, which is a contributing factor to several kinds of CVD.

• Enhancing the function of the cells that line the arteries (endothelial cells).

• Reducing inflammation.

• Preventing obesity and type 2 diabetes, both of which contribute to CVD.

Details on various types of CVD, their associated risk factors, and lifestyle factors that can reduce your risk for developing CVD are discussed in Chapter 11. To learn more about atherosclerosis, the underlying disease process in CVD, see page T3-4 of the color transparency insert "Touring the Cardiorespiratory System" in this chapter.

Cancer Although the findings are not conclusive, some studies have shown a relationship between increased physical activity and a reduction in a person's risk of cancer. Exercise reduces the risk of colon cancer, and it may reduce the risk of cancers of the breast and reproductive organs. Physical activity during the high school and college years may be particularly important for preventing breast cancer later in life. Exercise may also reduce the risk of lung cancer, endometrial cancer, pancreatic cancer, and prostate cancer. (See Chapter 12 for more information on various types of cancer.)

Type 2 Diabetes Regular exercise helps prevent the development of type 2 diabetes, the most common form of diabetes. Exercise metabolizes (burns) excess sugar and makes cells more sensitive to the hormone insulin, which is involved in the regulation of blood sugar levels. Obesity is a key risk factor for diabetes, and exercise helps keep body fat at healthy levels. But even without fat loss, exercise improves control of blood sugar levels in many people with diabetes, and physical activity is an important part of treatment. (See Chapter 6 for more on diabetes and insulin resistance.)

Osteoporosis A special benefit of exercise, especially for women, is protection against osteoporosis, a disease that results in loss of bone density and strength. Weight-bearing exercise—particularly weight training—helps build bone during the teens and twenties. People with denser bones can better endure the bone loss that occurs with aging. With stronger bones and muscles and better balance, fit people are less likely to experience debilitating falls and bone fractures. (See Chapter 8 for more on osteoporosis.)

Deaths from All Causes Physically active people have a reduced risk of dying prematurely from all causes, with the greatest benefits found for people with the highest levels of physical activity (Figure 3.3). Physical inactivity is a predictor of premature death and is as important a risk factor as smoking, high blood pressure, obesity, and diabetes.

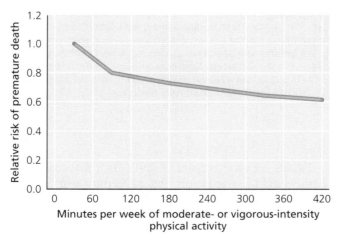

FIGURE 3.3 Doing only 150 minutes of moderate-intensity physical activity per week provides significant health benefits. As you exercise longer or more intensely, you reduce your risk of dying prematurely from a variety of causes.
SOURCE: Physical Activity Guidelines Advisory Committee. 2008. *Physical Activity Guidelines Advisory Committee Report, 2008.* Washington, D.C.: U. S. Department of Health and Human Services.

Fitness Tip

To prevent weight gain, you should exercise 150 to 250 minutes per week, which equals an energy expenditure of 1200 to 2000 calories per week. To lose weight, you should exercise at least 150 minutes per week and up to 420 minutes per week for significant weight loss.

Better Control of Body Fat

Too much body fat is linked to a variety of health problems, including CVD, cancer, and type 2 diabetes. Healthy body composition can be difficult to achieve and maintain—especially for someone who is sedentary—because a diet that contains all essential nutrients can be relatively high in calories. Excess calories are stored in the body as fat. Regular exercise increases daily calorie expenditure so that a healthy diet is less likely to lead to weight gain. Endurance exercise burns calories directly and, if intense enough, continues to do so by raising resting metabolic rate for several hours following an exercise session. A higher metabolic rate makes it easier for a person to maintain a healthy weight or to lose weight. However, exercise alone cannot ensure a healthy body composition. As described in Chapters 6 and 9, you will lose more weight more rapidly and keep it off longer if you decrease your calorie intake and boost your calorie expenditure through exercise.

Improved Immune Function

Exercise can have either positive or negative effects on the immune system, the physiological processes that protect us from diseases such as colds, bacterial infections, and even cancer. Moderate endurance exercise boosts immune function, whereas overtraining (excessive training) depresses it, at least temporarily. Physically fit people get fewer colds and upper respiratory tract infections than people who are not fit. Exercise affects immune function by influencing levels of specialized cells and chemicals involved in the immune response. In addition to getting regular moderate exercise, you can further strengthen your immune system by eating a well-balanced diet, managing stress, and getting 7–8 hours of sleep every night.

Improved Psychological and Emotional Well-Being

Most people who participate in regular endurance exercise experience social, psychological, and emotional benefits. Performing physical activities provides proof of skill mastery and self-control, thus enhancing self-image. Recreational sports provide an opportunity to socialize, have fun, and strive to excel. Endurance exercise lessens

Wellness Tip

If you have trouble sleeping, exercise could be the cure. Regular physical activity helps people fall asleep more easily; it also improves the quality of sleep.

Ask Yourself

QUESTIONS FOR CRITICAL THINKING AND REFLECTION

If you already follow an exercise program, how could you modify it to help improve your cellular metabolism? What specific activities (or changes to existing ones) could you incorporate into your program for this purpose?

anxiety, depression, stress, anger, and hostility, thereby improving mood and boosting cardiovascular health. Regular exercise also improves sleep.

ASSESSING CARDIORESPIRATORY FITNESS

The body's ability to maintain a level of exertion (exercise) for an extended time is a direct reflection of cardiorespiratory fitness. One's level of fitness is determined by the body's ability to take up, distribute, and use oxygen during physical activity. As explained earlier, the best quantitative measure of cardiorespiratory endurance is maximal oxygen consumption, expressed as $\dot{V}O_{2max}$, the amount of oxygen the body uses when a person reaches his or her maximum ability to supply oxygen during exercise (measured in milliliters of oxygen used per minute for each kilogram of body weight). Maximal oxygen consumption can be measured

pecisely in an exercise physiology laboratory through analysis of the air a person inhales and exhales when exercising to a level of exhaustion (maximum intensity). This procedure can be expensive and time-consuming, however, making it impractical for the average person.

Choosing an Assessment Test

Fortunately, several simple assessment tests provide reasonably good estimates of maximal oxygen consumption (within 10–15% of the results of a laboratory test). Three commonly used assessments are the following:

- *The 1-mile walk test.* This estimates your level of cardiorespiratory fitness (maximal oxygen consumption) based on the amount of time it takes you to complete 1 mile of brisk walking and your heart rate at the end of your walk. A fast time and a low heart rate indicate a high level of cardiorespiratory endurance.

- *The 3-minute step test.* The rate at which the pulse returns to normal after exercise is also a good measure of cardiorespiratory capacity; heart rate remains lower and recovers faster in people who are more physically fit. For the step test, you step continually at a steady rate and then monitor your heart rate during recovery.

- *The 1.5-mile run-walk test.* Oxygen consumption increases with speed in distance running, so a fast time on this test indicates high maximal oxygen consumption.

Lab 3.1 provides detailed instructions for each of these tests. An additional assessment, the 12-minute swim test, is also provided. To assess yourself, choose one of these methods based on your access to equipment, your current physical condition, and your own preference. Don't take any of these tests without checking with your physician if you are ill or have any of the risk factors for exercise discussed in Chapter 2 and Lab 2.1. Table 3.2 lists the fitness prerequisites and cautions recommended for each test.

Table 3.2	Fitness Prerequisites and Cautions for the Cardiorespiratory Endurance Assessment Tests
TEST	**FITNESS PREREQUISITES/CAUTIONS**
1-mile walk test	Recommended for anyone who meets the criteria for safe exercise. This test can be used by individuals who cannot perform other tests because of low fitness level or injury.
3-minute step test	If you suffer from joint problems in your ankles, knees, or hips or are significantly overweight, check with your physician before taking this test. People with balance problems or for whom a fall would be particularly dangerous, including older adults and pregnant women, should use special caution or avoid this test.
1.5-mile run-walk test	Recommended for people who are healthy and at least moderately active. If you have been sedentary, you should participate in a 4- to 8-week walk-run program before taking the test. Don't take this test in extremely hot or cold weather if you aren't used to exercising under those conditions.

NOTE: The conditions for exercise safety given in Chapter 2 apply to all fitness assessment tests. If you answered yes to any question on the PAR-Q in Lab 2.1, see your physician before taking any assessment test. If you experience any unusual symptoms while taking a test, stop exercising and discuss your condition with your instructor.

Monitoring Your Heart Rate

Each time your heart beats, it pumps blood into your arteries; this surge of blood causes a pulse that you can feel by holding your fingers against an artery. Counting your pulse to determine your exercise heart rate is a key part of most assessment tests for maximal oxygen consumption. Heart rate can also be used to monitor exercise intensity during a workout. (Intensity is described in more detail in the next section.)

The two most common sites for monitoring heart rate are the carotid artery in the neck and the radial artery in the wrist (Figure 3.4). To take your pulse, press your index and middle fingers gently on the correct site. You may have to shift position several times to find the best place to feel your pulse. Don't use your thumb to check your pulse; it has a pulse of its own that can confuse your count. (Use your middle and ring finger if you have a strong pulse in your index finger.) Be careful not to push too hard, particularly when taking your pulse in the

Ask Yourself

QUESTIONS FOR CRITICAL THINKING AND REFLECTION

Why do you think a relatively slow resting pulse rate is a sign of good cardiorespiratory fitness? What physical conditions or attributes are reflected in your pulse rate?

carotid artery (strong pressure on this artery may cause a reflex that slows the heart rate).

Heart rates are usually assessed in beats per minute (bpm). But counting your pulse for an entire minute isn't practical when you're exercising. And because heart rate slows rapidly when you stop exercising, a full minute's worth of counting can give inaccurate results. It's best to do a shorter count—10 seconds—and then multiply the result by 6 to get your heart rate in beats per minute. (You can also use a heart rate monitor to check your pulse. See the box "Heart Rate Monitors and GPS Devices" for more information.)

Interpreting Your Score

Once you've completed one or more of the assessment tests, use the table under "Rating Your Cardiovascular Fitness" in Lab 3.1 to determine your current level of cardiorespiratory fitness. As you interpret your score, remember that field tests of cardiorespiratory fitness are not precise scientific measurements and have up to a 10–15% margin of error.

You can use the assessment tests to monitor the progress of your fitness program by retesting yourself from time to time. Always compare scores for the *same* test: Your scores on different tests may vary considerably because of differences in skill and motivation and weaknesses in the tests themselves.

DEVELOPING A CARDIORESPIRATORY ENDURANCE PROGRAM

Cardiorespiratory endurance exercises are best for developing the type of fitness associated with good health, so they should serve as the focus of your exercise program. To create a successful endurance exercise program, follow these guidelines:

- Set realistic goals.
- Set your starting frequency, intensity, and duration of exercise at appropriate levels.
- Choose suitable activities.
- Warm up and cool down.
- Adjust your program as your fitness improves.

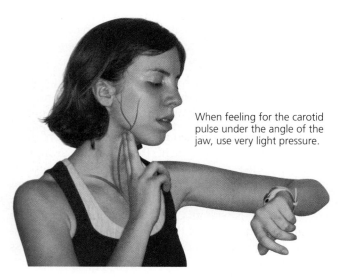

When feeling for the carotid pulse under the angle of the jaw, use very light pressure.

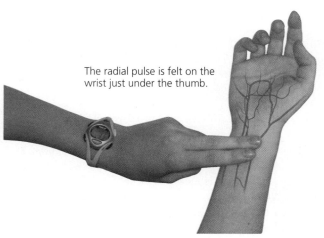

The radial pulse is felt on the wrist just under the thumb.

FIGURE 3.4 Checking your pulse.
The pulse can be taken at the carotid artery in the neck (top) or at the radial artery in the wrist (bottom).

Heart Rate Monitors and GPS Devices

A heart rate monitor is an electronic device that checks the user's pulse, either continuously or on demand. These devices make it easy to monitor your heart rate before, during, and after exercise. Some include global positioning system (GPS) receivers that help you track the distance you walk, run, or bike.

Wearable Monitors

Most consumer-grade monitors have two pieces—a strap that wraps around the user's chest and a wrist strap. The chest strap contains one or more small electrodes, which detect changes in the heart's electrical voltage. A transmitter in the chest strap sends this data to a receiver in the wrist strap. A small computer in the wrist strap calculates the wearer's heart rate and displays it on a small screen.

In a few low-cost monitors, the chest and wrist straps are connected together by a wire, but the most popular monitors use wireless technology to transmit data between the straps. In advanced wireless monitors, data is encoded so that it cannot be read by other monitors that may be nearby, as is often the case in a crowded gym. A one-piece (or "strapless") heart rate monitor does not include a chest strap; the wrist-worn device contains sensors that detect a pulse in the wearer's hand.

Monitors in Gym Equipment

Many pieces of workout equipment—including newer-model treadmills, stationary bikes, and elliptical trainers—feature built-in heart rate monitors. The monitor is usually mounted into the device's handles. To check your heart rate at any time while working out, simply grip the handles in the appropriate place; within a few seconds, your current heart rate will appear on the device's console.

Other Features

Heart rate monitors can do more than just check your pulse. For example, most monitors can tell you the following kinds of information:

- Highest and lowest heart rate during a session
- Average heart rate
- Target heart range, based on your age, weight, and other factors
- Time spent within the target range
- Number of calories burned during a session

Some monitors can upload their data to a computer, so information can be stored and analyzed. The analytical software can help you track your progress over a period of time or a number of workouts. Monitors with GPS provide an accurate estimate of distance traveled during a workout or over an entire day.

Advantages

Heart rate monitors are useful if very close tracking of heart rate is important in your program. They offer several advantages:

- They are accurate, and they reduce the risk of mistakes when checking your own pulse. (Note: Chest-strap monitors are considered more accurate than strapless models. If you use a monitor built into gym equipment, its accuracy will depend on how well the device is maintained.)
- They are easy to use, although a sophisticated, multifunction monitor may take some time to master.
- They do the monitoring for you, so you don't have to worry about checking your own pulse.

When shopping for a heart rate or exercise GPS monitor, do your homework. Quality, reliability, and warranties vary. Ask personal trainers in your area for their recommendations, and look for product reviews in consumer magazines or online.

Setting Goals

You can use the results of cardiorespiratory fitness assessment tests to set a specific oxygen consumption goal for your cardiorespiratory endurance program. Your goal should be high enough to ensure a healthy cardiorespiratory system, but not so high that it will be impossible to achieve. Scores in the fair and good ranges for maximal oxygen consumption suggest good fitness; scores in the excellent and superior ranges indicate a high standard of physical performance.

Through endurance training, an individual may be able to improve maximal oxygen consumption ($\dot{V}O_{2max}$) by about 10–30%. The amount of improvement possible depends on genetics, age, health status, and initial fitness level. People who start at a very low fitness level can improve by a greater percentage than elite athletes because the latter are already at a much higher fitness level, one that may approach their genetic physical limits. If you are tracking $\dot{V}O_{2max}$ by using the field tests described in this chapter, you may be able to increase your score by more than 30% due to improvements in other physical factors, such as muscle power, which can affect your performance on the tests.

Another physical factor you can track to monitor progress is resting heart rate—your heart rate at complete rest, measured in the morning before you get out of bed and move around. Resting heart rate may decrease by as much as 10–15 beats per minute in response to endurance training. Changes in resting heart rate may be noticeable after only about 4–6 weeks of training.

You may want to set other types of goals for your fitness program. For example, if you walk, jog, or cycle as part of your fitness program, you may want to set a time or distance goal—working up to walking 5 miles in one session, completing a 4-mile run in 28 minutes, or cycling a total of 35 miles per week. A more modest goal might be to achieve the U.S. Department of Health and Human Services and ACSM's recommendation of 150 minutes per week of moderate-intensity physical activity. Although it's best to base your program on "SMART" goals, you may also want to set more qualitative goals, such as becoming more energetic, sleeping better, and improving the fit of your clothes.

Applying the FITT Equation

As described in Chapter 2, you can use the acronym FITT to remember key parameters of your fitness program: Frequency, Intensity, Time (duration), and Type of activity.

Frequency of Training Accumulating at least 150 minutes per week of moderate-intensity physical activity (or at least 75 minutes per week of vigorous physical activity) is enough to promote health. Most experts recommend that people exercise 3 to 5 days per week to build cardiorespiratory endurance. Training more than 5 days per week can lead to injury and isn't necessary for the typical person on an exercise program designed to promote wellness. It is safe to do moderate-intensity activity such as walking and gardening every day. Training fewer than 3 days per week makes it difficult to improve your fitness (unless exercise intensity is very high) or to use exercise to lose weight. Remember, however, that some exercise is better than none.

Intensity of Training Intensity is the most important factor for increasing aerobic fitness. You must exercise intensely enough to stress your body so that fitness improves. Four methods of monitoring exercise intensity are described in the following sections; choose the method that works best for you. Be sure to make adjustments in your intensity levels for environmental or individual factors. For example, on a hot and humid day or on your first day back to your program after an illness, you should decrease your intensity level.

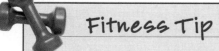

Fitness Tip

Listen to fast-paced music for a better workout! In a British study, students rode a stationary bike while listening to music at different tempos. The subjects rode harder when listening to faster music and performed less exercise in response to slower music.

TARGET HEART RATE ZONE One of the best ways to monitor the intensity of cardiorespiratory endurance exercise is to measure your heart rate. It isn't necessary to exercise at your maximum heart rate to improve maximal oxygen consumption. Fitness adaptations occur at lower heart rates with a much lower risk of injury.

According to the American College of Sports Medicine, your **target heart rate zone**—rates at which you should exercise to experience cardiorespiratory benefits—is between 65% and 90% of your maximum heart rate. To calculate your target heart rate zone, follow these steps:

1. Estimate your maximum heart rate (MHR) by subtracting your age from 220, or have it measured precisely by undergoing an exercise stress test in a doctor's office, hospital, or sports medicine lab. (*Note:* The formula to estimate MHR carries an error of about ±10−15 beats per minute and can be very inaccurate for some people, particularly older adults and young children. If your exercise heart rate seems inaccurate—that is, exercise within your target zone seems either too easy or too difficult—then use the perceived exertion method described in the next section, or have your maximum heart rate measured precisely.)

2. Multiply your MHR by 65% and 90% to calculate your target heart rate zone. (*Note:* Very unfit people should use 55% of MHR for their training threshold.)

For example, a 19-year-old would calculate her target heart rate zone as follows:

MHR = 220 − 19 = 201
65% training intensity = 0.65 × 201 = 131 bpm
90% training intensity = 0.90 × 201 = 181 bpm

To gain fitness benefits, the young woman in our example would have to exercise at an intensity that raises her heart rate to between 131 and 181 bpm.

An alternative method for calculating target heart rate range uses **heart rate reserve**, the difference between maximum heart rate and resting heart rate. Using this method, target heart rate is equal to resting heart rate plus between 50% (40% for very unfit people) and 85% of heart rate reserve. Although some people (particularly those with very low levels of fitness) will obtain more accurate results using this more complex method, both methods provide reasonable estimates of an appropriate target heart rate zone. Formulas for both methods of calculating target heart rate are given in Lab 3.2.

If you have been sedentary, start by exercising at the lower end of your target heart rate range (65% of maximum heart rate or 50% of heart rate reserve) for at least 4–6 weeks. Fast and significant gains in maximal oxygen consumption can be made by exercising closer to the top of the range, but you may increase your risk of injury and overtraining. You *can* achieve significant health benefits by exercising at the bottom of your target range, so don't feel pressure to exercise at an unnecessarily intense level. If you exercise at a lower intensity, you can increase the duration or frequency of training to obtain as much benefit to your health, as long as you are above the 65% training threshold. For people with a very low initial level of fitness, a lower training intensity of 55–64% of maximum heart rate or 40–49% of heart rate reserve may be sufficient to achieve improvements in maximal oxygen consumption, especially at the start of an exercise program. Intensities of 70–85% of maximum heart rate are appropriate for average individuals.

By monitoring your heart rate, you will always know if you are working hard enough to improve, not hard enough, or too hard. As your program progresses and your fitness improves, you will need to jog, cycle, or walk faster in order to reach your target heart rate zone. To monitor your heart rate during exercise, count your pulse while you're still moving or immediately after you stop exercising. Count beats for 10 seconds, then multiply that number by 6 to see if your heart rate is in your target zone. Table 3.3 shows target heart rate ranges and 10-second counts based on the maximum heart rate formula.

METS   One way scientists describe fitness is in terms of the capacity to increase metabolism (energy usage level) above rest. Scientists use METs to measure the metabolic cost of an exercise. One **MET** represents the body's resting metabolic rate—that is, the energy or calorie requirement of the body at rest. Exercise intensity is expressed in multiples of resting metabolic rate. For example, an exercise intensity of 2 METs is twice the resting metabolic rate.

METs are used to describe exercise intensities for occupational activities and exercise programs. Exercise intensities of less than 3–4 METs are considered low. Household chores and most industrial jobs fall into this category.

Table 3.4	Approximate MET and Caloric Costs of Selected Activities for a 154-Pound Person

ACTIVITY	METS	CALORIC EXPENDITURE (kilocalories/min)
Rest	1	1.2
Light housework	2–4	2.4–4.8
Bowling	2–4	2.5–5
Walking	2–7	2.5–8.5
Archery	3–4	3.7–5
Dancing	3–7	3.7–8.5
Hiking	3–7	3.7–8.5
Horseback riding	3–8	3.7–10
Cycling	3–8	3.7–10
Basketball (recreational)	3–9	3.7–11
Swimming	4–8	5–10
Tennis	4–9	5–11
Fishing (fly, stream)	5–6	6–7.5
In-line skating	5–8	6–10
Skiing (downhill)	5–8	6–10
Rock climbing	5–10	6–12
Scuba diving	5–10	6–12
Skiing (cross-country)	6–12	7.5–15
Jogging	8–12	10–15

NOTE: Intensity varies greatly with effort, skill, and motivation.

SOURCE: Adapted from American College of Sports Medicine. 2009. *ACSM's Guidelines for Exercise Testing and Prescription*, 8th ed. Philadelphia: Lippincott Williams and Wilkins.

Exercise at these intensities does not improve fitness for most people, but it will improve fitness for people with low physical capacities. Activities that increase metabolism by 6–8 METs are classified as moderate-intensity exercises and are suitable for most people beginning an exercise program. Vigorous exercise increases metabolic rate by more than 10 METs. Fast running or cycling, as well as intense play in sports like racquetball, can place people in this category. Table 3.4 lists the MET ratings for various activities.

METs are intended to be only an approximation of exercise intensity. Skill, body weight, body fat, and environment affect the accuracy of METs. As a practical matter, however, these limitations can be disregarded. METs are

Table 3.3	Target Heart Rate Range and 10-Second Counts

AGE (years)	TARGET HEART RATE RANGE (bpm)*	10-SECOND COUNT (beats)
20–24	127–180	21–30
25–29	124–176	20–29
30–34	121–171	20–28
35–39	118–167	19–27
40–44	114–162	19–27
45–49	111–158	18–26
50–54	108–153	18–25
55–59	105–149	17–24
60–64	101–144	16–24
65+	97–140	16–23

*Target heart rates lower than those shown here are appropriate for individuals with a very low initial level of fitness. Ranges are based on the following formula: target heart rate = 0.65 to 0.90 of maximum heart rate, assuming maximum heart rate = 220 − age. The heart rate range values shown here correspond to ratings of perceived exertion (rpe) values of about 12–18.

KEY TERMS

target heart rate zone   The range of heart rates that should be reached and maintained during cardiorespiratory endurance exercise to obtain training effects.

heart rate reserve   The difference between maximum heart rate and resting heart rate; used in one method for calculating target heart rate range.

MET   A unit of measure that represents the body's resting metabolic rate—that is, the energy requirement of the body at rest.

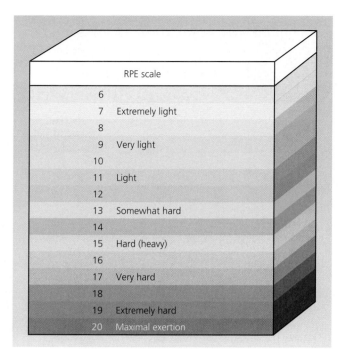

RPE scale

6	
7	Extremely light
8	
9	Very light
10	
11	Light
12	
13	Somewhat hard
14	
15	Hard (heavy)
16	
17	Very hard
18	
19	Extremely hard
20	Maximal exertion

FIGURE 3.5   Ratings of perceived exertion (RPE).
Experienced exercisers may use this subjective scale to estimate how near they are to their target heart rate zone.

SOURCE: *Psychology from Research to Practice* (1978), ed. H. L. Pick. Kluwer Academic/Plenum Publishing Corporation. With kind permission of Springer Science and Business Media and the author.

a good way to express exercise intensity because this system is easy for people to remember and apply.

RATINGS OF PERCEIVED EXERTION   Another way to monitor intensity is to monitor your perceived level of exertion. Repeated pulse counting during exercise can become a nuisance if it interferes with the activity. As your exercise program progresses, you will probably become familiar with the amount of exertion required to raise your heart rate to target levels. In other words, you will know how you feel when you have exercised intensely enough. If this is the case, you can use the scale of **ratings of perceived exertion (RPE)** shown in Figure 3.5 to monitor the intensity of your exercise session without checking your pulse.

To use the RPE scale, select a rating that corresponds to your subjective perception of how hard you are exercising when you are training in your target heart rate zone. If your target zone is about 135–155 bpm, exercise intensely enough to raise your heart rate to that level, and then associate a rating—for example, "somewhat hard" or "hard" (14 or 15)—with how hard you feel you are working. To reach and maintain a similar intensity in future workouts, exercise hard enough to reach what you feel is the same level of exertion. You should periodically check your RPE against

KEY TERM

ratings of perceived exertion (RPE)   A system of monitoring exercise intensity by assigning a number to the subjective perception of target intensity.

Table 3.5   Estimating Exercise Intensity

METHOD	MODERATE INTENSITY	VIGOROUS INTENSITY
Percentage of maximum heart rate	55–69%	70–90%
Heart rate reserve	40–59%	60–85%
Rating of perceived exertion	12–13 (somewhat hard)	14–16 (hard)
Talk test	Speech with some difficulty	Speech limited to short phrases

your target heart rate zone to make sure it's correct. RPE is an accurate means of monitoring exercise intensity, and you may find it easier and more convenient than pulse counting.

TALK TEST   Another easy method of monitoring exercise exertion—in particular, to prevent overly intense exercise—is the talk test. Although your breathing rate will increase during moderate-intensity cardiorespiratory endurance exercise, you should not work out so intensely that you cannot speak comfortably. Speech is limited to short phrases during vigorous-intensity exercise. The talk test is an effective gauge of intensity for many types of activities.

Table 3.5 provides a quick reference to each of the four methods of estimating exercise intensity discussed here.

Time (Duration) of Training   A total duration of 20–60 minutes per day is recommended; exercise can take place in a single session or in multiple sessions lasting 10 or more minutes. The total duration of exercise depends on its intensity. To improve cardiorespiratory endurance during a low- to moderate-intensity activity such as walking or slow swimming, you should exercise for 30–60 minutes. For high-intensity exercise performed at the top of your target heart rate zone, a duration of 20 minutes is sufficient.

Some studies have shown that 5–10 minutes of extremely intense exercise (greater than 90% of maximal oxygen consumption) improves cardiorespiratory endurance. However, training at high intensity, particularly during high-impact activities, increases the risk of injury. Also, because of the discomfort of high-intensity exercise, you are more likely to discontinue your exercise program. Longer-duration, low- to moderate-intensity activities generally result in more gradual gains in maximal oxygen consumption. In planning your program, start with less vigorous activities and gradually increase intensity.

Type of Activity   Cardiorespiratory endurance exercises include activities that involve the rhythmic use of large-muscle groups for an extended period of time, such as jogging, walking, cycling, aerobic dancing and other forms of group exercise, cross-country skiing, and swimming. Start-and-stop sports, such as tennis and racquetball, also qualify if you have enough skill to play continuously and intensely enough to raise your heart rate to target levels.

Other important considerations are access to facilities, expense, equipment, and the time required to achieve an adequate skill level and workout.

Warming Up and Cooling Down

It's important to warm up before every session of cardiorespiratory endurance exercise and to cool down afterward. Because the body's muscles work better when their temperature is slightly above resting level, warming up enhances performance and decreases the chance of injury. It gives the body time to redirect blood to active muscles and the heart time to adapt to increased demands. Warming up also helps spread protective fluid throughout the joints, preventing injury to their surfaces.

A warm-up session should include low-intensity, whole-body movements similar to those in the activity that will follow, such as walking slowly before beginning a brisk walk. An active warm-up of 5–10 minutes is adequate for most types of exercise. However, warm-up time will depend on your level of fitness, experience, and individual preferences.

Do not use stretching as part of your preexercise warm-up. Warm-up stretches do not prevent injury and have little or no effect on postexercise muscle soreness. Stretching before exercise can increase the energy cost of your workout and adversely affect strength, power, balance, reaction time, and movement time. Stretching interferes with muscle and joint receptors that are vital to performance of sport and movement skills. For these reasons, it is best to stretch at the end of your workout, while your muscles are still warm and your joints are lubricated. (See Chapter 5 for a detailed discussion of stretching and flexibility exercises.)

Cooling down after exercise is important for returning the body to a nonexercising state. A cool-down helps maintain blood flow to the heart and brain and redirects blood from working muscles to other areas of the body. This helps prevent a large drop in blood pressure, dizziness, and other potential cardiovascular complications. A cool-down, consisting of 5–10 minutes of reduced activity, should follow every workout to allow heart rate, breathing, and circulation to return to normal. Decrease the intensity of exercise gradually during your cool-down. For example, following a running workout, begin your cool-down by jogging at half speed for 30 seconds to a minute; then do several minutes of walking, reducing your speed slowly. A good rule of thumb is to cool down at least until your heart rate drops below 100 beats per minute.

Fitness Tip

Always make warming up and cooling down a part of your exercise routine! Doing so helps the body adapt to being more active, protects from certain injuries, and may make the health benefits of exercise last longer.

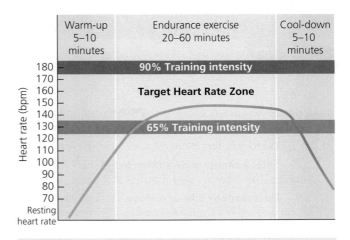

Frequency: 3–5 days per week

Intensity: 55/65–90% of maximum heart rate, 40/50–85% of heart rate reserve plus resting heart rate, or an RPE rating of about 12–18 (lower intensities—55–64% of maximum heart rate and 40–49% of heart rate reserve—are applicable to people who are quite unfit; for average individuals, intensities of 70–85% of maximum heart rate are appropriate)

Time (duration): 20–60 minutes (one session or multiple sessions lasting 10 or more minutes)

Type of activity: Cardiorespiratory endurance exercises, such as walking, jogging, biking, swimming, cross-country skiing, and rope skipping

FIGURE 3.6   The FITT principle for a cardiorespiratory endurance workout.
Longer-duration exercise at lower intensities can often be as beneficial for promoting health as shorter-duration, high-intensity exercise.

The general pattern of a safe and successful workout for cardiorespiratory fitness is illustrated in Figure 3.6.

Building Cardiorespiratory Fitness

Building fitness is as much an art as a science. Your fitness improves when you overload your body. However, you must increase the intensity, frequency, and duration of exercise carefully to avoid injury and overtraining.

For the initial stage of your program, which may last anywhere from 3 to 6 weeks, exercise at the low end of your target heart rate zone. Begin with a frequency of 3–4 days per week, and choose a duration appropriate for your fitness level: 12–15 minutes if you are very unfit, 20 minutes if you are sedentary but otherwise healthy, and 30–40 minutes if you are an experienced exerciser. Use this stage of your program to allow both your body and your schedule to adjust to your new exercise routine. Once you can exercise at the upper levels of frequency (4–5 days per week) and duration (30–40 minutes) without excessive fatigue or muscle soreness, you are ready to progress.

The next phase of your program is the improvement stage, lasting from 4 to 6 months. During this phase, slowly and gradually increase the amount of overload until you reach your target level of fitness (see the sample

Staying Active between Workouts

Many people who practice formal exercise programs do less activity during the rest of the day, which partially defeats the purpose of the exercise program. Below are some ideas for becoming more active during the day. Check which one you can work into your lifestyle:

1. _____ **Exercise before dinner:** Pre-meal exercise decreases appetite and promotes a feeling of fullness.

2. _____ **Enter a charity walk-a-thon:** Many charities make money by getting people to sign up as sponsors in walk-a-thons and fun runs. These events help charities and make you look better in a bikini.

3. _____ **Do errands by bike or on foot:** You are not chained to your car. Buy a grocery cart and walk to the store. Carts are small, so you won't buy as much food and will increase fitness at the same time.

4. _____ **Take the dog for a walk:** Do your dog and yourself a favor and go for a walk together.

5. _____ **Hit softballs or baseballs at the batting cage:** Hitting balls is a great way to get ready for springtime softball games and is a terrific total body exercise.

6. _____ **Hit a bucket of balls at the golf course:** Many people think golf is a wimpy sport. Hit a couple of hundred balls at the driving range and see how you feel the next day. This is a great way to burn calories and improve your game.

7. _____ **Do aerobics 30 to 90 minutes a day:** People who walk only 30 minutes, 5 times per week will lose an average of 5 pounds in 6 to 12 months—without dieting, watching what they eat, or exercising intensely.

8. _____ **Do calisthenics first thing in the morning**: Calisthenics are resistive exercises that use body weight as resistance. These are excellent for a person who wants to develop muscle strength but is unwilling to join a health club or devote too much time to the activity. Examples include push-ups, squats, curl-ups, chair dips, crunches, and jumping jacks.

9. _____ **Exercise in the housework gym:** A vacuum cleaner is actually a lunge machine. Use a little creativity and you can turn simple household chores into a weight and aerobics workout. Try wearing a weighted vest while you sweep or mop the floor. Don't walk up the stairs— run. Jog in place as you wash the dishes. Stretch while putting away the dishes.

10. _____ **Active shopping:** Go on a window-shopping hike. Walk through the mall and check out every single shop. If you live in a small town, check out each store twice. If you live near the Mall of America, cover the stores in four days.

11. _____**Trim the hedge**: Go to the hardware store and purchase hand hedge trimmers. This garden chore burns calories and builds chest, shoulder, leg, and core muscles.

12. _____ **Sweep the walkway**: Try interval sweeping: Pick a 10-yard strip of cement and sweep as fast and as hard as you can. Also, try lunge sweeping: Do a lunge every time you sweep the broom—first your left leg, then your right.

By themselves, few of these methods will make you physically fit. But combining two or three of these techniques gives you powerful tools that will help you build fitness and keep the fat off.

---

training progression in Table 3.6). Take care not to increase overload too quickly. It is usually best to avoid increasing intensity and duration during the same session or all three training variables in one week. Increasing duration in increments of 5–10 minutes every 2–3 weeks is usually appropriate. Signs that you are increasing overload too quickly include muscle aches and pains, lack of usual interest in exercise, extreme fatigue, and inability to complete a workout. Keep an exercise log or training diary to monitor your workouts and progress.

Maintaining Cardiorespiratory Fitness

You will not improve your fitness indefinitely. The more fit you become, the harder you must work to improve (see the box "Interval Training: Pros and Cons"). There are limits to the level of fitness you can achieve, and if you increase intensity and duration indefinitely, you are likely to become injured or overtrained. After an improvement stage of 4–6 months, you may reach your goal of an acceptable level of fitness. You can then maintain fitness by continuing to exercise at the same intensity at least 3 nonconsecutive days every week. If you stop exercising, you lose your gains in fitness fairly rapidly. If you take time off for any reason, start your program again at a lower level and rebuild your fitness in a slow and systematic way.

Fitness Tip

A 40-meter running track, found in almost any high school or college, is a great place to do interval training. Start by striding the straight-a-ways and walking the turns. Begin with just one lap and increase the number of laps until you can do 4 to 8 (1 to 2 miles).

Table 3.6	Sample Progression for an Endurance Program		
STAGE/WEEK	FREQUENCY (days/ week)	INTENSITY* (beats/ minute)	TIME (duration in minutes)
Initial stage			
1	3	120–130	15–20
2	3	120–130	20–25
3	4	130–145	20–25
4	4	130–145	25–30
Improvement stage			
5–7	3–4	145–160	25–30
8–10	3–4	145–160	30–35
11–13	3–4	150–165	30–35
14–16	4–5	150–165	30–35
17–20	4–5	160–180	35–40
21–24	4–5	160–180	35–40
Maintenance stage			
25+	3–5	160–180	20–60

*The target heart rates shown here are based on calculations for a healthy 20-year-old with a resting heart rate of 60 beats per minute; the program progresses from an initial target heart rate of 50% to a maintenance range of 70–85% of heart rate reserve.

SOURCE: Adapted from American College of Sports Medicine. 2009. *ACSM's Guidelines for Exercise Testing and Prescription*, 8th ed. Philadelphia: Lippincott Williams and Wilkins. Reprinted with permission from the publisher.

When you reach the maintenance stage, you may want to set new goals for your program and make some adjustments to maintain your motivation. Adding variety to your program can be a helpful strategy. Engaging in multiple types of endurance activities, an approach known as **cross-training**, can help boost enjoyment and prevent some types of injuries. For example, someone who has been jogging 5 days a week may change her program so that she jogs 3 days a week, plays tennis 1 day a week, and goes for a bike ride 1 day a week.

Ask Yourself

QUESTIONS FOR CRITICAL THINKING AND REFLECTION

Suppose you want to start a new cardiorespiratory exercise program. How do your age, health status, and current level of fitness affect the kind of program you design for yourself? For the first few weeks, how often would you exercise, at what intensity (heart rate), and for how long?

EXERCISE SAFETY AND INJURY PREVENTION

Exercising safely and preventing injuries are two important challenges for people who engage in cardiorespiratory endurance exercise. This section provides basic safety guidelines that can be applied to a variety of fitness activities. Chapters 4 and 5 include additional advice specific to strength training and flexibility training.

Hot Weather and Heat Stress

Human beings require a relatively constant body temperature to survive. A change of just a few degrees in body temperature can quickly lead to distress and even death. If you lose too much water or if your body temperature gets too high, you may suffer from heat stress. Problems associated with heat stress include dehydration, heat cramps, heat exhaustion, and heatstroke.

In a high-temperature environment, exercise safety depends on the body's ability to dissipate heat and maintain blood flow to active muscles. The body releases heat from exercise through the evaporation of sweat. This process cools the skin and the blood circulating near the body's surface. Sweating is an efficient process as long as the air is relatively dry. As humidity increases, however, the sweating mechanism becomes less efficient because extra moisture in the air inhibits the evaporation of sweat from the skin. This is why it takes longer to cool down in humid weather than in dry weather.

You can avoid significant heat stress by staying fit, avoiding overly intense or prolonged exercise for which you are not prepared, drinking adequate fluids before and during exercise, and wearing clothes that allow heat to dissipate.

Dehydration Your body needs water to carry out many chemical reactions and to regulate body temperature. Sweating during exercise depletes your body's water supply and can lead to **dehydration** if fluids aren't replaced. Although dehydration is most common in hot weather, it can occur even in comfortable temperatures if fluid intake is insufficient.

Dehydration increases body temperature and decreases sweat rate, plasma volume, cardiac output, maximal oxygen consumption, exercise capacity, muscular strength, and stores of liver glycogen. You may begin to feel thirsty when you have a fluid deficit of about 1% of total body weight.

Drinking fluids before and during exercise is important to prevent dehydration and enhance performance. Thirst receptors in the brain make you want to drink fluids, but during heavy or prolonged exercise or exercise

cross-training Alternating two or more activities to improve a single component of fitness.

dehydration Excessive loss of body fluid.

KEY TERMS

Interval Training: Pros and Cons

Few exercise techniques are more effective at improving fitness rapidly than *high-intensity interval training (HIT)*—a series of very brief, high-intensity exercise sessions interspersed with short rest periods. The four components of interval training are distance, repetition, intensity, and rest, defined as follows:

- *Distance* refers to either the distance or the time of the exercise interval.

- *Repetition* is the number of times the exercise is repeated.

- *Intensity* is the speed at which the exercise is performed.

- *Rest* is the time spent recovering between exercises.

Canadian researchers found that 6 sessions of high-intensity interval training on a stationary bike increased muscle oxidative capacity by almost 50%, muscle glycogen by 20%, and cycle endurance capacity by 100%. The subjects made these amazing improvements by exercising only 15 minutes in 2 weeks. Each workout consisted of 4–7 repetitions of high-intensity exercise (each repetition consisted of 30 seconds at near maximum effort) on a stationary bike. A follow-up study of moderately active women using the same training method showed that interval training increased the body's capacity for burning fat during exercise. These studies (and more than 20 others) showed the value of high-intensity training for building aerobic capacity and endurance.

You can use interval training in your favorite aerobic exercises. In fact, the type of exercise you select is not important as long as you exercise at a high intensity. HIT training can even be used to help develop sports skills. For example, a runner might do 4 to 8 repetitions of 200-meter sprints at near-maximum effort. A tennis player might practice volleys against a wall as fast as possible for 4 to 8 repetitions lasting 30 seconds each. A swimmer might swim 4 to 8 repetitions of 50 meters at 100% effort. It is important to rest from 3 to 5 minutes between repetitions, regardless of the type of exercise being performed.

If you add HIT to your exercise program, do not practice interval training more than 3 days per week. Intervals are exhausting and easily lead to injury. Let your body tell you how many days you can tolerate. If you become overly tired after doing interval training 3 days per week, cut back to 2 days. If you feel good, try increasing the intensity or volume of intervals (but not the number of days per week) and see what happens. As with any kind of exercise program, begin HIT training slowly and progress conservatively. Although the Canadian studies showed that HIT training produced substantial fitness improvements by themselves, it is best to integrate HIT into your total exercise program.

High-intensity interval training appears to be safe and effective in the short term, but there are concerns about the long-term safety and effectiveness of this type of training, so consider the following issues:

- Maximal-intensity training could be dangerous for some people. A physician might be reluctant to give certain patients the green light for this type of exercise.

- Always warm up with several minutes of low-intensity exercise before practicing HIT. Maximal-intensity exercise without a warm-up can cause cardiac arrhythmias (abnormal heart rhythms) even in healthy people.

- HIT might trigger overuse injuries in unfit people. For this reason, it is essential to start gradually, especially for someone at a low level of fitness. Exercise at sub-maximal intensities for at least 4 to 6 weeks before starting high-intensity interval training. Cut back on interval training or rest if you feel overly fatigued or develop overly sore joints or muscles.

---

in hot weather, thirst alone isn't a good indicator of how much you need to drink. As a rule of thumb, drink at least 2 cups (16 ounces) of fluid 2 hours before exercise, and then drink enough during exercise to match fluid loss in sweat. Drink at least 1 cup of fluid every 20–30 minutes during exercise, more in hot weather or if you sweat heavily. To determine if you're drinking enough fluid, weigh yourself before and after an exercise session; any weight loss is due to fluid loss that needs to be replaced.

Very rarely, active people consume too much water and develop *hyponatremia,* a condition characterized by lung congestion, muscle weakness, and nervous system problems. Following the guidelines presented here can help prevent this condition.

Bring a water bottle when you exercise so you can replace your fluids when they're being depleted. For exercise

sessions lasting less than 60–90 minutes, cool water is an excellent fluid replacement. For longer workouts, choose a sports drink that contains water and small amounts of electrolytes (sodium, potassium, and magnesium) and simple carbohydrates ("sugar," usually in the form of sucrose, glucose, lactate, or glucose polymers). Electrolytes, which are lost from the body in sweat, are important because they help regulate the balance of fluids in body cells and the bloodstream. The carbohydrates in typical sports drinks are rapidly digestible and can thus help maintain blood glucose levels. Choose a beverage with no more than 8 grams of simple carbohydrate per 100 milliliters. Nonfat milk or chocolate milk, for those who can tolerate dairy products, are excellent fluid replacement beverages because they promote long-term hydration. See Chapter 8 for more on diet and fluid recommendations for active people.

Heat Cramps Involuntary cramping and spasms in the muscle groups used during exercise are sometimes called **heat cramps.** Although depletion of sodium and potassium from the muscles is involved with the problem, the primary cause of cramps is muscle fatigue. Children are particularly susceptible to heat cramps, but the condition can also occur in adults, even those who are fit. The best treatment for heat cramps is a combination of gentle stretching, replacement of fluid and electrolytes, and rest.

Heat Exhaustion Symptoms of **heat exhaustion** include the following:

- Rapid, weak pulse
- Low blood pressure
- Headache
- Faintness, weakness, dizziness
- Profuse sweating
- Pale face
- Psychological disorientation (in some cases)
- Normal or slightly elevated core body temperature

Heat exhaustion occurs when an insufficient amount of blood returns to the heart because so much of the body's blood volume is being directed to working muscles (for exercise) and to the skin (for cooling). Treatment for heat exhaustion includes resting in a cool area, removing excess clothing, applying cool or damp towels to the body, and drinking fluids. An affected individual should rest for the remainder of the day and drink plenty of fluids for the next 24 hours.

Heatstroke **Heatstroke** is a major medical emergency involving the failure of the brain's temperature regulatory center. The body does not sweat enough, and body temperature rises dramatically to extremely dangerous levels. In addition to high body temperature, symptoms can include the following:

- Hot, flushed skin (dry or sweaty), red face
- Chills, shivering
- Very high or very low blood pressure
- Confusion, erratic behavior
- Convulsions, loss of consciousness

A heatstroke victim should be cooled as rapidly as possible and immediately transported to a hospital. To lower body temperature, get out of the heat, remove excess clothing, drink cold fluids, and apply cool or damp towels to the body or immerse the body in cold water. People experiencing heatstroke during exercise may still be sweating.

Cold Weather

In extremely cold conditions, problems can occur if a person's body temperature drops or if particular parts of the body are exposed. If the body's ability to warm itself through shivering or exercise can't keep pace with heat loss, the core body temperature begins to drop. This condition, known as **hypothermia**, depresses the central nervous system, resulting in sleepiness and a lower metabolic rate. As metabolic rate drops, body temperature declines even further, and coma and death can result. The risk of hypothermia is particularly great in cold water.

Frostbite—the freezing of body tissues—is another potential danger of exercise in extremely cold conditions. Frostbite most commonly occurs in exposed body parts like earlobes, fingers, and the nose, and it can cause permanent circulatory damage. Hypothermia and frostbite both require immediate medical treatment.

To exercise safely in cold conditions, don't stay out in very cold temperatures for too long. Take both the temperature and the wind into account when planning your exercise session. Frostbite is possible within 30 minutes in calm conditions when the temperature is colder than −5°F, or in windy conditions (30 mph) if the temperature is below 10°F. **Wind chill** values that reflect both the temperature and the wind speed are available as part of a local weather forecast and from the National Weather Service (http://www.weather.gov).

Appropriate clothing provides insulation and helps trap warm air next to the skin. Dress in layers so you can remove them as you warm up and can put them back on if you get cold. A substantial amount of heat loss comes from the head and neck, so keep these areas covered. In subfreezing temperatures, protect the areas of your body most susceptible to frostbite—fingers, toes, ears, nose, and cheeks—with warm socks, mittens or gloves, and a cap, hood, or ski mask. Wear clothing that breathes and will wick moisture away from your skin to avoid being cooled or overheated by trapped perspiration. Many types of comfortable, lightweight clothing that provide good insulation are available. It's also important to warm up thoroughly and to drink plenty of fluids.

KEY TERMS

heat cramps   Sudden muscle spasms and pain associated with intense exercise in hot weather.

heat exhaustion   Heat illness resulting from exertion in hot weather.

heatstroke   A severe and often fatal heat illness characterized by significantly elevated core body temperature.

hypothermia   Low body temperature due to exposure to cold conditions.

frostbite   Freezing of body tissues characterized by pallor, numbness, and a loss of cold sensation.

wind chill   A measure of how cold it feels based on the rate of heat loss from exposed skin caused by cold and wind; the temperature that would have the same cooling effect on a person as a given combination of temperature and wind speed.

| Table 3.7 | Care of Common Exercise Injuries and Discomforts |

INJURY	SYMPTOMS	TREATMENT
Blister	Accumulation of fluid in one spot under the skin	Don't pop or drain it unless it interferes too much with your daily activities. If it does pop, clean the area with antiseptic and cover with a bandage. Do not remove the skin covering the blister.
Bruise (contusion)	Pain, swelling, and discoloration	R-I-C-E: rest, ice, compression, elevation.
Fracture and/or dislocation	Pain, swelling, tenderness, loss of function, and deformity	Seek medical attention, immobilize the affected area, and apply cold.
Joint sprain	Pain, tenderness, swelling, discoloration, and loss of function	R-I-C-E; apply heat when swelling has disappeared. Stretch and strengthen affected area.
Muscle cramp	Painful, spasmodic muscle contractions	Gently stretch for 15–30 seconds at a time and/or massage the cramped area. Drink fluids and increase dietary salt intake if exercising in hot weather.
Muscle soreness or stiffness	Pain and tenderness in the affected muscle	Stretch the affected muscle gently; exercise at a low intensity; apply heat. Nonsteroidal anti-inflammatory drugs, such as ibuprofen, help some people.
Muscle strain	Pain, tenderness, swelling, and loss of strength in the affected muscle	R-I-C-E; apply heat when swelling has disappeared. Stretch and strengthen the affected area.
Plantar fascitis	Pain and tenderness in the connective tissue on the bottom of the foot	Apply ice, take nonsteroidal anti-inflammatory drugs, and stretch. Wear night splints when sleeping.
Shin splint	Pain and tenderness on the front of the lower leg; sometimes also pain in the calf muscle	Rest; apply ice to the affected area several times a day and before exercise; wrap with tape for support. Stretch and strengthen muscles in the lower legs. Purchase good-quality footwear and run on soft surfaces.
Side stitch	Pain on the side of the abdomen	Stretch the arm on the affected side as high as possible; if that doesn't help, try bending forward while tightening the abdominal muscles.
Tendinitis	Pain, swelling, and tenderness of the affected area	R-I-C-E; apply heat when swelling has disappeared. Stretch and strengthen the affected area.

Poor Air Quality

Air pollution can decrease exercise performance and negatively affect health, particularly if you smoke or have respiratory problems such as asthma, bronchitis, or emphysema. The effects of smog are worse during exercise than at rest because air enters the lungs faster. Polluted air may also contain carbon monoxide, which displaces oxygen in the blood and reduces the amount of oxygen available to working muscles. In a 2007 study, scientists from the ACSM found that exercise in polluted air could decrease lung function to the same extent as heavy smoking. Symptoms of poor air quality include eye and throat irritations, difficulty breathing, and possibly headache and malaise.

Do not exercise outdoors during a smog alert or if air quality is very poor. If you have any type of cardiorespiratory difficulty, you should also avoid exertion outdoors when air quality is poor. You can avoid some smog and air pollution by exercising in indoor facilities, in parks, near water (riverbanks, lakeshores, and ocean beaches), or in residential areas with less traffic (areas with stop-and-go traffic will have lower air quality than areas where traffic moves quickly). Air quality is also usually better in the early morning and late evening, before and after the commute hours.

Exercise Injuries

Most injuries are annoying rather than serious or permanent. However, an injury that isn't cared for properly can escalate into a chronic problem, sometimes serious enough to permanently curtail the activity. It's important to learn how to deal with injuries so they don't derail your fitness program. Strategies for the care of common exercise injuries and discomforts appear in Table 3.7; some general guidelines are given in the following sections.

When to Call a Physician Some injuries require medical attention. Consult a physician for the following:

- Head and eye injuries
- Possible ligament injuries
- Broken bones
- Internal disorders: chest pain, fainting, elevated body temperature, intolerance to hot weather

Also seek medical attention for ostensibly minor injuries that do not get better within a reasonable amount of time. You may need to modify your exercise program for a few weeks to allow an injury to heal.

Wellness Tip

It may be easy to nurse some injuries yourself, but if you aren't sure what to do, call your doctor.

Rehabilitation Following a Minor Athletic Injury

connect
ACTIVITY DO IT ONLINE

- Reduce the initial inflammation using the R-I-C-E principle (see text).

- After 36–48 hours, apply heat *if the swelling has disappeared completely.* Immerse the affected area in warm water or apply warm compresses, a hot water bottle, or a heating pad. As soon as it's comfortable, begin moving the affected joints slowly. If you feel pain, or if the injured area begins to swell again, reduce the amount of movement. Continue gently stretching and moving the affected area until you have regained normal range of motion.

- Gradually begin exercising the injured area to build strength and endurance. Depending on the type of injury, weight training, walking, and resistance training can all be effective.

- Gradually reintroduce the stress of an activity until you can return to full intensity. Don't progress too rapidly or you'll re-injure yourself. Before returning to full exercise participation, you should have a full range of motion in your joints, normal strength and balance among your muscles, normal coordinated patterns of movement (with no injury compensation movements, such as limping), and little or no pain.

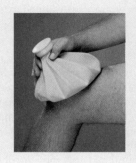

TAKE CHARGE

Managing Minor Exercise Injuries For minor cuts and scrapes, stop the bleeding and clean the wound. Treat injuries to soft tissue (muscles and joints) with the R-I-C-E principle: rest, ice, compression, and elevation.

- *Rest:* Stop using the injured area as soon as you experience pain. Avoid any activity that causes pain.

- *Ice:* Apply ice to the injured area to reduce swelling and alleviate pain. Apply ice immediately for 10–20 minutes, and repeat every few hours until the swelling disappears. Let the injured part return to normal temperature between icings, and do not apply ice to one area for more than 20 minutes. An easy method for applying ice is to freeze water in a paper cup, peel some of the paper away, and rub the exposed ice on the injured area. If the injured area is large, you can surround it with several bags of crushed ice or ice cubes, or bags of frozen vegetables. Place a thin towel between the bag and your skin. If you use a cold gel pack, limit application time to 10 minutes. Apply ice regularly for 36–48 hours or until the swelling is gone; it may be necessary to apply ice for a week or more if swelling persists.

- *Compression:* Wrap the injured area firmly with an elastic or compression bandage between icings. If the area starts throbbing or begins to change color, the bandage may be wrapped too tightly. Do not sleep with the wrap on.

- *Elevation:* Raise the injured area above heart level to decrease the blood supply and reduce swelling. Use pillows, books, or a low chair or stool to raise the injured area.

The day after the injury, some experts recommend also taking an over-the-counter medication, such as aspirin, ibuprofen, or naproxen, to decrease inflammation. To rehabilitate your body, follow the steps listed in the box "Rehabilitation Following a Minor Athletic Injury."

Preventing Injuries The best method for dealing with exercise injuries is to prevent them. If you choose activities for your program carefully and follow the training guidelines described here and in Chapter 2, you should be able to avoid most types of injuries. Important guidelines for preventing athletic injuries include the following:

- Train regularly and stay in condition.
- Gradually increase the intensity, duration, or frequency of your workouts.
- Avoid or minimize high-impact activities; alternate them with low-impact activities.
- Get proper rest between exercise sessions.
- Drink plenty of fluids.
- Warm up thoroughly before you exercise and cool down afterward.
- Achieve and maintain a normal range of motion in your joints.
- Use proper body mechanics when lifting objects or executing sports skills.
- Don't exercise when you are ill or overtrained.
- Use proper equipment, particularly shoes, and choose an appropriate exercise surface. If you exercise on a grass field, soft track, or wooden floor, you are less likely to be injured than on concrete or a hard track. (For information on athletic shoes, see the box "Choosing Exercise Footwear.")
- Don't return to your normal exercise program until any athletic injuries have healed. Restart your program at a lower intensity and gradually increase the amount of overload.

Choosing Exercise Footwear

Footwear is perhaps the most important item of equipment for almost any activity. Shoes protect and support your feet and improve your traction. When you jump or run, you place as much as six times more force on your feet than when you stand still. Shoes can help cushion against the stress that this additional force places on your lower legs, thereby preventing injuries. Some athletic shoes are also designed to help prevent ankle rollover, another common source of injury.

General Guidelines

When choosing athletic shoes, first consider the activity you've chosen for your exercise program. Shoes appropriate for different activities have very different characteristics.

Foot type is another important consideration. If your feet tend to roll inward excessively, you may need shoes with additional stability features on the inner side of the shoe to counteract this movement. If your feet tend to roll outward excessively, you may need highly flexible and cushioned shoes that promote foot motion. Most women will get a better fit if they choose shoes specifically designed for women's feet rather than downsized versions of men's shoes.

Successful Shopping For successful shoe shopping, keep the following strategies in mind:

- Shop late in the day or, ideally, following a workout. Your foot size increases over the course of the day and after exercise.

- Wear socks like those you plan to wear during exercise.

- Try on both shoes and wear them around for 10 or more minutes. Try walking on a noncarpeted surface. Approximate the movements of your activity: walk, jog, run, jump, and so on.

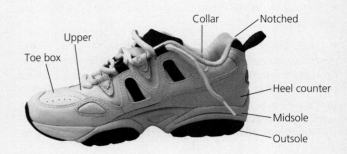

- Check the fit and style carefully:

  - Is the toe box roomy enough? Your toes will spread out when your foot hits the ground or you push off. There should be at least one thumb's width of space from the longest toe to the end of the toe box.

  - Do the shoes have enough cushioning? Do your feet feel supported when you bounce up and down? Try bouncing on your toes and on your heels.

  - Do your heels fit snugly into the shoe? Do they stay put when you walk, or do they slide up?

  - Are the arches of your feet right on top of the shoes' arch supports?

  - Do the shoes feel stable when you twist and turn on the balls of your feet? Try twisting from side to side while standing on one foot.

  - Do you feel any pressure points?

- If you exercise at dawn or dusk, choose shoes with reflective sections for added visibility and safety.

- Replace athletic shoes about every 3 months or 300–500 miles of jogging or walking.

? Ask Yourself

QUESTIONS FOR CRITICAL THINKING AND REFLECTION

Have you ever suffered an injury while exercising? If so, how did you treat the injury? Compare your treatment with the guidelines given in this chapter. Did you do the right things? What can you do to avoid such injuries in the future?

TIPS FOR TODAY AND THE FUTURE

Regular, moderate exercise, even in short bouts spread through the day, can improve cardiorespiratory fitness.

RIGHT NOW YOU CAN

- Assess your cardiorespiratory fitness by using one of the methods discussed in this chapter and in Lab 3.1.
- Do a short bout of endurance exercise, such as 10–15 minutes of walking, jogging, or cycling.
- If you have physical activity planned for later in the day, drink some fluids now to make sure you are fully hydrated for your workout.
- Consider the exercise equipment, including shoes, you currently have on hand. If you need new equipment, start researching your options to get the best equipment you can afford.

IN THE FUTURE YOU CAN

- Graduate to a different, more challenging fitness assessment as your cardiorespiratory fitness improves.
- Incorporate different types of exercises into your cardiorespiratory endurance training to keep yourself challenged and motivated.

Q Do I need a special diet for my endurance exercise program?

A No. For most people, a nutritionally balanced diet contains all the energy and nutrients needed to sustain an exercise program. Don't waste your money on unnecessary supplements. (Chapter 8 provides detailed information about putting together a healthy diet.)

Q How can I measure how far I walk or run?

A The simplest and cheapest way to measure distance is with a pedometer, which counts your steps. Although stride length varies among individuals, 2000 steps typically equals about 1 mile, and 10,000 steps equals about 5 miles. To track your distance and your progress using a pedometer, follow the guidelines in Lab 2.3.

Q How can I avoid being so sore when I start an exercise program?

A Postexercise muscle soreness is caused by muscle injury followed by muscle inflammation. Muscles get stronger and larger in response to muscle tension and injury. However, excessive injury can delay progress. The best approach is to begin conservatively with low-volume, low-intensity workouts, and gradually increase the severity of the exercise sessions. If you are currently sedentary, begin with 5 to 10 minutes of exercise and gradually increase the distance and speed you walk, run, cycle, or swim.

Q Is it OK to do cardiorespiratory endurance exercise while menstruating?

A Yes. There is no evidence that exercise during menstruation is unhealthy or that it has negative effects on performance. If you have headaches, backaches, and abdominal pain during menstruation, you may not feel like exercising. For some women, exercise helps relieve these symptoms. Listen to your body and exercise at whatever intensity is comfortable for you.

Q Will high altitude affect my ability to exercise?

A At high altitudes (above 1500 meters, or about 4900 feet), there is less oxygen available in the air than at lower altitudes. High altitude doesn't affect anaerobic exercise, such as stretching and weight lifting, but it does affect aerobic activities—that is, any type of cardiovascular endurance exercise—because the heart and lungs have to work harder, even when the body is at rest, to deliver enough oxygen to body cells. The increased cardiovascular strain of exercise reduces endurance. To play it safe when at high altitudes, avoid heavy exercise—at least for the first few days—and drink plenty of water. And don't expect to reach your normal lower-altitude exercise capacity.

For more Common Questions Answered about endurance training, visit the Online Learning Center at www.mhhe.com/fahey.

SUMMARY

• The cardiorespiratory system consists of the heart, blood vessels, and respiratory system; it picks up and transports oxygen, nutrients, and waste products.

• The body takes chemical energy from food and uses it to produce ATP and fuel cellular activities. ATP is stored in the body's cells as the basic form of energy.

• During exercise, the body supplies ATP and fuels cellular activities by combining three energy systems: immediate, for short periods of activity; nonoxidative (anaerobic), for intense activity; and oxidative (aerobic), for prolonged activity. Which energy system predominates depends on the duration and intensity of the activity.

• Cardiorespiratory endurance exercise improves cardiorespiratory functioning and cellular metabolism; it reduces the risk of chronic diseases such as heart disease, cancer, type 2 diabetes, obesity, and osteoporosis; and it improves immune function and psychological and emotional well-being.

• Cardiorespiratory fitness is measured by determining how well the cardiorespiratory system transports and uses oxygen. The upper limit of this measure, called maximal oxygen consumption, or $\dot{V}O_{2max}$, can be measured precisely in a laboratory, or it can be estimated reasonably well through self-assessment tests.

• To create a successful exercise program, set realistic goals, choose suitable activities, begin slowly, and always warm up and cool down. As fitness improves, exercise more often, longer, and/or harder.

• Intensity of training can be measured through target heart rate zone, METs, ratings of perceived exertion, or the talk test.

• With careful attention to fluid intake, clothing, duration of exercise, and exercise intensity, endurance training can be safe in hot and cold weather conditions.

- Serious injuries require medical attention. Application of the R-I-C-E principle (rest, ice, compression, elevation) is appropriate for treating many types of muscle or joint injuries.

FOR FURTHER EXPLORATION

BOOKS

American College of Sports Medicine. 2003. *ACSM Fitness Book.* 3rd ed. Champaign, Ill.: Human Kinetics. *Includes fitness assessment tests and advice on creating a complete fitness program.*

Centers for Disease Control and Prevention. 2010. *Promoting Physical Activity: A Guide for Community Action*, 2nd ed. Champaign, Ill.: Human Kinetics. *Presents a guide for community action that offers the tools and information you need to help people become more active.*

Coffman, S. 2007. *Successful Programs for Fitness and Health Clubs.* Champaign, Ill.: Human Kinetics. *Presents more than 100 ready-to-use programs for fitness centers, group exercise studios, pools, gyms, and classrooms.*

Edwards, S., and S. Reed. 2006. *Heart Zones Cycling: The Avid Cyclist's Guide to Riding Faster and Farther.* Boulder, Colo: VeloPress. *An excellent guide to using heart rate in endurance training written by a top athlete and scientist.*

Fenton, M. 2008. *The Complete Guide to Walking, New and Revised: For Health, Weight Loss, and Fitness.* Guilford, Conn.: Lyons Press. *Discusses walking as a fitness method and a way to avoid diseases such as diabetes.*

Gotlin, R. 2007. *Sports Injuries Guidebook.* Champaign, Ill.: Human Kinetics. *Provides information and care instructions on many types of sports-related injuries.*

Howley, E. T., and B. D. Franks. 2007. *Fitness Professional's Handbook,* 5th ed. Champaign, Ill.: Human Kinetics. *A comprehensive manual on physical training for professionals and people interested in exercise and sports.*

Maffetone, P. 2010. *The Big Book of Endurance Training and Racing.* New York: Skyhorse Publishing. *An excellent book for people of all levels interested in running, swimming, cycling, and triathlon.*

Marcus, B. H., and L. A. Forsyth. 2009. *Motivating People to be Physically Active,* 2nd ed. Champaign, Ill.: Human Kinetics. *Describes methods for helping people increase their level of physical activity.*

Nieman, D. C. 2010. *Exercise Testing and Prescription: A Health-Related Approach,* 7th ed. New York: McGraw-Hill. *A comprehensive discussion of the effect of exercise and exercise testing and prescription.*

Richmond, M. 2011. *The Physiology Storybook: An Owner's Manual for the Human Body.* Monterey, Calif.: Healthy Learning. *A discussion of human physiology and wellness written for the average person.*

Rothman, J., and T. LaFontaine. 2011. *The Exercise Professional's Guide to Optimizing Health: Strategies for Preventing and Reducing Chronic Disease.* Baltimore: Lippincott Williams & Wilkins. *Written for professionals in association with the American College of Sports Medicine, the book describes how exercise can help prevent and treat chronic disease.*

ORGANIZATIONS AND WEB SITES

American Academy of Orthopaedic Surgeons: Sports and Exercise. Provides fact sheets on many fitness and sports topics, including how to begin a program, how to choose equipment, and how to prevent and treat many types of injuries.
http://orthoinfo.aaos.org/menus/sports.cfm

American Cancer Society: Staying Active. Provides tools for managing an exercise program and discusses the links between cancer and lifestyle, including the importance of physical activity in preventing some cancers.
http://www.cancer.org/docroot/PED/ped_6.asp?sitearea-PED

American Heart Association: Exercise and Fitness. Provides information on cardiovascular health and disease, including the role of exercise in maintaining heart health and exercise tips for people of all ages.
http://www.americanheart.org/presenter.jhtml?identifier_1200013

Centers for Disease Control and Prevention: Physical Activity for Everyone. Explains the latest government recommendations on exercise and physical activity and provides strategies for getting the appropriate type and amount of exercise.
http://www.cdc.gov/physicalactivity/everyone/guidelines/adults.html

Dr. Pribut's Running Injuries Page. Provides information about running and many types of running injuries.
http://www.drpribut.com/sports/spsport.html

The Human Heart. An online museum exhibit with information on the structure and function of the heart, blood vessels, and respiratory system.
http://www.fi.edu/learn/heart/index.html

President's Challenge Adult Fitness Test: Aerobics. Provides step-by-step instructions for taking and interpreting standard tests of aerobic fitness.
http://www.adultfitnesstest.org/testInstructions/aerobicFitness/default.aspx

Runner's World Online. Contains a wide variety of information about running, including tips for beginning runners, advice about training, and a shoe buyer's guide.
http://www.runnersworld.com

Weight Control Information Network: Walking. An online fact sheet that explains the benefits of walking for exercise, tips for starting a walking program, and techniques for getting the most from walking workouts.
http://win.niddk.nih.gov/publications/walking.htm

Women's Sports Foundation. Provides information and links about training and about many specific sports activities.
http://www.womenssportsfoundation.org

SELECTED BIBLIOGRAPHY

Adler, P. A., and B. L. Roberts. 2009. The use of Tai Chi to improve health in older adults. *Orthopedic Nursing* 25(2): 122–126.

American College of Sports Medicine. 2009. *ACSM's Resource Manual for Guidelines for Exercise Testing and Prescription,* 6th ed. Philadelphia: Lippincott Williams and Wilkins.

American College of Sports Medicine. 2009. *ACSM's Guidelines for Exercise Testing and Prescription,* 8th ed. Philadelphia: Lippincott Williams and Wilkins.

American Heart Association. 2010. *Heart Disease and Stroke Statistics—2010 Update.* Dallas: American Heart Association.

Brooks, G. A., et al. 2005. *Exercise Physiology: Human Bioenergetics and Its Applications,* 4th ed. New York: McGraw-Hill.

Budde H., et al. 2008. Acute coordinative exercise improves attentional performance in adolescents. *Neuroscience Letters* 441(2): 219–223.

Cadore, E. L., et al. 2011. Effects of strength, endurance, and concurrent training on aerobic power and dynamic neuromuscular economy in elderly men. *J Strength Conditioning Research* 25(3): 758–766.

Courneya, K. S., and C. M. Friedenreich. 2011. Physical activity and cancer: an introduction. *Recent Results Cancer Research.* 186: 1–10.

Denadai, B. S., et al. 2006. Interval training at 95% and 100% of the velocity at $\dot{V}O_{2max}$: Effects on aerobic physiological indexes and running performance. *Applied Physiology, Nutrition, and Metabolism* 31(6): 737–743.

Erickson, K. I., et al. 2011. Exercise training increases size of hippocampus and improves memory. *Proceedings of the National Academy of Sciences.* 108(7): 3017–3022.

Garber, C. E., et al. 2011. Quantity and quality of exercise for developing and maintaining cardiorespiratory, musculoskeletal, and neuromotor fitness in apparently healthy adults: Guidance for prescribing exercise. *Medicine and Science in Sport and Exercise* 43(7):1334–1359.

Haskell, W. L., et al. 2007. Physical activity and public health: Updated recommendation for adults from the American College of Sports Medicine and the American Heart Association. *Medicine and Science in Sport and Exercise* 39(8): 1423–1434.

Hautala, A. J., et al. 2009. Individual responses to aerobic exercise: The role of the autonomic nervous system. *Neuroscience and Biobehavioral Reviews* 33(2): 107–115.

Keller, P., et al. 2011. A transcriptional map of the impact of endurance exercise training on skeletal muscle phenotype. *Journal of Applied Physiology* 110(1): 46–59.

Moien-Afshari, F., et al. 2009. Exercise restores endothelial function independently of weight loss or hyperglycaemic status in db/db mice. *Diabetologia* 51(7): 1327–1337.

Morikawa, M., et al. 2011. Physical fitness and indices of lifestyle-related diseases before and after interval walking training in middle-aged and older males and females. *British Journal Sports Medicine* 45(3): 216–224.

Murphy, M. H., et al. 2009. Accumulated versus continuous exercise for health benefit: A review of empirical studies. *Sports Medicine* 39(1): 29–43.

Netz, Y. T., et al. 2011. Aerobic fitness and multi-domain cognitive function in advanced age. *International Psychogeriatrics.* 23(1): 114–124.

Okura, T., et al. 2006. Effect of regular exercise on homocysteine concentrations: The HERITAGE Family Study. *European Journal of Applied Physiology* 98(4): 394–401.

Physical Activity Guidelines Advisory Committee. 2008. *Physical Activity Guidelines Advisory Committee Report, 2008.* Washington, D.C.: U.S. Department of Health and Human Services.

Ploughman, M. 2008. Exercise is brain food: The effects of physical activity on cognitive function. *Developmental Neurorehabilitation* 11(3): 236–240.

Reigle, B. S., and K. Wonders. 2009. Breast cancer and the role of exercise in women. *Methods in Molecular Biology* 472(1): 169–189.

Ruiz, J. R., et al. 2011. Strenuous endurance exercise improves life expectancy: It's in our genes. *British Journal of Sports Medicine* 45(3): 159–161.

Sui, X., et al. 2008. A prospective study of cardiorespiratory fitness and risk of type 2 diabetes in women. *Diabetes Care* 31(3): 550–555.

Suominen, H. 2006. Muscle training for bone strength. *Aging Clinical and Experimental Research* 18(2): 85–93.

U.S. Department of Health and Human Services. 2008. *Physical Activity Guidelines for Americans.* Washington, D.C.: U.S. Department of Health and Human Services.

Waterhouse, J., et al. 2010. Effects of music tempo upon submaximal cycling performance. *Scandinavian Journal of Medicine and Science in Sports* 20(4): 662–669.

Yeo, W. K., et al. 2011. Fat adaptation in well-trained athletes: effects on cell metabolism. *Applied Physiology Nutrition Metabolism* 36(1): 12–22.

Yung, L. M., et al. 2009. Exercise, vascular wall and cardiovascular diseases: An update (part 2). *Sports Medicine* 39(1): 45–63.

LAB 3.1 Assessing Your Current Level of Cardiorespiratory Endurance

Before taking any of the cardiorespiratory endurance assessment tests, refer to the fitness prerequisites and cautions given in Table 3.2. Choose one of the following four tests presented in this lab:

- 1-mile walk test
- 3-minute step test
- 1.5-mile run-walk test
- 12-minute swim test

For best results, don't exercise strenuously or consume caffeine the day of the test, and don't smoke or eat a heavy meal within about 3 hours of the test.

The 1-Mile Walk Test

Equipment

1. A track or course that provides a measurement of 1 mile
2. A stopwatch, clock, or watch with a second hand
3. A weight scale

Preparation

Measure your body weight (in pounds) before taking the test.
Body weight: _____ lb

Instructions

1. Warm up before taking the test. Do some walking, easy jogging, or calisthenics.
2. Cover the 1-mile course as quickly as possible. Walk at a pace that is brisk but comfortable. You must raise your heart rate above 120 beats per minute (bpm).
3. As soon as you complete the distance, note your time and take your pulse for 10 seconds.

   Walking time: _____ min _____ sec

   10-second pulse count: _____ beats
4. Cool down after the test by walking slowly for several minutes.

Determining Maximal Oxygen Consumption

1. Convert your 10-second pulse count into a value for exercise heart rate by multiplying it by 6.

   Exercise heart rate: _____ × 6 = _____ bpm
2. Convert your walking time from minutes and seconds to a decimal figure. For example, a time of 14 minutes and 45 seconds would be 14 + (45/60), or 14.75 minutes.

   Walking time: _____ min + (_____ sec ÷ 60 sec/min) = _____ min
3. Insert values for your age, gender, weight, walking time, and exercise heart rate in the following equation, where

   W = your weight (in pounds)

   A = your age (in years)

   G = your gender (male = 1; female = 0)

   T = your time to complete the 1-mile course (in minutes)

   H = your exercise heart rate (in beats per minute)

   $\dot{V}O_{2max} = 132.853 - (0.0769 \times W) - (0.3877 \times A) + (6.315 \times G) - (3.2649 \times T) - (0.1565 \times H)$

Mc Graw Hill **connect** http://www.mcgrawhillconnect.com/
FITNESS AND WELLNESS

For example, a 20-year-old, 190-pound male with a time of 14.75 minutes and an exercise heart rate of 152 bpm would calculate maximal oxygen consumption as follows:

$$\dot{V}O_{2max} = 132.853 - (0.0769 \times 190) - (0.3877 \times 20) + (6.315 \times 1) - (3.2649 \times 14.75) - (0.1565 \times 152) = 45 \text{ ml/kg/min}$$

$\dot{V}O_{2max}$ **= 132.853 − (0.0769 ×** _____ **) − (0.3877 ×** _____ **) + (6.315 ×** _____ **)**
weight (lb)   age (years)   gender

− (3.2649 × _____ **) − (0.1565 ×** _____ **) =** _____ **ml/kg/min**
walking time (min)   exercise heart rate (bpm)

4. Copy this value for $\dot{V}O_{2max}$ into the appropriate place in the chart on page 92.

The 3-Minute Step Test
Equipment

1. A step, bench, or bleacher step that is 16.25 inches from ground level
2. A stopwatch, clock, or watch with a second hand
3. A metronome

Preparation
Practice stepping up onto and down from the step before you begin the test. Each step has four beats: up-up-down-down. Males should perform the test with the metronome set for a rate of 96 beats per minute, or 24 steps per minute. Females should set the metronome at 88 beats per minute, or 22 steps per minute.

Instructions

1. Warm up before taking the test. Do some walking or easy jogging.
2. Set the metronome at the proper rate. Your instructor or a partner can call out starting and stopping times; otherwise, have a clock or watch within easy viewing during the test.
3. Begin the test and continue to step at the correct pace for 3 minutes.
4. Stop after 3 minutes. Remain standing and count your pulse for the 15-second period from 5 to 20 seconds into recovery.
   15-second pulse count: _____ beats
5. Cool down after the test by walking slowly for several minutes.

Determining Maximal Oxygen Consumption

1. Convert your 15-second pulse count to a value for recovery heart rate by multiplying by 4.
   Recovery heart rate: _____ × 4 = _____
   bpm 15-sec pulse count
2. Insert your recovery heart rate in the equation below, where
   H = recovery heart rate (in beats per minute)
   Males: $\dot{V}O_{2max}$ = 111.33 − (0.42 × H)
   Females: $\dot{V}O_{2max}$ = 65.81 − (0.1847 × H)

   For example, a man with a recovery heart rate of 162 bpm would calculate maximal oxygen consumption as follows:
   $$\dot{V}O_{2max} = 111.33 - (0.42 \times 162) = 43 \text{ ml/kg/min}$$

   Males: $\dot{V}O_{2max}$ = 111.33 − (0.42 × _____ **) =** _____ **ml/kg/min**
   recovery heart rate (bpm)

   Females: $\dot{V}O_{2max}$ = 65.81 − (0.1847 × _____ **) =** _____ **ml/kg/min**
   recovery heart rate (bpm)
3. Copy this value for $\dot{V}O_{2max}$ into the appropriate place in the chart on page 92.

The 1.5-Mile Run-Walk Test
Equipment

1. A running track or course that is flat and provides exact measurements of up to 1.5 miles
2. A stopwatch, clock, or watch with a second hand

Preparation

You may want to practice pacing yourself prior to taking the test to avoid going too fast at the start and becoming prematurely fatigued. Allow yourself a day or two to recover from your practice run before taking the test.

Instructions

1. Warm up before taking the test. Do some walking or easy jogging.
2. Try to cover the distance as fast as possible without overexerting yourself. If possible, monitor your own time, or have someone call out your time at various intervals of the test to determine whether your pace is correct.
3. Record the amount of time, in minutes and seconds, it takes you to complete the 1.5-mile distance.

   Running-walking time: _____ min _____ sec
4. Cool down after the test by walking or jogging slowly for about 5 minutes.

Determining Maximal Oxygen Consumption

1. Convert your running time from minutes and seconds to a decimal figure. For example, a time of 14 minutes and 25 seconds would be 14 + (25/60), or 14.4 minutes.

   Running-walking time: _____ min + (_____ sec ÷ 60 sec/min) = _____ min
2. Insert your running time into the equation below, where

   T = running time (in minutes)

   $\dot{V}O_{2max} = (483 \div T) + 3.5$

   For example, a person who completes 1.5 miles in 14.4 minutes would calculate maximal oxygen consumption as follows:

   $\dot{V}O_{2max} = (483 \div 14.4) + 3.5 = 37 \text{ ml/kg/min}$

   $\dot{V}O_{2max} = (483 \div \underline{\hspace{3cm}}_{\text{run-walk time (min)}}) + 3.5 = \underline{\hspace{3cm}} \text{ ml/kg/min}$
3. Copy this value for $\dot{V}O_{2max}$ into the appropriate place in the chart on page 92.

Rating Your Cardiovascular Fitness

Record your $\dot{V}O_{2max}$ score(s) and the corresponding fitness rating from the table below.

Women	Very Poor	Poor	Fair	Good	Excellent	Superior
Age: 18–29	Below 31.6	31.6–35.4	35.5–39.4	39.5–43.9	44.0–50.1	Above 50.1
30–39	Below 29.9	29.9–33.7	33.8–36.7	36.8–40.9	41.0–46.8	Above 46.8
40–49	Below 28.0	28.0–31.5	31.6–35.0	35.1–38.8	38.9–45.1	Above 45.1
50–59	Below 25.5	25.5–28.6	28.7–31.3	31.4–35.1	35.2–39.8	Above 39.8
60–69	Below 23.7	23.7–26.5	26.6–29.0	29.1–32.2	32.3–36.8	Above 36.8
Men						
Age: 18–29	Below 38.1	38.1–42.1	42.2–45.6	45.7–51.0	51.1–56.1	Above 56.1
30–39	Below 36.7	36.7–40.9	41.0–44.3	44.4–48.8	48.9–54.2	Above 54.2
40–49	Below 34.6	34.6–38.3	38.4–42.3	42.4–46.7	46.8–52.8	Above 52.8
50–59	Below 31.1	31.1–35.1	35.2–38.2	38.3–43.2	43.3–49.6	Above 49.6
60–69	Below 27.4	27.4–31.3	31.4–34.9	35.0–39.4	39.5–46.0	Above 46.0

SOURCE: Ratings based on norms from The Cooper Institute of Aerobic Research, Dallas, Texas; from *The Physical Fitness Specialist Manual*, Revised 2002. Used with permission.

	$\dot{V}O_{2max}$	Cardiovascular Fitness Rating
1-mile walk test		
3-minute step test		
1.5-mile run-walk test		

The 12-Minute Swim Test

If you enjoy swimming and prefer to build a cardiorespiratory training program around this type of exercise, you can assess your cardiorespiratory endurance by taking the 12-minute swim test. You will receive a rating based on the distance you can swim in 12 minutes. A complete fitness program based on swimming is presented in Chapter 7.

Note, however, that this test is appropriate only for relatively strong swimmers who are confident in the water. If you are unsure about your swimming ability, this test may not be appropriate for you. If necessary, ask your school's swim coach or a qualified swimming instructor to evaluate your ability in the water before attempting this test.

Equipment

1. A swimming pool that provides measurements in yards
2. A wall clock that is clearly visible from the pool, or someone with a watch who can time you

Preparation

You may want to practice pacing yourself before taking the test to avoid going too fast at the start and becoming prematurely fatigued. Allow yourself a day or two to recover from your practice swim before taking the test.

Instructions

1. Warm up before taking the test. Do some walking or light jogging before getting in the pool. Once in the water, swim a lap or two at an easy pace to make sure your muscles are warm and you are comfortable.
2. Try to cover the distance as fast as possible without overexerting yourself. If possible, monitor your own time, or have someone call out your time at various intervals of the test to determine whether your pace is correct.
3. Record the distance, in yards, that you were able to cover during the 12-minute period.
4. Cool down after the test by swimming a lap or two at an easy pace.
5. Use the following chart to gauge your level of cardiorespiratory fitness.

DISTANCE IN YARDS

Women	Needs Work	Better	Fair	Good	Excellent
Age: 13–19	Below 500	500–599	600–699	700–799	Above 800
20–29	Below 400	400–499	500–599	600–699	Above 700
30–39	Below 350	350–449	450–549	550–649	Above 650
40–49	Below 300	300–399	400–499	500–599	Above 600
50–59	Below 250	250–349	350–449	450–549	Above 550
60 and over	Below 250	250–299	300–399	400–499	Above 500
Men					
Age: 13–19	Below 400	400–499	500–599	600–699	Above 700
20–29	Below 300	300–399	400–499	500–599	Above 600
30–39	Below 250	250–349	350–449	450–549	Above 550
40–49	Below 200	200–299	300–399	400–499	Above 500
50–59	Below 150	150–249	250–349	350–449	Above 450
60 and over	Below 150	150–199	200–299	300–399	Above 400

100 yards = 91 meters

SOURCE: Cooper, K. H. 1982. *The Aerobics Program for Total Well-Being.* New York: Bantam Books.

Record your fitness rating:

	Cardiovascular Fitness Rating
12-minute swim test	

Using Your Results

How did you score? Are you surprised by your rating for cardiovascular fitness? Are you satisfied with your current rating?

If you're not satisfied, set a realistic goal for improvement: _____

_____

Are you satisfied with your current level of cardiovascular fitness as evidenced in your daily life—your ability to walk, run, bicycle, climb stairs, do yard work, or engage in recreational activities?

If you're not satisfied, set some realistic goals for improvement, such as completing a 5K run or 25-mile bike ride: _____

_____

What should you do next? Enter the results of this lab in the Preprogram Assessment column in Appendix C. If you've set goals for improvement, begin planning your cardiorespiratory endurance exercise program by completing the plan in Lab 3.2. After several weeks of your program, complete this lab again, and enter the results in the Postprogram Assessment column of Appendix C. How do the results compare? (Remember, it's best to compare $\dot{V}O_{2max}$ scores for the same test.)

SOURCES: Brooks, G. A., and T. D. Fahey. 1987. *Fundamentals of Human Performance.* New York: Macmillan. Kline, G. M., et al. 1987. Estimation of $\dot{V}O_{2max}$ from a one-mile track walk, gender, age, and body weight. *Medicine and Science in Sports and Exercise* 19(3): 253–259. McArdle, W. D., F. I. Katch, and V. L. Katch. 2010. *Exercise Physiology-. Energy, Nutrition, and Human Peformance.* Philadelphia: Lea and Febiger, pp. 243–246.

LAB 3.2 Developing an Exercise Program for Cardiorespiratory Endurance

1. *Goals.* List goals for your cardiorespiratory endurance exercise program. Your goals can be specific or general, short or long term. In the first section, include specific, measurable goals that you can use to track the progress of your fitness program. These goals might be things like raising your cardiorespiratory fitness rating from fair to good or swimming laps for 30 minutes without resting. In the second section, include long-term and more qualitative goals, such as improving self-confidence and reducing your risk for chronic disease.

Specific Goals: Current Status   Final Goals

_____   _____

_____   _____

_____   _____

Other goals: _____

_____

2. *Type of Activities.* Choose one or more endurance activities for your program. These can include any activity that uses large-muscle groups, can be maintained continuously, and is rhythmic and aerobic in nature. Examples include walking, jogging, cycling, group exercise such as aerobic dance, rowing, rope skipping, stair-climbing, cross-country skiing, swimming, skating, and endurance game activities such as soccer and tennis. Choose activities that are both convenient and enjoyable. Fill in the activity names on the program plan.

3. *Frequency.* On the program plan, fill in how often you plan to participate in each activity; the ACSM recommends participating in cardiorespiratory endurance exercise 3-5 days per week.

Program Plan

Type of Activity	Frequency (check ✓)							Intensity (bpm or RPE)	Time (min)
	M	T	W	Th	F	Sa	Su		

4. *Intensity.* Determine your exercise intensity using one of the following methods, and enter it on the program plan. Begin your program at a lower intensity and slowly increase intensity as your fitness improves, so select a range of intensities for your program,

a. Target heart rate zone: Calculate target heart rate zone in beats per minute and then calculate the corresponding 10-second exercise count by dividing the total count by 6. For example, the 10-second exercise counts corresponding to a target heart rate zone of 122–180 bpm would be 20–30 beats.

Maximum heart rate: 220 − _____ = _____ bpm
                                    age (years)

Maximum Heart Rate Method

65% training intensity = _____ bpm × 0.65 = _____ bpm
                                 maximum heart rate

90% training intensity = _____ bpm × 0.90 = _____ bpm
                                 maximum heart rate

Target heart rate zone = _____ to _____ bpm   **10-second count** = _____ to _____

McGraw Hill connect™ http://www.mcgrawhillconnect.com/ FITNESS AND WELLNESS

Heart Rate Reserve Method

Resting heart rate:_____ bpm (taken after 10 minutes of complete rest)

Heart rate reserve = _____ bpm − _____ bpm = _____ bpm
                      maximum heart rate   resting heart rate

50% training intensity = (_____ bpm × 0.50) + _____ bpm = _____ bpm
                           heart rate reserve   resting heart rate

85% training intensity = (_____ bpm × 0.85) + _____ bpm = _____ bpm
                           heart rate reserve   resting heart rate

Target heart rate zone = _____ to _____ **bpm**

10-second count = _____ to _____

b. Ratings of perceived exertion (RPE): If you prefer, determine an RPE value that corresponds to your target heart rate range (see p. 76 and Figure 3.5).

5. *Time (Duration).* A total time of 20–60 minutes is recommended; your duration of exercise will vary with intensity. For developing cardiorespiratory endurance, higher-intensity activities can be performed for a shorter duration; lower intensities require a longer duration. Enter a duration (or a range of duration) on the program plan.

6. *Monitoring Your Program.* Complete a log like the one below to monitor your program and track your progress. Note the date on top, and fill in the intensity and time (duration) for each workout. If you prefer, you can also track other variables such as distance. For example, if your cardiorespiratory endurance program includes walking and swimming, you may want to track miles walked and yards swum in addition to the duration of each exercise session.

Activity/Date													
1	Intentsity												
	Time												
	Distance												
2	Intentsity												
	Time												
	Distance												
3	Intentsity												
	Time												
	Distance												
4	Intentsity												
	Time												
	Distance												

7. *Making Progress.* Follow the guidelines in the chapter and Table 3.6 to slowly increase the amount of overload in your program. Continue keeping a log, and periodically evaluate your progress.

Progress Checkup: Week _____ of program

Goals: Original Status   Current Status

_____   _____

_____   _____

_____   _____

List each activity in your program and describe how satisfied you are with the activity and with your overall progress. List any problems you've encountered or any unexpected costs or benefits of your fitness program so far.

CHAPTER 8

Muscular Strength and Endurance

LOOKING AHEAD...

After reading this chapter, you should be able to:

- Describe the basic physiology of muscles and explain how strength training affects muscles
- Define muscular strength and endurance, and describe how they relate to wellness
- Assess muscular strength and endurance
- Apply the FITT principle to create a safe and successful strength training program
- Describe the effects of supplements and drugs that are marketed to active people and athletes
- Explain how to safely perform common strength training exercises using free weights and weight machines

TEST YOUR KNOWLEDGE

1. For women, weight training typically results in which of the following?
   a. bulky muscles
   b. significant increases in body weight
   c. improved body image

2. To maximize strength gains, it is a good idea to hold your breath as you lift a weight. True or false?

3. Regular strength training is associated with which of the following benefits?
   a. denser bones
   b. reduced risk of heart disease
   c. improved body composition
   d. fewer injuries
   e. improved metabolic health
   f. Increased longevity

Answers

1. **c.** Because the vast majority of women have low levels of testosterone, they do not develop large muscles or gain significant amounts of weight in response to a moderate-intensity weight training program. Men have higher levels of testosterone, so they can build large muscles more easily.

2. **False.** Holding one's breath while lifting weights can significantly elevate blood pressure; it also reduces blood flow to the heart and may cause faintness. You should breathe smoothly and normally while weight training. Some experts recommend that you exhale during the most difficult part of each exercise.

3. **All six.** Regular strength training has many benefits for both men and women.

connect http://www.mcgrawhillconnect.com
FITNESS AND WELLNESS

LearnSmart
GET A BETTER GRADE. TRY LEARNSMART.

uscles make up more than 40% of your body mass. You depend on them for movement, and, because of their mass, they are the site of a large portion of the energy reactions (metabolism) that take place in your body. Strong, well-developed muscles help you perform daily activities with greater ease, protect you from injury, and enhance your well-being in other ways.

As described in Chapter 2, muscular strength is the amount of force a muscle can produce with a single maximum effort; muscular endurance is the ability to hold or repeat a muscular contraction for a long time. This chapter explains the benefits of strength training (also called *resistance training* or *weight training*) and describes methods of assessing muscular strength and endurance. It then explains the basics of strength training and provides guidelines for setting up your own training program. The musculoskeletal system is depicted on pages T4-2 and T4-3 of the color transparency insert "Touring the Musculoskeletal System" in this chapter. You can refer to this illustration as you set up your program.

BASIC MUSCLE PHYSIOLOGY AND THE EFFECTS OF STRENGTH TRAINING

Muscles move the body and enable it to exert force because they move the skeleton. When a muscle contracts (shortens), it moves a bone by pulling on the tendon that attaches the muscle to the bone, as shown in Figure 4.1. When a muscle relaxes (lengthens), the tension placed on the tendon is released and the bone moves back to—or closer to—its starting position.

Muscle Fibers

Muscles consist of individual muscle cells, or **muscle fibers,** connected in bundles (see Figure 4.1). A single muscle is made up of many bundles of muscle fibers and is covered by layers of connective tissue that hold the fibers together. Muscle fibers, in turn, are made up of smaller protein structures called **myofibrils.** Myofibrils are made up of a series of contractile units called *sarcomeres,* which are composed largely of actin and myosin molecules. Muscle cells contract when the myosin molecules glide across the actin molecules in a ratchetlike movement.

Strength training increases the size and number of myofibrils, resulting in larger individual muscle fibers. Larger muscle fibers mean a larger and stronger muscle. The development of large muscle fibers is called **hypertrophy;** inactivity causes **atrophy,** the reversal of this process. For a depiction of the process of hypertrophy, see page T4-4 of the color transparency insert "Touring the Musculoskeletal System" in this chapter. In some species, muscles can increase in size through a separate process called **hyperplasia,** which involves an increase in the number of muscle fibers rather than the size of muscle fibers. In humans, hyperplasia is not thought to play a significant role in determining muscle size. Each muscle cell has many **nuclei** containing genes that direct the production of enzymes and structural proteins required for muscle contraction.

Muscle fibers are classified as slow-twitch or fast-twitch fibers according to their strength, speed of contraction, and energy source.

• **Slow-twitch muscle fibers** are relatively fatigue-resistant, but they don't contract as rapidly or strongly as fast-twitch fibers. The principal energy system that fuels slow-twitch fibers is aerobic (oxidative). Slow-twitch muscle fibers are typically reddish in color.

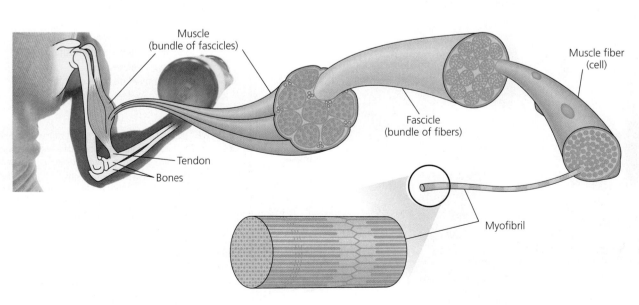

FIGURE 4.1   Components of skeletal muscle tissue.

Table 4.1 Physiological Changes and Benefits from Strength Training

CHANGE	BENEFITS
Increased muscle mass* and strength	Increased muscular strength Improved body composition Higher rate of metabolism Improved capacity to regulate fuel use with aging Toned, healthy-looking muscles Increased longevity Improved quality of life
Increased utilization of motor units during muscle contractions	Increased muscular strength and power
Improved coordination of motor units	Increased muscular strength and power
Increased strength of tendons, ligaments, and bones	Lower risk of injury to these tissues
Increased storage of fuel in muscles	Increased resistance to muscle fatigue
Increased size of fast-twitch muscle fibers (from a high-resistance program)	Increased muscular strength and power
Increased size of slow-twitch muscle fibers (from a high-repetition program)	Increased muscular endurance
Increased blood supply to muscles (from a high-repetition program) and improved blood vessel health	Increased delivery of oxygen and nutrients Faster elimination of wastes
Biochemical improvements (for example, increased sensitivity to insulin)	Enhanced metabolic health
Improved blood fat levels	Reduced risk of heart disease
Increased muscle endurance	Enhanced ability to exercise for long periods and maintain good body posture

*Due to genetic and hormonal differences, men will build more muscle mass than women, but both genders make about the same percent gains in strength through a good program.

• **Fast-twitch muscle fibers** contract more rapidly and forcefully than slow-twitch fibers but fatigue more quickly. Although oxygen is important in the energy system that fuels fast-twitch fibers, they rely more on anaerobic (nonoxidative) metabolism than do slow-twitch fibers. (See Chapter 3 for a discussion of energy systems.) Fast-twitch muscle fibers are typically whitish in color.

Most muscles contain both slow-twitch and fast-twitch fibers. The proportion of the types of fibers varies significantly among different muscles and different individuals, and that proportion is largely fixed at birth, although fibers can contract faster or slower following a period of training or a period of inactivity. The type of fiber that acts during a particular activity depends on the type of work required. Endurance activities like jogging tend to use slow-twitch fibers, whereas strength and **power** activities like sprinting use fast-twitch fibers. Strength training can increase the size and strength of both fast-twitch and slow-twitch fibers, although fast-twitch fibers are preferentially increased.

Motor Units

To exert force, a muscle recruits one or more motor units to contract. A **motor unit** is made up of a nerve connected to a number of muscle fibers. The number of muscle fibers in a motor unit varies from two to hundreds. Small motor units contain slow-twitch fibers, whereas large motor units contain fast-twitch fibers. When a motor unit calls on its fibers to contract, all fibers contract to their full capacity. The number of motor units recruited depends on the amount of strength required: When you pick up a small weight, you use fewer and smaller motor units than when picking up a large weight.

Strength training improves the body's ability to recruit motor units—a phenomenon called **muscle learning**—which increases strength even before muscle size increases. The physiological changes and benefits that result from strength training are summarized in Table 4.1.

KEY TERMS

muscle fiber   A single muscle cell, usually classified according to strength, speed of contraction, and energy source.

myofibrils   Protein structures that make up muscle fibers.

hypertrophy   An increase in the size of muscle fibers, usually stimulated by muscular overload, as occurs during strength training.

atrophy   A decrease in the size of muscle fibers.

hyperplasia   An increase in the number of muscle fibers.

nucleus   A cell structure containing DNA and genes that direct the production of proteins; plural, *nuclei.*

slow-twitch muscle fibers   Red muscle fibers that are fatigue resistant but have a slow contraction speed and a lower capacity for tension; usually recruited for endurance activities.

fast-twitch muscle fibers   White muscle fibers that contract rapidly and forcefully but fatigue quickly; usually recruited for actions requiring strength and power.

power   The ability to exert force rapidly.

motor unit   A motor nerve (one that initiates movement) connected to one or more muscle fibers.

muscle learning   The improvement in the body's ability to recruit motor units, brought about through strength training.

Does Muscular Strength Reduce the Risk of Premature Death?

THE EVIDENCE FOR EXERCISE

Strength training can make you stronger, but can it also help you live longer?

According to a growing body of evidence, the answer is yes—especially for men.

A number of studies have associated greater muscular strength with lower rates of death from all causes, including cancer and cardiovascular disease. According to the results of a study that followed nearly 9000 men over 18 years, the stronger a man is, the lower his risk of premature death from a variety of causes. This study gauged participants' strength through exercises such as bench and leg presses; other studies have measured strength using a handgrip test, with similar outcomes. The resulting data showed significant differences in death rates among the participants, with the strongest men having the lowest death rates. This effect was particularly important for older and overweight men.

When participants in the study died, researchers analyzed causes of death and correlated the numbers of dead and surviving participants with data about their muscular fitness, the amount of time they spent exercising, and other factors (such as metabolic data, cardiovascular health, smoking status, and age). The findings revealed that, compared to men with the lowest levels of muscular strength, stronger men were

- 1.5 times less likely to die from all causes
- 1.6 times less likely to die from cardiovascular disease
- 1.25 times less likely to die from cancer

These correlations held across all age groups (ranging from age 20 to 82) and body mass indexes. They were particularly striking in older men (age 60 and older), who were more than four times more likely to die from cancer than similar-age men with greater muscular strength.

Similarly, an earlier study of more than 3000 men demonstrated an inverse relationship between muscular strength and metabolic syndrome, a cluster of symptoms that includes high blood pressure, high blood glucose levels, high triglyceride levels, low HDL cholesterol levels, and abdominal obesity. Metabolic syndrome increases risk for diabetes, heart disease, and other illnesses. The results were true regardless of participants' age, weight, or waist circumference. The findings led researchers to suggest that weight training may be a valuable way for men to avoid metabolic syndrome. Protection against metabolic syndrome is also provided by cardiorespiratory fitness, according to a 2004 study of 8570 men, in which scientists measured

each participant's level of muscular strength and cardiorespiratory fitness.

You don't have to be a power lifter or bodybuilder to enjoy the benefits of strength training. In the first study, for example, participants were advised on basic fitness techniques and healthy lifestyle behaviors. Although participants were encouraged to incorporate weight training into their fitness routine, each man chose the type and amount of weight training he felt most comfortable doing. Many researchers believe that the basic minimum recommendation of doing weight training on 2 nonconsecutive days per week may be enough to lower the average male's risk of premature death, provided he is not obese and does not already have risk factors such as diabetes, hypertension, or preexisting cancer. At the same time, as noted in Chapter 3, strength training can have negative effects on the cardiovascular system in some men, at least temporarily, if not followed by aerobic exercise. To date, only small-scale studies have been performed on women, so more research is needed to see if the same conclusions apply to women.

SOURCES: Physical Activity Guidelines Advisory Committee. 2008. *Physical Activity Guidelines Advisory Committee Report, 2008*. Washington, D.C.: U.S. Department of Health and Human Services; Ruiz, J. R., et al. 2008. Association between muscular strength and mortality in men: Prospective cohort study. *BMJ* 337: a439; Ruiz, J. R., et al. 2009. Muscular strength and adiposity as predictors of adulthood cancer mortality in men. *Cancer Epidemiology, Biomarkers, and Prevention* 18: 1468; Rantanen, T., et al. 2011. Midlife muscle strength and human longevity up to age 100 years: A 44-year prospective study among a decedent cohort. *Age* published online: DOI 10.1007/s11357-011-9256-y.

BENEFITS OF MUSCULAR STRENGTH AND ENDURANCE

Enhanced muscular strength and endurance can lead to improvements in the areas of performance, injury prevention, body composition, self-image, lifetime muscle and bone health, and metabolic health. Most important, greater muscular strength and endurance reduce the

risk of premature death. Stronger people—particularly men—have a lower death rate due to all causes, including cardiovascular disease and cancer (see the box "Does Muscular Strength Reduce the Risk of Premature Death?"). The link between strength and death rate is independent of age, physical activity, smoking, alcohol intake, body composition, and family history of cardiovascular disease.

Improved Performance of Physical Activities

A person with a moderate to high level of muscular strength and endurance can perform everyday tasks—such as climbing stairs and carrying groceries—with ease. Increased strength can enhance your enjoyment of recreational sports by making it possible to achieve high levels of performance and to handle advanced techniques. Strength training also results in modest improvements in maximal oxygen consumption. People with poor muscle strength tire more easily and are less effective in both everyday and recreational activities.

Injury Prevention

Increased muscular strength and endurance help protect you from injury in two key ways:

- By enabling you to maintain good posture
- By encouraging proper body mechanics during everyday activities such as walking and lifting

Good muscle strength and, particularly, endurance in the abdomen, hips, lower back, and legs, maintain the spine in proper alignment and help prevent low-back pain, which afflicts more than 85% of Americans at some time in their lives. (Prevention of low-back pain is discussed in Chapter 5.)

Training for muscular strength and endurance also makes the **tendons, ligaments,** and **cartilage** cells stronger and less susceptible to injury. Resistance exercise prevents injuries best when the training program is gradual and progressive and builds all the major muscle groups.

Improved Body Composition

As Chapter 2 explained, healthy body composition means that the body has a high proportion of fat-free mass (composed primarily of muscle) and a relatively small proportion of fat. Strength training improves body composition by increasing muscle mass, thereby tipping the body composition ratio toward fat-free mass and away from fat.

Building muscle mass through strength training also helps with losing fat because metabolic rate is related to muscle mass: The greater your muscle mass, the higher your metabolic rate. A high metabolic rate means that a nutritionally sound diet coupled with regular exercise will not lead to an increase in body fat. Strength training

can boost resting metabolic rate by up to 15%, depending on how hard you train. Resistance exercise also increases muscle temperature, which in turn slightly increases the rate at which you burn calories over the hours following a weight training session.

Enhanced Self-Image and Quality of Life

Strength training leads to an enhanced self-image in both men and women by providing stronger, firmer-looking muscles and a toned, healthy-looking body. Women tend to lose inches, increase strength, and develop greater muscle definition. Men tend to build larger, stronger muscles. The larger muscles in men combine with high levels of the hormone **testosterone** for a strong tissue-building effect; see the box "Gender Differences in Muscular Strength."

Because strength training involves measurable objectives (pounds lifted, repetitions accomplished), a person can easily recognize improved performance, leading to greater self-confidence and self-esteem. Strength training also improves quality of life by increasing energy, preventing injuries, and making daily activities easier and more enjoyable.

Improved Muscle and Bone Health with Aging

Research has shown that good muscular strength helps people live healthier lives. A lifelong program of regular strength training prevents muscle and nerve degeneration that can compromise the quality of life and increase the risk of hip fractures and other potentially life-threatening injuries.

In the general population, people begin to lose muscle mass after age 30, a condition called *sarcopenia*. At first they may notice that they cannot play sports as well as they could in high school. After more years of inactivity and strength loss, people may have trouble performing even the simple movements of daily life, such as walking up a flight of stairs or doing yard work. By age 75, about 25% of men and 75% of women cannot lift more than 10 pounds overhead. Although aging contributes to decreased strength, inactivity causes most of the loss. Poor strength makes it much more likely that a person will be injured during everyday activities.

Wellness Tip

Circuit training involves a series of exercises with minimal rest in between. Circuits can include almost any kind of exercises. Circuit training is an excellent way to develop strength and endurance at the same time.

> **KEY TERMS**
>
> **tendon** A tough band of fibrous tissue that connects a muscle to a bone or other body part and transmits the force exerted by the muscle.
>
> **ligament** A tough band of tissue that connects the ends of bones to other bones or supports organs in place.
>
> **cartilage** Tough, resilient tissue that acts as a cushion between the bones in a joint.
>
> **testosterone** The principal male hormone, responsible for the development of secondary sex characteristics and important in increasing muscle size.

DIMENSIONS OF DIVERSITY

Gender Differences in Muscular Strength

Men are generally stronger than women because they typically have larger bodies and a larger proportion of their total body mass is made up of muscle. But when strength is expressed per unit of cross-sectional area of muscle tissue, men are only 1–2% stronger than women in the upper body and about equal to women in the lower body. Men have a larger proportion of muscle tissue in the upper body, so they can more easily build upper-body strength than women can. Individual muscle fibers are larger in men, but the metabolism of cells within those fibers is the same in both sexes.

Two factors that help explain these disparities are testosterone levels and the speed of nervous control of muscle. Testosterone promotes the growth of muscle tissue in both males and females. Testosterone levels are 5–10 times higher in men than in women, so men tend to have larger muscles. Also,

because the male nervous system can activate muscles faster, men tend to have more power.

Women are often concerned that they will develop large muscles from strength training. Because of hormonal differences, most women do not develop big muscles unless they train intensely over many years or take anabolic steroids. Women do gain muscle and improve body composition through strength training, but they don't develop bulky muscles or gain significant amounts of weight. A study of average women who weight trained 2–3 days per week for 8 weeks found that they gained about 1.75 pounds of muscle and lost about 3.5 pounds of fat. Losing muscle over time is a much greater health concern for women than small gains in muscle weight, especially because any gains in muscle weight are typically more than offset by loss of fat weight. Both men and women lose muscle mass and power as

they age, but because men start out with more muscle and don't lose power as quickly, older women tend to have greater impairment of muscle function than older men. This may partially account for the higher incidence of life-threatening falls in older women.

The bottom line is that both men and women can increase strength through strength training. Women may not be able to lift as much weight as men, but pound for pound of muscle, they have nearly the same capacity to gain strength as men.

As a person ages, motor nerves can become disconnected from the portion of muscle they control. By age 70, 15% of the motor nerves in most people are no longer connected to muscle tissue. Aging and inactivity also cause muscles to become slower and therefore less able to perform quick, powerful movements. Strength training helps maintain motor nerve connections and the quickness of muscles.

Osteoporosis (bone loss) is common in people over age 55, particularly postmenopausal women. Osteoporosis leads to fractures that can be life-threatening. Hormonal changes from aging account for much of the bone loss that occurs, but lack of bone mass due to inactivity and a poor diet are contributing factors. Strength training can lessen bone loss even if it is taken up later in life, and if practiced regularly, strength training may even build bone mass in postmenopausal women and older men. Increased muscle strength can also help prevent falls, which are a major cause of injury in people with osteoporosis.

Ask Yourself

QUESTIONS FOR CRITICAL THINKING AND REFLECTION

What benefits of strength training are most important to you? Are you more interested in improved physical performance? Better body composition and appearance? Long-term health benefits? How can you define your goals so they are most meaningful and motivating for you?

Metabolic and Heart Health

Strength training helps prevent and manage both cardiovascular disease (CVD) and diabetes by:

- Improving glucose metabolism
- Increasing maximal oxygen consumption
- Reducing blood pressure
- Increasing HDL cholesterol and reducing LDL cholesterol (in some people)
- Improving blood vessel health

Stronger muscles reduce the demand on the heart during ordinary daily activities such as lifting and carrying objects. The benefits of resistance exercise to the heart are so great that the American Heart Association recommends that healthy adults and many low-risk cardiac patients do strength training 2–3 days per week. Resistance training may not be appropriate for people with some types of heart disease.

ASSESSING MUSCULAR STRENGTH AND ENDURANCE

Muscular strength is usually assessed by measuring the maximum amount of weight a person can lift one time. This single maximum effort is called a **repetition maximum (RM).** You can assess the strength of your major muscle groups by taking the one–repetition maximum (1 RM) test

How Strong Are You?

Tests of strength have challenged humans since the dawn of history. Strength is highly specific; one type of strength does not necessarily predict another. Strength tests help you determine your current fitness level and help you set achievable goals. You could test your capacity doing almost any exercise. Test your maximum performance on as many of the following tests as you can.

TEST	MAXIMUM REPETITIONS OR TIME	GOAL
Push-ups (Modified Or Regular)		
Pull-ups or bent-arm bar hang		
One-arm kettlebell snatches		
Two-arm kettlebell swings		
Bench press for reps (at a specific weight; e.g., 135 pounds, 225 pounds)		

Write down your performance for each exercise in the second column of the list. (Note that you should wait at least a few minutes between tests.) If you aren't happy with the results, set a reasonable goal for each exercise in the third column. If you aren't sure what a reasonable goal would be, talk to your instructor or a certified personal trainer. Use these goals as a starting point for a broad-ranging strength training program.

for the bench press and by taking functional leg strength tests. You can measure 1 RM directly or estimate it by doing multiple repetitions with a submaximal (lighter) weight. It is best to train for several weeks before attempting a direct 1 RM test; once you have a baseline value, you can retest after 6–12 weeks to check your progress. See Lab 4.1 for guidelines on taking these tests. For more accurate results, avoid strenuous weight training for 48 hours beforehand.

Muscular endurance is usually assessed by counting the maximum number of **repetitions** of an exercise a person can do (such as in push-ups or kettlebell snatches) or the maximum amount of time a person can hold a muscular contraction (such as in the flexed-arm hang). You can test the muscular endurance of major muscle groups in your body by taking the curl-up test, the push-up test, and the squat endurance test. See Lab 4.2 for complete instructions on taking these assessment tests.

CREATING A SUCCESSFUL STRENGTH TRAINING PROGRAM

When the muscles are stressed by a greater load than they are used to, they adapt and improve their function. The type of adaptation that occurs depends on the type of stress applied.

Static Versus Dynamic Strength Training Exercises

Strength training exercises are generally classified as static or dynamic. Each involves a different way of using and strengthening muscles.

Static Exercise Also called **isometric** exercise, **static exercise** involves a muscle contraction without a change in the length of the muscle or the angle in the joint on which the muscle acts. In isometrics, the muscle contracts, but there is no movement. To perform an isometric exercise, a

Ask yourself

QUESTIONS FOR CRITICAL THINKING AND REFLECTION

Considering your lifestyle and the physical activities you most commonly do, which is more important to you—muscular strength or muscular endurance? Why is this the case? Do you think your priority may change some day?

repetition maximum (RM) The maximum amount of resistance that can be moved a specified number of times.

repetitions The number of times an exercise is performed during one set.

static (isometric) exercise Exercise involving a muscle contraction without a change in the muscle's length.

person can use an immovable object like a wall to provide resistance, or simply tighten a muscle while remaining still (for example, tightening the abdominal muscles while sitting at a desk). The spine extension and the side bridge, shown on pp. 119–120, are both isometric exercises.

Static exercises are not used as widely as dynamic exercises because they don't develop strength throughout a joint's entire range of motion. During almost all movements, however, some muscles contract statically to support the skeleton so that other muscles can contract dynamically. For example, when you throw, hit a ball, or ski, the core muscles in the abdomen and back stabilize the spine. This stability allows more powerful contractions in the lower- and upper-body muscles. The core muscles contract statically during dynamic exercises, such as squats, lunges, and overhead presses.

Static exercises are useful in strengthening muscles after an injury or surgery, when movement of the affected joint could delay healing. Isometrics are also used to overcome weak points in an individual's range of motion. Statically strengthening a muscle at its weakest point will allow more weight to be lifted with that muscle during dynamic exercise. Certain types of calisthenics and Pilates exercises (described in more detail later in the chapter) also involve static contractions. For maximum strength gains, hold the isometric contraction maximally for 6 seconds; do 2–10 repetitions.

Dynamic Exercise Also called **isotonic** exercise, **dynamic exercise** involves a muscle contraction with a change in the length of the muscle. Dynamic exercises are the most popular type of exercises for increasing muscle strength and seem to be most valuable for developing strength that can be transferred to other forms of physical activity. They can be performed with weight machines, free weights, or a person's own body weight (as in curl-ups or push-ups).

There are two kinds of dynamic muscle contractions:

- A **concentric muscle contraction** occurs when the muscle applies enough force to overcome resistance and shortens as it contracts.

- An **eccentric muscle contraction** (also called a *pliometric contraction*) occurs when the resistance is greater than the force applied by the muscle and the muscle lengthens as it contracts.

For example, in an arm curl, the biceps muscle works concentrically as the weight is raised toward the shoulder and eccentrically as the weight is lowered.

CONSTANT AND VARIABLE RESISTANCE Two of the most common dynamic exercise techniques are constant resistance exercise and variable resistance exercise.

- **Constant resistance exercise** uses a constant load (weight) throughout a joint's full range of motion. Training with free weights is a form of constant resistance exercise. A problem with this technique

A concentric contraction.   An eccentric contraction.

is that, because of differences in leverage, there are points in a joint's range of motion where the muscle controlling the movement is stronger and points where it is weaker. The amount of weight a person can lift is limited by the weakest point in the range.

- In **variable resistance exercise,** the load is changed to provide maximum load throughout the entire range of motion. This form of exercise uses machines that place more stress on muscles at the end of the range of motion, where a person has better leverage and can exert more force. Use elastic bands and chains with free weights to add variable resistance to the exercises.

Constant and variable resistance exercises are both extremely effective for building strength and endurance.

Pneumatic strength training machines use air pressure for resistance and are popular in many gyms and health clubs. They build strength in beginners but are less effective for more advanced strength trainers. The machines provide resistance only during the concentric (muscle shortening) phase of the exercise and not during the eccentric (muscle lengthening) phase. Such machines do not preload the muscles with resistance; they provide resistance only after the movement has been started.

OTHER DYNAMIC EXERCISE TECHNIQUES Athletes use four other kinds of isotonic techniques, primarily for training and rehabilitation.

- **Eccentric (pliometric) loading** involves placing a load on a muscle as it lengthens. The muscle contracts eccentrically in order to control the weight. Eccentric loading is practiced during most types of resistance training. For example, you are performing an eccentric movement as you lower the weight to your chest during a bench press in preparation for the active movement. You can also perform exercises designed specifically to overload muscle eccentrically, a technique called *negatives*.

- **Plyometrics** is the sudden eccentric loading and stretching of muscles followed by a forceful concentric contraction. An example would be the action of the lower-body muscles when jumping from a bench to the ground and then jumping back onto the bench. This type of exercise is used to develop explosive strength; it also helps build and maintain bone density.

- **Speed loading** involves moving a weight as rapidly as possible in an attempt to approach the speeds used in movements like throwing a softball or sprinting. In the bench press, for example, speed loading might involve doing five repetitions as fast as possible using a weight that is half the maximum load you can lift. You can gauge your progress by timing how fast you can perform the repetitions.

Training with **kettlebells** is a type of speed loading. Kettlebell training is highly ballistic, meaning that many exercises involve fast, pendulum-type motions, extreme decelerations, and high-speed eccentric muscle contractions. Kettlebell swings require dynamic concentric muscle contractions during the upward phase of the exercise followed by high-speed eccentric contractions to control the movement when returning to the starting position. Kettlebell training is very popular around the world, but more research is needed to better understand its effects on strength, power, and fitness.

- **Isokinetic** exercise involves exerting force at a constant speed against an equal force exerted by a special strength training machine. The isokinetic machine provides variable resistance at different points in the joint's range of motion, matching the effort applied by the individual while keeping the speed of the movement constant. Isokinetic exercises are excellent for building strength and endurance.

Comparing Static and Dynamic Exercise Static exercises require no equipment, so they can be done virtually

Kettlebells are growing in popularity. They provide a fast, effective workout when used properly.

Fitness Tip

As you create a personalized weight training program, focus on specificity and eliminate training methods that do not help you achieve your goal. Follow a well-designed training program that builds strength gradually and progressively. Don't adopt the program of the week just because it's popular.

anywhere. They build strength rapidly and are useful for rehabilitating injured joints. On the other hand, they have to be performed at several different angles for each joint to improve strength throughout its entire range of motion. Dynamic exercises can be performed without equipment (calisthenics) or with equipment (weight training). They are excellent for building strength and endurance, and they tend to build strength through a joint's full range of motion. Most people develop muscular strength and endurance using dynamic exercises. Ultimately, the type of exercise a person chooses depends on individual goals, preferences, and access to equipment.

Weight Machines Versus Free Weights

Muscles get stronger when made to work against resistance. Resistance can be provided by free weights, your own body weight, or exercise machines. Many people prefer weight machines because they are safe, convenient,

KEY TERMS

dynamic (isotonic) exercise Exercise involving a muscle contraction with a change in the muscle's length.

concentric muscle contraction A dynamic contraction in which the muscle gets shorter as it contracts.

eccentric muscle contraction A dynamic contraction in which the muscle lengthens as it contracts; also called a *pliometric contraction*.

constant resistance exercise A type of dynamic exercise that uses a constant load throughout a joint's full range of motion.

variable resistance exercise A type of dynamic exercise that uses a changing load, providing a maximum load at the strongest point in the affected joint's range of motion.

eccentric (pliometric) loading Loading the muscle while it is lengthening; sometimes called *negatives*.

plyometrics Rapid stretching of a muscle group that is undergoing eccentric stress (the muscle is exerting force while it lengthens), followed by a rapid concentric contraction.

speed loading Moving a load as rapidly as possible.

kettlebell A large iron weight with a connected handle; used for ballistic weight training exercises such as swings and one-arm snatches.

isokinetic The application of force at a constant speed against an equal force.

and easy to use. You just set the resistance, sit down at the machine, and start working. Machines make it easy to isolate and work specific muscles. You don't need a **spotter**—someone who stands by to assist when free weights are used—and you don't have to worry about dropping a weight on yourself. Many machines provide support for the back.

Free weights require more care, balance, and coordination to use, but they strengthen your body in ways that are more adaptable to real life. They are also more popular with athletes for developing functional strength for sports, especially sports that require a great deal of strength. Free weights are widely available, inexpensive, and convenient for home use.

Other Training Methods and Types of Equipment

You don't need a fitness center or expensive equipment to strength train. If you prefer to train at home or like low-cost alternatives, consider the following options.

Resistance Bands Resistance or exercise bands are elastic strips or tubes of rubber material that are inexpensive, lightweight, and portable. They are available in a variety of styles and levels of resistance. Some are sold with instructional guides or DVDs, and classes may be offered at

fitness centers. Many free weight exercises can be adapted for resistance bands. For example, you can do biceps curls by standing on the center of the band and holding one end of the band in each hand; the band provides resistance when you stretch it to perform the curl.

Exercise (Stability) Balls The exercise or stability ball is an extra-large inflatable ball. It was originally developed for use in physical therapy but has become a popular piece of exercise equipment for use in the home or gym. It can be used to work the entire body, but it is particularly effective for working the core stabilizing muscles in the abdomen, chest, and back—muscles that are important for preventing back problems. The ball's instability forces the exerciser to use the stability muscles to balance the body, even when just sitting on the ball. Moves such as crunches are more effective when performed with an exercise ball.

When choosing a ball, make sure that your thighs are parallel to the ground when you sit on it; if you are a beginner or have back problems, choose a larger ball so that your thighs are at an angle, with hips higher than knees. Beginners should use caution until they feel comfortable with the movements and take care to avoid poor form due to fatigue. See Chapter 7 for more on incorporating stability balls into a fitness program.

Pilates Pilates (*pil LAH teez*) was developed by German gymnast and boxer Joseph Pilates early in the twentieth

Resistance bands are a popular and inexpensive alternative to training with weights or machines.

Proper fit is an important factor in choosing and using a stability ball.

Fitness Tip

Think those resistance bands are just for beginners? Think again. Many serious weight trainers use elastic bands to provide variable resistance during large muscle lifts such as the squat and bench press. Bands might increase power, rate of force development, and speed.

century. It often involves the use of specially designed resistance training devices, although some classes feature just mat or floor work. Pilates focuses on strengthening and stretching the core muscles in the back, abdomen, and buttocks to create a solid base of support for whole-body movement; the emphasis is on concentration, control, movement flow, and breathing. Mat exercises can be done at home, but because there are hundreds of Pilates exercises, some of them strenuous, it is best to begin with some qualified instruction. The Pilates Method Alliance (www.pilatesmethodalliance.org) offers advice on finding a qualified teacher.

Medicine Balls, Suspension Training, Stones, and Carrying Exercises Almost anything that provides resistance to movement will develop strength. Rubber medicine balls weigh up to 50 pounds and can be used for a variety of functional movements, such as squats and overhead throws. Suspension training uses body weight as the resistance and involves doing exercises with ropes or cords attached to a hook, bar, door jam, or sturdy tree branch. Stones can provide resistance to almost any movement, are free, and can be found in many shapes and sizes. Walking while carrying dumbbells, farmer's bars, or heavy stones is an easy and effective way to develop whole body strength.

Medicine balls can be used in many ways to get an effective resistance workout.

No-Equipment Calisthenics You can use your own body weight as resistance for strength training. Exercises such as curl-ups, push-ups, squats, step-ups, heel raises, chair dips, and lunges can be done anywhere.

Applying the FITT Principle: Selecting Exercises and Putting Together a Program

A complete weight training program works all the major muscle groups. It usually takes about 8–10 different exercises to get a complete full-body workout. Use the FITT principle—frequency, intensity, time, and type—to set the parameters of your program.

Frequency of Exercise For general fitness, the American College of Sports Medicine (ACSM) recommends a frequency of at least 2 nonconsecutive days per week for weight training. Allow your muscles at least one day of rest between workouts; if you train too often, your muscles won't be able to work with enough intensity to improve their fitness, and soreness and injury are more likely to result. If you enjoy weight training and want to train more often, try working different muscle groups on alternate days—a training plan called a *split routine*. For example, work your arms and upper body one day, work your lower body the next day, and then return to upper-body exercises on the third day.

Intensity of Exercise: Amount of Resistance The amount of weight (resistance) you lift in weight training exercises is equivalent to intensity in cardiorespiratory endurance training. It determines how your body will adapt to weight training and how quickly these adaptations will occur.

Choose weights based on your current level of muscular fitness and your fitness goals. Choose a weight heavy enough to fatigue your muscles but light enough for you to complete the repetitions with good form. (For tips on perfecting your form, see the box "Improving Your Technique with Video.") To build strength rapidly, you should lift weights as heavy as 80% of your maximum capacity (1 RM). If you're more interested in building endurance, choose a lighter weight (perhaps 40–60% of 1 RM), and do more repetitions.

For example, if your maximum capacity for the leg press is 160 pounds, you might lift 130 pounds to build strength and 80 pounds to build endurance. For a general fitness program to develop both strength and endurance, choose a weight in the middle of this range, perhaps 70% of 1 RM. Or you can create a program that includes

spotter A person who assists with a weight training exercise done with free weights.

Improving Your Technique with Video

Want to get stronger? Then you need to focus on developing your skills at least as much as you focus on lifting more weight. Improving skill is the best way to increase strength during movements such as hitting a tennis ball or baseball, performing a bench press, driving a golf ball, skiing down a slope, or carrying a bag of groceries up a flight of stairs. In the world of weight training, skill means lifting weights with proper form; the better your form, the better your results.

The brain develops precise neural pathways as you learn a skill. As you improve, the pathways conduct nervous impulses faster and more precisely until the movement almost becomes reflexive. The best way to learn a skill is through focused practice that involves identifying mistakes, correcting them, and practicing the refined movement many times. However, simply practicing the skill is not enough if you want to improve and perform more powerful movements. You must perform the movements correctly instead of practicing mistakes or poor form over and over again.

Here's where technology can help. Watch videos of people performing weight-training movements correctly. You may be able to borrow videos from your instructor, purchase low-cost training videos through magazines and sporting goods stores, or find them on the Internet. If you watch training videos online, however, make sure they were produced by an authoritative source on weight training. Otherwise, you may be learning someone else's mistakes.

Film your movements using a phone camera or inexpensive video camera. Compare your movements with those of a more skilled person performing them correctly. Make a note of poor movement patterns and try to change your technique to make it more mechanically correct. Share your videos with your instructor or a certified personal trainer, who can help you identify poor form and teach you ways to correct your form.

---

both higher-intensity exercise (80% of 1 RM for 8–10 repetitions) and lower-intensity exercise (60% of 1 RM for 15–20 repetitions); this routine will develop both fast-twitch and slow-twitch muscle fibers.

Because it can be tedious and time-consuming to continually reassess your maximum capacity for each exercise, you might find it easier to choose a weight based on the number of repetitions of an exercise you can perform with a given resistance.

Time of Exercise: Repetitions and Sets To improve fitness, you must do enough repetitions of each exercise to fatigue your muscles. The number of repetitions needed to cause fatigue depends on the amount of resistance: The heavier the weight, the fewer repetitions to reach fatigue. In general, a heavy weight and a low number of repetitions (1–5) build strength and overload primarily fast-twitch fibers, whereas a light weight and a high number of repetitions (15–20) build endurance and overload primarily slow-twitch fibers.

For a general fitness program to build both strength and endurance, try to do about 8–12 repetitions of each exercise; a few exercises, such as abdominal crunches and calf raises, may require more. To avoid injury, older (approximately age 50–60 and above) and frailer people should perform more repetitions (10–15) using a lighter weight.

In weight training, a **set** refers to a group of repetitions of an exercise followed by a rest period. To develop strength and endurance for general fitness, you can make gains doing a single set of each exercise, provided you use enough resistance to fatigue your muscles. (You should just barely be able to complete the 8–12 repetitions—using good form—for each exercise.) Doing more than one set of each exercise will increase strength development, and most serious weight trainers do at least three sets of each exercise (see the section "More Advanced Strength Training Programs" for guidelines on more advanced programs).

If you perform more than one set of an exercise, you need to rest long enough between sets to allow your muscles to work with enough intensity to increase fitness. The length of the rest interval depends on the amount of resistance. In a program to develop a combination of strength and endurance for wellness, a rest period of 1–3 minutes between sets is appropriate. If you are lifting heavier loads to build strength, rest 3–5 minutes between sets. You can save time in your workouts by alternating sets of different exercises. One muscle group can rest between sets while you work on another group.

Training volume is one method of quantifying the total load lifted during weight training. Use this formula to calculate the training volume for a workout:

repetitions × weight × sets

For example, if you did three sets of 10 repetitions for biceps curls using 50 pounds, the training volume for the exercise would be 1500 pounds ($3 \times 10 \times 50 = 1500$). Do the same calculation for every exercise in your program and add the results together to determine the total training volume for the entire workout.

Overtraining—doing more exercise than your body can recover from—can occur in response to heavy resistance training. Possible signs of overtraining include lack of progress or decreased performance, chronic fatigue, decreased coordination, and chronic muscle soreness. The best remedy for overtraining is rest; add more days of recovery between workouts. With extra rest, chances are you'll be refreshed and ready to train again. Adding variety to your program, as discussed later in the chapter, can also help you avoid overtraining with resistance exercise.

Type or Mode of Exercise For overall fitness, you need to include exercises for your neck, upper back, shoulders, arms, chest, abdomen, lower back, thighs, buttocks, and calves—about 8–10 exercises in all. If you are also training for a particular sport, include exercises to strengthen the muscles important for optimal performance *and* the muscles most likely to be injured. Weight training exercises for general fitness are presented later in this chapter, on pp. 116–124.

It is important to balance exercises between **agonist** and **antagonist** muscle groups. When a muscle contracts, it is known as the agonist; the opposing muscle, which must relax and stretch to allow contraction by the agonist, is known as the antagonist. Whenever you do an exercise that moves a joint in one direction, also select an exercise that works the joint in the opposite direction. For example, if you do knee extensions to develop the muscles on the front of your thighs, also do leg curls to develop the antagonist muscles on the back of your thighs.

The order of exercises can also be important. Do exercises for large-muscle groups or for more than one joint before you do exercises that use small-muscle groups or single joints. This allows for more effective overload of the larger, more powerful muscle groups. Small-muscle groups fatigue more easily than larger ones, and small-muscle fatigue limits your capacity to overload large-muscle groups. For example, lateral raises, which work the shoulder muscles, should be performed after bench presses, which work the chest and arms in addition to the shoulders. If you fatigue your shoulder muscles by doing lateral raises first, you won't be able to lift as much weight and effectively fatigue all the key muscle groups used during the bench press.

Also, order exercises so that you work agonist and antagonist muscle groups in sequence, one after the other. For example, follow biceps curls, which work the biceps, with triceps extensions, which exercise the triceps—the antagonist muscle to the biceps.

Wellness Tip

A standard push-up is equivalent to bench-pressing 60% of your body weight. A set of 12 push-ups is a quick, effective upper-body workout. No gym required!

The Warm-Up and Cool-Down

As with cardiorespiratory endurance exercise, you should warm up before every weight training session and cool down afterward (Figure 4.2). You should do both a general warm-up—several minutes of walking or easy jogging—and a warm-up for the weight training exercises you plan

Warm-up 5–10 minutes	Strength training exercises for major muscle groups (8–10 exercises)		Cool-down 5–10 minutes
	Sample program		
	Exercise	*Muscle group(s) developed*	
	Bench press	Chest, shoulders, triceps	
	Pull-ups	Lats, biceps	
	Shoulder press	Shoulders, trapezius, triceps	
	Upright rowing	Deltoids, trapezius	
	Biceps curls	Biceps	
	Lateral raises	Shoulders	
	Squats	Gluteals, quadriceps	
	Heel raises	Calves	
	Abdominal curls	Abdominals	
	Spine extensions	Low- and mid-back spine extensors	
Start	Side bridges	Obliques, quadratus lumborum	*Stop*

Frequency: 2–3 nonconsecutive days per week

Intensity/Resistance: Weights heavy enough to cause muscle fatigue when exercises are performed with good form for the selected number of repetitions

Time: Repetitions: 8–12 of each exercise (10–15 with a lower weight for people over age 50–60); **Sets:** 1 (doing more than 1 set per exercise may result in faster and greater strength gains); rest 1–2 minutes between exercises.

Type of activity: 8–10 strength training exercises that focus on major muscle groups

FIGURE 4.2   The FITT principle for a strength training workout.

set   A group of repetitions followed by a rest period.

agonist   A muscle in a state of contraction, opposed by the action of another muscle, its *antagonist*.

antagonist   A muscle that opposes the action of a contracting muscle, its *agonist*.

KEY TERMS

to perform. For example, if you plan to do one or more sets of 10 repetitions of bench presses with 125 pounds, you might do one set of 10 repetitions with 50 pounds as a warm-up. Do similar warm-up exercises for each exercise in your program.

To cool down after weight training, relax for 5–10 minutes after your workout. Although this is controversial, a few studies have suggested that including a period of postexercise stretching may help prevent muscle soreness; warmed-up muscles and joints make this a particularly good time to work on flexibility.

Getting Started and Making Progress

The first few sessions of weight training should be devoted to learning the movements and allowing your nervous system to practice communicating with your muscles so you can develop strength effectively. To start, choose a weight that you can move easily through 8–12 repetitions, do only one set of each exercise, and rest 1–2 minutes between exercises. Gradually add weight and (if you want) sets to your program over the first few weeks until you are doing one to three sets of 8–12 repetitions of each exercise.

As you progress, add weight according to the "two-for-two" rule: When you can perform two additional repetitions with a given weight on two consecutive training sessions, increase the load. For example, if your target is to perform 8–10 repetitions per exercise, and you performed 12 repetitions in your previous two workouts, it would be appropriate to increase your load. If adding weight means you can do only 7 or 8 repetitions, stay with that weight until you can again complete 12 repetitions per set. If you can do only 4–6 repetitions after adding weight, or if you can't maintain good form, you've added too much and should take some off.

You can add more resistance in large-muscle exercises, such as squats and bench presses, than you can in small-muscle exercises, such as curls. For example, when you can complete 12 repetitions of squats with good form, you may be able to add 10–20 pounds of additional resistance; for curls, on the other hand, you might add only 3–5 pounds. As a general guideline, try increases of approximately 5%, which is half a pound of additional weight for each 10 pounds you are currently lifting.

You can expect to improve rapidly during the first 6–10 weeks of training—a 10–30% increase in the amount of weight lifted. Gains will then come more slowly. Your rate of improvement will depend on how hard you work and how your body responds to resistance training. Factors such as age, gender, motivation, and heredity also will affect your progress.

After you achieve the level of strength and muscularity you want, you can maintain your gains by training 2–3 days per week. You can monitor the progress of your program by recording the amount of resistance and the number of repetitions and sets you perform on a workout card like the one shown in Figure 4.3.

WORKOUT CARD FOR Sara Lopez

Exercise/Date		9/14	9/16	9/18	9/21	9/23	9/25	9/28	9/30	10/2
Bench press	Wt.	45	45	45	50	50	50	60	60	60
	Sets	1	1	1	1	1	1	1	1	1
	Reps.	10	12	12	10	12	12	10	9	12
Pull-ups (assisted)	Wt.	–	–	–	–	–	–	–	–	–
	Sets	1	1	1	1	1	1	1	1	1
	Reps.	5	5	5	6	6	6	7	7	7
Shoulder press	Wt.	20	20	20	25	25	25	30	30	30
	Sets	1	1	1	1	1	1	1	1	1
	Reps.	10	12	12	10	12	12	8	10	9
Upright rowing	Wt.	5	5	10	10	10	10	12	12	12
	Sets	1	1	1	1	1	1	1	1	1
	Reps.	12	12	8	10	11	12	9	10	12
Biceps curls	Wt.	15	15	15	20	20	20	25	25	25
	Sets	1	1	1	1	1	1	1	1	1
	Reps.	10	10	10	10	12	12	8	10	10
Lateral raise	Wt.	5	5	5	5	5	5	7.5	7.5	7.5
	Sets	1	1	1	1	1	1	1	1	1
	Reps.	8	8	10	10	12	12	8	10	10
Squats	Wt.	–	–	–	45	45	45	55	55	55
	Sets	1	1	1	1	1	1	1	1	1
	Reps.	10	12	15	8	12	12	8	12	12
Heel raises	Wt.	–	–	–	45	45	45	55	55	55
	Sets	1	1	1	1	1	1	1	1	1
	Reps.	15	15	15	8	12	12	10	12	12
Abdominal curls	Wt.	–	–	–	–	–	–	–	–	–
	Sets	1	1	1	1	1	1	1	1	1
	Reps.	20	20	20	20	20	20	25	25	25
Spine extensions	Wt.	–	–	–	–	–	–	–	–	–
	Sets	1	1	1	1	1	1	1	1	1
	Reps.	5	5	5	8	8	8	10	10	10
Side bridge	Wt.	–	–	–	–	–	–	–	–	–
	Sets	1	1	1	1	1	1	1	1	1
	Seconds	60	60	60	65	65	70	70	70	70

FIGURE 4.3 A sample workout card for a general fitness strength training program.

More Advanced Strength Training Programs

The program just described is sufficient to develop and maintain muscular strength and endurance for general fitness. Performing more sets and fewer repetitions with a heavier load will cause greater increases in strength. Such a program might include three to five sets of 4–6 repetitions each; the load should be heavy enough to cause fatigue with the smaller number of repetitions. Rest long enough after a set (3–5 minutes) to allow your muscles to recover and work intensely during the next set.

Experienced weight trainers often practice some form of cycle training, also called *periodization,* in which the exercises, number of sets and repetitions, and intensity vary within a workout and/or between workouts. For example, you might do a particular exercise more intensely during some sets or on some days than others. You might also vary the exercises you perform for particular muscle groups. For more detailed information on these more advanced training techniques, consult a strength coach certified by the National Strength and Conditioning Association or

Safe Weight Training

TAKE CHARGE

General Guidelines

- When beginning a program or trying new exercises or equipment, ask a qualified trainer or instructor to show you how to do exercises safely and correctly.

- Lift weights from a stabilized body position; keep weights as close to your body as possible.

- Protect your back by maintaining control of your spine and avoiding dangerous positions. Don't twist your body while lifting.

- Observe proper lifting techniques and good form at all times. Don't lift beyond the limits of your strength.

- Don't hold your breath while doing weight training exercises. Doing so causes a decrease in blood returning to the heart and can make you become dizzy and faint. It can also increase blood pressure to dangerous levels. Exhale when exerting the greatest force, and inhale when moving the weight into position for the active phase of the lift. Breathe smoothly and steadily.

- Don't use defective equipment. Be aware of broken collars or bolts, frayed cables, broken chains, or loose cushions.

- Don't exercise if you're ill, injured, or overtrained. Do not try to work through the pain.

Free Weights

- Make sure the bar is loaded evenly on both sides and that weights are secured with collars or spring clips.

- When you pick a weight up from the ground, keep your back straight and your head level. Don't bend at the waist with straight legs.

- Lift weights smoothly; don't jerk them. Control the weight through the entire range of motion.

- Do most of your lifting with your legs. Keep your hips and buttocks back. When doing standing lifts, maintain a good posture so that you protect your back. Bend at the hips, not with

the spine. Feet should be shoulder-width apart, heels and balls of the feet in contact with the floor, and knees slightly bent.

- Don't bounce weights against your body during an exercise.

Spotting

- Use spotters for free weights exercises in which the bar crosses the face or head (e.g., the bench press), is placed on the back (e.g., squats), or is racked in front of the chest (e.g., overhead press from the rack).

- If one spotter is used, the spotter should stand behind the lifter; if two spotters are used, one spotter should stand at each end of the barbell.

- For squats with heavy resistance, use at least three spotters—one behind the lifter (hands near lifter's hips, waist, or torso) and one at each end of the bar. Squatting in a power rack will increase safety during this exercise.

- Spot dumbbell exercises at the forearms, as close to the weights as possible.

- For over-the-face and over-the-head lifts, the spotter should hold the bar with an alternate grip (one palm up and one palm down) inside the lifter's grip.

- Ensure good communication between spotter and lifter by agreeing on verbal signals before the exercise.

---

another reliable source. If you decide to adopt a more advanced training regimen, start off slowly to give your body a chance to adjust and to minimize the risk of injury.

Fitness Tip

Doing three sets of resistance exercise is more anabolic than one set, meaning that doing multiple sets enhances muscle protein synthesis. If you're serious about strength training, do multiple sets of exercises to maximize muscle protein synthesis and muscle growth.

Weight Training Safety

Injuries happen in weight training. Maximum physical effort, elaborate machinery, rapid movements, and heavy weights can combine to make the weight room a dangerous place if proper precautions aren't taken. To help ensure that your workouts are safe and productive, follow the guidelines in the box "Safe Weight Training" and the following suggestions.

Use Proper Lifting Technique Every exercise has a proper technique that is important for obtaining maximum benefits and preventing injury. Your instructor or weight room attendant can help explain the specific techniques for different exercises and weight machines.

CRITICAL CONSUMER

Dietary Supplements: A Consumer Dilemma

Wading through manufacturers' claims can be tricky when you are considering taking a dietary supplement. Although drugs and food products undergo stringent government testing, dietary supplements can be freely marketed without testing for safety or effectiveness. There is no guarantee that advertisements about dietary supplements are accurate or true.

What's the difference between a drug—which must be approved by the Food and Drug Administration (FDA)—and a dietary supplement? In some cases, the only real difference is in how the product is marketed. Some dietary supplements are as potentially dangerous as potent prescription drugs. But because dietary supplements have a different classification, manufacturers do not have to prove they are safe and effective before being sold; the FDA can, however, take action against any unsafe supplement product after it reaches the market.

Supplement manufacturers often make glowing claims about their products, such as "Builds lean muscle fast" or "Burns fat and gives you energy." With all the hype, how can you determine if a particular supplement might be helpful? Ask yourself the following questions:

● **Do you really need a supplement at all?** Nutritional authorities agree that most athletes and young adults can obtain all the necessary ingredients for health and top athletic performance by eating a well-balanced diet and training appropriately. No dietary supplement outperforms

wholesome food and a good training regimen.

● **Is the product safe and effective?** The fact that a dietary supplement is available in your local store is no guarantee of safety. As described earlier, the FDA doesn't regulate supplements in the same way as drugs. The only way to determine if a supplement really works is to perform carefully controlled research on human subjects. Testimonials from individuals who claim to have benefited from the product don't count. Few dietary supplements have undergone careful human testing, so it is difficult to tell which of them may actually work.

● **Can you be sure that the product is of high quality?** There is no official agency that ensures the quality of dietary supplements. There is no guarantee that a supplement contains the desired ingredient, that dosages are appropriate, that potency is standardized, or that the product is free from contaminants. (See Chapter 8 for more information on dietary supplement labeling.)

Perform exercises smoothly and with good form. Lift or push the weight forcefully during the active phase of the lift and then lower it with control. Perform all lifts through the full range of motion and strive to maintain a neutral spine position during each exercise.

Use Spotters and Collars with Free Weights Spotters are necessary when an exercise has potential for danger; a weight that is out of control or falls can cause a serious injury. A spotter can assist you if you cannot complete a lift or if the weight tilts. A spotter can also help you move a weight into position before a lift and provide help or additional resistance during a lift. Spotting requires practice and coordination between the lifter and the spotter(s).

Collars are devices that secure weights to a barbell or dumbbell. Although people lift weights without collars, doing so is dangerous. It is easy to lose your balance or to raise one side of the weight faster than the other. Without collars, the weights can slip off and crash to the floor.

Be Alert for Injuries Report any obvious muscle or joint injuries to your instructor or physician, and stop exercising the affected area. Training with an injured joint or

muscle can lead to a more serious injury. Make sure you get the necessary first aid. Even minor injuries heal faster if you use the R-I-C-E principle of treating injuries described in Chapter 3.

Consult a physician if you have any unusual symptoms during exercise or if you're uncertain whether weight training is a proper activity for you. Conditions such as heart disease and high blood pressure can be aggravated during weight training. Immediately report symptoms such as headaches; dizziness; labored breathing; numbness; vision disturbances; and chest, neck, or arm pain.

A Caution About Supplements and Drugs

Many active people use nutritional supplements and drugs in the quest for improved performance and appearance. Table 4.2 lists a selective summary of "performance aids" along with their potential side effects. Most of these substances are ineffective and expensive, and many are dangerous (see the box "Dietary Supplements: A Consumer Dilemma"). A balanced diet should be your primary nutritional strategy.

| Table 4.2 | Performance Aids Marketed to Weight Trainers | | 255 |

SUBSTANCE	SUPPOSED EFFECTS	ACTUAL EFFECTS	SELECTED POTENTIAL SIDE EFFECTS
Adrenal androgens, such as dehydroepiandrosterone (DHEA), androstenedione	Increased testosterone, muscle mass, and strength; decreased body fat	Increased testosterone, strength, and fat-free mass; decreased fat in older subjects (more studies needed in younger people)	Gonadal suppression, prostate hypertrophy, breast development in males, masculinization in women and children; long-term effects unknown
Amino acids	Increased muscle mass	No effects if dietary protein intake is adequate; consuming before or after training may improve performance	Minimal side effects; unbalanced amino acid intake can cause problems with protein metabolism
Amphetamines	Prevention of fatigue; increased confidence and training intensity	Increased arousal, wakefulness, and confidence; feeling of enhanced decision-making ability	Depression and fatigue (after drug wears off), extreme confusion; neural and psychological effects including aggressiveness, paranoia, hallucinations, compulsive behavior, restlessness, irritability, heart arrhythmia, high blood pressure, and chest pain
Anabolic steroids	Increased muscle mass, strength, power, psychological aggressiveness, and endurance	Increased strength, power, fat-free mass, and aggression; no effects on endurance	Liver damage and tumors, decrease in high-density lipoprotein (good cholesterol), depressed sperm and testosterone production, high blood pressure, depressed immune function, problems with sugar metabolism, psychological disturbances, gonadal suppression, liver disease, acne, breast development in males, masculinization in women and children, heart disease, thicker blood, and increased risk of cancer; steroids are controlled substances*
Beta-agonists, such as clenbuterol, salmeterol, terbutaline	Enhanced performance; prevention of muscle atrophy; increased fat-free weight; decreased body fat	Used to treat asthma, including exercise-induced asthma	Insomnia, heart arrhythmia, anxiety, anorexia, nausea, heart enlargement, heart attack (particularly if used with steroids), and heart failure
Chromium picolinate	Increased muscle mass, decreased body fat; improved blood sugar control	Well-controlled studies show no significant effect on fat-free mass or body fat	Moderate doses (50–200 µg) appear safe; higher doses may cause DNA damage and other serious effects; long-term effects unknown
Creatine monohydrate	Increased creatine phosphate levels in muscles, muscle mass, and capacity for high-intensity exercise	Increased muscle mass and performance in some types of high-intensity exercise	Minimal side effects; long-term effects unknown
Diuretics	Promote loss of body fluid	Promote loss of body fluid to accentuate muscle definition; often taken with potassium supplements and very-low-calorie diets	Muscle cell destruction, low blood pressure, blood chemistry abnormalities, and heart problems
Energy drinks	Increased energy, strength, power	Increased training volume	Insomnia, increased blood pressure, heart palpitations
Ephedra	Decreased body fat; increased training intensity due to stimulant effect	Decreased appetite, particularly when taken with caffeine; some evidence for increased training intensity	Abnormal heart rhythms, nervousness, headache, gastrointestinal distress, and heatstroke; banned by the FDA
Erythropoietin, darbepoetin	Enhanced performance during endurance events	Stimulated growth of red blood cells; enhanced oxygen uptake and endurance	Increased blood viscosity (thickness); can cause potentially fatal blood clots

(Continued)

| Table 4.2 | Performance Aids Marketed to Weight Trainers (*continued*) |

SUBSTANCE	SUPPOSED EFFECTS	ACTUAL EFFECTS	SELECTED POTENTIAL SIDE EFFECTS
Ginseng	Decreased effects of physical and emotional stress; increased oxygen consumption	Most well-controlled studies show no effect on performance	No serious side effects; high doses can cause high blood pressure, nervousness, and insomnia
Green tea extract	Decreased body fat	Some studies show decreases in body fat	Insomnia, headache, nausea, heart palpitations
Growth hormone	Increased muscle mass, strength, and power; decreased body fat	Increased muscle mass and strength; decreased fat mass; studies show no effect on muscle or exercise performance	Elevated blood sugar, high insulin levels, and carpal tunnel syndrome; enlargement of the heart and other organs; acromegaly (disease characterized by increased growth of bones in hands and face); diseases of the heart, nerves, bones, and joints; an extremely expensive controlled substance*
Human chorionic gonadotrophin (HCG)	Increased testosterone production; prevention of muscle atrophy during steroid withdrawal	Increased testosterone production	Interferes with normal testosterone regulation; banned in most sports
Beta-hydroxy beta-methylbutyrate (HMB)	Increased strength and muscle mass; decreased body fat	Some studies show increased fat-free mass and decreased fat; more research needed	No reported side effects; long-term effects unknown
Insulin	Increased muscle mass	Effectiveness in stimulating muscle growth unknown	Insulin shock (characterized by extremely low blood sugar), which can lead to unconsciousness and death
Insulin-like growth factor (IGF)	Increased muscle mass; improved cellular function	Actual effects in healthy, active people unknown	Similar to side effects of growth hormone; long-term use promotes cancer
"Metabolic-optimizing" meals for athletes	Increased muscle mass and energy supply; decreased body fat	No proven effects beyond those of balanced meals	No reported side effets, extremely expensive
Over-the-counter stimulants, such as caffeine, phenylpropanolamine (PPA)	Weight loss; improved endurance; stimulant effect	Can be used for weight control; may improve endurance; does not appear to enhance short-term maximal exercise capacity	Increased risk of heart attack and stroke in some people (in high doses); increased incidence of abnormal heart rhythm and insomnia; caffeine is addictive
Prescription appetite suppressants, such as diethylproprion, phentermine, sibutramine, rimonabant	Weight control, weight loss	Weight loss; typically prescribed only for short-term use	Restlessness, anxiety, dizziness, depression, tremors, increased urination, diarrhea, constipation, vomiting, high blood pressure, swelling of legs or ankles, insomnia, seizures, fast or irregular heartbeat, heart palpitations, blurred vision, rashes, and difficulty breathing; can be habit-forming
Protein, amino acids, polypeptide supplements	Increased muscle mass and growth hormone release; accelerated muscle development; decreased body fat	No effects if dietary protein intake is adequate; may promote protein synthesis if taken immediately before or after weight training	Can be dangerous for people with liver or kidney disease; substituting amino acid or polypeptide supplements for protein-rich food can cause nutrient deficiencies

*Possession of a controlled substance is illegal without a prescription, and physicians are not allowed to prescribe controlled substances for the improvement of athletic performance. In addition, the use of anabolic steroids, growth hormone, or any of several other substances listed in this table is banned for athletic competition.

SOURCES: Brooks, G. A., et al. 2005. *Exercise Physiology: Human Bioenergetics and Its Applications*, 4th ed. New York: McGraw-Hill. Sports-supplement dangers. 2001. *Consumer Reports*, June. U.S. National Library of Medicine, National Institutes of Health. *MedlinePlus Medical Encyclopedia* (http://www.nlm.nih.gov/medlineplus/encyclopedia.html; retrieved).

Wellness Tip

The FDA has issued several consumer warnings about dietary supplements—particularly the kinds that are marketed to people who want to build muscle and lose fat. A number of products have been pulled off store shelves after the FDA found they were not safe. Talk to your doctor before considering any dietary supplement.

Ask Yourself

QUESTIONS FOR CRITICAL THINKING AND REFLECTION

Do you think athletes should be allowed to use drugs and supplements to improve their sports performance? Would you be tempted to use a banned performance-enhancing drug if you thought you could get away with it?

WEIGHT TRAINING EXERCISES

A general book on fitness and wellness cannot include a detailed description of all weight training exercises. The following pages present a basic program for developing muscular strength and endurance for general fitness using free weights and weight machines. Instructions for each exercise are accompanied by photographs and a listing of the muscles being trained. See pages T4-2 and T4-3 of the color transparency insert "Touring the Musculoskeletal System" in this chapter for a clear illustration of the deep and superficial muscles referenced in the exercises.

Labs 4.2 and 4.3 will help you assess your current level of muscular endurance and design your own weight training program. If you want to develop strength for a particular activity, your program should contain exercises for general fitness, exercises for the muscle groups most important for the activity, and exercises for muscle groups most often injured. Regardless of the goals of your program or the type of equipment you use, your program should be structured so that you obtain maximum results without risking injury.

TIPS FOR TODAY AND THE FUTURE

You don't need a complicated or heavy training program to improve strength: Just one set of 8–12 repetitions of 8–10 exercises, done at least two nonconsecutive days per week, is enough for general fitness.

RIGHT NOW YOU CAN

- Do a set of static (isometric) exercises. If you're sitting, try tightening your abdominal muscles as you press your lower back into the seat, or work your arms by placing the palms of your hands on top of your thighs and pressing down. Hold the contraction for 6 seconds and do 5–10 repetitions; don't hold your breath.
- Think of three things you've done in the past 24 hours that would have been easier or more enjoyable if you increased your level of muscular strength and endurance. Visualize improvements in your quality of life that could come from increased muscular strength and endurance.

IN THE FUTURE YOU CAN

- Make an appointment with a trainer at your campus or neighborhood fitness facility. A trainer can help you put together an appropriate weight training program and introduce you to the equipment at the facility.
- Invest in an inexpensive set of free weights, kettlebells, a stability ball, or a resistance band. Then make a regular appointment with yourself to use your new equipment.

EXERCISE 1   Bench Press

Instructions: (a) Lying on a bench on your back with your feet on the floor, grasp the bar with palms upward and hands shoulder-width apart. If the weight is on a rack, move the bar carefully from the supports to a point over the middle of your chest or slightly above it (at the lower part of the sternum). **(b)** Lower the bar to your chest. Then press it in a straight line to the starting position. Don't arch your back or bounce the bar off your chest. You can also do this exercise with dumbbells.

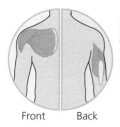

Muscles developed: Pectoralis major, triceps, deltoids

Front   Back

Note: *To allow an optimal view of exercise technique, a spotter does not appear in these demonstration photographs; however, spotters should be used for most exercises with free weights.*

EXERCISE 2   Pull-Up

Assisted pull-up: (c) This is done as described for a pull-up, except that a spotter assists the person by pushing upward at the waist, hips, or legs during the exercise.

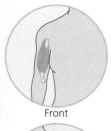

Front

Instructions: (a) Begin by grasping the pull-up bar with both hands, palms facing forward and elbows extended fully. **(b)** Pull yourself upward until your chin goes above the bar. Then return to the starting position.

Muscles developed: Latissimus dorsi, biceps

Back

EXERCISE 3 — Shoulder Press (Overhead or Military Press)

Instructions: This exercise can be done standing or seated, with dumbbells or a barbell. The shoulder press begins with the weight at your chest, preferably on a rack. **(a)** Grasp the weight with your palms facing away from you. **(b)** Push the weight overhead until your arms are extended. Then return to the starting position (weight at chest). Be careful not to arch your back excessively.

If you are a more advanced weight trainer, you can "clean" the weight (lift it from the floor to your chest). The clean should be attempted only after instruction from a knowledgeable coach; otherwise, it can lead to injury.

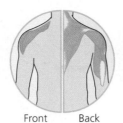

Front   Back

Muscles developed: Deltoids, triceps, trapezius

a

b

EXERCISE 4 — Upright Rowing

Instructions: From a standing position with arms extended fully, grasp a barbell with a close grip (hands about 6–12 inches apart) and palms facing the body. Raise the bar to about the level of your collarbone, keeping your elbows above bar level at all times. Return to the starting position.

This exercise can be done using dumbbells, a weighted bar (shown), or a barbell.

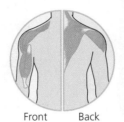

Front   Back

Muscles developed: Trapezius, deltoids, biceps

a

b

EXERCISE 5 — Biceps Curl

Instructions: **(a)** From a standing position, grasp the bar with your palms facing away from you and your hands shoulder-width apart. **(b)** Keeping your upper body rigid, flex (bend) your elbows until the bar reaches a level slightly below the collarbone. Return the bar to the starting position.

This exercise can be done using dumbbells, a curl bar (shown), or a barbell; some people find that using a curl bar places less stress on the wrists.

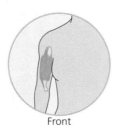

Front

Muscles developed: Biceps, brachialis

a

b

Mc Graw Hill **connect** http://www.mcgrawhillconnect.com/
FITNESS AND WELLNESS

EXERCISE 6   Lateral Raise

Instructions: (a) Stand with feet shoulder-width apart and a dumbbell in each hand. Hold the dumbbells in front of you and parallel to each other. **(b)** With elbows slightly bent, slowly lift both weights until they reach shoulder level. Keep your wrists in a neutral position, in line with your forearms. Return to the starting position.

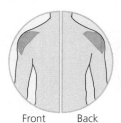

Front   Back

Muscles developed:
Deltoids

a   b

EXERCISE 7   Squat

Instructions: If the bar is racked, place the bar on the fleshy part of your upper back and grasp the bar at shoulder width. Keeping your back straight and head level, remove the bar from the rack and take a step back. Stand with feet slightly more than shoulder-width apart and toes pointed slightly outward. **(a)** Rest the bar on the back of your shoulders, holding it there with palms facing forward. **(b)** Keeping your head level and lower back straight and pelvis back, squat down until your thighs are below parallel with the floor. Let your thighs move laterally (outward) so that you "squat between your legs." This will help keep your back straight and keep your heels on the floor. Drive upward toward the starting position, hinging at the hips and keeping your back in a fixed position throughout the exercise.

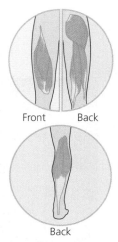

Front   Back

Back

Muscles developed:
Quadriceps, gluteus maximus, hamstrings, gastrocnemius

a   b

EXERCISE 8   Heel Raise

Instructions: Stand with feet shoulder-width apart and toes pointed straight ahead. **(a)** Rest the bar on the back of your shoulders, holding it there with palms facing forward. **(b)** Press down with your toes while lifting your heels. Return to the starting position.

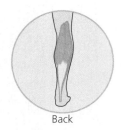

Back

Muscles developed:
Gastrocnemius, soleus

a   b

EXERCISE 9 — Curl-Up or Crunch

Instructions: **(a)** Lie on your back on the floor with your arms folded across your chest and your feet on the floor or on a bench. **(b)** Curl your trunk up, minimizing your head and shoulder movement. Lower to the starting position. Focus on using your abdominal muscles rather than the muscles in your shoulders, chest, and neck.

This exercise can also be done using an exercise ball (see p. 106).

Front

Muscles developed: Rectus abdominis, obliques

a

b

EXERCISE 10 — Spine Extension ("Bird Dog") (Isometric Exercise)

Instructions: Begin on all fours with your knees below your hips and your hands below your shoulders.

Unilateral spine extension:
(a) Extend your right leg to the rear and reach forward with your right arm. Keep your spine neutral and your raised arm and leg in line with your torso. Don't arch your back or let your hip or shoulder sag. Hold this position for 10–30 seconds. Repeat with your left leg and left arm.

Bilateral spine extension:
(b) Extend your left leg to the rear and reach forward with your right arm. Keep your spine neutral and your raised arm and leg in line with your torso. Don't arch your back or let your hip or shoulder sag. Hold this position for 10–30 seconds. Repeat with your right leg and left arm.

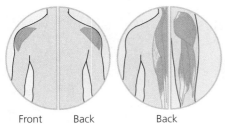

Front   Back   Back

Muscles developed: Erector spinae, gluteus maximus, hamstrings, deltoids

You can make this exercise more difficult by making box patterns with your arms and legs.

a

b

connect http://www.mcgrawhillconnect.com/ | FITNESS AND WELLNESS

Isometric Side Bridge

Instructions: Lie on the floor on your side with your knees bent and your top arm lying alongside your body. Lift and drive your hips forward so your weight is supported by your forearm and knee. Hold this position for 3–10 seconds, breathing normally. Repeat on the other side. Perform 3–10 repetitions on each side.

Variation: You can make the exercise more difficult by keeping your legs straight and supporting yourself with your feet and forearm (see Lab 5.3) or with your feet and hand (with elbow straight). You can also do this exercise on an exercise ball.

Muscles developed: Obliques, quadratus lumborum

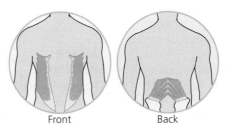

Front   Back

WEIGHT TRAINING EXERCISES   Weight Machines

EXERCISE 1

Bench Press (Chest or Vertical Press)

Instructions: Sit or lie on the seat or bench, depending on the type of machine and the manufacturer's instructions. Your back, hips, and buttocks should be pressed against the machine pads. Place your feet on the floor or the foot supports.

Muscles developed: Pectoralis major, anterior deltoids, triceps

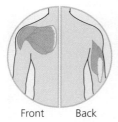

Front   Back

(a) Grasp the handles with your palms facing away from you; the handles should be aligned with your armpits.

(b) Push the bars until your arms are fully extended, but don't lock your elbows. Return to the starting position.

EXERCISE 2

Lat Pull

Instructions: Begin in a seated or kneeling position, depending on the type of lat machine and the manufacturer's instructions.

Note: *This exercise focuses on the same major muscles as the assisted pull-up (Exercise 3); choose an appropriate exercise for your program based on your preferences and equipment availability.*

Muscles developed: Latissimus dorsi, biceps

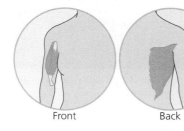

Front   Back

(a) Grasp the bar of the machine with arms fully extended.
(b) Slowly pull the weight down until it reaches the top of your chest. Slowly return to the starting position.

EXERCISE 3   Assisted Pull-Up

Instructions: Set the weight according to the amount of assistance you need to complete a set of pull-ups—the heavier the weight, the more assistance provided.

(a) Stand or kneel on the assist platform, and grasp the pull-up bar with your elbows fully extended and your palms facing away. **(b)** Pull up until your chin goes above the bar, and then return to the starting position.

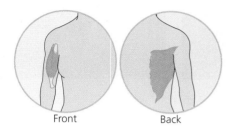

Front   Back

Muscles developed:
Latissimus dorsi, biceps

a   b

EXERCISE 4   Overhead Press (Shoulder Press)

Instructions: Adjust the seat so your feet are flat on the ground and the hand grips are slightly above your shoulders.

(a) Sit down, facing away from the machine, and grasp the hand grips with your palms facing forward. **(b)** Press the weight upward until your arms are extended. Return to the starting position.

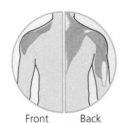

Front   Back

Muscles developed:
Deltoids, trapezius, triceps

a   b

EXERCISE 5   Biceps Curl

Instructions: **(a)** Adjust the seat so that your back is straight and your arms rest comfortably against the top and side pads. Place your arms on the support cushions and grasp the hand grips with your palms facing up. **(b)** Keeping your upper body still, flex (bend) your elbows until the hand grips almost reach your collarbone. Return to the starting position.

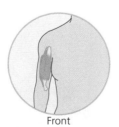

Front

Muscles developed:
Biceps, brachialis

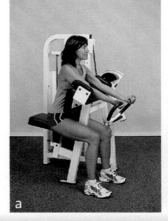

a   b

McGraw Hill **connect** http://www.mcgrawhillconnect.com/ |FITNESS AND WELLNESS

EXERCISE 6 Pullover

Instructions: Adjust the seat so your shoulders are aligned with the cams. Push down on the foot pads with your feet to bring the bar forward until you can place your elbows on the pads. Rest your hands lightly on the bar. If possible, place your feet flat on the floor. **(a)** To get into the starting position, let your arms go backward as far as possible. **(b)** Pull your elbows forward until the bar almost touches your abdomen. Return to the starting position.

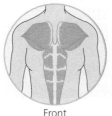

Front

Back

Muscles developed: Latissimus dorsi, pectoralis major and minor, triceps, rectus abdominis

a

b

EXERCISE 7 Lateral Raise

Instructions: **(a)** Adjust the seat so the pads rest just above your elbows when your upper arms are at your sides, your elbows are bent, and your forearms are parallel to the floor. Lightly grasp the handles. **(b)** Push outward and up with your arms until the pads are at shoulder height. Lead with your elbows rather than trying to lift the bars with your hands. Return to the starting position.

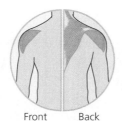

Front Back

Muscles developed: Deltoids, trapezius

a

b

EXERCISE 8 Triceps Extension

Note: *This exercise focuses on some of the same muscles as the assisted dip (Exercise 9); choose an appropriate exercise for your program based on your preferences and equipment availability.*

Instructions: **(a)** Adjust the seat so your back is straight and your arms rest comfortably against the top and side pads. Place your arms on the support cushions and grasp the hand grips with palms facing inward. **(b)** Keeping your upper body still, extend your elbows as much as possible. Return to the starting position.

Back

Muscles developed: Triceps

a

b

EXERCISE 9   Assisted Dip

Instructions: Set the weight according to the amount of assistance you need to complete a set of dips—the heavier the weight, the more assistance provided. **(a)** Stand or kneel on the assist platform with your body between the dip bars. With your elbows fully extended and palms facing your body, support your weight on your hands. **(b)** Lower your body until your upper arms are approximately parallel with the bars. Then push up until you reach the starting position.

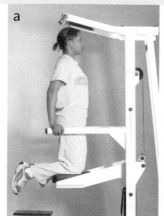

Front   Back

Muscles developed:
Triceps, deltoids, pectoralis major

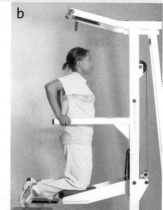

EXERCISE 10   Leg Press

Instructions: Sit or lie on the seat or bench, depending on the type of machine and the manufacturer's instructions. Your head, back, hips, and buttocks should be pressed against the machine pads. Loosely grasp the handles at the side of the machine. **(a)** Begin with your feet flat on the foot platform about shoulder-width apart. Extend your legs, but do not forcefully lock your knees. **(b)** Slowly lower the weight by bending your knees and flexing your hips until your knees are bent at about a 90-degree angle or your heels start to lift off the foot platform. Keep your lower back flat against the support pad. Then extend your knees and return to the starting position.

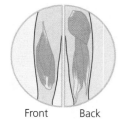

Front   Back

Muscles developed:
Gluteus maximus, quadriceps, hamstrings

EXERCISE 11   Leg Extension (Knee Extension)

Instructions: **(a)** Adjust the seat so the pads rest comfortably on top of your lower shins. Loosely grasp the handles. **(b)** Extend your knees until they are almost straight. Return to the starting position.

Knee extensions cause kneecap pain in some people. If you have kneecap pain during this exercise, check with an orthopedic specialist before repeating it.

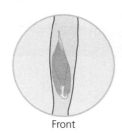

Front

Muscles developed:
Quadriceps

http://www.mcgrawhillconnect.com/
FITNESS AND WELLNESS

EXERCISE 12 — Seated Leg Curl

Instructions: (a) Sit on the seat with your back against the back pad and the leg pad below your calf muscles. **(b)** Flex your knees until your lower and upper legs form a 90-degree angle. Return to the starting position.

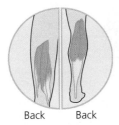

Back   Back

Muscles developed:
Hamstrings, gastrocnemius

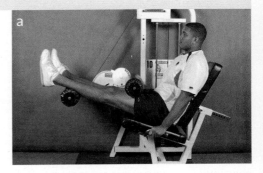

EXERCISE 13 — Heel Raise

Instructions: (a) Stand with your head between the pads and one pad on each shoulder. The balls of your feet should be on the platform. Lightly grasp the handles. **(b)** Press down with your toes while lifting your heels. Return to the starting position. Changing the direction your feet are pointing (straight ahead, inward, and outward) will work different portions of your calf muscles.

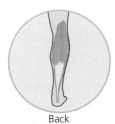

Back

Muscles developed:
Gastrocnemius, soleus

Note: *Abdominal machines, low-back machines, and trunk rotation machines are not recommended because of injury risk. Refer to the "Free Weights" exercise section for appropriate exercises to strengthen the abdominal and low-back muscles. For the rectus abdominus, obliques, and transvere abdominus, perform curl-ups (Exercise 9 in the "Free Weights" section), and for the erector spinae and quadratus lumborum, perform the spine extension and the isometric side bridge (Exercises 10 and 11 in the "Free Weights" section).*

Q Will I gain weight if I do resistance exercises?

A Your weight probably will not change significantly as a result of a general fitness program: one set of 8–12 repetitions of 8–10 exercises, performed on at least two nonconsecutive days per week. You will increase muscle mass and lose body fat, so your weight will stay about the same. You may notice a change in how your clothes fit, however, because muscle is denser than fat. Increased muscle mass will help you control body fat. Muscle increases your metabolism, which means you burn more calories every day. If you combine resistance exercises with endurance exercises, you will be on your way to developing a healthier body composition. Concentrate on fat loss rather than weight loss.

Q Do I need more protein in my diet when I train with weights?

A No. Although there is some evidence that power athletes involved in heavy training have a higher-than-normal protein requirement, there is no reason for most people to consume extra protein. Most Americans take in more protein than they need, so even if there is an increased protein need during heavy training, it is probably supplied by the average diet. Consuming a protein-rich snack before or after training may promote muscle hypertrophy.

Q What causes muscle soreness the day or two following a weight training workout?

A The muscle pain you feel a day or two after a heavy weight training workout is caused by injury to the muscle fibers and surrounding connective tissue. Contrary to popular belief, delayed-onset muscle soreness is not caused by lactic acid buildup. Scientists believe that injury to muscle fibers causes inflammation, which in turn causes the release of chemicals that break down part of the muscle tissue and cause pain. After a bout of intense exercise that causes muscle injury and delayed-onset muscle soreness, the muscles produce protective proteins that prevent soreness during future workouts. If you don't work out regularly, you lose these protective proteins and become susceptible to soreness again.

Q Will strength training improve my sports performance?

A Strength developed in the weight room does not automatically increase your power in sports such as skiing, tennis, or cycling. Hitting a forehand in tennis and making a turn on skis are precise skills that require coordination between your nervous system and muscles. For skilled people, movements become reflex; you don't think about them when you do them. Increasing strength can disturb this coordination. Only by simultaneously practicing a sport and improving fitness can you expect to become more powerful in the skill. Practice helps you integrate your new strength with your skills, which makes you more powerful. Consequently, you can hit the ball harder in tennis or make more graceful turns on the ski slopes. (Refer to Chapter 2 for more on the concept of specificity in physical training.)

Q Will I improve faster if I train every day?

A No. Your muscles need time to recover between training sessions. Doing resistance exercises every day will cause you to become overtrained, which will increase your chance of injury and impede your progress. If your strength training program reaches a plateau, try one of these strategies:

- Vary the number of sets. If you have been performing one set of each exercise, add sets.
- Train less frequently. If you are currently training the same muscle groups three or more times per week, you may not be allowing your muscles to fully recover from intense workouts.
- Change exercises. Using different exercises for the same muscle group may stimulate further strength development.
- Vary the load and number of repetitions. Try increasing or decreasing the loads you are using and changing the number of repetitions accordingly.
- If you are training alone, find a motivated training partner. A partner can encourage you and assist you with difficult lifts, forcing you to work harder.

Q If I stop training, will my muscles turn to fat?

A No. Fat and muscle are two different kinds of tissue, and one cannot turn into the other. Muscles that aren't used become smaller (atrophy), and body fat may increase if caloric intake exceeds calories burned. Although the result of inactivity may be smaller muscles and more fat, the change is caused by two separate processes.

Q Should I wear a weight belt when I lift?

A Until recently, most experts advised people to wear weight belts. However, several studies have shown that weight belts do not prevent back injuries and may, in fact, increase the risk of injury by encouraging people to lift more weight than they are capable of lifting with good form. Although wearing a belt may allow you to lift more weight in some lifts, you may not get the full benefit of your program because use of a weight belt reduces the effectiveness of the workout on the muscles that help support your spine.

For more Common Questions Answered about strength training, visit the Online Learning Center at www.mhhe.com/fahey.

- Hypertrophy (increased muscle fiber size) occurs when weight training causes the size and number of myofibrils to increase, thereby increasing total muscle size. Strength also increases through muscle learning. Most women do not develop large muscles from weight training.

- Improvements in muscular strength and endurance lead to enhanced physical performance, protection against injury, improved body composition, better self-image, improved muscle and bone health with aging, reduced risk of chronic disease, and decreased risk of premature death.

- Muscular strength can be assessed by determining the amount of weight that can be lifted in one repetition of an exercise. Muscular endurance can be assessed by determining the number of repetitions of a particular exercise that can be performed.

- Static (isometric) exercises involve contraction without movement. They are most useful when a person is recovering from an injury or surgery or needs to overcome weak points in a range of motion.

- Dynamic (isotonic) exercises involve contraction that results in movement. The two most common types are constant resistance (free weights) and variable resistance (many weight machines).

- Free weights and weight machines have pluses and minuses for developing fitness, although machines tend to be safer.

- Lifting heavy weights for only a few repetitions helps develop strength. Lifting lighter weights for more repetitions helps develop muscular endurance.

- A strength training program for general fitness includes at least one set of 8–12 repetitions (enough to cause fatigue) of 8–10 exercises, along with warm-up and cool-down periods. The program should be carried out at least 2 nonconsecutive days per week.

- Safety guidelines for strength training include using proper technique, using spotters and collars when necessary, and taking care of injuries.

- Supplements or drugs that are promoted as instant or quick "cures" usually don't work and are either dangerous, expensive, or both.

FOR FURTHER EXPLORATION

BOOKS

Baechle, T., and R. W. Earl. 2008. National Strength and Conditioning Association's *Essentials of Strength and Conditioning*. Champaign, Ill.: Human Kinetics. *A textbook of strength and conditioning for fitness professionals.*

Bjornlund, L. 2010. How Dangerous Are Performance-Enhancing Drugs? San Diego, Calif.: Referencepoint Press. *A discussion of the effects of performance-enhancing drugs on health, performance, and the integrity of sport. The author discusses the role of sports organizations in preventing drug use and whether they can be successful.*

Delavier, F. 2010. *Strength Training Anatomy*, 3rd ed. Champaign, Ill.: Human Kinetics. *Includes exercises for all major muscle groups as well as full anatomical pictures of the muscular system.* Women's Strength Training Anatomy, *a matching volume for women, was published in 2003.*

Fahey, T. D. 2011. *Basic Weight Training for Men and Women*, 8th ed. New York: McGraw-Hill. *A practical guide to developing training programs, using free weights, tailored to individual needs.*

Goldenberg, L., and P. Twist. 2007. *Strength Ball Training*. Champaign, Ill.: Human Kinetics. *A guide to incorporating exercise balls and medicine balls into a complete weight training program.*

Lethi, A., et al. 2007. *Free-Weight Training*. Berkeley, Calif.: Thunder Bay Press. *A complete guide to training with free weights, with special instructions for using weights with an exercise ball.*

Tsatsouline, P. 2010. *Enter the Kettlebell*. Minneapolis, Minn.: Dragon Door Publications. *A guide to basic strength training using kettlebells.*

ORGANIZATIONS AND WEB SITES

American College of Sports Medicine Position Stand: Progression Models in Resistance Training for Healthy Adults. Provides an in-depth look at strategies for setting up a strength training program and making progress based on individual program goals.
http://journals.lww.com/acsm-msse/Fulltext/2009/03000/Progression_Models_in_Resistance_Training_for.26.aspx

Dan John. An excellent Web site for people serious about improving strength and fitness, written by a world-class athlete and coach in track and field and Highland games.
http://danjohn.net

Georgia State University: Strength Training. Provides information about the benefits of strength training and ways to develop a safe and effective program; also includes illustrations of a variety of exercises.
http://www2.gsu.edu/~wwwfit/strength.html

Human Anatomy On-line. Provides text, illustrations, and animation about the muscular system, nerve-muscle connections, muscular contraction, and other topics.
http://www.innerbody.com/htm/body.html

Mayo Clinic: Weight Training: Improve Your Muscular Fitness. Provides a basic overview of weight training essentials along with links to many other articles on specific weight training-related topics.
http://www.mayoclinic.com/health/weight-training/HQ01627

National Strength and Conditioning Association. A professional organization that focuses on strength development for fitness and athletic performance.
http://www.nsca-lift.org

Pilates Method Alliance. Provides information about Pilates and about instructor certification; includes a directory of instructors.
http://www.pilatesmethodalliance.org

University of California, San Diego: Muscle Physiology Home Page. Provides an introduction to muscle physiology, including information about types of muscle fibers and energy cycles.
http://muscle.ucsd.edu/index.shtml

University of Michigan: Muscles in Action. Interactive descriptions of muscle movements.
http://www.med.umich.edu/lrc/Hypermuscle/Hyper.html
See also the listings in Chapter 2.

SELECTED BIBLIOGRAPHY

Ahtiainen, J. P., et al. 2011. Recovery after heavy resistance exercise and skeletal muscle androgen receptor and insulin-like growth factor-i isoform expression in strength trained men. *Journal of Strength and Conditioning Research* 25(3): 767–777.

American College of Sports Medicine. 2009. *ACSM's Guidelines for Exercise Testing and Prescription,* 8th ed. Philadelphia: Lippincott Williams and Wilkins.

American College of Sports Medicine. 2009. *ACSM's Resource Manual for Guidelines for Exercise Testing and Prescription,* 6th ed. Philadelphia: Lippincott Williams and Wilkins.

American College of Sports Medicine. 2009. American College of Sports Medicine position stand: Progression models in resistance training for healthy adults. *Medicine and Science in Sports and Exercise* 41(3): 687–708.

Arikawa, A. Y., et al. 2011. Adherence to a strength training intervention in adult women. *Journal of Physical Activity and Health* 8(1): 111–118.

Bellar, D. M., et al. 2011. The Effects of Combined Elastic- and Free-Weight Tension vs. Free-Weight Tension on One-Repetition Maximum Strength in the Bench Press. *Journal of Strength and Conditioning Research* 25(2): 459–463.

Blazevich, A. J., et al. 2007. Lack of human muscle architectural adaptation after short-term strength training. *Muscle and Nerve* 35(1): 78–86.

Bouchard, D. R., et al. 2011. Association between muscle mass, leg strength, and fat mass with physical function in older adults: Influence of age and sex. *Journal of Aging and Health* 23(2): 313–328.

Brentano, M. A., et al. 2011. A review on strength exercise-induced muscle damage: applications, adaptation mechanisms and limitations. *Journal of Sports Medicine and Physical Fitness* 51(1): 1–10.

Brooks, G. A., et al. 2005. *Exercise Physiology: Human Bioenergetics and Its Applications,* 4th ed. New York: McGraw-Hill.

Brooks, N., et al. 2006. Strength training improves muscle quality and insulin sensitivity in Hispanic older adults with type 2 diabetes. *International Journal of Medical Sciences* 4(1): 19–27.

Burt, J., et al. 2007. A comparison of once versus twice per week training on leg press strength in women. *Journal of Sports Medicine and Physical Fitness* 47(1): 13–17.

Cadore, E. L., et al. 2011. Effects of strength, endurance, and concurrent training on aerobic power and dynamic neuromuscular economy in elderly men. *Journal of Strength and Conditioning Research* 25(3): 758–766.

Carlsohn, A., et al. 2011. How much is too much? A case report of nutritional supplement use of a high-performance athlete. *British Journal Nutrition* 1–5.

Caserotti, P., et al. 2008. Explosive heavy-resistance training in old and very old adults: Changes in rapid muscle force, strength and power. *Scandinavian Journal of Medicine and Science in Sports* 18(6): 773–782.

Davis, W. J., et al. 2008. Concurrent training enhances athletes' strength, muscle endurance, and other measures. *Journal of Strength and Conditioning Research* 22(5): 1487–1502.

Dengel, D. R., et al. 2011. Gender differences in vascular function and insulin sensitivity in young adults. *Clinical Sciences* 120(4): 153–160.

Farrar, R. E., et al. 2010. Oxygen cost of kettlebell swings. *Journal of Strength and Conditioning Research* 24(4): 1034–1036.

Gee, T. I., et al. 2011. Strength and conditioning practices in rowing. *Journal of Strength and Conditioning Research* 25(3): 668–682.

Graham, M. R., et al. 2008. Anabolic steroid use: Patterns of use and detection of doping. *Sports Medicine* 38(6): 505–525.

Haskell, W. L., et al. 2007. Physical activity and public health: updated recommendation for adults from the American College of Sports Medicine and the American Heart Association. *Circulation* 116(9): 1081–1093.

Headley, S. A., et al. 2011. Effects of lifting tempo on one repetition maximum and hormonal responses to a bench press protocol. *Journal of Strength and Conditioning Research* 25(2): 406–413.

Heikkinen, A., et al. 2011. Use of dietary supplements in Olympic athletes is decreasing: A follow-up study between 2002 and 2009. *Journal of the International Society of Sports Nutrition* 8(1): 1.

Hoffman, J. R., et al. 2008. Nutritional supplementation and anabolic steroid use in adolescents. *Medicine and Science in Sports and Exercise* 40(1): 15–24.

Ikeda, E. R., et al. 2009. The valsalva maneuver revisited: The influence of voluntary breathing on isometric muscle strength. *Journal of Strength and Conditioning Research* 23(1): 127–132.

Jay, K., et al. 2010. Kettlebell training for musculoskeletal and cardiovascular health: A randomized controlled trial. *Scandinavian Journal of Work and Environmental Health.* Published online December 2010.

Kell, R. T. 2011. The influence of periodized resistance training on strength changes in men and women. *Journal of Strength and Conditioning Research* 25(3): 735–744.

Kirk, E. P., et al. 2007. Six months of supervised high-intensity low-volume resistance training improves strength independent of changes in muscle mass in young overweight men. *Journal of Strength and Conditioning Research* 21(1): 151–156.

Lindegaard, B., et al. 2008. The effect of strength and endurance training on insulin sensitivity and fat distribution in human immunodeficiency virus-infected patients with lipodystrophy. *Journal of Clinical Endocrinology and Metabolism* 93(10): 3860–3869.

Machado, M. V., et al. 2011. The dark side of sports: Using steroids may harm your liver. *Liver International* 31(3): 280–281.

Manore, M., et al. 2011. BJSM reviews: A-Z of nutritional supplements: dietary supplements, sports nutrition foods and ergogenic aids for health and performance—Part 16. *British Journal Sports Medicine* 45(1): 73–74.

Newsholme, P., et al. 2011. BJSM reviews: A to Z of nutritional supplements: dietary supplements, sports nutrition foods and ergogenic aids for health and performance—Part 18. *British Journal Sports Medicine* 45(3): 230–232.

Norrbrand, L., et al. 2008. Resistance training using eccentric overload induces early adaptations in skeletal muscle size. *European Journal of Applied Physiology* 102(3): 271–281.

Reitelseder, S., et al. 2011. Whey and casein labeled with L-[1-13C]leucine and muscle protein synthesis: Effect of resistance exercise and protein ingestion. *American Journal of Physiology, Endocrinology and Metabolism* 300(1): E231–242.

Ruiz, J. R., et al. 2008. Association between muscular strength and mortality in men: Prospective cohort study. *British Medical Journal* 337: a439, published online.

Saeterbakken, A. H., et al. 2011. A comparison of muscle activity and 1-RM strength of three chest-press exercises with different stability requirements. *Journal of Sports Science* 1–6.

Santos, E. J., et al. 2011. The effects of plyometric training followed by detraining and reduced training periods on explosive strength in adolescent male basketball players. *Journal of Strength and Conditioning Research* 25(2): 441–452.

Schick, E. E., et al. 2010. A comparison of muscle activation between a Smith machine and free weight bench press. *Journal of Strength and Conditioning Research* 24(3): 779–784.

Sedano, S., et al. 2011. Effects of plyometric training on explosive strength, acceleration capacity and kicking speed in young elite soccer players. *Journal of Sports Medicine and Physical Fitness* 51(1): 50–58.

Senchina, D. S., et al. 2011. BJSM reviews: A-Z of nutritional supplements: dietary supplements, sports nutrition foods and ergogenic aids for health and performance—Part 17. *British Journal Sports Medicine* 45(2): 150–151.

Wieser, M., and P. Haber. 2007. The effects of systematic resistance training in the elderly. *International Journal of Sports Medicine* 28(1): 59–65.

Winchester, J. B., et al. 2008. Eight weeks of ballistic exercise improves power independently of changes in strength and muscle fiber type expression. *Journal of Strength and Conditioning Research* 22(6): 1728–1734.

Young, W. B., et al. 2011. Enhancing foot velocity in football kicking: the role of strength training. *Journal of Strength and Conditioning Research* 25(2): 561–566.

LAB 4.1 Assessing Your Current Level of Muscular Strength

For best results, don't do any strenuous weight training within 48 hours of any test. Use great caution when completing 1-RM tests; do not take the maximum bench press test if you have any injuries to your shoulders, elbows, back, hips, or knees. In addition, do not take these tests until you have had at least one month of weight training experience.

The Maximum Bench Press Test

Equipment

The free weights bench press test uses the following equipment

1. Flat bench (with or without racks)
2. Barbell
3. Assorted weight plates, with collars to hold them in place
4. One or two spotters
5. Weight scale

If a weight machine is preferred, use the following equipment:

1. Universal Gym Dynamic Variable Resistance Machine
2. Weight scale

Maximum bench press test.

Preparation

Try a few bench presses with a small amount of weight so you can practice your technique, warm up your muscles, and, if you use free weights, coordinate your movements with those of your spotters. Weigh yourself and record the results.

Body weight: _____ lb

Instructions

1. Use a weight that is lower than the amount you believe you can lift. For free weights, men should begin with a weight about two-thirds of their body weight; women should begin with the weight of just the bar (45 lb).

2. Lie on the bench with your feet firmly on the floor. If you are using a weight machine, grasp the handles with palms away from you; the tops of the handles should be aligned with the tops of your armpits.

   If you are using free weights, grasp the bar slightly wider than shoulder width with your palms away from you. If you have one spotter, she or he should stand directly behind the bench; if you have two spotters, they should stand to the side, one at each end of the barbell. Signal to the spotter when you are ready to begin the test by saying "1, 2, 3." On "3," the spotter should help you lift the weight to a point over your midchest (nipple line).

3. Push the handles or barbell until your arms are fully extended. Exhale as you lift. If you are using free weights, the weight moves from a low point at the chest straight up. Keep your feet firmly on the floor, don't arch your back, and push the weight evenly with your right and left arms. Don't bounce the weight on your chest.

4. Rest for several minutes, then repeat the lift with a heavier weight. It will probably take several attempts to determine the maximum amount of weight you can lift (1 RM).

   1 RM: _____ lb   Check one: _____ Free weights _____ Universal _____ Other

5. If you used free weights, convert your free weights bench press score to an estimated value for 1 RM on the Universal bench press using the appropriate formula:

   Males: Estimated Universal 1 RM = (1.016 × free weights 1 RM _____ lb) + 18.41 = _____ lb

   Females: Estimated Universal 1 RM = (0.848 × free weights 1 RM _____ lb) + 21.37 = _____ lb

Rating Your Bench Press Result

1. Divide your Universal 1-RM value by your body weight.

   1 RM _____ lb ÷ body weight _____ lb = _____

2. Find this ratio in the table to determine your bench press strength rating. Record the rating here and in the chart at the end of this lab.

   Bench press strength rating: _____

Strength Ratings for the Maximum Bench Press Test

	Pounds Lifted/Body Weight (lb)					
Men	*Very Poor*	*Poor*	*Fair*	*Good*	*Excellent*	*Superior*
Age: Under 20	Below 0.89	0.89–1.05	1.06–1.18	1.19–1.33	1.34–1.75	Above 1.75
20–29	Below 0.88	0.88–0.98	0.99–1.13	1.14–1.31	1.32–1.62	Above 1.62
30–39	Below 0.78	0.78–0.87	0.88–0.97	0.98–1.11	1.12–1.34	Above 1.34
40–49	Below 0.72	0.72–0.79	0.80–0.87	0.88–0.99	1.00–1.19	Above 1.19
50–59	Below 0.63	0.63–0.70	0.71–0.78	0.79–0.89	0.90–1.04	Above 1.04
60 and over	Below 0.57	0.57–0.65	0.66–0.71	0.72–0.81	0.82–0.93	Above 0.93
Women						
Age: Under 20	Below 0.53	0.53–0.57	0.58–0.64	0.65–0.76	0.77–0.87	Above 0.87
20–29	Below 0.51	0.51–0.58	0.59–0.69	0.70–0.79	0.80–1.00	Above 1.00
30–39	Below 0.47	0.47–0.52	0.53–0.59	0.60–0.69	0.70–0.81	Above 0.81
40–49	Below 0.43	0.43–0.49	0.50–0.53	0.54–0.61	0.62–0.76	Above 0.76
50–59	Below 0.39	0.39–0.43	0.44–0.47	0.48–0.54	0.55–0.67	Above 0.67
60 and over	Below 0.38	0.38–0.42	0.43–0.46	0.47–0.53	0.54–0.71	Above 0.71

SOURCE: Based on norms from The Cooper Institute of Aerobic Research, Dallas, Texas; from *The Physical Fitness Specialist Manual*, revised 2002. Used with permission.

Predicting 1 RM from Multiple-Repetition Lifts Using Free Weights

Instead of doing the 1-RM maximum strength bench press test, you can predict your 1 RM from multiple-repetition lifts.

Instructions

1. Choose a weight you think you can bench press five times.

2. Follow the instructions for lifting the weight given in the maximum bench press test.

3. Do as many repetitions of the bench press as you can. A repetition counts only if done correctly

4. Refer to the chart on p. 131, or calculate predicted 1 RM using the Brzycki equation:

   1 RM = *weight* ÷ (1.0278 − [0.0278 × *number of repetitions*])

   1 RM = _____ lb ÷ (1.0278 − [0.0278 × _____ repetitions]) = _____

5. Divide your predicted 1-RM value by your body weight.

   1 RM _____ lb ÷ body weight _____ lb = _____

6. Find this ratio in the table above to determine your bench press strength rating. Record the rating here and in the chart at the end of the lab.

   Bench press strength rating: _____

RMs from the Multiple-Repetitions Bench Press Test

Weight Lifted (lb)	Repetitions											
	1	2	3	4	5	6	7	8	9	10	11	12
66	66	68	70	72	74	77	79	82	85	88	91	95
77	77	79	82	84	87	89	92	96	99	103	107	111
88	88	91	93	96	99	102	106	109	113	117	122	127
99	99	102	105	108	111	115	119	123	127	132	137	143
110	110	113	116	120	124	128	132	137	141	147	152	158
121	121	124	128	132	136	141	145	150	156	161	168	174
132	132	136	140	144	149	153	158	164	170	176	183	190
143	143	147	151	156	161	166	172	178	184	191	198	206
154	154	158	163	168	173	179	185	191	198	205	213	222
165	165	170	175	180	186	192	198	205	212	220	229	238
176	176	181	186	192	198	204	211	219	226	235	244	254
187	187	192	198	204	210	217	224	232	240	249	259	269
198	198	204	210	216	223	230	238	246	255	264	274	285
209	209	215	221	228	235	243	251	259	269	279	289	301
220	220	226	233	240	248	256	264	273	283	293	305	317
231	231	238	245	252	260	268	277	287	297	308	320	333
242	242	249	256	264	272	281	290	300	311	323	335	349
253	253	260	268	276	285	294	304	314	325	337	350	364
264	264	272	280	288	297	307	317	328	340	352	366	380
275	275	283	291	300	309	319	330	341	354	367	381	396
286	286	294	303	312	322	332	343	355	368	381	396	412
297	297	305	314	324	334	345	356	369	382	396	411	428
308	308	317	326	336	347	358	370	382	396	411	427	444

SOURCE: Brzycki, M. 1993. Strength testing—predicting a one-rep max from reps to fatigue. *The Journal of Physical Education, Recreation and Dance* 64: 88–90. January 1993, a publication of the American Alliance for Health, Physical Education, Recreation and Dance, www.aahperd.org. Reprinted with permission.

Functional Leg Strength Tests

The following tests assess functional leg strength using squats. Most people do squats improperly increasing their risk of knee and back pain. Before you add weight-bearing squats to your weight training program, you should determine your functional leg strength, check your ability to squat properly, and give yourself a chance to master squatting movements. The following leg strength tests will help you in each of these areas.

These tests are progressively more difficult, so do not move to the next test until you have scored at least a 3 on the current test. On each test, give yourself a rating of 0, 1, 3, or 5, as described in the instructions that follow the last test.

1. Chair Squat

Instructions

1. Sit up straight in a chair with your back resting against the backrest and your arms at your sides. Your feet should be placed more than shoulder-width apart so that you can get them under the body.

2. Begin the motion of rising out of the chair by flexing (bending) at the hips—not the back. Then squat up using a hip hinge movement (no spine movement). Stand without rocking forward, bending your back, or using external support, and keep your head in a neutral position.

Mc Graw Hill **connect** http://www.mcgrawhillconnect.com/ |FITNESS AND WELLNESS

3. Return to the sitting position while maintaining a straight back and keeping your weight centered over your feet. Your thighs should abduct (spread) as you sit back in the chair. Use your rear hip and thigh muscles as much as possible as you sit.

Do five repetitions.

Your rating: _____

(See rating instructions that follow.)

2. Single-Leg Step-Up

Instructions

1. Stand facing a bench, with your right foot placed on the middle of the bench, right knee bent at 90 degrees, and arms at your sides.
2. Step up on the bench until your right leg is straight, maximizing the use of the hip muscles.
3. Return to the starting position. Keep your hips stable, back straight, chest up, shoulders back, and head neutral during the entire movement.

Do five repetitions for each leg.

Your rating: _____

(See rating instructions that follow.)

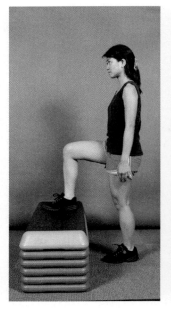 

3. Unweighted Squat

Instructions

1. Stand with your feet placed slightly more than shoulder-width apart, toes pointed out slightly, hands on hips or across your chest, head neutral, and back straight. Center your weight over your arches or slightly behind.
2. Squat down, keeping your weight centered over your arches and actively flexing (bending) your hips until your legs break parallel. During the movement, keep your back straight, shoulders back, and chest out, and let your thighs part to the side so that you are "squatting between your legs."
3. Push back up to the starting position, hinging at the hips and not with the spine, maximizing the use of the rear hip and thigh muscles, and maintaining a straight back and neutral head position.

Do five repetitions.

Your rating: _____

(See rating instructions that follow.)

4. Single-Leg Lunge-Squat with Rear-Foot Support

Instructions

1. Stand about 3 feet in front of a bench (with your back to the bench).

2. Place the instep of your left foot on the bench, and put most of your weight on your right leg (your left leg should be bent), with your hands at your sides.

3. Squat on your right leg until your thigh is parallel with the floor. Keep your back straight, chest up, shoulders back, and head neutral.

4. Return to the starting position.

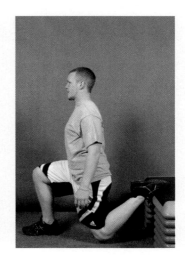

Do three repetitions for each leg.

Your rating: _____

(See rating instructions that follow.)

Rating Your Functional Leg Strength Test Results

5 points: Performed the exercise properly with good back and thigh position, weight centered over the middle or rear of the foot, chest out, and shoulders back; good use of hip muscles on the way down and on the way up, with head in a neutral position throughout the movement; maintained good form during all repetitions; abducted (spread) the thighs on the way down during chair squats and double-leg squats; for single-leg exercises, showed good strength on both sides; for single-leg lunge-squat with rear-foot support, maintained straight back, and knees stayed behind toes.

3 points: Weight was forward on the toes, with some rounding of the back; used thigh muscles excessively, with little use of hip muscles; head and chest were too far forward; showed little abduction of the thighs during double-leg squats; when going down for single-leg exercises, one side was stronger than the other; form deteriorated with repetitions; for single-leg lunge-squat with rear-foot support, could not reach parallel (thigh parallel with floor).

1 point: Had difficulty performing the movement, rocking forward and rounding back badly; used thigh muscles excessively, with little use of hip muscles on the way up or on the way down; chest and head were forward; on unweighted squats, had difficulty reaching parallel and showed little abduction of the thighs; on single-leg exercises, one leg was markedly stronger than the other; could not perform multiple repetitions.

0 points: Could not perform the exercise.

Summary of Results

Maximum bench press test from either the 1-RM test or the multiple-repetition test: Weight pressed: _____ lb Rating: _____

Functional leg strength tests (0–5): Chair squat: _____ Single-leg step-up: _____ Unweighted squat: _____

Single-leg lunge-squat with rear-foot support: _____

Remember that muscular strength is specific: Your ratings may vary considerably for different parts of your body.

Mc Graw Hill **connect** http://www.mcgrawhillconnect.com/
FITNESS AND WELLNESS

Using Your Results

How did you score? Are you surprised by your ratings for muscular strength? Are you satisfied with your current ratings?

If you're not satisfied, set realistic goals for improvement:

Are you satisfied with your current level of muscular strength as evidenced in your daily life—for example, your ability to lift objects, climb stairs, and engage in sports and recreational activities?

If you're not satisfied, set realistic goals for improvement:

What should you do next? Enter the results of this lab in the Preprogram Assessment column in Appendix C. If you've set goals for improvement, begin planning your strength training program by completing the plan in Lab 4.3. After several weeks of your program, complete this lab again and enter the results in the Postprogram Assessment column of Appendix C. How do the results compare?

LAB 4.2 Assessing Your Current Level of Muscular Endurance

For best results, don't do any strenuous weight training within 48 hours of any test. To assess endurance of the abdominal muscles, perform the curl-up test. To assess endurance of muscles in the upper body, perform the push-up test. To assess endurance of the muscles in the lower body, perform the squat endurance test.

The Curl-Up Test

Equipment

1. Four 6-inch strips of self-stick Velcro or heavy tape
2. Ruler
3. Partner
4. Mat (optional)

Preparation

Affix the strips of Velcro or long strips of tape on the mat or testing surface. Place the strips 3 inches apart.

Instructions

1. Start by lying on your back on the floor or mat, arms straight and by your sides, shoulders relaxed, palms down and on the floor, and fingers straight. Adjust your position so that the longest fingertip of each hand touches the end of the near strip of Velcro or tape. Your knees should be bent about 90 degrees, with your feet about 12–18 inches from your buttocks.

2. To perform a curl-up, flex your spine while sliding your fingers across the floor until the fingertips of each hand reach the second strip of Velcro or tape. Then return to the starting position; the shoulders must be returned to touch the mat between curl-ups, but the head need not touch. Shoulders must remain relaxed throughout the curl-up, and feet and buttocks must stay on the floor. Breathe easily exhaling during the lift phase of the curl-up; do not hold your breath.

3. Once your partner says "go," perform as many curl-ups as you can at a steady pace with correct form. Your partner counts the curl-ups you perform and calls a stop to the test if she or he notices any incorrect form or drop in your pace.

   Number of curl-ups: _____

 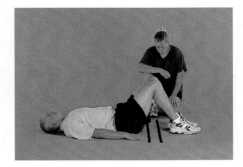

Rating Your Curl-Up Test Result

Your score is the number of completed curl-ups. Refer to the appropriate portion of the table for a rating of your abdominal muscular endurance. Record your rating below and in the summary at the end of this lab.

Rating: _____

Mc Graw Hill **connect** http://www.mcgrawhillconnect.com/
FITNESS AND WELLNESS

Ratings for the Curl-Up Test

	Number of Curl-Ups					
Men	*Very Poor*	*Poor*	*Average*	*Good*	*Excellent*	*Superior*
Age: 16–19	Below 48	48–57	58–64	65–74	75–93	Above 93
20–29	Below 46	46–54	55–63	64–74	75–93	Above 93
30–39	Below 40	40–47	48–55	56–64	65–81	Above 81
40–49	Below 38	38–45	46–53	54–62	63–79	Above 79
50–59	Below 36	36–43	44–51	52–60	61–77	Above 77
60–69	Below 33	33–40	41–48	49–57	58–74	Above 74
Women						
Age: 16–19	Below 42	42–50	51–58	59–67	68–84	Above 84
20–29	Below 41	41–51	52–57	58–66	67–83	Above 83
30–39	Below 38	38–47	48–56	57–66	67–85	Above 85
40–49	Below 36	36–45	46–54	55–64	65–83	Above 83
50–59	Below 34	34–43	44–52	53–62	63–81	Above 81
60–69	Below 31	31–40	41–49	50–59	60–78	Above 78

SOURCE: Ratings based on norms calculated from data collected by Robert Lualhati on 4545 college students, 16–80 years of age, at Skyline College, San Bruno, California. Used with permission.

The Push-Up Test

Equipment: Mat or towel (optional)

Preparation

In this test, you will perform either standard push-ups or modified push-ups, in which you support yourself with your knees. The Cooper Institute developed the ratings for this test with men performing push-ups and women performing modified push-ups. Biologically, males tend to be stronger than females; the modified technique reduces the need for upper-body strength in a test of muscular endurance. Therefore, for an accurate assessment of upper-body endurance, men should perform standard push-ups and women should perform modified push-ups. However, in using push-ups as part of a strength training program, individuals should choose the technique most appropriate for increasing their level of strength and endurance—regardless of gender.

Instructions

1. *For push-ups:* Start in the push-up position with your body supported by your hands and feet. *For modified push-ups:* Start in the modified push-up position with your body supported by your hands and knees. *For both positions*, keep your arms and your back straight and your fingers pointed forward.

2. Lower your chest to the floor with your back straight, and then return to the starting position.

3. Perform as many push-ups or modified push-ups as you can without stopping.

   Number of push-ups: _____ or number of modified push-ups: _____

Rating Your Push-Up Test Result

Your score is the number of completed push-ups or modified push-ups. Refer to the appropriate portion of the table for a rating of your upper-body endurance. Record your rating below and in the summary at the end of this lab.

Rating: _____

Ratings for the Push-Up and Modified Push-Up Tests

Number of Push-Ups

Men	Very Poor	Poor	Fair	Good	Excellent	Superior
Age: 18–29	Below 22	22–28	29–36	37–46	47–61	Above 61
30–39	Below 17	17–23	24–29	30–38	39–51	Above 51
40–49	Below 11	11–17	18–23	24–29	30–39	Above 39
50–59	Below 9	9–12	13–18	19–24	25–38	Above 38
60 and over	Below 6	6–9	10–17	18–22	23–27	Above 27

Number of Modified Push-Ups

Women	Very Poor	Poor	Fair	Good	Excellent	Superior
Age: 18–29	Below 17	17–22	23–29	30–35	36–44	Above 44
30–39	Below 11	11–18	19–23	24–30	31–38	Above 38
40–49	Below 6	6–12	13–17	18–23	24–32	Above 32
50–59	Below 6	6–11	12–16	17–20	21–27	Above 27
60 and over	Below 2	2–4	5–11	12–14	15–19	Above 19

SOURCE: Based on norms from The Cooper Institute of Aerobic Research, Dallas, Texas; from *The Physical Fitness Specialist Manual,* revised 2002. Used with permission.

The Squat Endurance Test

Instructions

1. Stand with your feet placed slightly more than shoulder width apart, toes pointed out slightly hands on hips or across your chest, head neutral, and back straight. Center your weight over your arches or slightly behind.

2. Squat down, keeping your weight centered over your arches, until your thighs are parallel with the floor. Push back up to the starting position, maintaining a straight back and neutral head position.

3. Perform as many squats as you can without stopping.

   Number of squats: _____

Rating Your Squat Endurance Test Result

Your score is the number of completed squats. Refer to the appropriate portion of the table for a rating of your leg muscular endurance. Record your rating below and in the summary at the end of this lab. Rating: _____

Ratings for the Squat Endurance Test

Number of Squats Performed

Men	Very Poor	Poor	Below Average	Average	Above Average	Good	Excellent
Age: 18–25	<25	25–30	31–34	35–38	39–43	44–49	>49
26–35	<22	22–28	29–30	31–34	35–39	40–45	>45
36–45	<17	17–22	23–26	27–29	30–34	35–41	>41
46–55	<9	13–17	18–21	22–24	25–38	29–35	>35
56–65	<9	9–12	13–16	17–20	21–24	25–31	>31
65 +	<7	7–10	11–14	15–18	19–21	22–28	>28

Women	Very Poor	Poor	Below Average	Average	Above Average	Good	Excellent
Age: 18–25	<18	18–24	25–28	29–32	33–36	37–43	>43
26–35	<20	13–20	21–24	25–28	29–32	33–39	>39
36–45	<7	7–14	15–18	19–22	23–26	27–33	>33
46–55	<5	5–9	10–13	14–17	18–21	22–27	>27
56–65	<3	3–6	7–9	10–12	13–17	18–24	>24
65+	<2	2–4	5–10	11–13	14–16	17–23	>23

SOURCE: www.topendsports.com/testing/tests/home-squat.htm

http://www.mcgrawhillconnect.com/
FITNESS AND WELLNESS

Summary of Results

Curl-up test: Number of curl-ups: _____ Rating: _____

Push-up test: Number of push-ups: _____ Rating: _____

Squat endurance test: Number of squats: _____ Rating: _____

Remember that muscular endurance is specific: Your ratings may vary considerably for different parts of your body.

Using Your Results

How did you score? Are you surprised by your ratings for muscular endurance? Are you satisfied with your current ratings?

If you're not satisfied, set realistic goals for improvement:

Are you satisfied with your current level of muscular endurance as evidenced in your daily life—for example, your ability to carry groceries or your books, hike, and do yard work?

If you're not satisfied, set realistic goals for improvement:

What should you do next? Enter the results of this lab in the Preprogram Assessment column in Appendix C. If you've set goals for improvement, begin planning your strength training program by completing the plan in Lab 4.3. After several weeks of your program, complete this lab again and enter the results in the Postprogram Assessment column of Appendix C. How do the results compare?

Name _____ **Section** _____ **Date** _____

LAB 4.3 Designing and Monitoring a Strength Training Program

1. *Set goals.* List goals for your strength training program. Your goals can be specific or general, short or long term. In the first section, include specific, measurable goals that you can use to track the progress of your fitness program—for example, raising your upper-body muscular strength rating from fair to good or being able to complete 10 repetitions of a lat pull with 125 pounds of resistance. In the second section, include long-term and more qualitative goals, such as improving self-confidence and reducing your risk for back pain.

Specific Goals: Current Status

_____

_____

_____

Final Goals

_____

_____

_____

Other goals: _____

_____

2. *Choose exercises.* Based on your goals, choose 8–10 exercises to perform during each weight training session. If your goal is general training for wellness, use the sample program in Figure 4.2 on p. 109. List your exercises and the muscles they develop in your program plan.

3. *Frequency: Choose the number of training sessions per week.* Work out at least 2 nonconsecutive days per week. Indicate the days you will train in your program plan; be sure to include days of rest to allow your body to recover.

4. *Intensity: Choose starting weights.* Experiment with different amounts of weight until you settle on a good starting weight, one that you can lift easily for 10–12 repetitions. As you progress in your program, add more weight. Fill in the starting weight for each exercise in your program plan.

5. *Time: Choose a starting number of sets and repetitions.* Include at least 1 set of 8–12 repetitions of each exercise. (When you add weight, you may have to decrease the number of repetitions slightly until your muscles adapt to the heavier load.) If your program is focusing on strength alone, your sets can contain fewer repetitions using a heavier load. If you are over approximately age 50–60, your sets should contain more repetitions (10–15) using a lighter load. Fill in the starting number of sets and repetitions of each exercise in your program plan.

6. *Monitor your progress.* Use the workout card on the next page to monitor your progress and keep track of exercises, weights, sets, and repetitions.

Program Plan for Weight Training

| Exercise | Muscle(s) Developed | Frequency (check ✓) | | | | | | | Intensity: Weight (lb) | Time | |
		M	T	W	Th	F	Sa	Su		Repetitions	Sets

Mc Graw Hill **connect** http://www.mcgrawhillconnect.com/
FITNESS AND WELLNESS

WORKOUT CARD FOR _____

Exercise/Date	Wt	Sets	Reps	Wt	Sets	Reps	Wt	Sets	Reps	Wt	Sets	Reps	Wt	Sets	Reps	Wt	Sets	Reps	Wt	Sets	Reps	Wt	Sets	Reps	Wt	Sets	Reps	Wt	Sets	Reps	Wt	Sets	Reps	Wt	Sets	Reps

CHAPTER 9

Flexibility and Low-Back Health

LOOKING AHEAD...

After reading this chapter, you should be able to:

- Identify the potential benefits of flexibility and stretching exercises
- List the factors that affect a joint's flexibility
- Describe the different types of stretching exercises and how they affect muscles
- Describe the intensity, duration, and frequency of stretching exercises that will develop the most flexibility with the lowest risk of injury
- List safe stretching exercises for major joints
- Explain how low-back pain can be prevented and managed

TEST YOUR KNOWLEDGE

1. Stretching exercises should be performed
   a. at the start of a warm-up.
   b. first thing in the morning.
   c. after endurance exercise or strength training.

2. If you injure your back, it's usually best to rest in bed until the pain is completely gone. True or false?

3. It is better to hold a stretch for a short time than to "bounce" while stretching. True or false?

Answers

1. **c.** It's best to do stretching exercises when your muscles are warm. Intensely stretching muscles before exercise may temporarily reduce their explosive strength and interfere with neuromuscular control.

2. **False.** Prolonged bed rest may actually worsen back pain. Limit bed rest to a day or less, treat pain and inflammation with cold and then heat, and begin moderate physical activity as soon as possible.

3. **True.** "Bouncing" during stretching can damage your muscles. This type of stretching, called ballistic stretching, should be used only by well-conditioned athletes for specific purposes. A person of average fitness should stretch slowly, holding each stretch for 10–30 seconds.

Mc Graw Hill **connect** http://www.mcgrawhillconnect.com
FITNESS AND WELLNESS

Mc Graw Hill **LearnSmart**
GET A BETTER GRADE. TRY LEARNSMART.

Flexibility—the ability of a joint to move through its normal, full **range of motion**—is important for general fitness and wellness. Flexibility is a highly adaptable physical fitness component. It increases in response to a regular program of stretching exercises and decreases with inactivity. Flexibility is also specific: Good flexibility in one joint doesn't necessarily mean good flexibility in another. You can increase your flexibility by doing regular stretching exercises for all your major joints.

This chapter describes the factors that affect flexibility and the benefits of maintaining good flexibility. It provides guidelines for assessing your current level of flexibility and putting together a successful stretching program. It also examines the common problem of low-back pain.

TYPES OF FLEXIBILITY

There are two types of flexibility:

- *Static flexibility* is the ability to hold an extended position at one end or point in a joint's range of motion. For example, static flexibility determines how far you can extend your arm across the front of your body or out to the side. Static flexibility depends on your ability to tolerate stretched muscles; the structure of your joints; and the tightness of muscles, tendons, and ligaments.

- *Dynamic flexibility* is the ability to move a joint through its range of motion with little resistance. For example, dynamic flexibility affects your ability to pitch a ball or swing a golf club. Dynamic flexibility depends on static flexibility, but it also involves strength, coordination, and resistance to movement.

Dynamic flexibility is important for daily activities and sports. Because static flexibility is easier to measure and better researched, however, most assessment tests and stretching programs target that type of flexibility.

WHAT DETERMINES FLEXIBILITY?

The flexibility of a joint is affected by its structure, by muscle elasticity and length, and by nervous system regulation. Some factors, such as joint structure, can't be changed. Other factors, such as the length of resting muscle fibers, can be changed through exercise; these factors should be the focus of a program to develop flexibility.

Joint Structure

The amount of flexibility in a joint is determined in part by the nature and structure of the joint (Figure 5.1). Hinge joints such as those in your fingers and knees allow only limited forward and backward movement; they lock

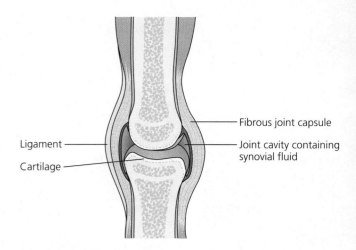

FIGURE 5.1 Basic joint structure.

when fully extended. Ball-and-socket joints like the hip enable movement in many different directions and provide for a greater range of motion. Major joints are surrounded by **joint capsules,** semielastic structures that give joints strength and stability but limit movement. The bone surfaces within the joint are lined with cartilage and separated by a joint cavity containing *synovial fluid,* which cushions the bones and reduces friction as the joint moves. Ligaments, both inside and outside the joint capsule, strengthen and reinforce the joint. For an illustration of the knee joint and more about its function, see page T4-5 of the color transparency insert "Touring the Musculoskeletal System," in Chapter 4.

Heredity plays a part in joint structure and flexibility. For example, although everyone has a broad range of motion in the hip joint, not everyone can do a split. Gender may also play a role. Some studies have found that women have greater flexibility in certain joints.

Muscle Elasticity and Length

Soft tissues—including skin, muscles, tendons, and ligaments—also limit the flexibility of a joint. Muscle tissue is the key to developing flexibility because it can be lengthened if it is stretched regularly. The most important component of muscle tissue related to flexibility is the connective tissue that surrounds and envelops every part of muscle tissue, from individual muscle fibers to entire muscles. Connective tissue provides structure, elasticity, and bulk and makes up about 30% of muscle mass. Two principal types of connective tissue are **collagen**—white fibers that provide structure and support—and **elastin**—yellow fibers that are elastic and flexible. Muscles contain both collagen and elastin, closely intertwined, so muscle tissue exhibits the properties of both types of fibers. A recently discovered structural protein in muscles called *titin* also has elastic properties and contributes to flexibility.

When a muscle is stretched, the wavelike elastin fibers straighten; when the stretch is relieved, they rapidly snap back to their resting position. This temporary lengthening

Wellness Tip

Muscles shrink after injury or surgery. Rehabilitation exercises can help muscles grow again. One caution: Overuse of drugs like ibuprofen can slow the regrowth process. Use such drugs only as prescribed by your doctor.

is called **elastic elongation.** If stretched gently and regularly, connective tissues may lengthen and flexibility may improve. This long-term lengthening is called **plastic elongation.** Without regular stretching, the process reverses: These tissues shorten, resulting in decreased flexibility. Regular stretching may contribute to flexibility by lengthening muscle fibers through the addition of contractile units called *sarcomeres.*

The amount of stretch a muscle will tolerate is limited, and as the limits of its flexibility are reached, connective tissue becomes more brittle and may rupture if overstretched. A safe and effective program stretches muscles enough to slightly elongate the tissues but not so much that they are damaged. Research has shown that flexibility is improved best by stretching when muscles are warm (following exercise or the application of heat) and the stretch is applied gradually and conservatively. Sudden, high-stress stretching is less effective and can lead to muscle damage.

Nervous System Regulation

Proprioceptors are nerves that send information about the muscular and skeletal systems to the nervous system. When these nerves detect any change in the position or force of muscles, tendons, and joints, they send signals to the spine and brain, which send signals back to coordinate muscle action in ways that protect muscles and tendons from injury. They help control the speed, strength, and coordination of muscle contractions.

When a muscle is stretched (lengthened), proprioceptors detect the amount and rate of the change in muscle length. The nerves send a signal to the spinal cord, which then sends a signal back to the muscle, triggering a muscle contraction that resists the change in muscle length. Another signal is sent to the antagonist muscle, causing it to relax and facilitate contraction of the stretched muscle. These reflexes occur frequently in active muscles and allow for fine control of muscle length and movement.

Small movements that only slightly stimulate these nerves cause small reflex actions. Rapid, powerful, and sudden changes in muscle length strongly stimulate the receptors and can cause large and powerful reflex muscle contractions. Thus, stretches that involve rapid, bouncy movements can be dangerous and cause injury because each bounce causes a reflex contraction, and so a muscle might be stretching at the same time it is contracting. Performing a gradual stretch and then holding it allows the

Ask Yourself

QUESTIONS FOR CRITICAL THINKING AND REFLECTION

Have you ever noticed that you are markedly more or less flexible than your friends or classmates? To what do you attribute these differences? Did you know that you could increase your flexibility with a regular stretching program? Would it be meaningful to you to do so?

proprioceptors to adjust to the new muscle length and to reduce the signals sent to the spine, thereby allowing muscles to lengthen and, over time, improving flexibility.

The stretching technique called *proprioceptive neuromuscular facilitation (PNF),* described later, takes advantage of nerve activity to improve flexibility. For example, contracting a muscle prior to stretching it can help allow the muscle to stretch farther. The advanced strength training technique called plyometrics (Chapter 4) also takes advantage of the nervous system action in stretching and contracting muscles.

Modifying nervous control through movement and specific exercises is the best way to improve the functional range of motion. Regular stretching trains the proprioceptors to allow greater lengthening of the muscles. Proprioceptors adapt quickly to stretching (or lack of stretching), so frequent training is beneficial for developing flexibility. Stretching before exercising, however, can disturb proprioceptors and interfere with motor control during exercise. This is another good reason to stretch after exercising.

BENEFITS OF FLEXIBILITY

Good flexibility provides benefits for the entire musculoskeletal system. It may also prevent injuries and soreness and improve performance in all physical activities.

KEY TERMS

range of motion The full motion possible in a joint.

joint capsules Semielastic structures, composed primarily of connective tissue, that surround major joints.

soft tissues Tissues of the human body that include skin, fat, linings of internal organs and blood vessels, connective tissues, tendons, ligaments, muscles, and nerves.

collagen White fibers that provide structure and support in connective tissue.

elastin Yellow fibers that make connective tissue flexible.

elastic elongation Temporary change in the length of muscles, tendons, and supporting connective tissues.

plastic elongation Long-term change in the length of muscles, tendons, and supporting connective tissues.

proprioceptor A nerve that sends information about the muscular and skeletal systems to the nervous system.

Does Physical Activity Increase or Decrease the Risk of Bone and Joint Disease?

Most college students don't worry much about developing fall-related fractures or chronic bone-related illnesses such as osteoporosis—loss of bone mass—or osteoarthritis—degeneration of the cartilage lining the bones inside joints. Even so, bone health should be a concern throughout life. This is because girls amass 85% of their adult bone mass by age 18, and boys build the same amount by age 20, but most people begin losing bone mass around age 30. For many, bone loss is accelerated by poor diet and lack of exercise. According to the National Osteoporosis Foundation, 10 million Americans have osteoporosis. Meantime, 34 million Americans are at risk of disease because of low bone mass. Overall, osteoporosis is a health threat for about 55% of Americans aged 50 and older.

In addition to getting enough nutrients that are important for bone health (see Chapter 8), there is mounting evidence that exercise can preserve or improve bone health. For example, several studies have shown an inverse relationship between physical activity and the risk for bone fractures. That is, the more you exercise, the less likely you are to suffer fractures, especially of the upper leg and hip. Research has not determined conclusively how much exercise is required to reduce fracture risk, but reduced risk seems to become apparent when people walk at least 4 hours per week and devote at least 1 hour per week to other forms of physical activity. These findings seem to be consistent for women and men, but some studies disagree on this point, meaning that further research is needed on the sex-related response to exercise as it relates to bone fractures.

Both men and women can prevent fractures and osteoporosis by maintaining or increasing their bone mineral density throughout life, and physical activity plays a significant role in this. One way exercise helps is by increasing the mineral density of bones, or at least by decreasing the loss of mineral density over time. Several one-year-long studies found that exercise can increase bone mineral density by 1–2% per year, which is significant—especially considering that the same amount of bone mineral density can be lost every 1–4 years in older persons. Currently, the American College of Sports Medicine recommends that adults perform weight-bearing physical activities (such as walking) 3–5 days per week and strength training exercises 2–3 days per week to increase bone mass or avoid loss of mineral density. Exercise is particularly important in lactating (breastfeeding) women for preventing bone loss.

When it comes to exercise and osteoarthritis, the evidence is less conclusive but still fairly positive. All experts agree that regular, moderate-intensity exercise is necessary for joint health. However, they also warn that vigorous or too-frequent exercise may contribute to joint damage and encourage the onset of osteoarthritis. For this reason, experts try to strike a balance in their exercise recommendations, especially for persons with a family history of osteoarthritis. Research seems to support this cautious approach. Some studies have found that regular physical activity (as recommended for general health) does not increase osteoarthritis risk. Other studies show that moderate activity may provide some protection against the disease, but this evidence is limited.

A few studies also reveal that the type of exercise you do may increase your risk. For example, competitive or strenuous sports such as ballet, orienteering, football, basketball, soccer, and tennis have been associated with the disease, whereas sports such as cross-country skiing, running, swimming, biking, and walking have not.

The bottom line is that the earlier in life you become physically active, the greater your protection against bone loss and bone-related diseases. However, if you have a family history of osteoporosis or osteoarthritis, or if you have already developed symptoms of one of these ailments, be sure to talk to your physician before beginning an exercise program.

SOURCES: Kemmler, W., and S. Stengel. 2011. Exercise and osteoporosis-related fractures: Perspectives and recommendations of the sports and exercise scientist. *Physician Sportsmedicine* 39(1): 142–157; Lovelady, et al. 2009. Effect of Exercise Training on Loss of Bone Mineral Density during Lactation. *Medicine and Science in Sports and Exercise* 41 (10): 1902–1907; American College of Sports Medicine. 2004. ACSM position stand: Physical activity and bone health. *Medicine and Science in Sports and Exercise* 36 (11): 1985–1996; National Osteoporosis Foundation. 2011. *Bone Basics: Fast Facts* (http://www.nof.org/node/40; retrieved March 23, 2011); Physical Activity Guidelines Advisory Committee. 2008. *Physical Activity Guidelines Advisory Committee Report, 2008.* Washington, D.C.: U.S. Department of Health and Human Services.

Joint Health

Good flexibility is essential to good joint health. When the muscles and other tissues that support a joint are tight, the joint is subject to abnormal stresses that can cause joint deterioration. For example, tight thigh muscles cause excessive pressure on the kneecap, leading to pain in the knee joint. Poor joint flexibility can also cause abnormalities in joint lubrication, leading to deterioration of the sensitive cartilage cells lining the joint; pain and further joint injury can result.

Improved flexibility can greatly improve your quality of life, particularly as you get older. People tend to exercise less as they age, leading to loss of joint mobility and increased incidence of joint pain. Aging also decreases the natural elasticity of muscles, tendons, and joints, resulting in stiffness. The problem is often compounded by arthritis (see the box "Does Physical Activity Increase or Decrease the Risk of Bone and Joint Disease?"). Good joint flexibility may prevent arthritis, and stretching may lessen pain in people who have the condition. Another benefit of good flexibility for older adults is that it increases balance and stability.

Prevention of Low-Back Pain and Injuries

Low-back pain can be related to poor spinal stability, which puts pressure on the nerves leading out from the spinal column. Strength and flexibility in the back, pelvis, and thighs may help prevent this type of back pain but may or may not improve back health or reduce the risk of injury. Good hip and knee flexibility protects the spine from excessive motion during the tasks of daily living.

Although scientific evidence is limited, people with either high or low flexibility seem to have an increased risk of injury. Extreme flexibility reduces joint stability, and poor flexibility limits a joint's range of motion. Persons of average fitness should try to attain normal flexibility in joints throughout the body, meaning each joint can move through its normal range of motion with no difficulty. Stretching programs are particularly important for older adults, people involved in high-power sports involving rapid changes in direction (such as football and tennis), workers involved in brief bouts of intense exertion (such as police officers and firefighters), and people who sit for prolonged periods (such as office workers and students).

However, stretching before a high-intensity activity (such as sprinting or basketball) may increase the risk of injury by interfering with neuromuscular control and reducing muscles' natural ability to stretch and contract. When injuries occur, flexibility exercises can be used in treatment: They reduce symptoms and help restore normal range of motion in affected joints.

Additional Potential Benefits

• *Relief of aches and pains.* Studying or working in one place for a long time can make your muscles tense. Stretching helps relieve tension and joint stiffness, so you can go back to work refreshed and effective. Stretching reduces the symptoms of exercise-induced muscle damage, and flexible muscles are less susceptible to the damage.

• *Relief of muscle cramps.* Recent research suggests that exercise-related muscle cramps are caused by increased electrical activity within the affected muscle. The best treatment for muscle cramps is gentle stretching, which reduces the electrical activity and allows the muscle to relax.

• *Improved body position and strength for sports (and life).* Good flexibility lets you assume more efficient body positions and exert force through a greater range of motion. For example, swimmers with more flexible shoulders have stronger strokes because they can pull their arms through the water in the optimal position. Some studies also suggest that flexibility training enhances strength development.

Fitness Tip

Many people have stopped stretching after hearing mixed results from research studies. This may be a mistake. Stretching after an intense workout can relieve soreness, in addition to providing all the other benefits listed here.

Ask Yourself

QUESTIONS FOR CRITICAL THINKING AND REFLECTION

When you think about the health-related components of fitness, how do you rank flexibility? Is it less important to you than cardiorespiratory endurance or muscular strength? If you place a low priority on flexibility, what can you do to increase your motivation to stretch?

• *Maintenance of good posture and balance.* Good flexibility also contributes to body symmetry and good posture. Bad posture can gradually change your body structures. Sitting in a slumped position, for example, can lead to tightness in the muscles in the front of your chest and overstretching and looseness in the upper spine, causing a rounding of the upper back. This condition, called *kyphosis*, is common in older people. It may be prevented by stretching regularly.

• *Relaxation.* Flexibility exercises, particularly when practiced in combination with yoga or tai chi, reduce mental tension, slow your breathing rate, and reduce blood pressure.

• *Improving impaired mobility.* Stretching often decreases pain and improves functional capacity in people with arthritis, stroke, or muscle and nerve diseases and in people who are recovering from surgery or injury.

ASSESSING FLEXIBILITY

Because flexibility is specific to each joint, there are no tests of general flexibility. The most commonly used flexibility test is the sit-and-reach test, which rates the flexibility of the muscles in the lower back and hamstrings. To assess your flexibility and identify inflexible joints, complete Lab 5.1.

CREATING A SUCCESSFUL PROGRAM TO DEVELOP FLEXIBILITY

A successful program for developing flexibility includes safe exercises executed with the most effective techniques. Your goal should be to attain normal flexibility

connect
ACTIVITY
DO IT ONLINE

Safe Stretching

TAKE CHARGE

- Do stretching exercises statically. Stretch to the point of mild discomfort, hold the position for 10–30 seconds, rest for 30–60 seconds, and then repeat, trying to stretch a bit farther.

- Do not stretch to the point of pain. Any soreness after a stretching workout should be mild and last no more than 24 hours. If you are sore for a longer period, you stretched too intensely.

- Relax and breathe easily as you stretch. Inhale through the nose and exhale through pursed lips during the stretch. Try to relax the muscles being stretched.

- Perform all exercises on both sides of your body.

- Wear loose-fitting clothing that won't inhibit movement when you're stretching.

- To prevent falls, wear athletic shoes when stretching, or stretch on a no-slip surface.

- Increase intensity and duration gradually over time. Improved flexibility takes many months to develop.

- Stretch when your muscles are warm. Do gentle warm-up exercises such as easy jogging or calisthenics before doing a stretching routine.

- There are large individual differences in joint flexibility. Don't feel you have to compete with others during stretching workouts.

- Engage in a variety of physical activities to help you develop well-rounded functional physical fitness and allow you to perform all types of training more safely and effectively.

in the major joints. Balanced flexibility (not too much or too little) provides joint stability and facilitates smooth, economical movement patterns. You can achieve balanced flexibility by performing stretching exercises regularly and by using a variety of stretches and stretching techniques.

Applying the FITT Principle

As with other programs, the acronym FITT can be used to remember key components of a stretching program: Frequency, Intensity, Time, and Type of exercise.

Frequency The ACSM recommends that stretching exercises be performed at least 2–3 days per week, but more often is even better. It's best to stretch when your muscles are warm, so try incorporating stretching into your cool-down after cardiorespiratory endurance exercise or weight training.

Never stretch when your muscles are cold; doing so can increase your risk of injury as well as limit the amount of flexibility you can develop. Although stretching before exercise is a time-honored ritual practiced by athletes in many sports, many studies have found that preexercise stretching decreases muscle strength and performance and disturbs neuromuscular control. If your workout involves participation in a sport or high-performance activity, you may be better off stretching after your workout. For moderate-intensity activities like walking or cycling, stretching before your workout is unlikely to impair your performance.

Intensity and Time (Duration) For each exercise, slowly stretch your muscles to the point of slight tension or mild discomfort—but not to the point of pain. Hold the stretch for 10–30 seconds. As you hold the stretch, the feeling of slight tension should slowly subside; at that point, try to stretch a bit farther. Throughout the stretch, try to relax and breathe easily. Rest for about 30–60

seconds between each stretch, and do 2–4 repetitions of each stretch. A complete flexibility workout usually takes about 10–30 minutes (Figure 5.2).

Types of Stretching Techniques Stretching techniques vary from simply stretching the muscles during the course of normal activities to sophisticated methods based on patterns

Warm-up 5–10 minutes or following an endurance or strength training workout	Stretching exercises for major joints **Sample program**	
	Exercise	*Areas stretched*
	Head turns and tilts	Neck
	Towel stretch	Triceps, shoulders, chest
	Across-the-body and overhead stretches	Shoulders, upper back, back of arm
	Upper-back stretch	Upper back
	Lateral stretch	Trunk muscles
	Step stretch	Hip, front of thigh
	Side lunge	Inner thigh, hip, calf
	Inner-thigh stretch	Inner thigh, hip
	Hip and trunk stretch	Trunk, outer thigh, hip, buttocks, lower back
	Modified hurdler stretch	Back of thigh, lower back
	Alternate leg stretcher	Back of thigh, hip, knee, ankle, buttocks
	Lower-leg stretch	Calf, soleus, Achilles tendon

Frequency: 2–3 days per week (minimum); 5–7 days per week (ideal)

Intensity: Stretch to the point of mild discomfort, not pain

Time (duration): All stretches should be held for 15–30 seconds and performed 2–4 times

Type of activity: Stretching exercises that focus on major joints

FIGURE 5.2 The FITT principle for a flexibility program.

of muscle reflexes. Improper stretching can do more harm than good, so it's important to understand the different types of stretching exercises and how they affect the muscles (see the box "Safe Stretching"). Four common techniques are static stretches, ballistic stretches, dynamic stretches, and PNF. These techniques can be performed passively or actively.

STATIC STRETCHING   In **static stretching**, each muscle is gradually stretched, and the stretch is held for 10–30 seconds. A slow stretch prompts less reaction from proprioceptors, and the muscles can safely stretch farther than usual. Static stretching is the type most often recommended by fitness experts because it is safe and effective.

The key to this technique is to stretch the muscles and joints to the point where a pull is felt, but not to the point of pain. (One note of caution: Excess static stretching can decrease joint stability and increase the risk of injury. This may be a particular concern for women, who naturally have joints that are less stable and more flexible than men.) The sample stretching program presented later in this chapter features static stretching exercises.

BALLISTIC STRETCHING   In **ballistic stretching**, the muscles are stretched suddenly in a forceful bouncing movement. For example, touching the toes repeatedly in rapid succession is a ballistic stretch for the hamstrings. A problem with this technique is that the heightened activity of proprioceptors caused by the rapid stretches can continue for some time, possibly causing injuries during any physical activities that follow. Another concern is that triggering strong responses from the nerves can cause a reflex muscle contraction that makes it harder to stretch. For these reasons, ballistic stretching is usually not recommended, especially for people of average fitness.

Ballistic stretching trains the muscle dynamically, so it can be an appropriate stretching technique for some well-trained athletes. For example, tennis players stretch their hamstrings and quadriceps ballistically when they lunge for a ball during a tennis match. Because this movement is part of their sport, they might benefit from ballistic training of these muscle groups.

DYNAMIC (FUNCTIONAL) STRETCHING   The emphasis in **dynamic stretching** is on functional movements. Dynamic stretching is similar to ballistic stretching in that it includes movement, but it differs in that it does not involve rapid bouncing. Instead, dynamic stretching involves moving the joints through the range of motion used in a specific exercise or sport in an exaggerated but controlled manner; movements are fluid rather than jerky. An example of a dynamic stretch is the lunge walk, in which a person takes slow steps with an exaggerated stride length and reaches a lunge stretch position with each step.

Slow dynamic stretches can lengthen the muscles in many directions without developing high tension in the tissues. These stretches elongate the tissues and train the neuromuscular system. Because dynamic stretches are based on sports movements or movements used in daily life, they develop functional flexibility that translates well into activities.

Dynamic stretches are more challenging than static stretches because they require balance and coordination and may carry a greater risk of muscle soreness and injury. People just beginning a flexibility program might want to start off with static stretches and try dynamic stretches only after they are comfortable with static stretching techniques and have improved their flexibility. It is also a good idea to seek expert advice on dynamic stretching technique and program development.

Serious athletes may use dynamic stretches as part of their warm-up before a competitive event or a high-intensity training session in order to move their joints through the range of motion required for the activity. Functional flexibility training can also be combined with functional strength training. For example, lunge curls, which combine dynamic lunges with free weights biceps curls, stretch the hip, thigh, and calf muscles; stabilize the core muscles in the trunk; and build strength in the arm muscles. Many activities build functional flexibility and strength at the same time, including yoga, Pilates, taijiquan, Olympic weight lifting, plyometrics, stability training (including Swiss and Bosu ball exercises), medicine ball exercises, and functional training machines (for example, Life Fitness and Cybex).

PROPRIOCEPTIVE NEUROMUSCULAR FACILITATION (PNF)   PNF techniques use reflexes initiated by both muscle and joint nerves to cause greater training effects. The most popular PNF stretching technique is the contract-relax stretching method, in which a muscle is contracted before it is stretched. The contraction activates proprioceptors, causing relaxation in the muscle about to be stretched. For example, in a seated stretch of calf muscles, the first step in PNF is to contract the calf muscles. The individual or a partner can provide resistance for an isometric

Wellness Tip

You don't have to be at the gym to stretch. There are lots of simple, small-movement stretches you can do anywhere—even at your desk. For some examples, visit a good health Web site such as MayoClinic.com and search for "stretching exercises."

static stretching   A technique in which a muscle is slowly and gently stretched and then held in the stretched position.

ballistic stretching   A technique in which muscles are stretched by the force generated as a body part is repeatedly bounced, swung, or jerked.

dynamic stretching   A technique in which muscles are stretched by moving joints slowly and fluidly through their range of motion in a controlled manner; also called *functional stretching*.

KEY TERMS

contraction. Following a brief period of relaxation, the next step is to stretch the calf muscles by pulling the tops of the feet toward the body. A duration of six seconds for the contraction and 10–30 seconds for the stretch is recommended. PNF appears to be most effective if the individual pushes hard during the isometric contraction.

Another example of a PNF stretch is the contract-relax-contract pattern. In this technique, begin by contracting the muscle to be stretched and then relaxing it. Next, contract the opposing muscle (the antagonist). Finally, stretch the first muscle. For example, using this technique to stretch the hamstrings (the muscles in the back of the thigh) would require the following steps: Contract the hamstrings, relax the hamstrings, contract the quadriceps (the muscles in the front of the thigh), then stretch the hamstrings.

PNF appears to allow more effective stretching and greater increases in flexibility than static stretching, but it tends to cause more muscle stiffness and soreness. It also usually requires a partner and takes more time.

PASSIVE VERSUS ACTIVE STRETCHING   Stretches can be done either passively or actively. In **passive stretching**, an outside force or resistance provided by yourself, a partner, gravity, or a weight helps your joints move through their range of motion. For example, a seated stretch of the hamstring and back muscles can be done by reaching the hands toward the feet until a pull is felt in those muscles. You can achieve a greater range of motion (a more intense stretch) using passive stretching. However, because the stretch is not controlled by the muscles themselves, there is a greater risk of injury. Communication between partners in passive stretching is important to ensure that joints aren't forced outside their normal functional range of motion.

In **active stretching**, a muscle is stretched by a contraction of the opposing muscle (the muscle on the opposite side of the limb). For example, an active seated stretch of the calf muscles occurs when a person actively contracts the muscles on the top of the shin. The contraction of this opposing muscle produces a reflex that relaxes the muscles to be stretched. The muscle can be stretched farther with a low risk of injury.

The only disadvantage of active stretching is that a person may not be able to produce enough stress (enough stretch) to increase flexibility using only the contraction of opposing muscle groups. The safest and most convenient technique is active static stretching, with an occasional passive assist. For example, you might stretch your calves both by contracting the muscles on the top of your shin and by pulling your feet toward you. This way you combine the advantages of active stretching—safety and

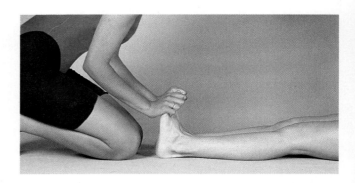

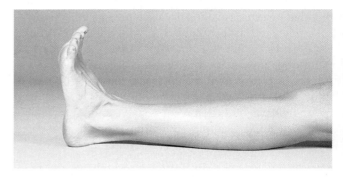

In passive stretching (top), an outside force—such as pressure exerted by another person—helps move the joint and stretch the muscles. In active stretching (bottom), the force to move the joint and stretch the muscles is provided by a contraction of the opposing muscles.

the relaxation reflex—with those of passive stretching—greater range of motion. People who are just beginning flexibility training may be better off doing active rather than passive stretches. For PNF techniques, it is particularly important to have a knowledgeable partner.

Making Progress

As with any type of training, you will make progress and improve your flexibility if you stick with your program. Judge your progress by noting your body position while stretching. For example, note how far you can lean forward during a modified hurdler stretch. Repeat the assessment tests that appear in Lab 5.1 periodically and be sure to take the test at the same time of day each time. You will likely notice some improvement after only 2–3 weeks of stretching, but you may need at least 2 months to attain significant improvements. By then, you can expect flexibility increases of about 10–20% in many joints.

Exercises to Improve Flexibility: A Sample Program

There are hundreds of exercises that can improve flexibility. Your program should include exercises that work all the major joints of the body by stretching their associated muscle groups (refer back to Figure 5.2). The exercises illustrated here are simple to do and pose a minimum risk of injury. Use these exercises to create a well-rounded program for developing flexibility. Be sure to perform each stretch using the proper technique. Hold each position

KEY TERMS

passive stretching   A technique in which muscles are stretched by force applied by an outside source.

active stretching   A technique in which muscles are stretched by the contraction of the opposing muscles.

EXERCISE 1   Head Turns and Tilts

Instructions:

Head turns: Turn your head to the right and hold the stretch. Repeat to the left.

Head tilts: Tilt your head to the right and hold the stretch. Repeat to the left.

Areas stretched: Neck

Variation: Place your right palm on your right cheek; try to turn your head to the right as you resist with your hand. Repeat on the left side.

EXERCISE 2   Towel Stretch

Instructions: Roll up a towel and grasp it with both hands, palms down. With your arms straight, slowly lift the towel back over your head as far as possible. The closer together your hands are, the greater the stretch.

Areas stretched: Triceps, shoulders, chest

Variation: Repeat the stretch with your arms down and the towel behind your back. Grasp the towel with your palms forward and thumbs pointing out. Gently raise your arms behind your back. This exercise can also be done without a towel.

EXERCISE 3   Across-the-Body and Overhead Stretches

Instructions: (a) Keeping your back straight, cross your right arm in front of your body and grasp it with your left hand. Stretch your arm, shoulders, and back by gently pulling your arm as close to your body as possible. Hold.
(b) Bend your right arm over your head, placing your right elbow as close to your right ear as possible. Grasp your right elbow with your left hand over your head. Stretch the back of your arm by gently pulling your right elbow back and toward your head. Hold. Repeat both stretches on your left side.

Areas stretched:
Shoulders, upper back, back of the arm (triceps)

EXERCISE 4   Upper-Back Stretch

Instructions: Stand with your feet shoulder-width apart, knees slightly bent, and pelvis tucked under. Lace your fingers in front of your body and press your palms forward.

Areas stretched: Upper back

Variation: In the same position, wrap your arms around your body as if you were giving yourself a hug.

McGraw Hill **connect** http://www.mcgrawhillconnect.com/
|FITNESS AND WELLNESS

EXERCISE 5 — Lateral Stretch

Instructions: Stand with your feet shoulder-width apart, knees slightly bent, and pelvis tucked under. Raise one arm over your head and bend sideways from the waist. Support your trunk by placing the hand or forearm of your other arm on your thigh or hip for support. Be sure you bend directly sideways and don't move your body below the waist. Repeat on the other side.

Areas stretched: Trunk muscles

Variation: Perform the same exercise in a seated position.

EXERCISE 6 — Step Stretch

Instructions: Step forward and bend your forward knee, keeping it directly above your ankle. Stretch your other leg back so that your shin is parallel to the floor. Press your hips forward and down to stretch. Your arms can be at your sides, on top of your knee, or on the ground for balance. Repeat on the other side.

Areas stretched: Hip, front of thigh (quadriceps)

EXERCISE 7 — Side Lunge

Instructions: Stand in a wide straddle with your legs turned out from your hip joints and your hands on your thighs. Lunge to one side by bending one knee and keeping the other leg straight. Keep your bent knee directly over your ankle; do not bend it more than 90 degrees. Repeat on the other side.

Areas stretched: Inner thigh, hip, calf

Variation: In the same position, lift the heel of the bent knee to provide additional stretch. The exercise may also be performed with your hands on the floor for balance.

EXERCISE 8 — Inner Thigh Stretch

Instructions: Sit with the soles of your feet together. Push your knees toward the floor using your hands or forearms.

Areas stretched: Inner thigh, hip

Variation: When you first begin to push your knees toward the floor, use your legs to resist the movement. Then relax and press your knees down as far as they will go.

EXERCISE 9 — Hip and Trunk Stretch

Instructions: Sit with your left leg straight, right leg bent and crossed over the left knee, and right hand on the floor next to your right hip. Turn your trunk as far as possible to the right by pushing against your right leg with your left forearm or elbow. Keep your right foot on the floor. Repeat on the other side.

Areas stretched: Trunk, outer thigh and hip, buttocks, lower back

EXERCISE 10 — Modified Hurdler Stretch (Seated Single-Leg Hamstring)

Instructions: Sit with your left leg straight and your right leg tucked close to your body. Reach toward your left ankle as far as possible. Repeat for the other leg.

Areas stretched: Back of the thigh (hamstring), lower back

Variation: As you stretch forward, alternately flex and point the foot of your extended leg.

EXERCISE 11 — Alternate Leg Stretcher

Instructions: Lie flat on your back with both legs straight. **(a)** Grasp your left leg behind the thigh, and pull it in to your chest. **(b)** Hold this position, and then extend your left leg toward the ceiling. **(c)** Hold this position, and then bring your left knee back to your chest and pull your toes toward your shin with your left hand. Stretch the back of the leg by attempting to straighten your knee. Repeat for the other leg.

Areas stretched: Back of the thigh (hamstring), hip, knee, ankle, buttocks

Variation: Perform the stretch on both legs at the same time.

a

b

c

EXERCISE 12 — Lower-Leg Stretch

Instructions: Stand with one foot about 1–2 feet in front of the other, with both feet pointing forward. **(a)** Keeping your back leg straight, lunge forward by bending your front knee and pushing your rear heel backward. Hold. **(b)** Then pull your back foot in slightly, and bend your back knee. Shift your weight to your back leg. Hold. Repeat on the other side.

Areas stretched: Back of the lower leg (calf, soleus, Achilles tendon)

Variation: Place your hands on a wall and extend one foot back, pressing your heel down to stretch, or stand with the balls of your feet on a step or bench and allow your heels to drop below the level of your toes.

a

b

Ask Yourself

QUESTIONS FOR CRITICAL THINKING AND REFLECTION

Why do you think improper stretching can do more harm than good? How can stretching cause injury? Of all the types of stretches described, which ones do you think would be safest for you? Which ones appeal to you most?

for 10–30 seconds and perform 2–4 repetitions of each exercise. Avoid exercises that put excessive pressure on your joints (see the box "Stretches to Avoid"). Complete Lab 5.2 when you're ready to start your program.

PREVENTING AND MANAGING LOW-BACK PAIN

More than 85% of Americans experience back pain by age 50. Low-back pain is the second most common ailment in the United States—headache tops the list—and the second most common reason for absences from work and visits to a physician. Low-back pain is estimated to cost as much as $50 billion a year in lost productivity, medical and legal fees, and disability insurance and compensation.

Back pain can result from sudden traumatic injuries, but it is more often the long-term result of weak and inflexible muscles, poor posture, or poor body mechanics during activities like lifting and carrying. Any abnormal strain on the back can result in pain. Most cases of low-back pain clear up within a few weeks or months, but some people have recurrences or suffer from chronic pain.

Function and Structure of the Spine

The spinal column performs many important functions in the body.

- It provides structural support for the body, especially the thorax (upper-body cavity).
- It surrounds and protects the spinal cord.
- It supports much of the body's weight and transmits it to the lower body.
- It serves as an attachment site for a large number of muscles, tendons, and ligaments.
- It allows movement of the neck and back in all directions.

The spinal column is made up of bones called **vertebrae** (Figure 5.3). The spine consists of 7 cervical vertebrae in the neck, 12 thoracic vertebrae in the upper

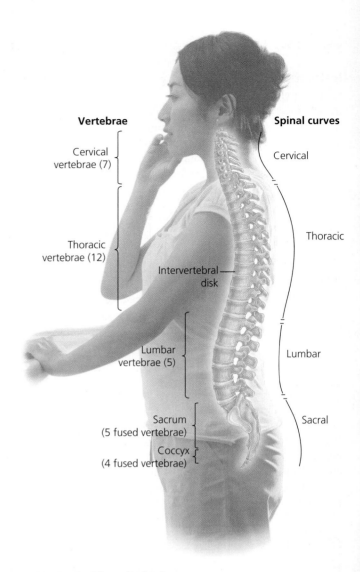

FIGURE 5.3 The spinal column.
The spine is made up of five separate regions and has four distinct curves. An intervertebral disk is located between adjoining vertebrae.

back, and 5 lumbar vertebrae in the lower back. The 9 vertebrae at the base of the spine are fused into two sections and form the sacrum and the coccyx (tailbone). The spine has four curves: the cervical, thoracic, lumbar, and sacral curves. These curves help bring the body weight supported by the spine in line with the axis of the body.

Although the structure of vertebrae depends on their location on the spine, the different types of vertebrae share common characteristics. Each consists of a body, an arch, and several bony processes (Figure 5.4). The vertebral body is cylindrical, with flattened surfaces where **intervertebral disks** are attached. The vertebral body is designed to carry the stress of body weight and physical activity. The vertebral arch surrounds and protects the spinal cord. The bony processes serve as joints for adjacent vertebrae and attachment sites for muscles and ligaments. **Nerve roots** from the spinal cord pass through notches in the vertebral arch.

Intervertebral disks, which absorb and disperse the stresses placed on the spine, separate vertebrae from each

Stretches to Avoid

The safe alternatives listed under each stretch are described and illustrated on pp. 149–151 as part of a complete program of safe flexibility exercises.

Standing Toe Touch

Problem: Puts excessive strain on the spine.

Alternatives: Modified hurdler stretch (Exercise 10), alternate leg stretcher (Exercise 11), and lower-leg stretch (Exercise 12).

Standing Ankle-to-Buttocks Quadriceps Stretch

Problem: Puts excessive strain on the ligaments of the knee.

Alternative: Step stretch (Exercise 6).

Full Squat with Bent Back

Problem: Puts excessive strain on the ankles, knees, and spine.

Alternatives: Alternate leg stretcher (Exercise 11) and lower-leg stretch (Exercise 12).

Prone Arch

Problem: Puts excessive strain on the spine, knees, and shoulders.

Alternatives: Towel stretch (Exercise 2) and step stretch (Exercise 6).

Standing Hamstring Stretch

Problem: Puts excessive strain on the knee and lower back.

Alternatives: Modified hurdler stretch (Exercise 10) and alternate leg stretcher (Exercise 11).

Yoga Plow

Problem: Puts excessive strain on the neck, shoulders, and back.

Alternatives: Head turns and tilts (Exercise 1), across-the-body and overhead stretches (Exercise 3), and upper-back stretch (Exercise 4).

Hurdler Stretch

Problem: Turning out the bent leg can put excessive strain on the ligaments of the knee.

Alternative: Modified hurdler stretch (Exercise 10).

Neck Circles

Problem: Puts excessive strain on the neck and cervical disks.

Alternatives: Head turns and tilts (Exercise 1).

NOTE: Prone leg extensions, in which a person lifts both the chest and the legs while lying on the stomach but without grabbing the ankles, should also be avoided; spine extensions (p. 160) are a safe alternative.

TAKE CHARGE

---

other. Disks are made up of a gel- and water-filled nucleus surrounded by a series of fibrous rings. The liquid nucleus can change shape when it is compressed, allowing the disk to absorb shock. The intervertebral disks also help maintain the spaces between vertebrae where the spinal nerve roots are located.

Core Muscle Fitness

The **core muscles** include those in the abdomen, pelvic floor, sides of the trunk, back, buttocks, hip, and

vertebrae Bony segments composing the spinal column that provide structural support for the body and protect the spinal cord.

intervertebral disk An elastic disk located between adjoining vertebrae, consisting of a gel- and water-filled nucleus surrounded by fibrous rings; serves as a shock absorber for the spinal column.

nerve root The base of each of the 31 pairs of spinal nerves that branch off the spinal cord through spaces between vertebrae.

core muscles The trunk muscles extending from the hips to the upper back.

KEY TERMS

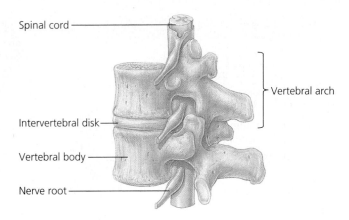

Spinal cord

Vertebral arch

Intervertebral disk

Vertebral body

Nerve root

FIGURE 5.4 Vertebrae and an intervertebral disk.

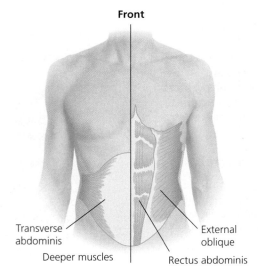

Front

Transverse abdominis

Deeper muscles

External oblique

Rectus abdominis

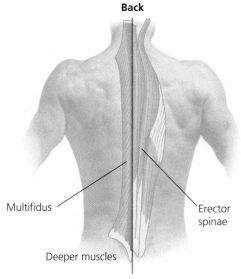

Back

Multifidus

Erector spinae

Deeper muscles

FIGURE 5.5 Major core muscles.

pelvis (Figure 5.5). There are 29 of these muscles, attaching to the ribs, hips, spinal column, and other bones in the trunk of the body. As described in Chapter 4, the core muscles stabilize the spine and help transfer force

Fitness Tip

Swiss ball exercises are great for building core muscles. Swiss ball training increases trunk flexion and extension, strength, abdominal endurance, lower back flexibility, and balance.

between the upper body and lower body. They stabilize the midsection when you sit, stand, reach, walk, jump, twist, squat, throw, or bend. The muscles on the front, back, and sides of your trunk support your spine when you sit in a chair and fix your midsection as you use your legs to stand up. When hitting a forehand in tennis or batting a softball, most of the force is transferred from the legs and hips, across the core muscles, to the arms. Strong core muscles make movements more forceful and help prevent back pain.

During any dynamic movement, the core muscles work together. Some shorten to cause movement, while others contract and hold to provide stability, lengthen to brake the movement, or send signals to the brain about the movements and positions of the muscles and bones (proprioception). When specific core muscles are weak or tired, the nervous system steps in and uses other muscles. This substitution causes abnormal stresses on the joints, decreases power, and increases the risk of injury.

The best exercises for low-back health are whole-body exercises that force the core muscles to stabilize the spine in many different directions. The low-back exercises presented later in this chapter include several exercises that focus on the core muscles, including the step stretch (lunge), side bridges, and spine extensions. These exercises are generally safe for beginning exercisers and, with physician approval, people with some back pain. More challenging core exercises utilize stability balls or free weights. Stability ball exercises require the core muscles to stabilize the ball (and the body) while performing nearly any type of exercise. Many traditional exercises with free weights can strengthen the core muscles if you do them in a standing position. Weight machines train muscles in isolation, while exercises with free weights done while standing help train the body for real-world movements—an essential principle of core training.

Causes of Back Pain

Back pain can occur at any point along your spine. The lumbar area, because it bears the majority of your weight, is the most common site. Any movement that causes excessive stress on the spinal column can cause injury and pain. The spine is well equipped to bear body weight and the force or stress of body movements along its long axis. However, it is less capable of bearing loads at an angle to its long axis or when the trunk is flexed (bent). You do not have to carry a heavy load or participate in a vigorous contact sport to injure your back. Picking a pencil up from the floor while using poor body mechanics—reaching too far out in front of you or bending over with your knees straight, for example—can also result in back pain.

Risk factors associated with low-back pain include age greater than 34 years, degenerative diseases such as arthritis or osteoporosis, a family or personal history of back pain or trauma, a sedentary lifestyle, low job satisfaction, and low socioeconomic status. Smoking increases risk because smoking appears to hasten degenerative changes in the spine. Excess body weight also increases strain on the back, and psychological stress or depression can cause muscle tension and back pain. Occupations and activities associated with low-back pain are those involving physically hard work, such as frequent lifting, twisting, bending, standing up, or straining in forced positions; those requiring high concentration demands (such as computer programming); and those involving vibrations affecting the entire body (such as truck driving).

Underlying causes of back pain include poor muscle endurance and strength in the core muscles; excess body weight; poor posture or body position when standing, sitting, or sleeping; and poor body mechanics when performing actions like lifting and carrying, or sports movements. Strained muscles, tendons, or ligaments can cause pain and can, over time, lead to injuries to vertebrae, intervertebral disks, and surrounding muscles and ligaments.

Stress can cause disks to break down and lose some of their ability to absorb shock. A damaged disk may bulge out between vertebrae and put pressure on a nerve root, a condition commonly referred to as a *slipped disk*. Painful pressure on nerves can also occur if damage to a disk narrows the space between two vertebrae. With age, you lose fluid from the disks, making them more likely to bulge and put pressure on nerve roots. Depending on the amount of pressure on a nerve, symptoms may include numbness in the back, hip, leg, or foot; radiating pain; loss of muscle function; depressed reflexes; and muscle spasm. If the pressure is severe enough, loss of function can be permanent.

Preventing Low-Back Pain

Incorrect posture is responsible for many back injuries. Strategies for maintaining good posture are presented in the box "Good Posture and Low-Back Health." Follow the same guidelines when you engage in sports or recreational activities. Control your movements, and warm up thoroughly before you exercise. Take special care when lifting weights.

The role of exercise in preventing and treating back pain is still being investigated. However, many experts recommend exercise, especially for people who have already experienced an episode of low-back pain.

Regular exercise aimed at increasing muscle endurance and strength in the back and abdomen is often recommended to prevent back pain, as is lifestyle physical activity such as walking. Movement helps lubricate your spinal joints and increases muscle fitness in your trunk and legs. Other lifestyle recommendations for preventing back pain include the following:

- Maintain a healthy weight. Excess fat contributes to poor posture, which can place harmful stresses on the spine.
- Stop smoking, and reduce stress.
- Avoid sitting, standing, or working in the same position for too long. Stand up every hour or half-hour and move around.
- Use a supportive seat and a medium-firm mattress.
- Use lumbar support when driving, particularly for long distances, to prevent muscle fatigue and pain.
- Warm up thoroughly before exercising.
- Progress gradually when attempting to improve strength or fitness.

Managing Acute Back Pain

Sudden (acute) back pain usually involves tissue injury. Symptoms may include pain, muscle spasms, stiffness, and inflammation. Many cases of acute back pain go away by themselves within a few days or weeks. You may be able to reduce pain and inflammation by applying cold and then heat (see Chapter 3). Apply ice several times a day; once inflammation and spasms subside, you can apply heat using a heating pad or a warm bath. If the pain is bothersome, an over-the-counter, nonsteroidal anti-inflammatory medication such as ibuprofen or naproxen may be helpful. Stronger pain medications and muscle relaxants are available by prescription.

Bed rest immediately following the onset of back pain may make you feel better, but it should be of very short duration. Prolonged bed rest—5 days or more—was once thought to be an effective treatment for back pain, but most physicians now advise against it because it may weaken muscles and actually worsen pain. Limit bed rest to one day and begin moderate physical activity as soon as possible. Exercise can increase muscular endurance and flexibility and protect disks from loss of fluid. Three of the back exercises discussed later in the chapter may be particularly helpful following an episode of acute back pain: curl-ups, side bridges, and spine extensions ("bird dogs").

See your physician if acute back pain doesn't resolve within a short time. Other warning signals of a more severe problem that requires a professional evaluation include severe pain, numbness, pain that radiates down one or both legs, problems with bladder or bowel control, fever, and rapid weight loss.

Keeping Your Back Pain-Free

About 85% of Americans suffer from back pain at some point in their lives. Back pain can be annoying and even disabling, and every day, many Americans miss school and work because of their pain. Luckily, you can minimize the risk of back problems by doing a few simple exercises every day. Keep a personal back pain prevention journal and do the following exercises on as many days of the week as possible.

EXERCISE	MON.	TUES.	WEDS.	THUR.	FRI.	SAT.	SUN.
Curl-ups: one set of 10 reps	✓		✓		✓		✓
Side bridge: five sets, 3-second hold, each side	✓		✓		✓		✓
Bird dog: five sets, 3-second hold, each side	✓		✓		✓		✓
Walking: 15–60 minutes		✓	✓		✓		✓
Kettlebell swings: one set 20 repetitions	✓				✓	✓	✓

Make a chart like the one shown above, and place a new copy in your training log each week. Enter a check mark every time you do the exercise. Try to enter a check mark for each exercise as often as you can during the week. In this one-week example, the person didn't do all the exercises every day, but she tried to do something on as many days a week as she could. Regularity is the key; if you miss a day, try not to miss the next one.

Managing Chronic Back Pain

Low-back pain is considered chronic if it persists for more than 3 months. Symptoms vary—some people experience stabbing or shooting pain, and others a steady ache accompanied by stiffness. Sometimes pain is localized; in other cases, it radiates to another part of the body. Underlying causes of chronic back pain include injuries, infection, muscle or ligament strains, and disk herniations.

Because symptoms and causes are so varied, different people benefit from different treatment strategies, and researchers have found that many treatments have only limited benefits. Potential treatments include over-the-counter or prescription medications; exercise; physical therapy, massage, yoga, or chiropractic care; acupuncture; percutaneous electrical nerve stimulation (PENS), in which acupuncture-like needles are used to deliver an electrical current; education and advice about posture, exercise, and body mechanics; and surgery (see the box "Yoga for Relaxation and Pain Relief").

Psychological therapy may also be beneficial in some cases. Reducing emotional stress that causes muscle tension can provide direct benefits, and other therapies can help people deal better with chronic pain and its effects on their daily lives. Support groups and expressive writing are beneficial for people with chronic pain and other conditions.

Exercises for the Prevention and Management of Low-Back Pain

The tests in Lab 5.3 can help you assess low-back muscular endurance. The exercises that follow are designed to help you maintain a healthy back by stretching and strengthening the major muscle groups that affect the back—the abdominal muscles, the muscles along your spine and sides, and the muscles of your hips and thighs. If you have back problems, check with your physician before beginning any exercise program. Perform the exercises slowly and progress very gradually. Stop and consult your physician if any exercise causes back pain. General guidelines for back exercise programs include the following:

- Do low-back exercises at least 3 days per week. Most experts recommend daily back exercises.

- Emphasize muscular endurance rather than muscular strength—endurance is more protective.

- Don't do spine exercises involving a full range of motion early in the morning. Your disks have a high fluid content early in the day and injuries may result.

- Engage in regular endurance exercise such as cycling or walking in addition to performing exercises that specifically build muscular endurance and flexibility. Brisk walking with a vigorous arm swing may help relieve back pain. Start with fast walking if your core muscles are weak or you have back pain.

- Be patient and stick with your program. Increased back fitness and pain relief may require as long as 3 months of regular exercise.

- The adage "no pain, no gain" does not apply to back exercises. Always use good form and stop if you feel pain.

Good Posture and Low-Back Health

Changes in everyday posture and behavior can help prevent and alleviate low-back pain.

- **Lying down.** When resting or sleeping, lie on your side with your knees and hips bent. If you lie on your back, place a pillow under your knees. However, do not elevate your knees so much that the curve in your lower spine is flattened. Don't lie on your stomach. Use a medium-firm mattress.

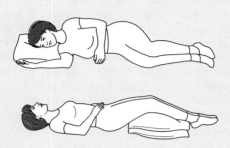

- **Sitting at a computer.** Sit in a slightly reclined position of 100–110 degrees, not an upright 90-degree position. Adjust your chair so your knees are slightly lower than your hips. If your back flattens as you sit, try using a lumbar roll to maintain your back's natural curvature. Place your feet flat on the floor or on a footrest. Place the monitor directly in front of you and adjust it so your eyes are level with the top of the screen; you should be looking slightly downward at the middle of the screen. Adjust the keyboard and mouse so your forearms and wrists are in a neutral position, parallel with the floor.

- **Lifting.** If you need to lower yourself to grasp an object, bend at the knees and hips rather than at the waist. Your feet should be about shoulder-width apart. Lift gradually, keeping your arms straight, by standing up or by pushing with your leg muscles. Keep the object close to your body. Don't twist; if you have to turn with the object, change the position of your feet.

- **Standing.** When you are standing, a straight line should run from the top of your ear through the center of your shoulder, the center of your hip, the back of your kneecap, and the front of your ankle bone. Support your weight mainly on your heels, with one or both knees slightly bent. Don't let your pelvis tip forward or your back arch. Shift your weight back and forth from foot to foot. Avoid prolonged standing.

  To check your posture, stand normally with your back to a wall. Your upper back and buttocks should touch the wall; your heels may be a few inches away. Slide one hand into the space between your lower back and the wall. It should slide in easily but should almost touch both your back and the wall. Adjust your posture as needed, and try to hold this position as you walk away from the wall.

- **Walking.** Walk with your toes pointed straight ahead. Keep your back flat, head up and centered over your body, and chin in. Swing your arms freely. Don't wear tight or high-heeled shoes. Walking briskly is better for back health than walking slowly.

Yoga for Relaxation and Pain Relief

Certain types of exercise can provide relief from back pain, depending on the pain's underlying cause. Effective exercises stretch the muscles and connective tissue in the hips, stabilize the spine, and strengthen and build endurance in the core muscles of the back and abdomen.

Yoga may be an option for many back pain sufferers because it offers a variety of exercises that target the spine and the core muscles. Yoga is an ancient practice involving slow, gentle movements performed with controlled breathing and focused attention. Yoga practitioners slowly move into a specific posture (called an *asana*) and hold the posture for up to 60 seconds. There are hundreds of asanas, many of which are easy to do and provide good stretches.

Yoga also involves simple breathing exercises that gently stretch the muscles of the upper back while helping the practitioner focus. Yoga experts say that breathing exercises not only encourage relaxation but also clear the mind and can help relieve mild to moderate pain. Yoga enthusiasts end their workouts energized and refreshed but calm and relaxed.

Many medical professionals now recommend yoga for patients with back pain, particularly postures that involve arching and gently stretching the back, such as the cat pose (similar to the cat stretch shown on p. 159) and the child pose (shown here). These are basic asanas that most people can perform repeatedly and hold for a relatively long time.

Because asanas must be performed correctly to be beneficial, qualified instruction is recommended. For those with back pain, physicians advise choosing an instructor who is not only accomplished in yoga but also knowledgeable about back pain and its causes. Such instructors can steer students away from exercises that do more harm than good. It is especially important to choose postures that will benefit the back without worsening the underlying problem. Some asanas can aggravate an injured or painful back if they are performed incorrectly or too aggressively. In fact, a few yoga postures should not be done at all by people with back pain.

If you have back pain, see your physician to determine its cause before beginning any type of exercise program. Even gentle exercise or stretching can be bad for an already injured back, especially if the spinal disks or nerves are involved. For some back conditions, rest or therapy may be better options than exercise, at least in the short term.

Ask Yourself

QUESTIONS FOR CRITICAL THINKING AND REFLECTION

Do you know anyone who suffers from chronic back pain? If so, how has it affected that person's life? Have you ever had back pain? Do you have any of the risk factors listed in the text? If so, what can you do to lower your risk and avoid developing chronic back problems?

TIPS FOR TODAY AND THE FUTURE

To improve and maintain your flexibility, perform stretches that work the major joints at least twice a week.

RIGHT NOW YOU CAN

- Stand up and stretch—do either the upper-back stretch or the across-the-body stretch shown in the chapter.
- Practice the recommended sitting and standing postures described in the chapter. If needed, adjust your chair or find something to use as a footrest.

IN THE FUTURE YOU CAN

- Build up your flexibility by incorporating more sophisticated stretching exercises into your routine.
- Increase the frequency of your flexibility workouts to 5 or more days per week.
- Increase the efficiency of your workouts by adding stretching exercises to the cool-down period of your endurance or strength workouts.

SUMMARY

- Flexibility, the ability of joints to move through their full range of motion, is highly adaptable and specific to each joint.

- Range of motion can be limited by joint structure, muscle inelasticity, and proprioceptor activity.

- Developing flexibility depends on stretching the elastic tissues within muscles regularly and gently until they lengthen. Overstretching can make connective tissue brittle and lead to rupture.

- Signals sent between muscle and tendon nerves and the spinal cord can enhance flexibility.

- The benefits of flexibility include preventing abnormal stresses that lead to joint deterioration and possibly reducing the risk of injuries.

- Stretches should be held for 10–30 seconds; perform 2–4 repetitions. Flexibility training should be done a minimum of 2–3 days per week, preferably following activity, when muscles are warm.

- Static stretching is done slowly and held to the point of mild tension; ballistic stretching consists of bouncing stretches and can lead to injury. Dynamic stretching involves moving joints slowly and fluidly through their range of motion. Proprioceptive neuromuscular facilitation uses muscle receptors in contracting and relaxing a muscle.

- Passive stretching, using an outside force in moving muscles and joints, achieves a greater range of motion (and has a higher injury risk) than active stretching, which uses opposing muscles to initiate a stretch.

EXERCISE 1   Cat Stretch

Instructions: Begin on all fours with your knees below your hips and your hands below your shoulders. Slowly and deliberately move through a cycle of extension and flexion of your spine. **(a)** Begin by slowly pushing your back up and dropping your head slightly until your spine is extended (rounded). **(b)** Then slowly lower your back and lift your chin slightly until your spine is flexed (relaxed and slightly arched). *Do not press at the ends of the range of motion.* Stop if you feel pain. Do 10 slow, continuous cycles of the movement.

Target: Improved flexibility, relaxation, and reduced stiffness in the spine

EXERCISE 2   Step Stretch *(See Exercise 6 in the flexibility program, p. 150)*

Instructions: Hold each stretch for 10–30 seconds and do 2–4 repetitions on each side.

Target: Improved flexibility, strength, and endurance in the muscles of the hip and the front of the thigh

EXERCISE 3   Alternate Leg Stretcher *(See Exercise 11 in the flexibility program, p. 151)*

Instructions: Hold each stretch for 10–30 seconds and do 2–4 repetitions on each side.

Target: Improved flexibility in the back of the thigh, hip, knee, and buttocks

EXERCISE 4   Trunk Twist

Instructions: Lie on your side with top knee bent, lower leg straight, lower arm extended in front of you on the floor, and upper arm at your side. Push down with your upper knee while you twist your trunk backward. Try to get your shoulders and upper body flat on the floor, turning your head as well. Return to the starting position, and then repeat on the other side. Hold the stretch for 10–30 seconds and do 2–4 repetitions on each side.

Target: Improved flexibility in the lower back and sides

http://www.mcgrawhillconnect.com/
FITNESS AND WELLNESS

EXERCISE 5 — Curl-Up

Instructions: Lie on your back with one or both knees bent and arms crossed on your chest or hands under your lower back. Maintain a neutral spine. Tuck your chin in and slowly curl up, one vertebra at a time, as you use your abdominal muscles to lift your head first and then your shoulders. Stop when you can see your knees and hold for 5–10 seconds before returning to the starting position. Do 10 or more repetitions.

Target: Improved strength and endurance in the abdomen

Variation: Add a twist to develop other abdominal muscles. When you have curled up so that your shoulder blades are off the floor, twist your upper body so that one shoulder is higher than the other; reach past your knee with your upper arm. Hold and then return to the starting position. Repeat on the opposite side. Curl-ups can also be done using an exercise ball.

EXERCISE 6 — Isometric Side Bridge *(See Exercise 11 in the free weights program in Chapter 4, p. 120)*

Instructions: Hold the bridge position for 10 seconds, breathing normally. Work up to a 60-second hold. Perform one or more repetitions on each side.

Target: Increased strength and endurance in the muscles along the sides of the abdomen

Variation: You can make the exercise more difficult by keeping your legs straight and supporting yourself with your feet and forearm (see Lab 5.3) or with your feet and hand (with elbow straight).

EXERCISE 7 — Spine Extensions *("Bird dogs"; see Exercise 10 in the free weights program in Chapter 4, p. 119)*

Instructions: Hold each position for 10–30 seconds. Begin with one repetition on each side, and work up to several repetitions.

Target: Increased strength and endurance in the back, buttocks, and back of the thighs

Variation: If you have experienced back pain in the past or if this exercise is difficult for you, do the exercise with both hands on the ground rather than with one arm lifted. You can make this exercise more difficult by doing it balancing on an exercise ball. Find a balance point on your chest while lying face down on the ball with one arm and the opposite leg on the ground. Tense your abdominal muscles while reaching and extending with one arm and reaching and extending with the opposite leg. Repeat this exercise using the other arm and leg.

EXERCISE 8   Wall Squat (Phantom Chair)

Instructions: Lean against a wall and bend your knees as though you are sitting in a chair. Support your weight with your legs. Begin by holding the position for 5–10 seconds. Squeeze your gluteal muscles together as you do the exercise. Build up to 1 minute or more. Perform one or more repetitions.

Target: Increased strength and endurance in the lower back, thighs, and abdomen

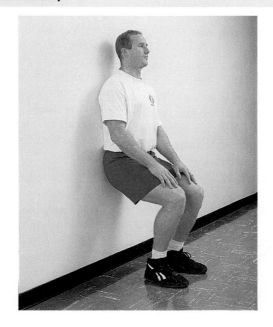

EXERCISE 9   Pelvic Tilt

Instructions: Lie on your back with knees bent and arms extended to the side. Tilt your pelvis under and try to flatten your lower back against the floor. Tighten your buttock and abdominal muscles while you hold this position for 5–10 seconds. Don't hold your breath. Work up to 10 repetitions of the exercise. Pelvic tilts can also be done standing or leaning against a wall.

Note: *Although this is a popular exercise with many therapists, some experts question the safety of pelvic tilts. Stop if you feel pain in your back at any time during the exercise.*

Target: Increased strength and endurance in the abdomen and buttocks

EXERCISE 10   Back Bridge

Instructions: Lie on your back with knees bent and arms extended to the side. Tuck your pelvis under, contract your gluteal muscles, and then lift your tailbone, buttocks, and lower back from the floor. Hold this position for 5–10 seconds with your weight resting on your feet, arms, and shoulders, and then return to the starting position. Work up to 10 repetitions of the exercise.

Target: Increased strength and endurance in the hips and buttocks

McGraw Hill **connect**™ http://www.mcgrawhillconnect.com/
FITNESS AND WELLNESS

Q Is stretching the same as warming up?

A No. They are two distinct activities. A warm-up is light exercise that involves moving the joints through the same motions used during a more intense activity; it increases body temperature so your metabolism works better when you're exercising at high intensity. Stretching increases the movement capability of your joints, so you can move more easily with less risk of injury. It is best to stretch at the end of your aerobic or weight training workout, when your muscles are warm. Warmed muscles stretch better than cold ones and are less prone to injury.

Q How much flexibility do I need?

A This question is not always easy to answer. If you're involved in a sport such as gymnastics, figure skating, or ballet, you are often required to reach extreme joint motions to achieve success. However, nonathletes do not need to reach these extreme joint positions. In fact, too much flexibility may, in some cases, create joint instability and increase your risk of injury. As with other types of fitness, moderation is the key. You should regularly stretch your major joints and muscle groups but not aspire to reach extreme flexibility.

Q Can I stretch too far?

A Yes. As muscle tissue is progressively stretched, it reaches a point where it becomes damaged and may rupture. The greatest danger occurs during passive stretching when a partner is doing the stretching for you. It is critical that your stretching partner not force your joint outside its normal functional range of motion.

Q Can physical training limit flexibility?

A Weight training, jogging, or any physical activity will decrease flexibility if the exercises are not performed through a full range of motion. When done properly, weight training increases flexibility. However, because of the limited range of motion used during the running stride, jogging tends to compromise flexibility. It is important for runners to do flexibility exercises for the hamstrings and quadriceps regularly.

Q Does stretching affect muscular strength?

A Flexibility training increases muscle strength over time, but preexercise stretching can cause short-term decreases in strength and power. Several recent studies have found that stretching decreases strength, power, and motor control following the stretch. This is one reason some experts suggest that people not stretch as part of their exercise warm-up. It is important to warm up before any workout by engaging in 5–10 minutes of light exercise such as walking or slow jogging.

For more Common Questions Answered about flexibility and low-back health, visit the Online Learning Center at www.mhhe.com/fahey.

- The spinal column consists of vertebrae separated by intervertebral disks. It provides structure and support for the body and protects the spinal cord. The core muscles stabilize the spine and transfer force between the upper and lower body.

- Acute back pain can be treated as a soft tissue injury, with cold treatment followed by application of heat (once swelling subsides); prolonged bed rest is not recommended. A variety of treatments have been suggested for chronic back pain, including regular exercise, physical therapy, acupuncture, education, and psychological therapy.

- In addition to good posture, proper body mechanics, and regular physical activity, a program for preventing low-back pain includes exercises that develop flexibility, strength, and endurance in the muscle groups that affect the lower back.

FOR FURTHER EXPLORATION

BOOKS

Anderson, B., and J. Anderson. 2010. *Stretching,* 30th anniv. ed. Bolinas, Calif.: Shelter Publications. *A best-selling exercise book, updated with more than 200 stretches for 60 sports and activities.*

Armiger, P., and M. A. Martyn. 2010. *Stretching for Functional Flexibility.* Philadelphia: Lippincott Williams & Wilkins. *Presents stretching methods for fitness, athletics, and rehabilitation.*

Blahnik, J. 2011. *Full-Body Flexibility,* 2nd ed. Champaign, Ill.: Human Kinetics. *Presents a blend of stretching techniques derived from sports training, martial arts, yoga, and Pilates.*

McGill, S. 2007. *Low Back Disorders: Evidence-Based Prevention and Rehabilitation,* 2nd ed. Champaign, Ill.: Human Kinetics. *A comprehensive guide to the prevention, diagnosis, and treatment of back pain.*

McGill, S. 2009. *Ultimate Back Fitness and Performance,* 4th ed. Waterloo, Canada: Backfit Pro. *Written by one of the premier researchers in the world on back biomechanics and back pain; describes mechanisms of back pain and exercises and movement patterns for preventing it.*

McGill, S. 2010. *Ultimate Back: Enhancing Performance* (DVD). Waterloo, Canada: Backfit Pro. *A video by the authors of* Ultimate Back Fitness and Performance.

Nelson, A. G., et al. 2006. *Stretching Anatomy.* Champaign, Ill.: Human Kinetics. *A guide to stretching that features highly detailed illustrations of the muscles that are affected by each exercise.*

ORGANIZATIONS AND WEB SITES

American Academy of Orthopaedic Surgeons. Provides information about a variety of joint problems.
   http://orthoinfo.aaos.org

Back Fit Pro. A Web site maintained by Dr. Stuart McGill, a professor of spine biomechanics at the University of Waterloo, which provides evidence-based information on preventing and treating back pain.

http://www.backfitpro.com

CUErgo: Cornell University Ergonomics Web Site. Provides information about how to arrange a computer workstation to prevent back pain and repetitive strain injuries, as well as other topics related to ergonomics.

http://ergo.human.cornell.edu

Georgia State University: Flexibility. Provides information about the benefits of stretching and ways to develop a safe and effective program; includes illustrations of stretches.

http://www2.gsu.edu/~wwwfit/flexibility.html

Mayo Clinic: Focus on Flexibility. Presents an easy-to-use program of basic stretching exercises for beginners, with a focus on the benefits of greater flexibility.

http://www.mayoclinic.com/health/stretching/HQ01447

NIH Back Pain Fact Sheet. Provides basic information on the prevention and treatment of back pain.

http://www.ninds.nih.gov/disorders/backpain/backpain.htm

Southern California Orthopedic Institute. Provides information on a variety of orthopedic problems, including back injuries; also has illustrations of spinal anatomy.

http://www.scoi.com

Stretching and Flexibility. Provides information on the physiology of stretching and different types of stretching exercises.

http://www.ifafitness.com/stretch/index.html

See also the listings for Chapters 2 and 4.

SELECTED BIBLIOGRAPHY

American College of Sports Medicine. 2009. *ACSM's Guidelines for Exercise Testing and Prescription,* 8th ed. Philadelphia: Lippincott Williams and Wilkins.

American College of Sports Medicine. 2009. *ACSM's Resource Manual for Guidelines for Exercise Testing and Prescription,* 6th ed. Philadelphia: Lippincott Williams and Wilkins.

Aquino, C. F., et al. 2010. Stretching versus strength training in lengthened position in subjects with tight hamstring muscles: a randomized controlled trial. *Manual Therapy* 15(1): 26–31.

Ayala, F., et al. 2010. Effect of active stretch on hip flexion range of motion in female professional futbal players. *The Journal of Sports Medicine and Physical Fitness* 50(4): 428–435.

Bacurau, R. F., et al. 2009. Acute effect of a ballistic and a static stretching exercise bout on flexibility and maximal strength. *Journal of Strength and Conditioning Research* 23(1): 304–308.

Bazett-Jones, D. M., et al. 2008. Sprint and vertical jump performances are not affected by six weeks of static hamstring stretching. *Journal of Strength and Conditioning Research* 22(1): 25–31.

Bogduk, N. 2010. A cure for back pain? *Pain* 149(1): 7–8.

Carpes, F. P., et al. 2008. Effects of a program for trunk strength and stability on pain, low back and pelvis kinematics, and body balance: A pilot study. *Journal of Bodywork and Movement Therapies* 12(1): 22–30.

Chen, C. H., et al. 2011. Effects of flexibility training on eccentric exercise-induced muscle damage. *Medicine and Science in Sports and Exercise* 43(3): 491–500.

Chen, K. M., et al. 2008. Physical fitness of older adults in senior activity centers after 24-week silver yoga exercises. *Journal of Clinical Nursing* 17(19): 2634–2646.

Christiansen, C. L. 2008. The effects of hip and ankle stretching on gait function of older people. *Archive of Physical Medicine and Rehabilitation* 89(8): 1421–1428.

Costa, P. B., et al. 2009. The acute effects of different durations of static stretching on dynamic balance performance. *Journal of Strength and Conditioning Research* 23(1): 141–147.

Davis, D. S., et al. 2008. Concurrent validity of four clinical tests used to measure hamstring flexibility. *Journal of Strength and Conditioning Research* 22(2): 583–588.

Deleget, A. 2010. Overview of thigh injuries in dance. *Journal of Dance Medicine and Science* 14(3): 97–102.

Duehring, M. D., et al. 2009. Strength and conditioning practices of United States high school strength and conditioning coaches. *Journal of Strength and Conditioning Research* 23(8): 2188–2203.

Duque, I., et al. 2011. Maximal aerobic power in patients with chronic low back pain: A comparison with healthy subjects. *European Spine Journal* 20(1): 87–93.

Fasen, J. M., et al. 2009. A randomized controlled trial of hamstring stretching: comparison of four techniques. *Journal of Strength and Conditioning Research.* 23(2): 660–667.

Favero, J. P., et al. 2009. Effects of an acute bout of static stretching on 40 m sprint performance: Influence of baseline flexibility. *Research in Sports Medicine* 17(1): 50–60.

Feland, J. B., et al. 2010. Whole body vibration as an adjunct to static stretching. *International Journal of Sports Medicine* 31(8): 584–589.

Fenwick, C. M., et al. 2009. Comparison of different rowing exercises: Trunk muscle activation and lumbar spine motion, load, and stiffness. *Journal of Strength and Conditioning Research* 23(5): 1408–1417.

Field, T. 2011. Yoga clinical research review. *Complementary Therapies in Clinical Practice* 17(1): 1–8.

Garber, C. E., et al. 2011. Quantity and quality of exercise for developing and maintaining cardiorespiratory, musculoskeletal, and neuromotor fitness in apparently healthy adults: guidance for prescribing exercise. *Medicine and Science in Sports and Exercise* 43(7): 1334–1359.

Gergley, J. C. 2010. Latent effect of passive static stretching on driver club-head speed, distance, accuracy, and consistent ball contact in young male competitive golfers. *Journal of Strength and Conditioning Research* 24(12): 3326–3333.

Guidetti, L., et al. 2009. Precompetition warm-up in elite and subelite rhythmic gymnastics. *Journal of Strength and Conditioning Research.* 23(6): 1877–1882.

Guillot, A., et al. 2010. Does motor imagery enhance stretching and flexibility? *Journal of Sports Sciences* 28(3): 291–298.

Gurjao, A. L., et al. 2009. Acute effect of static stretching on rate of force development and maximal voluntary contraction in older women. *Journal of Strength and Conditioning Research* 23(7): 2149–2154.

Henchoz, Y., and A. Kai-Lik So. 2008. Exercise and nonspecific low back pain: A literature review. *Joint Bone Spine* 75(5): 533–539.

Herman, S. L., et al. 2008. Four-week dynamic stretching warm-up intervention elicits longer-term performance benefits. *Journal of Strength and Conditioning Research* 22(4): 1286–1297.

Heuser, M., et al. 2010. The effects of stretching on knee flexor fatigue and perceived exertion. *Journal of Sports Sciences* 28(2): 219–226.

Higgs, F., et al. 2009. The effect of a four-week proprioceptive neuromuscular facilitation stretching program on isokinetic torque production. *Journal of Strength and Conditioning Research* 23(5): 1442–1447.

Jaggers, J. R., et al. 2008. The acute effects of dynamic and ballistic stretching on vertical jump height, force, and power. *Journal of Strength and Conditioning Research* 22(6): 1844–1849.

Jenkins, J., et al. 2010. Flexibility for runners. *Clinics in Sports Medicine* 29(3): 365–377.

Judge, L. W., et al. 2009. An examination of the stretching practices of Division I and Division III college football programs in the midwestern United States. *Journal of Strength and Conditioning Research* 23(4): 1091–1096.

Keller, A., et al. 2008. Predictors of change in trunk muscle strength for patients with chronic low back pain randomized to lumbar fusion or cognitive intervention and exercises. *Pain Medicine* 9(6): 680–687.

Kiecolt-Glaser, J. K., et al. 2010. Stress, inflammation, and yoga practice. *Psychosomatic Medicine* 72(1): 113–121.

Lariviere, C., et al. 2010. Poor back muscle endurance is related to pain catastrophizing in patients with chronic low back pain. *Spine* 35(22): E1178–E1186.

LaRoche, D. P., et al. 2008. Chronic stretching and voluntary muscle force. *Journal of Strength and Conditioning Research* 22(2): 589–596.

McGill, S. M., et al. 2009. Comparison of different strongman events: trunk muscle activation and lumbar spine motion, load, and stiffness. *Journal of Strength and Conditioning Research* 23(4): 1148–1161.

McHugh, M. P., and M. Nesse. 2008. Effect of stretching on strength loss and pain after eccentric exercise. *Medicine and Science in Sports and Exercise* 40(3): 566–573.

Meroni, R., et al. 2010. Comparison of active stretching technique and static stretching technique on hamstring flexibility. *Clinical Journal of Sport Medicine* 20(1): 8–14.

Molacek, Z. D., et al. 2010. Effects of low- and high-volume stretching on bench press performance in collegiate football players. *Journal of Strength and Conditioning Research* 24(3): 711–716.

Monteiro, W. D., et al. 2008. Influence of strength training on adult women's flexibility. *Journal of Strength and Conditioning Research* 22(3): 672–677.

Morse, C. I., et al. 2008. The acute effect of stretching on the passive stiffness of the human gastrocnemius muscle tendon unit. *Journal of Physiology* 586(1): 97–106.

Nieman, D. C. 2011. *Exercise Testing and Prescription: A Health-Related Approach,* 7th ed. New York: McGraw-Hill.

Purcell, L. 2009. Causes and prevention of low back pain in young athletes. *Paediatrics and Child Health* 14(8): 533–538.

Rancour, J., et al. 2009. The effects of intermittent stretching following a 4-week static stretching protocol: A randomized trial. *Journal of Strength and Conditioning Research* 23(8): 2217–2222.

Rasmussen-Barr, E., et al. 2009. Graded exercise for recurrent low-back pain: A randomized, controlled trial with 6-, 12-, and 36-month follow-ups. *Spine* 34(3): 221–228.

Ryan, E. D., et al. 2008. Do practical durations of stretching alter muscle strength? A dose-response study. *Medicine and Science in Sports and Exercise* 40(8): 1529–1537.

Saeed, S. A., et al. 2010. Exercise, yoga, and meditation for depressive and anxiety disorders. *American Family Physician* 81(8): 981–986.

Samuel, M. N., et al. 2008. Acute effects of static and ballistic stretching on measures of strength and power. *Journal of Strength and Conditioning Research* 22(5): 1422–1428.

Scannell, J. P., et al. 2009. Disc prolapse: Evidence of reversal with repeated extension. *Spine* 34(4): 344–350.

Small, K., et al. 2008. A systematic review into the efficacy of static stretching as part of a warm-up for the prevention of exercise-related injury. *Research in Sports Medicine* 16(3): 213–231.

Tekur, P., et al. 2008. Effect of short-term intensive yoga program on pain, functional disability and spinal flexibility in chronic low back pain: A randomized control study. *Journal of Alternative and Complementary Medicine* 14(6): 637–644.

Torres, E. M., et al. 2008. Effects of stretching on upper-body muscular performance. *Journal of Strength and Conditioning Research* 22(4): 1279–1285.

Verbunt, J. A., et al. 2010. Cause or effect? Deconditioning and chronic low back pain. *Pain* 149(3): 428–430.

Weil, R. 2008. Exercising the aging body. Part 2: Flexibility, balance, and diabetes control. *Diabetes Self-Management* 25(1): 42–52.

Werner, G. 2010. Strength and conditioning techniques in the rehabilitation of sports injury. *Clinics in Sports Medicine* 29(1): 177–191.

Winchester, J. B., et al. 2008. Static stretching impairs sprint performance in collegiate track and field athletes. *Journal of Strength and Conditioning Research* 22(1): 13–19.

Winke, M. R., et al. 2010. Moderate static stretching and torque production of the knee flexors. *Journal of Strength and Conditioning Research* 24(3): 706–710.

Ylinen, J., et al. 2009. Effect of stretching on hamstring muscle compliance. *Journal of Rehabilitation Medicine* 41(1): 80–84.

LAB 5.1 Assessing Your Current Level of Flexibility

Part I Sit-and-Reach Test

Equipment

Use a modified Wells and Dillon flexometer or construct your own measuring device using a firm box or two pieces of wood about 30 centimeters (12 inches) high attached at right angles to each other. Attach a metric ruler to measure the extent of reach. With the low numbers of the ruler toward the person being tested, set the 26-centimeter mark of the ruler at the footline of the box. Individuals who cannot reach as far as the footline will have scores below 26 centimeters; those who can reach past their feet will have scores above 26 centimeters. Most studies show no relationship between performance on the sit-and-reach test and the incidence of back pain.

Preparation

Warm up your muscles with a low-intensity activity such as walking or easy jogging. Then perform slow stretching movements.

Instructions

1. Remove your shoes and sit facing the flexibility measuring device with your knees fully extended and your feet flat against the device about 10 centimeters (4 inches) apart.

2. Reach as far forward as you can, with palms down, arms evenly stretched, and knees fully extended; hold the position of maximum reach for about 2 seconds.

3. Perform the stretch 2 times, recording the distance of maximum reach to the nearest 0.5 centimeters: _____ cm

Rating Your Flexibility

Find the score in the table below to determine your flexibility rating. Record it here and on the final page of this lab.
Rating: _____

Ratings for Sit-and-Reach Test

Men	Rating/Score (cm)*				
	Needs Improvement	Fair	Good	Very Good	Excellent
Age: 15–19	Below 24	24–28	29–33	34–38	Above 38
20–29	Below 25	25–29	30–33	34–39	Above 39
30–39	Below 23	23–27	28–32	33–37	Above 37
40–49	Below 18	18–23	24–28	29–34	Above 34
50–59	Below 16	16–23	24–27	28–34	Above 34
60–69	Below 15	15–19	20–24	25–32	Above 32
Women					
Age: 15–19	Below 29	29–33	34–37	38–42	Above 42
20–29	Below 28	28–32	33–36	37–40	Above 40
30–39	Below 27	27–31	32–35	36–40	Above 40
40–49	Below 25	25–29	30–33	34–37	Above 37
50–59	Below 25	25–29	30–32	33–38	Above 38
60–69	Below 23	23–26	27–30	31–34	Above 34

*Footline is set at 26 cm.

SOURCE: *The Canadian Physical Activity, Fitness & Lifestyle Approach: CSEP-Health & Fitness Program's Health-Related Appraisal and Counselling Strategy,* 3rd edition, 2003. Adapted with permission from the Canadian Society for Exercise Physiology.

http://www.mcgrawhillconnect.com/
FITNESS AND WELLNESS

Part II   Range-of-Motion Assessment

This portion of the lab can be completed by doing visual comparisons or by measuring joint range of motion with a goniometer or other instrument.

Equipment

1. A partner to do visual comparisons or to measure the range of motion of your joints. (You can also use a mirror to perform your own visual comparisons.)

2. For the measurement method, you need a goniometer, flexometer, or other instrument to measure range of motion.

Preparation

Warm up your muscles with some low-intensity activity such as walking or easy jogging.

Instructions

On the following pages, the average range of motion is illustrated and listed quantitatively for some of the major joints. Visually assess the range of motion in your joints, and compare it to that shown in the illustrations. For each joint, note (with a check mark) whether your range of motion is above average, average, or below average and in need of improvement. Average values for range of motion are given in degrees for each joint in the assessment. You can also complete the assessment by measuring your range of motion with a goniometer, flexometer, or other instrument. If you are using this measurement method, identify your rating (above average, average, or below average) and record your range of motion in degrees next to the appropriate category. Although the measurement method is more time-consuming, it allows you to track the progress of your stretching program more precisely and to note changes within the broader ratings categories (below average, above average).

   Record your ratings on the following pages and on the chart on the final page of this lab. (Ratings were derived from several published sources.)

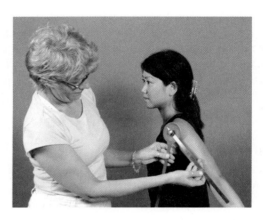

Assessment of range of motion using a goniometer

1. Shoulder Abduction and Adduction

For each position and arm, check one of the following; fill in degrees if using the measurement method.

Shoulder abduction—raise arm up to the side.

Right	Left	
_____	_____	Below average/needs improvement
_____	_____	Average (92–95°)
_____	_____	Above average

Shoulder abduction—move arm down and in front of body.

Right	Left	
_____	_____	Below average/needs improvement
_____	_____	Average (124–127°)
_____	_____	Above average.

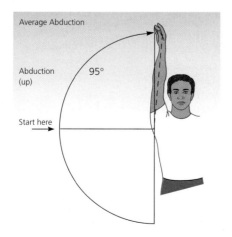

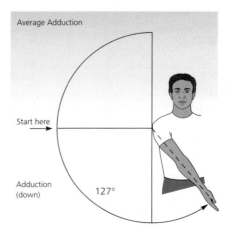

2. Shoulder Flexion and Extension

For each position and arm, check one of the following; fill in degrees if using the measurement method.

Shoulder flexion—raise arm up in front of the body.

Right   Left

_____ _____   Below average/needs improvement

_____ _____   Average (92–95°)

_____ _____   Above average

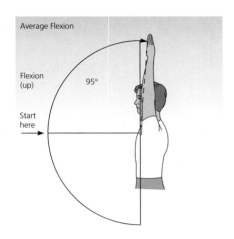

Shoulder extension—move arm down and behind the body.

Right   Left

_____ _____   Below average/needs improvement

_____ _____   Average (145–150°)

_____ _____   Above average

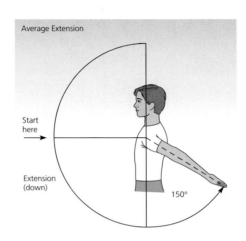

3. Trunk/Low-Back Lateral Flexion

Bend directly sideways at your waist. To prevent injury, keep your knees slightly bent, and support your trunk by placing your hand or forearm on your thigh. Check one of the following for each side; fill in degrees if using the measurement method.

Right   Left

_____ _____   Below average/needs improvement

_____ _____   Average (36–40°)

_____ _____   Above average

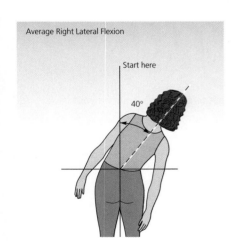

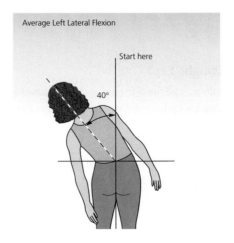

4. Hip Abduction

Raise your leg to the side at the hip. Check one of the following for each leg; fill in degrees if using the measurement method.

Right   *Left*

_____   _____   Below average/needs improvement

_____   _____   Average (40–45°)

_____   _____   Above average

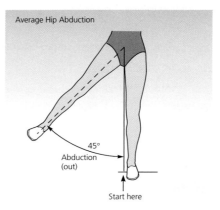

5. Hip Flexion (Bent Knee)

With one leg flat on the floor, bend the other knee and lift the leg up at the hip. Check one of the following for each leg; fill in degrees if using the measurement method.

Right   *Left*

_____   _____   Below average/needs improvement

_____   _____   Average (121–125°)

_____   _____   Above average

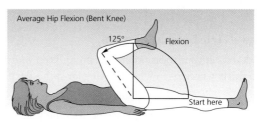

6. Hip Flexion (Straight Leg)

With one leg flat on the floor, raise the other leg at the hip, keeping both legs straight. Take care not to put excess strain on your back. Check one of the following for each leg; fill in degrees if using the measurement method.

Right   *Left*

_____   _____   Below average/needs improvement

_____   _____   Average (79–81°)

_____   _____   Above average

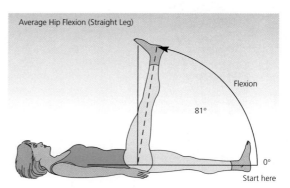

7. Ankle Dorsiflexion and Plantar Flexion

For each position and foot, check one of the following; fill in degrees if using the measurement method.

Ankle dorsiflexion—pull your toes toward your shin.

Right   Left

_____	_____	Below average/needs improvement
_____	_____	Average (9–13°)
_____	_____	Above average

Plantar flexion—point your toes.

Right   Left

_____	_____	Below average/needs improvement
_____	_____	Average (50–55°)
_____	_____	Above average

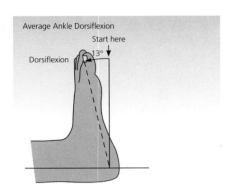

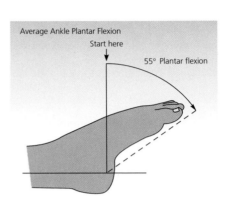

Rating Your Flexibility

Sit-and-reach test: Score: _____ cm   Rating: _____

Range-of-Motion Assessment

Identify your rating for each joint on each side of the body. If you used the comparison method, put check marks in the appropriate categories; if you measured range of motion, enter the degrees for each joint in the appropriate category.

Joint/Assessment		Right			Left		
		Below Average	Average	Above Average	Below Average	Average	Above Average
1. Shoulder abduction and adduction	Abduction						
	Adduction						
2. Shoulder flexion and extension	Flexion						
	Extension						
3. Trunk/low-back lateral flexion	Flexion						
4. Hip abduction	Abduction						
5. Hip flexion (bent knee)	Flexion						
6. Hip flexion (straight leg)	Flexion						
7. Ankle dorsiflexion and plantar flexion	Dorsiflexion						
	Plantar flexion						

Mc Graw Hill connect™ http://www.mcgrawhillconnect.com/ | FITNESS AND WELLNESS

Using Your Results

How did you score? Are you surprised by your ratings for flexibility? Are you satisfied with your current ratings?

If you're not satisfied, set a realistic goal for improvement.

Are you satisfied with your current level of flexibility as expressed in your daily life—for example, your ability to maintain good posture and move easily and without pain?

If you're not satisfied, set some realistic goals for improvement:

What should you do next? Enter the results of this lab in the Preprogram Assessment column in Appendix C. If you've set goals for improvement, begin planning your flexibility program by completing the plan in Lab 5.2. After several weeks of your program, complete this lab again and enter the results in the Postprogram Assessment column of Appendix C. How do the results compare?

LAB 5.2 Creating a Personalized Program for Developing Flexibility

1. *Goals.* List goals for your flexibility program. On the left, include specific, measurable goals that you can use to track the progress of your fitness program. These goals might be things like raising your sit-and-reach score from fair to good or your bent-leg hip flexion rating from below average to average. On the right, include long-term and more qualitative goals, such as reducing your risk for back pain.

Specific Goals: Current Status   Final Goals

_____   _____

_____   _____

_____   _____

Other Goals: _____

_____

2. *Exercises.* The exercises in the program plan below are from the general stretching program presented in Chapter 5. You can add or delete exercises depending on your needs, goals, and preferences. For any exercises you add, fill in the areas of the body affected.

3. *Frequency.* A minimum frequency of 2–3 days per week is recommended; 5–7 days per week is ideal. You may want to do your stretching exercises the same days you plan to do cardiorespiratory endurance exercise or weight training, because muscles stretch better following exercise, when they are warm.

4. *Intensity.* All stretches should be done to the point of mild discomfort, not pain.

5. *Time/duration.* All stretches should be held for 15–30 seconds. (PNF techniques should include a 6-second contraction followed by a 10–30-second assisted stretch.) All stretches should be performed 2–4 times.

Program Plan for Flexibility

Exercise	Areas Stretched	Frequency (check ✓)						
		M	T	W	Th	F	Sa	Su
Head turns and tilts	Neck							
Towel stretch	Triceps, shoulders, chest							
Across-the-body and overhead stretches	Shoulders, upper back, back of the arm							
Upper-back stretch	Upper back							
Lateral stretch	Trunk muscles							
Step stretch	Hip, front of thigh							
Side lunge	Inner thigh, hip, calf							
Inner-thigh stretch	Inner thigh, hip							
Trunk rotation	Trunk, outer thigh and hip, lower back							
Modified hurdler stretch	Back of the thigh, lower back							
Alternate leg stretcher	Back of the thigh, hip, knee, ankle, buttocks							
Lower-leg stretch	Back of the lower leg							

You can monitor your program using a chart like the one on the next page.

Flexibility Program Chart

Fill in the dates you perform each stretch, the number of seconds you hold each stretch (should be 15–30), and the number of repetitions of each (should be 2–4). For an easy check on the duration of your stretches, count "one thousand one, one thousand two," and so on. You will probably find that over time you'll be able to hold each stretch longer (in addition to being able to stretch farther).

Exercise/Date																					
	Duration																				
	Reps																				
	Duration																				
	Reps																				
	Duration																				
	Reps																				
	Duration																				
	Reps																				
	Duration																				
	Reps																				
	Duration																				
	Reps																				
	Duration																				
	Reps																				
	Duration																				
	Reps																				
	Duration																				
	Reps																				
	Duration																				
	Reps																				
	Duration																				
	Reps																				
	Duration																				
	Reps																				
	Duration																				
	Reps																				
	Duration																				
	Reps																				
	Duration																				
	Reps																				
	Duration																				
	Reps																				
	Duration																				
	Reps																				

LAB 5.3 Assessing Muscular Endurance for Low-Back Health

The three tests in this lab evaluate the muscular endurance of major spine-stabilizing muscles.

Side Bridge Endurance Test

Equipment

1. Stopwatch or clock with a second hand
2. Exercise mat
3. Partner

Preparation

Warm up your muscles with some low-intensity activity such as walking or easy jogging. Practice assuming the side bridge position described below.

Instructions

1. Lie on the mat on your side with your legs extended. Place your top foot in front of your lower foot for support. Lift your hips off the mat so that you are supporting yourself on one elbow and your feet (see photo). Your body should maintain a straight line. Breathe normally; don't hold your breath.

2. Hold the position as long as possible. Your partner should keep track of the time and make sure that you maintain the correct position. Your final score is the total time you are able to hold the side bridge with correct form—from the time you lift your hips until your hips return to the mat.

3. Rest for 5 minutes and then repeat the test on the other side. Record your times here and on the chart at the end of the lab. Right side bridge time: _____ sec   Left side bridge time: _____ sec

Trunk Flexors Endurance Test

Equipment

1. Stopwatch or clock with a second hand
2. Exercise mat or padded exercise table
3. Two helpers
4. Jig angled at 60 degrees from the floor or padded bench (optional)

Preparation

Warm up with some low-intensity activity such as walking or easy jogging.

Instructions

1. To start, assume a sit-up posture with your back supported at an angle of 60 degrees from the floor; support can be provided by a jig, a padded bench, or a spotter (see photos). Your knees and hips should both be flexed at 90 degrees, and your arms should be folded across your chest with your hands placed on the opposite shoulders. Your toes should be secured under a toe strap or held by a partner.

2. Your goal is to hold the starting position (isometric contraction) as long as possible after the support is pulled away. To begin the test, a helper should pull the jig or other support back about 10 centimeters (4 inches). The helper should keep track of the time; if a spotter is acting as your support, she or he should be ready to support your weight as soon as your torso begins to move back. Your final score is the total time you are able to hold the contraction—from the time the support is removed until any part of your back touches the support. Remember to breathe normally throughout the test.

3. Record your time here and on the chart at the end of the lab. Trunk flexors endurance time: _____ sec

Mc Graw Hill **connect**™ http://www.mcgrawhillconnect.com/
|FITNESS AND WELLNESS

Back Extensors Endurance Test

Equipment

1. Stopwatch or clock with a second hand
2. Extension bench with padded ankle support or any padded bench
3. Partner

Preparation

Warm up with some low-intensity activity such as walking or easy jogging.

Instructions

1. Lie face down on the test bench with your upper body extending out over the end of the bench and your pelvis, hips, and knees flat on the bench. Your arms should be folded across your chest with your hands placed on the opposite shoulders. Your feet should be secured under a padded strap or held by a partner.

2. Your goal is to hold your upper body in a straight horizontal line with your lower body as long as possible. Keep your neck straight and neutral; don't raise your head and don't arch your back. Breathe normally. Your partner should keep track of the time and watch your form. Your final score is the total time you are able to hold the horizontal position—from the time you assume the position until your upper body drops from the horizontal position.

3. Record your time here and on the chart below. Back extensors endurance time: _____ sec

Rating Your Test Results for Muscular Endurance for Low-Back Health

The table below shows mean endurance test times for healthy young college students with a mean age of 21 years. Compare your scores with the times shown in the table. (If you are older or have suffered from low-back pain in the past, these ratings are less accurate; however, your time scores can be used as a point of comparison.)

| | Mean Endurance Times (sec) | | | |
	Right side bridge	Left side bridge	Trunk flexors	Back extensors
Men	95	99	136	161
Women	75	78	134	185

SOURCE: Adapted with permission from S. M. McGill, 2007, *Low Back Disorders: Evidence-Based Prevention and Rehabilitation,* 2nd ed., p. 211. Champaign, IL: Human Kinetics.

Right side bridge: _____ sec   Rating (above mean, at mean, below mean): _____

Left side bridge: _____ sec   Rating (above mean, at mean, below mean): _____

Trunk flexors: _____ sec   Rating (above mean, at mean, below mean): _____

Back extensors: _____ sec   Rating (above mean, at mean, below mean): _____

Using Your Results

How did you score? Are you surprised by your scores for the low-back tests? Are you satisfied with your current ratings?

If you're not satisfied, set a realistic goal for improvement. The norms in this lab are based on healthy young adults, so a score above the mean may or may not be realistic for you. Instead, you may want to set a specific goal based on time rather than rating; for example, set a goal of improving your time by 10%. Imbalances in muscular endurance have been linked with back problems, so if your rating is significantly lower for one of the three tests, you should focus particular attention on that area of your body.
Goal:

What should you do next? Enter the results of this lab in the Preprogram Assessment column in Appendix C. If you've set a goal for improvement, begin a program of low-back exercises such as that suggested in this chapter. After several weeks of your program, complete this lab again and enter the results in the Postprogram Assessment column of Appendix C. How do the results compare?

CHAPTER 10

Putting Together a Complete Fitness Program

LOOKING AHEAD...

After reading this chapter, you should be able to:

- List the steps you can follow to put together a successful personal fitness program
- Describe strategies that can help you maintain a fitness program over the long term
- Tailor a fitness program to accommodate different life stages

TEST YOUR KNOWLEDGE

1. Which of the following physical activities is considered a high-intensity exercise?
   a. hiking uphill
   b. singles tennis
   c. jumping rope
2. Older adults should avoid exercise to protect themselves against falls and injuries. True or false?
3. Swimming is a total fitness activity that develops all the components of health-related fitness. True or false?

Answers

1. **All Three.** According to the U.S. Department of Health and Human Services, you can perform any of these activities for 75 minutes per week to obtain health and wellness benefits.
2. **False.** Older adults receive the same health benefits from exercise as younger adults, including improvements in strength, body composition, cardiorespiratory health, flexibility, balance, stability, and cognitive functioning. A far greater danger is posed by inactivity.
3. **False.** Swimming is excellent for developing cardiorespiratory endurance and muscular endurance, but because it is not a weight-bearing activity, it tends to reduce bone density. Swimmers are advised to include weight training in their exercise program to maintain bone mass.

connect http://www.mcgrawhillconnect.com
FITNESS AND WELLNESS

LearnSmart
GET A BETTER GRADE. TRY LEARNSMART.

nderstanding the benefits of physical fitness, as explained in Chapters 1–6, is the first step toward creating a well-rounded exercise program. The next challenge is to choose activities and combine them into a program that develops all the components of fitness and helps you stay motivated. This chapter presents a step-by-step plan for creating and maintaining a well-rounded fitness program. At the end of this chapter, you'll find sample programs based on popular activities. These programs provide structure that can be helpful if you're beginning an exercise program for the first time.

DEVELOPING A PERSONAL FITNESS PLAN

If you're ready to create a complete fitness program based on the activities you enjoy most, begin by preparing the program plan and contract in Lab 7.1. By carefully developing your plan and signing a contract, you'll increase your chances of success. The step-by-step procedure outlined here will guide you through the steps of Lab 7.1 to create an exercise program that's right for you. (See Figure 7.1 for a sample personal fitness program plan and contract.)

If you'd like additional help in setting up your program, choose one of the sample programs at the end of this chapter. Sample programs are provided for walking/jogging/running, cycling, swimming, and rowing. They include detailed instructions for starting a program and developing and maintaining fitness.

1. Set Goals

Ask yourself, "What do I want from my fitness program?" Develop different types of goals—general and specific, long term and short term. General or long-term goals might include lowering your risk for chronic disease, improving posture, having more energy, or improving the fit of your clothes.

It's also a good idea to develop some specific, short-term goals based on measurable factors. Specific goals might be:

- Raising cardiorespiratory capacity ($\dot{V}O_{2max}$) by 10%.
- Reducing the time it takes you to jog 2 miles from 22 minutes to 19 minutes.
- Increasing the number of push-ups you can do from 15 to 25.
- Lowering your BMI from 26 to 24.5.

Having specific goals will allow you to track your progress and enjoy the measurable changes brought about by your fitness program. Finally, break your specific goals into several smaller steps (mini-goals), such as those shown in Figure 7.1. (For detailed discussions of goals and goal setting in a behavior change or fitness program, refer back to Chapters 1 and 2.)

An overall fitness program includes activities to develop all the components of physical fitness.

Physical fitness assessment tests—as described in Chapters 3–6—are essential to determining your goals. They help you decide which types of exercise you should emphasize, and they help you understand the relative difficulty of attaining specific goals. If you have health problems, such as high blood pressure, heart disease, obesity, or serious joint or muscle disabilities, see your physician before taking assessment tests. Measure your progress by taking these tests about every 3 months.

2. Select Activities

If you have already chosen activities and created separate program plans for different fitness components in

Fitness Tip

Although some research indicates that pre-workout stretching can reduce muscle power and interfere with motor control, there are benefits to stretching after running. You can increase flexibility by doing stretching exercises as part of your cool-down.

A. I [Tracie Kaufman] am contracting with myself to follow a physical
(name)
fitness program to work toward the following goals:

Specific or short-term goals

1. Improving cardiorespiratory fitness by raising my $\dot{V}O_{2max}$ from 34 to 37 ml/kg/min
2. Improving upper body muscular strength and endurance rating from fair to good
3. Improving body composition (from 28% to 25% body fat)
4. Improving my tennis game (hitting 20 playable shots in a row against the ball machine)

General or long-term goals

1. Developing a more positive attitude about myself
2. Improving the fit of my clothes
3. Building and maintaining bone mass to reduce my risk of osteoporosis
4. Increasing my life expectancy and reducing my risk for diabetes and heart disease

B. **My program plan is as follows:**

	Components (Check X)						Frequency (Check X)							Intensity*
Activities	CRE	MS	ME	F	BC	Time	M	Tu	W	Th	F	S	S	
Swimming	X	X	X	X	X	35min	X		X		X			140–170 bpm
Tennis	X	X	X	X	X	90min						X		RPE = 13–16
Weight training		X	X	X	X	30min		X		X		X		see Lab 4.3
Stretching				X		25min	X		X		X	X		—

*List your target heart rate range or an RPE value if appropriate.

C. My program will begin on [Sept. ⬍] [21 ⬍] My program includes the following schedule
of mini-goals. For each step in my program, I will give myself the reward listed.

Completing 2 full weeks of program (mini-goal 1)	Oct. ⬍ 5 ⬍	movie with friends (reward)
$\dot{V}O_{2max}$ of 35 ml/kg/min (mini-goal 2)	Nov. ⬍ 2 ⬍	new CD (reward)
Completing 10 full weeks of program (mini-goal 3)	Nov. ⬍ 30 ⬍	new sweater (reward)
Percent body fat of 27% (mini-goal 4)	Dec. ⬍ 22 ⬍	weekend away (reward)
$\dot{V}O_{2max}$ of 36 ml/kg/min (mini-goal)	Jan. ⬍ 18 ⬍	new CD (reward)

D. My program will include the addition of physical activity to my daily routine (such
as climbing stairs or walking to class):

1. Walking to and from campus job
2. Taking the stairs to dorm room instead of elevator
3. Bicycling to the library instead of driving
4. Doing one active chore a day
5.

E. I will use the following tools to monitor my program and my progress toward
my goals:

I'll use a chart that lists the number of laps and minutes I swim and the
charts for strength and flexibility from Labs 4.3 & 5.2.

I sign this contract as an indication of my personal commitment to reach my goal.

_____*Tracie Kaufman*_____   Sep. ⬍ 10 ⬍
(your signature)

I have recruited a helper who will witness my contract and

swim with me three days per week

(list any way your helper will participate in your program)

_____*Russell Walker*_____   Sep. ⬍ 10 ⬍
(witness's signature)

FIGURE 7.1   A sample personal fitness program plan and contract.

Table 7.1	Examples of Different Aerobic Activities and Their Intensities

MODERATE-INTENSITY ACTIVITIES	VIGOROUS-INTENSITY ACTIVITIES
• Walking briskly (3 miles per hour or faster, but not race-walking)	• Race-walking, jogging, or running
• Water aerobics	• Swimming laps
• Bicycling slower than 10 miles per hour	• Singles tennis
• Doubles tennis	• Aerobic dancing
• Ballroom dancing	• Bicycling 10 miles per hour or faster
• General gardening	• Jumping rope
	• Heavy gardening (continuous digging or hoeing)
	• Hiking uphill or with a heavy backpack

SOURCES: Physical Activity Guidelines Advisory Committee. 2008. *Physical Activity Guidelines Advisory Committee Report,* 2008. Washington, D.C.: U.S. Department of Health and Human Services.

Chapters 3–5, you can put those plans together into a single program. It's usually best to include exercises to develop each of the health-related components of fitness, as follows:

- Cardiorespiratory endurance is developed by activities that involve continuous rhythmic movements of large-muscle groups, like those in the legs (see Chapter 3).
- Muscular strength and endurance are developed by training against resistance (see Chapter 4).
- Flexibility is developed by stretching the major muscle groups (see Chapter 5).
- Healthy body composition can be developed by combining a sensible diet and a program of regular exercise, including cardiorespiratory endurance exercise to burn calories and resistance training to build muscle mass (see Chapter 6).

Table 7.1 shows the intensity levels of several popular activities that promote health. Check the intensity levels of the activities you're considering to make sure the program you put together will help you achieve your goals.

If you select activities that support your commitment rather than activities that turn exercise into a chore, your program will provide plenty of incentive for continuing. Consider the following factors in making your choices:

- ***Fun and interest.*** Your fitness program is much more likely to be successful if you choose activities that you currently engage in and enjoy. Often you can modify your current activities to fit your fitness program. If you want to add a new activity to your program, it is a good idea to try it for

a while before committing to it. (See the box "Can Stability Balls Be Part of a Safe and Effective Fitness Program?")

- ***Your current skill and fitness level.*** Although many activities are appropriate for beginners, some sports and activities require a certain level of skill to obtain fitness benefits. For example, if you are a beginning tennis player, you will probably not be able to sustain rallies long enough to develop cardiorespiratory endurance. A better choice might be a walking program while you improve your tennis game. To build skill for a particular activity, consider taking a class or getting some instruction from a coach or fellow participant.
- ***Time and convenience.*** You are more likely to maintain a long-term exercise program if you can easily fit exercise into your daily routine. As you consider activities, think about whether a special location or facility is required. Can you participate in the activity close to your home, school, or job? Are the necessary facilities available at convenient times (see Lab 7.2)? Can you participate in the activity year-round, or will you need to find an alternative during the summer or winter? Would a home treadmill make you more likely to exercise regularly?
- ***Cost.*** Some sports and activities require equipment, fees, or some type of membership investment. If you are on a tight budget, limit your choices to activities that are inexpensive or free. Investigate the facilities on your campus, which you may be able to use at little or no cost. Many activities require no equipment beyond an appropriate pair of shoes.
- ***Special health needs.*** If you have special exercise needs due to a particular health problem, choose activities that will conform to your needs and enhance your ability to cope. Ask your physician about how to tailor an exercise program to your needs and goals. Appendix B provides guidelines and safety tips for exercisers with common chronic conditions.

3. Set a Target Frequency, Intensity, and Time (Duration) for Each Activity

The next step is to apply the FITT principle and set a starting frequency, intensity, and time (duration) for each type

? Ask yourself

QUESTIONS FOR CRITICAL THINKING AND REFLECTION

Consider the list of physical activities and sports in Table 7.1. Given your current fitness and skill level, which ones could you reasonably incorporate into your exercise program?

Can Stability Balls Be Part of a Safe and Effective Fitness Program?

As you create a personalized exercise program, you might consider incorporating a stability ball into your workouts. Stability balls add variety and challenge to a workout and can help you target certain muscle groups more effectively than is possible with some other workout strategies. But what is the real purpose of stability balls, and what is the best way to use them?

When most people think of exercising with stability balls, they think of *core training*—exercises that target the muscles of the trunk. These core muscles, as described in Chapter 5, surround your internal organs and provide support for your spine. The core muscles enable you to stand straight, sit up, twist and bend, and perform countless types of movements, both large and small. If you play any type of competitive sport, from golf to figure skating, your core muscles are essential to your performance. In everyday living, a strong, stable core helps you maintain good posture and balance and provides some protection against injuries.

Core training can be done on a stable surface, such as a floor or bench, or on an unstable surface, such as a stability ball. A stability ball—which is actually an unstable platform—gets its name from the fact that it forces the user's body to stabilize itself to compensate for the ball's instability. Using a stability ball, therefore, is sometimes called *instability training*. Stability ball exercises activate muscle and nerve groups that might not otherwise get involved in the exercise. Depending on the specific exercises being done, instability training improves core strength and enhances the stability of supporting joints throughout the body.

There are many ways to incorporate a stability ball into a typical workout. For example, you can perform crunches or curl-ups while lying on a ball instead of on the floor. Lying face-down across a ball provides different leverage points for push-ups. A variety of resistance training exercises can be performed on a stability ball, but experts recommend using dumbbells rather than barbells when lifting weights on a ball.

Although stability balls are an excellent workout tool, they have drawbacks. For example, if you lift weights while resting on a ball instead of on a stable bench, much of your muscles' effort is devoted to keeping your body stable, reducing the muscles' ability to exert force. This effort can enhance your overall stability, but it can also slow your gains in strength. Research has shown that some exercises (such as curl-ups) can be more

stressful to certain joints and muscles when performed on a ball, at least in some people. Further, there is always a risk of falling off an unstable surface; this can cause serious injury, especially if you are holding weights in your hands.

Finally, while instability training is a valuable aid in building up the core stabilizing muscles, it contributes little to the development of dynamic strength or power in the core. This strength and power are essential to total core fitness (especially in athletes) and must be developed through other types of exercise. For these reasons, many experts recommend instability training as part of an overall exercise program but do not suggest that all exercises be performed on a ball. For example, it's probably more effective to do curl-ups on the floor 2 days per week and on a ball 1 day per week, instead of using the ball every day. If you want to work with stability balls, it's a good idea to join a class where you can learn about this method from a qualified instructor and make sure instability training is appropriate for you.

SOURCES: Behm, D. G., et al. 2010. Canadian Society for Exercise Physiology position stand: The use of instability to train the core in athletic and non-athletic conditioning. *Applied Physiology Nutrition and Metabolism.* 35(1): 109–112; Marshall, P. W., et al. 2010. Electromyographic analysis of upper body, lower body, and abdominal muscles during advanced Swiss ball exercises. *Journal of Strength and Conditioning Research.* 24(6): 1537–1545; Okada, T., et al. 2011. Relationship between core stability, functional movement, and performance. *Journal of Strength and Conditioning Research.* 25(1): 252–261.

of activity you've chosen (see the summary in Figure 7.2 and the sample in Figure 7.1).

Cardiorespiratory Endurance Exercise As noted in earlier chapters, based on more than 50 years of research on exercise and health, the U.S. Department of Health and Human Services concluded that most health benefits occur with at least 150 minutes per week of moderate-intensity physical activity (such as brisk walking) or 75 minutes per week of vigorous-intensity activity (such as jogging). Additional benefits occur with more exercise. An appropriate frequency for cardiorespiratory endurance exercise is 3–5 days per week. For intensity, note your target heart rate

zone or RPE value. Your target total workout time (duration) should be about 20–60 minutes per day, depending on the intensity of the activity. You can exercise in a single session or in multiple sessions of 10 or more minutes.

Muscular Strength and Endurance Training A frequency of at least 2 nonconsecutive days per week for strength training is recommended. As described in Chapter 4, a general fitness strength training program includes 1 or more sets of 8–12 repetitions of 8–10 exercises that work all major muscle groups. For intensity, choose a weight that is heavy enough to fatigue your muscles but not so heavy that you cannot complete the full number of repetitions

	Cardiorespiratory endurance training	Strength training	Flexibility training
Frequency	3–5 days per week	2–3 nonconsecutive days per week	2–3 days per week (minimum); 5–7 days per week (ideal)
Intensity	55/65–90% of maximum heart rate	Sufficient resistance to fatigue muscles	Stretch to the point of tension
Time	20–60 minutes in sessions lasting 10 minutes or more	8–12 repetitions of each exercise, 1 or more sets	2–4 repetitions of each exercise, held for 15–30 seconds
Type	Continuous rhythmic activities using large muscle groups	Resistance exercises for all major muscle groups	Stretching exercises for all major joints

FIGURE 7.2   A summary of the FITT principle for the health-related components of fitness.

Fitness Tip

Want to lift weights without going to a gym? Try using resistance bands. Research shows that—especially for young women—resistance bands are just as effective as weight machines or free weights for increasing muscular strength.

with proper form. Exercises that use body weight for resistance also build strength and muscle endurance.

Flexibility Training Stretches should be performed when muscles are warm at least 2–3 days per week (5–7 days per week is ideal). Stretches should be performed for all major muscle groups. For each exercise, stretch to the point of slight tension or mild discomfort, and hold the stretch for 10–30 seconds; do 2–4 repetitions of each exercise.

4. Set Up a System of Mini-Goals and Rewards

To keep your program on track, set up a system of goals and rewards. Break your specific goals into several steps, and set a target date for each step. For example, if one of the goals of an 18-year-old male student's program is to improve upper-body strength and endurance, he could use the push-up test in Lab 4.2 to set intermediate goals. If he can currently perform 15 push-ups (for a rating of "very poor"), he might set intermediate goals of 17, 20, 25, and 30 push-ups (for a final rating of "fair"). By allowing several weeks between mini-goals and specifying rewards, he'll be able to track his progress and reward himself as he moves toward his final goal. Reaching a series of small goals is more satisfying than working toward a single, more challenging goal that may take months to achieve. For more on choosing appropriate rewards, see Chapter 1 and Activity 4 in the Behavior Change Workbook at the end of the text.

5. Include Lifestyle Physical Activity in Your Program

Daily physical activity is a simple but important way to improve your overall wellness. As part of your fitness program plan, specify ways to be more active during your daily routine. You may find it helpful to first use your health journal to track your activities for several days. Review the records in your journal, identify routine opportunities to be more active, and add these to your program plan in Lab 7.1.

6. Develop Tools for Monitoring Your Progress

A record that tracks your daily progress will help remind you of your ongoing commitment to your program and give you a sense of accomplishment. Figure 7.3 shows you how to create a general program log and record the activity type, frequency, and times (durations). Or, if you wish, complete specific activity logs like those in Labs 3.2, 4.3, and 5.2 in addition to, or instead of, a general log. Post your log in a place where you'll see it often as a reminder and as an incentive for improvement. If you have specific, measurable goals, you can also graph your weekly or monthly progress toward your goal (Figure 7.4). To monitor the overall progress of your fitness program, you may choose to reassess your fitness every 3 months or so during the improvement phase of your program. Because the results of different fitness tests vary, be sure to compare results for the same assessments over time.

7. Make a Commitment

Your final step in planning your program is to make a commitment by signing a contract. Find a witness for your contract—preferably someone who will be actively involved in your program. Keep your contract in a visible spot to remind you of your commitment.

Name Tracie Kaufman

Enter time, distance, or another factor (such as heart rate or perceived exertion) to track your progress.

Activity/Date	M	Tu	W	Th	F	S	S	Weekly Total	M	Tu	W	Th	F	S	S	Weekly Total
1 Swimming	800 yd		725 yd		800 yd			2325 yd	800 yd		800 yd		850 yd			2450 yd
2 Tennis						90 min		90 min					95 min			95 min
3 Weight Training		X		X		X				X		X		X		
4 Stretching	X		X		X	X						X	X	X	X	

FIGURE 7.3 A sample program log.

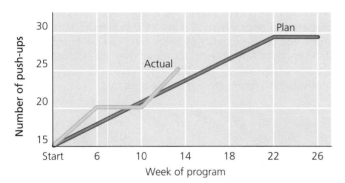

FIGURE 7.4 A sample program progress chart.

PUTTING YOUR PLAN INTO ACTION

Once you've developed a detailed plan and signed your contract, you are ready to begin your fitness program. Refer to the specific training suggestions provided in Chapters 2–5 for advice on beginning and maintaining your program. Many people find it easier to plan a program than to put their plan into action and stick with it over time. For that reason, adherence to healthy lifestyle programs has become an important area of study for psychologists and health researchers. The guidelines below and in the next section reflect research into strategies that help people succeed in sticking with an exercise program.

• **Start slowly and increase fitness gradually.** Overzealous exercising can result in discouraging discomforts and injuries. Your program is meant to last a lifetime. The important first step is to break your established pattern of inactivity. Be patient and realistic. Once your body has adjusted to your starting level of exercise, slowly increase the amount of overload. Small increases are the key—achieving a large number of small improvements will eventually result in substantial gains in fitness. It's usually best to increase duration and frequency before increasing intensity.

• **Find an exercise buddy.** The social side of exercise is an important factor for many regular exercisers. Working out with a friend will make exercise more enjoyable and increase your chances of sticking with your program.

Find an exercise partner who shares your goals and general fitness level. On days when a partner isn't available, a smartphone or MP3 player can be your workout buddy; see the box "Digital Motivation" for more information.

• **Ask for support from others.** You have a much greater chance of exercising consistently if you have the support of important people in your life, such as parents, spouse, partner, and friends. Talk with them about your program, and let them know the importance of exercise and wellness in your life. Exercise needs to be a critical component of your day (just like sleeping and eating). Good communication will help others become more supportive of and enthusiastic about the time you spend on your wellness program.

• **Vary your activities.** You can make your program more fun over the long term if you participate in a variety of activities that you enjoy. You can also add interest by varying the routes you take when walking, finding a new tennis partner, or switching to a new volleyball or basketball court. Varying your activities, a strategy known as *cross-training*, has other benefits. It can help you develop balanced, total-body fitness. For example, by alternating running with swimming, you build both upper- and lower-body strength. Cross-training can reduce the risk of injury and overtraining because the same muscles, bones, and joints are not continuously subjected to the stresses of the same activity. Cross-training can be done either by choosing different activities on different days or by alternating activities within a single workout.

• **Cycle the duration and intensity of your workouts.** Olympic athletes use a technique called periodization of training, meaning that they vary the duration and intensity of their workouts. Sometimes they exercise very intensely; other times they train lightly or rest. You can use the same technique to improve fitness more quickly and make your training program more varied and enjoyable. For example, if your program consists of walking, weight training, and stretching, pick one day a week for each activity to train a little harder or longer than you normally do. If you usually walk 2 miles at 16 minutes per mile, increase the pace to 15 minutes per mile once a week. If you lift weights twice a week, train more intensely during one of the workouts by using more resistance or performing multiple sets.

• **Adapt to changing environments and schedules.** Most people are creatures of habit and have trouble adjusting to

Digital Motivation

If you ever have trouble getting inspired to work out, motivation may be as close as your smartphone.

Since the iPhone's advent, dozens of interactive motivational applications ("apps") have been developed for use on smart cell phones. Coaching and motivational recordings are available for use on MP3 players, as well. These apps and recordings can substitute for an exercise partner when your workout buddy isn't around and can inspire you to keep your program on track. Some smartphone apps can monitor your workouts, track your progress, and even provide on-the-spot coaching to help you keep going.

Here are just a few examples of low-cost or free smartphone apps that can help you keep exercising:

- **The "Fu" series.** Featuring titles like "CrunchFu," "Push-upFu," and others, each app in this series focuses on one type of exercise and motivates you to excel at it. Using the accelerometers built into your smartphone, these apps can count your reps and monitor your speed as you exercise. A built-in coach offers suggestions and can challenge you to improve your performance.

- **RunKeeper.** This app works with a variety of activities, including walking, running, cycling, skiing, and others. The app uses your phone's built-in GPS to tell you how far and fast you are moving and to calculate your average and overall pace. The coaching feature offers tips and advice in real time, and you can listen to your favorite music while RunKeeper functions in the background. When you're finished exercising, the program can automatically upload data about your session to the RunKeeper Web site, which offers more tools for tracking your fitness program.

- **BeatBurn Trainer.** If you like to exercise in time to music, this app can be a big help. BeatBurn features coaching and tracking capabilities like many other smartphone apps, but it also includes beat-tracking technology. The app analyzes the pace (in beats per minute) of your music, and automatically speeds or slows the music to keep it in time with your movement. Music quality is not affected by the speed shifting.

If you don't have a smartphone—or don't want to risk breaking your phone while exercising—look for motivational albums and podcasts to play on an inexpensive MP3 player. Hundreds of titles, many of them free, can be found online and already in MP3 format. Although they are not interactive, albums can provide music that inspires you to keep moving, motivational commentary, and coaching tips.

Wellness Tip

Are you into intervals? Interval training can dramatically boost muscle performance and maximal oxygen consumption, but it doesn't do that much for certain measures of heart health. This is one reason it's important to vary your workouts; blend intervals with higher-volume workouts for optimal results.

Ask Yourself

QUESTIONS FOR CRITICAL THINKING AND REFLECTION

How do you typically deal with setbacks? For example, if you have trouble getting motivated to study for exams, what strategies do you use to get back on track? Could those strategies work for keeping your fitness program moving forward? If so, how?

change. Don't use bad weather or a new job as an excuse to give up your exercise program. If you walk in the summer, put on a warm coat and walk in the winter. If you can't go out because of darkness, join a gym and walk on a treadmill.

- **Expect fluctuations and lapses.** On some days, your progress will be excellent, but on others, you'll barely be able to drag yourself through your scheduled activities. Don't let off-days or lapses discourage you or make you feel guilty (see the box "Getting Your Fitness Program Back on Track").

- **Choose other healthy lifestyle behaviors.** Exercise provides huge benefits for your health, but other behaviors are also important. Choose a nutritious diet, and avoid harmful habits like smoking and overconsumption of alcohol. Be sure to stay hydrated with water or other healthy beverages (see the box "Choosing Healthy Beverages"). Don't skimp on sleep, which has a mutually beneficial relationship with exercise. Physical activity improves sleep, and adequate sleep can improve physical performance.

EXERCISE GUIDELINES FOR LIFE STAGES

A fitness program may need to be adjusted to accommodate the requirements of different life stages.

Getting Your Fitness Program Back on Track

 connect ACTIVITY DO IT ONLINE

Lapses are a normal part of any behavior change program. The important point is to move on and avoid becoming discouraged. Try again and keep trying. Know that continued effort will lead to success. Here are some tips to help you keep going:

● Don't judge yourself too harshly. Some people make faster gains in fitness than others. Focus on the improvements you've already made from your program and how good you feel after exercise—both physically and mentally.

● Visualize what it will be like to reach your goals. Keep these images in mind as an incentive to stick with your program.

● Use your exercise journal to identify thoughts and behaviors that are causing noncompliance. Devise strategies to combat these problematic patterns. If needed, make additional changes in your environment or find more social support. For example, call a friend to walk with you, or keep exercise clothes in your car or backpack.

● Make changes in your plan and reward system to help renew your enthusiasm for and commitment to your program. Try changing fitness activities or your exercise schedule. Build in more opportunities to reward yourself.

● Plan ahead for difficult situations. Think about what circumstances might make it tough to keep up your fitness routine. Develop strategies to increase your chances of sticking with your program. For example, figure out ways to continue your program during vacation, travel, bad weather, and so on.

● If you're in a bad mood or just don't feel like exercising, remind yourself that physical activity is probably the one thing you can do that will make you feel better. Even if you can only do half your scheduled workout, you'll boost your energy, improve your mood, and help keep your program on track.

TAKE CHARGE

People of all ages benefit from exercise. Simply by playing actively with their children, parents can set a positive example that will lead to a lifetime of physical activity.

Children and Adolescents

Lack of physical activity has led to alarming increases in overweight and obesity in children and adolescents. If you have children or are in a position to influence children, keep these guidelines in mind:

• Provide opportunities for children and adolescents to exercise every day. Minimize sedentary activities, such as watching television. Children and adolescents should aim for at least 60 minutes of moderate activity every day. Less fit kids should start with 30 minutes a day until their fitness improves and they can exercise longer.

• During family outings, choose dynamic activities. For example, go for a walk or park away from a mall, and then walk to the stores.

• For children younger than 12, emphasize skill development and fitness rather than excellence in competitive sports. For adolescents, combine participation and training in lifetime sports with traditional, competitive sports.

• Make sure children are developmentally capable of participating in an activity. For example, catching skills are difficult for young children because their nervous system is not developed enough to fully master the skill. Gradually increase the complexity of the skill once the child has mastered the simpler skill.

• Make sure children get plenty of water when exercising in the heat. Make sure they are dressed properly when exercising in the cold.

connect
ACTIVITY
DO IT ONLINE

Choosing Healthy Beverages

As discussed in other chapters, it's important to stay hydrated at all times, but especially when you are exercising. Too little water intake can leave you feeling fatigued, reduce your body's performance, and leave you vulnerable to heat-related sicknesses in hot weather. But *what* you drink is as significant as how much you drink, both when you are exercising and when you are going about your normal routine.

The Great Water Controversy

Wherever you see people exercising, you will see bottled water in abundance. For several years, a debate has been raging about the quality and safety of commercially bottled water. Recently, new evidence has emerged showing that most bottled waters are no better for you than regular tap water, and some bottled waters may actually be bad for you. To make matters worse, bottled water costs up to 1900 times more than tap water.

In a 2011 analysis of 173 bottled water products, the Environmental Working Group, found 38 different contaminants in ten popular brands of bottled water. Contaminants included heavy metals such as arsenic, pharmaceutical residues and other pollutants commonly found in urban wastewater, and a variety of industrial chemicals. Bottled water companies are notoriously secretive about their products. Overall, 18% of bottled waters failed to list the location of their source,

and 32% disclosed nothing about the treatment or purity of the water.

Many commercially bottled water products are tap water drawn from municipal water systems. Such revelations have caused some bottlers to put statements on their products' labels, identifying them as having been drawn from a standard water supply. Although these products are priced many times higher than water from a residential tap, they provide no benefit over standard tap water.

An even bigger issue is that plastic water bottles have become a huge environmental problem, with billions of bottles now filling landfills and floating in the world's oceans. Many kinds of plastic bottles will never decompose at all; at best, some types of plastic take years to biodegrade. Newer types of plastic bottles can decompose significantly faster than older bottles, but fast-degrading plastics have not yet come into widespread use in the bottled water industry.

Experts say that when you're exercising, the cheapest and safest way to stay hydrated is to drink filtered tap water. If you need to carry water with you, buy a reusable container (preferably made of stainless steel) that can be cleaned after each use. If you drink from plastic bottles, be sure they are recyclable, and dispose of them by recycling.

Other Choices

Instead of water, many people choose to drink sodas, juice, tea, or flavored water.

While these kinds of beverages have their place, it's important not to drink them too often or in large amounts, especially if they are high in sugar or caffeine. Sugary drinks add empty calories to your diet, and caffeine is a psychoactive drug with a variety of side effects.

Regular (nondiet) sodas are now the leading source of calories in the American diet; most people don't count the calories from beverages as part of their daily caloric intake, leading them to underestimate their total intake. For this reason and others, many experts believe that soda consumption is a major factor in the increasing levels of obesity, metabolic syndrome, diabetes, and other chronic diseases among Americans.

If you're concerned that the liquid portion of your diet is not as healthy as it should be, choose water, fat-free milk, or unsweetened herbal tea more often. Avoid regular soda, sweetened bottled iced tea, flavored water, and fruit beverages made with little fruit juice. To make water more appealing, try adding slices of citrus fruit with sparkling water. With some imagination, you can make sure you stay hydrated without consuming excess calories, spending money unnecessarily, or hurting the environment.

SOURCE: Leiba, N., et. al. 2011. The Environmental Working Group's 2011 Bottled Water Scorecard (http://www.ewg.org/bottled-water -2011-home; retrieved April 5, 2011).

Pregnant Women

Exercise is important during pregnancy, but women should be cautious because some types of exercise can pose increased risk to the mother and the unborn child. The following guidelines are consistent with the recommendations of the American College of Obstetrics and Gynecology:

- See your physician about possible modifications needed for your particular pregnancy.

- Continue mild to moderate exercise routines at least three times a week. (For most women, this means maintaining an exercise heart rate of 100–160 beats per minute.) Avoid exercising vigorously or to exhaustion, especially in the third trimester. Monitor exercise intensity by assessing how you feel rather than by monitoring your heart rate; RPE levels of 11–13 are appropriate.

- Favor non- or low-weight-bearing exercises such as swimming or cycling over weight-bearing exercises, which can carry increased risk of injury.

- Avoid exercise in a supine position—lying on your back—after the first trimester. This position restricts blood flow to the uterus. Also avoid prolonged periods of motionless standing.

- Avoid exercise that could cause loss of balance, especially in the third trimester, and exercise that might injure the abdomen, stress the joints, or carry a risk of falling (such as contact sports, vigorous racquet sports, skiing, and in-line skating).

- Avoid activities involving extremes in barometric pressure, such as diving and mountain climbing.

- Especially during the first trimester, drink plenty of fluids and exercise in well-ventilated areas to avoid heat stress.

Q Should I exercise every day?

A Some daily exercise is beneficial, but if you train intensely every day without giving yourself a rest, you will likely get injured or become over-trained. When strength training, for example, rest at least 48 hours between workouts before exercising the same muscle group. For cardiorespiratory endurance exercise, rest or exercise lightly the day after an intense or lengthy workout. Balancing the proper amount of rest and exercise will help you feel better and improve your fitness faster.

Q If exercise is so good for my health, why hasn't my physician ever mentioned it to me?

A A recent study by the ACSM suggests that most people would benefit from getting a physician's advice about exercising. According to the study, 65% of patients said they would be more interested in exercising if their physicians suggested it. About 40% of physicians said they talk to their patients about exercise.

To encourage physicians and patients to talk more often about exercise and its benefits, the ACSM and the American Medical Association have launched the Exercise Is Medicine program. The program advises physicians to give more guidance to patients about exercise and suggests that everyone try to exercise at least 5 days each week. For more information on the program, visit www.exerciseismedicine.org.

For more Common Questions Answered about developing and maintaining a fitness program, visit the Online Learning Center at www.mhhe.com/fahey.

- Do 3–5 sets of 10 Kegel exercises daily. These exercises involve tightening the muscles of the pelvic floor for 5–15 seconds per repetition. Kegel exercises are thought to help prevent incontinence (involuntary loss of urine) and speed recovery after giving birth.
- After giving birth, resume prepregnancy exercise routines gradually, based on how you feel.

Older Adults

Older people readily adapt to endurance exercise and strength training. Exercise principles are the same as for younger people, but some specific guidelines apply:

- According to the American College of Sports Medicine (ACSM), older adults should follow the same guidelines for aerobic exercise as younger adults, but they should judge intensity on a 10-point scale of perceived exertion rather than by heart rate.
- For strength training, older adults should use a lighter weight and perform more (10–15) repetitions than young adults.
- Older adults should perform flexibility exercises at least 2 days per week for at least 10 minutes. Exercises that improve balance should also be performed 2 days per week.
- Drink plenty of water and avoid exercising in excessively hot or cold environments. Wear clothes that speed heat loss in warm environments and prevent heat loss in cold environments.

- Warm up slowly and carefully. Increase intensity and duration of exercise gradually.
- Cool down slowly, continuing very light exercise until the heart rate is below 100.
- Older adults with physical disabilities or limitations who cannot meet the recommendation of at least 150 minutes of moderate-intensity exercise should do as much exercise as they can.

TIPS FOR TODAY AND THE FUTURE

A complete fitness program includes activities to build and maintain cardiorespiratory endurance, muscular strength and endurance, and flexibility.

RIGHT NOW YOU CAN
- Get a journal to track your daily physical activity and exercise routine.
- Put away your remote control devices—every bit of physical activity can benefit your health.
- Set up your next workout with your training partner.
- Plan to go to bed 15 minutes earlier than usual.

IN THE FUTURE YOU CAN
- Create a schedule that incorporates your workouts into your daily routine. Each week, update the schedule for the upcoming week.
- Develop strategies for dealing with setbacks in your exercise program. Having strategies in place ahead of time can prepare you to cope with lapses as they occur.

SUMMARY

- Steps for putting together a complete fitness program include (1) setting realistic goals; (2) selecting activities to develop all the health-related components of fitness; (3) setting a target frequency, intensity, and time (duration) for each activity; (4) setting up a system of mini-goals and rewards; (5) making lifestyle physical activity a part of the daily routine; (6) developing tools for monitoring progress; and (7) making a commitment.

- In selecting activities, consider fun and interest, your current skill and fitness levels, time and convenience, cost, and any special health concerns.

- Keys to beginning and maintaining a successful program include starting slowly, increasing intensity and duration gradually, finding a buddy, varying the activities and intensity of the program, and expecting fluctuations and lapses.

- Regular exercise is appropriate and beneficial for people in particular stages of life, although program modifications may be necessary for safety.

FOR FURTHER EXPLORATION

BOOKS, ORGANIZATIONS, AND WEB SITES

American Academy of Orthopaedic Surgeons. Provides information about injuries, treatment, and rehabilitation along with exercise guidelines for people with bone, muscle, and joint pain.

http://www.aaos.org

American College of Obstetricians and Gynecologists. Provides guidelines for promoting a healthy pregnancy and postpartum recovery, including exercise during pregnancy.

http://www.acog.org

American Diabetes Association. Promotes diabetes education, research, and advocacy; includes guidelines for diet and exercise for people with diabetes.

http://www.diabetes.org

American Heart Association. Includes information on fitness for kids as well as diet, exercise, fitness, and weight management for adults.

http://www.americanheart.org

For additional listings, see Chapters 2–6.

SELECTED BIBLIOGRAPHY

Almstedt, H. C., et al. 2011. Changes in bone mineral density in response to 24 weeks of resistance training in college-age men and women. *Journal of Strength and Conditioning Research* 25(4): 1098–1103.

American College of Sports Medicine. 2009. *ACSM's Guidelines for Exercise Testing and Prescription*, 8th ed. Philadelphia: Lippincott Williams and Wilkins.

American College of Sports Medicine. 2009. *ACSM's Resource Manual for Guidelines for Exercise Testing and Prescription*, 6th ed. Philadelphia: Lippincott Williams and Wilkins.

Behm, D. G., et al. 2010. Canadian Society for Exercise Physiology position stand: The use of instability to train the core in athletic and nonathletic conditioning. *Applied Physiology, Nutrition and Metabolism* 35(1): 109–112.

Behm, D. G., et al. 2010. The use of instability to train the core musculature. *Applied Physiology, Nutrition and Metabolism* 35(1): 91–108.

Boarnet, M. G., et al. 2011. Retrofitting the suburbs to increase walking: Evidence from a land-use-travel study. *Urban Studies* 48(1): 129–159.

Boone-Heinonen, J., et al. 2011. Neighborhood socioeconomic status predictors of physical activity through young to middle adulthood: The CARDIA study. *Social Science and Medicine* 72(5): 641–649.

Canadian Society for Exercise Physiology. 2011. *Public Health Agency of Canada Physical Activity Guidelines* (www.publichealth.gc.ca; retrieved April 6, 2011).

Clark, P. G., et al. 2011. Maintaining exercise and healthful eating in older adults: The SENIOR project II: Study design and methodology. *Contemporary Clinical Trials* 32(1): 129–139.

Finkelstein, E. A., et al. 2008. A randomized study of financial incentives to increase physical activity among sedentary older adults. *Preventive Medicine* 47(2): 182–187.

Hamer, M., and Y. Chida. 2008. Walking and primary prevention: A meta-analysis of prospective cohort studies. *British Journal of Sports Medicine* 42(4): 238–243.

Hurley, B. F., et al. 2011. Strength training as a countermeasure to aging muscle and chronic disease. *Sports Medicine* 41(4): 289–306.

Ingham, S. A., et al. 2008. Physiological and performance effects of low-versus mixed-intensity rowing training. *Medicine and Science in Sports and Exercise* 40(3): 579–584.

Kilpatrick, M. W., et al. 2009. Heart rate and metabolic responses to moderate-intensity aerobic exercise: A comparison of graded walking and ungraded jogging at a constant perceived exertion. *Journal of Sports Sciences* 27(5): 509–516.

Kokkinos, P. 2008. Physical activity and cardiovascular disease prevention: Current recommendations. *Angiology* 59(2 Supplement): 26S–29S.

Levine, J. A., et al. 2008. The role of free-living daily walking in human weight gain and obesity. *Diabetes* 57(3): 548–554.

Marshall, P. W., et al. 2010. Electromyographic analysis of upper body, lower body, and abdominal muscles during advanced Swiss ball exercises. *Journal of Strength and Conditioning Research* 24(6): 1537–1545.

McGinn, A. P., et al. 2008. Walking speed and risk of incident ischemic stroke among postmenopausal women. *Stroke* 39(4): 1233–1239.

Mozumdar, A., et al. 2011. Persistent increase of prevalence of metabolic syndrome among U.S. adults: NHANES III to NHANES 1999–2006. *Diabetes Care* 34(1): 216–219.

Okada, T., et al. 2011. Relationship between core stability, functional movement, and performance. *Journal of Strength and Conditioning Research* 25(1): 252–261.

Pascual, C., et al. 2009. Socioeconomic environment, availability of sports facilities, and jogging, swimming and gym use. *Health and Place* 15(2): 553–561.

Plisiene, J., et al. 2008. Moderate physical exercise: A simplified approach for ventricular rate control in older patients with atrial fibrillation. *Clinical Research in Cardiology* 97(11): 820–826.

Reis, J. P., et al. 2008. Prevalence of total daily walking among US adults, 2002–2003. *Journal of Physical Activity and Health* 5(3): 337–346.

Richardson, C. R., et al. 2008. A meta-analysis of pedometer-based walking interventions and weight loss. *Annals of Family Medicine* 6(1): 69–77.

Suminski, R. R., et al. 2008. Observing physical activity in suburbs. *Health and Place* 14(4): 894–899.

Troped, P. J., et al. 2008. Prediction of activity mode with global positioning system and accelerometer data. *Medicine and Science in Sports and Exercise* 40(5): 972–978.

U.S. Department of Health and Human Services. 2008. *Physical Activity Guidelines for Americans.* Washington, D.C.: U.S. Department of Health and Human Services.

Westhoff, T. H., et al. 2008. The cardiovascular effects of upper-limb aerobic exercise in hypertensive patients. *Journal of Hypertension* 26(7): 1336–1342.

Xu, D. Q., et al. 2008. Tai Chi exercise and muscle strength and endurance in older people. *Medicine and Sports Science* 52: 20–29.

Yabroff, K. R., et al. 2008. Walking the dog: Is pet ownership associated with physical activity in California? *Journal of Physical Activity and Health* 5(2): 216–228.

SAMPLE PROGRAMS FOR POPULAR ACTIVITIES

The following sections present four sample programs based on different types of cardiorespiratory activities—walking/jogging/running, bicycling, swimming, and rowing. Each sample program includes regular cardiorespiratory endurance exercise, resistance training, and stretching. Read the descriptions of the programs you're considering, and decide which will work best for you based on your present routine, the potential for enjoyment, and adaptability to your lifestyle. If you choose one of these programs, complete the personal fitness program plan in Lab 7.1, just as if you had created a program from scratch.

No program will produce enormous changes in your fitness level in the first few weeks. Follow the specifics of the program for 3–4 weeks. Then, if the exercise program doesn't seem suitable, make adjustments to adapt it to your particular needs. But retain the basic elements of the program that make it effective for developing fitness.

GENERAL GUIDELINES

The following guidelines can help make the activity programs more effective for you:

- **Frequency and time.** To improve physical fitness, exercise for 20–60 minutes at least three times a week.

- **Intensity.** To work effectively for cardiorespiratory endurance training or to improve body composition, raise your heart rate into its target zone. Monitor your pulse or use rates of perceived exertion to monitor your intensity. If you've been sedentary, begin very slowly. Give your muscles

a chance to adjust to their increased workload. It's probably best to keep your heart rate below target until your body has had time to adjust to new demands. At first you may not need to work very hard to keep your heart rate in its target zone, but as your cardiorespiratory endurance improves, you will probably need to increase intensity.

- **Interval training.** Some of the sample programs involve continuous activity. Others rely on interval training, which calls for alternating a relief interval with exercise (walking after jogging, for example, or coasting after biking uphill). Interval training is an effective method of progressive overload and improves fitness rapidly (see the box "Interval Training: Pros and Cons" in Chapter 3).

- **Resistance training and stretching guidelines.** For the resistance training and stretching parts of the program, remember the general guidelines for safe and effective exercise. See the summary of guidelines in Figure 7.2.

- **Warm-up and cool-down.** Begin each exercise session with a 10-minute warm-up. Begin your activity at a slow pace, and work up gradually to your target heart rate. Always slow down gradually at the end of your exercise session to bring your system back to its normal state. It's a good idea to do stretching exercises to increase your flexibility after cardiorespiratory exercise or strength training because your muscles will be warm and ready to stretch.

Follow the guidelines presented in Chapter 3 for exercising in hot or cold weather. Drink enough liquids to stay adequately hydrated, particularly in hot weather.

- **Record keeping.** After each exercise session, record your daily distance or time on a progress chart.

WALKING/JOGGING/RUNNING SAMPLE PROGRAM

Walking is the perfect exercise. It increases longevity, builds fitness, expends calories, prevents weight gain, and protects against heart disease, stroke, and back pain. You don't need to join a gym, and you can walk almost anywhere. People who walk 30 minutes five times per week will lose an average of 5 pounds in 6–12 months—without dieting, watching what they eat, or exercising intensely.

Jogging takes walking to the next level. Jogging only 75 minutes per week will increase fitness, promote weight control, and provide health benefits that will prevent disease and increase longevity. Your ultimate goal for promoting wellness is to walk at a moderate intensity for 150–300 minutes per week or jog at 70% effort or more for 75–150 minutes per week.

It isn't always easy to distinguish among walking, jogging, and running. For clarity and consistency, we'll consider walking to be any on-foot exercise of less than 5 miles per hour, jogging any pace between 5 and 7.5 miles per hour, and running any pace faster than that. The faster

your pace or the longer you exercise, the more calories you burn (Table 1). The greater the number of calories burned, the higher the potential training effects of these activities. Table 2 contains a sample walking/jogging program.

Equipment and Technique

These activities require no special skills, expensive equipment, or unusual facilities. Comfortable clothing, well-fitted walking or running shoes (see Chapter 3), and a stopwatch or ordinary watch with a second hand are all you need.

When you advance to jogging, use proper technique:

- Run with your back straight and your head up. Look straight ahead, not at your feet. Shift your pelvis forward and tuck your buttocks in.

- Hold your arms slightly away from your body. Your elbows should be bent so that your forearms are parallel to the ground. You may cup your hands, but do not clench

Table 1	Estimated Calories Expended by a 165-pound Adult at Different Intensities of Walking and Running for 150 and 300 minutes per week (min/wk)

	SPEED (MILES PER HOUR)	SPEED (MINUTES PER MILE)	CALORIES EXPENDED EXERCISING 150 MIN/WK	CALORIES EXPENDED EXERCISING 300 MIN/WK
Walking	Rest	—	190	380
	2.5	24	565	1130
	3.0	20	620	1240
	4.0	15	940	1880
	4.3	14	1125	2250
Jogging/Running	5.0	12	1500	3000
	6.0	10	1875	3750
	7.0	8.6	2155	4310
	8.0	6.7	2530	5060
	10.0	6	3000	6000

NOTE: Heavier people will expend slightly more calories, while lighter people will expend slightly fewer.

SOURCE: Adapted from Physical Activity Guidelines Advisory Committee. 2008. *Physical Activity Guidelines Advisory Committee Report, 2008.* Washington, D. C.: U.S. Department of Health and Human Services.

Table 2	Sample Walking/Jogging Fitness Program

DAY	ACTIVITIES
Monday	• **Walking/Jogging:** Walk briskly for 30 minutes or jog for 25 minutes. • **Stretching:** Stretch major muscle groups for 10 minutes after exercise. Do each exercise 2 times; hold stretch for 10–30 seconds.
Tuesday	• **Resistance workout:** Using body weight for resistance, perform the following exercises: • Push-ups: 2 sets, 20 reps per set • Pull-ups: 2 sets, 5 reps per set • Unloaded squats: 2 sets, 10 reps per set • Curl-ups: 2 sets, 20 reps per set • Side bridges: 3 sets, 10-second hold (left and right sides) • Spine extensions: 3 sets, 10-second hold (left and right sides)
Wednesday	• Repeat Monday activities.
Thursday	• Repeat Tuesday activities.
Friday	• Repeat Monday activities.
Saturday	• **Rest.**
Sunday	• **Rest.**

your fists. Allow your arms to swing loosely and rhythmically with each stride.

• Let your heel hit the ground first in each stride. Then roll forward onto the ball of your foot and push off for the next stride. If you find this difficult, you can try a more flat-footed style, but don't land on the balls of your feet.

• Keep your steps short by allowing your foot to strike the ground in line with your knee. Keep your knees bent at all times.

• Breathe deeply through your mouth. Try to use your abdominal muscles rather than just your chest muscles to take deep breaths.

• Stay relaxed.

Find a safe, convenient place to walk or jog. Exercise on a trail, path, or sidewalk to stay clear of bicycles and cars. Make sure your clothes are brightly colored so others can see you easily.

Beginning A Walking/Jogging Program

Start slowly if you have not been exercising, are overweight, or are recovering from an illness or surgery. At first, walk for 15 minutes at a slow pace, below your target heart rate zone. Gradually increase to 30-minute sessions. You will probably cover 1 to 2 miles. At the beginning, walk every other day.

You can gradually increase to walking 5 days per week or more if you want to expend more calories (which is helpful if you want to change body composition). Depending on your weight, you will expend ("burn") 90–135 calories during each 30-minute walking session. To increase the calories that you expend, walk for a longer time or for a longer distance instead of sharply increasing speed.

Start at the level of effort that is most comfortable for you. Maintain a normal, easy pace and stop to rest as often as you need to. Never prolong a walk past the point of comfort. When walking with a friend (a good motivator), let a comfortable conversation be your guide to pace. If you find that you cannot carry on a conversation without getting out of breath, you are walking too quickly.

Once your muscles have become adjusted to the exercise program, increase the duration of your sessions by no more than 10% each week. Keep your heart rate just below your target zone. Don't be discouraged by a lack of immediate progress, and don't try to speed things up by overdoing it. Remember that pace and heart rate can vary with the terrain, the weather, and other factors.

Advanced Walking

Advanced walking involves walking more quickly for longer times. You should feel an increased perception of effort, but the exercise intensity should not be too stressful. Vary your pace to allow for intervals of slow, medium, and fast walking. Keep your heart rate toward the lower end of your target zone with brief periods in the upper levels. At first, walk for 30 minutes and increase your walking time gradually until eventually you reach 60 minutes at a brisk pace and can walk 2–4 miles. Try to walk at least 5 days per week. Vary your program by changing the pace and distance or by walking routes with different terrains and views. You can expect to burn 200–350 calories or more during each advanced walking session.

Making the Transition to Jogging

Increase the intensity of exercise by gradually introducing jogging into your walking program. During a 2-mile walk, for example, periodically jog for 100 yards and then resume walking. Increase the number and distance of your jogging segments until you can jog continuously for the entire distance. More physically fit people may be capable of jogging without walking first. However, people unaccustomed to jogging should initially combine walking with short bouts of jogging.

A good strategy is to exercise on a 400-meter track at a local high school or college. Begin by jogging the straightaways and walking the turns for 800 meters (two laps). Progress to walking 200 meters (half lap) and jogging 200 meters; jogging 400 meters and walking 200 meters; jogging 800 meters, walking 800 meters; and jogging 1200

meters, walking 400 meters. Continue until you can run 2 miles without stopping.

During the transition to jogging, adjust the ratio of walking to jogging to keep within your target heart rate zone as much as possible. Most people who sustain a continuous jog/run program will find that they can stay within their target heart rate zone with a speed of 5.5–7.5 miles per hour (8–11 minutes per mile). Exercise at least every other day. Increasing frequency by doing other activities on alternate days will place less stress on the weight-bearing parts of your lower body than will a daily program of jogging/running.

Developing Muscular Strength and Endurance and Flexibility

Walking, jogging, and running provide muscular endurance workouts for your lower body; they also develop muscular strength of the lower body to a lesser degree. If you'd like to increase your running speed and performance, you might want to focus your program on lower-body exercises. (Don't neglect upper-body strength. It is important for overall wellness.) For flexibility, pay special attention to the hamstrings and quadriceps, which are not worked through their complete range of motion during walking or jogging.

Staying with Your Walking/Jogging Program

Health experts have found that simple motivators such as using a pedometer, walking a dog, parking farther from the office or grocery store, or training for a fun run help people stay with their programs. Use a pedometer or GPS exercise device to track your progress and help motivate you to increase distance and speed. Accurate pedometers for walking, such as those made by Omron, Yamax, and New Lifestyles, cost $20–40 and are accurate to about 5%. Sophisticated GPS-based devices made by Polar and Garmin keep track of your exercise speed and distance via satellite, monitor heart rate, and store data that can be downloaded wirelessly to your computer. Several of these units can be plugged into programs such as Google Earth, which give you a satellite view of your walking or jogging route.

A pedometer can also help you increase the number of steps you walk each day. Most sedentary people take only 2000 to 3000 steps per day. Adding 1000 steps per day and increasing gradually until you reach 10,000 steps can increase fitness and help you manage your weight. The nonprofit organization Shape Up America! has developed the 10,000 Steps program to promote walking as a fitness activity (www.shapeup.org).

BICYCLING SAMPLE PROGRAM

Bicycling can also lead to large gains in physical fitness. For many people, cycling is a pleasant and economical alternative to driving and a convenient way to build fitness.

Equipment and Technique

Cycling has its own special array of equipment, including helmets, lights, safety gear, and biking shoes. The bike is the most expensive item, ranging from about $100 to $1000 or more. Avoid making a large investment until you're sure you'll use your bike regularly. While investigating what the marketplace has to offer, rent or borrow a bike. Consider your intended use of the bike. Most cyclists who are interested primarily in fitness are best served by a sturdy 10-speed rather than a mountain bike or sport bike. Stationary cycles are good for rainy days and areas that have harsh winters.

Clothing for bike riding shouldn't be restrictive or binding; nor should it be so loose that it catches the wind and slows you down. Shirts made from materials that wick moisture away from your skin and padded biking shorts make for a more comfortable ride. Wear glasses or goggles to protect your eyes from dirt, small objects, and irritation from wind. Wear a pair of well-padded gloves if your hands tend to become numb while riding or if you begin to develop blisters or calluses.

To avoid saddle soreness and injury, choose a soft or padded saddle, and adjust it to a height that allows your legs to almost reach full extension while pedaling. To prevent backache and neck strain, warm up thoroughly and periodically shift the position of your hands on the handlebars and your body in the saddle. Keep your arms relaxed and don't lock your elbows. To protect your knees from strain, pedal with your feet pointed straight ahead or very slightly inward, and don't pedal in high gear for long periods.

Bike riding requires a number of precise skills that practice makes automatic. If you've never ridden before, consider taking a course. In fact, many courses are not just for beginners. They'll help you develop skills in braking, shifting, and handling emergencies, as well as teach you ways of caring for and repairing your bike. For safe cycling, follow these rules:

- Always wear a helmet.
- Keep on the correct side of the road. Bicycling against traffic is usually illegal and always dangerous.
- Obey all the same traffic signs and signals that apply to autos.
- On public roads, ride in single file, except in low-traffic areas (if the law permits). Ride in a straight line; don't swerve or weave in traffic.
- Be alert; anticipate the movements of other traffic and pedestrians. Listen for approaching traffic that is out of your line of vision.
- Slow down at street crossings. Check both ways before crossing.
- Use hand signals—the same as for automobile drivers—if you intend to stop or turn. Use audible signals to warn those in your path.
- Maintain full control. Avoid anything that interferes with your vision. Don't jeopardize your ability to steer by carrying anything (including people) on the handlebars.

- Keep your bicycle in good shape. Brakes, gears, saddle, wheels, and tires should always be in good condition.
- See and be seen. Use a headlight at night and equip your bike with rear reflectors. Use side reflectors on pedals, front and rear. Wear light-colored clothing or use reflective tape at night; wear bright colors or use fluorescent tape by day.
- Be courteous to other road users. Anticipate the worst and practice preventive cycling.
- Use a rear-view mirror.

Developing Cardiorespiratory Endurance

Cycling is an excellent way to develop and maintain cardiorespiratory endurance and a healthy body composition.

FIT—frequency, intensity, and time: If you've been inactive for a long time, begin your cycling program at a heart rate that is 10–20% below your target zone. Beginning cyclists should pedal at about 80–100 revolutions per minute; adjust the gear so you can pedal at that rate easily. You can equip your bicycle with a cycling computer that displays different types of useful information, such as speed, distance traveled, heart rate, altitude, and revolutions per minute.

Once you feel at home on your bike, try cycling 1 mile at a comfortable speed, and then stop and check your heart rate. Increase your speed gradually until you can cycle at 12–15 miles per hour (4–5 minutes per mile), a speed fast enough to bring most new cyclists' heart rate into their target zone. Allow your pulse rate to be your guide: More highly fit individuals may need to ride faster to achieve their target heart rate. Cycling for at least 20 minutes 3 days per week will improve your fitness.

At the beginning: It may require several outings to get the muscles and joints of your legs and hips adjusted to this new activity. Begin each outing with a 10-minute warm-up. When your muscles are warm, stretch your hamstrings and your back and neck muscles. Until you become a skilled cyclist, select routes with the fewest hazards and avoid heavy automobile traffic.

As you progress: Interval training is also effective with bicycling. Simply increase your speed for periods of 4–8 minutes or for specific distances, such as 1–2 miles. Then coast for 2–3 minutes. Alternate the speed intervals and slow intervals for a total of 20–60 minutes, depending on your level of fitness. Biking over hilly terrain is also a form of interval training.

Developing Muscular Strength and Endurance and Flexibility

Bicycling develops a high level of endurance and a moderate level of strength in the muscles of the lower body. If one of your goals is to increase your cycling speed and performance, be sure to include exercises for the quadriceps, hamstrings, and buttocks muscles in your strength training program. For flexibility, pay special attention to the hamstrings and quadriceps, which are not worked through their complete range of motion during bike riding, and to the muscles in your lower back, shoulders, and neck.

SWIMMING SAMPLE PROGRAM

Swimming works every major muscle group in the body. It increases upper- and lower-body strength, promotes cardiovascular fitness, and is excellent for rehabilitating athletic injuries and preventing day-to-day aches and pains. It promotes weight control; builds powerful lungs, heart, and blood vessels; and promotes metabolic health. People weigh only 6–10 pounds in the water, so swimming places less stress on the knees, hips, and back than jogging, hiking, volleyball, or basketball.

Swimming is one of the most popular recreational and competitive sports in the world. Over 120 million Americans swim regularly. More than 165,000 of these are competitive age-group swimmers (ages 5–18), and over 30,000 competitors are over 19 years of age. You don't need a backyard pool to swim. Almost every town and city in America has a public pool. Pools are standard in many health clubs, YMCAs, and schools. Ocean and lake swimming may be options in the summer. High-tech wet suits make it possible to swim outdoors even in the middle of winter in many parts of the country.

Training Methods

Improved fitness from swimming depends on the quantity, quality, and frequency of training. Most swimmers use interval training to increase swimming fitness, speed, and endurance. Interval training involves repeated fast swims at fixed distances followed by rest. Distance or endurance training builds stamina, mental toughness, and endurance. Interval and distance training each play important and different roles in improving fitness for swimming. Interval training improves overall swimming speed and the ability to swim fast at the beginning of a swim. Endurance training helps to maintain a faster average pace during a swim without becoming overly fatigued. Endurance training becomes more important when you want to compete in long, open-water swims or triathlons.

In swimming workouts, however, quality is better than quantity. Thirty years ago, elite swimmers from East Germany sometimes swam as much as 20,000 meters in a single workout (more than 12 miles). Recent studies found that competitive athletes who swam 4000 to 6000 meters per workout produced results similar to those who swam much farther. Likewise, recreational swimmers can improve fitness, strength, and power by swimming around 1000–2000 meters (approximately 1100–2200 yards) per workout. Swim fast to get maximum benefits, but maintain good technique to maximize efficiency and minimize the risk of injury.

Interval training: Interval training involves repeated fast swims at fixed distances, followed by rest. Interval training increases sprinting speed so that swimmers can accelerate faster at the beginning of a swim. It also helps the body cope with metabolic waste products so that you can maintain your speed during the workout. To increase speed, swim intervals between 25 and 200 meters (or yards) at 80–90% effort. An example of a beginning program might be to swim four sets of 50 meters using the sidestroke at 70% of maximum effort, with a 1-minute rest between sets. A more advanced program would be to swim ten sets of 100 meters using the freestyle stroke at 85–95% maximum effort with 30 seconds of rest between sets.

Endurance training: Include longer swims—1000 meters or more at a time—to build general stamina for swimming. Endurance training will improve aerobic capacity and help your cells use fuels and clear metabolic wastes. This will allow you to swim faster and longer. Longer swims promote metabolic health and build physical fitness.

Cross-training: Cross-training combines more than one type of endurance exercise, such as swimming and jogging, in your program at a time. It is a good training method for people who prefer swimming but don't have daily access to a swimming pool or open water. Including multiple exercises, such as swimming and running, stair stepping, or cycling, adds variety to the program. It also prepares you for a greater variety of physical challenges.

Technique: The Basic Swimming Strokes for General Conditioning

The best strokes for conditioning are the freestyle and sidestroke. Competitive athletes also swim the breaststroke, butterfly, and backstroke (but not the sidestroke). Learning efficient swimming strokes helps increase enjoyment and results in better workouts. Take a class from the Red Cross, local recreation department, or private coach if you are not a strong swimmer or need help with the basic strokes.

Freestyle: While freestyle technically includes any unregulated stroke (such as the sidestroke), it generally refers to the front (Australian) crawl or overhand stroke. Freestyle is the fastest stroke and is best for general conditioning. Swim this stroke in a prone (face-down) position with arms stretched out in front and legs extended to the back. Move through the water by pulling first with the right arm and then with the left, while performing a kicking motion generated from the hips. During the stroke, rotate the thumb and palm 45 degrees toward the bottom of the pool. Pull in a semicircle downward toward the center of the body with the elbow higher than the hand. When the hand reaches the beginning of the ribcage, push the palm backward underneath the body as far as possible. Don't begin to stroke with the other hand until the first stroke is completed. Maximize the distance with each stroke by pulling fully and maintaining good posture.

The crawl uses a flutter kick, which involves moving the legs alternately with the force generated from the hips and a slight bend of the knees. Maintain a neutral spine during the stroke. A strong kick is important to minimize body roll during the stroke. For this reason, some of your training should include kicking without using the arms.

Breathing is almost always a problem for novice swimmers. Don't hold your breath! You will fatigue rapidly if you have poor air exchange during swimming. Breathe by turning the head to the side of a recovering stroke. Do not lift the head out of the water. Exhale continuously through the nose and mouth in between breaths. Beginners should breathe on the same side following each stroke cycle (left and right arm strokes).

Sidestroke: Even novices can get a good workout with minimal skill using the sidestroke. This is a good choice for beginners because you keep your head out of water and can swim great distances without fatigue. Lie in the water on your right side and stretch your right arm and hand in front of you in the direction you want to swim and place your left hand across your chest. Draw your right arm toward you, pulling at the water until your hand reaches your waist. At the same time, make a scissors kick with your legs. Repeat the stroke as your forward speed slows. Swim half the distance on your right side and the rest on your left side.

Beginning Swim Program

Take swimming lessons from a certified teacher or coach if you are a nonswimmer or have not used swimming as your primary form of exercise. A swim teacher can help you develop good technique, make more rapid progress, and avoid injuries.

To assess your starting fitness, take the 12-minute swim test described in Lab 3.1. Use the swim test table to help you measure progress in your program. Take the test every 1 or 2 months to help establish short-term goals.

Start your program by swimming one-half lap at a time, using either freestyle or sidestroke. If you can't swim the length of a standard pool (25 meters or yards), begin by swimming the width. As soon as you can, swim one length of the pool, rest for 30 seconds, and then repeat. Build up your capacity until you can swim 20 lengths with a short rest interval between each length. If you start your program with the sidestroke, try to switch to the freestyle stroke as quickly as you can.

Increase the distance of each swim to a full lap (50 meters or yards) with 30 seconds to 1 minute of rest between laps. Build up until you can swim 20 sets of 50-meter swims with 30 seconds of rest between sets. Gradually increase the distance of each set to 100-meter swims. You are ready for the next level when you can swim 10 sets of 100 meters with 30 seconds of rest between sets.

Swimming Program for Higher Levels of Fitness

This program includes a warm-up, specific conditioning drills for strokes and kicking, and a cool-down. It involves interval training 3 days a week and distance training 2 days per week.

Warm up before each workout by swimming 2–4 laps at an easy pace. It is also a good idea to warm up your legs and hips by holding on to the side of the pool and gently moving your legs using a flutter-kick motion. At the end of the workout, cool down by swimming 100–200 meters at a slow pace.

On Monday, Wednesday, and Friday, do interval training. Your goal is to swim intervals totaling 2000 meters per workout (20 sets of 100 meters each) at a fast pace with 30 seconds of rest between intervals. Every fifth interval, swim 25 meters using your legs alone, with your arms extended in front of you. Have someone watch you during the legs-only swims to make sure you are kicking mainly from the hips and maintaining a neutral spine. Add variety to your interval training workouts by using gloves, swim paddles, or fins.

If you are unable to do the interval workout at first, modify it by increasing rest intervals, decreasing speed, or decreasing the number of sets as you gradually increase the volume and intensity.

On Tuesday and Thursday, do distance training. Swim 1000–2000 meters continuously at a comfortable pace. Although distance days will help develop endurance, they are used mainly to help you recover from intense interval training days.

Rest on Saturday and Sunday. Rest is very important to help your muscles and metabolism recover and build fitness. Rest will also prevent overtraining and overuse injuries. Include 2 rest days per week. Rest days can be consecutive (such as Saturday and Sunday) or interspersed during the normal workout schedule.

Integrating Swimming into a Total Fitness Program

You will develop fitness best and maintain interest in continuing your exercise program by varying the structure of your workouts. Incorporate kick boards, pull-buoys, hand paddles, and fins into some of your training sessions. Cross-training is a good option for developing well-rounded fitness. Swimming results in moderate gains in strength and large gains in endurance.

Table 3	Sample Swimming Program

DAY	ACTIVITIES
Monday	• **Warm-up:** Swim 100–200 meters (2–4 laps of a standard pool) at an easy pace. • **Intervals:** Swim 10–20 sets of 100-meter swims at 90% effort, with 30 seconds of rest between sets. After every 5 sets, swim 25 meters using your legs alone. • **Cool-down:** Swim 100–200 meters at a slow pace. • **Weight training:** Do at least 1 set of 10 repetitions of 8–10 exercises that work the body's major muscle groups. • **Flexibility:** Do standard stretching exercises for the shoulders, chest, back, hips, and thighs.
Tuesday	• **Distance:** Swim 1000–2000 meters continuously at a comfortable pace.
Wednesday	• Repeat Monday activities.
Thursday	• Repeat Tuesday activities.
Friday	• Repeat Monday activities.
Saturday	• **Rest.**
Sunday	• **Rest.**

Because swimming is not a weight-bearing activity and is not done in an upright position, it elicits a lower heart rate per minute. Therefore, swimmers need to adjust their target heart rate zone. To calculate your target heart rate for swimming, use this formula:

Maximum swimming heart rate (MSHR) = 205 − age

Target heart rate zone = 65–90% of MSHR

For example, a 19-year-old swimmer would calculate his or her target heart rate zone for swimming as follows:

MSHR: 205 − 19 = 186 bpm

65% intensity: 0.65 × 186 = 121 bpm

90% intensity: 0.90 × 186 = 167 bpm

Swimming tends to reduce bone density, so swimmers are advised to include weight training in their exercise program. Do at least one set of 10 repetitions for 8–10 exercises that use the major muscle groups in the body. To improve swimming performance, include exercises that work key muscles. For example, if you primarily swim the freestyle stroke, include exercises to increase strength in your shoulders, arms, upper back, and hips. Training the muscles you use during swimming can also help prevent injuries. In your flexibility training, pay special attention to the muscles you use during swimming, particularly the shoulders, hips, and back. Table 3 shows a basic sample swimming program that incorporates all these types of exercises.

ROWING MACHINE SAMPLE PROGRAM

Rowing is a whole-body exercise that overloads the cardiorespiratory system and strengthens the major muscles of the body. The beauty and serenity of rowing on flat water in the morning is indescribable, but few people have access to a lake and rowing shell. Fortunately, sophisticated rowing machines simulate the rowing motion and make it possible to do this exercise at the fitness center or at a health club.

Modern rowing machines are very much like the real thing. They provide resistance with hydraulic pistons, magnets, air, or water. The best machines are solid and comfortable, provide a steady stroke, and allow you to maintain a neutral spine so you don't injure your back. Many rowing machines come with LCD displays that show heart rate, stroke rate, power output, and estimated caloric expenditure. They are also preprogrammed with workouts for interval training, cardiovascular conditioning, and moderate-intensity physical activity. Good rowing mechanics are essential because, if done incorrectly, rowing can cause severe overuse injuries that can damage the back, hips, knees, elbows, and shoulders.

Technique: Basic Rowing Movement

Most of the power for rowing comes from the thigh and hip muscles and finishes with a pulling motion with the upper body. Maintain a neutral spine (that is, with normal curves) during the movement. Hinge at the hips and not at the back during the rowing motion.

The rowing movement includes the following phases:

• ***The catch.*** The catch involves sliding the seat forward on the track with arms straight as far as you can while keeping the spine neutral.

- **The drive.** The drive begins by pushing with the legs and keeping your arms straight.
- **The finish.** Finish by leaning back slightly (still maintaining a neutral spine) and pulling the handle to your abdomen.
- **The recovery.** Recover by extending your arms forward, hinging forward at the hips with a neutral spine, and sliding forward again on the seat for another "catch."

Training Methods

Your rowing program should include both continuous training and interval training. Continuous training involves rowing for a specific amount of time—typically 20–90 minutes without stopping. Most people enjoy rowing at about 70% of maximum heart rate.

Interval training involves a series of exercise bouts followed by rest. The method manipulates distance, intensity, repetitions, and rest. An example of an interval workout would be to row for eight sets of 4-minute exercise bouts at 85% effort with 2 minutes of rest between intervals. During interval training, changing one factor affects the others. For example, if you increase the intensity of exercise, you will need more rest between intervals and won't be able to do as many repetitions. High-intensity exercise builds fitness best but also increases the risk of injury and loss of motivation. Make intervals challenging but not so difficult that you get injured or discouraged.

Beginning Rowing Program

During the first few workouts, start conservatively by rowing for 10 minutes at a rate of about 20 strokes per minute with a moderate resistance. Exercise at about 60% effort. Do this workout three times during the first week. The movement is deceptively easy and invigorating. You are, however, using all the major muscle groups in the body and are probably not ready for a more intense exercise program.

After the first workout, do a series of 5-minute intervals during the first few weeks of training. For example, row for 5 minutes, rest 3 minutes, row 5 minutes, then rest 3 minutes. Build up until you can do 4–6 repetitions of 5-minute exercise intervals, resting only 1 minute between sets. Gradually, increase the time for each interval to 15 minutes and vary the rowing cadence from 20 to 25 strokes per minute. Your first short-term goal is to complete 30 minutes of continuous rowing without stopping.

Rowing Program for Higher Levels of Fitness

Vary your training methods after you can row continuously for 30 minutes, gain some fitness, and get used to the technique. Alternate between interval training and distance training. Doing both will help you develop fitness rapidly and improve rowing efficiency. A good strategy is to row continuously at about 70% effort for 30-60 minutes 3 days per week and practice interval training at 80–90% effort for 2 days per week. Do resistance and flexibility training 2–3 days per week. A basic but complete rowing machine program that includes continuous and interval training as well as resistance and flexibility exercises is shown in Table 4.

Table 4	Sample Rowing Machine Fitness Program

DAY	ACTIVITIES
Monday	• **Warm-up:** Row at low intensity for 2 minutes. • **Continuous rowing:** Row for 30 minutes at 70% effort (20–22 strokes per minute). • **Weight training (1–2 sets of 10 repetitions):** Squats, leg curls, bench press, lat pulls, raises, biceps curls, triceps extensions, curl-ups, side bridge (10 seconds per side), spine extensions (10 seconds per side). • **Stretching:** Do static stretching exercises for the shoulders, chest, back, hips, and thighs. Hold each stretch for 10–30 seconds.
Tuesday	• **Warm-up:** Row at low intensity for 2 minutes. • **Continuous rowing:** Row at 60–70% of maximum effort for 5 minutes. Rest for 3 minutes. • **Interval rowing:** Row 6 sets, for 5 minutes per set, at 25 strokes per minute (90% effort). Rest for 3 minutes between intervals.
Wednesday	• **Warm-up:** Row at low intensity for 2 minutes. • **Continuous rowing:** Row for 45 minutes at 70% effort (20–22 strokes per minute). • **Stretching:** Repeat Monday stretches.
Thursday	• **Warm-up:** Row at low intensity for 2 minutes. • **Continuous rowing:** Row for 30 minutes at 70% effort (20–22 strokes per minute). • **Weight training (1–2 sets of 10 repetitions):** Repeat Monday weight training exercises.
Friday	• **Warm-up:** Row at low intensity for 2 minutes. • **Continuous rowing:** Row for 30 minutes at 70% effort (20–22 strokes per minute). • **Stretching:** Repeat Monday stretches.
Saturday	• **Rest.**
Sunday	• **Rest.**

Name _____ Section _____ Date _____

LAB 7.1   A Personal Fitness Program Plan and Contract

A. I, _____, am contracting with myself to follow a physical fitness program to
                        (name)
work toward the following goals:

Specific or short-term goals (include current status for each):

1. _____

2. _____

3. _____

4. _____

General or long-term goals:

1. _____

2. _____

3. _____

4. _____

B. My program plan is as follows:

Activities	Components (Check ✓)					Frequency (Check ✓)							Intensity*	Time (duration)
	CRE	MS	ME	F	BC	M	Tu	W	Th	F	Sa	Su		

*Conduct activities for achieving CRE goals in your target range for heart rate or RPE.

C. My program will begin on _____. My program includes the following schedule of mini-goals. For each step in my
                                    (date)
program, I will give myself the reward listed.

_____	_____	_____
(mini-goal 1)	(date)	(reward)
_____	_____	_____
(mini-goal 2)	(date)	(reward)
_____	_____	_____
(mini-goal 3)	(date)	(reward)
_____	_____	_____
(mini-goal 4)	(date)	(reward)
_____	_____	_____
(mini-goal 5)	(date)	(reward)

Mc Graw Hill **connect** http://www.mcgrawhillconnect.com/
|FITNESS AND WELLNESS

D. My program will include the addition of physical activity to my daily routine (such as climbing stairs or walking to class):

1. _____

2. _____

3. _____

4. _____

5. _____

E. I will use the following tools to monitor my program and my progress toward my goals:

_____

(list any charts, graphs, or journals you plan to use)

_____

_____

I sign this contract as an indication of my personal commitment to reach my goal.

_____   _____

(your signature)   (date)

I have recruited a helper who will witness my contract and _____

_____

(list any way your helper will participate in your program)

_____

_____   _____

(witness's signature)   (date)

LAB 7.2 Getting to Know Your Fitness Facility

To help create a successful training program, take time to learn more about the fitness facility you plan to use.

Basic Information

Name and location of facility: _____

Hours of operation: _____

Times available for general use: _____

Times most convenient for your schedule: _____

Can you obtain an initial session or consultation with a trainer to help you create a program? _____ yes _____ no

If so, what does the initial planning session involve? _____

_____

Are any of the staff certified? Do any have special training? If yes, list/describe: _____

_____

What types of equipment are available for the development of cardiorespiratory endurance? Briefly list/describe: _____

_____

_____

_____

Are any group activities or classes available? If so, briefly describe: _____

_____

_____

What types of weight training equipment are available for use? _____

_____

Yes	No	
_____	_____	Is there a fee for using the facility? If so, how much? $ _____
_____	_____	Is a student ID required for access to the facility?
_____	_____	Do you need to sign up in advance to use the facility or any of the equipment?
_____	_____	Is there typically a line or wait to use the equipment during the times you use the facility?
_____	_____	Is there a separate area with mats for stretching and/or cool-down?
_____	_____	Do you need to bring your own towel?
_____	_____	Are lockers available? If so, do you need to bring your own lock? _____ yes _____ no
_____	_____	Are showers available? If so, do you need to bring your own soap and shampoo? _____ yes _____ no
_____	_____	Is drinking water available? (If not, be sure to bring your own bottle of water.)

What other amenities, such as vending machines or saunas, are available at the facility? Briefly list/describe: _____

_____

Information About Equipment

Fill in the specific equipment and exercise(s) that you can use to develop cardiorespiratory endurance and each of the major muscle groups. For cardiorespiratory endurance, list the type(s) of equipment and a sample starting workout: frequency, intensity, time, and other pertinent information (such as a setting for resistance or speed). For muscular strength and endurance, list the equipment and exercises, and indicate the order in which you'll complete them during a workout session.

Cardiorespiratory Endurance Equipment

Equipment	Sample Starting Workout

Muscular Strength and Endurance Equipment

Order	Muscle Groups	Equipment	Exercise(s)
	Neck		
	Chest		
	Shoulders		
	Upper back		
	Front of arms		
	Back of arms		
	Buttocks		
	Abdomen		
	Lower back		
	Front of thighs		
	Back of thighs		
	Calves		
	Other:		
	Other:		

Aging: A Vital Process

After reading this chapter, you should be able to

- List strategies for healthy aging

- Identify key physical, social, and mental changes that may accompany aging and explain how people can best confront these changes

- Describe practical considerations for older adults and caregivers, including housing, finances, health care, communication, and transportation

TEST YOUR KNOWLEDGE

1. **Women do not need to take preventive measures against osteoporosis until after menopause.**
   True or false?

2. **What is the leading cause of disability in the United States?**
   a. Heart disease
   b. Arthritis
   c. Dementia

3. **On average, a woman will spend more time caring for an aging relative than raising children.**
   True or false?

4. **Exercise is beneficial for older people because it**
   a. Protects against osteoporosis
   b. Maintains alertness and intelligence
   c. Prevents falls

5. **When Social Security was initiated in 1935, the average life expectancy was**
   a. 58
   b. 63
   c. 70

ANSWERS

1. **FALSE.** All people—but especially women—need to pay attention to diet and exercise in their younger years in order to build bone mass.

2. **B.** According to the Centers for Disease Control and Prevention, arthritis is the leading cause of disability in the United States.

3. **TRUE.** The average woman will spend 17 years raising children and 18 years caring for an aging relative.

4. **ALL THREE.** Even for people over 80, exercise can improve physical functioning and balance and reduce falls and injuries.

5. **B.** Life expectancy has increased by about 15 years since 1935 due to medical advances and improvements in diet and personal habits.

Aging is the process of becoming older, a process that is genetically determined but profoundly affected by one's environment. Your grandparents or great-grandparents may be examples of how these two determinants play a role in the aging process.

Aging does not begin at some specific point in life, and there is no precise age at which a person becomes "old." Rather, aging is a normal process of development that occurs throughout life. It happens to everyone, but at different rates for different people. Some people are "old" at 25, and others are still "young" at 75.

Although youth is not entirely a state of mind, your attitude toward life and your attention to your health significantly influence the satisfaction you will get from life. This is especially true when new physical, mental, and social challenges occur in later years. If you optimize wellness during young adulthood, you can exert great control over the physical and mental aspects of aging, and you can better handle your response to events that might be out of your control.

This chapter discusses the aging process and describes some of the major effects increasing age can have on our lives.

GENERATING VITALITY AS YOU AGE

As we age, physical and mental changes occur gradually over a lifetime. Biological aging includes all the normal, progressive, irreversible changes to our bodies that begin at birth and continue until death. Psychological aging and social aging usually involve more abrupt changes in circumstance and emotion: relocating, changing homes, losing a spouse and friends, retiring, having a lower income, and changing roles and social status. These changes represent opportunities for growth throughout life.

Not all of these changes happen to everybody, and their timing varies, partly depending on how we have prepared for our later years. Some people never have to leave their homes and appear to be in good health until they die. Others have tremendous adjustments to make—to entirely new surroundings with fewer financial resources, to new acquaintances, to the changing physical condition of their bodies and new health problems, and possibly to loneliness and loss of self-esteem.

Successful aging requires preparation. People need to establish good health habits in their teens and twenties. During their twenties and thirties, they usually develop important relationships and settle into a particular lifestyle. By their mid-forties, they generally know how much money they need to support the lifestyle they've chosen. At this point, they must assess their financial status and perhaps adjust their savings in order to continue enjoying that lifestyle after retirement. In their mid-fifties, they need to reevaluate their health insurance plans and may want to think about retirement housing. In their seventies and beyond, they need to consider ways of sharing their legacy with the next generation. Throughout life, people should cultivate interests and hobbies they enjoy, both alone and with others.

What Happens as You Age?

A significant number of older Americans describe themselves as being in poor health (Table 22.1). Many of the characteristics

> The aging process is genetically determined but **profoundly affected by our environment.**

QUICK STATS

One of the nation's fastest-growing groups, the **90-plus population** is projected to reach 8 million by 2050, representing 2 percent of the U.S. population.

—National Institute on Aging

associated with aging, however, are not due to aging at all. Rather, they result from the neglect and abuse of our bodies and minds. These assaults lay the foundation for later psychological problems and chronic conditions like arthritis, heart disease, diabetes, hearing loss, vision problems, and hypertension. We sacrifice our health by smoking, ignoring our nutritional needs, overeating, abusing alcohol and drugs, bombarding our ears with excessive noise, and exposing our bodies to too much ultraviolet radiation from the sun. We also jeopardize our bodies through inactivity, encouraging our muscles and even our bones to wither and deteriorate. And we endure abuse from the toxic chemicals in our environment.

But even with the healthiest behavior and environment, aging inevitably occurs. It results from biochemical processes we don't yet fully understand. The physiological changes in organ systems are caused by a combination of gradual aging and impairment from disease. Because of redundancy in most organ systems, the body's ability to function is not affected until damage is fairly extensive. Studies of healthy people indicate that functioning remains essentially constant until after age 70. Further research may help pinpoint the causes of aging and aid in the development of therapies to repair damage to aging organs.

Life-Enhancing Measures: Age-Proofing

You can prevent, delay, lessen, or even reverse some of the changes associated with aging through good habits. Simple things you can do daily will make a vast difference to your level of energy and vitality—your overall wellness. The following suggestions have been mentioned throughout this text. But because they are profoundly related to health in later life, we highlight them here.

Challenge Your Mind Numerous studies show that older adults who stay mentally active have lower levels of the brain protein linked to Alzheimer's and dementia. Reading, writing, doing puzzles, learning language, and studying music are good ways to stimulate the brain. The more complex the activity, the more protective it may be.

Develop Physical Fitness Exercise significantly enhances both psychological and physical health. A review of more than 70 scientific studies cited in the 2008 *Physical Activity Guidelines Advisory Committee Report* found that physically active people have about a 30% lower risk of dying prematurely compared with inactive people. Poor fitness and

Table 22.1	Americans Who Rate Their Health as Fair or Poor
AGE GROUP	**PERCENTAGE**
18–24	9.1%
25–34	9.9%
35–44	12.0%
45–54	16.8%
55–64	22.2%
65–74	25.5%
75 and older	31.7%

SOURCE: Centers for Disease Control and Prevention, National Center for Chronic Disease Prevention and Health Promotion. 2010. *Health Related Quality of Life* (http://www.cdc.gov/hrqol).

Regular exercise is a key to successful, healthy aging.

low physical activity levels were found to be better predictors of premature death than smoking, diabetes, or obesity. The committee found that about 150 minutes (2.5 hours) of physical activity per week is sufficient to decrease all-cause mortality and that it is the overall volume of energy expended, regardless of what kinds of activities produce the energy expenditure, that makes a difference in risk of premature death.

The positive effects of exercise include the following:

- Lower blood pressure and healthier cholesterol levels.

- Better protection against heart attacks and an increased chance of survival should one occur.

- Sustained or increased lung capacity.

- Weight control through less accumulation of fat.

- Maintenance of strength, flexibility, and balance.

- Improved sleep.

- Longer life expectancy.

- Protection against osteoporosis and type 2 diabetes.

- Increased effectiveness of the immune system.

- Maintenance of mental agility and flexibility, response time, memory, and hand–eye coordination.

The stimulus that exercise provides also seems to protect against the loss of **fluid intelligence,** which is the ability to

find solutions to new problems. Fluid intelligence depends on rapidity of responsiveness, memory, and alertness. Individuals who exercise regularly are also less susceptible to depression and dementia.

Regular physical activity also fends off *sarcopenia*, which is age-related loss of muscle mass, strength, and function (see Chapter 13). The weaker a person becomes, the less he or she can do; this condition can rob one of self-sufficiency and lead to greater dependence on others. The muscle wasting that occurs in sarcopenia also leads to weight gain because muscle burns more calories than fat, even at rest.

Regular physical activity is essential for healthy aging, as it is throughout life. The *2008 Physical Activity Guidelines for Americans* include recommendations for older adults that are the same as for all adults:

- All older adults should avoid inactivity. Some physical activity is better than none.

- For substantial health benefits, older adults should do at least 150 minutes a week of moderate-intensity activity, or 75 minutes a week of vigorous-intensity activity, or a combination of both. For additional and more extensive health benefits, older adults should increase their aerobic physical activity to 300 minutes a week of moderate-intensity, or 150 minutes a week of vigorous-intensity, aerobic physical activity.

- Older adults should also do muscle-strengthening activities that are moderate or high intensity and involve all major muscle groups on two or more days a week because these activities provide additional health benefits.

There are also guidelines just for older adults:

- When older adults cannot do 150 minutes of moderate-intensity aerobic activity a week because of chronic conditions, they should be as physically active as their abilities and conditions allow.

- Older adults should do exercises that maintain or improve balance if they are at risk of falling.

- Older adults with chronic conditions should understand whether and how their conditions affect their ability to do regular physical activity safely.

- Older adults should maintain the flexibility necessary for regular physical activity and activities of daily life.

For more about the beneficial effects of exercise for older adults, see the box "Can Exercise Delay the Effects of Aging?"

Eat Wisely   Good health at any age is enhanced by eating a varied diet full of nutrient-rich foods (see Chapter 12). For many adults, that means eating more fruits, vegetables, and whole grains while eating fewer foods high in saturated and

| **fluid intelligence**   The ability to develop a solution when confronted with a new problem. | TERMS |

As people age, they often experience declines in functional health—the ability to perform the tasks of everyday life—and related declines in the quality of life. According to the CDC, more than 25% of Americans over age 65 report their health as only "fair" or "poor." Similarly, according to a Medicare survey, 31% of men and 42% of women aged 65–74 reported some sort of mobility limitation in 2003 (meaning they had difficulty walking one-quarter mile).

Can physical activity and exercise combat the degenerative effects of aging in middle-aged and older adults? The evidence indicates that they can. In reviewing the research, the U.S. government's Physical Activity Guidelines Advisory Committee concluded that physical activity can prevent or delay the onset of limitations and declines in functional health in older adults, can maintain or improve functional health in those who already have limitations, and can reduce the incidence of falls and fall-related injuries.

One mechanism by which physical activity prevents declines in functional health is through maintenance or improvement of the physiological capacities of the body, such as aerobic power, muscular strength, and balance—in other words, through improvements in physical fitness. Declines in these physiological capacities occur with biological aging and are often compounded by disease-related disability. But evidence shows that older adults who participate in regular aerobic exercise are 30% less likely than inactive individuals to develop functional limitations (such as a limited ability to walk or climb stairs) or role limitations (such as a limited ability to be the family grocery shopper). Although studies found that both physical activity and aerobic fitness were associated with reduced risk of functional limitations, aerobic fitness was associated with a greater reduction of risk. Evidence also suggests that regular physical activity is safe and beneficial for older adults who already have functional limitations.

Numerous studies have shown that regular exercise—particularly strength training, balance training, and flexibility exercises—can improve muscular strength, muscular endurance, and stability and provide some protection against falls. Aerobic activity, especially walking, also helps reduce risk of falls, and some evidence indicates that t'ai chi exercise programs are beneficial as well. Regular exercise not only reduces the incidence of falls but also greatly enhances mobility, allowing older people to live more independently and with greater confidence. Research also shows that regular physical activity can reduce anxiety and depression in older adults. Exercise stimulates blood flow to the brain and can even increase brain mass, helping the brain to function more efficiently and improving memory. There is some evidence that exercise may stave off mental decline and the occurrence of age-related dementia.

Current physical activity recommendations for older adults from the American Heart Association and the American College of Sports Medicine include moderate- to vigorous-intensity aerobic activity, strength training, and flexibility exercises, as well as balance exercises for older adults at risk for falls. Unfortunately more than 75% of Americans aged 65 and older do not get the recommended amounts of physical activity, and many get no exercise at all beyond the activities of daily living. Older adults are the least active group of Americans. Although it is important to exercise throughout life, the evidence indicates that older adults who become more active even late in life can experience improvements in physical fitness and functional health.

SOURCES: Centers for Disease Control and Prevention. 2007. Prevalence of regular physical activity among adults—United States, 2001 and 2005. *Morbidity and Mortality Weekly Report* 56 (46): 1209–1212; Physical Activity Guidelines Advisory Committee. 2008. *Physical Activity Guidelines Advisory Committee Report, 2008.* Washington, DC: U.S. Department of Health and Human Services; Simonsick, E. M., et al. 2005. Just get out the door! Importance of walking outside the home for maintaining mobility: findings from the Women's Health and Aging Study. *Journal of the American Geriatrics Society* 53(2): 198–203.

trans fats and added sugars. Special guidelines for older adults include the following:

- Get enough vitamin B-12 and extra vitamin D from fortified foods or supplements.

- Limit sodium intake to 1500 mg per day, and get enough potassium (4700 mg per day). Older adults tend to have higher blood pressure and to be salt-sensitive.

- Eat foods rich in dietary fiber and drink plenty of water to help prevent constipation.

- Pay special attention to food safety. Older adults are often more susceptible to foodborne illness.

Maintain a Healthy Weight   Weight management is especially difficult if you have been overweight most of your life. A sensible program of expending more calories through exercise, cutting calorie intake, or a combination of both will work for most people who want to lose weight, but there is no magic formula. Obesity is not physically healthy, and it leads to premature aging (see Chapter 14).

Control Drinking and Overdependence on Medications   Alcohol abuse ranks with depression as a common hidden mental health problem, affecting about 10% of older adults. (The ability to metabolize alcohol decreases with age.) The problem is often not identified because the effects of alcohol or drug dependence can mimic disease, such as Alzheimer's disease.

Signs of potential alcohol or drug dependence include unexplained falls or frequent injuries, forgetfulness, depression, and malnutrition. Older people who retire or lose a spouse are especially at risk. Problems can be avoided by not using alcohol to relieve anxiety or emotional pain and not taking medication when safer forms of treatment are available.

Don't Smoke   The average pack-a-day smoker can expect to live about 13–14 fewer years than a nonsmoker. Furthermore, smokers suffer more illnesses that last longer, and they are subject to respiratory disabilities that limit their total vigor for many years before their death. Premature balding, skin wrinkling, and osteoporosis have been linked to cigarette

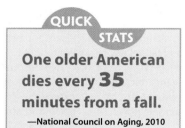

QUICK STATS

One older American dies every 35 minutes from a fall.

—National Council on Aging, 2010

smoking. Smokers at age 50 often have wrinkles resembling those of a person of 60.

Schedule Physical Examinations to Detect Treatable Diseases   When detected early, many diseases, including hypertension, diabetes, and many types of cancer, can be successfully controlled by medication and lifestyle changes. Regular testing for **glaucoma** after age 40 can prevent blindness from this eye disease. Recommended screenings and immunizations can protect against preventable chronic and infectious diseases (see Chapters 14–17).

Recognize and Reduce Stress   Stress-induced physiological changes increase wear and tear on your body. Cut down on the stresses in your life. Don't wear yourself out through lack of sleep, substance abuse or misuse, or overwork. Take five minutes every so often throughout the day to close your eyes and focus on your breathing. Practice relaxation using the techniques described in Chapter 2. If you contract a disease, consider it your body's attempt to interrupt your life pattern; reevaluate your lifestyle, and perhaps slow down.

DEALING WITH THE CHANGES OF AGING

As we age, we experience many losses. Loss is painful—whether it's a loss of independence, mobility, health, your long-time career, or someone you love. The changes that occur with aging have repercussions that must be grappled with and resolved. Just as you can act now to prevent or limit the physical changes of aging, you can also begin preparing yourself psychologically, socially, and financially for changes that may occur later in life. If you have aging parents, grandparents, and friends, the following information may give you insight into their lives and encourage you to begin cultivating appropriate and useful behaviors now.

Planning for Social Changes

Retirement marks a major change in the second half of life. As Americans' longevity has increased, people spend a larger proportion of their lives—17 years or more—in retirement. This has implications for reestablishing important relationships, developing satisfying interests outside work, and saving for an adequate retirement income. People who have well-developed leisure pursuits adjust better to retirement than those with few interests outside work.

Ask Yourself

QUESTIONS FOR CRITICAL THINKING AND REFLECTION

How do you feel about the prospect of growing old? Would you say that you look forward to it, or are you anxious about it? What influences have shaped your feelings about aging?

glaucoma   A disease in which fluid inside the eye is under abnormally high pressure; can lead to the loss of peripheral vision and blindness.

TERMS

Changing Roles and Relationships Changes in social roles are a major feature of life as we age. Children become young adults and leave home, putting an end to daily parenting. Parents experiencing this empty-nest syndrome must adapt to changes in their customary responsibilities and personal identities. And although retirement may be a desirable milestone for most people, it may also be viewed as a threat to prestige, purpose, and self-respect—the loss of a valued or customary role—and often requires some adjustment.

Retirement and the end of child rearing also bring about changes in the relationship between marriage partners. The amount of time a couple spends together will increase, and activities will change. Couples may need a period of adjustment in which they get to know each other as individuals again. Discussing what types of activities each partner enjoys can help couples set up a mutually satisfying routine of shared and independent activities.

> Financial planning for retirement should begin early in life—**as early as your twenties.**

Increased Leisure Time Although retirement confers the advantages of leisure time and freedom from deadlines, competition, and stress, many people do not know how to enjoy their free time. If you have developed diverse interests, retirement can be a joyful and fulfilling period of your life. It

can provide opportunities for expanding your horizons by giving you the chance to try new activities, take classes, and meet new people. Volunteering in your community can enhance self-esteem and allow you to be a contributing member of society.

The Economics of Retirement Retirement is usually accompanied by a new economic situation. It may mean a severely restricted budget or possibly even financial disaster if you don't take stock of your finances and plan ahead. Financial planning for retirement should begin early in life. People in their twenties and thirties should estimate how much money they need to support their standard of living, calculate their projected income, and begin a savings program. The earlier people begin such a program, the more money they will have at retirement.

Financial planning for retirement is especially critical for women. American women are much less likely than men to be covered by pension plans, reflecting the fact that many women have lower-paying jobs or work part-time during their childbearing years. They tend to have less money vested in other types of retirement plans as well. Although the gap is narrowing, women currently outlive men by about five to six years, and they are more likely to develop chronic conditions that impair their daily activities later in life. The net result of these factors is that older women are almost twice as likely as older men to live in poverty. Women should investigate their retirement plans and take charge of their finances to be sure they will be provided for as they get older.

Adapting to Physical Changes

As described earlier in the chapter, there are many things a person can do to avoid or minimize the effects of the physical changes associated with aging. However, some changes in physical functioning are inevitable, and successful aging involves anticipating and accommodating these changes.

Decreased energy and changes in health mean that older people have to develop priorities for how to use their energy. Rather than curtailing activities to conserve energy, they need to learn how to generate energy. This usually involves saying yes to enjoyable activities and paying close attention to the need for rest and sleep.

Adapting, rather than giving up, favorite activities may be the best strategy for dealing with physical limitations. For example, if arthritis interferes with playing an instrument, a person can continue to enjoy music by taking up a different instrument or attending concerts.

Hearing Loss The loss of hearing is a common physical change that can have a particularly strong effect on the lives of older adults. Some people lose their hearing slowly as they age—a condition known as *presbycusis*. Hearing loss affects a person's ability to interact with others and can lead to a sense of isolation and depression. Hearing loss should be assessed and

The retirement years can be the best part of one's life socially, with increased opportunities to meet and interact with new and different people.

treated by a health care professional. In some cases hearing can be completely restored by dealing with the underlying cause of hearing loss. In other cases hearing aids may be prescribed; but many older adults, especially women, resist wearing hearing aids. The cost of hearing aids may be another limiting factor.

Protect your hearing by avoiding exposure to noises above 90 decibels, such as lawnmowers, motorcycles, gunshots, and loud music (see Chapter 19). Wear earplugs when you must be around loud noises, limit your time of exposure, and stay as far as possible from the sound's source.

Vision Changes   Vision usually declines with age. For some individuals this can be traced to conditions such as **glaucoma** or **age-related macular degeneration (AMD)** that can be treated medically. For others, the effects of a decline in vision can be managed using strategies to make the most of remaining vision.

Glaucoma is caused by increased pressure within the eye due to built-up fluid. The optic nerve can be damaged by this increased pressure, resulting in a loss of side vision and, if untreated, blindness. Medication can relieve the pressure by decreasing the amount of fluid produced or by helping it drain more efficiently. Laser and conventional surgery are other options. Of the 4 million Americans with glaucoma, only half know that they have it;

others lose the opportunity to control it and preserve their sight. People over 60, African Americans over 40, and anyone with a family history of glaucoma are at risk.

AMD is a slow disintegration of the *macula*—the tissue at the center of the retina where fine, straight-ahead detail is distinguished. AMD affects more than 1.5 million Americans over 40 and is the leading cause of blindness in people over age 75. Losing this vision makes it difficult to read, drive, or perform other close-up activities. Risk factors for AMD are age, gender (women may be at higher risk than men), smoking, elevated cholesterol levels, and family history. Some cases of AMD can be treated with laser surgery. Both glaucoma and AMD can be detected with regular screening.

Vision can also be affected by conditions that are products of aging. By the time they reach their forties, many people have developed **presbyopia**—a gradual decline in the ability to focus on objects close to them. This occurs because the lens of the eye no longer expands and contracts as readily. **Cataracts,** a clouding of the lens caused by lifelong oxidation damage (a byproduct of normal body chemistry), may dim vision by the sixties.

Arthritis   More than 46 million American adults are estimated to have some form of **arthritis.** This degenerative disease causes joint inflammation leading to chronic pain, swelling, and loss of mobility. Its symptoms include swelling, pain, redness, warmth, tenderness, changes in joint mobility, early-morning stiffness, and unexplained weight loss, fever, or weakness in combination with joint pain. Arthritis is a disease that affects people of all ages, although it affects older adults and women more often.

There are more than 100 different types of arthritis; osteoarthritis (OA) is by far the most common. (Rheumatoid arthritis, an autoimmune disorder, is described in Chapter 17.) In a person with OA, the cartilage that caps the bones in joints wears away, forming sharp spurs (Figure 22.1). It most

> **QUICK STATS**
>
> **120,000 Americans are blind due to glaucoma, accounting for 9–12% of all blindness.**
>
> —Glaucoma Research Foundation, 2010

Inflamed joints

Eroded cartilage

Inflamed tissues

Excess synovial fluid

FIGURE 22.1 Osteoarthritis. When cartilage wears away within a joint, sharp spurs form and the amount of fluid increases, causing pain and swelling.

SOURCE: Clayman, C., ed. 1995. *The Human Body: An Illustrated Guide to Its Structure, Function, and Disorders.* New York: DK.

> **TERMS**
>
> **glaucoma**   An increase in pressure in the eye due to fluid buildup that can result in loss of side vision and, if left untreated, blindness.
>
> **age-related macular degeneration (AMD)**   A deterioration of the macula (the central area of the retina) leading to blurred vision and sensitivity to glare; some cases can lead to blindness.
>
> **presbyopia**   The inability of the eyes to focus sharply on nearby objects, caused by a loss of elasticity of the lens that occurs with advancing age.
>
> **cataracts**   Opacity of the lens of the eye that impairs vision and can cause blindness.
>
> **arthritis**   Inflammation and swelling of a joint or joints, causing pain and swelling.

often affects the hands and weight-bearing joints of the body—the knees, ankles, and hips.

Strategies for reducing the risk of arthritis and, for those who already have OA, for managing it include exercise, weight management, and avoidance of heavy or repetitive muscle use. Weakness of the muscles around joints is linked to arthritis. This is why exercising is helpful. Exercise lubricates joints and strengthens the muscles around them, protecting them from further damage. Swimming, walking, cross-country skiing, cycling, and t'ai chi are good low-impact exercises; knitting and crocheting are excellent for the hands. Maintaining an appropriate weight is important to avoid placing stress on the hips, knees, and ankles. Assistive devices such as kitchen utensils and repair tools with large handles can also help.

It is also important to visit a physician as soon as arthritis symptoms occur so appropriate treatment can be started to reduce pain and swelling, keep joints moving safely, and prevent further joint damage. If joints are severely damaged and activity is limited, surgery to repair or replace joints may be considered, but medication is usually the first treatment. Many people with OA take medication to relieve inflammation and reduce pain. Because arthritis is a chronic condition, researchers are trying to find medications that are effective and safe when used over the long term. Nonsteroidal anti-inflammatory drugs like ibuprofen can help but can irritate the digestive tract; prescription drugs that relieve pain without damaging the stomach have been found to have other dangerous side effects. Acetaminophen can also reduce pain without upsetting the stomach, but exceeding the recommended dosage can cause liver damage.

> A key to avoiding osteoporosis is to **build as much bone mass as you can while you're young.**

Menopause   The natural process of menopause usually occurs during a woman's forties or fifties. The ovaries gradually stop functioning, estrogen levels drop, and eventually menstruation ceases. Several years before a woman stops menstruating, her periods usually become irregular, and she may experience hot flashes, vaginal dryness, sleep disturbances, and mood swings. This period, called *perimenopause*, can be troublesome for many women, some more than others.

Lifestyle strategies to reduce menopause-related problems include many of the healthy habits discussed throughout the text: stop smoking, exercise, eat a healthful diet, lose excess weight, and perform relaxation techniques regularly. For more information about menopause, refer to Chapters 5, 15, and 16.

Sexual Functioning   The ability to enjoy sex can continue well into old age, particularly if people make the effort to understand and respond to the various changes that age brings to the natural pattern of sexual response. All too often, older people give up intercourse because they mistakenly interpret these changes as signs of impending impotence. Lovemaking may become a more leisurely affair as a couple gets older, but the benefits of maintaining the sexual aspect of the relationship into old age can be great. It is important for the older adult, now exploring new sexual horizons after divorce or death of a spouse, to practice safe sex. A growing number of adults over age 50 have STIs.

Osteoporosis   As described in Chapter 12, **osteoporosis** is a condition in which bones become dangerously thin and fragile over time. Fractures are the most serious consequence of osteoporosis; up to 20% of all people who suffer a hip fracture die within a year. Other problems associated with osteoporosis are loss of height and a stooped posture due to vertebral fractures, severe back and hip pain, and breathing problems caused by changes in the shape of the skeleton.

Osteoporosis affects about 12 million Americans, 80% of whom are women. Women are at greater risk than men for osteoporosis because they have 10–25% less bone in their skeletons. As they lose bone mass with age, women's bones become dangerously thin sooner than men's bones (although more men will probably develop osteoporosis in the future as they live into their eighties and nineties). Bone loss accelerates in women during the first 5–10 years after the onset of menopause because of the drop in estrogen production. (Estrogen improves calcium absorption and reduces the amount of calcium the body excretes.) Black or Latino women have higher bone density and fewer fractures than white or Asian women but may be at increased risk of osteoporosis due to lack of vitamin D (a condition caused by high levels of melatonin). Other risk factors include a family history of osteoporosis, early menopause (before age 45), abnormal or irregular menstruation, a history of anorexia, and a thin, small frame. Regular consumption of more than two alcoholic drinks a day increases the risk of osteoporosis, possibly because alcohol can interfere with the body's ability to absorb calcium. Thyroid medication, corticosteroid drugs for arthritis or asthma, and long-term use of certain contraceptives can also have a negative effect on bone mass.

Preventing osteoporosis requires building as much bone as possible during your young years and then maintaining it as you age. Girls aged 9–18 are in their critical bone-building years, and it is recommended that they eat more foods rich in calcium and vitamin D and get adequate exercise. Weight-bearing aerobic activities must be performed regularly throughout life to have lasting effects. Strength training improves bone density, muscle mass, strength, and balance, protecting against both bone loss and falls, a major cause of fractures. Even for people in their seventies, low-intensity strength training has been shown to improve bone density.

---

osteoporosis   The loss of bone density, causing bones to become weak, porous, and more prone to fractures.   **TERMS**

Two other lifelong strategies for reducing the effects of osteoporosis are avoiding tobacco use and managing depression and stress. Smoking reduces the body's estrogen levels and is linked to earlier menopause and more rapid postmenopausal bone loss. Some women with depression experience significant bone loss. Researchers have not identified the reason, but it may be linked to increases in the stress hormone cortisol.

Bone mineral density testing can be used to gauge an individual's risk of fracture and help determine if any treatment is needed. It is recommended for all women over age 65 and for younger postmenopausal women who have a fracture or one or more risk factors. Below-normal bone density may be classified as *osteopenia*, which is usually treated with medication, exercise, and nutrition. A greater loss of bone mass is classified as full-blown osteoporosis and is often treated with medications.

Handling Psychological and Mental Changes

Many people associate old age with forgetfulness, and slowly losing one's memory was once considered an inevitable part of growing old. However, we now know that most older adults in good health remain mentally alert and retain their full capacity to learn and remember new information. Occasional confusion or forgetfulness may indicate only a temporary information overload, fatigue, or response to medications. Many people become smarter as they become older and more experienced in life.

Dementia Dementia is a loss of brain function that occurs with certain diseases. It affects memory, thinking, language, judgment, and behavior. About 4–5 million people in the United States have some degree of dementia, and that number will increase over the next few decades with the aging of the population. Dementia affects about 1% of people aged 60–64 years and as many as 30–50% of people older than 85 years. Early symptoms of dementia include slight disturbances in a person's ability to grasp the situation he or she is in. As dementia progresses, memory failure becomes apparent, and the person may forget conversations, the events of the day, or how to perform simple tasks. It is important to have any symptoms evaluated by a health care professional because some of the over 50 known causes of dementia are treatable (for example, depression, dehydration, malnutrition, vitamin B-12 deficiency, alcoholism, and misuse of medications).

The most common forms of dementia among older people—**Alzheimer's disease,** Lewy-Body disease, and multi-infarct dementia—are irreversible. The most common, **Alzheimer's disease** (AD), is a progressive brain disorder that damages and eventually destroys brain cells, leading to loss of memory, thinking, and other brain functions. Alzheimer's is not a part of normal aging, but results from a complex pattern of abnormal changes. It usually develops slowly and gradually gets worse as more brain cells wither and die. As the brain's nerve cells are destroyed, the system that produces the neurotransmitter acetylcholine breaks down, and communication among parts of the brain deteriorates. Autopsies reveal that the interiors of the affected neurons are filled with clusters of proteins known as *tangles*; the spaces between the neurons are filled with protein deposits called *amyloid plaques*. Ultimately Alzheimer's is fatal, and currently there is no cure.

About 5.3 million Americans have Alzheimer's disease, and that number is expected to quadruple in the next 50 years as more people live into their eighties and nineties. AD usually occurs in people over 60 but can occur in people as young as 40.

Early symptoms include trouble remembering new information; Alzheimer's changes typically begin in the part of the brain that affects learning. As Alzheimer's advances through the brain, it leads to increasingly severe symptoms, including disorientation; mood and behavior changes; deepening confusion about events, time, and place; unfounded suspicions about family, friends, and professional caregivers; more serious memory loss and behavior changes (hallucinations with major personality changes); and difficulty speaking, swallowing, and walking. Scientists do not yet know what causes Alzheimer's disease. Both age and genetics have been identified as risk factors, but many questions still remain.

Lewy-Body dementia is an umbrella term for a form of dementia that resembles Alzheimer's disease but has two or more distinctive features. Symptoms that differentiate Lewy-Body dementia from Alzheimer's include unpredictable levels of cognitive ability, attention, or alertness; changes in walking or movement; visual hallucinations; and a sleep disorder called REM sleep behavior disorder, in which people physically act out their dreams.

Multi-infarct dementia results from a series of small strokes or changes in the brain's blood supply that deprive the

> **QUICK STATS**
>
> Alzheimer's is the **sixth leading cause of death** in the United States and the only cause of death among the top 10 that cannot currently be prevented, cured, or even slowed.

TERMS

dementia Deterioration of mental functioning (including memory, concentration, and judgment) resulting from a brain disorder; often accompanied by emotional disturbances and personality changes.

Alzheimer's disease A disease characterized by a progressive loss of mental functioning (dementia), caused by a degeneration of brain cells.

brain of oxygen and destroy brain tissue. Symptoms may appear suddenly and worsen with additional strokes; they include disorientation in familiar locations; walking with rapid, shuffling steps; incontinence; laughing or crying inappropriately; difficulty following instructions; and problems handling money. High blood pressure, cigarette smoking, and high cholesterol are some of the risk factors for stroke that may be controlled to prevent vascular dementia. Even for these incurable forms of dementia, treatment can improve an affected person's quality of life.

There is evidence that some cases of dementia are hereditary, but experts say genetics are not always a sure sign that a person will develop the disease. You can also take lifestyle steps to help ward off dementia, such as controlling weight and blood pressure, eating a balanced diet (including adequate B vitamins and omega-3 fatty acids), exercising, not smoking, moderating your use of alcohol, practicing stress reduction techniques, maintaining social contacts, and cultivating a variety of mental pursuits, such as doing crossword puzzles. Strong evidence links the Mediterranean diet with reduced risk of these diseases.

Grief Another psychological and emotional challenge of aging is dealing with grief and mourning. Aging is associated with loss—the loss of friends, family and spouse, peers, physical appearance, possessions, and health. Grief is the process of getting through the pain of loss, and it can be one of the loneliest and most emotionally intense times in a person's life. It can take years to completely come to terms with the loss of a loved one. (See Chapter 23 for more information about responses to loss and how to support a grieving person.)

Unresolved grief can have serious physical and psychological or emotional health consequences and may require professional help. Signs of unresolved grief include hostility toward people connected with the death (physicians or nurses, for example), talking about the death as if it occurred yesterday, and unrealistic or harmful behavior (such as giving away all of one's own belongings). Many people become depressed after the loss of a loved one or when confronted with retirement or a chronic illness. But after a period of grieving, people are generally able to resume their lives.

Depression Unresolved grief can lead to depression, a common problem in older adults (see Chapter 3). If you notice

Suicide rates are relatively high among the elderly, and depression should be taken seriously.

the signs of depression in yourself or someone you know, consult a mental health professional. A marked loss of interest in usually pleasurable activities, decreased appetite, insomnia, fatigue, and feelings of worthlessness are signs of depression. Listen carefully when an older friend or relative complains about being depressed; it may be a request for help. Suicide rates are relatively high among the elderly, and depression should be taken seriously.

Suicide Elderly Americans are more than twice as likely to commit suicide as any other demographic group. White males over age 65 have particularly high rates of suicide. Among men over age 65, the rate of suicide among whites is more than double that of any other group. Women and minorities of all ages have much lower rates of suicide than older white men.

The act of completing suicide is rarely preceded by only one cause or one reason. Factors include the recent death of a loved one; physical illness, uncontrollable pain, or the fear of a prolonged illness; perceived poor health; social isolation and loneliness; and major changes in social roles (such as retirement). Depression is probably the single most significant factor associated with suicidal behavior in older adults.

AGING AND LIFE EXPECTANCY

Life expectancy is the average length of time we can expect to live. It is calculated by averaging mortality statistics—the ages at death of a group of people over a certain period. In 2009 life

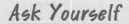

Ask Yourself

QUESTIONS FOR CRITICAL THINKING AND REFLECTION

If scientists discovered the gene that causes Alzheimer's disease or other debilitating forms of dementia, would you want to know whether you carried this gene?

life expectancy   The average length of time a person is expected to live.

TERMS

DIVERSITY MATTERS
Why Do Women Live Longer?

Women live longer than men in most countries around the world, even in places where maternal mortality rates are high. In the United States, women on average can expect to live about five years longer than men (see the table in this box). Worldwide, among people over age 100, women outnumber men about nine to one.

The reason for the gender gap in life expectancy is not entirely understood but may be influenced by biological, social, and lifestyle factors. Estrogen production and other factors during a woman's younger years may protect her from early heart disease and from age-related declines in the heart's pumping power. Women may have lower rates of stress-related illnesses because they cope more positively with stress.

The news for women is not all good, however, because not all their extra years are likely to be healthy years. They are more likely than men to suffer from chronic conditions like arthritis and osteoporosis. Women's longer life spans, combined with the facts that men tend to marry younger women and that widowed men remarry more often than widowed women, mean there are many more single older women than men. Older men are more likely to live in family settings, whereas older women are more likely to live alone. Older women are also less likely to be covered by a pension or to have

retirement savings, so they are more likely to be poor.

Increased male mortality can be traced in part to higher rates of behaviors such as smoking and alcohol and drug abuse. Testosterone production may be partly responsible in that it is linked to aggressive and risky behavior and to unhealthy cholesterol levels. Men have much higher rates of death than women from car crashes and other unintentional injuries, firearm-related deaths, homicide, suicide, AIDS, and early heart attack. Gender roles that promote risky behavior among young men are a factor in many of these

causes of death. Indeed, among people who have made it to age 65, the gender longevity gap is smaller.

Social and behavioral factors may be more important than physiological causes in explaining the gender gap; for example, among the Amish, a religious sect that has strict rules against smoking and drinking, men usually live as long as women. This suggests that the longevity gap could be substantially narrowed through lifestyle changes.

Life Expectancy

Year	Men	Women
At birth		
1900	46.3	48.3
1950	65.6	71.1
2000	74.1	79.3
2007	75.4	80.4
At age 65		
1900	11.5	12.2
1950	12.8	15.0
2000	16.0	19.0
2007	17.2	19.9

SOURCES: U.S. Census Bureau. 2005. *We the People: Women and Men in the United States.* Washington, DC: U.S. Census Bureau; National Center for Health Statistics. 2009. *Health, United States, 2009.* Hyattsville, MD: National Center for Health Statistics; World Health Organization. 2003. *Gender, Health, and Aging.* Geneva: World Health Organization.

ACTIVITY
DO IT ONLINE

expectancy for the total population was 78.5 years, but those who reach age 65 can expect to live even longer—18.5 more years or longer—because they have already survived hazards to life in the younger years. Women have a longer life expectancy than men do (see the box "Why Do Women Live Longer?"). Life expectancy also varies among ethnic groups; reasons for these differences include socioeconomic, genetic, and lifestyle factors.

Life expectancy in the United States increased dramatically in the 20th century, as described in Chapter 1. This does not mean that every American lives longer now than in 1900. Rather, far fewer people die young now because childhood and infectious diseases are better controlled and diet and sanitation are much improved. Only 30% of people born in 1900 would live to age 70; of those born in 2004, closer to 77% can expect to live that long.

How long can humans expect to live in the best of circumstances? It now seems possible that our maximum potential **life span** is 100–120 years. Our **health span,** by contrast, is the period of life when we are generally healthy and free from chronic or serious disease. The major difference between life span (how long we live) and health span (how long we stay

TERMS

life span   A theoretically projected length of life based on the maximum potential of the human body in the best environment.

health span   The period of life when one is generally healthy and free from chronic or serious disease.

healthy) is freedom from chronic or disabling disease. Failure to achieve our life span in good health results to some degree from destructive environmental and behavioral factors—factors over which we can exert considerable control. Longevity appears to be influenced little by genetics. Studies of identical twins and other research suggest that life span is only about 3% heritable, meaning that the age at which our parents die has only a 3% effect on our own age at death.

Long life does not necessarily mean a longer period of disability, either. People often live longer because they have been well longer. A healthy old age is very often an extension of a healthy middle age. However, behavior changes cannot extend the maximum human life span, which seems to be built into our genes.

No one really knows how and why people change as they get older. Different theories claim that aging is caused by accumulated injuries from ultraviolet light, wear and tear on the body, by-products of metabolism, and so on. Other theories view aging as a predetermined, genetically programmed process.

No theory, however, sufficiently explains all the changes of the aging process. Aging is complex and varies in how it affects different people and even different organs. Most gerontologists (scientists who study aging and its effects) feel that aging is the cumulative result of the interaction of many lifelong influences, including heredity, environment, culture, diet, exercise and leisure, past illnesses, and many other factors.

LIFE IN AN AGING AMERICA

As life expectancy increases, a larger proportion of Americans will be in their later years. This change will necessitate

> ### QUICK STATS
> The life expectancy of white Americans is **78.6** years; the life expectancy of black Americans is **74.3** years; and the life expectancy of Hispanic Americans is **80.9** years.
> —National Center for Health Statistics, 2010

> There are many theories about aging, but **none fully explains all the changes** of the aging process.

new government policies and changes in our general attitudes toward older adults.

America's Aging Minority

People over age 65 are a large minority in the American population—over 40.1 million people and about 13% of the total population in 2010. That number is expected to nearly double by the year 2030 (Figure 22.2). Many older people are happy, healthy, and self-sufficient. Changes that come with age, including negative ones, normally occur so gradually that most people adapt, some even gracefully.

The enormous increase in the over-65 population is markedly affecting our stereotypes of what it means to grow old. The misfortunes associated with aging—frailty, forgetfulness, poor health, isolation—occur in fewer people in their sixties and seventies and are shifting instead to burden the very old: those over age 85.

More than 80% of older Americans own their homes. Their living expenses are lower after retirement because they no longer support children and have fewer work-related expenses; they consume and buy less food. They are more likely to continue practicing their expertise for years after retirement: thousands of retired consultants, teachers, technicians, and craftspeople work until their middle and late seventies. They receive greater amounts of assistance, such as Medicare, pay proportionately lower taxes, and have greater net worth from lifetime savings.

Even so, according to the Administration on Aging (AOA), nearly 9% (3.4 million) of elderly people live below the poverty level; another 5.4% (2.1 million) are "near poor," with incomes reaching 125% of the poverty level. Older women are more likely to live in poverty than older men.

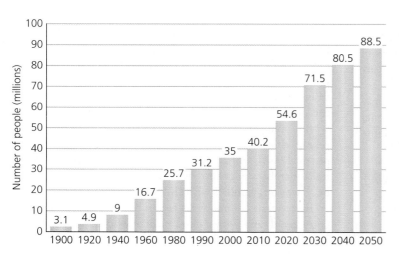

FIGURE 22.2 Increase in Americans over age 65, 1900–2050. Federal Interagency Forum on Aging-Related Statistics. 2010. *Older American 2010: Key Indicators of Well-Being.* Washington, DC: Federal Interagency Forum on Aging-Related Statistics.

People over 65 who live alone are much more likely to be poor than those who live with families.

As the aging population increases proportionately, however, the number of older people who are ill and dependent rises. Health care remains the largest expense for older adults. On average, they visit a physician 10–12 times a year, are hospitalized more frequently, and require twice as many prescription drugs as the general population. Most older Americans have at least one chronic condition; many have more than one.

Retirement finds many older people with their incomes reduced to subsistence levels. This is especially true of the very old and women. The majority of older Americans live with fixed sources of income, such as pensions, that are eroded by inflation. Expenses tend to increase more rapidly, especially those due to circumstances over which people have little or no control, such as deteriorating health. **Social Security** is the major source of income for most of the elderly. Social Security was intended to serve as a supplement to personal savings and private pensions, not as a sole source of income. It is vital to plan for an adequate retirement income.

Family and Community Resources for Older Adults

With help from friends, family members, and community services, people in their later years can remain active and independent. Over half of noninstitutionalized older Americans live with a spouse (Figure 22.3); some live with a family member other than a spouse, and 30% live alone. Only 4% live in institutional settings, but among those over age 85, about 15% live in a nursing home.

Family Involvement in Caregiving
Studies show that in about three out of four cases, a spouse, a grown daughter, or a daughter-in-law assumes a caregiving role for elderly relatives. With more parents living into their eighties and with fewer children per family, many people, especially women, will face the dilemma of how best to care for an aging relative. Surveys indicate that the average woman will spend about 17 years raising children and 18 years caring for an aging relative.

Caregiving can be rewarding, but it is also hard work. If the experience is stressful and long-term, family members may become emotionally exhausted. Corporations are increasingly responsive to the needs of their employees who are family caregivers by providing services such as referrals, flexible schedules and leaves, and on-site adult care. Professional health care advice is another critical part of successful home

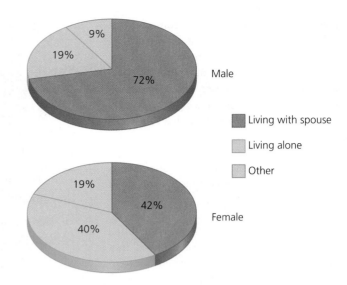

FIGURE 22.3 Living arrangements of Americans aged 65 and older, 2008.

SOURCE: Federal Interagency Forum on Aging-Related Statistics. 2010. *Older American 2010: Key Indicators of Well-Being.* Washington, DC: Federal Interagency Forum on Aging-Related Statistics.

care. Caregivers need to give special consideration to issues such as hearing and vision loss, which can make an elderly person feel disconnected or isolated, and dementia, which can make caregiving extremely challenging.

The caregiver must work with the older person's doctors and pharmacists to ensure that medication is available and taken as prescribed. (Studies show that older adults commonly skip their cholesterol and blood pressure medications, for example.) The caregiver may need to acquire a legal status called *medical power of attorney*, which enables him or her to make decisions about the patient's medical care.

The best thing a family can do is talk honestly about the obligations, time, and commitment required by caregiving. Families should also explore the community resources and professional assistance that may be available to reduce the stress in this difficult job.

Other Living and Care Options   If living together is not possible for aging parents and adult children, other living and care options are available. There are agencies that recruit and match like-minded individuals for shared living situations. Homesharing offers older adults who are in fairly good health the opportunity for new relationships, either with peers or with a younger family. Intergenerational homesharing may relieve elders of transportation problems and demanding physical tasks, which can be taken care of by younger household members. Conversely, elders in good health can help busy, working families with child care and household chores.

Retirement communities are an option for individuals in good health and with a good income who want to maintain home ownership. Other types of facilities are available for

QUICK STATS

The average American spends 20 years in retirement.

—U.S. Social Security Administration

Social Security   A government program that provides financial assistance to people who are unemployed, disabled, or retired (and over a certain age); financed through taxes on business and workers.

TERMS

Later in life, many older people need help with everyday activities like shopping, cooking, walking, or bathing. Help from family and friends may be all some people need to stay active and healthy in their own homes, while others may choose to move to a place that offers more services. A variety of options are available:

• *Retirement communities* allow maximum independence with very little supervision. They may offer transportation, activities, and other services but do not routinely offer assistance with basic needs.

• *Residential care homes* are licensed to provide services to three or more residents in a smaller environment, typically in a private home. They may provide assistance with medications, bathing, dressing, transportation, daily laundry, daily housekeeping, and meals.

• *Assisted living facilities* allow independence with supervision and are licensed by the state. They provide some meals, housekeeping and laundry, transportation, and activities.

• *Nursing homes* provide 24-hour medical care and rehabilitation for residents, who are mostly very frail or suffer from the later stages of dementia.

Some providers offer all levels of care at one site. These continuing care communities allow people to move from one level to another as their needs change.

Finding the right place to live takes some investigation. Because the best homes often have a waiting list, plan ahead. Don't wait until your family member is too sick to function. Once you have an initial list of facilities in your area, start visiting the homes, keeping the following evaluation points in mind:

• Ask questions about specific facilities. Doctors, friends, relatives, local hospital discharge planners, social workers, and religious organizations can help. The ombudsperson at your state's office of long-term care can let you know if there have been problems in a particular nursing home. Residential care homes and assisted living facilities do not follow the same licensing requirements as nursing homes. Talk to people in the community to find out about these options.

• Contact the places that interest you. Ask basic questions about vacancies, number of residents, cost, and any services of interest to you, such as transportation and meals.

• Visit several places. Talk to the staff, residents, and, if possible, family members of residents. Set up an appointment, but also go unannounced and at different times of the day. Make sure residents are clean, well groomed, involved in activities, and treated with respect.

• Evaluate the facility's financial agreements. Have a lawyer look them over before you sign. Nursing homes may accept Medicare or Medicaid, but most other facilities are private-pay only. Costs can range from $1500 per month to $5500 per month or more.

• Moving is a big change that affects the whole family. Talk about how you feel. Once a family member has moved to a new home, visit often and pay attention to the quality of care. Say something nice when care is good, and speak up when care is poor. If you have trouble resolving a complaint, your local ombudsperson or citizen advocacy groups may be able to help.

people who need more assistance with daily living (see the box "Choosing a Place to Live").

Community Resources Community resources are available to help older adults remain active and in their own homes. Typical services include the following:

• *Senior citizens' centers or adult day care centers* provide meals, social activities, and health care services for those unable to be alone during the day.

• *Homemaker services* offer housekeeping, cooking, errand running, and escort service.

• *Visiting nurses* provide basic health care.

• *Household services* perform household repairs.

• *Friendly visitor or daily telephone reassurance services* provide contacts for older people who live alone.

• *Home food delivery services* such as "Meals on Wheels" provide meals to homebound people.

- *Adult day hospital care* provides day care plus physical therapy and treatment for chronic illnesses.
- *Low-cost legal aid* helps manage finances and health care.
- *Transportation services* offer rides at low rates.
- *Case management* helps seniors navigate confusing health care services.

Transportation   Older drivers usually have safe driving records compared with young adults because they tend to be more cautious; however, crashes in the older age group are more likely to be fatal. Many states require special driver's testing for people over age 70 and may restrict some drivers as to the time, area, and distances they may drive. Because of changes in vision or other health problems, some older drivers may be required to give up their licenses before they feel ready. Elderly people report that the loss of a driver's license, and the loss of independence it brings, is one of the most severe hardships they face.

Government Aid and Policies

The federal government helps older Americans through several programs, such as food stamps, housing subsidies, Social Security, Medicare, and Medicaid. Social Security, the life insurance and old-age pension plan, has saved many from destitution, although it is intended not as a sole source of income but as a supplement to other income. Social Security funds have been used to cover other government financial deficits, so the future solvency of the program is uncertain.

Medicare is a major health insurance program for older adults and disabled persons. Medicare Part A is financed by part of the payroll (FICA) tax that also pays for Social Security. Medicare Part B is financed by monthly premiums paid by people who choose to enroll. Part A helps pay for inpatient hospital care, some inpatient care in a skilled nursing facility, and some types of home and hospice care. Medicare Part B helps pay for physicians' services and other services not covered by Part A. Medicare Part D is a prescription drug coverage plan.

Medicare pays about 28% of the medical costs of older Americans. It provides basic health care coverage for acute episodes of illness that require skilled professional care; it pays for some preventive services, including an initial physical exam, vaccinations, and screenings for CVD, certain cancers, osteoporosis, diabetes, and glaucoma. It does not pay for many office visits, dental care, and dentures. Over 1.6 million older people currently live in nursing homes, but Medicare pays less than 2% of nursing home costs, and private insurers pay less than 1%, creating a tremendous financial burden for nursing home residents and their families.

When their financial resources are exhausted, people may apply for Medicaid. A 1965 amendment to the Social Security Act, Medicaid provides medical insurance to low-income people of any age. Funded by state and federal contributions,

Some individuals defy all preconceived ideas about age and continue to live vigorous and productive lives into their seventies, eighties, and beyond.

QUICK STATS

In 2005 Social Security benefits accounted for **38%** of the aggregate income of the older population.

—AOA, 2008

the services vary from state to state but typically include hospital, nursing home, and home health care; physician services; and some medical supplies and services.

A crucial question regarding aid for the elderly is who will pay for it. The government picks up many of these health care expenses, primarily through Medicare and Medicaid. Total health care expenditures are 16–17% of the U.S. gross domestic product; about one-third of these expenditures go to care for older Americans.

Health care policy planners hope that rising medical costs for older adults will shrink dramatically through education and prevention. Health care professionals, including **gerontologists** and **geriatricians,** are

TERMS

gerontologist   One who studies the biological, psychological, and social phenomena associated with aging and old age.

geriatrician   A physician specializing in the diseases, disabilities, and care of older adults.

beginning to practice preventive medicine, just as pediatricians do. They advise older people about how to avoid and, if necessary, how to manage disabilities.

Changing the Public's Idea of Aging

Aging people may be one of our least used and least appreciated resources. How can we use the knowledge and productivity of our growing numbers of older citizens, particularly those now leaving the work force through mandatory early retirement?

To start, we must change our thinking about what aging means. We must learn to judge productivity rather than age. Capacity to function should replace age as a criterion for usefulness. Instead of singling out 65 as a magic number, we could consider ages 50–75 as the third quarter of life. Changes occur around 50 that signal a new era: Children are usually grown and gone, and a person has often achieved a level in career, earnings, and accomplishments that meets his or her ambitions. The upper end of this quarter is determined by the fact that most people today are vigorous, in good health, mentally alert, and capable of making a productive contribution until they are at least in their seventies.

However we define old age, the costs of losing what older adults can contribute to our national productivity and quality of life are too high. Through their early retirement, we forfeit substantial income tax and Social Security tax revenues on their earnings. Those who retire at 62 start using their Social Security benefits earlier than they otherwise would, and they receive lower monthly benefit amounts.

A far better arrangement would be to make available full-time and part-time volunteer and paid employment. We would benefit by providing retraining programs for both occupational and leisure activities. Volunteer opportunities, such as preparing recordings for the blind, helping with activities for the disabled, and performing necessary tasks in hospitals, could be expanded. At the same time, we could possibly change both public and private pension programs to make partial retirement possible. In such cases we could allow people to borrow against their Social Security benefits to finance retraining or enrollment in new educational programs.

There can be benefits to aging, but they don't come automatically. They require planning and wise choices earlier in life. One octogenarian, Russell Lee, founder of a medical clinic in California, perceived the advantages of aging as growth: "The limitations imposed by time are compensated by the improved taste, sharper discretion, sounder mental and esthetic judgment, increased sensitivity and compassion, clearer focus—which all contribute to a more certain direction in living. . . . The later years can be the best of life for which the earlier ones were preparation."

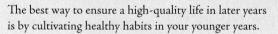

Connect to Your Choices

Have you ever thought about where you get your attitudes toward aging and older adults? Many factors can influence our attitudes, some not as obvious as others. Were your grandparents part of your life when you were growing up? Do your parents express negative feelings about growing older and aging? Are older adults present and visible in your community, or are you surrounded primarily by young adults? How susceptible are you to ageism, and how strongly are you influenced by the youth orientation of the media?

What are the external factors that influence your attitudes toward aging? What are your inner motivations and core values, and how do they affect your choices? Based on what you learned in this chapter, will you make some different choices in the future? If so, what will they be?

Go online to Connect to complete this activity: www.mcgraw-hillconnect.com

TIPS FOR TODAY AND THE FUTURE

The best way to ensure a high-quality life in later years is by cultivating healthy habits in your younger years.

RIGHT NOW YOU CAN:
- Review your financial situation, and start thinking about a plan for the future.
- Think about any unhealthy habits you have and resolve to change them. Review the information in this text to devise strategies for change.
- If you know any older people, speak to them about what aging has meant to them, and see what lessons you can learn from them.

IN THE FUTURE YOU CAN:
- Learn a new skill, such as a language or a game of strategy.
- Volunteer with a nonprofit group in your community; consider a literacy campaign, a soup kitchen, a youth mentoring program, or a group that helps the elderly in some manner.

Ask Yourself

QUESTIONS FOR CRITICAL THINKING AND REFLECTION

What do you want your life to be like when you are old? Do you hope to retire, or keep working indefinitely? Where would you like to live? How much time do you spend thinking about these questions? Have you done any planning yet for old age?

SUMMARY

- People who take charge of their health during their youth have greater control over the physical and mental aspects of aging.

- Biological aging takes place over a lifetime, but some of the other changes associated with aging are more abrupt.

- A lifetime of interests and hobbies helps maintain creativity and intelligence.

- Exercise and a healthful diet throughout life enhance physical and psychological health.

- Alcohol abuse is a common but often hidden problem, as is over-dependence on medications. Tobacco use not only shortens life but also may cause severe health impairment for many years.

- Regular physical examinations help detect conditions that can shorten life and make old age less healthy.

- Stress increases wear and tear on the body; getting enough sleep, avoiding drugs, and practicing relaxation help reduce stress.

- Retirement can be a fulfilling and enjoyable time of life for those who adjust to their new roles, enjoy participating in a variety of activities, and have planned ahead for financial stability.

- Successful aging involves anticipating and accommodating physical changes and limitations.

- Slight confusion and forgetfulness are not signs of a serious illness; however, severe symptoms may indicate Alzheimer's disease or another form of dementia.

- Resolving grief and mourning and dealing with depression are important tasks for older adults.

- Older adults can be role models for the successful integration of life's experiences and the ability to adapt to challenges.

- People over age 65 form a large minority in the United States, and their status is improving. But older adults who are ill and dependent—often those who were already poor—experience major social and economic problems.

- Family and community resources can help older adults stay active and independent.

- Government aid to the elderly includes food stamps, housing subsidies, Social Security, Medicare, and Medicaid.

FOR MORE INFORMATION

BOOKS

Beers, M. H. 2005. *Merck Manual of Health and Aging: The Complete Home Guide to Healthcare and Healthy Aging for Older People and Those Who Care about Them.* New York: Ballantine. *Provides information about fundamentals of aging and preventive care.*

Buettner, Dan. 2010. *Thrive: Finding Happiness the Blue Zones Way.* National Geographic. *Explores the world in search of those who live the longest and seeks to answer why.*

Hyams, J. 2011. *Time to Help Your Parents.* London: Piatkus. *A sympathetic overview of the many challenges facing adult children who must care for their aging parents.*

Johns Hopkins Medical Center. 2007. *The Johns Hopkins Medical Guide to Health after 50.* New York: Black Dog & Leventhal. *A practical guide to healthy aging for all wellness dimensions.*

National Institute on Aging. 2010. *Exercise & Physical Activity: Your Everyday Guide from the National Institute on Aging*, book and DVD ed. New York: Hatherleigh Press. *A practical guide to physical activity and exercise, with specific guidelines for safe exercise for older adults.*

Weil, A. 2007. *Healthy Aging: A Lifelong Guide to Your Physical and Spiritual Well-Being.* New York: Anchor. *One of America's best-known complementary care physicians discusses the aging process and explains methods for maintaining health during the latter years of life.*

ORGANIZATIONS AND WEBSITES

AARP. Provides information about all aspects of aging, including health promotion, health care, and retirement planning.

http://www.aarp.org

Aging Well. A practical resource for seniors that includes information about diet, exercise, safety, and medical care.

http://www.aging.ny.gov

Alliance for Aging Research. A nonprofit organization supporting medical and psychological research on aging.

http://www.agingresearch.org

Alzheimer's Association. Offers tips for caregivers and patients and information on the causes and treatment of Alzheimer's disease.

http://www.alz.org

Arthritis Foundation. Provides information about arthritis, including free brochures, referrals to local services, and research updates.

http://www.arthritis.org

LeadingAge. Provides information about living and care arrangements available for older adults.

http://www.leadingage.org/
http://www.arthritis.org

Medicare. Provides information about Medicare.

http://www.medicare.gov

National Council on Aging. Provides helpful information about retirement planning, health promotion, and lifelong learning.

http://www.ncoa.org

National Institute on Aging. Provides fact sheets and brochures about aging-related topics.

http://www.nia.nih.gov
http://nihseniorhealth.gov

National Osteoporosis Foundation. Provides information about the causes, prevention, detection, and treatment of osteoporosis.

http://www.nof.org

U.S. Administration on Aging. Provides fact sheets, statistical information, and Internet links to other resources on aging.

http://www.aoa.gov

SELECTED BIBLIOGRAPHY

Alzheimer's Association. 2012. *2012 Alzheimer's Disease Facts and Figures.* Chicago: Alzheimer's Association.

Americans over 50 at risk for bone fractures. 2005. *FDA Consumer,* January/ February.

Beyond menopause: life after estrogen. 2005. *Mayo Clinic Health Letter Supplement,* February.

Centers for Disease Control and Prevention. 2005. Racial/ethnic differences in the prevalence and impact of doctor-diagnosed arthritis—United States, 2002. *Morbidity and Mortality Weekly Report* 54(5): 119–123.

Centers for Disease Control and Prevention. 2006. Prevalence of doctor-diagnosed arthritis and arthritis-attributable activity limitation—United States, 2003–2005. *Morbidity and Mortality Weekly Report* 55(40): 1089–1092.

Cirillo, D., et al. 2005. Effect of estrogen therapy on gallbladder disease. *Journal of the American Medical Association* 293(3): 330–339.

Harvard Medical School. 2006. Minding your mind: 12 ways to keep your brain young with proper care and feeding. *Harvard Men's Health Watch* 10(10): 1–4.

Heyn, P. C., et al. 2008. Endurance and strength training outcomes on cognitively impaired and cognitively intact older adults: A meta-analysis. *Journal of Nutrition, Health & Aging* 12(6): 401–409.

Jager, R. D., et al. 2008. Age-related macular degeneration. *New England Journal of Medicine* 258(24): 2606–2617.

Kado, D. M., et al. 2005. Homocysteine versus the vitamins folate, B(6), and B(12) as predictors of cognitive function and decline in older high-functioning adults: MacArthur Studies of Successful Aging. *American Journal of Medicine* 118(2): 161–167.

Kirkwood, Thomas. Why women live longer: stress alone does not explain the longevity gap. *Scientific American* October 21, 2010: http://www.scientificamerican.com/article.cfm?id=why-women-live-longer.

Kolata, G. 2006. Live long? Die young? Answer isn't just in genes. *The New York Times*, 31 August.

Mudge, A. M., et al. 2008. Exercising body and mind: an integrated approach to functional independence in hospitalized older people. *Journal of the American Geriatrics Society* 56(4): 630–635.

Nelson, H. D., et al. 2006. Nonhormonal therapies for menopausal hot flashes: systematic review and meta-analysis. *Journal of the American Medical Association* 295(17): 2057–2071.

Rosengren, A., et al. 2005. Body mass index, other cardiovascular risk factors, and hospitalization for dementia. *Archives of Internal Medicine* 165(3): 321–326.

Scarmeas, N., et al. 2006. Mediterranean diet, Alzheimer disease, and vascular mediation. *Archives of Neurology* 63: December.

Sorrell, J. M. 2008. As good as it gets? Rethinking old age. *Journal of Psychosocial Nursing and Mental Health Services* 46(5): 21–24.

Stern, C., and Z. Munn. 2010. Cognitive leisure activities and their role in preventing dementia: a systematic review. *International Journal of Evidence-Based Healthcare* 8(1): 2–17.

Syed, F. A., and A. C. Ng. 2010. The pathophysiology of the aging skeleton. *Current Osteoporosis Reports* 8(4): 235–240.

Tufts University. 2006. Pendulum swings on estrogen and women's heart health risk. *Tufts University Health & Nutrition Letter* 24(3): 1–2.

Ward, E. M. 2006. A weekly to-do list to help delay or prevent dementia. *Environmental Nutrition* 29(5): 2.

Welland, D. 2006. Keeping an eye on your diet may help save your sight. *Environmental Nutrition* 29(5): 1, 6.

Whitmer, R. A., et al. 2005. Midlife cardiovascular risk factors and risk of dementia in late life. *Neurology* 64(2): 277–281.

Wilson, R. S., et al. 2005. Proneness to psychological distress and risk of Alzheimer disease in a biracial community. *Neurology* 64(2): 380–382.

Wolfe, M. S. 2006. Shutting down Alzheimer's. *Scientific American* 294(5): 72–79.

Yuhas, D. 2012. Cracks in the plaques: Mysteries of Alzheimer's slowly yielding to new research. *Scientific American*: February.

APPENDIXES

NUTRITIONAL CONTENT OF COMMON FOODS

If you are developing a behavior change plan to improve your diet, or if you simply want to choose healthier foods, you may want to know more about the nutritional content of common food items. An appendix with this information is available on the *Fit and Well* Online Learning Center at **www.mhhe.com/fahey.**

You can track your daily food intake, calculate your nutrient intake from foods, and compare your intake with the U.S. Department of Agriculture's recommendations for your age, sex, height, and weight at the MyPlate Web site (**www.choosemyplate.gov**).

You can also look up the nutrient content of the foods you eat in the USDA Agricultural Research Service National Nutrient Database, which lists foods both by description and by nutrient content (**www.ars.usda.gov/Services/docs.htm?docid=17477**). For example, under "protein," you can find out how much protein there is in a chicken pot pie or what foods have the most protein per serving. Although cumbersome, the database is comprehensive.

Nutritional Content of Popular Items from Fast-Food Restaurants

Although most foods served at fast-food restaurants are high in calories, fat, saturated fat, cholesterol, sodium, and sugar, some items are healthier than others. If you eat at fast-food restaurants, knowing the nutritional content of various items can help you make better choices. Fast-food restaurants provide nutritional information both online and in print brochures available at most restaurant locations. To learn more about the items you order, visit the restaurants' Web sites:

Arby's:	www.arbysrestaurant.com
Burger King:	http://www.bk.com/en/us/index.html
Domino's Pizza:	www.dominos.com
Hardees:	www.hardees.com
KFC:	www.kfc.com
McDonald's:	www.mcdonalds.com
Papa John's Pizza:	http://www.papajohns.com/index.html
Pizza Hut:	http://www.pizzahut.com
Subway:	http://www.subway.com/subwayroot/default.aspx
Taco Bell:	www.tacobell.com
Wendy's:	www.wendys.com
White Castle:	www.whitecastle.com

INJURY PREVENTION AND PERSONAL SAFETY

Unintentional injuries are the fifth leading cause of death among Americans overall and the leading killer of people under age 35. Injuries affect all segments of the population, but they are particularly common among minorities and people with low incomes, primarily due to social, environmental, and economic factors. The economic cost of injuries in the United States is high, with more than $650 billion spent each year for medical care and rehabilitation of injured people.

Injuries are generally classified into four categories, based on where they occur: motor vehicle injuries, home injuries, leisure injuries, and work injuries.

MOTOR VEHICLE INJURIES

According to the CDC, more than 36,000 Americans were killed and 2.3 million injured in motor vehicle crashes in 2009. Motor vehicle accidents are a leading cause of paralysis due to spinal injury and the leading cause of severe brain injury.

Factors in Motor Vehicle Injuries

Driving Habits Nearly 63% of motor vehicle injuries are caused by bad driving, especially speeding. As speed increases, momentum and force of impact increase and the time available for the driver to react decreases. Speed limits are posted to establish the safest *maximum* speed limit for a given area under *ideal* conditions. Aggressive driving—characterized by speeding, frequent and abrupt lane changes, tailgating, and passing on the shoulder—also increases the risk of crashes.

Distratcted driving contributes to 8000 crashes every day in the United States. Anything that distracts a driver—sleepiness, bad mood, children or pets in the car, use of a cell phone—can increase the risk of a crash. Sleepiness reduces reaction time, coordination, and speed of information processing and can be as dangerous as drug and alcohol use. Even mild sleep deprivation causes a deterioration in driving ability comparable to that caused by a 0.05% blood alcohol concentration.

Cell phone users respond to hazards about 20% slower than undistracted drivers and are about twice as likely to rear-end a braking car in front of them. According to 2011 statistics from the AAA Foundation for Traffic Safety, drivers who use cell phones are nearly four times as likely to be involved in a crash as drivers who don't. Hands-free devices do not help significantly; the mental distraction of talking is the factor in crashes rather than holding a phone. Newer research shows that text-messaging (texting) on a cell phone while driving is even more dangerous than talking. Several cities and states have outlawed the use of cell phones while driving; similar laws are being considered in many parts of the United States.

Safety Belts and Air Bags A person who doesn't wear a safety belt is twice as likely to be injured in a crash as a person who does wear one. Safety belts not only prevent occupants from being thrown from the car at the time of the crash but also provide protection from the "second collision," which occurs when the occupant of the car hits something inside the car, such as the steering column or windshield. The safety belt also spreads the stopping force of a collision over the body.

Since 1998, all new cars have been equipped with dual air bags—one for the driver and one for the front passenger seat. Air bags provide supplemental protection in a collision but are most useful in head-on collisions. (Many newer vehicles feature side air bags to offer protection in a side-impact crash.) They also deflate immediately after inflating and so do not provide protection in collisions involving multiple impacts. To ensure that air bags work as intended, follow these guidelines:

- Place infants in rear-facing infant seats in the back seat.
- Transport children age 12 and under in the back seat.
- Always use safety belts or appropriate safety seats.
- Keep at least 10 inches between the air bag cover and the breastbone of the driver or passenger.

If you cannot comply with these guidelines, you can apply to the National Highway Traffic Safety Administration for permission to install an on-off switch that temporarily disables the air bag.

Alcohol and Other Drugs Alcohol is involved in about 40% of all fatal crashes. Alcohol-impaired driving, defined by blood alcohol concentration (BAC), is illegal. The legal BAC limit is 0.08% in all states, but driving ability is impaired at much lower BACs. All psychoactive drugs have the potential to impair driving ability.

Preventing Motor Vehicle Injuries

About 75% of all motor vehicle collisions occur within 25 miles of home and at speeds lower than 40 mph. These crashes often occur because the driver believes safety measures are not necessary for short trips. Clearly, the statistics prove otherwise.

To prevent motor vehicle injuries:

- Obey the speed limit. If you have to speed to get to your destination on time, you're not allowing enough time.
- Always wear a safety belt and ask passengers to do the same. Strap infants and toddlers into government-approved

car seats in the back seat. Children who have outgrown child safety seats but who are still too small for adult safety belts alone (usually age 4–8) should be secured using booster seats. All children under 12 should ride in the back seat.

- Never drive under the influence of alcohol or other drugs or with a driver who is.
- Do not drive when you are sleepy or have been awake for 18 or more hours.
- Avoid using your cell phone while driving—your primary obligation is to pay attention to the road. If you do make calls, follow laws set by your city or state. Place calls when you are at a stop, and keep them short. Pull over if the conversation is stressful or emotional.
- Never text while driving.
- Keep your car in good working order. Regularly inspect tires, oil and fluid levels, windshield wipers, spare tire, and so on.
- Always allow enough following distance. Follow the "3-second rule": When the vehicle ahead passes a reference point, count out 3 seconds. If you pass the reference point before you finish counting, drop back and allow more following distance.
- Always increase following distance and slow down if weather or road conditions are poor.
- Choose major highways rather than rural roads. Highways are much safer because of better visibility, wider lanes, fewer surprises, and other factors.
- Always signal before turning or changing lanes.
- Stop completely at stop signs. Follow all traffic laws.
- Take special care at intersections. Always look left, right, and then left again. Make sure you have plenty of time to complete your maneuver in the intersection.
- Don't pass on two-lane roads unless you are in a designated passing area and have a clear view ahead.

Motorcycles and Scooters

About 1 out of every 10 traffic fatalities among people age 15–34 involves someone riding a motorcycle. Injuries from motorcycle collisions are generally more severe than those involving automobiles because motorcycles provide little, if any, protection. Scooter riders face additional challenges. Motorized scooters usually have a maximum speed of 30–35 mph and have less power for maneuverability.

To prevent motorcycle and scooter injuries:

- Make yourself easier to see by wearing light-colored clothing, driving with your headlights on, and correctly positioning yourself in traffic.
- Develop the necessary skills. Lack of skill, especially when evasive action is needed to avoid a collision, is a major factor in motorcycle and moped injuries. Skidding from improper braking is the most common cause of loss of control.
- Wear a close-fitting helmet, one marked with the symbol DOT (for Department of Transportation).

- Protect your eyes with goggles, a face shield, or a windshield.
- Drive defensively and never assume that other drivers see you.

Pedestrians and Bicycles

Injuries to pedestrians and bicyclists are considered motor vehicle–related because they usually involve motor vehicles. About 1 in 8 motor vehicle deaths each year involves a pedestrian; more than 70,000 pedestrians are injured each year.

To prevent injuries when walking or jogging:

- Walk or jog in daylight.
- Make yourself easier to see by wearing light-colored, reflective clothing.
- Face traffic when walking or jogging along a roadway, and follow traffic laws.
- Avoid busy roads or roads with poor visibility.
- Cross only at marked crosswalks and intersections.
- Don't use headphones while walking or jogging.
- Don't hitchhike. Hitchhiking places you in a potentially dangerous situation.

Bicycle injuries result primarily from not knowing or understanding the rules of the road, failing to follow traffic laws, and not having sufficient skill or experience to handle traffic conditions. Bicycles are considered vehicles; bicycle riders must obey all traffic laws that apply to automobile drivers, including stopping at traffic lights and stop signs.

To prevent injuries when riding a bike:

- Wear safety equipment, including a helmet, eye protection, gloves, and proper footwear. Secure the bottom of your pant legs with clips and secure your shoelaces so they don't get tangled in the chain.
- Make yourself easier to see by wearing light-colored, reflective clothing. Equip your bike with reflectors and use lights, especially at night or when riding in wooded or other dark areas.
- Ride with the flow of traffic, not against it, and follow traffic laws. Use bike paths when they are available.
- Ride defensively; never assume that drivers can see you. Be especially careful when turning or crossing at corners and intersections. Watch for cars turning right.
- Stop at all traffic lights and stop signs. Know and use hand signals.
- Continue pedaling at all times when moving (don't coast) to help keep the bike stable and to maintain your balance.
- Properly maintain your bike.

Aggressive Driving

Aggressive driving, known as *road rage,* has increased more than 50% since 1990. Aggressive drivers increase the risk of crashes for themselves and others. They further increase the risk of injuries if they stop their vehicles and confront each other. Even if you are successful at controlling your own aggressive driving impulses, you may still encounter an aggressive driver.

To avoid being the victim of an aggressive driver:

- Always keep distance between your car and others. If you are behind a very slow driver and can't pass, slow down to increase distance in case that driver does something unexpected. If you are being tailgated, do not increase your speed; instead, let the other driver pass you. If you are in the left lane when being tailgated, signal and pull over to let the other driver go by, even if you are traveling at the speed limit. When you are merging, make sure you have plenty of room. If you are cut off by a merging driver, slow down to make room.
- Be courteous, even if the other driver is not. Use your horn rarely, if ever. Avoid making gestures of irritation, even shaking your head. When parking, let the other driver have the space that both of you found.
- Refuse to join in a fight. Avoid eye contact with an angry driver. If someone makes a rude gesture, ignore it. If you think another car is following you and you have a cell phone, call the police. Otherwise, drive to a public place and honk your horn to get someone's attention.
- If you make a mistake while driving, apologize. Raise or wave your hand or touch or knock your head with the palm of your hand to indicate "What was I thinking?" You can also mouth the words "I'm sorry."

HOME INJURIES

Contrary to popular belief, home is one of the most dangerous places to be. The most common fatal home injuries are caused by falls, poisoning, fires, suffocation and choking, and incidents involving firearms.

Falls

About 90% of fatal falls involve people age 45 and older, but falls are a significant cause of unintentional death for people under age 25. Most deaths occurring from falls involve falling on stairs or steps or from one level to another. Falls also occur on the same level, from tripping, slipping, or stumbling. Alcohol is a contributing factor in many falls.

To prevent injuries from falls:

- Install handrails and nonslip surfaces in the shower and bathtub. Place skidproof backing on rugs and carpets.
- Keep floors, stairs, and outside areas clear of objects or conditions that could cause slipping or tripping, such as heavy wax coating, electrical cords, and toys.
- Put a light switch by the door of every room so no one has to walk across a room to turn on a light. Use night lights in bedrooms, halls, stairways, and bathrooms.
- Outside the house, clear dangerous surfaces created by ice, snow, fallen leaves, or rough ground.
- Install handrails on stairs. Keep stairs well lit and clear of objects.
- When climbing a ladder, use both hands. Never stand higher than the third step from the top. When using a stepladder, make sure the spreader brace is in the locked

position. With straight ladders, set the base out 1 foot for every 4 feet of height. Don't stand on chairs to reach things.
- If there are small children in the home, place gates at the top and bottom of stairs. Never leave a baby unattended.

Poisoning

More than 2.4 million poisonings and over 30,000 poison-related deaths occur every year in the United States.

To prevent poisoning:

- Store all medicines out of the reach of children. Use medicines only as directed on the label or by a physician.
- Use cleaners, pesticides, and other dangerous substances only in areas with proper ventilation. Store them out of the reach of children.
- Never operate a vehicle in an enclosed space. Have your furnace inspected yearly. Use caution with any substance that produces potentially toxic fumes, such as kerosene. If appropriate, install carbon monoxide detectors.
- Keep poisonous plants out of the reach of children. These include azalea, oleander, rhododendron, wild mushrooms, daffodil and hyacinth bulbs, mistletoe berries, apple seeds, morning glory seeds, wisteria seeds, and the leaves and stems of potato, rhubarb, and tomato plants.

To be prepared in case of poisoning:

- Keep the number of the nearest Poison Control Center (or emergency room) in an accessible location. A call to the national poison control hotline (800-222-1222) will be routed to a local center.

Emergency first aid for poisonings:

1. Remove the poison from contact with eyes, skin, or mouth, or remove the victim from contact with poisonous fumes or gases.
2. Call the Poison Control Center immediately for instructions. Have the container with you.
3. Do not follow emergency instructions on labels. Some may be out-of-date and carry incorrect treatment information.
4. If you are instructed to go to an emergency room, take the poisonous substance or its container with you.

Guidelines for specific types of poisons:

- *Swallowed poisons.* Call the Poison Control Center or a physician for advice. Do not induce vomiting.
- *Poisons on the skin.* Remove any affected clothing. Flood affected parts of the skin with warm water, wash with soap and water, and rinse. Then call for advice.
- *Poisons in the eye.* For children, flood the eye with lukewarm water poured from a pitcher held 3–4 inches above the eye for 15 minutes; alternatively, irrigate the eye under a faucet. For adults, get in the shower and flood the eye with a gentle stream of lukewarm water for 15 minutes. Then call for advice.
- *Inhaled poisons.* Immediately carry or drag the person to fresh air and, if necessary, give rescue breaths (Figure A.1). If the victim is not breathing easily, call 9-1-1 for help. Ventilate the area. Then call the Poison Control Center for advice.

EMERGENCY CARE FOR CHOKING

- If the victim is coughing, encourage the coughing to clear the object from the airway.
- If the victim is not coughing, follow the steps in "Choking Care for Responsive Adult or Child."

Choking Care for Responsive Adult or Child

Stand behind an adult victim with one leg forward between the victim's legs. (With a child, kneel behind the victim.) Keep your head slightly to one side. Reach around the abdomen with both arms. Make a fist with one hand and place the thumb side of the fist against the abdomen just above the navel.

Grasp your fist with your other hand and thrust inward and upward into the victim's abdomen with quick jerks. Continue abdominal thrusts until the victim expels the object or becomes unresponsive. If the victim becomes unresponsive while you are administering abdominal thrusts, lower the victim to the floor onto his or her back, and follow the steps in "Choking Care for Unresponsive Adult or Child."

Choking Care for Unresponsive Adult or Child: CPR

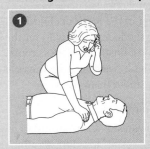 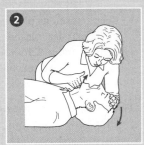 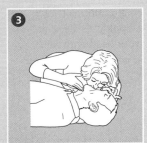 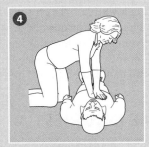

Call 911 and begin CPR.

Open the airway to see if the victim is breathing. Use the "head tilt–chin lift" maneuver to open the airway: Push down on the forehead and lift the chin.

If the victim is not breathing, give two rescue breaths, each lasting 1 second. Pinch the victim's nose shut and blow a normal breath into the victim's mouth. If the first breath does not go in (the chest does not rise), reposition the head to open the airway and try again. Each time you give a rescue breath, look for an object in the victim's mouth and remove it if present.

If the obstruction remains, begin chest compressions. Place the heel of one hand in the center of the chest between the nipples and the other hand on top of the first. Position your shoulders over your hands and lock your elbows. Give 30 chest compressions at a rate of 100 per minute. The chest should go down by 1½ to 2 inches. Then give two breaths, looking in the mouth for an expelled object. Continue chest compressions until help arrives. **Remember: Push hard and push fast at a rate of 100 compressions per minute.**

EMERGENCY CARE FOR CARDIAC ARREST

For cardiac arrest, the American Heart Association's revised (2005) Emergency Cardiac Care guidelines are as follows:

1 Call 911.

2 Start CPR (100 compressions per minute, stopping every 30 to 60 seconds to give two rescue breaths).

3 If an automated external defibrillator (AED) is available, or when one arrives, give one shock to restart the victim's heart.

4 Go back to CPR immediately after the shock.

Hands-Only CPR

In 2008, the American Heart Association reported that hands-only (compression-only) CPR can be as effective as conventional CPR. There are only two steps:

 Call 911.

 Push hard and fast in the center of the chest.

Don't wait for an emergency to learn how to use an AED or perform CPR.
To find a course in your area, contact the American Heart Association (800 242-8721) or the American Red Cross (202 303-4498).

FIGURE A.1 Emergency care for choking and for cardiac arrest.

SOURCES: Adapted from American Heart Association. 2008. Hands-only (compression-only) cardiopulmonary resuscitation: A call to action for bystander response to adults who experience out-of-hospital sudden cardiac arrest. *Circulation* 117: 2162–2167; National Safety Council. 2007. *First Aid: Taking Action.* New York: McGraw-Hill; American Heart Association. 2005. Adult basic life support. *Circulation* 112: 19–34; New CPR guidelines: Simplicity to the rescue. 2006. *Harvard Health Letter*, March, Streamlined CPR guidelines a life-saving move. 2006. *Harvard Heart Letter*, February.

Fires

Each year, about 80% of fire deaths and 65% of fire injuries occur in the home. Careless smoking is the leading cause of home fire deaths. Cooking is the leading cause of home fire injuries.

To prevent fires:

- Dispose of all cigarettes in ashtrays. Never smoke in bed.
- Do not overload electrical outlets. Do not place extension cords under rugs or where people walk. Replace worn or frayed extension cords.
- Place a wire screen in front of fireplaces and woodstoves. Remove ashes carefully and store them in airtight metal containers, not paper bags.
- Properly maintain electrical appliances, kerosene heaters, and furnaces. Clean flues and chimneys annually.
- Keep portable heaters at least 3 feet away from curtains, bedding, towels, or anything that might catch fire. Never leave operating heaters unattended.

To be prepared for a fire:

- Plan at least two escape routes out of each room. Designate a location outside the home as a meeting place. Stage a home fire drill.
- Install a smoke detection device on every level of your home. Clean the detectors and test batteries once a month, and replace the batteries at least once a year.
- Keep a fire extinguisher in your home and know how to use it.

To prevent injuries from fire:

- Get out as quickly as possible and go to the designated meeting place. Don't stop for a keepsake or a pet. Never hide in a closet or under a bed. Once outside, count heads to see if everyone is out. If you think someone is still inside the burning building, tell the firefighters. Never go back inside a burning building.
- If you're trapped in a room, feel the door. If it is hot or if smoke is coming in through the cracks, don't open it; use the alternative escape route. If you can't get out of a room, go to the window and shout or wave for help.
- Avoid inhaling smoke. Smoke inhalation is the largest cause of death and injury in fires. To avoid inhaling smoke, crawl along the floor away from the heat and smoke. Cover your mouth and nose, ideally with a wet cloth, and take short, shallow breaths.
- If your clothes catch fire, don't run. Drop to the ground, cover your face, and roll back and forth to smother the flames. Remember: Stop-drop-roll.

Suffocation and Choking

Suffocation and choking account for about 5000 deaths annually in the United States. Children can suffocate if they put small items in their mouths, get tangled in their crib bedding, or get trapped in airtight appliances like old refrigerators. Keep small objects out of reach of children under age 3, and don't give them raw carrots, hot dogs, popcorn, peanuts, or hard candy. Examine toys carefully for small parts that could come loose; don't give plastic bags or balloons to small children.

Adults can also become choking victims, especially if they fail to chew food properly, eat hurriedly, or try to talk and eat at the same time. Many choking victims can be saved with abdominal thrusts, also called the Heimlich maneuver (see Figure A.1). Infants who are choking can be saved with blows to the upper back, followed by chest thrusts if necessary.

Incidents Involving Firearms

Firearms pose a significant threat of unintentional injury, especially to people between ages 5 and 29.

To prevent firearm injuries:

- Always treat a gun as though it were loaded, even if you know it isn't.
- Never point a gun—loaded or unloaded—at something you do not intend to shoot.
- Always unload a firearm before storing it. Store unloaded firearms under lock and key, away from ammunition.
- Inspect firearms carefully before handling them.
- If you own a gun, buy and use a gun lock designed specifically for that weapon.
- If you ever plan to handle a gun, take a firearms safety course first.

LEISURE INJURIES

Leisure injuries take place in public places but do not involve motor vehicles. Many injuries in this category involve such recreational activities as boating and swimming, playground activities, in-line skating, and sports.

Drowning and Boating Injuries

Although most drownings are reported in lakes, ponds, rivers, and oceans, more than half the drownings of young children take place in residential pools. Among adolescents and adults, alcohol plays a significant role in many boating injuries and drownings.

To prevent drowning and boating injuries:

- Develop adequate swimming skill and make sure children learn to swim.
- Make sure residential pools are fenced and that children are never allowed to swim without supervision.
- Don't swim alone or in unsupervised places.
- Use caution when swimming in unfamiliar surroundings or for an unusual length of time. To avoid being chilled, don't swim in water colder than 70°F.
- Don't swim or boat under the influence of alcohol or other drugs. Don't chew gum or eat while in the water.
- Check the depth of water before diving.
- When on a boat, use a life jacket (personal flotation device).

In-Line Skating and Scooter Injuries

Most in-line skating injuries occur because users are not familiar with the equipment and do not wear appropriate safety gear. Injuries to the wrist and head are the most common. To prevent injuries while skating, wear a helmet, elbow and knee pads, wrist guards, a long-sleeved shirt, and long pants.

Wearing a helmet and knee and elbow pads is also important for preventing scooter injuries. The rise in popularity of lightweight scooters has seen a corresponding increase in associated injuries. Scooters should not be viewed as toys, and young children should be closely supervised. Be sure that handlebars, steering column, and all nuts and bolts are securely fastened. Ride on smooth, paved surfaces away from motor vehicle traffic. Avoid streets and surfaces with water, sand, gravel, or dirt.

Sports Injuries

Since more people have begun exercising to improve their health, there has been an increase in sports-related injuries.

To prevent sports injuries:

- Develop the skills required for the activity. Recognize and guard against the hazards associated with it.
- Always warm up and cool down.
- Make sure facilities are safe.
- Follow the rules and practice good sportsmanship.
- Use proper safety equipment, including, where appropriate, helmets, eye protection, knee and elbow pads, and wrist guards. Wear correct footwear.
- When it is excessively hot and humid, avoid heat stress by following the guidelines given in Chapter 3.

WORK INJURIES

Many aspects of workplace safety are monitored by the Occupational Safety and Health Administration (OSHA), a federal agency. The highest rate of work-related injuries occurs among laborers, whose jobs usually involve extensive manual labor and lifting—two areas not addressed by OSHA safety standards. Back injuries are the most common work injury.

To protect your back when lifting:

- Don't try to lift beyond your strength. If you need it, get help.
- Get a firm footing, with your feet shoulder-width apart. Get a firm grip on the object.
- Keep your torso in a relatively upright position and crouch down, bending at the knees and hips. Avoid bending at the waist. To lift, stand up or push up with your leg muscles. Lift gradually, keeping your arms straight. Keep the object close to your body.
- Don't twist. If you have to turn with an object, change the position of your feet.
- Put the object down gently, reversing the rules for lifting.

Another type of work-related injury is damage to the musculoskeletal system from repeated strain on the hand, arm, wrist, or other part of the body. Such repetitive-strain injuries are proliferating due to increased use of computers. One type, carpal tunnel syndrome, is characterized by pain and swelling in the tendons of the wrists and sometimes numbness and weakness.

To prevent carpal tunnel syndrome:

- Maintain good posture at the computer. Use a chair that provides back support and place the feet flat on the floor or on a footrest.
- Position the screen at eye level and the keyboard so the hands and wrists are straight.
- Take breaks periodically to stretch and flex your wrists and hands to lessen the cumulative effects of stress.

VIOLENCE AND INTENTIONAL INJURIES

According to the Federal Bureau of Investigation (FBI), nearly 1.3 million violent crimes occurred in the United States in 2009. Violence includes assault, sexual assault, homicide, domestic violence, suicide, and child abuse. Compared with rates of violence in other industrialized countries, U.S. rates are unusually high in two areas: homicide and firearm-related deaths.

Assault

Assault is the use of physical force to inflict injury or death on another person. Most assaults occur during arguments or in connection with another crime, such as robbery. Poverty, urban settings, and the use of alcohol and drugs are associated with higher rates of assault. The FBI estimates that about 807,000 aggravated assaults occurred in 2009, and 15,200 Americans were murdered that year. Homicide victims are most likely to be male, between ages 19 and 24, and members of minority groups. Most homicides are committed with a firearm; the murderer and the victim usually know each other.

To protect yourself at home:

- Secure your home with good lighting and effective locks, preferably deadbolts. Make sure that all doors and windows are securely locked.
- Get a dog, or post "Beware of Dog" signs.
- Don't hide keys in obvious places, and don't give anyone the chance to duplicate your keys.
- Install a peephole in your front door. Don't open your door to people you don't know.
- If you or a family member owns a weapon, store it securely. Store guns and ammunition separately.
- If you are a woman living alone, use your initials rather than your full name in the phone directory. Don't use a greeting on your answering machine that implies you live alone or are not home.
- Teach everyone in the household how to get emergency assistance.
- Know your neighbors. Work out a system for alerting each other in case of an emergency.
- Establish a neighborhood watch program.

To protect yourself on the street:

- Avoid walking alone, especially at night. Stay where people can see and hear you.

- Walk on the outside of the sidewalk, facing traffic. Walk purposefully. Act alert and confident. If possible, keep at least two arm lengths between yourself and a stranger.
- Know where you are going. Appearing to be lost increases your vulnerability.
- Carry valuables in a fanny pack, pants pocket, or shoulder bag strapped diagonally across the chest.
- Always have your keys ready as you approach your vehicle or home.
- Carry a whistle to blow if you are attacked or harassed. If you feel threatened, run and/or yell. Go into a store or knock on the door of a home. If someone grabs you, yell for help.

To protect yourself in your car:

- Keep your car in good working condition, carry emergency supplies, and keep the gas tank at least half full.
- When driving, keep doors locked and windows rolled up at least three-quarters of the way.
- Park your car in well-lighted areas or parking garages, preferably those with an attendant or a security guard.
- Lock your car when you leave it, and check the interior before opening the door when you return.
- Don't pick up strangers. Don't stop for vehicles in distress; drive on and call for help.
- Note the location of emergency call boxes along highways and in public facilities. Carry a cell phone.
- If your car breaks down, raise the hood and tie a white cloth to the antenna or door handle. Wait in the car with the doors locked and windows rolled up. If someone approaches to offer help, open a window only a crack and ask the person to call the police or a towing service.
- When you stop at a light or stop sign, leave enough room to maneuver if you need an escape route.
- If you are involved in a minor automobile crash and you think you have been bumped intentionally, don't leave your car. Motion to the other driver to follow you to the nearest police station.
- If confronted by a person with a weapon, give up your car.

To protect yourself on public transportation:

- While waiting, stand in a populated, well-lighted area.
- Make sure that the bus, subway, or train is bound for your destination before you board it. Sit near the driver or conductor in a single seat or an outside seat.
- If you flag down a taxi, make sure it's from a legitimate service. When you reach your destination, ask the driver to wait until you are safely inside the building.

To protect yourself on campus:

- Make sure that door and window locks are secure and that halls and stairwells have adequate lighting.
- Don't give dorm or residence keys to anybody.
- Don't leave your door unlocked or allow strangers into your room.
- Avoid solitary late-night trips to the library or laundry room. Take advantage of on-campus escort services.
- Don't exercise outside alone at night. Don't take shortcuts across campus that are unfamiliar or seem unsafe.

- If security guards patrol the campus, know the areas they cover and stay where they can see or hear you.

Sexual Assault—Rape and Date Rape

The use of force and coercion in sexual relationships is one of the most serious problems in human interactions. The most extreme manifestation of sexual coercion—forcing a person to submit to another's sexual desires—is rape. Taking advantage of circumstances that render a person incapable of giving consent (such as when drunk) is also considered sexual assault or rape. Coerced sexual activity in which the victim knows or is dating the rapist is often referred to as date rape.

An estimated 700,000 females are raped annually in the United States, and some males—perhaps 10,000 annually—are raped each year by other males. However, only a fraction of rapes are actually reported to authorities. For example, the FBI states that only 88,000 forcible rapes were reported to authorities in 2009. Rape victims suffer both physical and psychological injury. The psychological pain can be substantial and long-lasting.

To protect yourself against rape:

- Follow the guidelines listed earlier for protecting yourself against assault.
- Trust your gut feeling. If you feel you are in danger, don't hesitate to run and scream.
- Think out in advance what you would do if you were threatened with rape. However, no one knows what he or she will do when scared to death. Trust that you will make the best decision at the time—whether to scream, run, fight, or give in to avoid being injured or killed.

To protect yourself against date rape:

- Believe in your right to control what you do. Set limits and communicate them clearly, firmly, and early. Be assertive; men often interpret passivity as permission.
- If you are unsure of a new acquaintance, go on a group date or double date. If possible, provide your own transportation.
- Remember that some men think flirtatious behavior or sexy clothing indicates an interest in having sex.
- Remember that alcohol and drugs interfere with judgment, perception, and communication about sex. In a bar or at a party, don't leave your drink unattended, and don't accept opened beverages; watch your drinks being poured. At a party or club, check on friends and ask them to check on you.
- Use the statement that has proved most effective in stopping date rape: "This is rape and I'm calling the cops!"

If you are raped:

- Tell what happened to the first friendly person you meet.
- Call the police. Tell them you were raped and give your location.
- Try to remember everything you can about your attacker and write it down.
- Don't wash or douche before the medical exam. Don't change your clothes, but bring a new set with you if you can.
- Be aware that at the hospital you will have a complete exam. Show the physician any bruises or scratches.

- Tell the police exactly what happened. Be honest and stick to your story.
- If you do not want to report the rape to the police, see a physician as soon as possible. Be sure you are checked for pregnancy and STDs.
- Contact an organization with skilled counselors so you can talk about the experience. Look in the telephone directory under "Rape" or "Rape Crisis Center" for a hotline number.

Guidelines for men:

- Be aware of social pressure. It's OK not to score.
- Understand that "No" means "No." Stop making advances when your date says to stop. Remember that she has the right to refuse sex.
- Don't assume that flirtatious behavior or sexy clothing means a woman is interested in having sex, that previous permission for sex applies to the current situation, or that your date's relationships with other men constitute sexual permission for you.
- Remember that alcohol and drugs interfere with judgment, perception, and communication about sex.

Stalking and Cyberstalking

Stalking is characterized by harassing behaviors such as following or spying on a person and making verbal, written, or implied threats. It is estimated that 1 million U.S. women and 400,000 men are stalked each year; nearly 90% of stalkers are men. Cyberstalking, the use of electronic communications devices to stalk another person, is becoming more common. Cyberstalkers may send harassing or threatening e-mails or chat room messages to the victim, or they may encourage others to harass the victim by posting inflammatory messages and personal information on bulletin boards or chat rooms.

To protect yourself online:

- Never use your real name as an e-mail user name or chat room nickname. Select an age- and gender-neutral identity.
- Avoid filling out profiles for accounts related to e-mail use or chat room activities with information that could be used to identify you.
- Do not share personal information in public spaces anywhere online or give it to strangers.
- Learn how to filter unwanted e-mail messages.
- If you experience harassment online, do not respond to the harasser. Log off or surf elsewhere. Save all communications for evidence. If harassment continues, report it to the harasser's Internet service provider, your Internet service provider, and the local police.
- Don't agree to meet someone you've met online face-to-face unless you feel completely comfortable about it. Schedule a series of phone conversations first. Meet initially in a very public place and bring along a friend to increase your safety.

Coping After Terrorism, Mass Violence, or Natural Disasters

Certain areas of the United States are prone to natural disasters like Hurricane Irene, which wreaked havoc along the East Coast in 2011. Other natural disasters include tornadoes, floods, and earthquakes. Less frequent in the United States are episodes of mass violence or terrorist events such as those that occurred in Oklahoma in April 1995 and on September 11, 2001. When such events occur, some people suffer direct physical harm and/or the loss of relatives, friends, or possessions; many others experience emotional distress and are robbed of their sense of security.

Each person reacts differently to traumatic disaster, and it is normal to experience a variety of responses. Reactions may include disbelief and shock, fear, anger and resentment, anxiety about the future, difficulty concentrating or making decisions, mood swings, irritability, sadness and depression, panic, guilt, apathy, feelings of isolation or powerlessness, and many of the behaviorial signs such as headaches or insomnia that are associated with excess stress (see Chapter 10). Reactions may occur immediately or may be delayed until weeks or months after the event.

Taking positive steps can help you cope with powerful emotions. Consider the following strategies:

- Share your experiences and emotions with friends and family members. Be a supportive listener. Reassure children and encourage them to talk about what they are feeling.
- Take care of your mind and body. Choose a healthy diet, exercise regularly, get plenty of sleep, and practice relaxation techniques. Don't turn to unhealthy coping techniques such as using alcohol or other drugs.
- Take a break from media reports and images, and try not to develop nightmare scenarios for possible future events.
- Reestablish your routines at home, school, and work.
- Find ways to help others. Donating money, blood, food, clothes, or time can ease difficult emotions and give you a greater sense of control.

Everyone copes with tragedy in a different way and recovers at a different pace. If you feel overwhelmed by your emotions, seek professional help. Additional information about coping with terrorism and violence is available from the Federal Emergency Management Agency (www.fema.gov), the U.S. Department of Justice (www. usdoj.gov), and the National Mental Health Association (www.nmha.org).

Emergency Preparedness

Most prevention and coping activities related to terrorism, mass violence, and natural disasters occur at the federal, state, and community levels. However, one step you can take is to put together an emergency plan and kit for your family or household that can serve for any type of emergency or disaster.

Emergency Supplies   Your kit of emergency supplies should include everything you'll need to make it on your own for at least 3 days. You'll need nonperishable food, water, first-aid and sanitation supplies, a battery-powered radio, clothing, a flashlight, cash, keys, copies of important documents, and supplies for sleeping outdoors in any weather. Remember special-needs items for infants, seniors, and pets. Supplies for a basic emergency kit are listed in Figure A.2; add to your kit based on your family situation and the type of problems most likely to occur in your area.

Basic emergency supplies

Map of the area for locating evacuation routes or shelters	Signal flares	Shutoff wrench for gas and water supplies
Cash, coins, and credit cards	Fire extinguisher (small A-B-C type)	Shovel, hammer, pliers, screwdriver, and other tools
Copies of important documents stored in watertight container	Whistle	Compass
	Ladder	
Emergency contact list and phone numbers	Tube tent and rope	Matches in a waterproof container
Extra sets of house and car keys	Sleeping bags or warm blankets	Aluminum foil
Flashlights or lightsticks	Foam pads, pillows, baby bed	Plastic storage containers, bucket
Battery- or solar-powered radio	Complete change of warm clothing, footwear, outerware (jacket or coat, long pants, long-sleeved shirt, sturdy shoes, hat, gloves, raingear, extra socks and underwear, sunglasses)	Duct tape, utility knife, and scissors
Battery-powered alarm clock		Paper, pens, pencils
Extra batteries and bulbs		Needles and thread
Cell phone or prepaid phone card	Work gloves	

First aid kit

First aid manual	Insect repellent	Anti-diarrhea medication
Thermometer	Antibiotic ointment	Laxative
Scissors	Burn ointment	Antacid
Tweezers	Petroleum jelly or another lubricant	Activated charcoal (use if advised by Poison Control Center)
Safety pins, safety razor blades	Sterile adhesive bandages, several sizes	
Needle	Sterile rolled bandages and triangular bandages	Potassium iodide (use following radiation exposure if advised by local health authorities)
Latex or other sterile gloves	Cotton balls	
Sterile gauze pads	Eyewash solution	Prescription medications and prescribed medical supplies
Cleansing agents (soap, isopropyl alcohol, antiseptic towelettes)	Chemical heat and cold packs	
	Aspirin or nonaspirin pain reliever	List of medications, dosages, and any allergies
Sunscreen		Medicine dropper

Special needs items

Infant care needs (formula, bottles, diapers, powdered milk, diaper rash ointment)	Feminine hygiene supplies	Pet care supplies, including leash, pet carrier, copy of vaccination history, and tie-out stakes
	Denture needs	
Books or toys	Hearing aid or wheelchair batteries; other special equipment	Other (list)
Extra eyeglasses, contact lenses and supplies		

Food and related supplies

Manual (nonelectric) can opener	Eating utensils: Mess kits, or paper cups and plates and utensils	Small cooking stove and cooking fuel (if food must be cooked)
Utility knife		
Paper towels	Plastic garbage bags and resealing bags	Water purification tablets

Water: Three-day-supply, at least 1 gallon of water per person per day, stored in plastic containers:

Number of people: _____ x _1 gallon_ x _3 days_ = _____ total minimum gallons of water

Store additional water if you live in a hot climate or if your household includes infants, pregnant women, or people with special health needs. Don't forget to store water for pets. Containers can be sterilized by rinsing them with a diluted bleach solution (one part bleach to ten parts water). Replace your water supply every six months.

Food: At least a three-day supply of nonperishable foods—those requiring no refrigeration, preparation, or cooking and little or no water. Choose foods from the following list and add foods that members of your household will eat. Replace items in your food supply every six months.

Ready-to-eat canned meats, fruits, soups, and vegetables	Dried fruit	High-energy foods
	Nuts	Comfort/stress foods
Protein or fruit bars	Crackers	MREs (military rations)
Dry cereal or granola	Canned, powdered, or boxed juices	Infant formula and baby foods
Peanut butter	Nonperishable pasteurized milk or powered milk	Pet foods
Sugar, salt, pepper	Coffee, tea, sodas	

Sanitation

Plastic garbage bags (and ties)	Personal hygiene items (toothbrush, shampoo, deodorant, comb, shaving cream, and so on)	Household chlorine bleach, disinfectant
Toilet paper		Powdered lime
Moist towelettes or hand soap	Plastic bucket with tight lid	Small shovel for digging latrine
Washcloth and towel		

For a clean air supply

Face masks or several layers of dense-weave cotton material (handkerchiefs, t-shirts, towels) that fit snugly over your nose and mouth.

Shelter-in-place supplies, to be used in an interior room to create a barrier between you and potentially contaminated air outside: Heavyweight plastic garbage bags or plastic sheeting; duct tape; scissors; and if possible, a portable air purifier with a HEPA filter.

Family emergency plan

Plan places where your family will meet; choose one location near your home and one outside your neighborhood.

Local _____ Outside neighborhood _____

Have one local and one out-of-state contact person for family members to call if separated during a disaster. (It may be easier to make long-distance calls than local calls.)

Local _____ Out-of state _____

FIGURE A.2 Sample emergency preparedness kit and plan.

You may want to create several kinds of emergency kits. The primary one would contain supplies for home use. Put together a smaller, lightweight version that you can take with you if you are forced to evacuate your residence. Smaller kits for your car and your workplace are also recommended.

A Family or Household Plan   You and your family or household members should have a plan about where to meet and how to communicate. Choose at least two potential meeting places—one in your neighborhood and one or more in other areas. Your community may also have set locations for community shelters. Where you go may depend on the circumstances of the emergency situation. Use your common sense, and listen to the radio or television for instructions from emergency officials about whether to evacuate or stay in place. In addition, know all the transportation options in the vicinity of your home, school, and workplace; roadways and public transit may be affected, so a sturdy pair of walking shoes is a good item to keep in your emergency kit.

Everyone in the family or household should also have the same emergency contact person to call, preferably someone who lives outside the immediate area and won't be affected by the same local disaster. Local phone service may be significantly disrupted, so long-distance calls may be more likely to go through. Everyone should carry the relevant phone numbers and addresses at all times.

It is also important to check into the emergency plans at any location where you or family members spend time, including schools and workplaces. For each location, know the safest place to be for different types of emergencies—for example, near load-bearing interior walls during an earthquake or in the basement during a tornado. Also know how to turn off water, gas, and electricity in case of damaged utility lines; keep the needed tools next to the shutoff valves.

Other steps you can take to help prepare for emergencies include taking a first-aid class and setting up an emergency response group in your neighborhood, residential building, or office. Talk with your neighbors: Who has specialized equipment (for example, a power generator) or expertise that might help in a crisis? Do older or disabled neighbors have someone to help them? More complete information about emergency preparedness is available from local government agencies and from the following:

American Academy of Pediatrics
(www.aap.org)

American Red Cross
(www.redcross.org)

Federal Emergency Management Agency
(www.fema.gov)

U.S. Department of Homeland Security
(www.ready.gov)

PROVIDING EMERGENCY CARE

You can improve someone else's chances of surviving if you are prepared to provide emergency help. A course in first aid offered by the American Red Cross and on many college campuses can teach you to respond appropriately when someone needs help. Emergency rescue techniques can save the lives of people who have stopped breathing, who are choking, or whose hearts have stopped beating. Pulmonary resuscitation (also known as rescue breathing, artificial respiration, or mouth-to-mouth resuscitation) is used when a person is not breathing (refer back to Figure A.1). Cardiopulmonary resuscitation (CPR) is used when a pulse can't be found. Training is required before a person can perform CPR. Significant changes were made to the guidelines for lay rescue CPR in 2005. Courses are offered by the American Red Cross and the American Heart Association.

When You Have to Provide Emergency Care   Remain calm and act sensibly. The basic pattern for providing emergency care is *check-call-care*:

1. *Check the situation.* Make sure the scene is safe for both you and the injured person. Don't put yourself in danger; if you get hurt too, you will be of little help to the injured person.
2. *Check the victim.* Conduct a quick head-to-toe examination. Assess the victim's signs and symptoms, such as level of responsiveness, pulse, and breathing rate. Look for bleeding and any indications of broken bones or paralysis.
3. *Call for help.* Call 9-1-1 or a local emergency number. Identify yourself and give as much information as you can about the condition of the victim and what happened.
4. *Care for the victim.* If the situation requires immediate action (no pulse, shock, etc.), provide first aid if you are trained to do so (refer back to Figure A.1).

Selected Bibliography

Bren, L. 2005. Prevent your child from choking. *FDA Consumer,* September/ October.

Central Intelligence Agency. 2011. *The World Factbook.* Washington, D.C.: Central Intelligence Agency.

Federal Bureau of Investigation. 2009. *Hate Crime Statistics,* 2008. Washington, D.C.: U.S. Department of Justice.

Federal Bureau of Investigation. 2010. *Crime in the United States:* 2009. Washington, D.C.: U.S. Department of Justice.

Insurance Information Institute. 2007. *Road Rage* (http://www.iii.org/individuals/auto/lifesaving/roadrage; retrieved August 31, 2011).

Iudice, A., et al. 2005. Effects of prolonged wakefulness combined with alcohol and hands-free cell phone divided attention tasks on simulated driving. *Human Psychopharmacology* 20(2): 125–132.

National Center for Health Statistics. 2011. Deaths: Preliminary Data for 2009. *National Vital Statistics Reports* 59(4).

National Center for Health Statistics. 2011. *Health, United States,* 2010. Hyattsville, Md.: National Center for Health Statistics.

National Safety Council. 2011. *Injury Facts* 2011. Itasca, Ill.: National Safety Council.

U.S. Department of Homeland Security. 2005. *Ready America* (www.ready.gov; retrieved August 31, 2011).

As explained in Chapters 2–7, regular, appropriate exercise is safe and beneficial for many people with chronic conditions or other special health concerns. In fact, for many people with special health concerns, the risks associated with not exercising are far greater than those associated with a moderate program of regular exercise.

The fitness recommendations made throughout this book are intended for the general population and can serve as basic guidelines for any exercise program. If you have a chronic health condition, however, you may need to modify your exercise program to accommodate your situation. This appendix presents precautions and specialized recommendations for people with a variety of special health concerns.

These recommendations, however, are not intended to replace a physician's advice. If you have a special health concern, talk to your physician before starting any exercise program.

ARTHRITIS

- Begin an exercise program as early as possible in the course of the disease.
- Warm up thoroughly before each workout to loosen stiff muscles and lower the risk of injury.
- For cardiorespiratory endurance exercise, avoid high-impact activities that may damage arthritic joints. Consider swimming, water walking, or another type of exercise that can be done in a warm pool.
- Strength train the whole body. Pay special attention to muscles that support and protect affected joints. For example, build the quadriceps, hamstrings, and calf muscles to support and protect arthritic knees. Start with small amounts of weight and gradually increase the intensity of your workouts.
- Perform flexibility exercises daily to maintain joint mobility.

ASTHMA

- Exercise regularly. Acute attacks are more likely to occur if you exercise only occasionally.
- Carry medication during workouts and avoid exercising alone. Use your inhaler as recommended by your physician.
- Warm up and cool down slowly to reduce the risk of acute attacks.
- When starting an exercise program, choose self-paced endurance activities, especially those involving interval training (short bouts of exercise followed by a rest period). Gradually increase the intensity of your cardiorespiratory endurance workouts.

- Educate yourself about situations that can trigger an asthma attack and act accordingly when exercising. For example, cold, dry air can trigger or worsen an attack. Pollen, dust, and polluted air can also trigger an attack. To avoid attacks in dry air, drink water before, during, and after a workout to moisten your airways. In cold weather, cover your mouth with a mask or scarf to warm and humidify the air you breathe. Also, avoid outdoor activities during pollen season or when the air is polluted or dusty.

DIABETES

- Don't begin an exercise program unless your diabetes is under control and you have discussed exercise safety with your physician. Because people with diabetes have an increased risk for heart disease, an exercise stress test may be recommended.
- Don't exercise alone. Wear a bracelet that identifies you as someone with diabetes.
- If you take insulin or another medication, adjust the timing and amount of each dose as needed. Work with your physician and check your blood sugar level regularly so you can learn to balance your energy intake and output and your medication dosage.
- To prevent abnormally rapid absorption of injected insulin, inject it over a muscle that will not be exercised, and wait at least an hour before exercising.
- Check your blood sugar before, during, and after exercise. Adjust your diet and insulin dosage as needed. Keep high-carbohydrate foods on hand during a workout. Avoid exercise if your blood sugar level is above 250 mg/dl; if your blood sugar level is below 100 mg/dl, eat some carbohydrate-rich food before exercising.
- If you have poor circulation or numbness in your extremities, check your skin regularly for blisters and abrasions, especially on your feet. Avoid high-impact activities and wear comfortable shoes.
- For maximum benefit and minimum risk, choose moderate-intensity activities.

HEART DISEASE AND HYPERTENSION

- Check with your physician about exercise safety before increasing your activity level. Your doctor may recommend that you take an exercise stress test before starting your program.

- Exercise at moderate intensity rather than high intensity. Keep your heart rate below the level at which abnormalities appear on an exercise stress test.
- Warm up and cool down gradually. Every warm-up and cool-down session should last at least 10 minutes.
- Monitor your heart rate during exercise, and stop if you experience dizziness or chest pain.
- If your physician prescribes nitroglycerin, carry it with you during exercise. If you take a beta-blocker to manage hypertension, use RPE rather than heart rate to monitor your exercise intensity (beta-blockers reduce heart rate). Exercise at an RPE level of "fairly light" to "somewhat hard." Your breathing should be unlabored, and you should be able to talk during exercise.
- Don't hold your breath when exercising. Doing so can cause sudden, steep increases in blood pressure. Take special care during weight training and do not lift heavy loads. Exhale during the exertion phase of each lift.
- Increase exercise frequency, intensity, and time very gradually.

OBESITY

- For maximum benefit and minimum risk, begin by choosing low- to moderate-intensity activities. Increase intensity slowly as your fitness improves. Studies of overweight people show that exercising at moderate to high intensities causes more fat loss than training at low intensities.
- People who want to lose weight or maintain weight loss should exercise moderately for 60 minutes or more every day. To get the benefit of 60 minutes of exercise, you can exercise all at once or divide your total activity time into sessions of 10, 20, or 30 minutes.

- Choose non- or low-weight-bearing activities such as swimming, water exercises, cycling, or walking. Low-impact activities are less likely to cause joint problems or injuries.
- Stay alert for symptoms of heat-related problems during exercise (as described in Chapter 3). Obese people are vulnerable to heat intolerance.
- Ease into your exercise program and increase overload gradually. Increase time and frequency of exercise before increasing intensity.
- Include strength training in your fitness program to build or maintain muscle mass.
- Try to include as much lifestyle physical activity in your daily routine as possible.

OSTEOPOROSIS

- For cardiorespiratory endurance activities, exercise at the maximum intensity that causes no significant discomfort. If possible, choose low-impact, weight-bearing exercises to help safely maintain bone density. (See Chapter 8 for strategies for building and maintaining bone density.)
- To prevent fractures, avoid any activity or movement that stresses the back or carries a risk of falling.
- Include weight training in your exercise program to improve strength and balance and to reduce the risk of falls and fractures. Always use proper exercise technique and avoid lifting heavy loads.
- Include muscle-strengthening exercises 3 days per week.
- Include bone-strengthening exercises, such as jumping, at least 3 days per week.

NAME _____ **SECTION** _____ **DATE** _____

As you completed the labs listed below, you entered the results in the Preprogram Assessment column of this appendix. Now that you have been involved in a fitness and wellness program for some time, do the labs again and enter your new results in the Postprogram Assessment column. You will probably notice improvement in several areas. Congratulations! If you are not satisfied with your progress thus far, refer to the tips for successful behavior change in Chapter 1 and throughout this book. Remember—fitness and wellness are forever. The time you invest now in developing a comprehensive, individualized program will pay off in a richer, more vital life in the years to come.

	Preprogram Assessment	Postprogram Assessment
LAB 2.3 Pedometer	Daily steps: _____	Daily steps: _____
LAB 3.1 Cardiorespiratory Endurance		
1-mile walk test	$\dot{V}O_{2max}$: _____ Rating: _____	$\dot{V}O_{2max}$: _____ Rating: _____
3-minute step test	$\dot{V}O_{2max}$: _____ Rating: _____	$\dot{V}O_{2max}$: _____ Rating: _____
1.5-mile run-walk test	$\dot{V}O_{2max}$: _____ Rating: _____	$\dot{V}O_{2max}$: _____ Rating: _____
12-minute swim test	Rating: _____	Rating: _____
LAB 4.1 Muscular Strength		
Maximum bench press test	Weight: _____ lb Rating: _____	Weight: _____ lb Rating: _____
LAB 4.2 Muscular Endurance		
Curl-up test	Number: _____ Rating: _____	Number: _____ Rating: _____
Push-up test	Number: _____ Rating: _____	Number: _____ Rating: _____
Squat endurance test	Number: _____ Rating: _____	Number: _____ Rating: _____
LAB 5.1 Flexibility		
Sit-and-reach test	Score: _____ cm Rating: _____	Score: _____ cm Rating: _____
LAB 5.3 Low-Back Muscular Endurance		
Side bridge endurance test	Right: _____ sec. Rating: _____	Right: _____ sec. Rating: _____
	Left: _____ sec. Rating: _____	Left: _____ sec. Rating: _____
Trunk flexors endurance test	Trunk flexors: _____ sec. Rating: _____	Trunk flexors: _____ sec. Rating: _____
Back extensors endurance test	Back extensors: _____ sec. Rating: _____	Back extensors: _____ sec. Rating: _____

	Preprogram Assessment	Postprogram Assessment
LAB 6.1 Body Composition Body mass index Skinfold measurements (or other methods for determining percent body fat) Waist circumference Waist-to-hip ratio	BMI: _____ kg/m2 Rating: _____ Sum of 3 skinfolds: _____ mm % body fat: _____% Rating: _____ Circumf.: _____ Rating: _____ Ratio: _____ Rating: _____	BMI: _____ kg/m2 Rating: _____ Sum of 3 skinfolds: _____ mm % body fat: _____% Rating: _____ Circumf.: _____ Rating: _____ Ratio: _____ Rating: _____
LAB 8.1 Daily Diet Number of oz-eq Number of cups Number of cups Number of cups Number of oz-eq Number of tsp Number of g Number of g or tsp	Grains: _____ Vegetables: _____ Fruits: _____ Milk: _____ Meat or beans: _____ Oils: _____ Solid fats: _____ Added sugars: _____	Grains: _____ Vegetables: _____ Fruits: _____ Milk: _____ Meat or beans: _____ Oils: _____ Solid fats: _____ Added sugars: _____
LAB 8.2 Dietary Analysis Percentage of calories Percentage of calories Percentage of calories Percentage of calories	From protein: _____ % From fat: _____ % From saturated fat: _____ % From carbohydrate: _____ %	From protein: _____ % From fat: _____ % From saturated fat: _____ % From carbohydrate: _____ %
LAB 9.1 Daily Energy Needs	Daily energy needs: _____ cal/day	Daily energy needs: _____ cal/day
LAB 10.1 Identifying Stressors	Average weekly stress score: _____	Average weekly stress score: _____
LAB 11.1 Cardiovascular Health CVD risk assessment Hostility assessment	Score: _____ Estimated risk: _____ Score: _____ Rating: _____	Score: _____ Estimated risk: _____ Score: _____ Rating: _____
LAB 12.1 Cancer Prevention Diet: Number of servings Skin cancer	Fruits/vegetables: _____ Score: _____ Risk: _____	Fruits/vegetables: _____ Score: _____ Risk: _____

BEHAVIOR CHANGE WORKBOOK

This workbook is designed to take you step by step through a behavior change program. The first eight activities in the workbook will help you develop a successful plan—beginning with choosing a target behavior, moving through the planning steps described in Chapter 1, and completing and signing a behavior change contract. The final seven activities will help you work through common obstacles to behavior change and maximize your program's chances of success.

Part 1 Developing a Plan for Behavior Change and Completing a Contract

1. Choosing a Target Behavior
2. Gathering Information About Your Target Behavior
3. Monitoring Your Current Patterns of Behavior
4. Setting Goals
5. Examining Your Attitudes About Your Target Behavior
6. Choosing Rewards
7. Breaking Behavior Chains
8. Completing a Contract for Behavior Change

Part 2 Overcoming Obstacles to Behavior Change

9. Building Motivation and Commitment
10. Managing Your Time Successfully
11. Developing Realistic Self-Talk
12. Involving the People Around You
13. Dealing with Feelings
14. Overcoming Peer Pressure: Communicating Assertively
15. Maintaining Your Program over Time

ACTIVITY 1 CHOOSING A TARGET BEHAVIOR

Use your knowledge of yourself and the results of Lab 1.2 (Lifestyle Evaluation) to identify five behaviors that you could change to improve your level of wellness. Examples of target behaviors include smoking cigarettes, not exercising regularly, eating candy bars every night, not getting enough sleep, getting drunk frequently on weekends, and not wearing a safety belt when driving or riding in a car. List your five behaviors below.

1. _____
2. _____
3. _____
4. _____
5. _____

For successful behavior change, it's best to focus on one behavior at a time. Review your list of behaviors and select one to start with. Choose a behavior that is important to you and that you are strongly motivated to change. If this will be your first attempt at behavior change, start with a simple change, such as wearing your bicycle helmet regularly, before tackling a more difficult change, such as quitting smoking. Circle the behavior on your list that you've chosen to start with; this will be your target behavior throughout this workbook.

ACTIVITY 2 GATHERING INFORMATION ABOUT YOUR TARGET BEHAVIOR

Take a close look at what your target behavior means to your health, now and in the future. How is it affecting your level of wellness? What diseases or conditions does this behavior place you at risk for? What will changing this behavior mean to you? To evaluate your behavior, use information from this text, from the resources listed in the For Further Exploration section at the end of each chapter, and from other reliable sources.

Health behaviors have short-term and long-term benefits and costs associated with them. For example, in the short term, an inactive lifestyle allows for more time to watch TV and hang out with friends but leaves a person less able to participate in recreational activities. In the long term, it increases the risk of cardiovascular disease, cancer, and premature death. Fill in the blanks below with the benefits and costs of continuing your current behavior and of changing to a new, healthier behavior. Pay close attention to the short-term benefits of the new behavior—these are an important motivating force behind successful behavior change programs.

Target (current) behavior _____

Benefits   *Short-Term*   *Long-Term*

_____   _____

_____   _____

_____   _____

Costs   *Short-Term*   *Long-Term*

_____   _____

_____   _____

_____   _____

New behavior _____

Benefits   *Short-Term*   *Long-Term*

_____   _____

_____   _____

_____   _____

Costs   *Short-Term*   *Long-Term*

_____   _____

_____   _____

_____   _____

ACTIVITY 3   MONITORING YOUR CURRENT PATTERNS OF BEHAVIOR

To develop a successful behavior change program, you need detailed information about your current behavior patterns. You can obtain this information by developing a system of record keeping geared toward your target behavior. Depending on your target behavior, you may want to monitor a single behavior, such as your diet, or you may want to keep daily activity records to determine how you could make time for exercise or another new behavior. Consider tracking factors such as the following:

- What the behavior was
- When and for how long it occurred
- Where it occurred
- What else you were doing at the time
- What other people you were with and how they influenced you
- What your thoughts and feelings were
- How strong your urge for the behavior was (for example, how hungry you were or how much you wanted to watch TV)

Figure 1.6 shows a sample log for tracking daily diet. Below, create a format for a sample daily log for monitoring the behavior patterns relating to your target behavior. Then use the log to monitor your behavior for a day. Evaluate your log as you use it. Ask yourself if you are tracking all the key factors that influence your behavior; make any necessary adjustments to the format of your log. Once you've developed an appropriate format, use a separate notebook (your health journal) to keep records of your behavior for a week or two. These records will provide solid information about your behavior that will help you develop a successful behavior change program. Later activities in this workbook will ask you to analyze your records.

ACTIVITY 4   SETTING GOALS

For your behavior change program to succeed, you must set meaningful, realistic goals. In addition to an ultimate goal, set some intermediate goals—milestones that you can strive for on the way to your final objective. For example, if your overall goal is to run a 5K road race, an intermediate goal might be to successfully complete 2 weeks of your fitness program. If you set a final goal of eating 7 servings of fruits and vegetables every day, an intermediate goal would be to increase your daily intake from 3 to 4 servings. List your intermediate and final goals below. Don't strive for immediate perfection. Allow an adequate amount of time to reach each of your goals.

Intermediate Goals   **Target Date**

_____   _____

_____   _____

_____   _____

_____   _____

_____   _____

Final Goals

_____   _____

ACTIVITY 5   EXAMINING YOUR ATTITUDES ABOUT YOUR TARGET BEHAVIOR

Your attitudes toward your target behavior can determine whether your behavior change program will be successful. Consider your attitudes carefully by completing the following statements about how you think and feel about your current behavior and your goal.

1. I like _____ because _____
         (current behavior)
   _____.

2. I don't like _____ because _____
           (current behavior)
   _____.

3. I like _____ because _____
         (behavior goal)
   _____.

4. I don't like _____ because _____
           (behavior goal)
   _____.

5. I don't _____ now because _____
         (behavior goal)
   _____.

6. I would be more likely to _____ if _____
           (behavior goal)
   _____.

If your statements indicate that you have major reservations about changing your behavior, work to build your motivation and commitment before you begin your program. Look carefully at your objections to changing your behavior. How valid and important are they? What can you do to overcome them? Can you adopt any of the strategies you listed under statement 6? Review the facts about your current behavior and your goals.

ACTIVITY 6   CHOOSING REWARDS

Make a list of objects, activities, and events you can use as rewards for achieving the goals of your behavior change program. Rewards should be special, relatively inexpensive, and preferably unrelated to food or alcohol—for example, tickets to a ball game, a CD, or a long-distance phone call to a family member or friend—whatever is meaningful for you. Write down a variety of rewards you can use when you reach milestones in your program and your final goal.

_____   _____

_____   _____

_____   _____

_____   _____

Many people also find it helpful to give themselves small rewards daily or weekly for sticking with their behavior change program. These could be things like a study break, a movie, or a Saturday morning bike ride. Make a list of rewards for maintaining your program in the short term.

_____   _____

_____   _____

_____   _____

And don't forget to congratulate yourself regularly during your behavior change program. Notice how much better you feel. Savor how far you've come and how you've gained control of your behavior.

ACTIVITY 7   BREAKING BEHAVIOR CHAINS

Use the records you collected about your target behavior in Activity 3 and in your health journal to identify what leads up to your target behavior and what follows it. By tracing these chains of events, you'll be able to identify points in the chain where you can make a change that will lead to your new behavior. The sample behavior chain on the next page shows a sequence of events for a person who wants to add exercise to her daily routine—but who winds up snacking and watching TV instead. By examining the chain carefully, you can identify ways to break it at every step. After you review the sample, go through the same process for a typical chain of events involving your target behavior. Use the blank behavior chain on the following page.

Some general strategies for breaking behavior chains include the following:

- **Control or eliminate environmental cues that provoke the behavior.** Stay out of the room where your television is located. Go out for an ice cream cone instead of keeping a half gallon of ice cream in your freezer.
- **Change behaviors or habits that are linked to your target behavior.** If you always smoke in your car when you drive to school, try taking public transportation instead.
- **Add new cues to your environment to trigger your new behavior.** Prepare easy-to-grab healthy snacks and carry them with you to class or work. Keep your exercise clothes and equipment in a visible location.

See also the suggestions in Chapter 1.

Chain of Events	Strategies for Breaking the Chain
Come home from class	You had planned an afternoon walk as part of your exercise program.
Feel tired, not like exercising	Tell yourself you'll feel better and more alert after working out.
Look for walking shoes; can't find them	Put shoes and clothes for exercise in an obvious place the night before.
Feel annoyed	Remind yourself of your program goals, and tell yourself that you can stick with your program.
Go to kitchen, see food	Stay out of the kitchen unless you will be fixing or eating a planned meal or snack.
Feel hungry	Look at the picture of a healthy exercise that you've put on the refrigerator to remind you of your goals.
Grab a soda and bag of chips	Have a glass of water or a pre-prepared healthy snack.
Turn on TV and sit down	Turn on the radio instead; listen to news or music while you get ready to exercise.
Eat chips, watch TV	If you really like to watch TV in the afternoon, plan to work out in the morning or exercise on a stationary bike or treadmill in front of the TV.
Feel guilty	Even if you do have occasional lapses, don't beat yourself up. Think positively about how you'll resume your program the next day.

Chain of Events

Strategies for Breaking the Chain

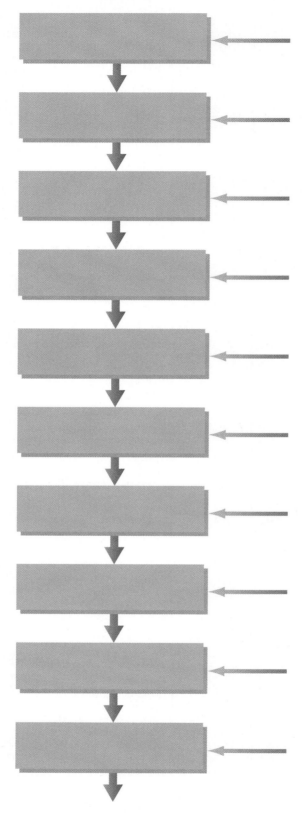

Your next step in creating a successful behavior change program is to complete and sign a behavior change contract. Your contract should include details of your program and indicate your commitment to changing your behavior. Use the information from previous activities in this workbook to complete the following contract. (If your target behavior relates to exercise, you may want to use the program plan and contract for a fitness program in Lab 7.1.)

1. I, _____, agree to _____
   (name)   (specify behavior you want to change)
   _____.

2. I will begin on _____ and plan to reach my goal of _____
   (start date)   (specify final goal)
   _____ by _____.

3. To reach my final goal, I have devised the following schedule of mini-goals. For each step in my program, I will give myself the reward listed.

(mini-goal 1)	(target date)	(reward)
(mini-goal 2)	(target date)	(reward)
(mini-goal 3)	(target date)	(reward)
(mini-goal 4)	(target date)	(reward)
(mini-goal 5)	(target date)	(reward)

   My overall reward for reaching my final goal will be _____

4. I have gathered and analyzed data on my target behavior and have identified the following strategies for changing my behavior: _____
   _____
   _____

5. I will use the following tools to monitor my progress toward reaching my final goal:

   _____
   (list any charts, graphs, or journals you plan to use)
   _____

   I sign this contract as an indication of my personal commitment to reach my goal.

   _____   _____
   (your signature)   (date)

   I have recruited a helper who will witness my contract and _____
   _____
   (list any way in which your helper will participate in your program)
   _____

   _____   _____
   (helper's signature)   (date)

Describe in detail any special strategies you will use to help change your behavior (refer to Activity 7).

Create a plan for any charts, graphs, or journals you will use to monitor your progress. The log format you developed in Activity 3 may be appropriate, or you may need to develop a more detailed or specific record-keeping system. Examples of journal formats are included in Labs 3.2, 4.3, 5.2, 8.1, and 10.1. You might also want to develop a graph to show your progress; posting such a graph in a prominent location can help keep your motivation strong and your program on track. Depending on your target behavior, you could graph the number of push-ups you can do, the number of servings of vegetables you eat each day, or your average daily stress level.

ACTIVITY 9   BUILDING MOTIVATION AND COMMITMENT

Complete the following checklist to determine whether you are motivated and committed to changing your behavior. Check the statements that are true for you.

_____ I feel responsible for my own behavior and capable of managing it.

_____ I am not easily discouraged.

_____ I enjoy setting goals and then working to achieve them.

_____ I am good at keeping promises to myself.

_____ I like having a structure and schedule for my activities.

_____ I view my new behavior as a necessity, not an optional activity.

_____ Compared with previous attempts to change my behavior, I am more motivated now.

_____ My goals are realistic.

_____ I have a positive mental picture of the new behavior.

_____ Considering the stresses in my life, I feel confident that I can stick to my program.

_____ I feel prepared for lapses and ups-and-downs in my behavior change program.

_____ I feel that my plan for behavior change is enjoyable.

_____ I feel comfortable telling other people about the change I am making in my behavior.

Did you check most of these statements? If not, you need to boost your motivation and commitment. Consider these strategies:

- Review the potential benefits of changing your behavior and the costs of not changing it (see Activity 2). Pay special attention to the short-term benefits of changing your behavior, including feelings of accomplishment and self-confidence. Post a list of these benefits in a prominent location.

- Visualize yourself achieving your goal and enjoying its benefits. For example, if you want to manage time more effectively, picture yourself as a confident, organized person who systematically tackles important tasks and sets aside time each day for relaxation, exercise, and friends. Practice this type of visualization regularly.

- Put aside obstacles and objections to change. Counter thoughts such as "I'll never have time to exercise" with thoughts like "Lots of other people do it, and so can I."

- Bombard yourself with propaganda. Take a class dealing with the change you want to make. Read books and watch television shows on the subject. Post motivational phrases or pictures on your refrigerator or over your desk. Talk to people who have already made the change.

- Build up your confidence. Remind yourself of other goals you've achieved. At the end of each day, mentally review your good decisions and actions. See yourself as a capable person, as being in charge of your behavior.

List two strategies for boosting your motivation and commitment; choose from the list above, or develop your own. Try each strategy, and then describe how well it worked for you.

Strategy 1: _____

How well it worked: _____

_____

Strategy 2: _____

How well it worked: _____

_____

ACTIVITY 10   MANAGING YOUR TIME SUCCESSFULLY

"Too little time" is a common excuse for not exercising or engaging in other healthy behaviors. Learning to manage your time successfully is crucial if you are to maintain a wellness lifestyle. The first step is to examine how you are currently spending your time; use the following grid to track your activities.

Time	Activity	Time	Activity
6:00 A.M.		6:00 P.M.	
6:30 A.M.		6:30 P.M.	
7:00 A.M.		7:00 P.M.	
8:00 A.M.		8:00 P.M.	
9:00 A.M.		9:00 P.M.	
10:00 A.M.		10:00 P.M.	
11:00 A.M.		11:00 P.M.	
12:00 P.M.		12:00 A.M.	
1:00 P.M.		1:00 A.M.	
2:00 P.M.		2:00 A.M	
3:00 P.M.		3:00 A.M.	
4:00 P.M.		4:00 A.M.	
5:00 P.M.		5:00 A.M.	

Next, list each type of activity and the total time you engaged in it on a given day in the chart below (for example, sleeping, 7 hours; eating, 1.5 hours; studying, 3 hours; working, 3 hours; and so on). Take a close look at your list of activities. Successful time management is based on prioritization. Assign a priority to each of your activities according to how important it is to you: essential (A), somewhat important (B), or not important (C). Based on these priority rankings, make changes in your schedule by adding and subtracting hours from different categories of activities; enter a duration goal for each activity. Add your new activities to the list and assign a priority and duration goal to each.

Activity	Current Total Duration	Priority (A, B, or C)	Goal Total Duration

Prioritizing in this manner will involve trade-offs. For example, you may choose to reduce the amount of time you spend watching television, listening to music, and chatting on the telephone while you increase the amount of time spent sleeping, studying, and exercising. Don't feel that you have to miss out on anything you enjoy. You can get more from less time by focusing on what you are doing. Strategies for managing time more productively and creatively are described in Chapter 10.

ACTIVITY 11 DEVELOPING REALISTIC SELF-TALK

Self-talk is the ongoing internal dialogue you have with yourself throughout much of the day. Your thoughts can be accurate, positive, and supportive, or they can be exaggerated and negative. Self-talk is closely related to self-esteem and self-concept. Realistic self-talk can help maintain positive self-esteem, the belief that you are a good and competent person, worthy of friendship and love. A negative internal dialogue can reinforce negative self-esteem and can make behavior change difficult. Substituting realistic self-talk for negative self-talk can help you build and maintain self-esteem and cope better with the challenges in your life.

First, take a closer look at your current pattern of self-talk. Use your health journal to track self-talk, especially as it relates to your target behavior. Does any of your self-talk fall into the common patterns of distorted, negative self-talk shown in Chapter 10? If so, use the examples of realistic self-talk from Chapter 10 to develop more accurate and rational responses. Write your current negative thoughts in the left-hand column, and then record more realistic thoughts in the right-hand column.

Current Self-Talk About Target Behavior

More Realistic Self-Talk

Your behavior change program will be more successful if the people around you are supportive and involved—or at least are not sabotaging your efforts. Use your health journal to track how other people influence your target behavior and your efforts to change it. For example, do you always skip exercising when you're with certain people? Do you always drink or eat too much when you socialize with certain friends? Are friends and family members offering you enthusiastic support for your efforts to change your behavior, or do they make jokes about your program? Have they even noticed your efforts? Summarize the reactions of those around you in the chart below.

Target behavior _____

Person	Typical Effect on Target Behavior	Involvement in/Reaction to Program

It may be difficult to change the actions and reactions of the people who are close to you. For them to be involved in your program, you may need to develop new ways of interacting with them (for example, taking a walk rather than going out to dinner as a means of socializing). Most of your friends and family members will want to help you—if they know how. Ask for exactly the type of help or involvement you want. Do you want feedback, praise, or just cooperation? Would you like someone to witness your contract or to be involved more directly in your program? Do you want someone to stop sabotaging your efforts by inviting you to watch TV, eat rich desserts, and so on? Look for ways that the people who are close to you can share in your behavior change program. They can help to motivate you and to maintain your commitment to your program. Develop a way that each individual you listed above can become involved in your program in a positive way.

Person	Target Involvement in Behavior Change Program

Choose one person on your list to tackle first. Talk to that person about her or his current behavior and how you would like her or him to be involved in your behavior change program. Below, describe this person's reaction to your talk and her or his subsequent behavior. Did this individual become a positive participant in your behavior change program?

_____

_____

_____

_____

_____

Long-standing habits are difficult to change in part because many of them represent ways people have developed to cope with certain feelings. For example, people may overeat when bored, skip their exercise sessions when frustrated, or drink alcoholic beverages when anxious. Developing new ways to deal with feelings can help improve the chance that a behavior change program will succeed.

Review the records on your target behavior that you kept in your health journal. Identify the feelings that are interfering with the success of your program, and develop new strategies for coping with them. Some common problematic feelings are listed below, along with one possible coping strategy for each. Put a check mark next to those that are influencing your target behavior, and fill in additional strategies. Add the other feelings that are significant roadblocks in your program to the bottom of the chart, along with coping strategies for each.

✔	Feeling	Coping Strategies
	Stressed out	Go for a 10-minute walk.
	Anxious	Do one of the relaxation exercises described in Chapter 10.
	Bored	Call a friend for a chat.
	Tired	Take a 20-minute nap.
	Frustrated	Identify the source of the feeling and deal with it constructively.

Consider the following situations:

- Julia is trying to give up smoking; her friend Marie continues to offer her cigarettes whenever they are together.
- Emilio is planning to exercise in the morning; his roommates tell him he's being antisocial by not having breakfast with them.
- Tracy's boyfriend told her that in high school he once experimented with drugs and shared needles; she wants him to have an HIV test, but he says he's sure the people he shared needles with were not infected.

Peer pressure is the common ingredient in these situations. To successfully maintain your behavior change program, you must develop effective strategies for resisting peer pressure. Assertive communication is one such strategy. By communicating assertively—firmly, but not aggressively—you can stick with your program even in the face of pressure from others.

Review your health journal to determine how other people affect your target behavior. If you find that you often give in to peer pressure, try the following strategies for communicating more assertively:

- Collect your thoughts, and plan in advance what you will say. You might try out your response on a friend to get some feedback.
- State your case—how you feel and what you want—as clearly as you can.
- Use "I" messages—statements about how you feel—rather than "you" statements.
- Focus on the behavior rather than the person. Suggest a solution, such as asking the other person to change his or her behavior toward you. Avoid generalizations. Be specific about what you want.
- Make clear, constructive requests. Focus on your needs ("I would like . . .") rather than the mistakes of others ("You always . . .").
- Avoid blaming, accusing, and belittling. Treat others with the same respect you'd like to receive yourself.
- Ask for action ahead of time. Tell others what you would like to have happen; don't wait for them to do the wrong thing and then get angry at them.
- Ask for a response to what you have proposed. Wait for an answer and listen carefully to it. Try to understand other people's points of view, just as you would hope that others would understand yours.

With these strategies in mind, review your health journal and identify three instances in which peer pressure interfered with your behavior change program. For each instance, write out what you might have said to deal with the situation more assertively. (If you can't think of three situations from your experiences, choose one or more of the three scenarios described at the beginning of this activity.)

1. _____
   _____

2. _____
   _____

3. _____
   _____

Assertive communication can help you achieve your behavior change goals in a direct way by helping you keep your program on track. It can also provide a boost for your self-image and increase your confidence in your ability to successfully manage your behavior.

ACTIVITY 15 MAINTAINING YOUR PROGRAM OVER TIME

If you maintain your new behavior for at least 6 months, you've reached the maintenance stage, and your chances of lifetime success are greatly increased. However, you may find yourself sliding back into old habits at some point. If this happens, there are some things you can do to help maintain your new behavior.

- Remind yourself of the goals of your program (list them here).

  _____

  _____

  _____

  _____

  _____

- Pay attention to how your new pattern of behavior has improved your wellness status. List the major benefits of changing your behavior, both now and in the future.

  _____

  _____

  _____

  _____

  _____

- Consider the things you enjoy most about your new pattern of behavior. List your favorite aspects.

  _____

  _____

  _____

  _____

  _____

- Think of yourself as a problem solver. If something begins to interfere with your program, devise strategies for dealing with it. Take time out now to list things that have the potential to derail your program and develop possible coping mechanisms.

Problem   **Solution**

_____   _____

                       _____

_____   _____

                       _____

_____   _____

                       _____

_____   _____

- Remember the basics of behavior change. If your program runs into trouble, go back to keeping records of your behavior to pinpoint problem areas. Make adjustments in your program to deal with new disruptions. Don't feel defeated if you lapse. The best thing you can do is renew your commitment and continue with your program.

CREDITS

Title page

Thomas Northcut/Getty Images

Chapter 1

p. 1, © Odilon Dimier/PhotoAlto Agency RF Collections/Getty Images; p. 5, Ryan McVay/Getty Images; p. 8, © The McGraw-Hill Companies, Inc./Lars A. Niki, photographer; p. 10, Dynamic Graphics/JupiterImages; p. 12, © Stockdisc/PunchStock; p. 14, Blend Images/Getty Images; p. 19, Photodisc/Getty Images

Chapter 2

p. 29, RubberBall Productions/Getty Images; p. 31, © moodboard/Alamy; p. 35, © Erik Isakson/Blend Images/Getty Images; p. 37, © Ezra Shaw/Getty Images; p. 38, © Harold Cunningham/Getty Images; p. 39, Comstock Images/Jupiterimages; p. 42, © Kevin Fleming/Corbis; p. 43, Man in white chair: © Stockbyte/PunchStock, weight lifter arm: Ryan McVay/Getty Images, stretching: The McGraw-Hill Companies, Inc/Ken Karp photographer, bicycling: Joaquin Palting/Getty Images, walking: Doug Menuez/Getty Images, raking: UpperCut Images/Alamy; p. 44, Dancing, RubberBall Productions, Biking, © Royalty-Free/Corbis, weightlifting, © Thinkstock Images/Jupiterimages; p. 47, © IT Stock/PunchStock

Chapter 3

p. 61, © Caetano Barreira/X01990/Reuters/Corbis; p. 66, © Bill Varie/Workbook Stock/Getty Images; p. 68, © altrendo images/Stockbyte/Getty Images; p. 69, © Paul Burns/Digital Vision/Getty Images; p. 72, Courtesy Robin Mouat; p. 80, Ingram Publishing; p. 83, © Royalty-Free/Corbis; p. 84, © Siede Preis/PhotoDisc/Getty Images

Chapter 4

p. 97, © Paul Bradbury/The Image Bank/Getty Images; p. 100, © Terry Vine/Stone/Getty Images; p. 102, © TMI/Alamy; p. 104, Courtesy Neil A. Tanner; p. 105, © Elie Gardner/MCT /Landov; p. 106L, © The McGraw-Hill Companies, Inc./John Flournoy, photographer; p. 106R, Ingram Publishing; p. 107, © Royalty-Free/Corbis; p. 108, © Comstock Images/Alamy; p. 111, Courtesy Neil A. Tanner; p. 112, © Charles D. Winters/Photo Researchers, Inc.; p. 116T, © Wayne Glusker; p. 116B, © Taylor Robertson Photography; p. 117T, Courtesy Joseph Quever; p. 117M, © Wayne Glusker; p. 117B, Courtesy Joseph Quever; p. 118T, Courtesy Neil A.Tanner; p. 118M, © Taylor Robertson Photography; p. 118B, Courtesy Shirlee Stevens; p. 119T, Courtesy Neil A. Tanner; p. 119B, © Wayne Glusker; p. 120T, Courtesy Joseph Quever; p. 120M, © Taylor Robertson Photography; p. 120B, Courtesy Neil A. Tanner; p. 121T, © Wayne Glusker; pp. 121M, 121B, Courtesy Joseph Quever; p. 122T, Courtesy Neil A. Tanner; pp. 122M, 122B, Courtesy Joseph Quever; p. 123T, © Taylor Robertson Photography; p. 123M, © Wayne Glusker; p. 123B, Courtesy Joseph Quever; p. 124T, © Wayne Glusker; p. 124B, Courtesy Joseph Quever; p. 129, © Wayne Glusker; p. 131, Courtesy Tom Fahey; pp. 132, 133, © Wayne Glusker; pp. 135, 136, Courtesy Neil A. Tanner; p. 137, © Wayne Glusker

Chapter 5

p. 141, © Chris Clinton/Lifesize/Getty Images; p. 144, © Thinkstock Images/Jupiterimages; p. 148, Courtesy Shirlee Stevens; p. 149T, © Taylor Robertson Photography; pp. 149MT, 149MB, © Wayne Glusker; pp. 149B, 150T, © Taylor Robertson Photography; pp. 150MT, 150MB, Courtesy Neil A. Tanner; p. 150B, © Taylor Robertson Photography; p. 151T, 151MT, © Wayne Glusker; p. 151MB, Courtesy Shirlee Stevens; p. 151B, Courtesy Neil A. Tanner; p. 158, © Reggie Casagrande/Workbook Stock/Getty Images; p. 159T, © Wayne Glusker; pp. 159B, 160, © Taylor Robertson Photography; p. 161T, Courtesy Neil A. Tanner; pp. 161M, 161B, © Taylor Robertson Photography; p. 165, Courtesy Shirlee Stevens; p. 166, © Wayne Glusker; p. 173T, Courtesy Joseph Quever; p. 173B, © Taylor Robertson Photography; p. 174, © Wayne Glusker

Chapter 6

p. 175, © Robin Nelson/Alamy; p. 177, © Ocean/Corbis; p. 181, © EyeWire Collection/Getty Images; p. 183, Courtesy Life Measurement, Inc.; p. 184T, Courtesy Salter Housewares Ltd.; p. 184B, © Julie Brown/Custom Medical Stock Photo; p. 185, © Tony Santo, Ph.D., R.D., CSSD/tonysantophotography.com; p. 192, Courtesy Shirlee Stevens

Chapter 7

p. 199, Ingram Publishing; p. 200, © Assembly/Getty Images; p. 203, Comstock Images/Jupiterimages; p. 206, © Thinkstock Images/Jupiterimages; p. 207, © Zia Soleil/Iconica/Getty Images

Chapter 8

p. 223, © Valery Rizzo/Botanica/Getty Images; p. 227, © I. Rozenbaum/F. Cirou/Photo Alto; p. 231, © Brand X Pictures/PunchStock; p. 233, © Nathan Benn/Ottochrome/Corbis; p. 235, © Richard Levine/Alamy; p. 240, © Steven Miric/Photodisc/Getty Images; p. 247, ©Stewart Cohen/Blend Images/Getty Images; p. 249, © David Young-Wolff/PhotoEdit; p. 250, © Patrick Murphy-Racey/Sports Illustrated/Getty Images; p. 254, © Dave King/Dorling Kindersley/Getty Images; p. 255, © Royalty-Free/Corbis

Chapter 9

p. 273, Ingram Publishing; p. 276, Scale: Ryan McVay/Getty Images, Orange: © Stockdisc/PunchStock, Cheese: © Photodisc/PunchStock, Beans: C Squared Studios/Getty Images, Cookie: © Brand X Pictures/PunchStock, Broccoli: © Stockdisc/PunchStock, Tomato: © Comstock/Jupiter Images, Bike: © Royalty-Free/Corbis; p. 278, © Rennie Solis/Workbook Stock/Getty Images; p. 281, © David Madison/Stone/Getty Images; p. 282, © Susan Van Etten/PhotoEdit; p. 283, © Fancy Photography/Veer; p. 286, © Tim Boyle/Getty Images; p. 287, © Rick Gomez/Corbis; p. 289, © ZenShui/Alix Minde/PhotoAlto Agency RF Collections/Getty Images; p. 290, © David Oliver/Photographer's Choice/Getty Images

Chapter 10

p. 301, © Doug Pensinger/Getty Images; p. 305, © Purestock/PunchStock; p. 309, © Brand X Pictures/PunchStock; p. 310, © Stockbyte/Getty Images; p. 313, Ingram Publishing; p. 317, © Image Source/Getty Images; p. 321, Tetra Images/Getty Images

Chapter 11

p. 331, © Stockbroker/Alamy; p. 335, © iStockphoto.com/webphotographeer; p. 336, © David Buffington/Blend Images/Getty Images; p. 338, © Burke/Triolo Productions/Botanica/Getty Images; p. 343L, © Jessica Peterson/Rubberball Productions/Getty Images; p. 343R, © Stockbyte/PunchStock; p. 344, Ingram Publishing

Chapter 12

p. 351, © Hollandse Hoogte/Redux; p. 357, © Daniel Simon/Westend61/Corbis; p. 359, © Chuck Franklin/Alamy; p. 361, © Brandi Simons/Getty Images; p. 363, Ed Carey/Cole Group/Getty Images; p. 364, © Andersen Ross/Blend Images LLC; p. 365, Steve Cole/Getty Images

Chapter 13

p. 373, © Ingram Publishing/SuperStock; p. 375, © Dex Images/Photolibrary; p. 379, Courtesy DEA; p. 380, © David Young-Wolff/PhotoEdit; p. 384, © Sean Murphy/Stone/Getty Images; p. 388, © Brand X Pictures/PunchStock; p. 392, © Jupiterimages/Brand X Pictures/Getty Images

Chapter 14

p. 401, © AP Photo/Tina Fineberg; p. 403, © Erik Isakson/Getty Images; p. 406, © Jenny Matthews/Alamy; p. 407, © Joel Gordon

Chapter 15

p. 421, Courtesy NASA; p. 422, © AP Photo/Kyodo News; p. 426, Digital Vision/PunchStock; p. 431, © MadmàT/Flickr/Getty Images; p. 437, © Piccell/Photographer's Choice RF/Getty Images; p. 438T, © Tony Freeman/PhotoEdit; p. 438B, TV: Imagery Majestic/Cutcaster, iPhone: McGraw-Hill Companies, Microwave: © Stockbyte/PictureQuest, Eye: Barbara Penoyar/Getty Images, Sunglases: © Stockbyte/Getty Images, X-ray: © Royalty-Free/Corbis, Radiation symbol: Martin Diebel/Getty Images

Box photos

man on mountaintop with arms up, © RubberBall Productions/the Agency Collection/Getty Images; girl with magnifying glass, © Lane Oatey/Getty Images; various adults, different races, © David Young-Wolff/Photographer's Choice/Getty Images; woman in white doing yoga, © Science Photo Library/Getty Images; scale with food, © Alex Max/istockphoto.com; pad on clipboard, © Photodisc/Getty Images; purple dumbbells, Image Source; running shoes, © Comstock Images/Alamy; apple with tape measure, Ingram Publishing/SuperStock; scale with tape measure, © iStockphoto; woman reaching for the sky, © iStockphoto/Jacob Wackerhausen

Transparency inserts

Mountain biker: Joaquin Palting/Getty Images; Jumping jacks: Mike Powell/Getty Images; Climbing wall: Victoria Snowber/Getty Images; Lifting weights with trainer, Getty Images; Young girl eating: © iStockphoto.com/webphotographeer; Girl running: Rubberball Productions/Getty Images, Alan Bailey photographer; Bicep curl: Ryan McVay/Getty Images; Lifting dumbell, side view: Ryan McVay/Getty Images

Text/Line Art Credits

Chapter 1

Figure 1.5 Adapted from J.O. Prochaska, C.C. Diclemente & J.C. Norcross, 1992, "In search of how people change," American Psychologist, 47(9), 1102–1114. Copyright © 1992 by the American Psychological Association. Reprinted by permission.

Chapter 2

Lab 2.1 Source: Physical Activity Readiness Questionnaire (PAR-Q) Copyright © 2002. Used with permission from the Canadian Society for Exercise Physiology. www.csep.ca/forms.asp.

Chapter 3

Table 3.1 Adapted from G.A. Brooks, et al., 2005, Exercise Physiology: Human Bioenergetics and Its Applications, 4th ed. New York: McGraw-Hill. Copyright © 2005 The McGraw-Hill Companies, Inc. Reproduced with permission. Figure 3.5 Source: Psychology: from Research to Practice (1978), ed. H.L. Pick. Kluwer Academic/Plenum Publishing Corporation. Reprinted with kind permission of Springer Science and Business Media and the author. Table 3.6 Adapted with permission from American College of Sports Medicine, 2006. ACSM's Guidelines for Exercise Testing and Prescription, 7th ed. Philadelphia: Lippincott

Williams & Wilkins. Reprinted with permission from the publisher.
Lab 3., p. 91 (Rating Your Cardiovascular Fitness) Source: Ratings based on norms from The Cooper Institute for Aerobics, Dallas, TX; from The Physical Fitness Specialist Manual, Revised 2002. Used with permission.

Chapter 4

Lab 4.1, p. 130 Source: Based on norms from The Cooper Institute for Aerobics, Dallas, TX, from The Physical Fitness Specialist Manual, Revised 2002. Used with permission.
Lab 4.1, p. 131 Source: Brzycki, M. 1993. "Strength Testing-Predicting a One-Rep Max from Reps to Fatigue," Reprinted with permission from the January 1993 issue of The Journal of Physical Education, Recreation and Dance, 64:88–90, a publication of the American Alliance for Health, Physical Education, Recreation & Dance, 1900 Association Drive, Reston, VA 20191 (www.aahperd.org).
Lab 4.2, p. 136 Source: Ratings based on norms calculated from data collected by Dr. Robert Lualhati on 4545 college students, 16–80 years of age, at Skyline College, San Bruno, CA. Used with permission.
Lab 4.2, p. 137 Ratings for the Push-Up and Modified Push-Up Tests, based on norms from The Physical Fitness Specialist Manual, Revised 2002. The Cooper Institute for Aerobics, Dallas, TX. Reprinted by permission.
Lab 4.2, p. 137 Ratings for the Squat Endurance Test. Source: www.topendsports.com/testing.tests/home-squat.htm. Reprinted by permission.

Chapter 5

Lab 5.1, p. 165 Assessing Your Current Level of Flexibility, Sit & Reach Test: Source: The Canadian Physical Activity, Fitness & Lifestyle Approach: CSEP-Health & Fitness Program's Appraisal and Counseling Strategy, 3rd Edition, © 2003. Adapted with permission from the Canadian Society for Exercise Physiology.
Lab 5.3, p. 174 Adapted with permission from S. M. McGill, 2007, Low Back Disorders: Evidence-Based Prevention and Rehabilitation, 2nd Edition, p. 211. Champaign, IL: Human Kinetics.

Chapter 8

Take Charge Box, p. 230: Source: Food and Nutrition Board, Institute of Medicine, National Academies. 2002. Dietary Reference Intakes: Applications in Dietary Planning. Washington, DC: National Academies Press. Copyright © 2003 National Academy of Sciences. Reprinted with permission from the National Academies Press.
pp. 263–265 Nutrition Resources, Table 1: Source: Food and Nutrition Board, Institute of Medicine, National Academies, 2004. Dietary Reference Intakes Tables. Washington, D.C. Reprinted with permission from the National Academies Press. Copyright © 2004 National Academy of Sciences.
p. 266 Reprinted by permission of Simon & Schuster Inc. from Eat, Drink, and Be Healthy: The Harvard Medical School Guide to Healthy Eating by Walter C. Willett, M.D. Copyright © 2001, 2005 by President and Fellows of Harvard College. All rights reserved.
Lab 8., p. 272 Source: P.M. Insel & W.T. Roth, Wellness Worksheet 66, Core Concepts in Health, 11th Edition. Copyright © 2010 The McGraw-Hill Companies, Inc. Reprinted with permission.

Chapter 9

p. 284 The National Weight Control registry, www.nwcr.ws. Reprinted by permission.
Lab 9.1, p. 296 Estimating Daily Energy Requirements Using Food and Nutrition Board Formulas Part II: Reprinted with permission from Dietary Reference Intakes for Energy, Carbohydrate, Fiber, Fat, Fatty Acids, Cholesterol, Protein, and Amino Acids (Macronutrients). Reprinted with permission from the National Academies Press, Copyright 2005, National Academy of Sciences.
Lab 9.3, p. 299 J.D. Nash, 1997, The New Maximize Your Body Potential. Palo Alto, CA: Bull Publishing. Reprinted with permission from Bull Publishing. All rights reserved.
Lab 9.3, p. 300 "Eating Disorder Checklist" from D.M. Garner, M. Olmstead & J. Polivy, 1983, "Development and Validation of a Multidimensional Eating Disorder Inventory for Anorexia Nervosa and Bulimia," International Journal of Eating Disorders, 2(2), 15–34. Copyright © 1983 John Wiley & Sons. Reprinted with permission of John Wiley & Sons, Inc.

Chapter 10

p. 318 "Realistic Self-Talk, Cognitive Distortion, Negative Self-Talk" based on W. Schafer. 1999. Stress Management for Wellness, 4e. Copyright © 2000 Wadsworth, a part of Cengage Learning, Inc. Reproduced by permission. www.cengage.com/permissions.

Chapter 11

p. 341 American Heart Association, 2011, Heart Attack, Stroke, and Cardiac Arrest Warning Signs. Copyright © 2011 American Heart Association, Inc. www.heart.org. Reprinted with permission.
Lab 11.1, Part II Hostility Quiz from LifeSkills by Virginia Williams and Redford Williams. New York: Times Books. Reprinted by permission of the authors.

Chapter 12

p. 356 Adapted and reprinted by permission of the American Cancer Society, Inc. from www.cancer.org. Copyright © 2011 American Heart Association. All rights reserved.
Table 12.2 From American Cancer Society, Cancer Facts and Figures, 2011. Adapted and reprinted by permission of the American Cancer Society, Inc. from www.cancer.org. All rights reserved.
Lab 12.1, p. 372, Part II: Skin Cancer Risk Assessment adapted from Neil Shear, 1996. "What's Your UV-Risk Score?" Copyright © 1996 by the Consumers Union of the United States, Inc. Yonkers, NY 10703-1057. Reprinted with permission of the author.

Chapter 13

Lab 13.1, p. 398, Part I: From J.B. Saunders, et al., 1993, "Development of the Alcohol Use Disorders Identification Test (AUDIT): WHO Collaborative Project on Early Detection of Persons with Harmful Alcohol Consumption-II," Addiction, 88(6), 791-804, June, p. 803. Carfax Publishing Ltd. Reprinted by permission of Blackwell Publishing via Rightslink.
Lab 13., p. 398 Part II: From "Are You Troubled by Someone's Drinking?" http://www.al-anon.alateen.org/quiz.html. Copyright © 1980 Al-Anon Family Group Headquarters, Inc. Reprinted by permission of Al-Anon Family Group Headquarters, Inc.